Wine Atlas
OF CALIFORNIA

Wine Atlas OF CALIFORNIA

JAMES HALLIDAY

VIKING

Editorial Consultant
BRUCE CASS

VIKING
Published by the Penguin Group
Penguin Books USA Inc., 375 Hudson Street,
New York, New York 10014, U.S.A.
Penguin Books Ltd, 27 Wrights Lane
London W8 5TZ, England
Penguin Books Australia Ltd, Ringwood,
Victoria, Australia
Penguin Books Canada Ltd, 10 Alcorn Avenue, Suite 300,
Toronto, Ontario, Canada M4V 3B2
Penguin Books (N.Z.) Ltd, 182–190 Wairau Road,
Auckland 10, New Zealand

Penguin Books Ltd, Registered Offices:
Harmondsworth, Middlesex, England

First American Edition
Published in 1993 by Viking Penguin,
a division of Penguin Books USA Inc.

1 3 5 7 9 10 8 6 4 2

Published in association with Collins/Angus & Robertson
Publishers, Sydney, Australia

ISBN 0-670-84950-2
(CIP data available)
Printed in Australia

The following photographs appear courtesy of:
James Halliday: pages 51 and 357
George Rose of Fetzer: pages 49, 198–9, 203, 211 and 217
Illustrations: Jenny Phillips
Line diagrams: Russell Jeffrey
Graphs and California map: Colin Bardill
Maps: Donald Grahame and High Q Resolutions

FOREWORD

When Frank Schoonmaker and Tom Marvel wrote *The Wines of America,* in the 1940s, it was considered a curiosity. An entire book on American wines? Could there be that much to say? There was, but just barely.

As late as the 1960s, when President Lyndon Johnson, for the first time, ordered American embassies around the world to serve only American wines, self-styled connoisseurs shuddered. They called him an unschooled chauvinist, and worse. American wine was for immigrants and college kids. Then, suddenly, thanks to a new generation of vintners and a new generation of consumers, everyone wanted to know about American wine. Wine writers scrambled to fill the demand.

There are fashions in wine books, as there are in hemlines and politics. The early 1960s was the time for the big books — the wine encyclopedias and the wine picture books, coffee-table version.

The encyclopedias were global: a chapter on Italy, a chapter on Germany, two on France and, somewhere near the back, a few pages called "Other Wines of the World". Alas, in those days, that's often where American wines were to be found. Some of the coffee-table books were more generous. They were mostly picture books and the beautiful California wine country lent itself easily to pictures. The texts of those books were minimal at best and often pretentious, but a few at least conveyed the sense of excitement and discovery that was so much a part of the wine scene in those days.

Gradually, the wine literature became more specific. Even books for general readers became narrower in scope but deeper in interpretation. Instead of The Wines of the World, we got books on Napa or Sonoma, on specific grapes and on people who had influenced the wine industry. The cheerleading of the early days was, thank God, replaced by some good history and serious analysis.

Of course there has been almost from the start a succession of influential books that are both learned, beautiful and exciting to read. Hugh Johnson's *World Atlas of Wine* comes immediately to mind. Now with James Halliday's *Wine Atlas of California,* we can say the wheel has come full circle. Mr. Halliday combines immense knowledge of his subject — expressed in disarmingly clear prose — with years of hands-on experience and a formidable capacity for legwork.

James Halliday started out as a lawyer, became absorbed in wine, as an amateur, as an investor and ultimately as a winemaker, winery owner and prominent wine writer. For years he juggled two careers. Finally, he pulled down his shingle and became a wineman *tout court.* Today he is known for his prolific writing, his skill as a wine judge, and as the owner and winemaker of Coldstream Hills, an award-winning winery in the Yarra Valley of the state of Victoria in Australia.

Wine writing is plagued by hyperbole; a sort of phylloxera of the written word that spreads fast and is tough to root out. Competent winemakers become "geniuses", so-so wines are "superb", merely good becomes "truly magnificent" and even the dullest become "great for everyday drinking".

The same holds for wine writing. Any ink- — or wine- — stained scribbler can sound off on, just to give an example, the relative merits of mountain-grown grapes. Halliday can say this: ". . . my own vineyards are steep hillside, with gradients of 25 degrees in part. I took the decision to buy the land and was physically involved in the planting. Indeed, one horrendous spring, I knelt before almost every one of the 30,000 new planted vines on one block, pulling away weeds by hand . . . ."

How many wine writers can top that? Mr. Halliday brings not just his knowledge and passion to this beautiful study of California wine but a critical eye and a unique perspective.

I enjoy tasting with James Halliday; I enjoy reading him even more.

FRANK PRIAL
The New York Times

ABOVE ~ *Renaissance Vineyard, looking towards Lake Tahoe and the Sierras.*

CONTENTS

SODA CANYON
DELI

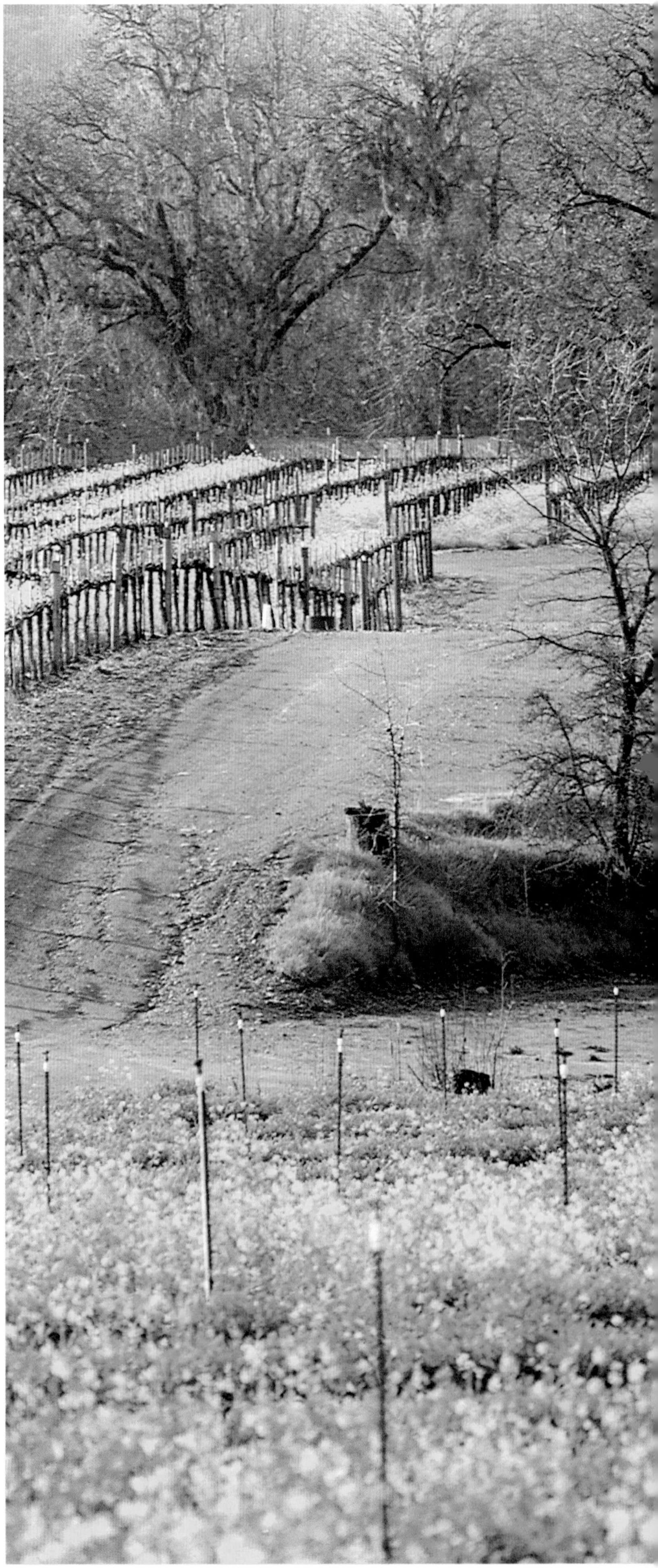

CONTENTS

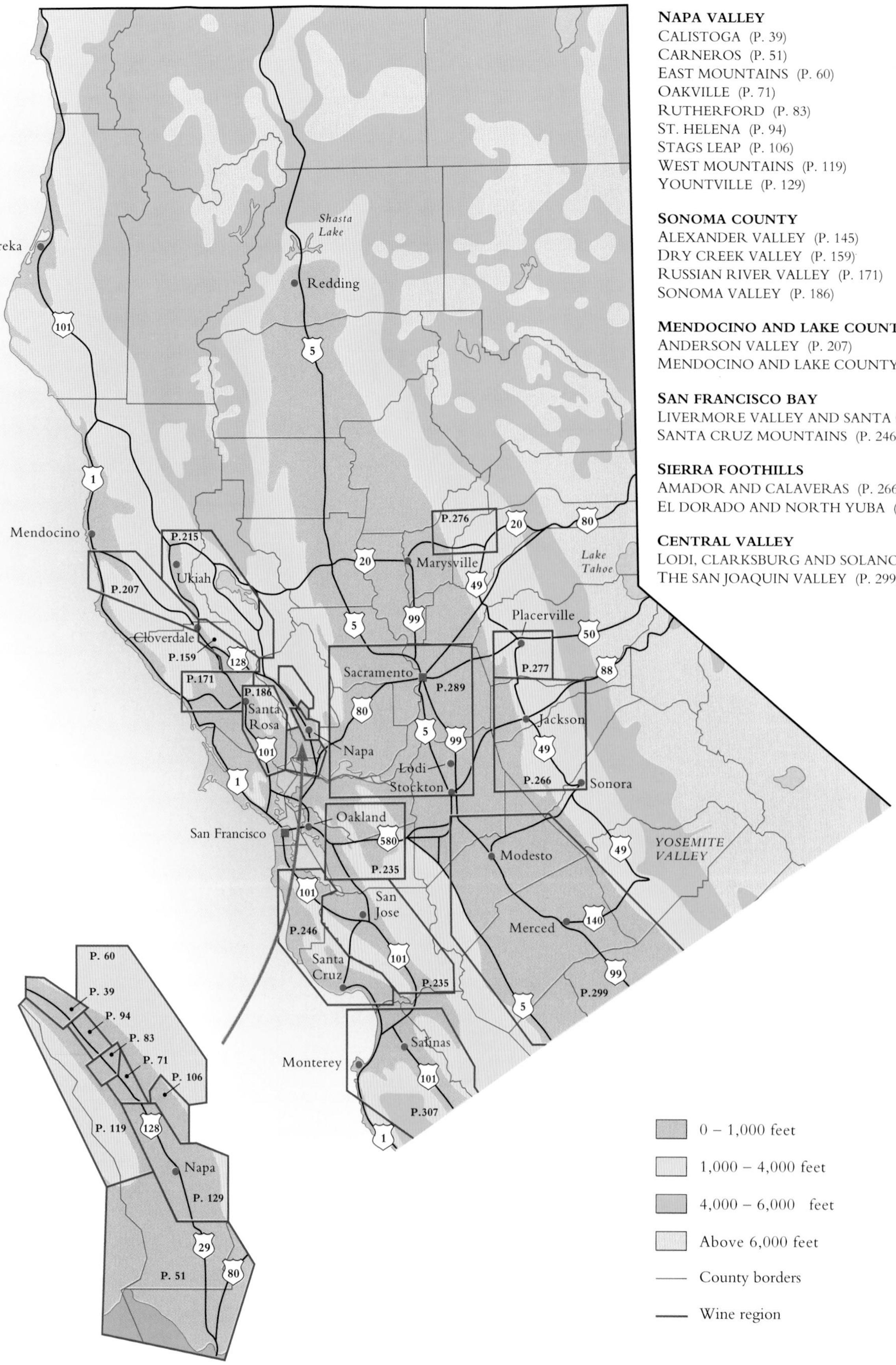
Eureka
Shasta Lake
Redding
Mendocino
Ukiah
Cloverdale
Santa Rosa
Napa
Marysville
Lake Tahoe
Placerville
Sacramento
Jackson
Lodi
Stockton
Sonora
Oakland
San Francisco
Modesto
YOSEMITE VALLEY
San Jose
Santa Cruz
Merced
Salinas
Monterey
P.215
P.207
P.159
P.171
P.186
P.276
P.277
P.289
P.266
P.235
P.246
P.299
P.307
P. 60
P. 39
P. 94
P. 83
P. 71
P. 106
P. 119
P. 129
P. 51
0 – 1,000 feet
1,000 – 4,000 feet
4,000 – 6,000 feet
Above 6,000 feet
County borders
Wine region

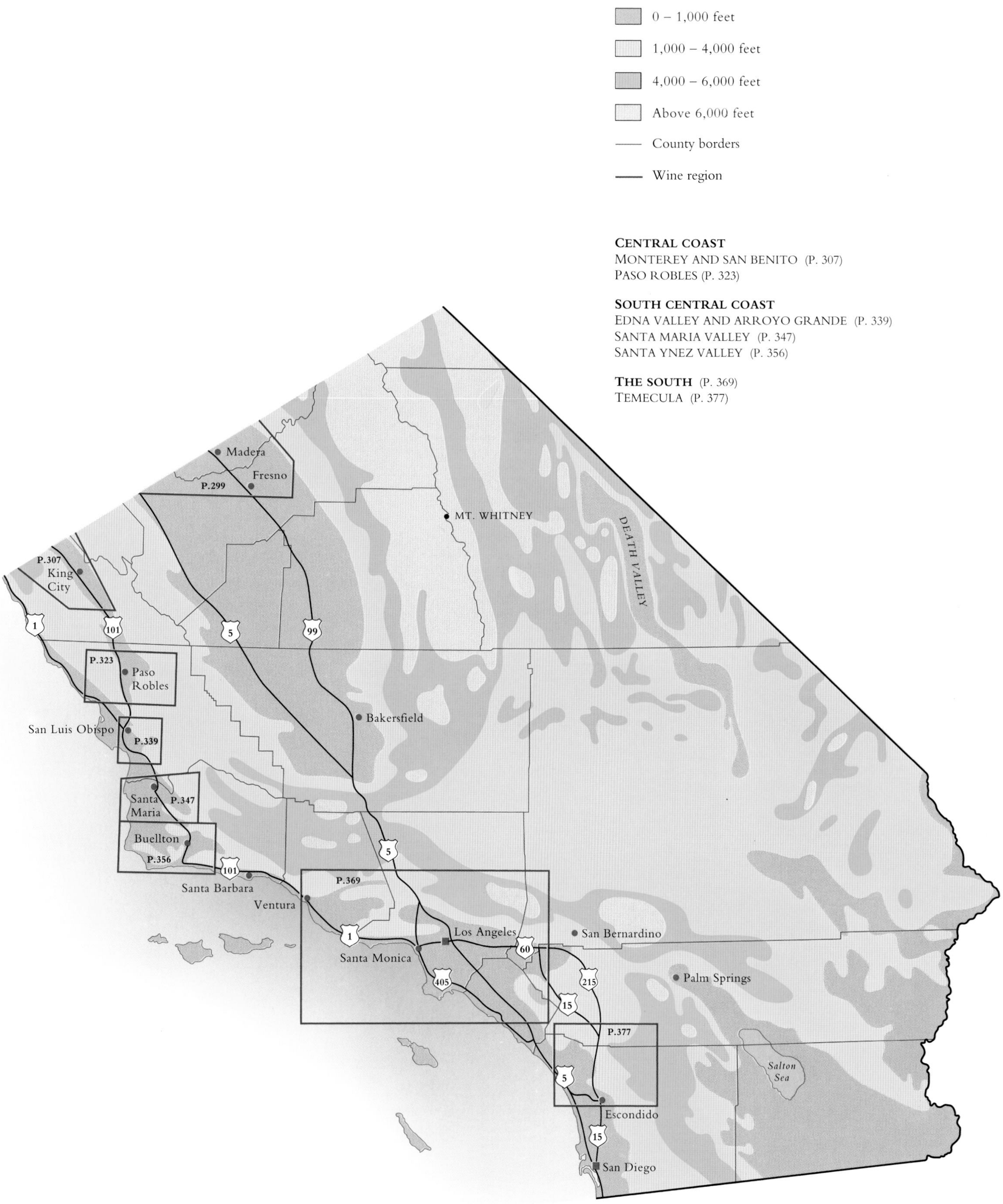
0 – 1,000 feet
1,000 – 4,000 feet
4,000 – 6,000 feet
Above 6,000 feet
County borders
Wine region
CENTRAL COAST
MONTEREY AND SAN BENITO (P. 307)
PASO ROBLES (P. 323)
SOUTH CENTRAL COAST
EDNA VALLEY AND ARROYO GRANDE (P. 339)
SANTA MARIA VALLEY (P. 347)
SANTA YNEZ VALLEY (P. 356)
THE SOUTH (P. 369)
TEMECULA (P. 377)
Madera
Fresno
P.299
MT. WHITNEY
DEATH VALLEY
P.307
King City
1
101
5
99
P.323
Paso Robles
San Luis Obispo
P.339
Bakersfield
Santa Maria
P.347
Buellton
P.356
101
Santa Barbara
Ventura
P.369
5
1
Los Angeles
60
Santa Monica
405
San Bernardino
215
Palm Springs
15
P.377
5
Salton Sea
Escondido
15
San Diego

ACKNOWLEDGMENTS

Writing a book such as this inevitably involves the contribution of many people. Most obvious is that of the winemakers, and I would customarily acknowledge their fundamental role at the outset. But this book posed special problems, and only one person was able to provide the answers: my editorial consultant and long-time friend, Bruce Cass. It was he who organized the interminable tastings, planned the broad framework of my itineraries, and ultimately sat by the telephone for weeks on end arranging up to a dozen winery visits for each succeeding day. It was he who ensured I visited wineries across the broadest spectrum — from tiny to large, from obscure to famous — and in so doing reached every corner of California in which grapes are grown and wine is made. I cannot thank him enough.

But I do not mean to diminish the contribution of the many hundreds of winemakers who so courteously received me and who so unhesitatingly answered my questions. If any regarded me as an interloper, they gave no sign of doing so. Many extended hospitality, and many more offered to do so, not taking offense when the schedule demanded I press on. To those with whom I stayed or dined, my special thanks.

Next, Oliver Strewe — assisted by Kathy Gerrard — had the near-impossible task of anticipating my path on his first photographic visit in winter, and following my erratic footsteps during the vintage session. The exceptionally beautiful photographs in this book show just how well he succeeded; they capture the very essence of one of the great wine regions of the world.

Which leads me to the production team at Angus & Robertson, headed by Nonfiction Publisher Kim Anderson, responsible for the all-important editorial and design functions. You, as reader, are entitled to take their contribution for granted; I as author, rely on it absolutely. Finally, my thanks to Michael Jacobs, then President of Viking Penguin, who had the courage to believe I could write this book. I can only hope his judgment is vindicated.

JAMES HALLIDAY

ABOVE ~ *Silverado Trail, Napa Valley.*

Introduction

I am a rare and possibly endangered species, both poacher and gamekeeper, hands-on winemaker and winewriter. I planted my first vineyard in the winter of 1971 and made my first wine in 1973. My vineyard and winery partners were, like me, Sydney lawyers with no technical qualifications. But — with help from our friends — we did it all ourselves: clearing the land, planting the grapes, pruning, summer training, winemaking, bottling, and marketing the 150 cases of that first vintage. The marketing was easy: we sent letters to fellow lawyers and other acquaintances, telling them to send their money quickly for the single case available for each. They duly did.

As the years went by, production increased and the marketing became rather more difficult as dozens of other wineries opened for business in the Hunter Valley, where Brokenwood Winery was situated. But for the next ten vintages an expanded partnership, which I effectively managed, continued to handle all aspects of viticulture, winemaking and marketing. It took virtually every weekend and all of my holidays, but it was fun even though production had neared 3,000 cases.

Even as I was engaged in the search for the land at the end of the 1960s, I was writing my first wine articles, initially for wine and food magazines (*Epicurean* and *Australian Gourmet*) and then for a national daily newspaper. One thing led to another, and in 1978 I was commissioned to write my first book, which was published by McGraw Hill in 1979. *The Wines and History of the Hunter Valley* was the first of 24 books. As I recall, I wrote most of it during the Easter of 1978, although I had previously spent a considerable amount of time researching the history in the New South Wales public library.

The compressed time frame was due to the fact that I was by then managing partner of a substantial and rapidly growing Sydney law firm and also carried on an active practice in public company takeovers and leveraged leasing of aircraft for major international airlines. The compensation was that I was in no sense dependent on winewriting as a source of income and could afford the expensive pastime of running a boutique winery. Without my being aware of it, it also insulated me from the conflict of interest pressures which might have otherwise taken their toll.

Somehow or other I managed to help make wine in Bordeaux (in Graves, making both dry red and Sauternes) in 1979 and in Burgundy (at Domaine Dujac) in 1983. During the latter part of the 1970s and into the 1980s I became actively involved in importing wine, chiefly as a consultant. I came to California on several occasions, first in 1979, and selected the first container of super-premium wines to be imported into Australia. Later that year I met Bruce Cass, without whose help this book could not have been written. My attention switched increasingly to France (and Italy), and I became a regular visitor to Europe.

In 1983 I moved to Melbourne to start the Melbourne office of my law firm. Brokenwood had hired a winemaker and general manager prior to that vintage, and it was in good hands (and has since flourished). Having sold my interest in Brokenwood my plan was to start making wine in the Yarra Valley (one-and-a-half hours east of Melbourne) from the 1985 vintage and onwards, buying grapes and using custom crush facilities. By 1988, when I planned to retire, I would have a nest egg of four vintages to cushion the blow of lost legal income as I then established my own vineyard and winery. I duly made the 1985 vintage — all 400 cases of it — at another winery, relying chiefly on grapes grown by one of my law partners. But later that same year an exceptionally beautiful 40-acre hillside property and house came on the market: I heard about it in early August, purchased it two weeks later (with 100% borrowed funds) and went to Europe on a long planned six-week sabbatical leave. Four weeks after my return I planted 12 acres of vineyard, forming the nucleus of what is now Coldstream Hills.

For the next two-and-a-half years I commuted daily to Melbourne, leaving home around 6:15 A.M. and seldom returning before 7:30 P.M., writing my wine column (and even books) on the train each day. From the verandah of my house I could see (and can still see) the building which housed my law office: as I looked out from my 31st floor office to the distant hills I knew that if I had the eyes of an eagle I could see my house and vineyard. It wasn't an easy time, particularly when I was getting up before dawn to begin pruning for an hour from first light before heading off for the office.

When, five months before my 50th birthday, I retired from my legal practice, it was not before time. By a quirk of fate, an adjoining property had come onto the market in late 1987 just as a 30,000-case capacity winery was being built at the vineyard. Coldstream Hills became Coldstream Winemakers Limited, a small second board company listed on the stock exchange, the only way I could raise the money to acquire the 36-acre property and plant a further 25 acres of vines (the rest of the property being taken up with dams, a house and farm buildings which are now insulated warehouses).

The poacher and gamekeeper role has also surfaced in my 20-year career as a wine show judge, although by and large I declined to enter wines in shows which I judged. I am a fervent supporter of the Australian wine show system, which has no parallel anywhere else in the world and which has played a very important role in developing the quality and style of Australian wine.

I relate this personal history to explain why I should have the gall to imagine that I could write a book about the California wine industry without having lived in the United States. It also explains how I approached the subject.

During my time in California I visited over 300 wineries, driving 15,000 miles and tasting 1,500 wines, primarily in blind tastings in San Francisco. I visited every wine region from the Anderson Valley to Temecula, from the Santa Cruz Mountains to the Sierra Foothills. I taped countless hours of interviews, sent one 44-pound U.S. mail bag back to Australia full of printed information, and broke all records with the weight of my suitcase, filled with more books and papers.

As I crisscrossed the state, Bruce Cass sat in San Francisco making endless phone calls to set up the schedule for the following day, which would typically cover 200 miles and ten wineries, faxing it through to my last port of call on the previous day. The days started at 8 A.M. and finished late; winemaker interviews were conducted in verbal shorthand, but were immensely informative and rewarding.

Unfailingly I was greeted with the friendship and cooperation which are the hallmark of the wine industry everywhere in the world. In what other industry could you walk onto the premises and say, "I am a winemaker, and hence in competition with you. Tell me all you know, how you make your wine, and what changes you have in mind."? Yet the international brotherhood of wine is such that you will be welcomed and your questions will be answered. This, indeed, is one of the chief reasons why wine has drawn so many doctors, lawyers, scientists and others with tertiary qualifications into its web.

To say I enjoyed my time in California is a masterly understatement. Notwithstanding the ravages of phylloxera, the California wine industry is alive and well. It has its stereotypes, be they winemakers, wines or winery edifices. So does any business, and it is all too easy to lampoon those stereotypes. The reality is quite different: there is tremendous diversity, originality and vibrancy. There are the Taj Mahals, but there are far more simple, functional wineries run by owner-winemakers driven by a burning desire to make better wine this vintage than ever before. The sadness is that some will fail, not because of lack of skill or commitment, but because hand-crafting fine wine is an expensive pastime, a fact insufficiently recognized by either the media or the public.

Wine is an increasingly international product. Hitherto, California has basically been content to sell its wine within the United States, and — thanks to archaic state laws — primarily within California. While the United States may be unable to disassemble its internal trade barriers against wine by the end of this century, the many great wines of California will surely appear on the best wine lists of the world and in the top cellars of Europe. They deserve no less.

ABOVE ~ *Artist's studio, Calistoga.*

Climate

The more I learn, the less I know: this has been observed in many disciplines over many centuries by people far wiser than I. It applies with particular force to our attempts to describe and quantify climate, or at least climate as it affects grape growing. My uncertainty stems in part from over 20 years as a vineyard owner (and winemaker) in two utterly different parts of Australia, an experience which has brought me face to face with the daily realities of grape growing and the knowledge that the climate of one part of a relatively small vineyard can be distinctly different from that of another part.

At the risk of digressing, I should give here three definitions. *Microclimate* is a term which (properly speaking) refers to the climate within or immediately adjacent to the canopy of the vine. *Mesoclimate* is the climate of a limited area, unified by its altitude and particular topographic characteristics: it may or may not be synonymous with "site climate," which is also used to denote a vineyard or part of a vineyard within a mesoclimate. (Site climate and microclimate are often confused, but shouldn't be.) Finally, there is *macroclimate,* which is that of a general region or American Viticultural Area (AVA), derived from one or more official recording sites.

While I am on the subject of definitions, I should also draw the distinction between climate and weather. Climate is the aggregation of the weather of a given region collected on an hour by hour, day by day basis and averaged over a long period of time. Meteorologists and climatologists are openly contemptuous of those who see the weather as being unusual simply because it does not accord with the experience of last year, or the last five years. It is precisely such variations which go to make up the climate and which explain the differences both in ten-year and 100-year accumulations.

Since I have ventured down this track, let me go further. In the midst of the debate about climate change and the greenhouse effect, a remarkable book entitled *Times of Feast, Times of Famine: A History of Climate Since the Year 1000* by Emmanuel Le Roy

ABOVE ~ *Early morning fog shrouds the Napa Valley floor, but will be gone before noon.*

Ladurie should be compulsory reading for any journalist or media commentator trying to present a balanced view of the issues. By studying the advance and retreat of the European glaciers, the start of the harvest in French vineyards (immaculately recorded by the monasteries which dominated viticulture for the first half of this millennium), and the growth rings in California redwoods, Ladurie has presented a detailed picture of the climate of the past 1,000 years.

Ladurie demonstrates periods of warming greater than the one projected by the prophets of greenhouse doom and periods of drought in California which make those of recent times (the mid 1980s for example) pale into insignificance. His research was supported by a French-Soviet team at Vostok Antarctic research station, which drilled a 6,560-foot deep ice-core. It shows that between 150,000 and 130,000 years ago there was a massive warming of the earth from temperatures well below those of today to above those predicted by the most radical greenhouse prophets, matched by a rise in carbon dioxide concentrations in the atmosphere from 190 parts per million to 300 parts per million (concentrations which declined, along with temperature, to 175 parts per million 45,000 years ago). We have (figuratively) seen it all before.

My uncertainty about describing climate was intensified by my research for various books including my *Wine Atlas of Australia and New Zealand*. In that book I attempted to describe and define the climate of the wine regions of Australia through a multi-faceted system developed by Dr. Richard Smart (then an academic but now an international viticultural consultant well known in California) and Peter Dry.

This approach measures the heat degree day summation (which I return to shortly); the mean July temperature (January for Australia); the mean annual range or continentality index (which is the difference between the mean July temperature and the mean January temperature, with the highest figures denoting a continental climate, the lowest a maritime climate); mean sunshine hours during the growing period; aridity (the difference between growing season rainfall and 50% evaporation); and humidity, calculated as the mean for July at 9 A.M.

All of these factors are acknowledged by expert viticulturists and enologists to affect the way the vine grows, the way it ripens its grapes, and the color and flavor it bestows on those grapes. But at the end of the day, I really doubt whether such a maze of figures is of much use to the average reader or even to the average viticulturist: how one determines the relative importance of each is a threshold question, and there are many more.

So in describing climate in this book I have elected to do as the Romans do and used the tried and true Winkler and Amerine heat degree summation system, which works as follows:

Region I	less than 2,500°F
Region II	2,501–3,000°F
Region III	3,001–3,500°F
Region IV	3,501–4,000°F
Region V	4,001–4,500°F

The summation system derives from the observation in 1855 by a French scientist, A.P. de Candolle, that vines start their active growth in the spring when the mean air temperature reaches 50°F. Winkler and Amerine calculated the effective heat available for growth over the seven-month growing season from April to October inclusive by measuring the difference between 50°F and the mean temperature for each day and then aggregating the monthly totals.

The system has been criticized by many: Australian scientist J.T.O. Kirk has described it as "a one-dimensional blurring or obliteration of climate dissimilarities." Furthermore, the mean temperature is calculated by adding the maximum and minimum temperatures and dividing by two. This gives a different result from taking the average of the temperature measured continuously over the 24-hour period, realistically at hourly intervals but theoretically at even closer intervals.

The distinction between mean and true average temperature becomes important when considering the difference between (say) the climate of the Napa Valley floor and the adjacent mountain tops or between the North Coast and the Central Coast. Thus if St. Helena has a daily range of 95°F and 50°F, but with fog in the morning, sea breezes in the afternoon, and only a short period of temperature above 85°F, it will nonetheless have a higher mean temperature than the mountain top which has a lower maximum, a similar minimum but — because of the absence of fog — more effective heat during the day.

This, I am sorry to say, is only the beginning. In the most up-to-date and thought-provoking book on the whole subject, *Viticulture and Environment* by Dr. John Gladstones (Winetitles, Australia 1992, but available in the United States through the *Practical Winery Magazine*), he suggests that the optimum mean temperature for ripening grapes is between 68°F and 72°F and that vines reach their maximum rate of photosynthesis (and hence growth) between 73°F and 77°F. The higher the temperature above that level, the lower the rate of growth. The reason is that the vine seeks to protect itself against dehydration by progressively shutting down its photosynthetic system. Wind causes a similar effect, leading to closure of the vine's stomata and hence the photosynthetic system. From these observations he has developed a highly sophisticated concept of biologically effective degree days, in part by eliminating the top end of the temperature scale just as Winkler and Amerine cut off the bottom end.

Yet for all its imperfections, the Winkler and Amerine system does give a simple, single-unit description of climate which certainly gives a valid relative guide, and I have not hesitated to use it, along with rainfall, as the basic climate index.

But what of the climate of California, both in its own right and compared to other winemaking countries around the world? It seems to me that relatively few Californians — be they winemakers, wine writers or consumers — fully realize what an extraordinary climate California has. Certainly, I know of no correlative elsewhere. (In speaking of the climate of California, I am talking of that from Santa Barbara to Mendocino, and hence deliberately engaging in broad generalizations.)

Were it not for the Pacific Ocean, and in particular the current which sweeps down from Alaska, there would not be a premium wine industry at all, or at least not a table wine industry. It would simply be too hot; indeed, it is the heat of the Central Valley (and corresponding areas further south) which

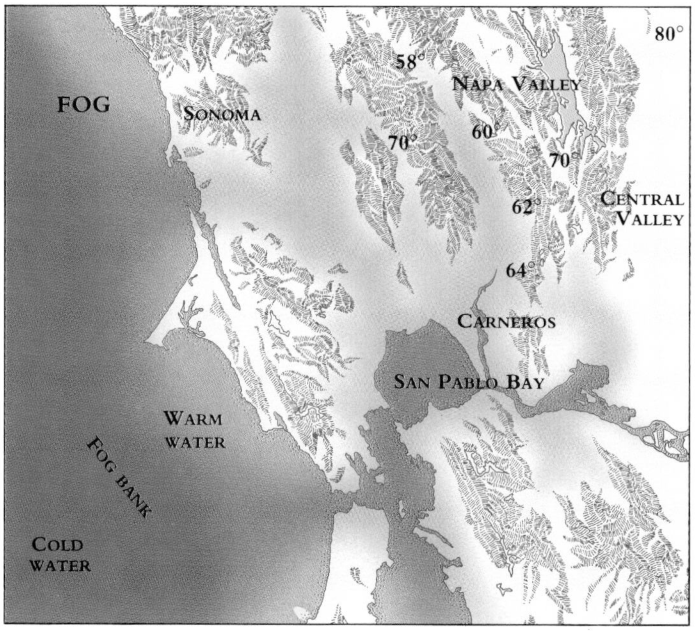
FOG
SONOMA
NAPA VALLEY
CENTRAL VALLEY
CARNEROS
SAN PABLO BAY
WARM WATER
FOG BANK
COLD WATER
80°
58°
70°
60°
70°
62°
64°

8 a.m. — Fog has moved in overnight through Petaluma gap and from San Pablo Bay, pulled inwards by warm air rising from Central Valley. Hillside (1,500') temperatures are warmer as they are above the level of the fog.

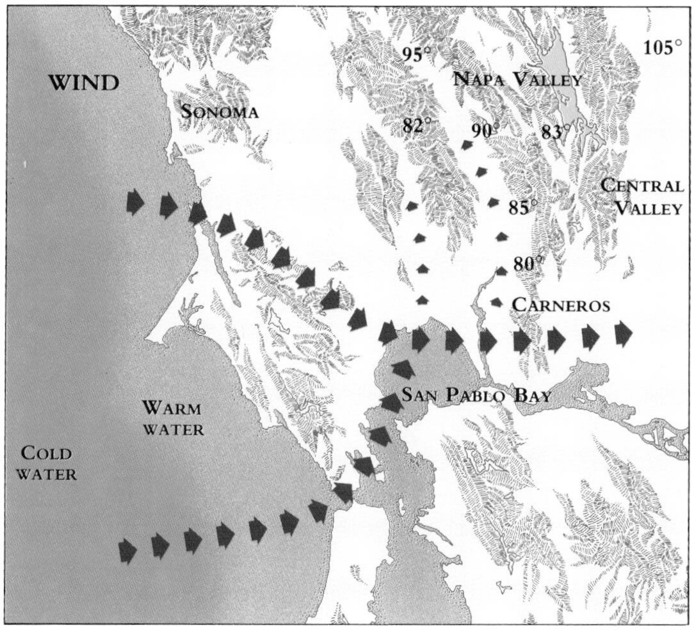
WIND
SONOMA
NAPA VALLEY
CENTRAL VALLEY
CARNEROS
SAN PABLO BAY
WARM WATER
COLD WATER
105°
95°
82°
90°
83°
85°
80°

Noon — Fog has burnt off between 10 and 11 a.m. leading to a rise in Napa Valley temperatures. Wind has started to sweep across Carneros, drawn by Central Valley air rising. Marine influence wanes as the valleys go north, often leading to a one-degree-per-mile temperature increase. The hillsides are cooler because of the effect of elevation.
4 p.m. — Marine influence extends up the valley to cool temperatures with afternoon breezes.

provides the energy to drive what can best be described as a massive air-conditioning system.

Actually, this is the first of two energy sources. The second is the high pressure systems which move north up the Pacific Ocean and out to sea. These cause westerly winds to blow over long distances, picking up moisture from the ocean. They also — as they veer south towards the coast because of the Coriolis Force — cause a strong southward-running surface current which moves away from the coast at a 45-degree angle. This in turn causes a continuous upwelling of cold water from depths of 200 to 300 feet throughout spring and summer. This is 10°F to 15°F colder than the water it replaces and makes the warm air above condense, producing the North Coast marine fog layer which forms a menacing wall out to sea, day after day.

Meanwhile, as the season starts to warm, the days grow longer and the sun's arc moves to the north, the inland valleys — and most of all the massive bladder of the Central Valley — heat up during the day. As the heat intensifies, the air rises, causing the atmospheric pressure to drop. Two forces are now at work. One is the prevailing northwesterly wind which does the pushing; the other is the vacuum or sucking effect of the interior valleys. The net result is a huge inflow of cold, foggy marine air through the San Francisco and Monterey Bays and the various gaps (notably the Petaluma Gap in the north) in the coastal mountain ranges. For the outsider who does not take the phenomenon for granted, being on or near the Golden Gate Bridge late on a summer's afternoon is a near-apocalyptic experience: winds spring up from nowhere, the fog cascades down the hillsides and the temperature drops like a stone.

From a distance, the fog appears on ridge lines and starts to slip down like a tablecloth pulled by a giant, unseen hand. As evening falls, the fog continues to flood inland, filling all of the coastal valleys. Early one morning in mid August, Randy Dunn flew me over the Napa Valley in his plane: I had driven up from a gray-skied valley, through the fog on the sides of Howell Mountain, and then to the airstrip at Angwin above the fog. As we took off and climbed higher, we had a view of a continuous sea of fog from Healdsburg in the north to Santa Clara and Monterey in the south, made dramatic and beautiful by the mountains rending the damask cloth of the fog, their jewel-like vineyards thrown into sharp relief by the sun's early rays.

By 10 or 11 A.M. the heat of the sun burns the fog away: it does not move upward or out to sea, but simply disappears. Because it normally lies above the valley floor level it does not actually wet the vines, it certainly increases the humidity and (of course) reduces the temperature. In the afternoon sea breezes will follow, relatively gently if they precede another foggy night, stronger if they do not.

For this cycle works in phases. When the Central Valley has sucked in enough fog and marine air, its temperatures abate and an equilibrium exists with the ocean coast. The system rests; the fog remains offshore; the Central Valley commences to build up heat once again, and the coastal regions experience northwesterly winds in advance of the fog cycle starting once again.

To say that the topography of California is convoluted is a masterly understatement; the series of north-south running valleys of the North Coast with their intervening mountain ranges are almost as impressive on the digital relief maps produced by the U.S. Geological Survey for the Department of the Interior as they are in the flesh. It is easy to see why the coastal influence diminishes rapidly as one valley succeeds another and why the temperature gradient within each of the valleys operates as it does.

Whether one is talking of California's usual north-south (or south-north) alignment, there is a rule of thumb which holds remarkably true. For each mile up (or down) a valley that the marine air travels, add 1°F to the temperature. (The same holds true, moving inland, for the east-west valleys of Santa Barbara.) In the simplest terms, it explains why Carneros has a Region I climate, Calistoga a Region IV climate; why Maison Deutz at the western end of the little Arroyo Grande AVA has a sub-region I climate, that of Saucelito Canyon at the eastern end a Region III climate.

The only regions not significantly affected by the marine influence are the northern and southern ends of the Central Valley (only the area south of Stockton grows grapes, if you accept Lodi as significantly marine-influenced), along with Clear Lake AVA in Mendocino — which, like Mendocino proper is said to be a transitionary climate between marine and continental. Even the Sierras claim a moderating influence, but one suspects that here (as at Clear Lake) altitude plays as big a role as the marine breezes.

But for Sonoma, and the Napa Valley, western Mendocino (notably the Russian River), Monterey, Paso Robles and the Edna, Santa Maria and Santa Ynez Valleys, it is the Pacific fogs and breezes which fundamentally shape the climate. It is why, indeed, one has the curious phenomenon that as you move south from San Francisco towards the equator, and towards the latitudes which worldwide mark the limits of wine grape growing, the climate (of those short east-west valleys in Santa Barbara County) is no warmer than that of the Willamette Valley, so far to the north in Oregon.

The other feature of the majority of the North Coast regions of California is the high daily (or diurnal) temperature range. It is the deeply embedded belief of every grape grower in these regions that the cold nights are essential and beneficial, as they inhibit the respiration of acid. This extreme diurnal range, coupled with the abnormally high sunshine hours throughout the growing season, constitutes a combination unique to California.

If one accepts the scientific research which suggests that intermediate temperatures best promote the ripening of the grapes and the creation of coloring and flavoring components through enzyme activity, and that ripening can continue unabated during the night, you come to the conclusion that the best climate is that which provides the most even accumulation of heat. Indeed, Australian viticulturists and researchers suggest that the best site within a given region will be the one which ripens its grapes the most quickly, a view paralleled by the European experience that the early vintages are the best. Thus, if one had a climate in which the accumulation of sugar and pigments in the grapes continued unabated, that accumulation would very likely keep pace with the decrease in acidity — but without the stop-start sequence of very cold nights and very hot days. It is almost certainly one of the reasons why the Santa Barbara climate produces such high quality Chardonnay and Pinot Noir.

Of course, the climate of the North Coast works particularly well for some varieties, but a consequence does appear to be the necessity of achieving relatively high sugar levels (and hence alcohol) before adequate flavor develops, and likewise the retention of fairly high malic acid levels in varieties such as Chardonnay.

Finally, there are California's bone-dry growing seasons. Almost everywhere in California, 80% of the rainfall falls between October and February. That rainfall varies between six inches and 30 inches (a few mountain regions receive more), with the greatest percentage of land under vine receiving between six inches and 16 inches. Technically, much of the Central Valley and Monterey's Salinas Valley is desert.

The aridity of the growing season has two major consequences: utter reliance on irrigation in the major valleys, and a climate ideally suited to the development of organic viticulture. Even areas such as Sonoma and the Napa Valley, which receive enough rainfall to make irrigation necessary, are nonetheless conducive to organic viticulture. It is a situation which California growers will surely turn to their advantage.

ABOVE ~ *Cabernet Sauvignon at Beckstoffer, Rutherford.*

SOIL

The soils of California reflect its tortured and still highly active geology as well as the unimaginable forces created by the movements of the Pacific Plate, the Farralon Plate and the North American Plate. One hundred and fifty million years ago the West Coast ended at the Sierra Mountains (which were then much lower than they are today). The present three series of coastal ranges north of San Francisco were originally formed as a submarine accretion of the shells of microscopic plankton a mile thick.

Eventually, however, massive volcanic activity (especially at fault lines), constant erosion and the offsetting rise in the Sierra Mountains caused by plate movements broke up the simple marine accretion. One major geological influence was the occurrence of submarine slides (also known as turbidity currents). These were created when massive earthquakes caused sand and rock which had loosened and eroded from the western sides of the Sierras to slide downhill underwater. It is estimated these huge slurries could travel 100 miles in 10 hours, creating the alluvial fans of today.

As the North American Plate moved west, overriding the Farallon Plate, the sea bottom was thrust up, initially leaving inland seas. Ultimately these, too, drained. Even this was not a simple or peaceful process, with tipping, faulting, volcanic eruptions and erosion all breaking up the surface. These processes explain why the soils of the Sonoma and Napa Valleys are constituted of deformed and faulted sandstone and shale; pieces of oceanic crust; blocks of oceanic sediment basically composed of radiolarion (plankton) shells in the form of silica; and the Franciscan Melange, which is a mixture of all of the above. In the last 30 million years the North American Plate completely overrode the Farallon Plate, and now meets (and overrides) the Pacific Plate at the San Andreas fault. All of the land west of the San Andreas fault is moving northwest at the rate of half an inch a year.

The east-west valleys of Santa Barbara County and the Salinas Valley were likewise once marine, and calcareous (lime) deposits make up a large portion of their structure. So when would-be vignerons go searching for coveted limestone (in one form or another) they should find it without undue difficulty. Only the oldest mountain soils, leached by millennia of rain, are acidic: most of California's soil is either close to neutral or alkaline, conditions which greatly favor the growth of the vine. (Australia's far more ancient soils and subsoils are significantly more acidic.)

These ancient forces which shaped the landscape were modified by changes wrought in the soil patterns during the last few hundred thousand years — a mere speck in geological time.

ABOVE ~ *New plantings, northwest of Napa township.*

Rivers have waxed and waned and wandered back and forth across valleys, moving sand, earth and rock from mountains, and from one place in the valley to another. Then in the last few hundred years humans have damaged the topsoil in ways that nature could not have achieved in a million years. The dustbowls of the Midwest are the most shameful examples, but the long-term consequences of the massive reshaping of California's water resources may be equally dire, whatever the short-term gain.

So much for the background. What specific influences do the California soils have on vine growth and grape quality? Is the California (and Australian) belief that climate is more important than soils justified? And, if it is, how much less important is soil? In order to deal with this issue, it is necessary to introduce the concept of *terroir,* a key French term which incorporates soil. Bruno Prats, the owner of Chateau Cos-d'Estournel in Bordeaux, has given the best single definition of *terroir:* "The very French notion of the *terroir* looks at all the natural conditions which influence the biology of the vinestock and thus the composition of the grape itself. The *terroir* is the coming together of the climate, the soil and the landscape. It is the combination of an infinite number of factors: temperatures by night and by day, rainfall distribution, hours of sunlight, soil acidity, presence of minerals, depth, water-retention, exposure to sunlight, slope and drainage, to name but a few. All these factors react with each other to form, in each part of the vineyard, what Fench wine growers call a *terroir.*"

If the concept of terroir is properly understood, and if one ignores the unscientific propaganda trotted out by public relations personnel on both sides of the Atlantic, there is a surprising measure of agreement: soil structure (and to a lesser degree soil texture) is the most important factor; soil type (in terms of mineralogical and organic composition) is the least important.

Take the Burgundian belief that limestone is all-important in the production of great Burgundy. It is true that limestone is the basic soil type, and no less true that the Burgundians can indeed produce the greatest Pinot Noir and Chardonnay. But are the chemical or the mechanical properties of limestone most important? Soil pH can be adjusted, and in any event most authorities agree that there is no direct relationship between soil minerals and grape flavor.

The answer lies in the high growing season rainfall of Burgundy and in the free-draining nature of limestone. Why on earth should limestone be critical in the bone dry summer hillsides of Mount Harlan, where Josh Jensen has his vineyards? I am not for a moment suggesting that the soils are a disadvantage or in any way unsuitable, but I strongly suspect other mountain soils could do the job equally well.

Monsieur G. Seguin, from the Institute of Enology at the University of Bordeaux, makes two fundamental points:

In the climate-soil-vine ecosystem it is difficult, when studying soil in isolation, to determine its influence on the constitution and the quality of grapes and wines. Moreover, human factors must be added to the natural factors, since the wine grower may happen to transform the characteristics and properties of the soil with soil conditioners, chemical manures and sometimes with irrigation. For any given mesoclimate, plant and soil, he can, by means of training systems, modify the forwardness, quantity and quality of the harvest.

(I would also add that the winemaker can fundamentally modify grape character during winemaking by practices such as removing part of the free-run juice from red musts prior to fermentation, acid additions, partial or total whole bunch fermentation, malolactic fermentation, use of new oak, choice of yeasts, and so on and so forth.)

Seguin's second point is that it is the water control qualities of the soil (and subsoil) structure which determine the quality of a given site. He argues that a steady, moderate availability of moisture is essential for the production of the highest quality grapes, and that this is best achieved in free-draining, well-aerated soils which promote deep root growth and which have moderate water retention capacities. In these circumstances the vine's reaction to periods of drought or excess rainfall will be minimized.

Gravelly alluvial soils, clay loams and limestone and chalk subsoils and rubbles can all provide such environments. Dr. John Gladstones' *Viticulture and Environment* also emphasizes the importance of gravelly, rocky or cobbly soils: not only are these well drained and aerated, but they store heat by day and re-radiate it at night, providing a thermal blanket which aids vine growth.

Both Gladstones and Seguin agree that the best soils are typically found on the lower slopes of hills and valley sides, and on terraces and alluvial, gravelly fans. It is here, indeed, that the broader aspects of *terroir* come into play, for the topographic characteristics of the best vineyard sites can be summarized thus:

- They are on slopes with good air drainage and are typically situated above the fog level.
- They are usually on the slopes of projecting or isolated hills, or on benchlands.
- Even in hot areas, they face the sun directly during at least some part of the day.
- If inland, they tend to be close to substantial rivers or lakes.

A word, too, on irrigation. Research in California by the Robert Mondavi viticulturists, among others, suggests there is a large difference between vines grown on sandy soils in a hot climate (such as the Central Valley) or a cool climate (such as the Monterey Valley), and those grown in stronger, better structured soils. If the vine commences its spring growth in soils which have been taken to what is called field capacity (that is, saturated) by winter-spring rainfall, their roots will forage deep. When drip irrigation is applied later in the season, surface root growth will have ceased and will not directly respond to the water — which if applied by drip, in any event penetrates in an inverted cone-shaped pattern to some depth. So the idea that all irrigated vines are surface rooted is simply not correct. But, if they are grown in excessively well-drained, sandy soils, they will be surface rooted.

So, soil — as the principal component of *terroir* — is most important in determining the way the vine grows and the way in which it ripens its grapes. Some sites will be more suited to a given grape variety than to another, the degree of suitability being a complex function of *terroir* and climate. But there is no one soil which is so well suited to a given grape variety that one is able to construct general rules. Given the incredibly complex and fragmented nature of the California soil map, this is probably just as well.

AMERICAN VITICULTURAL AREAS

When I sat in Australia thinking about the planning of this atlas, it seemed to me that American Viticultural Areas (or AVAs) would be the fulcrum for the book. I am now wiser, if not sadder: I have certainly used them, but have discovered for myself the limitations, the inconsistencies, and the sheer irrationalities which virtually every commentator has exposed.

But first, what are AVAs, and when did they come into existence? They have been created pursuant to regulations set up by the Bureau of Alcohol, Tobacco and Firearms (which throughout this book I shall call the BATF) in 1978. Prior to that time, California wineries complied with a series of vague regulatory standards which permitted the use of various geographic names or indicators on their labels.

In ascending order of precision, the BATF recognizes the following appellations of origin for American wine:

1. The United States.
2. Two or three states which are all contiguous.
3. A state.
4. Two or three counties in the same state.
5. A county.
6. A viticultural area (AVA).

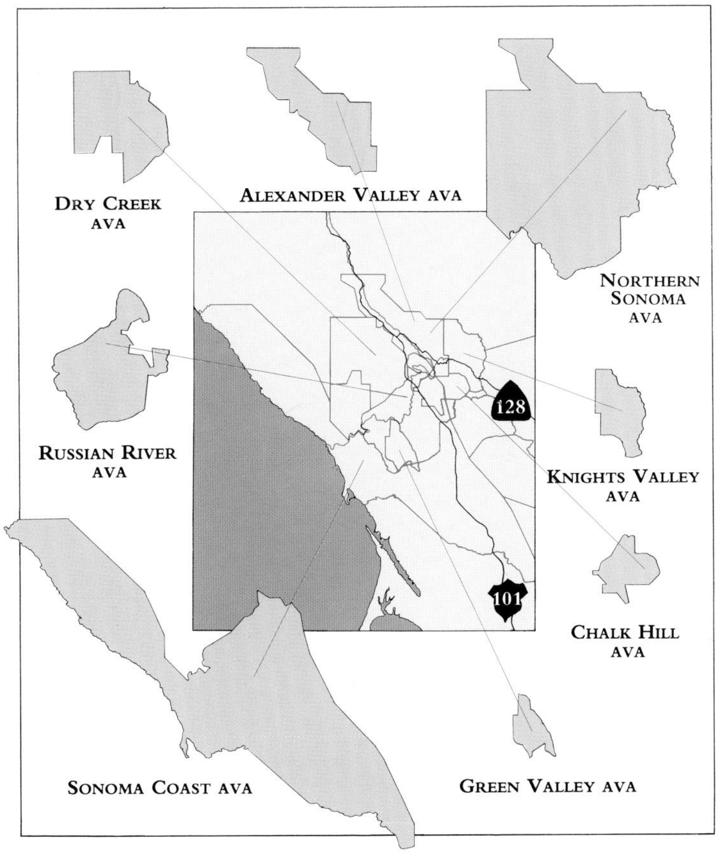
DRY CREEK AVA
ALEXANDER VALLEY AVA
NORTHERN SONOMA AVA
RUSSIAN RIVER AVA
128
KNIGHTS VALLEY AVA
101
CHALK HILL AVA
SONOMA COAST AVA
GREEN VALLEY AVA

An AVA is defined under the regulations as "a delimited grape growing region distinguished by geographical features, the boundaries of which have been recognized and defined ...." Anyone may petition for the establishment of an AVA, but must provide, among other things:

- evidence that the proposed name of the AVA is locally and/or nationally already known and recognized as referring to the area specified in the application;
- evidence relating to the geographical features (notably climate, soil, elevation and physical characteristics) which distinguish the viticultural features of the proposed AVA from the surrounding areas;
- the specific boundaries of the area, based on features which can be found on U.S. geological survey maps.

But if the BATF approves an AVA, it invariably makes four statements and disclaimers:

1. "BATF believes that the establishment of viticultural areas and the subsequent use of viticultural area names as appellations of origin in wine labeling and advertising will help consumers better identify the wines they purchase."

2. "The establishment of viticultural areas also allows wineries to specify more accurately the origin of wines they offer for sale to the public."

3. "BATF does not wish to give the impression by approving a viticultural area that it is approving or endorsing the quality of the wine from this area."

4. "BATF approves a viticultural area by finding that the area is distinct from surrounding areas, but not better than other areas."

As Dick Steltzner of the Napa Valley summarizes the implications and consequences: "The BATF cannot sustain or endorse quality in any manner; therefore they have written rules which preclude real examination. Thus if you accept these criteria, it becomes a me-too game. If anyone starts an AVA, others can say me-too and will always be added on. Infighting doesn't get you anywhere, because it is a granting of rights by an agency. The end result is that all areas are larger than they should be, and have physical boundaries (such as roads) which make no sense from a viticultural viewpoint."

A classic example of the me-too syndrome is the Alexander Valley AVA saga. In the ruling of November 23, 1984, which created the Alexander Valley, the BATF dilated at length on the opposing views of what is identified as group A (which argued for more restrictive boundaries) and group B (which argued for wider boundaries). Predictably, it ruled in favor of group B, but took it upon itself to conclude "that the eastern and northwestern boundaries proposed by group B encompass mountainous areas which lie outside the actual geographical and viticultural limits of the Alexander Valley ... and that the historical or current boundaries of the Alexander Valley have never included these areas. Accordingly the boundaries proposed by group B are modified to exclude these mountainous areas."

Between that time and September 10, 1990, the BATF underwent a frontal lobotomy. On receiving a petition from Gauer Ranch (and another mountain vineyard) situated high in the eastern mountains and having nothing to do with the valley floor viticulture, the BATF said it "mistakenly believed that there were no vineyards planted in the mountainous areas to the east of the eastern boundary line." It then proceeded to demonstrate that the soils throughout the valley and the mountainside are so varied and complex it is difficult to distinguish among them (although it did make the distinction, again erroneously it says, in its original ruling), and granted the petition.

Wendell Lee, counsel for the Wine Institute, then poses the question: "Without any government quality standards, does a label statement which indicates an AVA help the consumers better identify the wines they purchase? Many commentators have answered that question in the negative."

The reality is, of course, that even if the BATF wanted to venture into the realms of quality, and even more nebulously, into questions of style, it could not do so without retaining a bevy of specialist consultants. So evidence is trotted up to the BATF which goes through the motions of showing the area is distinct and different; objections are usually dealt with by including the objector (who is typically someone excluded by the application) in the area; and the application is granted.

But how, then, can there be multiple overlapping AVAs? And how can it possibly be said that these help consumers better identify the wines they purchase? Nowhere does this come into more chaotic, almost comical, relief than in Sonoma County. The map shows the end result of the following sequence of events:

AVA	**Date Approved**
Sonoma Valley	1.4.82
North Coast	10.21.83
Russian River Valley	11.21.83
Knights Valley	11.21.83
Chalk Hill	11.21.83
Sonoma Green Valley	12.21.83
Alexander Valley	11.23.84
Sonoma Mountain	2.22.85
Northern Sonoma	6.17.85
Alexander Valley Revision	9.25.86
Sonoma Coast	7.12.87
Alexander Valley Revision	9.10.90

Accepting the crazy patchwork quilt thus created, the most obvious feature is that there has not been, as one might expect, a progression from larger to smaller areas. Other than Sonoma County (which was not, of course, required to go through the AVA procedure), the largest designation is the most recent, the oddly shaped Sonoma Coast AVA.

So it is that a winery and vineyard situated just to the east of the town of Windsor could elect to label its wine in any one of the following ways: California, Sonoma County, Northern Sonoma, Sonoma Coast, Russian River Valley, or Chalk Hill. The intellectual nonsense that this makes of the system really needs no elaboration.

Chalk Hill and Sonoma Coast are examples of special interest AVAs, created to fit the specific needs of a particular winery. But there are other even more extreme examples of AVAs created for a single grape grower, such as the Cienega Valley, Lime Kiln Valley, and Paicines AVAs within the San Benito AVA.

Many intelligent winemakers have despaired of the system. Says Francis Mahoney of Carneros Creek, "We got too commercial, too quickly, before we could sit down and be honest with each other — and then we sat and watched water go uphill as they proclaimed the limits of the Napa Valley." He is referring to the fact that the Napa Valley's boundaries coincide with those of the county and include all manner of mountains and valleys as disconnected — in every way — as the Pope Valley.

The Napa Valley, of course, has seen the greatest argument and political intrigue, chiefly centered over the Rutherford Bench, an appellation recognized by authorities such as Hugh Johnson and Jancis Robinson before it was still-born. The continued fragmentation of the valley will continue, counterbalanced by the curious piece of California State legislation which requires any AVA situated entirely within Napa County (in other words, every AVA other than Carneros) to use the expression Napa Valley in direct conjunction with the AVA in typeface not smaller than 1 mm less than that used for the AVA.

Those who have despaired believe that specific vineyard or winery designations are the way of the future. If they are correct, the wheel will have turned full circle. In the meantime, and for better or worse, I have broadly followed — and certainly referred to — the existing AVA system in the structure of this atlas.

ABOVE ~ *The first Chardonnay and Pinot Noir to be planted in the Sonoma Valley, at Hanzell.*

GRAPE VARIETIES

California

1971, 1981 AND 1991 ACREAGE/GRAPE VARIETIES

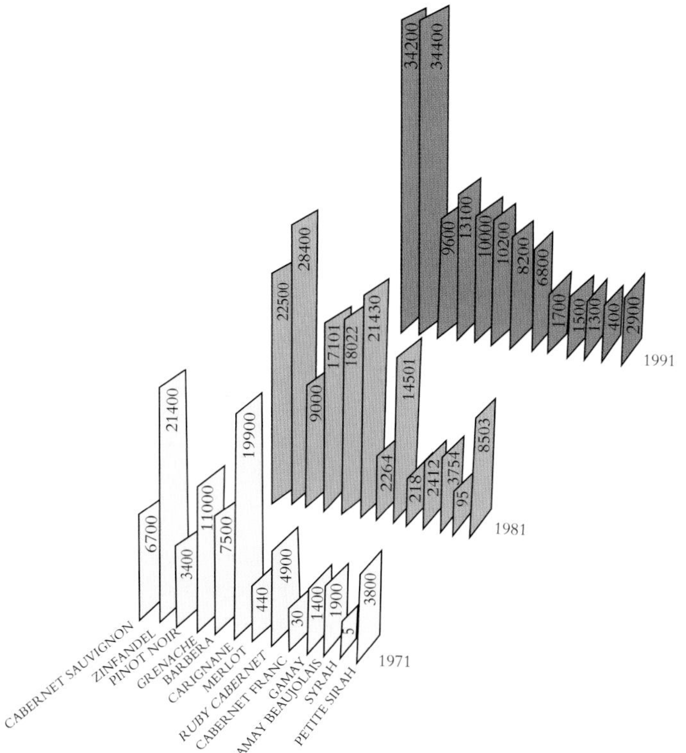
CABERNET SAUVIGNON
ZINFANDEL
PINOT NOIR
GRENACHE
BARBERA
CARIGNANE
MERLOT
RUBY CABERNET
CABERNET FRANC
GAMAY
GAMAY BEAUJOLAIS
SYRAH
PETITE SIRAH
1971
6700
21400
3400
11000
7500
19900
440
4900
30
1400
1900
5
3800
1981
22500
28400
9000
17101
18022
21430
2264
14501
218
2412
3754
95
8503
1991
34200
34400
9600
13100
10000
10200
8200
6800
1700
1500
1300
400
2900

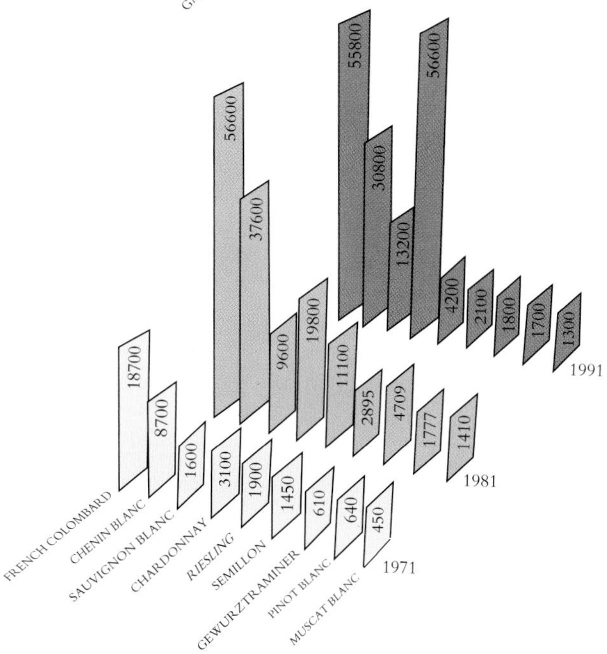
FRENCH COLOMBARD
CHENIN BLANC
SAUVIGNON BLANC
CHARDONNAY
RIESLING
SEMILLON
GEWURZTRAMINER
PINOT BLANC
MUSCAT BLANC
1971
18700
8700
1600
3100
1900
1450
610
640
450
1981
56600
37600
9600
19800
11100
2895
4709
1777
1410
1991
55800
30800
13200
56600
4200
2100
1800
1700
1300

Chardonnay

Chardonnay acreage finally overtook that of French Colombard in 1991, but the writing had been on the wall since 1985. From that year on, it had been the most widely planted variety, and it is now represented in 35 of the 42 counties in which wine grapes are planted.

Its performance in California is precisely the same as it has been worldwide over the past 20 years. The reasons lie in part with the worldwide swing from red wine to white wine, and in part with the inherent qualities of the variety. Those inherent qualities include its capacity to produce a wine which the public is

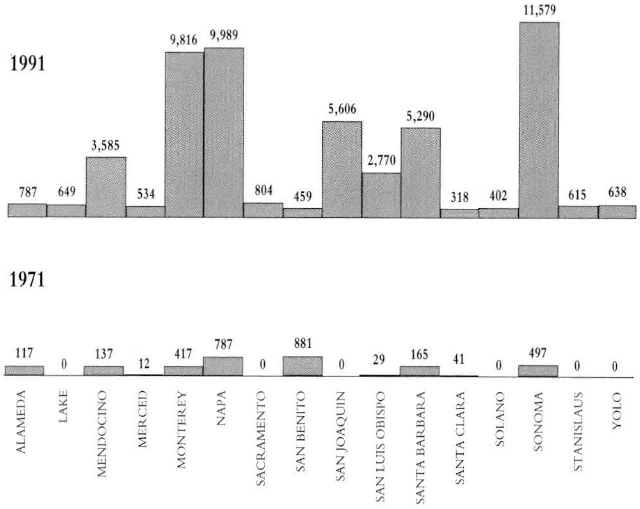
1991
787
649
3,585
534
9,816
9,989
804
459
5,606
2,770
5,290
318
402
11,579
615
638
1971
117
0
137
12
417
787
0
881
0
29
165
41
0
497
0
0
ALAMEDA
LAKE
MENDOCINO
MERCED
MONTEREY
NAPA
SACRAMENTO
SAN BENITO
SAN JOAQUIN
SAN LUIS OBISPO
SANTA BARBARA
SANTA CLARA
SOLANO
SONOMA
STANISLAUS
YOLO

prepared to accept as being of premium quality in almost any climate; its generous yield; and its flexibility in the winery, which is greater than that of any other variety.

It is possible to argue that this very flexibility is Chardonnay's Achilles heel, that familiarity may breed contempt. As I suggest on pages 340–1, it has become synonymous with white wine in the minds of many consumers. That argument does not impress me, any more than the oft-repeated statement that the public is tiring of Chardonnay. Just ask any retailer or restaurateur which white wine sells best and you will get the same answer whether you are in London, Sydney, Los Angeles or New York.

All that has happened is that Chardonnay is in the process of losing its God-given right automatically to command disproportionately high prices as a grape and as a wine. Increasingly, growers will have to ask themselves the question how much, if any, Chardonnay should they be growing, and winemakers will have to stop winemaking by formula (or peer group pressure).

French Colombard

California, South Africa, and lately Australia have taken this grape to their bosom for two reasons: its ability to retain acidity when grown in very warm climates, and its enormous yields. Therefore, in 1990 the average California yield was 11.7 tons per acre, a truly extraordinary figure. As the statistics show, it is a Central Valley variety; it is thus not surprising that it is seldom identified on the label of table wine, and even less frequently found as a cork finished, varietally identified product. For those who are interested in the taste of the wine, its acidity has a very particular oily characteristic. Incidentally, it is a fast-disappearing, third-ranked variety in its native Cognac in France. As the years go by in California, it is certain it will continue to decline in importance, even if it has proved more suitable than any of the crosses or hybrids bred for the ovens of the Central Valley.

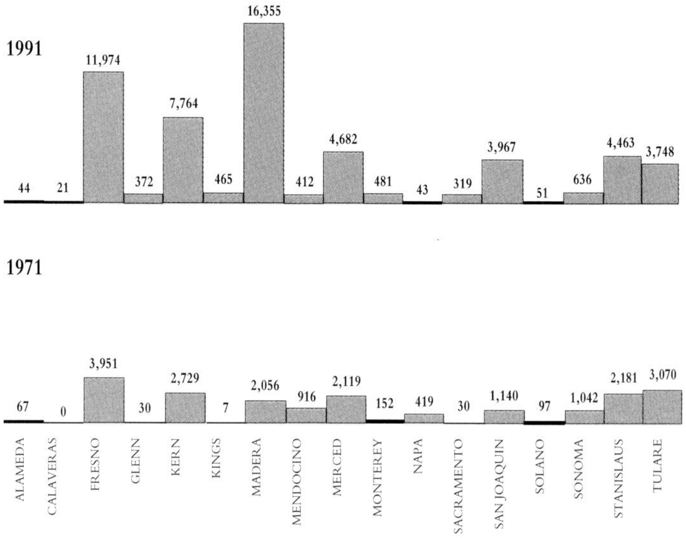
1991
44
21
11,974
372
7,764
465
16,355
412
4,682
481
43
319
3,967
51
636
4,463
3,748
1971
67
0
3,951
30
2,729
7
2,056
916
2,119
152
419
30
1,140
97
1,042
2,181
3,070
ALAMEDA
CALAVERAS
FRESNO
GLENN
KERN
KINGS
MADERA
MENDOCINO
MERCED
MONTEREY
NAPA
SACRAMENTO
SAN JOAQUIN
SOLANO
SONOMA
STANISLAUS
TULARE

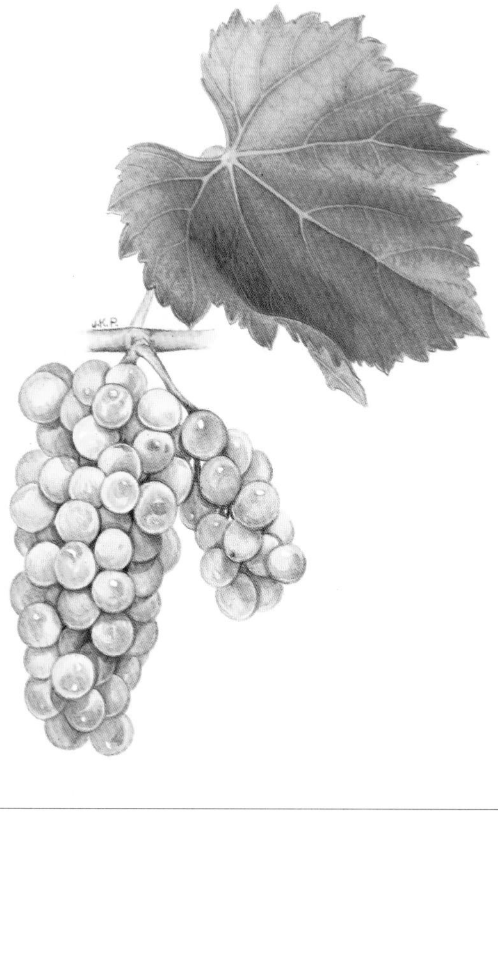

Chenin Blanc

In some ways Chenin Blanc is an alter ego of Colombard. Certainly, its role in California, South Africa (where it is dominant, traveling under its local name of Steen), and Australia is by and large on a par with French Colombard. It is in France that it shows its noble lineage, producing the fabulously long-lived (up to 100 years) and exceptionally complex wines of Vouvray and Bonnezaux in the Loire Valley, often aided by botrytis. It does not have the acid-retention capacity of Colombard but certainly yields generously — a capacity which has endeared it to Central Valley growers.

For all this damning by faint praise, it does have two homes-away-from-home in California: the Clarksburg AVA and Dry Creek Winery. To be fair, Monterey is also capable of producing pleasant wines. But even these most favored places and producers

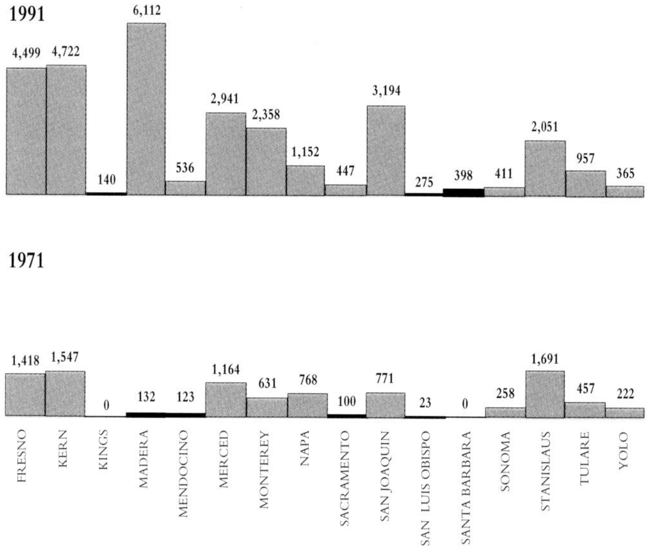
1991
4,499
4,722
140
6,112
536
2,941
2,358
1,152
447
3,194
275
398
411
2,051
957
365
1971
1,418
1,547
0
132
123
1,164
631
768
100
771
23
0
258
1,691
457
222
FRESNO
KERN
KINGS
MADERA
MENDOCINO
MERCED
MONTEREY
NAPA
SACRAMENTO
SAN JOAQUIN
SAN LUIS OBISPO
SANTA BARBARA
SONOMA
STANISLAUS
TULARE
YOLO

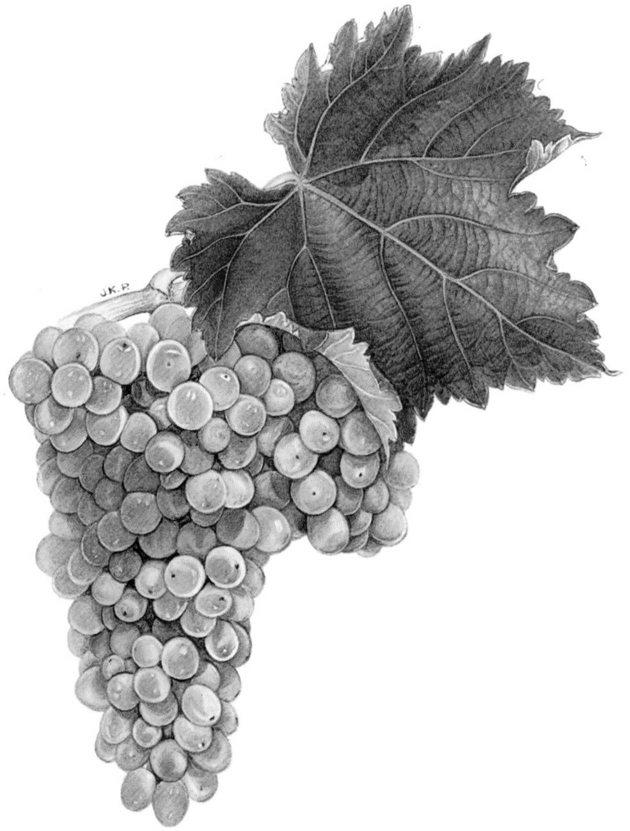

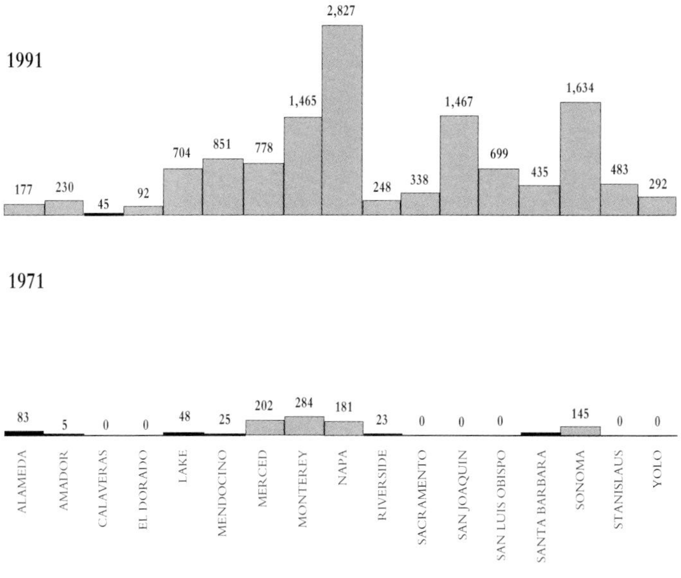
1991
177
230
45
92
704
851
778
1,465
2,827
248
338
1,467
699
435
1,634
483
292
1971
83
5
0
0
48
25
202
284
181
23
0
0
0
145
0
0
ALAMEDA
AMADOR
CALAVERAS
EL DORADO
LAKE
MENDOCINO
MERCED
MONTEREY
NAPA
RIVERSIDE
SACRAMENTO
SAN JOAQUIN
SAN LUIS OBISPO
SANTA BARBARA
SONOMA
STANISLAUS
YOLO

provide wines more notable for their softness and complaisance than their character, and no one (other, perhaps, than Gene Kirkham of Casa Nuestra in the Napa Valley) claims that the wine is especially ageworthy.

Sauvignon Blanc

While a long way short of French Colombard and Chenin Blanc in terms of acreage, it ranks second to Chardonnay in the premium white wine area. But it is fair to say that over the decades both California producers and the American wine buying public have had an uneasy relationship with the variety. When Robert Mondavi stepped in to grab it by the scruff of the neck in the 1970s, much of it was made with distinct residual sugar from grapes grown in the Central Valley and had no particular varietal character.

Mondavi took the sugar out and introduced new oak and a percentage of Semillon, calling the wine Fumé Blanc. Mondavi has constantly refined the style and basically marked the path for others to follow. Interestingly, the standard Fumé Blanc has become softer and less overtly varietal, although one could never accuse the Mondavi Reserve To-Kalon Fumé Blanc of lacking character. When makers such as Rochioli in the Russian River produce a crisp, unoaked, varietally exact wine with distinct herbaceous characteristics, opinions polarize. It is quite clear that a body of opinion either does not like or does not recognize (or both) the true flavor of Sauvignon Blanc. The argument, if you wish, is akin to that between White Bordeaux and Sancerre/Pouilly Fumé.

It may be partly for this reason that the vignerons of so many districts look you straight in the eye and say, "This is the greatest place for Sauvignon Blanc in California." Notable contenders include Lake County (with Clear Lake and the Potter Valley disputing regional leadership), the Napa Valley, the Livermore Valley, Monterey, the Russian River — and just about anywhere else you care to name.

Overall plantings have decreased slightly since 1985; I think this is more a reflection of market uncertainty than a comment on what is an underrated variety which produces far better wine than most Californians realize.

Riesling

Right around the world, Riesling has suffered from the dreadful mistakes made by the Germans both in growing the grapes and in marketing the wine. In the latter part of the nineteenth century, top class dry German Riesling was more expensive than First Growth Clarets and was often cellared for far longer. In the twentieth century yields have increased tenfold, Germany developed byzantine label laws and label designs, and Blue Nun became emblematic of German white wine — and hence Riesling — in the mind of the public, even though it was in fact largely Sylvaner.

The fact is that Riesling is a noble variety which, if grown in appropriate climates and not over-cropped, can make great wine. Nor is it necessary that the climate be as cold as that of Germany, as California and Australia (where the variety still vies with Chardonnay) have shown. Monterey and the Santa Ynez Valley are the two most significant producing areas, both in terms of quantity and quality, with Firestone leading the way. The Anderson Valley does well in a minor way, and the Russian River might do so if given a chance.

California has also shown it can produce superlative late harvest wines: Joseph Phelps, Chateau St. Jean, Renaissance and (from time to time) Firestone are among the best.

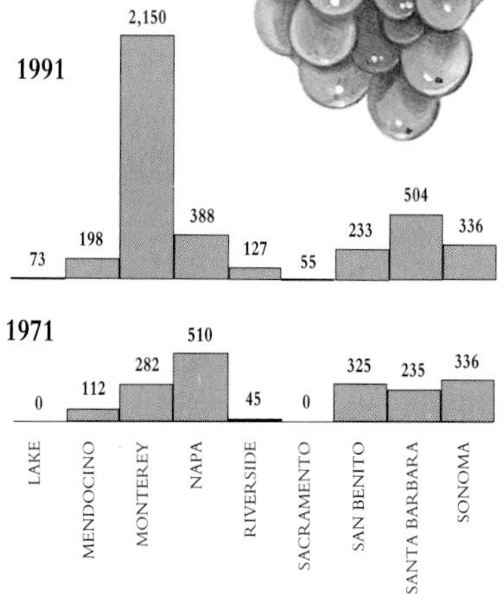
1991
73
198
2,150
388
127
55
233
504
336
1971
0
112
282
510
45
0
325
235
336
LAKE
MENDOCINO
MONTEREY
NAPA
RIVERSIDE
SACRAMENTO
SAN BENITO
SANTA BARBARA
SONOMA

Semillon

Semillon is grown in a surprisingly large number of counties but is nowhere dominant. While this no doubt partially reflects its climatic adaptability, it more importantly underscores its role in life as an often unmentioned component in Sauvignon Blanc, Fumé Blanc and Meritage wines. It seldom appears as a varietal in its own right.

Australia's experience with the grape suggests it deserves a better fate; the cynical might suggest it would help if its home were the Rhone Valley rather than Bordeaux. Pending a miracle rebirth, there is little suggestion it will escape the shackles. Kalin Cellars, Graeser and a few other small wineries join a couple of major makers such as Wente as significant producers.

Gewurztraminer

In many ways, this is the little brother — or sister — of Riesling, being a bit harder to sell through retail outlets and a bit easier to sell through the cellar door or mailing list — as the Anderson Valley's Navarro Winery so handsomely demonstrates. Incidentally, the best botrytised, late harvest Gewurztraminers I have ever tasted have been from California.

Pinot Blanc

This mutation of Pinot Noir lives a shadowy existence in many parts of the world, and California is no exception. What is notable is the amount used in the production of premium sparkling wine, with Deutz and Domaine Chandon among those who have espoused its cause. Chalone — in minuscule quantities — is the most prominent producer of table wine.

Muscat Blanc

It mystifies me why more of this variety has not been grown: it produces intensely fruity wines which are an ideal entry point for the novice consumer. It can be used in dry, semi-sweet and sparkling wines which are as cheerful as they are unpretentious.

Zinfandel

I have to admit to a certain degree of perverse pleasure in finding that as of 1991, California's most unique grape still held a tiny lead over Cabernet Sauvignon, and no less in finding that its plantings continue to increase at a rate much greater than even the high flying Merlot. However, when the 1992 figures come out I am sure Cabernet Sauvignon will be on top. What is more, much of the demand for Zinfandel — and hence the increased plantings — has derived from the phenomenal increase in the sales of Blush Zinfandel throughout the second half of the 1980s. But, as I say on page 269, the rate of increase has slowed to a crawl and future significant growth in Zinfandel plantings seems unlikely. It also seems unnecessary to point out that the massive San Joaquin plantings are largely devoted to the production of blush wines, however high the quality of Lodi Zinfandel may be.

The producers of red Zinfandel continue to fight the good fight; I discuss their problems — and their successes — on page 160. All I can do here is briefly restate my view that Zinfandel not only makes California's most unique wine but also one of its best.

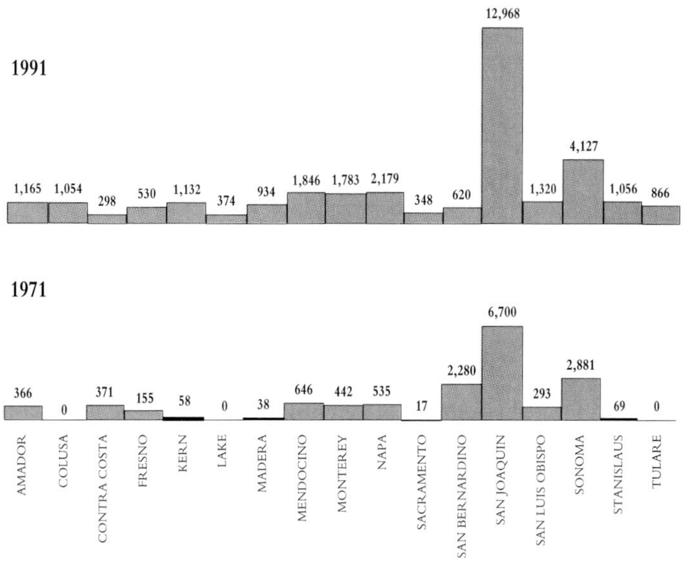
1991
1,165 1,054 298 530 1,132 374 934 1,846 1,783 2,179 348 620 12,968 1,320 4,127 1,056 866
1971
366 0 371 155 58 0 38 646 442 535 17 2,280 6,700 293 2,881 69 0
AMADOR
COLUSA
CONTRA COSTA
FRESNO
KERN
LAKE
MADERA
MENDOCINO
MONTEREY
NAPA
SACRAMENTO
SAN BERNARDINO
SAN JOAQUIN
SAN LUIS OBISPO
SONOMA
STANISLAUS
TULARE

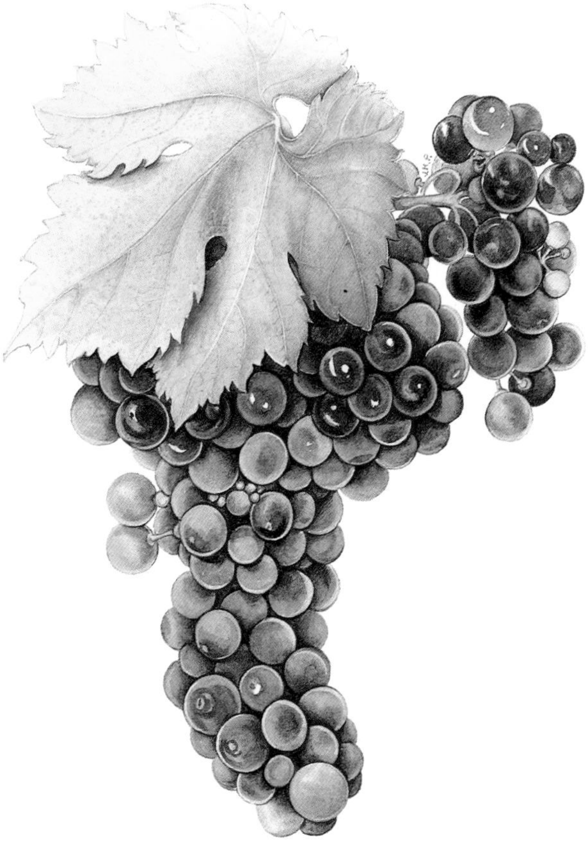

Cabernet Sauvignon

There is a natural affinity between Cabernet Sauvignon and much of the California North Coast growing conditions. It is perhaps partly for this reason that for 100 years Cabernet and quality — the best quality — have been regarded as synonymous. It is perfectly true that for the first 60 years of that symbiotic bond there wasn't much Cabernet Sauvignon, but quality has nothing to do with quantity. Of course, it must also be said that Cabernet Sauvignon is one of the world's great travelers, the polar opposite of Pinot Noir. Its thick skins, loose bunch formation and relatively small berries mean it stands up to rain and resists rot; the consequences of overcropping are unhappy but not disastrous; and while it produces a range of flavors reflecting the input of *terroir* and climate, it always retains a form of identifiable varietal character. In other words, presented with a glass of unknown wine anywhere in the world (assuming it to be well made and in sound condition) you will identify it first as Cabernet Sauvignon and second as California (or Napa Valley, or whatever).

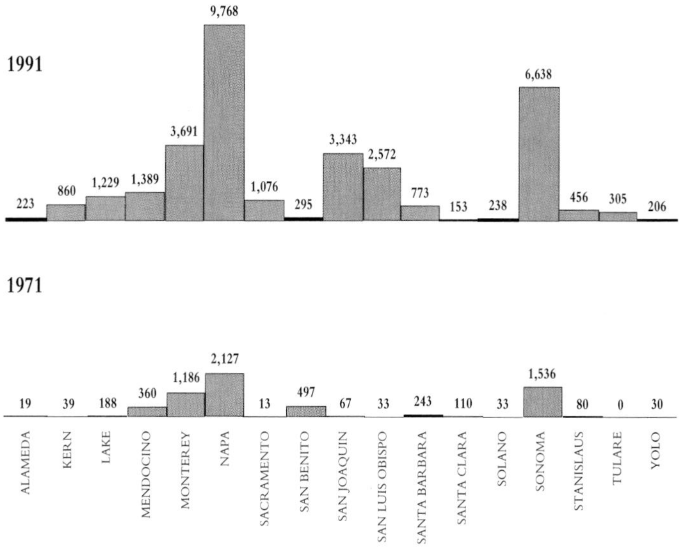
1991
223 860 1,229 1,389 3,691 9,768 1,076 295 3,343 2,572 773 153 238 6,638 456 305 206
1971
19 39 188 360 1,186 2,127 13 497 67 33 243 110 33 1,536 80 0 30
ALAMEDA
KERN
LAKE
MENDOCINO
MONTEREY
NAPA
SACRAMENTO
SAN BENITO
SAN JOAQUIN
SAN LUIS OBISPO
SANTA BARBARA
SANTA CLARA
SOLANO
SONOMA
STANISLAUS
TULARE
YOLO

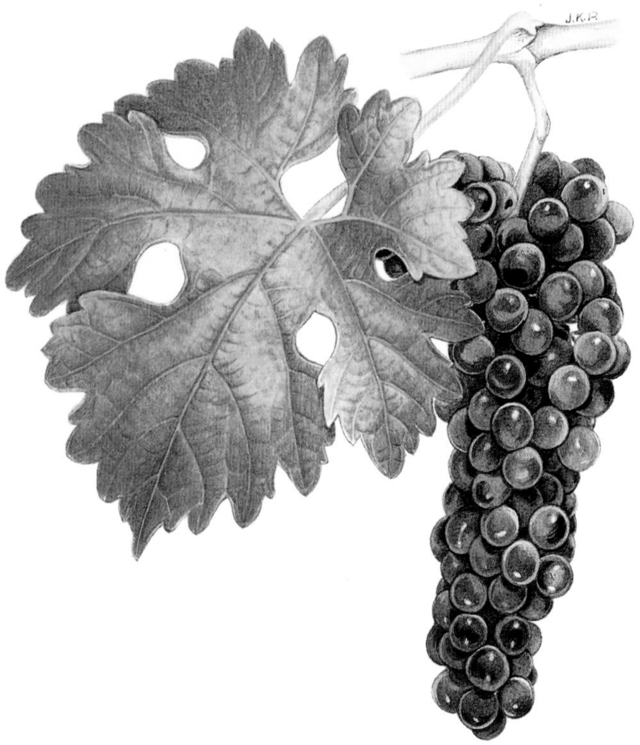

Grenache

A Central Valley workhorse, producing millions of gallons of soft, light, gently fruity jug wine in red, rosé or blush form. Unlike the other two workhorses, Barbera and Carignane, there have been significant plantings over the past ten years in the Central Valley, suggesting a (relatively) better performance there. How much the tentative development of the Rhone-styled wines will focus attention on the potential quality of the variety remains to be seen. But if grown in a high Region II to low Region III climate under dryland or controlled irrigation to produce a crop of around three tons an acre, it can produce a voluptuously fruity and spicy wine with very soft tannins but good structure. As in the Rhone, it is most commonly blended with other varieties, usually with synergistic results.

It would take a braver and more iconoclastic person than I to deny the Napa Valley's preeminence with Cabernet Sauvignon; I look at the style of Napa Cabernet in detail on pages 110–11. For better or worse, it has molded American perceptions of what Cabernet Sauvignon should taste like and has caused much confusion and debate about wines which are more European in style, with the Cabernet Franc of Chinon in the Loire Valley an extreme example. (The same debate exists in Australia.) Many tasters and critics rear back in horror at any sign of vegetal/herbaceous/green olive/green pepper character, particularly when these are associated with a lighter bodied, less tannic structure.

Cabernet Sauvignon should not be thick, jammy and tannic; nor should it be thin, soapy and vegetal. The wine should tell you it has been made from physically ripe grapes, be dominated by dark berry fruit flavors, and be balanced and harmonious in the mouth. It benefits from a small measure of astringency: this may come from a hint of herbal/olive character, or from tannins, or both. The Napa Valley, obviously enough, produces many such wines, as does most of the Sonoma Valley. The Santa Cruz Mountains, Mendocino, parts of Santa Ynez and the Sierra Foothills can and do produce good to very good Cabernet, but not with ease and regularity of the Napa Valley and Sonoma. If it has a particular home-away-from-home, it is in Paso Robles, although in a soft, lush and relatively early maturing style. The continuing controversy lies with Monterey and the Monterey "veggies." Specific site selection, viticultural practices and location within the valley are the keys. Whatever Monterey growers may believe to the contrary, they have a way to go.

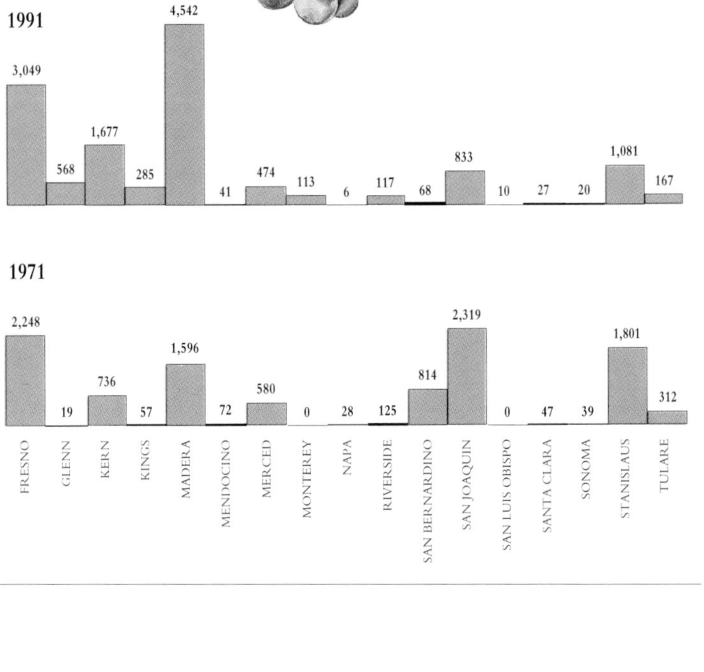
1991
3,049
568
1,677
285
4,542
41
474
113
6
117
68
833
10
27
20
1,081
167
1971
2,248
19
736
57
1,596
72
580
0
28
125
814
2,319
0
47
39
1,801
312
FRESNO
GLENN
KERN
KINGS
MADERA
MENDOCINO
MERCED
MONTEREY
NAPA
RIVERSIDE
SAN BERNARDINO
SAN JOAQUIN
SAN LUIS OBISPO
SANTA CLARA
SONOMA
STANISLAUS
TULARE

Barbera

Over 10,000 of the 10,243 acres of this variety are grown in the Central Valley; what is more, at one point plantings approached 20,000 acres. Its chief virtue is its ability to retain good acidity when grown in a hot climate and heavily cropped; the result may impress the pH meter but not the palate. As I say on page 326, it can do better if given the chance, however unlikely it is that it will be given the opportunity to do so on any meaningful scale.

Carignane

In *Wine Grapes and Vines,* Jancis Robinson makes an extremely interesting comment about the variety. "Although it is grown in quantity only in France and California, Carignan [sic] probably produces more red wine than any other vine variety in the world. The much more widely dispersed Trebbiano is its only serious rival as the most productive vine in the world." But the fall from grace of Carignane in the Central Valley has precisely tracked that of Barbera, with its present plantings barely more than half of those at its peak. It can be argued that, like Barbera, it deserves a better fate; the chances of its achieving this are, if anything, even less than those of Barbera.

Pinot Noir

If Cabernet Sauvignon is one of the great travelers, Pinot Noir is one of the great stay-at-homes. Its checkered career in California is no different from its performance everywhere outside Burgundy — indeed, all things considered, it has emerged in remarkably good shape. It owes significant part of its statistical health to the growth in the premium sparkling wine industry, growth which for the time being at least has slowed to a crawl. But as in Australia, its use in sparkling wine has to a degree reflected the need to make a virtue of necessity. If the grape will not produce a still red table wine of merit, why not use it to make sparkling wine? As long as sparkling wine makers cannot obtain sufficient Pinot grown in an appropriately cool climate (where the chances are it will produce a meritorious red wine), necessity will prevail, and in the meantime the shift in plantings from less suitable to more suitable climates will continue.

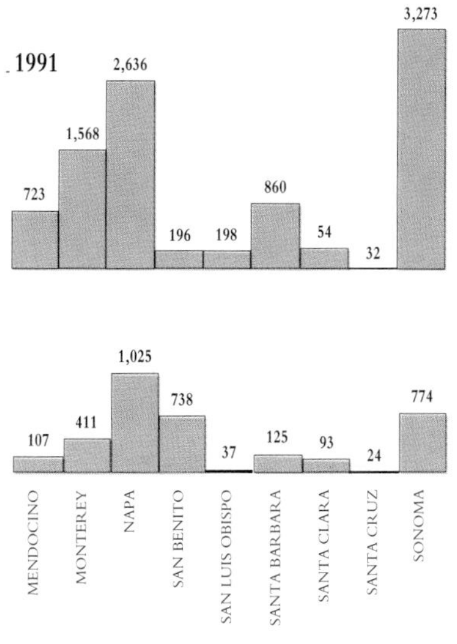

1991
723
1,568
2,636
196
198
860
54
32
3,273
107
411
1,025
738
37
125
93
24
774
MENDOCINO
MONTEREY
NAPA
SAN BENITO
SAN LUIS OBISPO
SANTA BARBARA
SANTA CLARA
SANTA CRUZ
SONOMA

I discuss Pinot Noir in the context of red table wine on pages 348–9. Suffice it to say here that the potential for selected regions of California to produce great Pinot Noir is every bit as good as that of Oregon or Washington State, and that the fat lady hasn't even begun to sing.

Merlot

The percentage growth in the plantings of Merlot between 1971 and 1991 is as great as that of Chardonnay, even if Chardonnay has galloped away from the field since 1985. When phylloxera has run its course in the Napa and Sonoma Valleys, the figures may be even more interesting. In the course of my 320 winery visits researching this book, I lost track of the number of vignerons who indicated their intention to replace Chardonnay with Merlot (or, in some instances, allied varieties).

For all that, the rise of Merlot as a varietal wine has very much been a phenomenon of the latter part of the 1980s. Initially, it was used as a blend component (typically 15%) in wines labeled Cabernet Sauvignon; then came the move to more complex Bordeaux-style blends and to the creation of the name Meritage; and finally came the popularity of varietal Merlots. Even here the story is still being written; there are those who see Merlot as a subtly altered form of Cabernet Sauvignon and who will routinely add the maximum permissable percentage of Cabernet, sometimes in the form of pressings. A lesser number are content to present Merlot unassisted and effectively to contrast it with Cabernet Sauvignon. Issues of both flavor and structure underlie these differing approaches: Merlot is an earlier ripening variety than Cabernet Sauvignon and the classicists would argue that it therefore requires a somewhat cooler climate than Cabernet.

While I agree with that view, a disproportionately large percentage of the most enjoyable Cabernet-family wines I tasted

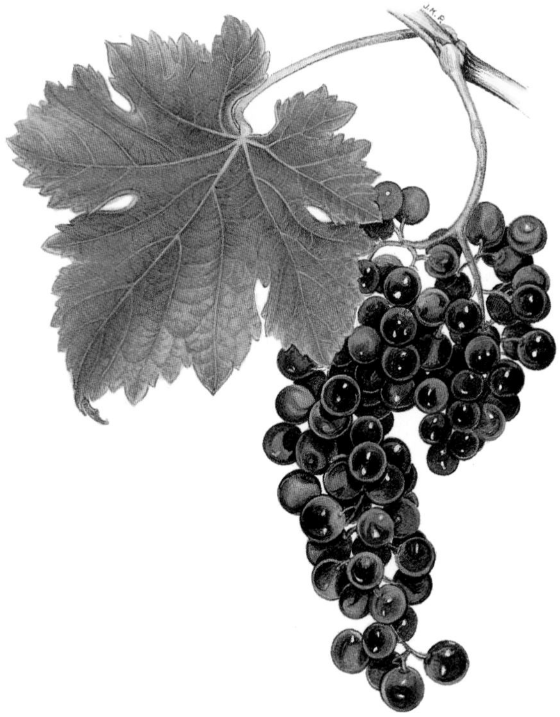

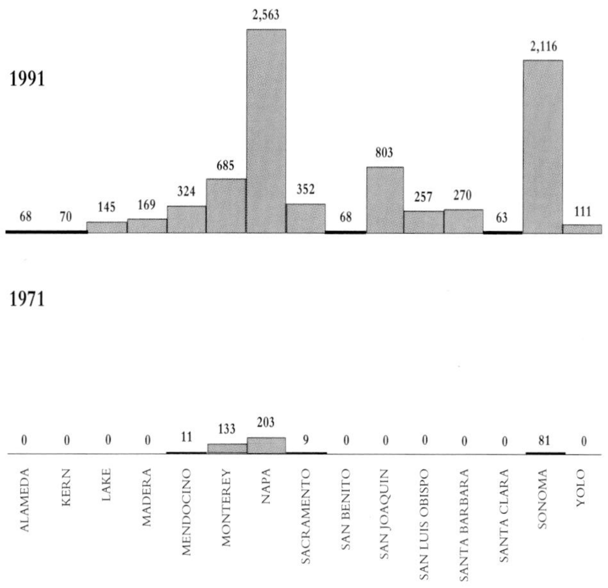
1991
68
70
145
169
324
685
2,563
352
68
803
257
270
63
2,116
111
1971
0
0
0
0
11
133
203
9
0
0
0
0
0
81
0
ALAMEDA
KERN
LAKE
MADERA
MENDOCINO
MONTEREY
NAPA
SACRAMENTO
SAN BENITO
SAN JOAQUIN
SAN LUIS OBISPO
SANTA BARBARA
SANTA CLARA
SONOMA
YOLO

were Merlots; the North Coast is doing wonderfully well with the variety. Some of the same flavor issues arise with Merlot as they do with Cabernet Sauvignon: I see all of the wines of the eastern or right bank of the Gironde in Bordeaux (other than Chateau Petrus) as having a certain greenness in most vintages. It is a matter of personal taste whether you welcome a touch of that in California Merlot. I do, and hence particularly enjoy the Merlots of the southern Sonoma and southern Napa Valleys (including, of course, Carneros).

Ruby Cabernet

This cross between Carignane and Cabernet Sauvignon was bred by Professor H.P. Olmo at U.C. Davis in 1948. The good news is that it is the most successful of the ambitious and extensive breeding program; the bad news is that it proves (once again) that the human hand has been unable to improve on, or even equal, nature. As the market becomes progressively more sophisticated, and as Cabernet Sauvignon becomes ever more widely planted, the highly colored but structurally empty Ruby Cabernet will continue its decline.

Petite Sirah

While the variety was bred in the Rhone Valley by a Dr. Durif around 1880, Petite Sirah has no connection with Syrah and is given this name only in California: its correct name is that of its creator — Durif. Whether the apparent connection with the Rhone Valley will help arrest the decline in plantings is debatable, but it certainly does have its ardent supporters among winemakers and consumers. If given even half a chance, it will produce a dark colored, massive, tough, long-lived wine, requiring a supremely sensitive touch by the maker to invest the wine with enough fruit to provide balance. It is used to advantage in generic blends and by makers such as Paul Draper of Ridge Vineyards with Zinfandel.

Cabernet Franc

The plantings of Cabernet Franc have grown at much the same rate as those of Merlot, although from a much smaller base. It is also very tentatively following the path of Merlot in its progression from junior blend partner to varietally labeled wine. Its supporters point to its fragrance and its slightly lighter and more supple texture; its detractors suggest it lacks richness and mid-palate weight. One obvious blend is the St. Emilion/Pomerol pattern of Cabernet Franc and Merlot (with a touch of Cabernet Sauvignon to appease those for whom the world begins and ends with that variety). Another model is the red wine of

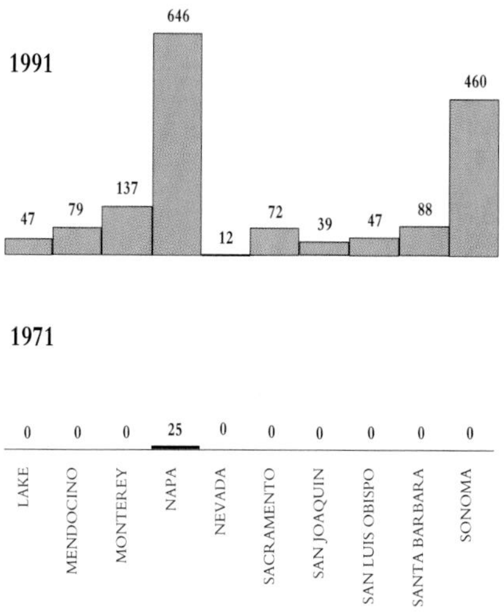
1991
47
79
137
646
12
72
39
47
88
460
1971
0
0
0
25
0
0
0
0
0
0
LAKE
MENDOCINO
MONTEREY
NAPA
NEVADA
SACRAMENTO
SAN JOAQUIN
SAN LUIS OBISPO
SANTA BARBARA
SONOMA

Chinon in the Loire Valley, but I suspect the process of education has a long way to go before a California version of Chinon would be well received. For what it is worth, I agree with those commentators and winemakers who think it may have a special place in the Santa Ynez Valley.

Gamay

The sooner Gamay is given its proper name of Valdigue (however hard to spell and pronounce) and the sooner Gamay Beaujolais is given its proper name of Pinot Noir, the sooner the hopeless confusion which reigns will be sorted out. Gamay, a variety which can produce a very pleasant wine if made so as to emphasize its sweet fruit (notably by using carbonic maceration), would then be allowed to assume its true identity. Frankly, I think confusion will continue to reign; the power of the marketers should never be underestimated.

Gamay Beaujolais

This high-yielding clone of Pinot Noir predictably makes undistinguished wine in most places and its plantings are steadily declining, which should worry no one very much.

Syrah

It is not hard to achieve a growth rate of 1000% if plantings start at four acres in 1971, but it is difficult to understand why there is such interest in a variety which in 1991 had only 160 acres in bearing. Perhaps the fact that 253 acres had been planted between 1989 to 1991 gives the clue: it really is one of the hot varieties (along with Viognier). I prognosticate on the future of the variety on page 327 and point to the adaptability of the grape when grown in a wide range of climates in Australia. The limited California experience suggests (as one would expect) that it will perform in the same way here, with pronounced black pepper and spice aromas and flavors appearing in cooler regions and red cherry and earth characters in warmer regions. Paso Robles (where Gary Eberle pioneered the variety at Estrella River) and Santa Barbara will produce Syrah at opposite ends of the spectrum; the role of Chateau Beaucastel in the mid-range climate around Adelaida in Paso Robles will be fascinating to watch.

ABOVE ~ *On Geysers Road, Alexander Valley.*

NAPA VALLEY

Much though the vignerons in other parts of California wish it were otherwise, the Napa Valley is the symbol of California wine throughout the world. In various ways, it embodies many of the finest features of the American way of life, and some of the least appealing. Its most obvious face is that of wealth and social position, but behind this facade there is a far more attractive and real world in which the winemakers (the *real* winemakers that is) live and work. It is also a valley in transition: a golden age has ended, and the future is not entirely certain. There is a realization that money alone does not guarantee success, while phylloxera raises previously unasked questions and offers choices and opportunities which must be correctly addressed.

Yet Napa did not always occupy the center of the stage. For a brief period the Sonoma Valley held sway, but the departure from Sonoma of Colonel Agoston Haraszthy for Nicaragua in 1868 (where he was eaten by an alligator) had been preceded by the arrival of Charles Krug at St. Helena in 1861. From this point on, the two regions took divergent paths, with Sonoma always treading several steps behind, and not sharing in the two Napa Valley booms. The golden ages of the Napa Valley were between 1860 and 1899, and from 1966 to 1988. These were times of expansion, of the building of great monuments, and of unbounded faith and optimism.

Seminal events in the first era (following Charles Krug) were the establishment of Schramsberg in 1862, the arrival of H.W. Crabb at what was to become To-Kalon in 1868, the building of Beringer's Rhine House in 1877, of Inglenook in 1879, of Christian Brothers Greystone Cellars in 1888, and of Beaulieu in 1899. The end of this phase came with the devastating arrival of phylloxera; in 1890 there were over 18,000 acres of vines, but by 1900 there were only 3,000 acres. Next, the World War and then Prohibition finally brought the momentum of the nineteenth century to an end, although Beaulieu and Inglenook kept the flame aflutter during those dark days.

Although 1966 is a somewhat arbitrary date for the start of the second golden age, it can be justified (although I guess one or two might challenge this) by the establishment of Robert Mondavi Winery in that year. Whether one puts the starting date a few years earlier (for example 1961 and Heitz Cellars) is not important; the next 25 years were to witness a tidal wave of investment and development which by 1988 had reached its logical and logistical conclusion, and which also happened to coincide with the first real scars of the second phylloxera invasion (through the agency of phylloxera Biotype B).

What more can one say of the Napa Valley which has not already been written or is not patently obvious? Nothing much, so please bear with me. For a start, what the ordinary visitor to the Napa will see is a valley 35 miles long, varying in width between one and four miles. On the western side (or southwestern, to be precise) is the Mayacamas Range, on the opposite side the Vaca Range, with the Napa River meandering down the center of the valley in a particularly unobtrusive fashion. But this vista bears no relationship to the Napa Valley AVA, which encompasses almost the entire county and includes not only the mountain ranges on both sides (which in turn incorporate a number of AVAs) but a whole series of valleys hidden in the folds of the Vaca Range. Those with AVAs are the Wild Horse Valley and Pope Valley, but vines are also planted in the Chiles, Gordon and Wooden Valleys.

That the creation of the Napa Valley AVA in this form was an act of sheer political expediency on the part of the BATF hardly

Napa Valley
1971 AND 1991 ACREAGE/GRAPE VARIETIES

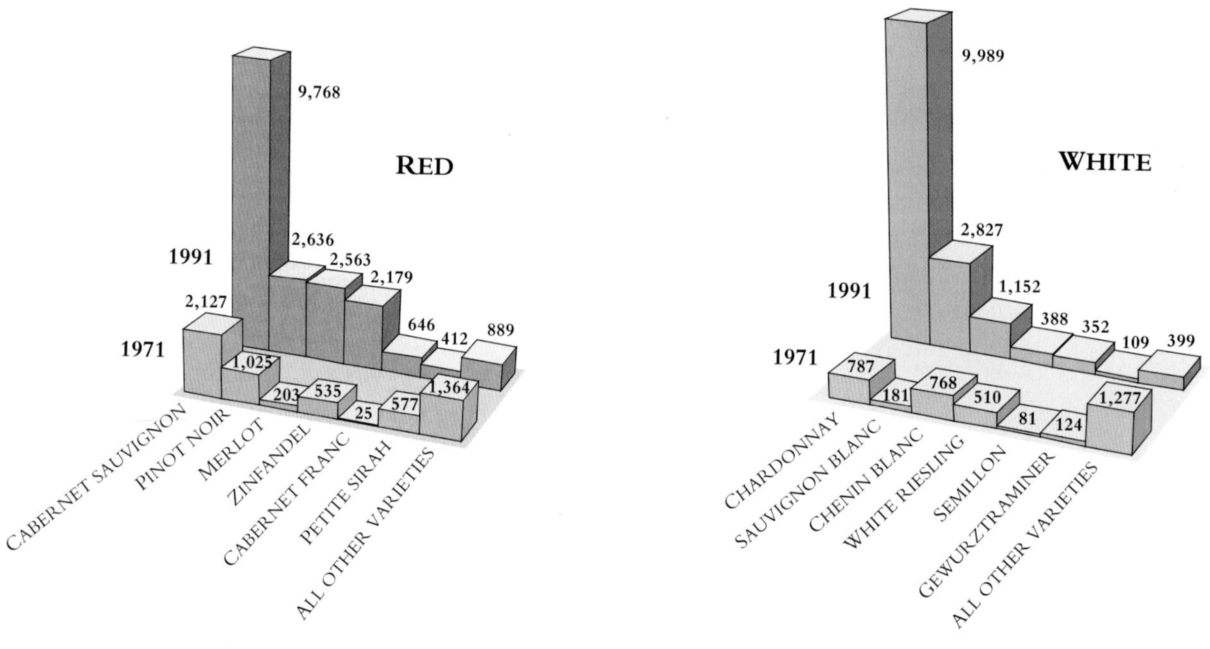
RED
1991
1971
9,768
2,636
2,563
2,179
646
412
889
2,127
1,025
203
535
25
577
1,364
CABERNET SAUVIGNON
PINOT NOIR
MERLOT
ZINFANDEL
CABERNET FRANC
PETITE SIRAH
ALL OTHER VARIETIES
WHITE
1991
1971
9,989
2,827
1,152
388
352
109
399
787
181
768
510
81
124
1,277
CHARDONNAY
SAUVIGNON BLANC
CHENIN BLANC
WHITE RIESLING
SEMILLON
GEWURZTRAMINER
ALL OTHER VARIETIES

PREVIOUS PAGE ~ *The complex topography of the Vaca Range ripples like waves in the setting sun.*

Napa Valley
1982–91 ACREAGE

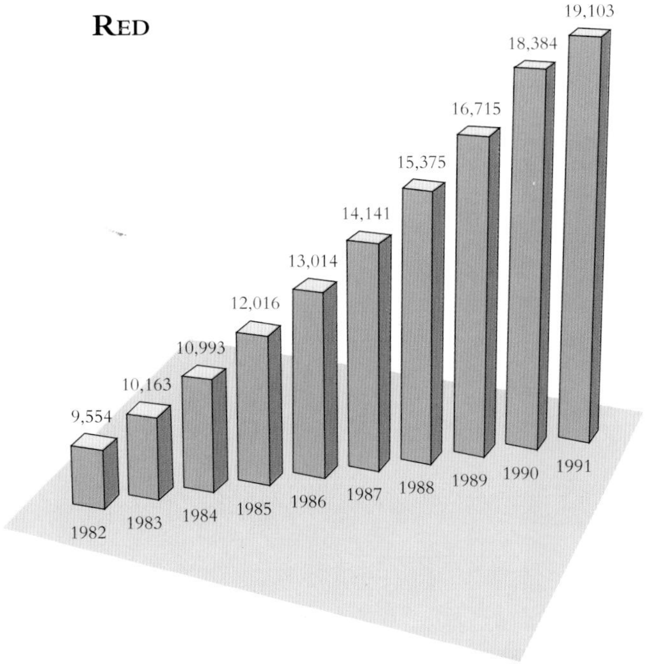
RED
9,554
10,163
10,993
12,016
13,014
14,141
15,375
16,715
18,384
19,103
1982
1983
1984
1985
1986
1987
1988
1989
1990
1991

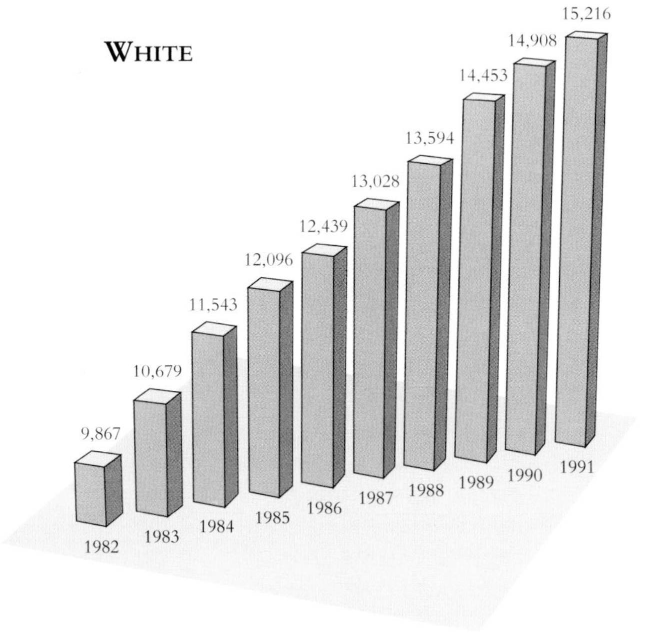
WHITE
9,867
10,679
11,543
12,096
12,439
13,028
13,594
14,453
14,908
15,216
1982
1983
1984
1985
1986
1987
1988
1989
1990
1991

needs be said. But it was followed by a piece of California legislation which was no less political. There is an ever-proliferating number of subappellations (or AVAs) within the Napa Valley, but none (other than Carneros which is partly in Napa County and partly in Sonoma County) may use the subappellation without also appending the name Napa Valley.

So much for the mechanics, as it were. In physical terms the Napa Valley proper is a place of great beauty, beauty which changes dramatically with the seasons. The vivid yellow of the mustard flowers of early spring carpeting the vine rows, the emerald-green vines of summer and straw bleached grass, and the gold and red hues of fall are set within the unchanging framework of the dark green fir, redwood, oak and madrone forested mountainsides. Wineries of every shape, size and description dot the landscape, some with sensitivity, some without.

There is everything for the tourist; indeed, much of the debate since 1988 has been centered on the proposition that there is altogether too much. There is the highly controversial wine-train, the fate of which hung in the balance in 1992. There is S. Claus, a shop selling Christmas gifts, decorations and so forth 365 days a year. There are many very fine restaurants, and accommodation ranging from humble to grand. And there is traffic, which in the summer holidays and weekends can test the patience of the most hardened Los Angeles or San Francisco commuter.

The Napa Valley is capable of producing some of California's greatest wines (and does so), and in the same breath some of its most boring and banal. Prices may not so much reflect quality as the cost of the monuments in which the wines are made, not to mention the exorbitant land values. But it is the Mecca to which all wine pilgrims must come sooner or later. And those who seek in the right places will find fine people, great wines and much beauty.

ABOVE ~ *The valley looking north as the eye of the ever-circling buzzard might see it.*

ROBERT MONDAVI

The biographical entry in a who's who might read thus:

> *Robert Gerald Mondavi b. 1913 to Cesare and Rosa Mondavi in Minnesota. Educated Lodi High School and Stanford University, the latter in business and economics. Joined family wine business, which in 1943 purchased a rundown Charles Krug Winery. Here he developed business from bulk to own brand, and introduced many technical innovations through the later 1950s and early 1960s, pioneering the cold fermentation of Chenin Blanc, use of inert gases in bottles and tanks, and vacuum corking. A well-publicized family feud led to his departure from Charles Krug and the establishment of Robert Mondavi Winery in 1966. Formed joint venture with Baron Philippe de Rothschild in 1979. Retired from active management of Robert Mondavi Winery in 1991, with sons Tim (Enology) and Michael (Administration), and daughter Marcia (Marketing) in key management positions.*

ABOVE ~ *Few winemakers understand the interaction between wine and barrel better than Robert Mondavi.*

Such an entry obscures as much as it tells about a man of truly remarkable talent, vision, energy, impetuosity and generosity. Cyril Ray's book *Robert Mondavi of the Napa Valley* leaves the reader in no doubt where Mondavi inherited most of these characteristics from: his mother Rosa, who arrived from Italy as an illiterate 19-year-old bride, and who for the next 12 years single-handedly ran a combined house and boarding home for her husband and 14 other men, seldom finishing work before 11 P.M. and rising every morning at 4:30 A.M. During this time she had borne Cesare four children, never missing a beat in the running of the home.

I first met Robert Mondavi in the latter part of the 1970s during one of his many visits to Australia where, for a period, he was involved as a consultant to a Margaret River (Western Australia) winery called Leeuwin Estate. By that time he was approaching 70, but had the drive and enthusiasm of a 20-year-old. His intellect is formidable, and his curiosity endless: his pioneering days at Charles Krug were but a foretaste of what was to come at his own winery.

Throughout his 25 years at the helm of Robert Mondavi Winery, one of the keynotes was his generosity. In the 1970s the winery undertook an immensely complicated, computer-monitored and controlled examination of the differing effects from different oak types of varying levels of toast (or charring) at varying storage temperatures. Few other wineries in the world could have duplicated the research even if they wished to, and none in fact did. Instead of keeping the results of the research as closely guarded and immensely valuable trade secrets, Mondavi shared them with all who wished to know.

In the 1980s much attention was devoted to the development of the Mondavi vineyard holdings, spanning the Napa Valley, Carneros, and Santa Barbara. In particular, much work was done on trellising and vine density patterns in conjunction with sustainable viticultural practices. All of the independent grape growers who sell to Mondavi (some purely on a handshake basis) are given full access to the results of this work, and are encouraged to attend regular seminars at which information is disseminated in the context of experimental or illustrative wines made from varying viticultural techniques.

One of Robert Mondavi's earliest achievements was the resuscitation of Sauvignon Blanc. Plantings of 2,000 acres had dwindled to only 700 acres in 1965 in the face of complete disinterest on the part of the public — disinterest which was hardly surprising given the simple, appreciably sweet wine made at that time from the grape. In 1967 Mondavi took it by the scruff of the neck, fermenting it cool, taking it through to dryness, and then maturing it in French oak. He also invented the name Fumé Blanc, and quite deliberately did not protect that name by trademark registration. He was content that not only should others copy his winemaking style, but use the name as well. By 1982 there were 9,000 acres of Sauvignon Blanc planted in California, by 1992 13,275 acres, and Mondavi still points the way with its Reserve Sauvignon Blanc from its To-Kalon vineyard.

The more recent achievements with Pinot Noir are no less remarkable — if anything, even more so. Throughout California, Australia, New Zealand, South Africa and South America the larger wineries have shied away from Pinot Noir. They find it temperamental to grow, difficult to make and nearly impossible to market. In California a massive surge in plantings in the early 1970s was followed by a decade of disillusionment as grape prices fell to levels as low as those for Thompsons Seedless, largely reflecting the fact that the grape was planted in all the wrong places (far too warm) and no one knew how to make the wine. Only the sparkling wine industry managed to keep the 1991 plantings at the same level as those of 1975.

Every aspect of Pinot Noir demands attention to detail, and much more sensitive (and labor intensive) handling in the winery than any other variety. Mondavi started serious attempts to make

good Pinot Noir in 1972, introducing the Burgundian practice of returning stems to the fermenter and deliberately increasing fermentation temperatures, among other things. (It is true some similar research was undertaken at U.C. Davis in the mid 1970s.) But all in all, there was as much disappointment as there was success, and a less committed winery would have simply given up.

Not Mondavi: at the very time that the winery grew to over 600,000 cases of total wine production, it made a major breakthrough with its Pinot Noir. This came about in part through sourcing the grapes from Carneros and various parts of the Central Coast, and in part through the relentless on-going experiments. In 1988, 1990 and 1992, I attended the winemakers' Pinot Noir Conference at Steamboat in Oregon; every year (and for that matter in the intervening years) Tim Mondavi or other senior winemakers from the winery were present, sharing the knowledge gained from their experiments. And while Pinot Noir sales are relatively small in the Mondavi scheme of things, I have no doubt that since 1985 the Reserve Pinot Noirs are the best made anywhere in the world by a winery of this size.

The Opus One joint venture (pages 72-3) is of itself the ultimate tribute to Robert Mondavi's skills as an ambassador, not just for his own wines but those of the Napa Valley as a whole. Those skills have been at work both abroad and at home: together with wife Margrit Biever, he has welded wine, food, music and art in the exceptional functions held throughout the year at the Mondavi Winery. And when he plays host to private groups or individuals, you are likely to end up tasting a first growth Bordeaux or a great Burgundy alongside his own wines. Robert Mondavi's generosity of spirit shines through everything he has ever done.

TOP ~ *Statues abound in the gardens and precincts of the Robert Mondavi visitors' centre.*

ABOVE ~ *Tim (left) and Michael (right) Mondavi showing that ties are not, after all, unheard of in the Napa Valley.*

CALISTOGA

Calistoga's first vigneron was one of those larger-than-life characters who strode across the West in the mid nineteenth century. Sam Brannan was a hard drinking renegade Mormon who arrived in Calistoga in 1859 determined to invest a large part of his considerable wealth in turning it into a major health resort, based upon its geysers, mineral waters, hot springs and mud baths.

Almost as an afterthought, it seems, he collected thousands of vine cuttings from France, Spain, Germany and Italy, and established 200 acres of vineyards. His grand plan for the health resort failed, as did his marriage (in 1870), and he died penniless in the arms of an Indian squaw 30 years after he first strode into Calistoga.

The vineyards, at least, were a success, and in 1882 the industrialist Alfred L. Tubbs built Chateau Montelena, said by Leon Adams to have been partly inspired by Chateau Lafite, while the Grimm brothers winery was dug into the mountainside north of Calistoga on the site of what is now Storybook Mountain.

Brannan, it seems, was simply ahead of his time, for these days Calistoga is the busiest of the towns in the Napa Valley, bristling with restaurants, hotels, hot springs and mud baths. Yet it also has a feeling of mountain wilderness: the Palisades rear skyward on the eastern side, and one can visualize grizzly bears still prowling through the redwoods and craggy rock outcrocks, while the Petrified Forest Road and Diamond Mountain on the western side are no less evocative. Mount St. Helena, to the north, is the largest mountain of all, and completes the feeling of being hemmed in on all sides other than the south, emphasizing that the width of the valley has narrowed from four miles in the south to only one mile at Calistoga, and is about to end abruptly.

CALISTOGA AND JUICE
TOYOTA

ABOVE ~ *The cellars at Storybook Mountain were tunnelled more than 100 years ago.*

TOP ~ *An evocation of bygone decades, appropriate given the rich history of Calistoga.*

OPPOSITE ~ *Old bush-pruned vines in the quaintly named Two Dog Vineyard at Calistoga.*

THE REGION IN BRIEF

Climate, Soil and Viticulture

CLIMATE

With the usual caveat about seasonal and site variation, the climate of Calistoga is the warmest in the Napa Valley with summations varying between 3,360 degree days (high Region III) and 3,765 degree days (mid Region IV). This is explained and put into perspective on page 42 "The Temperature Gradient." However, the diurnal temperature range during the growing season is normally extreme; the night cooling by marine fog intrusions is augmented by (or in the absence of fog, replaced by) cold air draining down the sides of the mountains which surround it. This extreme diurnal range is both blessing and bane: it helps delay otherwise excessively quick ripening and assists acid retention, but it also makes spring frosts a common occurrence, with frost protection (through wind machines, smudge pots or spray irrigation) essential for the valley floor vineyards.

SOIL

The soils at the extreme northern end of the valley floor are very different from those in the middle and south, and (relatively speaking) are more uniform. The highly geothermal nature of the district attests to the adjacent volcanic mountains, and it is hardly surprising that the soils are volcanic in origin. They are very deep, very gravelly and at times bouldery sandy to sandy clay loams. Recognizing, too, that the headwaters of the Napa River rise here, the sediments have been transported relatively short distances, with a high percentage of coarse clasts (or boulders) yet with sand dominating the fine fraction of the soil.

Calistoga
VINTAGE CHART 1981-91

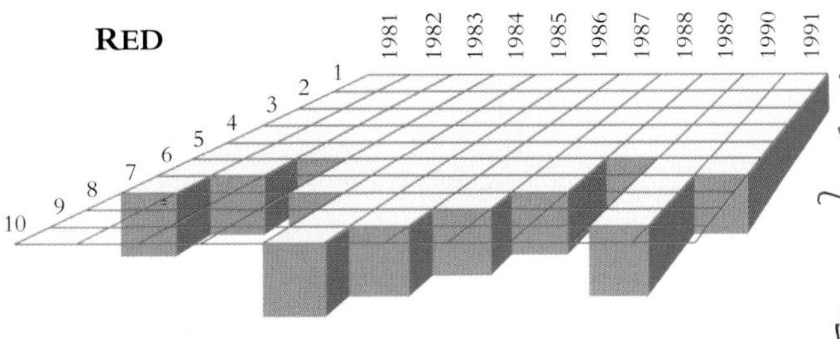
RED
1981
1982
1983
1984
1985
1986
1987
1988
1989
1990
1991
1
2
3
4
5
6
7
8
9
10

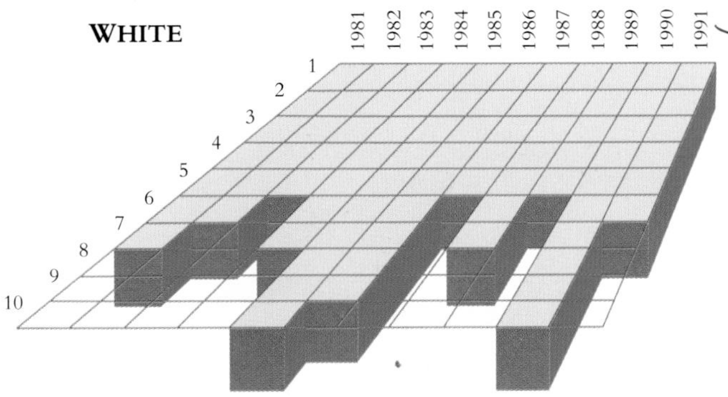
WHITE
1981
1982
1983
1984
1985
1986
1987
1988
1989
1990
1991
1
2
3
4
5
6
7
8
9
10

THE GROWING SEASON

The valley rises from a mere 12 feet around the city of Napa to 365 feet at Calistoga, but unless one moves up into the foothills of the surrounding mountains, elevation does not play a significant role in shortening the growing season. In those foothills, afternoon breezes may intensify (Storybook Mountain is typically 10 to 12°F cooler than the town of Calistoga) and the risks of frost decrease. The heat — which in terms of summation is less than Florence in Chianti — is always moderated by the afternoon sea breezes, and a second moderating influence comes from the bouldery fan soils, which decrease vine vigor and slow the ripening process yet intensify and concentrate the grape biosynthates, which are responsible for red wine color and flavor.

ABOVE ~ *The Robert Pecota winery buildings merge quietly into the Calistoga landscape.*

Contract Growers

Canard Vineyard Twenty-four acres, including ten acres of Napa Gamay, six acres of Zinfandel (including three acres of 100-year-old Zinfandel which is purchased by Ravenswood) together with Cabernet Franc and Merlot. Some wine is made under the Canard Winery name.

Eisele Vineyard Thirty-nine acres planted between 1964 and 1991 to Cabernet Sauvignon, Cabernet Franc, Petit Verdot and Sauvignon Blanc. The entire production of this important vineyard (not to be confused with Volker Eisele's Vineyard in the Chiles Valley) was previously purchased by Joseph Phelps, but by 1992 it had begun the establishment of its own winery.

Principal Wine Styles

Cabernet Sauvignon

Growers such as Robert Pecota are quick to tell you that Calistoga is not as hot as its high Region III–low Region IV rating would suggest. Certainly it produces Cabernet Sauvignon which has strong, rich, almost voluptuous fruit flavors but which avoid jammy or baked overtones and retain distinctive varietal character. Indeed, unless the tannins are carefully managed, the wines can assume some of the characters of mountain grown Cabernet, so strong are the flavors. In the skilled hands of Sterling, Robert Pecota, Chateau Montelena, Clos Pegase and Joseph Phelps (using the Eisele Vineyard grapes), Calistoga Cabernet Sauvignon produces some of the most enjoyable of all Napa's reds, an ideal match for the thickest, juiciest char-grilled rump steak.

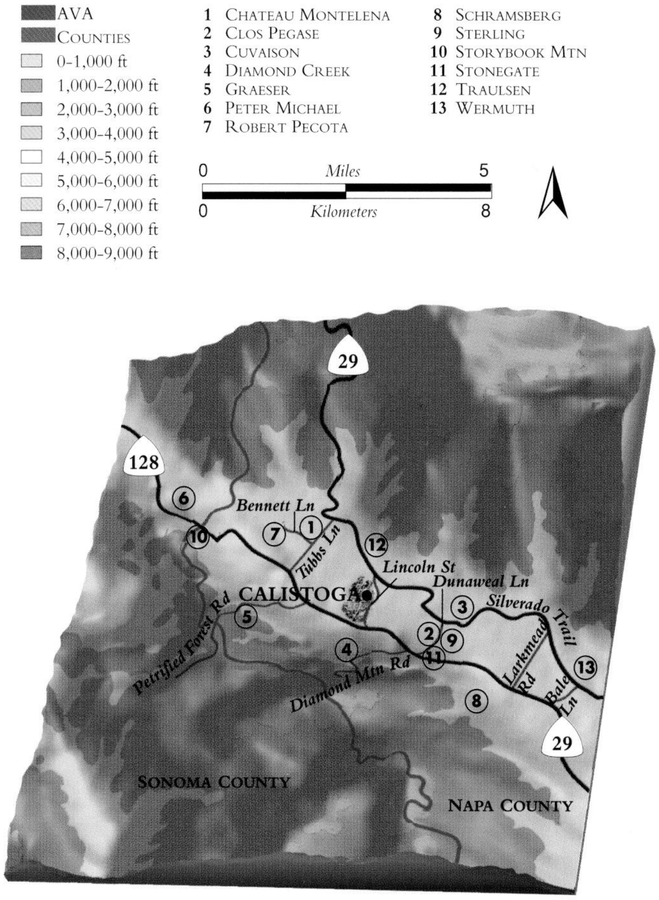
AVA
Counties
0-1,000 ft
1,000-2,000 ft
2,000-3,000 ft
3,000-4,000 ft
4,000-5,000 ft
5,000-6,000 ft
6,000-7,000 ft
7,000-8,000 ft
8,000-9,000 ft
1 Chateau Montelena
2 Clos Pegase
3 Cuvaison
4 Diamond Creek
5 Graeser
6 Peter Michael
7 Robert Pecota
8 Schramsberg
9 Sterling
10 Storybook Mtn
11 Stonegate
12 Traulsen
13 Wermuth
0 Miles 5
0 Kilometers 8
29
128
Bennett Ln
Tubbs Ln
Lincoln St
Dunaweal Ln
Silverado Trail
CALISTOGA
Petrified Forest Rd
Diamond Mtn Rd
Larkmead Rd
Bale Ln
Sonoma County
Napa County

Conway
CASTRO VALLEY

ABOVE ~ *Controversy has surrounded Clos Pegase since its inception, and is unlikely to diminish.*

TOP ~ *Calistoga map.*

ABOVE ~ *Classic wooden farmhouse in the foothills of the Mayacamas Range at the head of the valley.*

ZINFANDEL

If Storybook Mountain were the only producer of this variety — and it isn't — Zinfandel would still have to rate highly, so spectacular is the flavor (and the longevity) of these wines. The flavors here run from dark cherry to briary, and are supported by fine tannins which run right through the structure of the wine. The peppery, spicy characters of cooler-grown Zinfandel are not frequently encountered, nor are the jammy/boiled flavors which can sometimes surface in such highly regarded areas as Amador County.

SYRAH, PETITE SIRAH AND OTHERS

It is perhaps no coincidence that when Robert Pecota purchased his vineyard in 1977, it was planted entirely to Petite Sirah. Whether this turns out to be Durif, it is not one of the most distinguished of the Rhone varieties — if it can be classed as one at all — but this region seems on its face to be ideally suited to the better Rhone varieties. It will be interesting to see the final outcome once phylloxera Biotype B has finished its work, and the replanted vineyards have taken shape.

Notwithstanding that both Schramsberg and Hanns Kornell (the latter in receivership in late 1992) are both situated in the region, this is red wine country, not white wine (and certainly not sparkling wine — to be fair to Schramsberg, much of its grape intake comes from the southern third of the valley). The point has already been made about the Rhone varietals, but what of the Italian varieties (other than Zinfandel, if indeed it is a descendant of Primitivo)? Calistoga has a similar heat summation — slightly cooler indeed — to Florence in Chianti. There must surely be as much scope for selected Italian varieties (many of them as yet untried outside their native habitat) as there is for those of the Rhone. The early Italian pioneers with their plantings of "mixed black" may have had a far better instinctive feel for *terroir* and climate than the technocrats who followed.

PETIT VERDOT

Theoretically this very late ripening variety should do well in such a warm climate, and it is no surprise that Sterling has invested more than a little effort in growing it in its Three Palms Vineyard. More interesting still is the discovery that the original plantings were of a lesser clone called Verdot Rosso by the Bordelaise, and that the most recent plantings are of a true, high quality clone. The Eisele Vineyard, too, has Petit Verdot planted.

ABOVE ~ *The father–son team which has tended the vines at Storybook Mountain since 1976.*

Bush trained, 2 bud spur. But trained pretty high

The Temperature Gradient

If you avoid the weekend madhouse, the infuriatingly slow Winnebago, and the periodic traffic jams which make you wonder whether you are in St. Helena or Los Angeles, you can drive up Highway 29 from the city of Napa to Calistoga in little more than 40 minutes. (If you are clever, you won't drive up Highway 29 at all, but take the Silverado Trail: it is just that for the purposes of this particular trip, I want to take you up Highway 29.)

The road is mainly straight, albeit of varying and unpredictable width. It also seems to be completely flat: the climb of a little over 300 feet is accomplished as if a laser beam had cut the incline over the entire 35 miles. The roadside topography is the same: vines stretching in all directions, dotted with numerous wineries and the occasional restaurant or roadside stall, and only once seriously interrupted by the town of St. Helena (Yountville hides modestly on the eastern side of the highway, Oakville boasts one of the world's great grocery stores but little else, and Rutherford is more a town in name than in fact).

ABOVE ~ *Punching down the cap; a labor-intensive method of red winemaking, but worth the effort.*

The distance is little different from that between Santenay and Dijon, and if you take the N70 (rather than the autoroute) the feeling (and some of the frustrations) of the trip will not be dissimilar. The climate of Santenay is little different from that of Dijon: the weather on any given day may be different, hail or frost may hit here but not there, but in climatological terms it is much the same. Pinot Noir and Chardonnay flourish in Santenay, and both could flourish in Marsannay (the first vineyards south of Dijon). It is more an accident — or design, if your prefer — of history that Pinot Noir has a virtual stranglehold on the northern end of the Cote d'Or.

The Burgundians would also point out with utter conviction the differences in *terroir*, and no one in his or her right mind would suggest that the style of a Santenay Pinot Noir is the same as that of a Gevrey-Chambertin, and a regular consumer of Burgundy should have little or no difficulty in identifying which is which in a blind tasting. But the core of Pinot Noir is present in both places: the climate (to the extent that it can be divorced from *terroir*) is not only favorable in both places, but largely identical.

Yet the difference between the climate of the city of Napa and of Calistoga is so extreme that in viticultural terms one might as well be talking of different countries. To the immediate south or north of Napa city you are in Pinot Noir and Chardonnay country: Region I on the Winkler Scale. Only with the most careful site selection and viticultural practices will you be able to ripen Cabernet Sauvignon, and even then in a style which is not to everyone's taste.

By the time you reach Rutherford and Oakville, you are into Region III, and some of the world's greatest and most classic Cabernets are produced on the best of the alluvial fan soils deposited by mountain creeks. Chardonnay — that ever-flexible white grape — has changed character quite dramatically, and the early efforts (in the 1970s) to grow Pinot Noir were soon abandoned as being hopeless. The white Bordeaux varieties also do well here: witness Mondavi's magnificent Reserve Sauvignon Blanc from the To-Kalon Vineyard.

Saint Helena sees a distinct temperature leap (to 3,500 degree days, at the bottom end of Region IV), and by the time you have reached Calistoga you are in a climate that makes luscious and tannic Cabernets of a particular style, but which is a region that I suggest may be equally well (if not better) suited to the late ripening Rhone and Italian varietals.

Why is this so? Well, there is a rule of thumb which seems to apply in all of the coastal valleys of California, whether they run north–south (as most do) or east–west (those of the Central Coast). It is that for every mile you travel away from the valley mouth at the sea there will be a half to one degree rise in average growing season temperature. In the case of the longer north–south valleys, the gradient is closer to half than one degree, but the principle holds.

It is of course due to the all-important influence of the cold oceans which run down the California coast, and which is discussed and explained in the broader context in the introductory section on climate. But it is fundamental to understanding the amazing diversity of wine styles produced within a relatively small area (particularly if you take the narrowest definition of the Napa Valley and exclude the hillsides and extraneous side valleys) which is often thought of as a wine region in the same fashion as the Medoc or Cote d'Or — when nothing could be further from the truth.

WINERIES *of* CALISTOGA

CHATEAU MONTELENA 1882

A: 1429 Tubbs Lane, Calistoga, CA 94515
T: (707) 942 5105 **V**: 10–4 daily **P**: 30,000
W: Bo Barrett

The establishment date of 1882 constitutes a little poetic license: when a syndicate headed by attorney Jim Barrett acquired the property in 1969 neither vineyards nor winery had been in production for many decades, and the first vintage under the new ownership (from purchased grapes) was made in 1972 by the then relatively unknown Mike Grgich. The estate vineyard had been planted to 72 acres of Cabernet Sauvignon in 1969–70, and the intention was to focus on this variety. When the 1973 Chardonnay took first place in a famous tasting in Paris in 1976, the game plan altered significantly, and today two Chardonnays (one from Napa Valley, the other Alexander Valley) account for 18,000 cases, the 100% estate-grown Cabernet Sauvignon for 10,000 cases, with 1,500 cases of Zinfandel presumably made to relieve the boredom (but without great distinction).

It seems to me the Napa Valley Chardonnay lives in part on its reputation, and in part on the general acceptance of the Napa style, a style about which I have grave reservations. Having said that, I must confess a sneaking regard for the simple but well-constructed '90 Chardonnay. When it comes to the Cabernet Sauvignons, I have no reservations, particularly in those years in which Bo Barrett (son of Jim Barrett) backs off the tannins. The '87 Cabernet Sauvignon is as close to perfection as one could hope for: voluptuous, chewy dark cassis/blackcurrant fruit with tannins under control (though certainly present) and with wonderful balance and structure.

CLOS PEGASE 1984

A: 1060 Dunaweal Lane, Calistoga, CA 94515 **T**: (707) 942 4981 **V**: 10:30–5 daily **P**: 30,000 **W**: Bob Masyczek

What can one say about Clos Pegase, that ultimate expression of the edifice complex? Perhaps the extraordinary career of owner Jan Shrem gives some clue. He was born in Colombia in 1930; moved to Jerusalem in 1932 and to New York in 1944 where he finished high school at night while working as a messenger boy during the day; thence to the University of Utah on a scholarship, emerging with a degree in Political Science in 1954. In 1955, while studying for his Master's degree at UCLA, he took a vacation in Japan, fell in love

CLOS PEGASE
1990
CHARDONNAY
NAPA VALLEY

with the culture and simply stayed on, building a publishing empire which he sold in 1968; with his Japanese wife-to-be Mitsuko, he then went to Europe, establishing new publishing firms in Italy and then France. He traveled extensively through Asia and the Mediterranean, studying art, architecture and history, particularly Mycenaean Greek history; in 1980 he sold his European publishing business and enrolled in enology at the University of Bordeaux; in 1983, having engaged Andre Tchelistcheff as consultant, purchased a 50-acre vineyard on Dunaweal Lane. He then caused the San Francisco Museum of Modern Art to sponsor a competition (won by Princeton architect Michael Graves) for the design of what is part-winery, part-museum and part-Parthenon, and which makes Domain Carneros, Groth and Opus One look like country weekenders.

The wines are in one sense incidental, in another quite remarkable, for they are as restrained and understated as the building is flamboyant. The white wines — Sauvignon Blanc and Chardonnay — border on the vapid, but the '87 Cabernet Sauvignon was an excellent wine, still holding lovely fresh sweet fruit flavors and an intriguing touch of spice. The 1992 appointment of Bob Masyczek, who spent five years with John Thacher at Cuvaison (coupled with the establishment of a major Carneros vineyard), as winemaker could well herald a white wine renaissance.

CUVAISON 1970

A: 4550 Silverado Trail, Calistoga, CA 94515
T: (707) 942 6266 **V**: 10–5 daily **P**: 50,000
W: John Thacher

The Cuvaison of today bears no resemblance whatsoever to that of the 1970s. The winery's location in Calistoga may be an undeniable fact but is entirely misleading, for all of its 284 acres

CUVAISON
Cabernet Sauvignon
Napa Valley
1989
ALC. 13.0% BY VOL.

of vines (Chardonnays, Pinot Noir and Merlot) are established on its 400-acre property in Carneros, while its Cabernet Sauvignon is made from grapes purchased in the Oakville and Rutherford areas. The big change came in 1979: in that year the Swiss Schmidheiny family purchased both the winery and the then unplanted Carneros site, appointing Manfred Esser as president. The modest, quietly spoken but supremely talented winemaker John Thacher had become winemaker in 1977, but it was not until 1982 that the grape sources began to take their present shape, and the mid 1980s before the increasing flow of accolades for Cuvaison began — and for every good reason this shows no sign of slackening. The winemaking skills of Thacher perfectly complement the marketing genius of Esser, making a formidable team.

The core of the business is the 35,000–40,000 cases of typically elegant and beautifully balanced Carneros Chardonnay produced every year, and for which demand seems to be growing rather than diminishing. Merlot and Cabernet Sauvignon account for around 5,000–6,000 cases each; while the vicissitudes of the 1989 vintage had their effect on the Merlot of that year, the Cabernet Sauvignon was exemplary in its complexity and balance, signifying the progressive softening in the tannin profile which has taken place in the second half of the 1980s. In the wings are some exceptional Pinot Noirs (200 cases in 1990, 1,200 in 1991 and possibly 2,000 in 1992) which Thacher has been developing in his typically quiet but disciplined fashion. 1992 also marked the initial releases of a second label, Calistoga Vineyards, which will add an additional 10,000 cases to the 50,000 cases under the Cuvaison label, and help underwrite the consistency and quality of the latter.

DIAMOND CREEK VINEYARDS 1972

A: 1500 Diamond Mountain Road, Calistoga, CA 94515 **T**: (707) 942 6926 **V**: By appointment **P**: 3,000 **W**: Al Brounstein

Ex-pharmacist Al Brounstein reminds me of a nineteenth-century Australian viticulturist who, at the height of the gold mining fever which gripped Australia at much the same time as California, said, "To get gold, you need dig only about 18 inches and plant vines." It also helps to have the super sales flair which Brounstein shares with Dick Grace, but few others.

The 79-acre property on the lower slopes of the Diamond Mountain was originally planted in three blocks simply because the topography demanded it, but which immediately showed their radically different soil types. Volcanic Hill, at eight acres, is the largest block, its gray crumbly soil producing the densest and darkest wine — and in the context of Diamond Creek, one is talking of the density and darkness of a black hole in space. Red Rock Terrace is seven acres, its soil stained a vivid red by iron impurities, and grudgingly allows some fruit to express itself. Gravelly Meadow's five acres have a brown–black mixture which produces wines reflecting the name of the block: hard, gravelly and exceptionally slow maturing. A fourth one-acre block, Winery Lake, is usually blended with Gravelly Meadow, but when released as a vineyard wine brings stratospheric prices: in 1992, $150 a bottle, easily outdoing Grace Family.

The landscaping of the man-made mini-lakes and the springs which meander through the vineyards has all the beauty and precision of a Japanese garden; the wines have all the subtlety and finesse of a Panzer tank brigade. If more is good, and tannin is better, these wines are the best. Almost all is sold by mailing list and all on allocation, so any criticism is superfluous.

GRAESER WINERY 1985

A: 255 Petrified Forest Road, Calistoga, CA 94515 **T**: (707) 942 4437 **V**: 11–5 Thurs–Mon **P**: Variable **W**: Dick Graeser

Dick Graeser is a battler, doing it hard in a remote but beautiful location in the hills east of Calistoga, but it hasn't always been that way: in the 1970s he was, in his words, "making heaps" as a fruit grower, packer and shipper in Southern California before bankers and an ex-wife left him with just enough money for a five-week holiday in France. He returned with no occupation, no money and no plan for the future, but when his father died, moved into the house to help his mother; within months she, too, died, leaving Dick Graeser the house

1990
PETER MICHAEL
WINERY
'MON PLAISIR'
WHITE TABLE WINE • FROM SONOMA COUNTY CHARDONNAY
PRODUCED AND BOTTLED BY PETER MICHAEL
CALISTOGA, CA USA

and buildings which had been built by a San Francisco surgeon in 1886 on a ranch he called "La Perlita Del Monte." Today as one drives up through the giant redwoods to the house and rudimentary winery, it is not hard to see why it was called "The Pearl of the Mountain."

Graeser has planted six and a half acres of Cabernet Sauvignon, two acres of Cabernet Franc and one acre of Merlot, and the vines bear exceptionally well in the rich mountain soil — indeed, vigor control is a problem. Graeser has also purchased Semillon in most years since 1985, and made a series of flavorful if somewhat rustic wines from this variety. Financial pressures have led to the sale of the estate red wines in some years, and if the 1988 estate-bottled Cabernet Franc is any guide, the purchasers may be well pleased. The wine has considerable fragrance, with rose and tobacco aromas intermingling, and an appropriate delicacy to its structure and texture.

PETER MICHAEL WINERY 1988

A: 12400 Ida Clayton Road, Calistoga, CA 94515 **T**: (707) 942 4459 **V**: By appointment **P**: 10,000 **W**: Mark Aubert

Despite its address, Peter Michael Winery is not within the Calistoga area or, for that matter, even within the Napa Valley. It is the only winery situated in the Knights Valley AVA of Sonoma, a region which has a far closer geographic nexus to the Napa Valley than does the Pope Valley, but which simply happens to fall north of the county line. Wherever the winery is included, it will accordingly appear something of an orphan.

The property was acquired in the early 1980s purely as a holiday and relaxation venture, but in 1984 establishment of the vineyards began. These now total 75 acres, at elevations of between 800 and 1,800 feet, planted primarily to Cabernet Sauvignon. The winery, wine storage building and administrative offices have been built to emulate a town hall, an old barn, and a school house of 100 years ago.

Two Chardonnays are made, one from Gauer Ranch in the Alexander Valley called Mon Plaisir, and the other from Liparita Vineyard on Napa's Howell Mountain. The Cabernet Sauvignon, called Les Pavots, comes from the estate plantings. The initial Chardonnay release from Gauer Estate was accorded rave reviews, but subsequent releases, while sound, have been rather less exciting.

ROBERT PECOTA 1978

A: 3299 Bennett Lane, Calistoga, CA 94515 **T**: (707) 942 6625 **V**: By appointment **P**: 20,000 **W**: Robert Pecota

Bob Pecota learned about every nook and cranny of the Napa Valley during his decade with Beringer, first as a vineyard purchaser, then as a grape buyer and vineyard manager — with a dash of public relations to provide variation. In 1978 he acquired a 35-acre Petite Sirah vineyard of his own and built a no-frills but highly functional winery, and removed half the Petite Sirah, replacing it with Cabernet Sauvignon (a field selection with a little virus rather than heat treated) and Sauvignon Blanc. While the Cabernet Sauvignon has been an unqualified success, the Sauvignon Blanc has not: Bob Pecota frankly says he doesn't like it particularly, even though its 7,000 case volume has been a major part of his overall production.

Responding to suggestions that his Kara's

ABOVE ~ *Smudge pots are the traditional method of combating spring frosts.*

ABOVE ~ *View from the Silverado Trail as it approaches the Calistoga end of the valley.*

Vineyard Cabernet Sauvignon (3,000 cases) is excessively tannic, Pecota has stopped using any press wine since 1990 (selling it in bulk) and increased the amount of sweet French oak. And his absolutely delicious 1991 Gamay Beaujolais shows Pecota knows all about fruit: this wholly seductive wine, redolent with pepper, spice and red cherries, is a classic example of the style.

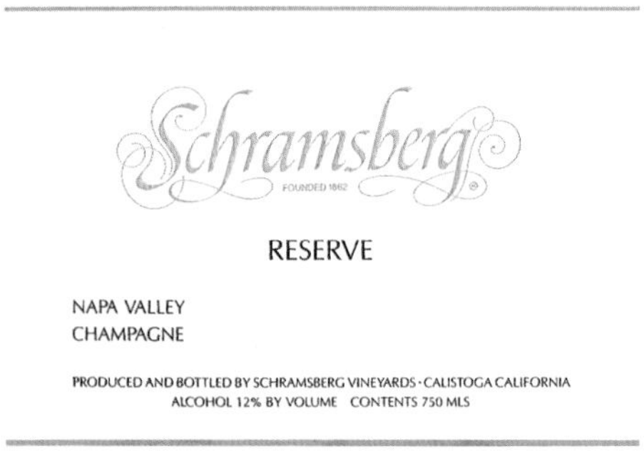
Schramsberg
FOUNDED 1862
RESERVE
NAPA VALLEY
CHAMPAGNE
PRODUCED AND BOTTLED BY SCHRAMSBERG VINEYARDS · CALISTOGA CALIFORNIA
ALCOHOL 12% BY VOLUME CONTENTS 750 MLS

SCHRAMSBERG 1862

A: 1400 Schramsberg Road, Calistoga, CA 94515 **T**: (707) 942 4558 **V**: By appointment **P**: 42,000 **W**: Alan Tenscher

This is another historic winery with a major hiatus between its nineteenth-century heyday and its rebirth in 1965 in the hands of Jack Davies and wife Jamie. Unlike the vast majority of Americans who have come to the Napa Valley to establish wineries during or after successful business careers and who have been content to provide the dollars — often by the millions — and let others do the work, the Davies attempted the impossible by doing it themselves, and succeeded in making sparkling wine with no prior experience, lurching with indomitable humor and courage from one crisis to the next, making do with Heath Robinson equipment which (obeying the first law of vintage) broke down at the worst possible moment. Yet within four years their wine was served at the Great Hall of the People as President Nixon toasted Premier Chou En-lai at that epochal 1969 meeting. The rest — that of Schramsberg and that of China — is history.

The estate itself is of great beauty, still rich with the history dating back to Jacob Schram and Robert Louis Stevenson's praise of Schram's wines. Small wonder it is open only by appointment (the Davies' house is near the center of the operational area), but a large number of people seem to make the appropriate appointments every day of the week.

There are five wines: Blanc de Blancs, Blanc de Noirs, Cuvee de Pinot, Cremant Demi-Sec and Reserve, all being vintage dated, and all with extended lees contact (up to five years for the Reserve). As if to acknowledge that while the quality of Schramsberg has not waned, that of the opposition has improved out of sight. Schramsberg released its new super prestige Cuvee Schram in London on October 7, 1992, in its custom-designed bottle and artistic label along the lines of the Taittinger Art Collection. This wine to one side, my vote goes to the creamy, gently citric 1987 Blanc de Blancs, a blend of Chardonnay and Pinot Blanc I would be happy to drink any time, any day.

STERLING 1969

A: 1111 Dunaweal Lane, Calistoga, CA 94515 **T**: (707) 942 3464 **V**: 10:30–4:30 daily **P**: 200,000 **W**: Bill Dyer

It is impossible to miss the Mediterranean-white Sterling Winery, perched on top of the 300-foot high knoll which rears out of the center of the valley and which is reached by an aerial tram servicing the valley-floor parking area. The four principals of the Sterling Paper Group who established the winery reasoned this would attract thousands of visitors a day who would then buy all the winery's production on the spot. They were wrong, notwithstanding the abundant skills of first winemaker Ric Forman, and Coca Cola became the owners in 1977, expanding the vineyard holdings by purchasing the 307-acre Diamond Mountain

ABOVE ~ *The hillside mountains of Storybook Mountain produce some of California's finest Zinfandel.*

Ranch, but tiring of the wine business and selling to Seagram in 1983.

Of all Seagram's worldwide wine investments, Sterling must be one of the best. In Bill Dyer, chief winemaker since 1985, it not only has one of the nicest executives in the industry, but one of the most competent. He is able to draw on 14 estate vineyards totaling 1,180 acres and spread from one end of the valley to the other. The most famous are the Diamond Mountain Ranch, with 199 acres of Chardonnay, Cabernet Sauvignon, Merlot and Cabernet Franc; the Three Palms Vineyard adjacent to the winery which has some precious plantings of Petit Verdot; and Winery Lake Vineyard in Carneros.

Opinions differ as to which are Sterling's best wines, but everyone agrees they are of great quality given the scale of overall production. The Sterling Reserve Meritage is my choice, showing all of the complexity and style one would expect of a blend which in 1988 (for example) was 40% Cabernet Sauvignon, 38% Merlot, 14% Cabernet Franc and 8% Petit Verdot and which spent 20 months on new French Allier oak, while the 1989 Winery Lake Chardonnay — redolent with toasty barrel ferment oak — was one of the best Carneros Chardonnays of that vintage. While not especially luscious on the mid-palate, it has great length. And just to show that big companies need not be boring, visitors to the winery can (exclusively) buy Semillon, and in the near future a Zinfandel made from old mountain vines — each made in less than 500-case lots.

STORYBOOK MOUNTAIN 1976

A: 3835 Highway 128, Calistoga, CA 94515
T: (707) 942 5310 **V**: By appointment
P: 8,500 **W**: Dr. J. Bernard Seps

Why erstwhile Stanford University professor of history lists himself as J. Bernard Seps when he is universally called Jerry I do not know, but I do know that over ten years ago he forever changed my then somewhat patronising view about Zinfandel, and I have not the slightest hesitation in naming him as the world's foremost producer of this variety. When he decided to close his history books in 1976 and purchase a historic 90-acre mountainside vineyard and winery which had been abandoned in 1964, he knew he wanted to re-establish a vineyard and reopen the cave cellars which had been dug by the Grimm brothers in 1880. The selection of the name was far easier than the choice of grape: he talked to Andre Tchelistcheff and whoever else would listen. All said the clay loam and mountainside topography, together with the high Region II climate, was red grape country. But which? The choice fell on Zinfandel, and Seps has spent the ensuing 17 years endeavoring to persuade a largely sceptical world that it (Zinfandel) should be treated with the same respect as a Cabernet or a Pinot of equal quality.

In 1992 I tasted his 1980, 1984, 1985 and 1987 Reserves: all were superb, easily scoring gold medal points, the 1980 still showing fresh fruit, depth and an exceptionally long finish — and looking like taking the next decade in its stride. The 1984 was ready, the 1985 and 1987 nowhere near. All have a remarkable intensity of complex dark cherry/briary/cedary flavors, with flashes of spice exploding here and there. Yet they are not the least bit heavy, jammy or tannic: put simply, they are great wines with superb balance. And yes, I did taste his 1990 standard, which was in the same class, and left me wondering just how good the 1990 Reserve will turn out to be.

OTHER WINERIES

STONEGATE 1973
A: 1183 Dunaweal Lane, Calistoga, CA 94515
T: (707) 942 6500 **W**: David B. Spaulding

TRAULSEN
A: 2250 Lake County Highway, Calistoga, CA 94515 **T**: (707) 942 0283
W: John Traulsen

WERMUTH 1982
A: 3942 Silverado Trail, Calistoga, CA 94515
T: (707) 942 5924 **W**: Ralph Wermuth

TOP ~ *Sterling Winery sits atop its knoll, gleaming like a Moorish palace, an irresistible lure to tourists.*

ABOVE ~ *The cellars at Storybook Mountain were tunneled more than 100 years ago.*

CARNEROS

ABOVE ~ *The patterns of the grapevine leaf are as complicated — and precise — as electronic circuitry.*

Los Carneros (or Carneros, as it is usually called) is one of the relatively few AVAs which withstand scrutiny from all viticultural viewpoints, yet it must have been a desolate and unfriendly place when the first settlers traveled through in 1823 to establish the mission town of Sonoma, a few critical miles to the north.

For even with its ever increasing acreage of vines — 6,200 acres in 1991 — Carneros can lay no claim to the sort of beauty wantonly displayed by so many wine regions. Such trees as there are huddle in the insignificant valleys, while the very hills themselves seem to have been cowed by the remorseless wind which howls across the landscape every afternoon. Says Kent Rasmussen, "The wind is what makes the Carneros, whether it is fun to live in it or not."

I discuss the daily wind cycle in more detail in the description of climate; here I briefly explain its significance for the way the vines grow and the quality (and quantity) of the grapes they produce. At high wind speeds young shoots will simply break off, or the growing tip will be severed as it hits a foliage wire. Likewise, during flowering, winds can interrupt the delicate fertilization process, leading to poor set and significantly reduced crop levels.

Such consequences are observable by the naked eye; more recently, however, research has uncovered a less visible impact of wind at lower speeds than previously thought important. A vine "breathes" by consuming carbon dioxide and water, the latter through uptake from its roots, and exhaling oxygen and water through its leaves. This is a central part of the process of photosynthesis, in which the energy of sunlight is converted into the energy of carbohydrate and — ultimately — sugar in the grapes.

In conditions of extreme heat (90°F or above) there will be a progressive shut-down of the vine's photosynthetic system as it seeks to protect itself against dehydration. The vine's stomata likewise shut down during windy conditions — but at far lower temperatures — for much the same reason.

So one can conjecture that Carneros would grow vines and produce grapes of a very different kind if all other conditions (soil, temperature, fog and so forth) were identical, but the wind were absent. It is yet another matter to guess whether the grapes would be better, but my feeling is that the wind is indeed far more of a friend than a foe.

Certain it is that the vignerons of Carneros have been crusaders within the broader scope of the Napa Valley in improving all aspects of viticulture: row orientation, row and vine spacing, trellis design, canopy management, site/varietal selection, clonal selection, and water management. Why? Because Carneros is the one truly marginal viticultural area within the Napa/Sonoma Valleys, and each of these aspects has to be intelligently and skillfully addressed if the full potential of each vineyard is to be realized.

OPPOSITE ~ *Carneros has many faces, not all as calm and verdant as that of a late summer evening in the vineyards behind Domaine Carneros.*

THE REGION IN BRIEF

Climate, Soil and Viticulture

CLIMATE

This is unequivocally Region I, strongly maritime influenced by the San Pablo Bay and by a second marine intrusion through the Petaluma Gap. It has the usual foggy mornings — typically dissipating at around 10:30–11 A.M. — followed by an hour or two of crisp and sunny weather (still significantly cooled by the nearby water mass) before the wind starts to blow from the west, whistling across the Carneros Plains, through American Canyon in the east, on to the Sacramento Delta and thence up the San Joaquin Valley. As evening comes, the Central Valley cools, the vacuum cleaner ceases to suck, and the winds are replaced by the fog which builds through the night.

Carneros
VINTAGE CHART 1981-91

RED

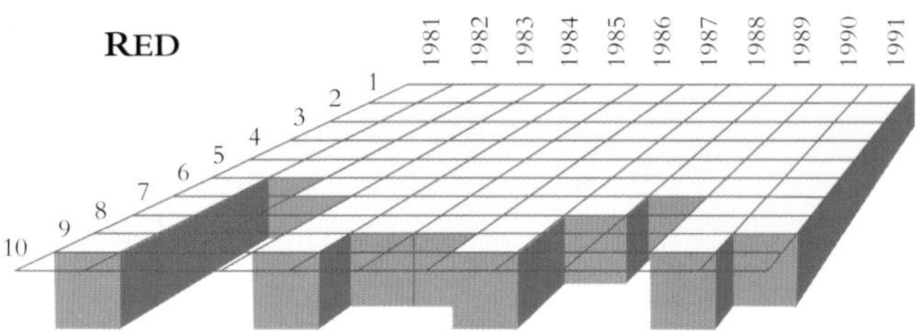
1981 1982 1983 1984 1985 1986 1987 1988 1989 1990 1991
1 2 3 4 5 6 7 8 9 10

WHITE

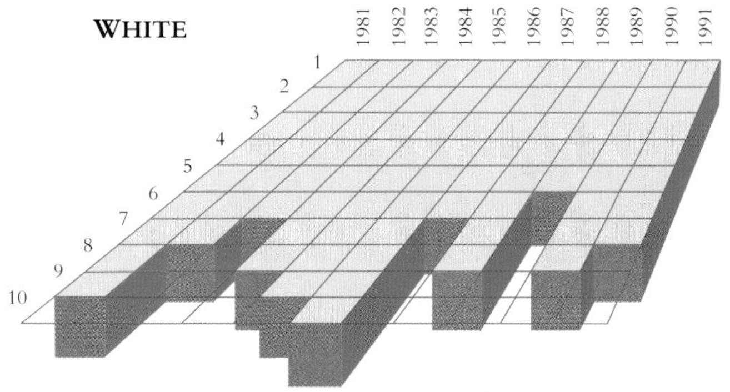
1981 1982 1983 1984 1985 1986 1987 1988 1989 1990 1991
1 2 3 4 5 6 7 8 9 10

If wind and cool temperatures are limiting factors on vine growth and grape ripening, so is the low rainfall, averaging around 22 inches compared to 30 inches at Rutherford in the Napa Valley and 40 inches at Healdsburg in the Alexander Valley. Until the advent of drip irrigation, it was the lack of effectively available moisture which was one of the principal limiting factors for viticulture (and horticulture of all kinds). A secondary constraint was (and is) limited underground water, requiring the installation and use of surface ponds or dams to store winter run-off rain, or slow-pumping bores which work all year round. On the plus side, spring frosts are not a significant risk, while the sparsely growing vines and strong winds reduce fungal diseases to a minimum.

SOIL

A quick drive through the 165-acre Truchard Vineyard will show you just how many soil types there are in even a small part of Carneros (not to mention the existence of some one-in-two slopes), but overall the pattern is far more simple than in many regions. For a start, the soils are thin, seldom more than three feet in depth, and often much less; they are of low to moderate fertility, and are underlaid by hard, relatively impermeable clay which, while having good water-holding capacity, is not readily penetrated by the roots of the vines.

There are two basic soil types, deposited within the last two million years during the ice ages by the receding waters of the San Pablo Bay. The first is the yellowish-brown Haire series derived from shallow tidal waters which had abundant marine life and whose innumerable sea shells can still be seen as fossils, adding calcium to the soil and lifting its pH to between seven and eight. The second series is the Diablo, formed by deeper marsh and bay sediments, with much less organic life. These black, fairly acidic soils have one particular redeeming feature: a high level of manganese, which promotes the formation of chlorophyll.

THE GROWING SEASON

The season is a particularly long one: the maritime influence promotes early budbreak (typically at the end of the first week of March) while harvest frequently runs into October. There is sufficient warmth to continue ripening grapes through to the end of October if the canopy has been properly maintained; the limitation is most likely to be the season break and the arrival of autumn rains.

Contract Growers

Beckstoffer Vineyards Thirty-six acres of Chardonnay and Pinot Noir; partly supplied to Schug.
Durrell Vineyards Principally Chardonnay and Pinot Noir; 155 acres falling partly in the Sonoma Valley and partly in Carneros, supplying (*inter alia*) Kistler and Kendall-Jackson.
Hyde Vineyard One hundred and fifty acres planted to five Bordeaux varieties (red and white) as well as Pinot Noir and Chardonnay.
Sangiacomo Nine hundred acres planted progressively since 1969 to Chardonnay, Pinot Noir and Merlot, supplying approximately 40 wineries, including many of the most prestigious makers in California.
Truchard One hundred and sixty-five acres planted on various blocks and varying *terroir* to Chardonnay, Pinot Noir, Merlot, Cabernet Franc, Cabernet Sauvignon, Syrah and Zinfandel; many

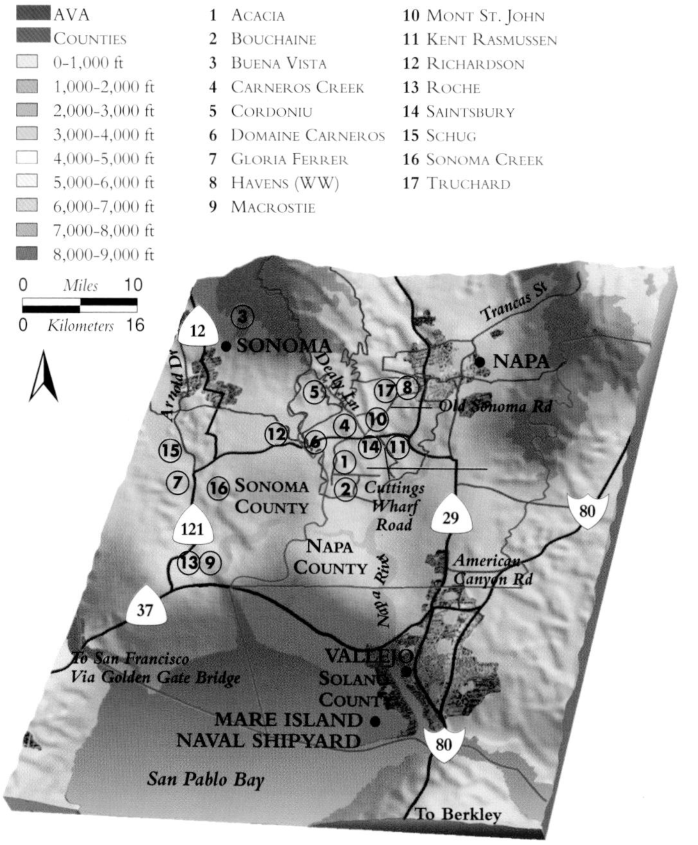
AVA
Counties
0-1,000 ft
1,000-2,000 ft
2,000-3,000 ft
3,000-4,000 ft
4,000-5,000 ft
5,000-6,000 ft
6,000-7,000 ft
7,000-8,000 ft
8,000-9,000 ft
1 Acacia
2 Bouchaine
3 Buena Vista
4 Carneros Creek
5 Cordoniu
6 Domaine Carneros
7 Gloria Ferrer
8 Havens (WW)
9 Macrostie
10 Mont St. John
11 Kent Rasmussen
12 Richardson
13 Roche
14 Saintsbury
15 Schug
16 Sonoma Creek
17 Truchard
0 Miles 10
0 Kilometers 16
SONOMA
NAPA
Old Sonoma Rd
Arnold Dr
Sonoma County
Cuttings Wharf Road
Napa County
American Canyon Rd
To San Francisco Via Golden Gate Bridge
VALLEJO
Solano County
MARE ISLAND NAVAL SHIPYARD
San Pablo Bay
To Berkley
12
121
37
29
80

purchasers including Michael Havens, but also makes wines on its (Truchard's) own account.

Principal Wine Styles

Chardonnay

Given the flexibility of Chardonnay as a grape in both vineyard and winery, it is hardly surprising that it should flourish here in climatic conditions which (on some perhaps simplistic measures) are not far removed from those of Burgundy. Neither is it surprising that it should produce a distinctive and immediately recognizable style: lean, tart, crisp, appley and intense in its youth, most obviously so where the winemaker has been content to let the grape (and its interaction with the *terroir*) speak for itself. The wines are slow developing, and always tend to elegance rather than opulence, with citrus-melon-apple flavors predominating over heavier, nutty/peachy characters. There are few, if any, poor producers; Acacia, Buena Vista, Kent Rasmussen, Saintsbury and Sonoma Creek have all produced wines of the highest quality.

Pinot Noir

If Chardonnay is the wine world's dashing groom, Pinot Noir is the reluctant bride — and Carneros is unquestionably one of the few areas in California (and for that matter in the world) which has at least enticed the bride to the altar and exchanged vows. Yet were it not for the experimental work of Francis Mahoney at Carneros Creek and the effective pragmatism of the Saintsbury team I might wonder whether the marriage had been consummated and borne fruit. For there is something virginal about many of the Carneros Pinot Noirs: the cherry/red berry flavors are consistently correct, pure and delicate, yet that wildness — an animal scent — and velvety textural opulence of the very greatest Pinot Noirs are (with the odd exception) still to manifest themselves. Carneros Creek seems likely to be the first to do so with regularity, without demeaning the consistently excellent wines of Saintsbury nor the deservedly praised Pinots of Acacia. Mont St. John and Schug, too, have joined the choir and deserve an audition.

Sparkling Wine

One-third of the Chardonnay and Pinot Noir grown in Carneros is used in making premium sparkling wine — so much so that I deal with it separately on page 53.

Other Varieties

Cabernet Sauvignon (6%) and Merlot (5%) attest to the fact that even in a topographically and climatically homogenous region such as Carneros pockets of mesoclimate and *terroir* can make the exception prove the rule. Of the two, the earlier ripening Merlot is catching the wave of excitement which the variety is generating state-wide, but in the warmer north-eastern sector of Carneros even Cabernet Sauvignon can avoid excessive green vegetable characters, while growers such as Dr. Tony Truchard are extending the argument even further with varieties such as Syrah and Zinfandel.

ABOVE ~ *Elaborate landscaping at Cordoniu in Carneros.*

ABOVE ~ *Carneros map.*

THE CARNEROS QUALITY ALLIANCE

While Carneros is the closest region to San Francisco, and Roche is the first winery you pass (immediately after you turn north off Highway 37 to head towards Sonoma), many people drive through on the way to the Napa or Sonoma Valleys without realizing they have done so. Yet most of those would know of Carneros, and — what is more — associate it with high quality grapes and wine.

The paradox of high reputation yet physical anonymity was both the cause and effect of the Carneros Quality Alliance: the anonymity led to the formation of the Alliance, and the reputation is in no small measure due to the efforts of the Alliance. One of its more recent achievements, the mid 1992 renaming of the 12/121 highway as the Carneros Highway, should also do much to alleviate the anonymity factor.

CARNEROS

QUALITY ALLIANCE

ABOVE ~ *Carneros Quality Alliance, promoting the reputation and alleviating the anonymity of the region.*

Carneros means "sheep," and this was grazing and mixed agricultural country; there is not now nor has there ever been a town by that name. While there were significant vineyards established in the late nineteenth century (Stanly Ranch had over 300 acres), viticulture all but disappeared under the dual assault of phylloxera (in the late 1870s and onwards) and of Prohibition.

John Garetto established the first post Prohibition winery in the early 1930s (it is now Bouchaine), and both the newly arrived (from Europe) Andre Tchelistcheff and the not-so-newly arrived Louis Martini started purchasing Carneros grapes around the same time, principally from part of the Stanly Ranch which had somehow survived the initial phylloxera attack. In 1942 Louis Martini purchased 200 acres of the Stanly Ranch, now known as La Loma Vineyard (following it with Las Amigas, purchased in two parcels in 1962 and 1972), while the 1960s saw the inception of Winery Lake Vineyard (by Rene di Rosa, now owned by Sterling) and the Sangiacomo Vineyards.

But even throughout the boom days of the 1970s relatively little attention was paid to Carneros, and land values remained low. Dr. Tony Truchard recalls being given departmental advice not to purchase one of his prime blocks because the soil was too shallow, and because of the general scepticism about the ability of the area to produce economic yields.

To this day there are only two wineries visible as you drive along the Carneros Highway: the relatively humble Mont St. John and the imposing edifice of Domaine Carneros. Far more grapes grown in Carneros are processed outside its boundaries than within.

So it was that the Carneros Quality Alliance was formed: in 1992 it had 26 winery members (not all of which are physically situated in Carneros nor even draw the majority of their grapes from Carneros) and 44 grower members. Members pay significant subscription fees, and the Alliance has an operating budget which makes other districts green with envy, but it has been conspicuously successful in lifting awareness of the region in the perception of both the consumer and the industry as a whole. Its distinctive green symbols with the words "Carneros Quality Alliance" abound along the roadsides; it produces exceptionally comprehensive information booklets for the public, and an equally comprehensive grower booklet for industry (winery purchase) use; and stands ever ready to help journalists, winemakers or others from any part of the world seeking information on the grapes or wines of Carneros. Its address, incidentally, is P.O. Box 178, Vineburg, CA 95487, telephone (707) 938 5906.

ABOVE ~ *The Domaine Carneros Winery and visitors facility is one of the most prominent landmarks in the region — some say too prominent.*

CALIFORNIA SPARKLING WINES

"There has been a more dramatic change in the style and quality of California sparkling wine over the past 20 years than for any other single wine category." The speaker is John Wright, Chairman of Domaine Chandon, and if the statement is true, the single most important catalyst for change has been none other than Domaine Chandon and its long term chief executive officer, John Wright himself.

So the cynical might dismiss or at least seek to qualify the statement, but cynics are not always right — if you will forgive the pun. For my money, the truth is that there has been such a change, and that it is in fact accelerating. Without denigrating the pioneering efforts of Schramsberg, Kornell and Scharffenberger, near ballistic improvement has come about largely through the influence — not to mention the massive investment — of the additional seven Champagne and the two Spanish houses which have followed the lead of Domaine Chandon and established California brands.

ABOVE ~ *Michel Salgues, chief executive and winemaker at Roederer, flamboyantly disgorging a bottle of sparkling wine.*

Roederer and Scharffenberger (the latter now owned by Pommery) have established themselves in the Anderson Valley at the northern extremity of California's wine regions, and Piper Sonoma in the Russian River, while Maison Deutz has headed south to the chilly ocean edge of the Arroyo Grande appellation (within San Luis Obispo). All the remainder of the foreign owned or controlled wineries have set themselves up in the Napa Valley (whether within Carneros or further north) while sourcing all or the major part of their grapes from Carneros.

In turn, all of the serious *methode champenoise* wines are principally wrought from the classic varieties of Chardonnay and Pinot Noir, with a little Pinot Meuniere and (occasionally) Pinot Blanc according to the whim of the maker.

The learning curve has been so steep for many reasons, with both viticultural and enological influences at work. For a start, California makers have had very similar experiences to their Australian counterparts in dealing with the relative performance and style contribution of Chardonnay and Pinot Noir compared to the way those varieties perform in France.

In France, Pinot Noir is predictable and is the component which provides the structure and grace to the cuvee; in both California and Australia, Pinot Noir has been altogether less predictable and harmonious. In the New World, Chardonnay has tended "to fatten up" too quickly in bottle, leading to rather heavy and coarse wines.

The initial response to this period of learning was to pick the grapes earlier, and to seek to balance the green, hard flavors which emerged with higher dosage levels at disgorgement, an approach which met with even less success. As viticultural techniques improved — directed to getting more flavor into the grapes at a given level of sugar accumulation — and as makers realized that achieving flavor was no less important for sparkling than for table wines, so did their winemaking approaches loosen up. Most paradoxically, it was found that riper grapes could benefit from higher, rather than lower, dosage levels.

Then there was the matching learning curve on the part of the consumer. Says Mumm chief winemaker Greg Fowler, "I grew up drinking French — it was the only champagne." Price and currency fluctuations, sudden export drives by houses not represented in California (notably Lanson) and labels which some might think insufficiently differentiated the real thing from the California wines added confusion to what originally was a justified prejudice. Yet still the houses arrived and commenced production: had the initial increases in consumption patterns been maintained, all would have been well. They were not, and it is now estimated that there is more sparkling wine on tirage in California than the annual consumption of the whole of the United States.

To make matters worse, most of the houses are operating at only a fraction of their capacity, and the newcomers, in particular, are necessarily projecting very slow growth.

The saving graces are twofold: first, the investment time-frame of the Champagne houses is almost Japanese in its scale (vast) and its patience (no less impressive). Second, the wines are being given far longer on their yeast lees before disgorgement than pure economics would dictate, but are all the better for that.

Thus in 1992 Domaine Chandon released its super-premium Etoile, a non-vintage blend of the 1984 (66.6%) and 1986 (33.3%) vintages, remarkable for its age but unique in that the blend was made long after the components had been champagnized, a technique which opens up fascinating opportunities for the future.

John Wright, with decades of first-hand experience of sparkling winemaking in four continents, has the next-to-last word. "Overall, there is a very definitive underlying flavor profile for California sparkling wines which transcends stylistic differences." I would only add that the quality of the wines released by the likes of Deutz, Domaine Chandon, Mumm, Roederer and Scharffenberger in the past few years has caused me to entirely reappraise my previously somewhat negative views of California sparkling wines.

WINERIES *of* CARNEROS

ACACIA WINERY 1979

A: 2750 Las Amigas Rd, Napa, CA 94559
T: (707) 226 9991 **V**: By appointment
P: 50,000 **W**: Larry Brooks

In 1986 Acacia become part of the Chalone Inc. group, which in turn has cross shareholdings with Chateau Lafite, but co-founder Mike Richmond and long-term winemaker Larry Brooks remain very much involved with the winery, which since inception has been a pacesetter for Chardonnay and Pinot Noir, and more recently has made a modest entry into the sparkling wine market. The greyhound-lean Brooks had a circuitous and non-technical entry into the wine industry, and retains a constantly enquiring mind untrammeled by conventional wisdom.

Chardonnay (75–80% of total production) is in mainstream Carneros style: clean, crisp and understated in its youth, but developing complex honeyed, nutty characters with several years' bottle age without becoming fat or blowsy. Pinot Noir, like Chardonnay, is offered both under Carneros and specific vineyard designations (notably St. Clair): again like Chardonnay, the philosophy is that the cherry/redcurrant fruit should not be over-elaborated, although sensitive use of spicy, charred oak does add a dimension to wines of finesse.

BOUCHAINE 1981

A: 1075 Buchli Station Road, Napa, CA 94558 **T**: (707) 252 9065 **V**: By appointment
P: 20,500 **W**: John Montero

Bouchaine is housed in an outsized redwood and concrete winery built in the unlikely year of 1931 by Italian-born Johnny Garetto, whose theory of counter-cyclical investment failed to produce the rewards one might have expected. In 1951 the winery was purchased by Beringer, and at one time was used as a major storage and blending facility. Thirty years later it was acquired and renovated by DuPont heir Gerret Copeland and publisher Austin Kiplinger, who renamed it Bouchaine. Even since 1981 it has had several changes in direction, but has now settled upon Carneros Chardonnay (12,000 cases), Carneros Pinot Noir (7,000 cases) and Russian River Gewurztraminer (500 cases and a sentimental reminder of winemaker John Montero's earlier years at Navarro).

Wine-style is direct, firm, oaky and fairly uncompromising, but on-going work with clonal selection of Pinot Noir, coupled with Montero's formidable technical qualifications, hold greater promise for the future. The Chardonnays are in ultra-reserved Carneros style, crisp, apple-scented and slow developing.

BUENA VISTA 1857

A: 18000 Old Winery Road, Sonoma, CA 95476 **T**: (707) 252 7117 **V**: 10–5 daily
P: 250,000 **W**: Jill Davis

Agoston Haraszthy founded Buena Vista in 1857, and by the 1870s it was claimed to be the largest vineyard in the world. A decline in the Haraszthy family fortunes followed by the 1906 earthquake closed the winery until the post-Second World War years, but it was not until 1968 that the renaissance began, and only in 1979 did the Buena Vista of today begin to take shape. In that year it was purchased by A. Racke Co. of Germany, with a still youthful Marcus Moller-Racke installed as chairman and enchanting wife Anne Moller-Racke as director of vineyard operations — 935 estate acres, of which 769 acres are organically farmed (230 acres are fully certified).

CARNEROS
Since 1857
Buena Vista
1989
Carneros
PINOT NOIR

The wines (spearheaded by Chardonnay, Cabernet Sauvignon, Merlot and Pinot Noir but with others) are produced in three tiers: at the bottom end, Domaine Buena Vista, then Estate Varietals, and next Private Reserve, with plans for occasional ultra-premium Vineyard Selection wines. Notwithstanding considerable expenditure and expertise being lavished on the vineyards, the wines so far do little more than reflect their modest price, although the 1990 Chardonnays fulfill the Carneros promise of crisp citrus/melon fruit, and have a real touch of elegance which augurs well for their development in bottle.

CARNEROS CREEK WINERY 1972

A: 1285 Dealy Lane, Napa, CA 94558
T: (707) 253 9463 **V**: 10–5 daily **P**: 25,000
W: Francis Mahoney and Melissa Moravec

FLEUR
de
CARNEROS
Carneros Pinot Noir
FLEUR DE CARNEROS IS PRODUCED AND BOTTLED BY
CARNEROS CREEK WINERY NAPA, CALIFORNIA
ALCOHOL 13.2% BY VOLUME

Co-owner Francis Mahoney has undertaken an odyssey of Homeric proportions since founding Carneros Creek and becoming totally dissatisfied with the Pinot Noir clonal selections then available from U.C. Davis. In 1975, together with Dr. C.J. Alley of Davis, he began one of the most painstaking clonal evaluation programs undertaken anywhere in the New World, and quite unique for a winery of this modest size. The first phase ran from 1975 to 1982; the second to 1988; and the third is now coming to fruition — precisely at the time phylloxera threatens to turn back the experimental clock by at least five heart (and bank) breaking years.

Mahoney is eerily calm and philosophical about the phylloxera threat to the 22-acre vineyard planted in 1988 to his six clones (on varied spacings) so painstakingly selected over almost 20 years. Perhaps he is consoled by the superb quality of the 1991 vintage wines made from this vineyard, wines which — if repeated — will make the name Carneros Creek famous around the Pinot wine world. Until 1991 the Pinots were released in three guises: Fleur de Carneros, effectively a second label wine (11,000 cases); the standard Blue Label; and (at three times the price of the Fleur de Carneros) limited quantities of Signature Reserve. 1991 will result in the first vineyard-designated ultra-premium wine, making the fascinating cellar releases of Napa Valley-sourced Cabernet Sauvignon back to the early '70s, and the ongoing Chardonnay, seem almost incidental.

CORDONIU 1989

A: 1345 Henry Road, Napa, CA 94558
T: (707) 224 1668 **V**: 10–5 Mon–Thurs; 10–3 Fri–Sun **P**: 10,000 **W**: Janet Papagano

Cordoniu made the first sparkling wine in Spain in 1872, and has gone on to become one of the giants of the worldwide sparkling wine industry. After a five-year search in a number of countries, it purchased 350 acres in Carneros, with vineyard plantings planned to grow from 110 to 225 acres, and wine production to rise gradually to the winery permit capacity of 180,000 cases, but being unlikely to exceed 100,000 cases before the year 2000. The winery is a striking architectural concept, designed to blend into the landscape rather than dominate it (as does Domaine Carneros), and the interior is a sheer delight — as well as being highly functional, and commanding breathtaking views of Carneros.

The initial release in 1992 was of a non-vintage Brut Cuvee (50% Pinot Noir, 50% Chardonnay) which is a fine, subtle yet distinctly fruity wine. It will be followed by a Carneros Cuvee (75% Pinot Noir, 25% Chardonnay, probably vintage-dated) and a Reserve Cuvee (styled with prolonged yeast-aging in mind).

DOMAINE CARNEROS 1987

A: 1240 Duhig Road, Napa, CA 94581
T: (707) 257 0101 **V**: 10:30–5:30 daily June–October **P**: 45,000 **W**: Eileen Crane

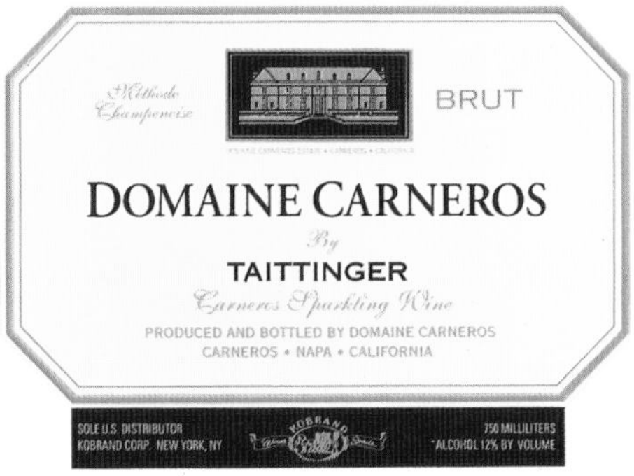
BRUT
DOMAINE CARNEROS
TAITTINGER
PRODUCED AND BOTTLED BY DOMAINE CARNEROS
CARNEROS • NAPA • CALIFORNIA

The winery and visitor center completed in the spring of 1989 is said to have been inspired by the Chateau de la Marquetterie owned by Taittinger, the French champagne house which is the major partner in Domaine Carneros. Those who think Disneyland is an appropriate adjunct to the suburbs of Paris will no doubt find the Domaine Carneros building no less aesthetically pleasing. It draws its grapes from 138 acres planted between 1982 and 1989; two-thirds to Chardonnay and one-third to Pinot Noir, with small plantings of Pinot Meuniere and Pinot Blanc. Production is planned to peak at 60,000 cases, but not in the immediate future. The non-vintage Brut Domaine Carneros (60% Pinot Noir, 35% Chardonnay and 5% Pinot Blanc) is a very fine and delicate wine, with a crisp, faintly green-grassy palate and excellent finish which deserves the lavish praise heaped on it from all quarters.

GLORIA FERRER 1982

A: 23555 Highway 121, Sonoma, CA 95476
T: (707) 996 7256 **V**: 10:30–5:30 daily
P: 65,000 **W**: Bob Iantosca

GLORIA FERRER
BRUT
SONOMA COUNTY MÉTHODE CHAMPENOISE

Freixenet, with a production of around three million cases, ranks second only to Cordoniu among the largest makers of sparkling wines in the world. By those standards, its investment in Carneros — named after the owner's wife — might seem modest; by almost any other yardstick it is a very substantial one. The strongly Spanish-influenced (in terms of design) winery was completed in 1988; prior to that time the wine had been made and stored at other facilities, but winemaking is now entirely under the control of Bob Iantosca at headquarters. There are 175 acres of estate grapes, 75% Pinot Noir and 25% Chardonnay, with a few more acres still to be planted. Once in full bearing, the possibility exists for 100% estate wines, but it is likely blending options will be kept open, particularly with Pinot Noir from as far north in Sonoma County as Healdsburg.

The wines being sold in 1992 all had very considerable age: 1985 Carneros Cuvee (60% Pinot Noir, 40% Chardonnay), 1987 Royal Cuvee (the same blend) and Gloria Ferrer Brut (90% Pinot Noir, 10% Chardonnay). The wines have been well reviewed, but I have to admit finding strange and not terribly pleasant flavors in all three.

MACROSTIE 1987

A: 17246 Woodland Avenue, Sonoma, CA 95476 **T**: (707) 996 4480 **V**: By appointment
P: 6,000 **W**: Steve MacRostie

By the fast-moving standards of the 1990s Steve MacRostie is an old hand in the wine industry, and certainly knows the southern end of the Sonoma Valley (which often merges imperceptibly with Carneros), having worked for 11 years as winemaker at Hacienda before moving on to establish his own label in 1987 and becoming a consultant to several small wineries, including Roche, where he has made his wines since 1989.

Chardonnay is the principal wine, first released in 1987, and with the '90 receiving high praise in numerous magazines including the *Wine Spectator*. MacRostie believes the vintage to be one of the finest he has encountered in 17 years of winemaking, but I find that the 100% malolactic fermentation through which the wine went tends to dominate and suppress the fruit without providing any softness or creaminess on the finish. A Hudson Vineyard Merlot was due for release in late 1992, and a Pinot Noir (like the Chardonnay from Sangiacomo) will make its appearance once MacRostie is satisfied with the style.

1990
MACROSTIE
CHARDONNAY
CARNEROS

MONT ST. JOHN 1978

A: 5400 Old Sonoma Road, Napa, CA 94559
T: (707) 257 2775 **V**: 10–5 daily **P**: 20,000
W: Buck Bartolucci

The Bartolucci family entered the wine industry in 1922, defying the constraints of Prohibition by purchasing a vineyard and winery at Oakville which was ultimately sold in 1971. Third generation Andrea "Buck" Bartolucci used his share of the sale proceeds to purchase 160 acres of Carneros vineyards on which he established the dry-farmed and now certified organic Madonna Vineyard. Chardonnay (74 acres), Pinot Noir (25 acres), Cabernet Sauvignon (12 acres) and Johannisberg Riesling (10 acres) provide the bulk of the 350–400 tonne production, which through the '70s and early '80s was largely sold to other wineries. In 1978 father Louis came out of retirement to join with his son Buck to build the Mont St. John Winery, and steadily increasing quantities of the estate grapes have been used for the Mont St. John label.

The excellent 1989 Pinot Noir, with strong, clean, dark cherry fruit and plenty of weight, shows just why buyers such as Acacia, Mondavi and Phelps had been so happy to acquire the Madonna Vineyard grapes. The Cabernet Sauvignon, too, demonstrates that with appropriate site selection and vineyard management this variety can produce Carneros wines with plenty of weight, extract and ripe, dark chocolate fruit flavor.

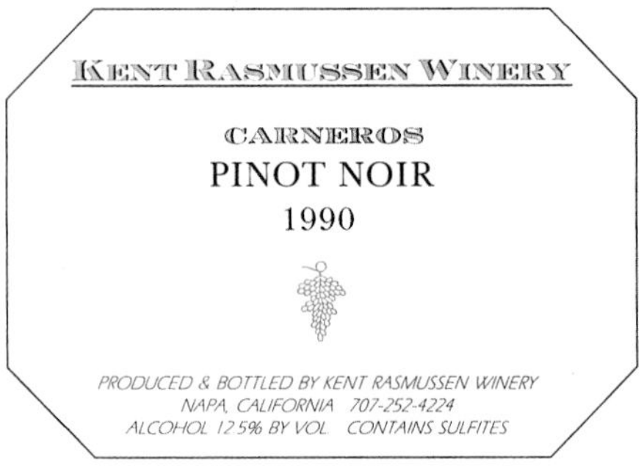
KENT RASMUSSEN WINERY
CARNEROS
PINOT NOIR
1990
PRODUCED & BOTTLED BY KENT RASMUSSEN WINERY
NAPA, CALIFORNIA 707-252-4224
ALCOHOL 12.5% BY VOL. CONTAINS SULFITES

KENT RASMUSSEN WINERY 1986

A: 2125 Cuttings Wharf Road, Napa, CA 94559 **T**: (707) 252 4224 **V**: By appointment **P**: 4,200 **W**: Kent Rasmussen

Kent Rasmussen cuts a distinctly Hobbit-like figure as he walks around his diminutive winery, filled with the odd batches of wine and odd pieces of equipment which any self-respecting hobbit would thoroughly approve of. After working in South Africa and Australia (as well as in other Napa Valley wineries) Rasmussen financed the construction of his winery by a complicated quasi co-operative scheme, which still results in significant wine dividends to his original backers. He has become an acknowledged Pinot Noir specialist (he also consults to other Pinot makers), but sells two-thirds of the grapes from his 12-acre Pinot vineyard, vinifying the remaining one-third under the Kent Rasmussen label, along with a Chardonnay made from Carneros fruit. Somewhat quixotically, he then purchases an odd and ever-changing assemblage of grapes from other regions including Alicante Bouschet, Dolcetto, Syrah and so forth for release (in tiny quantities) under his second label Ramsey, most of which is sold direct ex-winery.

The Chardonnay can be outstanding ('86 and '90 being great examples of a complex, barrel-fermented and richly oaky wine which has length and fruit freshness on the finish to give balance), while the Pinot Noir can be opulently plummy, even in difficult years such as 1989.

RICHARDSON VINEYARDS 1980

A: 2711 Knob Hill Road, Sonoma, CA 95476 **T**: (707) 938 2610 **V**: By appointment **P**: 3,000 **W**: Dennis Richardson

Dennis Richardson was a political science major, and I imagine he would be the first to acknowledge that a tertiary degree of this kind is the perfect training for someone who says the hell with it all — why don't I do something I really believe in, something I really enjoy, and to blazes with the money. The missing ingredient, as it were, was the money in the first place, but it didn't prevent him and his family purchasing a tiny house and erecting an equally tiny winery on a tiny and insignificant road which, with exquisite irony, is called Knob Hill Road. The original plan was to plant a vineyard on the surrounding ten acres of land, but even the smallest and most basic winery seems to have an insatiable appetite for whatever loose change happens to be around, so the vineyard (equally financially rapacious) remains as part of the business plan. Having taken the plunge, he also gained knowledge of the sharp end of the industry through a stint in retailing.

These salutory experiences notwithstanding, Dennis Richardson has made some outstanding wines, most from grapes from the Sangiacomo Vineyard. His 1989 Meritage could have come straight from a classed growth Bordeaux chateau so far as I am concerned, while both his '90 and '91 Pinots (from Sangiacomo, like the varietal Merlot) are wines with that touch of wildness which the perfectly sculpted Carneros Pinots sometimes lack, even if the appeal is more to the heart than the intellect.

ROCHE WINERY 1989

A: 28700 Arnold Drive, Sonoma, CA 95476 **T**: (707) 935 7846 **V**: 10–5 daily **P**: 6,000 **W**: Steve MacRostie

Dr. John Roche (still actively practicing medicine) and wife Genevieve purchased 2,500 acres of typical Carneros rolling pastureland in 1977 as an ultimate retirement investment, but without any particular thought of establishing a vineyard or winery. Indeed, current wisdom would have said this site (adjacent to the intersection of Highways 37 and 121, on the western side of the Sonoma Hills, and five miles closer to San Pablo Bay than the nearest vineyard) simply wouldn't ripen grapes. By 1985 the thinking of all concerned had changed; the Roches established 25 acres of Pinot Noir and Chardonnay and set up a winery to receive the

ABOVE ~ *The celebrated cows of Winery Lake give a new meaning to landscape art.*

1989 vintage, dubbed "The Gateway Winery" by the owners. Any doubts about the ability of the site to ripen grapes were comprehensively answered by the 1990 vintage: the Chardonnay was picked between September 8 and 23, the Pinot Noir on September 14 and 15, and both varieties were harvested at over 23° Brix, finishing with alcohol just under 14°.

The Chardonnay is in typical Carneros style — lean, racy and crisp with citrus, apple and melon fruit — and certainly doesn't betray its high alcohol. The Pinot Noir, by contrast, does, showing very ripe plummy fruit with abundant extract, suggesting all sorts of interesting possibilities for future vintages.

SAINTSBURY 1981

A: 1500 Los Carneros Avenue, Napa, CA 94559 **T**: (707) 252 0592 **V**: By appointment **P**: 42,000 **W**: William Knuttel

Saintsbury stands for success: success in perfecting the most difficult variety (Pinot Noir) in a most demanding climate; success in marketing exponentially increasing production in the middle-upper end of the price spectrum; success in neatly compressing the operation into a pleasantly functional but manifestly undersized winery; and (inevitably from the foregoing) financial success. Co-owners David Graves (for many Mr. Pinot Noir) and Dick Ward are as dedicated consumers as they are marketers of fine Chardonnay and Pinot Noir, and apply their skills in the area they know best, leaving the production magic to Bill Knuttel.

For the most extraordinary thing about this exceptional winery is that not only has production increased, but so has quality — yet the winemaking practices are far from exotic. Indeed, in the case of Pinot Noir they border on the banal. The answer to the paradox lies in the ever-increasing quality of the grapes, partly triggered by improved trellis and canopy management, clonal selection and yield limitation, and partly through the development of Saintsbury's own vineyards. There are two Chardonnays — regular and Reserve, and three Pinot Noirs — Garnet (light bodied and inexpensive), Carneros and Reserve. In 1990 these all hit new heights: the Reserve Chardonnay with melon/citric/stone fruit flavors and a seductive touch of spicy oak, the Carneros and Reserve Pinots with perfectly balanced plum/cherry fruit, the Reserve with an extra dimension of intensity and structure. The '91 Pinots are every bit as good, and one wonders if the Saintsbury juggernaut will ever stop.

SCHUG WINERY 1980

A: 602 Bonneau Road, CA 95476 **T**: (707) 939 9365 **V**: 10–5 daily **P**: 10,000 **W**: Walter Schug

If Walter Schug were a racehorse his breeding might be described as by Gallo out of

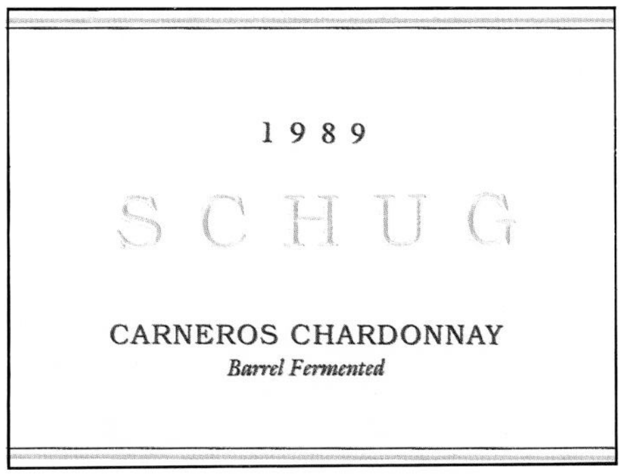
1989
SCHUG
CARNEROS CHARDONNAY
Barrel Fermented

Geisenheim. From a distinguished German winemaking family, he graduated from Geisenheim before moving to California in 1959 to work for several large wineries, including six years as grower liaison officer with the largest of them all, Gallo. He came into the public spotlight in 1973 when he was recruited to help design Joseph Phelps Winery, becoming chief winemaker; he remained until 1983. From the vast to the medium-sized winery was one major transition; in 1983 he began the final transition to a small, premium producer of strictly hand-made wines, a metamorphosis which continued in 1989 with the building of his 10,000 case Carneros winery and establishment of 38 acres of estate vineyards, planted two-thirds to Chardonnay (on the flats) and one-third Pinot Noir (on the hillsides), close spaced, with a vertical trellis, arched canes and moveable catch wires. Once those vineyards come into full production, and the wines made from them are released, the metamorphosis will be complete.

One of the reasons Schug left Joseph Phelps was his personal dislike for the big Californian style, and his Chardonnays cannot be accused of being big. On the contrary, they are lean, austere and flinty; the Pinot Noirs can fall into the same category, although the generous, complex, structured plum and cherry flavored '89 Beckstoffer Vineyard Pinot Noir shows Schug at his very best.

SONOMA CREEK WINERY 1987

A: 23355 Millerick Road, Sonoma, CA 95476 **T**: (707) 938 3031 **V**: 11–4:30 weekends; other by appointment **P**: 10,000 **W**: Dave Dobson

A retired veterinary surgeon and veterinary science lecturer (at Davis); an ex-Tahoe croupier who then put himself through Davis with a major in enology while practicing as a home winemaker and intermittent builder; and a Johns Hopkins graduate in chemical engineering with a career with DuPont and Adell Plastics before obtaining an enology Masters from Davis (triggered by his elder brother's feeble attempts at making rosehip and dandelion wine and bolstered by a part-time job as a brewer at a brew pub) have coalesced to form a formidable team at Sonoma Creek. The dramatis personae are, respectively, father and general manager Bob Larsen, son and partner Tom Larsen (briefly winemaker and now sales and marketing director), and winemaker Dave Dobson. If all this were not enough, the 40-acre Chardonnay estate vineyard is organically farmed, with Zinfandel, Cabernet Sauvignon, Muscat Canelli and Merlot purchased from Sonoma Valley vineyards. The winery, incidentally, is a testament to the anti-edifice complex: it is ultra-functional, spotlessly clean and production driven.

The best wines are exemplary: a peppery, spicy, lively Zinfandel (part 60-year-old vines and part Mayacamas Mountain); a juicy sweet fruit and appropriately tannic Cabernet from old vines at the southern end of the Sonoma Valley; and a wonderfully rich Estate Chardonnay (utilizing one of the best French coopers, Dargaud & Jaegle) which exemplifies the synergy between high quality fruit and oak. Sonoma Creek is slightly off the beaten track, but it is certainly worth finding.

1990
SONOMA
WINERY
ZINFANDEL
SONOMA VALLEY
CREEK
ALCOHOL 13.0% BY VOLUME

TRUCHARD VINEYARDS 1990

A: 3234 Old Sonoma Road, Napa, CA 94559 **T**: (707) 253 7153 **V**: By appointment **P**: 6,000 **W**: Michael Havens

When medical practitioner Tony Truchard and his wife purchased their first piece of land in Carneros in 1973 they did so simply because the price was right: in Truchard's words, "It was across the railroad tracks." Over the ensuing ten-year period they purchased a further five parcels averaging $3,000 to $4,000 an acre which, even in the recessionary market of 1992, were by then commanding $20,000 an acre or more. Those purchases have lifted Truchard's vineyard plantings (all established by him) to 170 acres, and includes one hillside block with old oak trees which must surely be the most beautiful site in the whole of Carneros. While remaining primarily grape sellers, the Truchards ventured into winemaking in 1989 (using custom crush facilities) and in 1990 restored — lavishly restored, indeed — an old barn on the property, lifting production from the 1990 level of 1,600 cases to 4,600 in 1991, ultimately aiming to level off at 12,000 cases.

The accent will be on Chardonnay, Pinot Noir and Merlot; the 1990 Pinot Noir showed the typical bright, crystal-clear cherry fruit for which Carneros is noted, and — given the vineyard base to chose from — one should expect Truchard's wines to gain a formidable reputation.

EAST MOUNTAINS

The East Mountains I describe in this chapter are essentially the western extremity of the Vaca Range: Mount St. Helena to the north of Calistoga being the dominant landmark at the northern end of the region; then The Palisades and Howell Mountain, due east of which is the Pope Valley, tenuously connected with what most people would call the Napa Valley by means of the Chiles Valley; next comes Mount Pritchard above Sage Canyon Road, then Atlas Peak, accessed by the long and winding Soda Canyon Road at the southern end; and finally that most obscure of all Napa Valley AVAs, Wild Horse Valley, boasting less than 200 acres of grapes in total, and lying in the hills which mark the border between Napa and Solano counties, due east of the city of Napa.

Most of the country is far too steep for cultivation (or even habitation) and vines make only intermittent intrusions into densely forested country — even if much of it is regrowth forest after the logging depradations of a century ago, and notwithstanding the establishment of vineyards on both Howell Mountain and Atlas Peak in the last quarter of the nineteenth century. Craggy outcrops, streams and lakes abound, many of the streams being significant Steelhead runs. Hawks, eagles and buzzards soar in perpetual motion, ever seeking food but so seldom being caught in the act, as it were.

In a county subject to so much regulation, it is quite extraordinary how little control there has been on the development and clearing of fragile mountainsides. Fortunately, the sheer cost (and technical difficulty) has meant that damage to date has been largely self-contained, and there are now regulations which should ensure any future development is subject to reasonable control.

Those who grow grapes and make wines in these hills would, I suspect, sooner quit the industry altogether than return to the Napa Valley floor. They are men and women of a different breed, and so are their wines.

ABOVE ~ *Salvador Guiterrez stands beside the Cabernet Sauvignon vines he tends on the slopes of Howell Mountain.*

OPPOSITE ~ *Trellis systems take many forms, creating at times surreal patterns such as the wide T-trellis at La Jota.*

The Region in Brief

Climate, Soil and Viticulture

Climate

The climate of the East Mountains differs significantly from that of the Napa Valley floor in many ways and for many reasons. Altitude is the principal differentiating factor, ranging between 600 and over 2,000 feet, but mostly over 1,200 feet. Unlike the valley floor, there is a lesser increase in average temperatures as one travels along the hills from Atlas Peak at the bottom end of the valley above Napa City to Howell Mountain at the top end above Calistoga. Only at lower elevations does morning fog play a role, and then infrequently (the fog line effectively marks the lower limit of the Howell Mountain AVA), but the maritime influence of the afternoon sea breezes is as important as it is on the valley floor. So the days are characterised by warmer mornings and significantly more hours of sunshine, yet much lower total heat summations. The daytime peak temperatures are 10°–15°F lower at Atlas Peak than Yountville, and the differential between Calistoga and Howell Mountain may sometimes be greater still. Atlas Peak, with a range of 2,000-2,600 heat degree days, is Region I; the range of Howell Mountain is slightly higher but within Region II. Rainfall is significantly higher, averaging 40.74 inches at Howell Mountain and 37.5 inches at Atlas Peak.

But the heat accumulation is much more even than on the valley floor: there are more hours each day with ideal ripening conditions, rather than extreme peaks and troughs. Night-time temperatures are often warmer (at Dunn Vineyards by as much as 15°–20°F), caused by what is termed temperature inversion: the warm air from the valley floor rises and the cold air from the mountaintops descends into the fog-shrouded valley. However, in certain weather conditions the clear night skies and absence of cloud/fog cover can give very low temperatures and frost problems in pockets. Overall, frosts on the mountain vineyards pose a far lower threat than they do on the valley floor, which is not what one might imagine to be the case. It is for this reason, and perhaps because of the lower yields and more open canopies, that even at Atlas Peak Cabernet Sauvignon will readily ripen, and it explains why it attains such exceptional concentration of flavor and color at Howell Mountain.

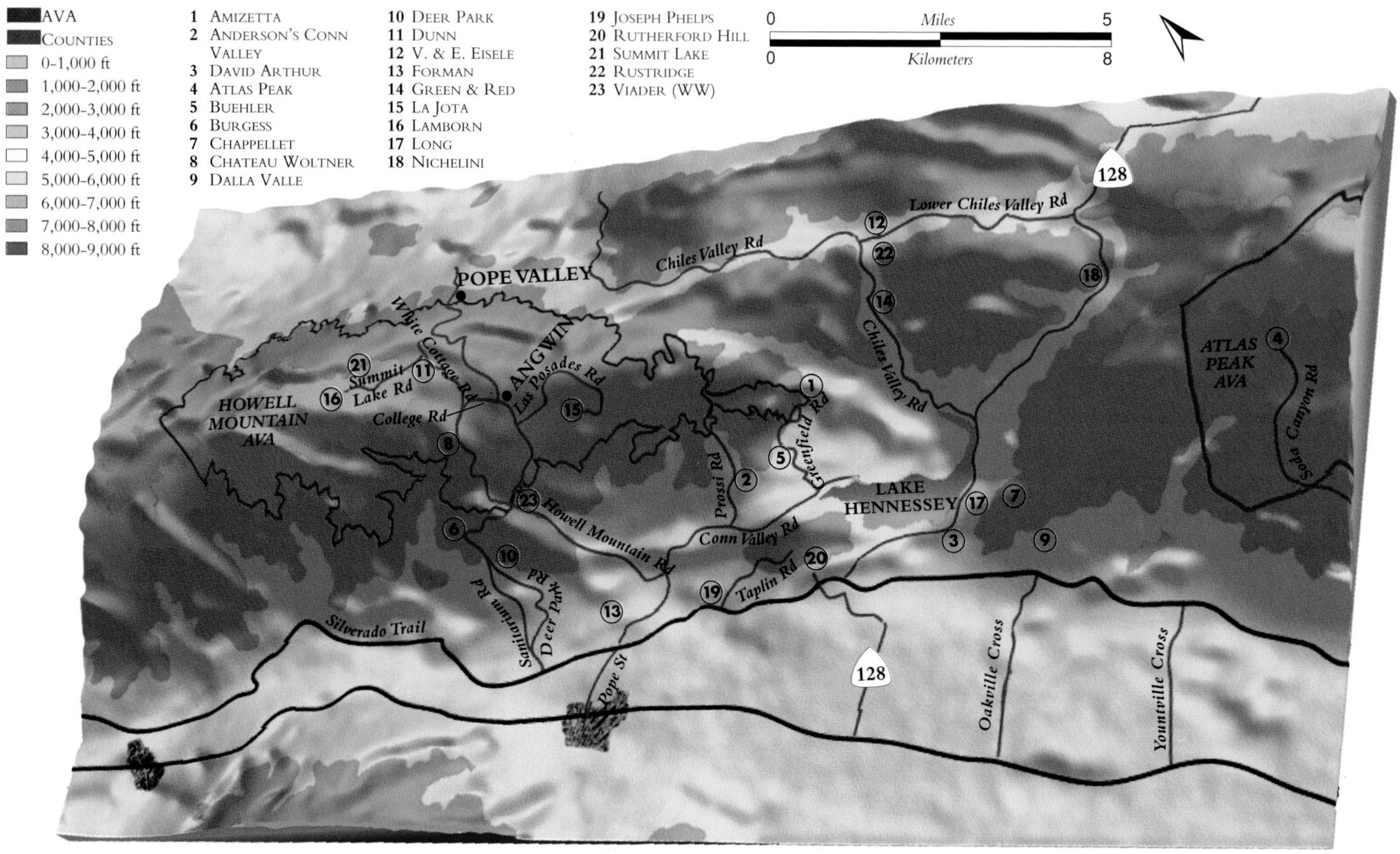
AVA
COUNTIES
0-1,000 ft
1,000-2,000 ft
2,000-3,000 ft
3,000-4,000 ft
4,000-5,000 ft
5,000-6,000 ft
6,000-7,000 ft
7,000-8,000 ft
8,000-9,000 ft
1 Amizetta
2 Anderson's Conn Valley
3 David Arthur
4 Atlas Peak
5 Buehler
6 Burgess
7 Chappellet
8 Chateau Woltner
9 Dalla Valle
10 Deer Park
11 Dunn
12 V. & E. Eisele
13 Forman
14 Green & Red
15 La Jota
16 Lamborn
17 Long
18 Nichelini
19 Joseph Phelps
20 Rutherford Hill
21 Summit Lake
22 Rustridge
23 Viader (WW)
0 Miles 5
0 Kilometers 8
128
Lower Chiles Valley Rd
Chiles Valley Rd
POPE VALLEY
White Cottage Rd
ANGWIN
Las Posadas Rd
Summit Lake Rd
HOWELL MOUNTAIN AVA
College Rd
Chiles Valley Rd
Greenfield Rd
Prossi Rd
LAKE HENNESSEY
ATLAS PEAK AVA
Soda Canyon Rd
Howell Mountain Rd
Conn Valley Rd
Taplin Rd
Silverado Trail
Sanitarium Rd
Deer Park Rd
Pope St
128
Oakville Cross
Yountville Cross

ABOVE ~ *East Mountains map.*

Soil
The soils are no less different from those of the valley floor, being almost entirely volcanic in origin. Those of Atlas Peak are in the Aiken group (derived from basalt) and the Forward group (derived from rhyolite); similar groups occur on Howell Mountain, and although the range increases here, only a small percentage are from a non-volcanic source. They are typically dark red in color, friable and well drained, but are often shallow, in stark contrast to the deep alluvial soils of the valley. Likewise, their water-retention capacity is limited, and even though rainfall is higher than on the floor, the need for irrigation has also been proved to be essential in many locations if the vines (and the grapes) are to be kept in balance and adequate yields obtained.

The Growing Season
The season starts later than on the valley floor, and lags behind throughout, on average by two to three weeks. Thus Atlas Peak normally picks Chardonnay around September 20, while the Howell Mountain vineyards typically range between the last week of August and the first week of September. The Cabernet Sauvignon harvest would normally be mid-September, Zinfandel a week or so earlier. But the twists and folds of mountain vineyards often lead to great variation in ripening patterns, while ultra-late vintages such as 1991 play havoc in the mountains as much as elsewhere. Thus Lamborn Zinfandel has been picked as early as August 15 and as late as October 15, Dunn Cabernet Sauvignon between September 10 and November 13.

Contract Growers

Birkmeyer Vineyard Eighteen acres in the Wild Horse Valley at an elevation of 1,500 feet planted to White Riesling and Chardonnay; first established 1964 and supplies Stag's Leap Wine Cellars.
Volker Eisele Vineyard Sixty acres established by Napa Valley activist Volker Eisele, whose battles to preserve the valley are so vividly portrayed in James Conway's book *Napa*. Cabernet Sauvignon, Cabernet Franc, Chardonnay, Semillon and Sauvignon Blanc are planted at around 1,000 feet in the Chiles Valley, an area likely to have been given its own AVA status by the time this book is published. Page Mill, Vichon and V. & E. Eisele use the name.
Liparita Vineyard Eighty acres at 1,700–1,850 feet on Las Posadas Road, planted to Cabernet Sauvignon, Chardonnay, Merlot and Sauvignon Blanc between 1985 and 1988; Peter Michael Winery and Liparita Cellars are users of the grapes.
Priest Ranch One of the largest (100 acres) in the Chiles Valley area, planted to Cabernet Sauvignon, Chenin Blanc, Johannisberg Riesling and Zinfandel at 2,200 feet. Rustridge is the principal winery name using the grapes.

Principal Wine Styles

Cabernet Sauvignon
The Cabernets of Howell Mountain are legends in their own lifetime, brooding, dark, intense wines with layer upon layer of flavor encased in a tightly woven skein of tannin. The problem for the makers of these wines has never been how to achieve color, intensity, depth of flavor and structure, but how to control the potential so as to achieve balance, and in particular to manage the anthocyanins and other tannins. It is an issue I examine in some detail on page 120; suffice it to say that Randy Dunn has shown it is possible to make Cabernet Sauvignon which, while of exceptional strength and intensity, does have that first prerequisite of great wine (balance) and does reward cellaring for ten years or more. At the other end of the spectrum, Ric Forman (who, incidentally, does not see himself as part of Howell Mountain) makes finer, leaner wines which have more grace and accessibility from the outset. The most conventional wines, which have devoted clienteles, come from Burgess, Chappellet, Joseph Phelps and Rutherford Hill, while Dalla Valle is bidding to outweigh them all (and Atlas Peak Vineyards has yet to show its hand).

Zinfandel
Historically, Zinfandel has always done well in these mountains — in the last century at Atlas Peak, and in more recent times in the Howell Mountain area, with Lamborn and Summit Lake setting the pace, and Green and Red, Buehler, Deer Park and Burgess doing nothing to harm the cause. While I remain convinced that most Zinfandel is at its most delicious during the first three or four years of its life, these mountain producers do provide a consistently impressive number of exceptions: 1978 Burgess (tasted 1992) was a wonderfully graceful wine with its structure still held together by soft tannins, while Summit Lake is clearly able to produce long-lived wines. Mountain Zinfandels are seldom jammy or oversweet these days; the tannins may be elevated, but not unduly so; the fruit flavors tend more to dark cherry than red cherry; and marked spicy/smoky characters sometimes add a layer of intrigue (and pleasure).

Chardonnay
The wines are frequently lean, tight and somehow disciplined by the often austere soils in which the vines grow and the cool climate in which the grapes ripen. Chateau Woltner is the leader of the band on Howell Mountain, and seems intent on a game of viticultural and enological minimalism, with time in the bottle the key to future greatness. Chappellet and Burgess fall into a similar (though different) category, providing rather hard and lean wines, the future of which I am less optimistic about. The exceptions are Long Vineyards (Chappellet's neighbor on Mount Pritchard) which in 1988 and 1990 — in particular — showed that spicy, barrel-ferment hazelnut characters and a soft richness in the mid-palate can be obtained; and Forman — whose Chardonnay doesn't come from Mountain vineyards anyway. Finally, there is the as yet undisclosed hand of Atlas Peak Vineyards.

Sangiovese
Atlas Peak Vineyard's plantings of 120 acres account for around half of California's total: given the care with which the clonal stock was selected (from Italy), the success or failure here will surely have a profound influence on the future of the variety in California — however much Sangiovese may prove itself to be influenced by site and climate. It is early days yet: the bright, cherry-flavored 1990 was much better than the somewhat light and astringent 1989, but I am sure still better things are in store. How much better, time will tell.

VARIETAL CHOICE

Modern California grape growers could well be forgiven for feeling they are damned if they do, and damned if they don't. On the one hand, they are criticized for (apparently) assuming that one can grow any variety anywhere, regardless of *terroir* and climate; yet on the other, they are accused of ignoring all varieties except two, Chardonnay and Cabernet Sauvignon. (Their bankers, it must be said, only want to know about the latter two varieties.)

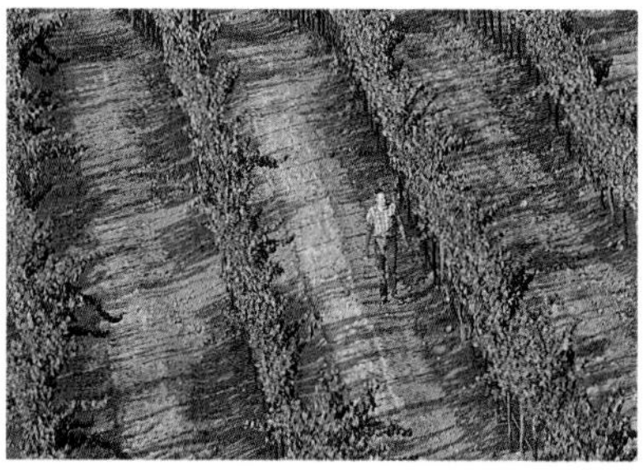

ABOVE ~ *Ted Lemon, winemaker at Chateau Woltner, among Chardonnay vines on the estate vineyards.*

Phylloxera type B has served to sharpen the horns of the dilemma: it provides unexpected choice (and the inherent pain of decision-making) on the one hand, yet for economic reasons pushes vignerons down the twin track of Chardonnay and Cabernet Sauvignon.

The East Mountains (which is strictly an invention of convenience, including two existing AVAs, Atlas Peak and Howell Mountain) have in fact always provided a scope of varietal choice far wider than conventional wisdom has proposed, and a choice acted upon to a greater degree than is generally recognized.

Take Howell Mountain AVA as an example: until Chateau Woltner came along it was accepted as holy writ that this was red grape country, with Cabernet Sauvignon as King, and Zinfandel as the King's bastard — in no way to pretend to the throne. Yet the Woltners gave up not only their Bordeaux chateau but their Bordeaux grapes, and chose the white grape of Burgundy — Chardonnay. When asked why (and they have been asked countless times) the answer is simple: their site is too cold to ripen Cabernet Sauvignon. Not far away at La Jota, Bill Smith is enjoying success with Viognier and doing battle with Marsanne and Roussanne, while Long Vineyards produces fine Johannisberg Riesling on Pritchard Mountain, and Joseph Phelps has made an impressive entry into the Rhone varieties — both white and red — with his Vin du Mistral range.

At the southern end of the East Mountains, Atlas Peak Vineyards has introduced a witch's brew of varieties with Sangiovese heading the large-scale commercial plantings (together with Cabernet Sauvignon and Chardonnay), but has added in Sauvignon Blanc, Semillon, Merlot, Cabernet Franc, Petit Verdot, Pinot Noir and Zinfandel.

One could go on with numerous other examples, and so I come back to the opening criticism that it is seen as legitimate to grow any grape anywhere. That criticism is born of European experience where the limiting factor is insufficient warmth (or sunshine) and the concomitant risk of mold and rot in an unduly extended growing season. In other words, Cabernet Sauvignon is not grown in Burgundy because it will not ripen there, Shiraz is not grown in Bordeaux because it will not ripen there. This has led to a system in which there has been a logical matching and maximization of the potential of *terroir* and climate at one end of the scale (the bottom end) and a neat differentiation of area, variety and style, which may have both quality and marketing advantages.

Yet when the French raise a supercilious eyebrow at the sight of Chardonnay and Cabernet Sauvignon growing next to each other, they forget (or ignore) the fact that were it not for their Appellation Control laws, the same situation could exist in Bordeaux.

In California, as in many New World wine regions, insufficient warmth and sunshine is seldom a relevant factor in determining varietal choice: rather it will be too much warmth, not because the vine will not grow and produce grapes, but because varietal character may be unacceptably altered or attenuated.

What will (or should) determine varietal choice is a complex matrix of physical growing conditions which are not capable of manipulation (and there are in fact surprisingly few of these); physical conditions which can be manipulated by human intervention; economic factors; and perceptions of desired style.

What the intelligent and open-minded vigneron is learning today is that *terroir*, water management, vine spacing, clonal selection and canopy design can radically alter the performance of a given variety in a given locality. All are important, none more so than *terroir* — being that factor least prone to human manipulation, unless one is Gallo reshaping the mountains of the Sonoma Valley.

Just to make life that little bit more difficult, experience shows that site selection can significantly alter the performance of a given grape variety within a geographic region. And by site, one may be talking of (say) a one-acre plot within a 15-acre vineyard in which the variety in question performs markedly better or markedly worse.

Nowhere is this more apparent than in the convoluted folds of mountain vineyards, where within 100 yards a south-facing slope can become north-facing, or a mini-valley forms into which cold air drains, or soils become abruptly deeper or thinner. Then there are the less obvious "secrets" of any vineyard site which are discovered only through long occupation — an underground rock shelf, a subterranean water drift, a wind tunnel which only operates under certain extreme weather conditions. So talking to one's neighbors, and observing which varieties historically have flourished may be a starting point, but will not necessarily provide the right answers.

Finally, some varieties — notably Chardonnay and Cabernet Sauvignon — are more resilient than others, whch is no doubt one of the reasons why they are so widely planted. Others — notably Pinot Noir — are temperamental in the extreme and no one is left wondering whether the choice was right or not.

Make the correct choices, and you will grow great grapes (and it is hoped, make great wine); make the wrong choices, and mediocrity will result, notwithstanding you have (for example) planted Chardonnay in the Napa Valley.

WINERIES *of* EAST MOUNTAINS

ATLAS PEAK VINEYARDS 1983

A: 3700 Soda Canyon Road, Napa, CA 94581
T: (707) 252 7971 **V**: By appointment
P: 30,000 **W**: Glen Salva

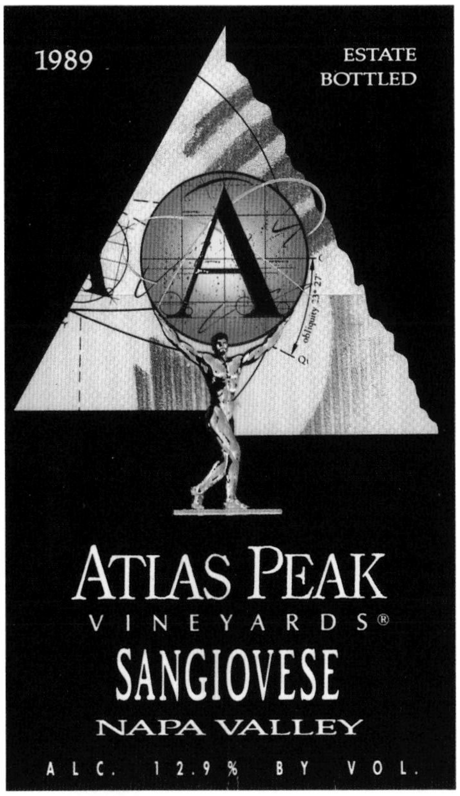
1989
ESTATE BOTTLED
ATLAS PEAK
VINEYARDS®
SANGIOVESE
NAPA VALLEY
ALC. 12.9% BY VOL.

When three D9, two D8 bulldozers, six 25-ton dump trucks, four earth movers and a continuous mine shaft driving machine — worth a collective $2 million — were at work in the formative days of Atlas Peak Vineyards, it was inevitable that the most lurid stories would emanate, chiefly written by those who had either not been to the site or who had visited but not understood. The caves are now built (at a lower cost than conventional above-ground insulated warehouse facilities, and aesthetically much more pleasant), the surface rocks impeding planting largely removed, and the dams (sufficient for a three-year drought, or ten to 15 years' irrigation if no frost protection is needed) completed. The machinery has been sold, and the 465 acres of vines are now growing in peace. If you have over $20 million to invest, and are not looking for a short-term payback, you might well be comforted by general manager Glen Salva's observation, "I think we are going to make some of the great wines of the Napa Valley here."

Approximately 120 acres each of Chardonnay, Sangiovese and Cabernet Sauvignon dominate the plantings; the rest is made up with smaller but commercial-sized blocks of Sauvignon Blanc, Semillon, Merlot, Cabernet Franc, Petit Verdot, Pinot Noir and Zinfandel, while there is an eclectic selection of Nebbiolo, Pinot Grigio and Muscadelle on an experimental level. The catholic nature of the mix gives a clue to the partnership: Hiram Walker of the United Kingdom, J. Bollinger of France and L.P. Antinori of Italy (the latter two having mercifully small shares). The vineyards are established in a shallow bowl at an elevation of 1,400–1,800 feet: Atlas Peak itself soars to 2,665 feet at the northern edge of the estate.

While the slopes are not steep, there is considerable microclimate variation, with heat summations ranging from 2,000 degree days on the floor of the bowl to 2,500–2,600 degree days on the sunniest slopes. The winters are cold, and budbreak is two to three weeks later than in Carneros (a distinct advantage for spring frosts) and remains two to three weeks later right through the growing season. Yet because it is above the fog line, it has significantly more sunshine hours than the floor of the Napa Valley, but without high daytime peaks. Says Glen Salva, "In six years I can count the 100°F days on one hand." The nine different soil types which have been identified are all of volcanic origin, many with that characteristic dark red hue. Glen Salva is an acutely observant and intelligent viticulturist, and I do not think for one moment that his confidence about the potential quality of Atlas Peak is misplaced. There is indeed every chance this site will produce some of the greatest Napa Valley wines.

For the moment, the concrete evidence is limited. The first wine released, a 1989 Sangiovese, was adequate but uninspiring. Sometimes a first crop wine will be great, sometimes not. This was not. The 1990 Sangiovese was a great deal more convincing; it has fresh redcurrant and cherry fruits, a sophisticated touch of charred oak, and wonderfully fresh acidity on a crisp but long finish. All in all, watch this space.

BUEHLER 1978

A: 820 Greenfield Road, St. Helena, CA 94574 **T**: (707) 963 2155
V: By appointment **P**: 30,000
W: John Buehler Jnr.

Bechtel Corporation is a very large company, but it seems to have made one of its principal corporate missions turning its retiring senior executives into vignerons. John Buehler Senior is just another to conform to the pattern, although only a construction engineer would view with equanimity the twisting and narrow road which ultimately leads one to his remote but beautiful vineyard above Lake Hennessy. It is planted to 27 acres of Zinfandel, 26 acres of Cabernet Sauvignon and eight acres of Pinot Blanc, which is supplemented by 100 tons of purchased grapes.

The end result is a curious production mix of almost 20,000 cases of White Zinfandel and two massive Howell Mountain red wines, Cabernet Sauvignon and Zinfandel, wines which are not for the faint of heart or tongue.

BURGESS CELLARS 1972

A: 1108 Deer Park Road, St. Helena, CA 94574 **T**: (707) 963 4766
V: By appointment **P**: 30,000
W: Bill Sorenson

Although situated on the steep slopes of Howell Mountain, it is below the 1,400 feet level which was adopted as the boundary of the Howell Mountain AVA. Yet any visitor to this exquisitely beautiful site — which has been in use for grape growing and winemaking since 1880, and was the legendary Lee Stewart's Souverain Winery — would surely regard it as a mountain winery.

It is true, also, that its split personality does not stop with the vagaries of AVAs; while its Vintage Selection Cabernet Sauvignon is made from non-irrigated steep hillside vineyards (replanted by former pilot Tom Burgess in the 1970s), the Chardonnay comes from his 50-acre Triere Vineyard at Yountville on the valley floor, which Burgess acquired in 1979. The third wine is a Zinfandel, partly estate-grown and all from hillside vineyards.

Because it is below the fog line, the climate is neither mountain nor valley floor, and the wines reflect this mid position. A 1978 Zinfandel tasted in 1992 was a wonderfully graceful wine, with soft tannins still holding the structure together, its 1990 counterpart with smoky/tangy overtones to the fruit, and finishing with crisp acid. The Cabernet Sauvignon can and does lack the concentration and abrasiveness of true Mountain Cabernet, but does have a long palate. The Chardonnay is highly regarded by some, but I found the 1990 hard and charmless. Which will not worry Burgess one whit: it does not seek publicity, and regularly sells out all of its production, other than the 15% deliberately held back as library stock and re-released when ten years old.

CHAPPELLET 1969

A: 1581 Sage Canyon Road, St. Helena, CA 94574 **T**: (707) 963 7136 **V**: By appointment **P**: 26,000 **W**: Phillip Corallo-Titus

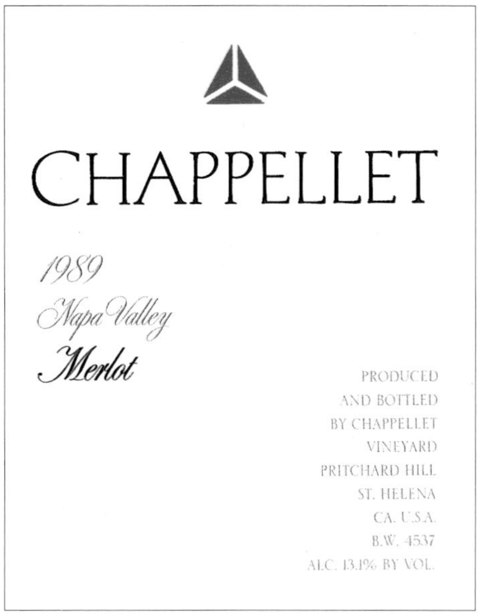
CHAPPELLET
1989
Napa Valley
Merlot
PRODUCED AND BOTTLED BY CHAPPELLET VINEYARD PRITCHARD HILL ST. HELENA CA. U.S.A. B.W. 4537
ALC. 13.1% BY VOL.

I first visited Chappellet on a fog-shrouded day in 1979 (and was much impressed by its Chenin Blanc), and returned five years later for one of those extraordinary Leroy tastings organised by Madame Lalou Bize-Leroy (36 Burgundies from the 1964 vintage), all of which may explain why I have had some difficulty in ever coming to terms with the winery's Chardonnay and Cabernet Sauvignon. This is real mountain viticulture, with all its attendant problems of yield (two to three tons per acre), tannins (also two to three tons per acre, it seems) and economics. For given the investment in the spectacular pyramid-shaped winery and 110 acres of painstakingly terraced vineyards at elevations of up to 1,700 feet, the return must be very different to that earned by Don Chappellet before he took early retirement from his industrial food vending business.

In recent years moves have been made to tame those tannins: throwing originally strongly held convictions to one side, drip irrigation has been progressively installed over the past decade, while the pressings (around 7%) are now sold in bulk. Another direction has been the establishment of eight acres of Sangiovese: says Cyril Chappellet, "I am most excited about it, the conditions here are very similar to those encountered in Italy, and it offers the prospect of faster cash flow. But it has only been in the ground for a couple of years, and it may be another five years before we have any available even for sampling." The Chappellets, it seems, have long-term investment criteria. Getting back to the Cabernet Sauvignon, and to those changes, I wish I could share in the *Wine Spectator*'s enthusiasm for the 1987, which it placed 21st in its top 100 wines for 1991, awarding it a near-celestial 94 points. I found the wine as astringent, unyielding and tannic as its predecessors. Since every bottle will have long been sold by the time these words appear in print, my dissenting voice will have little importance — but such is life.

CHATEAU WOLTNER 1980

A: 150 White Cottage Road South, Angwin, CA 94508 **T**: (707) 963 1744 **V**: By appointment **P**: 12,000 **W**: Ted Lemon

From majority ownership of Chateau La Mission Haut Brion (which had been in the family since 1919) producing one of the great classic Bordeaux reds (and a little Bordeaux white) to ownership of Chateau Woltner producing Chardonnay near the top of Howell Mountain (which conventional wisdom regarded as red wine country, pure and simple) was a highly controversial but very deliberate move by Francois and Francoise Dewavrin-Woltner. Seven million dollars later into a projected $12 million, 25-year development plan the Woltners do not give any indication of regretting their decision or their total change in lifestyle.

And there was at least a pre-existing French connection: in 1886 two Frenchmen, M. Brun and M. Chaix, built the three-story stone winery which is the focal point of the present day operations. It seems they, too, found that the vines grew slowly and produced sparingly at the 1,600–1,800 feet level on the 181-acre red mountain soil property. The Woltners grow only Chardonnay, in the "abundant" vintage of 1990 producing 1.6 tons per acre from the three distinct vineyard blocks: Frederique, St. Thomas and Titus, retailing between $35 and $50 a bottle in 1992. Then there is the Woltner Estate Reserve at $20, and (from 1992) a Howell Mountain Chardonnay at $12.

Winemaker Ted Lemon spent a number of years in charge of Guy Roulot in Meursault, and is able to draw on the experience of Ric Forman as consultant. The wines are, to say the least, controversial, flying in the face of almost everything which is California: no malolactic fermentation, only 20% new oak each year, and with bracing acidity. Yet these wines do have tremendous elegance, breed and length, with flavors running through a citric/minty/passionfruit spectrum, and the hand of the winemaker all but hidden. They certainly need many years in bottle, during which all manner of complex aromas and flavors will develop. I still have a sneaking question at the back of my mind: given the concentration of the grapes, should the winemaker not show his hand a little more at the outset?

DALLA VALLE 1982

A: 7776 Silverado Trail, Napa, CA 94558 **T**: (707) 944 2676 **V**: Nil **P**: 3,500 **W**: Gustav Dalla Valle

As the address might suggest, this is another of the contentious mountain vineyard inclusions, but I rest my case on two points. First, the monumental — indeed mountainous — weight and depth of the wines produced from the rocky mountainside vineyard surrounding the winery; and second, the spectacular views which the house, winery and vineyard enjoy of the valley floor 300–400 feet below. Italian-born Gustav was 70 before he and his much younger Japanese wife Naoko decided to abandon his deep sea diving business in favor of grape growing and winemaking on the craggy hills above the Silverado Trail.

The wines have been made with consultancy advice from Joe Cafaro, but seem to principally reflect the vineyard influence being given free reign. They have sent Robert Parker into orbit, and if you like wines of impenetrable color, immense extract, huge tannin, and masses of oak holding the fruit in a vice-like grip, and have 30 years or so to see which side wins the arm wrestle, by all means undertake the difficult task of tracking some down. Given Parker's endorsements, the tiny production, and distribution by the prestigious Wilson Daniels, that will be no easy task.

DEER PARK WINERY 1979

A: 1000 Deer Park Road, Deer Park, CA 94576 **T**: (707) 963 5411 **V**: By appointment **P**: 3,000 **W**: David Clark

The beautiful stone winery of Deer Park was built four years earlier than that at La Jota — in 1891 — attesting to the vigor and extent of

DEER PARK WINERY
1988
Beatty Ranch
Howell Mountain / Napa Valley
ZINFANDEL
PRODUCED & BOTTLED BY DEER PARK WINERY
DEER PARK, NAPA VALLEY, CALIFORNIA, U.S.A.
ALCOHOL 13.5% BY VOLUME CONTAINS SULFITES

Howell Mountain viticulture at the end of the last century. It is owned by David and Kinta Clark and Lila and Robert Knapp, who restored it in 1979 and established seven acres of steep hillside vineyard planted to Chardonnay and Sauvignon Blanc, supplemented by Zinfandel usually purchased from the Beatty Ranch and (previously) Petite Sirah from the Park Muscatine Vineyard now owned by Randy Dunn.

A range of Zinfandels (principally from the Beatty Ranch) tasted in 1992 left no doubt about the style preferred by winemaker David Clark: hugely concentrated, tannic and long-lived. The 1982 was wonderfully rich, spicy and complex, followed (in order of preference) by the 1990, 1985, 1984, 1987 and 1988. A 1988 Petite Sirah was equally concentrated and massive: strictly for those who like their mountain wines to be big. The Chardonnay could not be recommended on any basis.

DUNN VINEYARDS 1978

A: 805 White Cottage Road, Angwin, CA 94508 **T**: (707) 965 3642 **V**: Nil **P**: 5,000 **W**: Randy Dunn

They say that dogs look like their owners (or vice versa), and I must say I have often seen first-hand evidence of the truth of that statement. If the diminutive, gentle, quietly generous and clearly sensitive Randy Dunn is any example, the reverse holds true to winemakers and their wines. For when Dunn, winemaker at Caymus from 1975 to 1982, purchased a six-acre block 2,100 feet up on Howell Mountain in 1978, few would have guessed that he would provide the archetypal Howell Mountain Cabernet Sauvignon which many have sought to emulate but none have transcended. He made 660 cases of that wine, 28 cases of magnums and — through an amazing piece of prescience — 53 imperials. All Dunn wines have become collector's items of the first magnitude, none more so than the imperials, and all are famed for their longevity. By 1982 the time had come for Dunn to leave Caymus (on the best possible terms), as his own business expanded and as he became a consultant to others who over the years have included La Jota, Grace Family, Livingston and Pahlmeyer (currently only the latter two).

Dunn makes 2,500 cases a year each of Napa Valley and Howell Mountain Cabernets (not including those big bottles). Fifty per cent is marketed through a fanatically loyal mailing list: Dunn says he could sell 80–90% this way if he wished, but does not want to put his eggs in the one sale basket, releasing the rest to the trade in the traditionally quiet months of January and February. I personally suspect it is because he finds writing his newsletter so difficult that he treats the trade so generously.

I have to admit to two personal debts of gratitude to Randy Dunn. One for flying me over the Napa Valley on a brilliant morning when the low level cloud cover was like a skein of the finest wool, the mountains and mountain vineyards rearing jewel-like above; the other for making the 1982 Howell Mountain which Michael Broadbent served me at his country home in July 1992 along with 1987 and 1945 Chateaux Margaux — and which fitted like a glove between the young and not-so-young (I could never call it old) Margaux.

FORMAN VINEYARDS 1982

A: 1501 Big Rock Road, St. Helena, CA 94571 **T**: (707) 963 0234 **V**: By appointment **P**: 4,000 **W**: Ric Forman

Ric Forman has achieved more in his 50 years than most people would achieve in a lifetime, establishing a formidable reputation during his 1968–77 tenure as head winemaker at Sterling, before helping establish Newton (via a brief partnership) and then moving on to establish his own mountainside vineyards in 1982 while consulting to several well-known wineries. While on Howell Mountain, he is below the 1,400 foot elevation, and grows his 47 acres of Cabernet Sauvignon (plus some other bits and pieces) on Boomer Series volcanic gravels which are immensely deep and which (together with the more foggy mornings) result in grapes enabling Forman to produce Cabernet Sauvignon with the fruit and finesse he prizes so highly (and avoid the power and raw strength which he does not). It speaks much for the soils that despite four years of drought between 1987 and 1991 he has not used his irrigation system.

He was mowing the tiny patch of grass at the edge of his swimming pool the day I visited his immaculate winery and no less immaculate caves. He is driven by an obsession to detail, knowing it is this which differentiates good from great wine, and by a desire to do it himself alone. His Cabernet Sauvignons do justice to his high standards and philosophies, but his Chardonnays (such as the 1990), produced from a vineyard jointly owned with Charles Shaw at Rutherford, are the wines which for me, at least, show him to be a winemaker of genius. They are fragrant, scented, unforced and supremely elegant, yet have abundant fruit (citrus and melon) with a freshness and smoothness to the texture which so many makers talk about but seldom, if ever, achieve.

GREEN & RED VINEYARD 1977

A: 3208 Chiles Pope Valley Road, St. Helena, CA 94574 **T**: (707) 965 2346 **V**: By appointment **P**: 5,000 **W**: Jay Heminway

When former school teacher Jay Heminway purchased his 160-acre property in 1970, the vineyard which had existed there at the turn of the century was long since abandoned and overgrown, but miraculously a few vines still clung to life, producing a few bunches which told Jay Heminway they were red, and possibly Burger. He initially intended to plant Cabernet Sauvignon, but changed his mind, establishing seven acres of Zinfandel at around 1,000 feet, and ten low-yielding acres of Chardonnay up at 1,500 feet. The climate is relatively cool: fog and breezes both penetrate the canyon, and Chardonnay is normally picked around the first week of September, Zinfandel mid to late September.

Heminway is changing his techniques in handling Zinfandel, moving more to Rhone or

ABOVE ~ *The glorious century-old stone winery of Chateau Woltner guarded by Ted Lemon and Pinto.*

Burgundy practices, with 20% whole clusters and no extended maceration, aiming for a wine which will be most delicious at three to four years of age. In fact a 1977 Zinfandel tasted in 1992 had aged very well (made in the old style, of course) with good structure and length to the flavor, while the 1990 faithfully reflected the change in making style, with light, fresh, crisp cherry fruit and a clean, silky texture — the sort of wine that encourages the second bottle, rather than the second glass.

LA JOTA VINEYARD 1974

A: 1102 Las Posadas Road, Angwin, CA 94508 **T**: (707) 965 3020 **V**: By appointment **P**: 3,000 **W**: Bill Smith

Bill Smith became involved in the wine industry during the tax shelter bonanza days of the early 1970s when he was commissioned by an oil company to find vineyard land for a development investment. He did just that: a modest ranch of 4,500 acres in the Pope Valley, an investment which had much to do with Pope Valley ultimately being included in the Napa Valley AVA, although that is a story for another day. During his travels he noticed a vineyard on Las Posadas Road which he mistakenly thought was owned by Chappellet. It was not, it was for sale, and — most miraculously of all — had a quite beautiful stone winery built in 1895 by Frederick Hess.

History and beauty notwithstanding, the winery did not figure in Bill Smith's early plans: he intended simply to grow and sell grapes and it was only the grim economic realities of mountain grape growing which led him to the reality (or theory?) of the added value to be gained from turning one's grapes into wine, and selling that instead of grapes.

Once again the fine hand of Randy Dunn emerges with the production of La Jota's first wine, a 1982 Estate Cabernet Sauvignon, followed a year later by an Estate Zinfandel. Then came Merlot and Cabernet Franc (intended for blending but sometimes released as straight varietals) followed by Viognier, and most recently of all, Marsanne and Roussanne. A 1992 Chardonnay will also make its appearance, made from grapes grown in a neighboring estate.

The Cabernet Sauvignon, still the mainstay of production, is decidedly erratic in style and quality, but the 1989 was quite delicious, with full, ripe cassis/berry fruit, not overly tannic, and full of interest. Several commentators have described the wines as rustic, and I well understand the comment. The Viognier, too, is unpredictable: a 1991 tasted from bottle was unattractive, a different batch tasted from barrel was totally exciting and authentic. But then Bill Smith does things his own way: dissatisfied with sugar levels of his Marsanne and Roussanne, he intended to make a Vin de Paille from them in 1992 if conditions permitted.

ABOVE ~ *Bob Lamborn thoroughly at home in an old speakeasy bar in Oakland, with his beloved Zinfandel.*

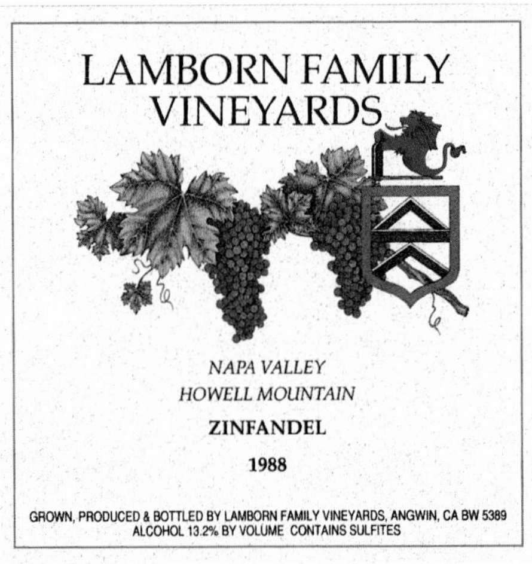
LAMBORN FAMILY VINEYARDS
NAPA VALLEY
HOWELL MOUNTAIN
ZINFANDEL
1988
GROWN, PRODUCED & BOTTLED BY LAMBORN FAMILY VINEYARDS, ANGWIN, CA BW 5389
ALCOHOL 13.2% BY VOLUME CONTAINS SULFITES

LAMBORN FAMILY VINEYARDS 1973

A: 2075 Summit Lake Drive, Angwin, CA 94508 **T**: (415) 547 4643 **V**: By appointment **P**: 2,200 **W**: Bob Lamborn

Bob Lamborn's major claim to fame is probably his role as a private investigator involved in the Patti Hearst kidnapping, but in a saner and more civilized world it should be his Howell Mountain Zinfandel vineyard and wine. I say vineyard and wine, because Lamborn is as accomplished a viticulturist as he is winemaker — and pretty damned good at both, self-taught though he may be (with some neighborly advice and help from Randy Dunn in the early years).

The 25-acre weekend retreat he purchased in 1973 for pure relaxation has become an immaculate nine-acre vineyard and 2,000-case winery, with some extra Zinfandel purchased from the nearby Beatty Ranch just to make quite sure there is no relaxation. The other rewards are there though. The 1988 was lavishly praised but I found it rather overblown in the old-fashioned style. By contrast, the 1990 Zinfandel is as close to perfection as they come: bursting with lively, spicy, crisp fruit making it irresistible now, but with the concentration and fine tannins to carry it for another five years if that is what you want.

LONG VINEYARDS 1967

A: 1535 Sage Canyon Road, St. Helena, CA 94574 **T**: (707) 963 2496 **V**: By appointment **P**: 3,000 **W**: Sandi Belcher

Zelma Long, then winemaker at Robert Mondavi, and Bob Long, then (but not now) married to Zelma, started planting their 17 acres of mountainside vineyards 700–1,200 feet above Lake Berryessa as some kind of busman's holiday — or could it have been aversion therapy? On county advice Johannisberg Riesling was planted first, and to this day it accounts for roughly 25% of production, the rest being Chardonnay utilizing a Martini clone selection which traces its ancestry back to

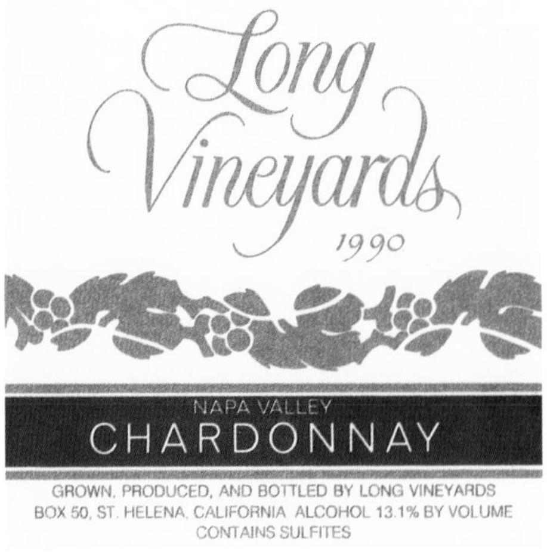
Long Vineyards
1990
NAPA VALLEY
CHARDONNAY
GROWN, PRODUCED, AND BOTTLED BY LONG VINEYARDS
BOX 50, ST. HELENA, CALIFORNIA ALCOHOL 13.1% BY VOLUME
CONTAINS SULFITES

Meursault via one of the original Wente importations of the 1930s. Six hundred cases (or thereabouts) of Sauvignon Blanc (with 20% Chardonnay blended in) and 200 cases of Cabernet Sauvignon made from grapes purchased from the famous U.C. Davis vineyard on the Rutherford Bench round out the selection.

The Johannisberg Riesling, made in a straightforward Late Harvest Spatlese style, is a clean, no-nonsense wine of above average quality; like the Sauvignon Blanc, there is plenty of fruit flavor. The Cabernet Sauvignon warrants its price more because of its rarity than its inherent quality, but the wine which really stands out is the Chardonnay. Francois Freres oak, barrel fermentation, fruit concentration and lees contact give some of that grilled hazelnut aroma which so distinguishes the Kistler Chardonnays. The palate may not quite live up to the excitement of the bouquet: in a full-blown Napa style, it does have good acidity (presumably the mountainside at work) and some intriguing side-light flavors.

JOSEPH PHELPS 1973

A: 200 Taplin Road, St. Helena, CA 94574
T: (707) 963 2745 **V**: By appointment
P: 80,000 **W**: Craig Williams

Joseph Phelps has one foot in the hills and one foot in the valley floor, with 350 acres under vine, 175 acres on the hillsides of Spring Valley, and 105 acres in three Napa floor parcels at Rutherford (on the west side of Highway 29) at Oakville and at Stag's Leap.

Phelps came from Colorado as a construction engineer to build wineries for others, but almost immediately purchased the 670-acre ranch on Taplin Road, building the winery the following year. Walter Schug became winemaker, and the early reputation of Phelps turned on its white wines, in particular some superb botrytised late harvest wines, including such exotics as Scheurebe and Gewurztraminer. This early reputation for the unusual has been continued with the recent development of the Vin du Mistral range of Rhone varietal wines, including a Viognier, a Grenache-Mouvedre Rosé, Syrah, and Mistral Rouge (a Syrah, Grenache, Mourvedre blend). For all that, two of the most highly regarded wines are the Eisele Vineyard Cabernet Sauvignon and Insignia, a Meritage-type blend, the composition of which varies from year to year. These reds (together with the Backus Cabernet Sauvignon) are massive in their weight and concentration, at times bordering on caricatures.

The 1990 Mistral Rouge shows why Joe Phelps is so enthusiastic about the future of the Rhone reds: it is redolent with sweet red berry fruit, hints of spice, and just the right amount of tannin. The 1991 Viognier has some genuine varietal character, with soft, lush tropical fruit flavors, even if it is slightly blowsy. Yet another wine of quality, this time with links in the past, is the 1991 Late Harvest White Riesling, with intense botrytis-induced apricot aroma and flavor, needing just a touch more acidity for greatness.

RUTHERFORD HILL WINERY 1976

A: 200 Rutherford Hill Road, St. Helena, CA 94573 **T**: (707) 96 3187 **V**: 10–4:30 Mon–Fri, 10–5 Sat–Sun **P**: 125,000
W: Jerry Luper

A close affiliate of Freemark Abbey (with a similar but not identical owning partnership) which was built and operated prior to 1976 as Souverain (not Lee Stewart's Souverain, but that of Pillsbury). Rutherford Hill Winery boasts an extraordinarily ornate and non-functional series of abstract wooden scaffold-like edifices to mark the entrance to the caves, which extend half a mile back into the mountainside. Schizophrenic? Yes, and so have been some of the wines, received with widely differing perceptions both in each year (for each wine) and from year to year. Despite endeavors to do so, I did not get to the point of tasting current releases (although I have tasted earlier wines) and am therefore ineligible to vote.

SUMMIT LAKE VINEYARD 1971

A: 2000 Summit Lake Drive, Angwin, CA 94508 **T**: (707) 465 248 **V**: By appointment
P: 2,000 cases **W**: Bob Brakesman

Others who have visited Summit Lake tell of the various animals which share the ever-varied Brakesman family life, including the golden labradors. One of those labradors found and commenced to devour my lunch within a microsecond of my opening the door of my car — a simple ham sandwich in a brown paper bag. Like Aesop's fox, I consoled myself with the knowledge I didn't have time to eat it anyway, and it was at least an appropriate introduction to one of the best loved (and more eccentric) Howell Mountain families.

Bob and Sue Brakesman are among those who are and always will be passionately devoted to Zinfandel (they allowed a few cases of Chardonnay once or twice, and contemplate the possibility of 150–200 cases of affordable Cabernet Sauvignon), and to long-lived Zinfandel at that. Only a few months before I visited them they had broached bottles of their 1975 and 1979, which they pronounced great, the 1972 also hanging in there like an old Cabernet. I tasted two youngsters, the 1988 and the 1986: the latter was still a baby, big, sweet, chewy and chunky with masses of dark, sweet, black cherry fruit flavor, and its bouquet still to evolve and open up. Carlo Farazzi, who established the 21-acre ranch in the late nineteenth century, must be resting easy in his grave, knowing how well his inheritance is being guarded.

OTHER WINERIES

AMIZETTA VINEYARDS 1984
A: 1099 Greenfield Road, St. Helena, CA 94574
T: (707) 963 1460 **W**: Spencer Clark

ANDERSON'S CONN VALLEY VINEYARDS 1984
A: 680 Rossi Road, St. Helena, CA 94574
T: (707) 963 8600 **W**: Gus Anderson

DAVID ARTHUR VINEYARDS 1985
A: 1521 Sage Canyon Road, St. Helena, CA 94574 **T**: (707) 963 5190 **W**: David Long

V. & E. EISELE 1992
A: 160 Lower Chiles Valley Road, St. Helena, CA 94574 **T**: (707) 965 2260

NICHELINI 1890
A: 2950 Sage Canyon Road, St. Helena, CA 94574 **T**: (707) 963 0717 **W**: Gregory Boeger

RUSTRIDGE 1985
A: 2910 Lower Chiles Valley Road, St. Helena, CA 94574 **T**: (707) 965 2871 **W**: Heidi Barrett

ABOVE ~ *Gordon's Highland Vineyard is one of several East Mountains vineyards above Lake Hennessey.*

OAKVILLE

H.W. Crabb — he is called this because no one is sure whether his first name was Henry, Hiram or Hamilton, although his second name was Walker — arrived near what is now known as Oakville in 1868, buying 240 acres on the south-western side of the valley, which he soon increased to 500 acres, and equally quickly established 360 acres of vines. Much of the plantings were of the classic *vitis vinifera* varieties, including Cabernet Sauvignon, and by 1880 he was producing 300,000 gallons (or 11% of the Napa Valley's total).

He was a pioneer of fine wine production, selling in bottle under his To-Kalon brand to merchants all over the United States. To-Kalon is Ancient Greek for "the highest good," and the business flourished until Crabb's death from apoplexy in 1899 and the onset of phylloxera. The final blow was a fire — started by an arsonist — which destroyed the winery and remaining cooperage in 1939.

The Oakville of today is (fittingly) dominated by Robert Mondavi, who purchased the To-Kalon Vineyard in 1965, and by the Mondavi-Rothschild joint venture of Opus One. In saying that, I am not seeking to diminish the importance of Caymus, Far Niente, Mumm or Silver Oak — but none of these are visible from Highway 29 as Mondavi and Opus One emphatically are. Nor, on a purely personal note, should I neglect mentioning the Oakville Grocery Store, the unpretentious front of which conceals an Aladdin's cave of gastronomic and vinous treasures which have delighted me on every visit to the valley since 1979.

Accepting the definition of Oakville given in the AVA application of September 1991, there are 5,760 acres in the region, densely planted to vineyards. It produces many famous Cabernet Sauvignons, none more so than Martha's Vineyard — unless it be Opus One. It is also sufficiently cool to produce distinguished white wines in an opulent, fruity style. In many ways, it can claim to be the very heart of the Napa Valley.

ABOVE ~ *Stone wineries, new and old, are very much part of the fabric of the Napa Valley.*

OPPOSITE ~ *Robert Pepi Winery is built on one of the knolls which unexpectedly rise out of the center of the valley.*

THE REGION IN BRIEF

Climate, Soil and Viticulture

CLIMATE

Whether the slightly cooler climate of Oakville or the slightly warmer climate of Rutherford is better suited to Cabernet Sauvignon is a question which can no doubt be debated at length, but has an air of unreality about it. What is more interesting are the relatively generous heat summations for Oakville, averaging between 3,039 and 3,124 degree days, both falling in Region III, significantly warmer than Bordeaux, and higher than many wineries situated in the region admit in their promotional material. So here, as elsewhere, the limitations of any statistical description of climate (see page 13) should be remembered. Rainfall averages 35 inches, but fluctuates wildly around that average.

SOIL

That the soils of Oakville change as one moves from the western side of the valley to the east is not in dispute: the gravelly fan soils of the western benchland are quite different to those found on the banks of the Napa River. But whether the bench finishes closer to Highway 29 or at the river is an unanswered question, and no doubt one of the reasons why the proposed Oakville Bench AVA application did not proceed. This apart, Professor Deborah Elliot-Fisk distinguishes the Oakville soils from those of Rutherford because of the high percentage of clasts from the Sonoma Volcanics in the former, and the higher pH of the latter.

THE GROWING SEASON

While the heat summation is generous, the cool evenings and morning fogs slow the ripening cycle and protect acidity — factors which apply in other parts of the Napa Valley, of course, but which are nonetheless crucial in shaping grape quality and wine style. Harvest is usually mid-season, Sauvignon Blanc coming in from mid to late August, Chardonnay from the third week of August through to the second week of September, and Cabernet Sauvignon usually being picked around the first week of October.

Contract Growers

Allais Vineyard Fifteen acres of Sauvignon Blanc planted 1970 east of Highway 29 adjacent to Cakebread Cellars. Purchasers include Bernard Pradel.

Backus Vineyard Seven acres of terraced vineyard on Silverado Trail just south of Oakville Cross Road planted to Cabernet Sauvignon and sold exclusively to Joseph Phelps for its Backus Vineyard label.

Martha's Vineyard The most famous of all Napa Valley vineyards,

OAKVILLE
GROCERY
DRINK
Coca-Cola
PRODUCE
PACIFIC BELL

ABOVE ~ *The exterior of the Oakville Grocery Store gives no hint of the sophisticated array of food and wine within.*

with 40 acres of Cabernet Sauvignon planted between 1964 and the early 1970s, it is sold exclusively to Heitz for its Martha's Vineyard label.

Tench Vineyard Twelve acres of hillside vineyard near the intersection of Oakville Cross Road and Silverado Trail planted late 1960s to Cabernet Sauvignon, Malbec, Merlot and Sauvignon Blanc and sold to Inglenook for the Gustav Niebaum Collection brand.

Principal Wine Styles

Cabernet Sauvignon

Oakville can surely claim to be the heartland of Napa Cabernet Sauvignon. Improbable though it might seem given the absence of any obvious physical or topographical features differentiating Oakville from its neighbors, its Cabernets are often distinctly different. James Laube aptly calls this "the mint belt," referring to the eucalypt mint character to be found in abundance in the wines of Heitz, Johnson Turnbull and (across the other side of the valley) Silver Oak. Yet it is not universal, although the equilibrium, ripeness and richness of the wines are common features of all the best producers. Those producers are as numerous as they are notable: Caymus, Conn Creek, Far Niente, Johnson Turnbull, Robert Mondavi, Opus One, Silver Oak and Villa Mt. Eden include some of the most famous names in the Cabernet lexicon. Of these I would single out Caymus, Mondavi and Opus One as consistently producing wines of the highest quality.

Red Meritage and Merlot

Cabernet country this may be, but it is highly probable that Meritage wines and Merlots will appear in greater numbers in the future. Conn Creek's Triomphe Meritage is aptly named, a wine of tremendous style and harmony, while Conn Creek produces Merlot of great distinction. These wines abound with sweet, generous cassis-accented fruit and a touch of district mint, and have appropriately soft tannins.

Zinfandel

Here, as elsewhere on Millionaires' Row, Zinfandel is very probably an endangered species, but able to produce opulently layered, dark cherry and spice-flavored wines with tannins which (just) stay within the bounds for those who like their Zinfandels young, but ensure longevity for those who seek it. Caymus is an outstanding producer.

Chardonnay

Most of the wineries produce at least one Chardonnay, some of them contributing a number. But all the best examples (notably those of Mondavi and Z D) come from far and wide — anywhere, in fact, other than Oakville itself. Far Niente is the most important estate producer, but its Chardonnay fails to convince me that it should be grown here.

Sauvignon Blanc

Robert Mondavi's To-Kalon Reserve Sauvignon Blanc is, quite simply, a superb wine, a tribute in equal proportions to outstanding viticultural and enological skills. Once again, many other makers include Sauvignon Blanc in their portfolio; only that of

Oakville
Vintage Chart 1981-91

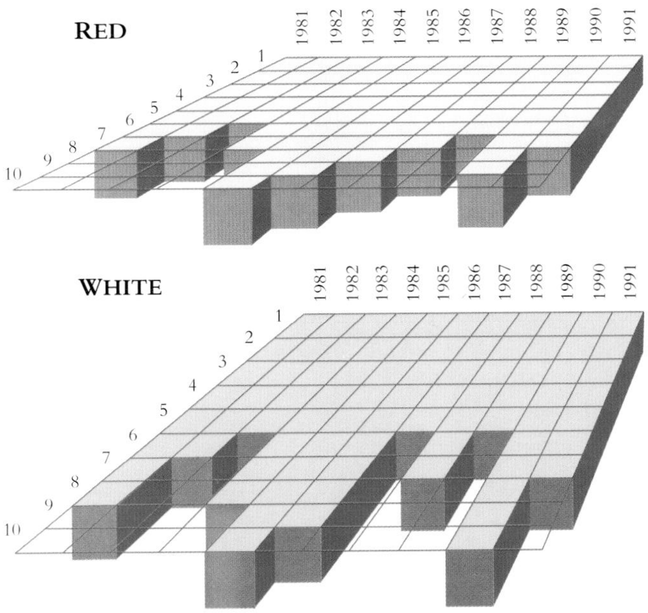
RED
1981
1982
1983
1984
1985
1986
1987
1988
1989
1990
1991
1
2
3
4
5
6
7
8
9
10
WHITE
1981
1982
1983
1984
1985
1986
1987
1988
1989
1990
1991
1
2
3
4
5
6
7
8
9
10

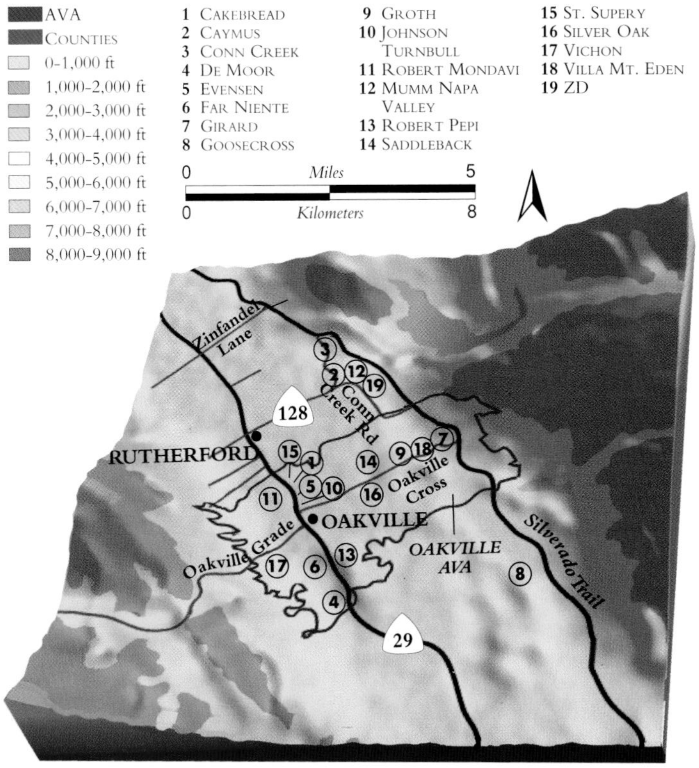
AVA
Counties
0-1,000 ft
1,000-2,000 ft
2,000-3,000 ft
3,000-4,000 ft
4,000-5,000 ft
5,000-6,000 ft
6,000-7,000 ft
7,000-8,000 ft
8,000-9,000 ft
1 Cakebread
2 Caymus
3 Conn Creek
4 De Moor
5 Evensen
6 Far Niente
7 Girard
8 Goosecross
9 Groth
10 Johnson Turnbull
11 Robert Mondavi
12 Mumm Napa Valley
13 Robert Pepi
14 Saddleback
15 St. Supery
16 Silver Oak
17 Vichon
18 Villa Mt. Eden
19 ZD
0
Miles
5
0
Kilometers
8
Zinfandel Lane
Conn Creek Rd
128
RUTHERFORD
Oakville Cross
OAKVILLE
Oakville Grade
OAKVILLE AVA
Silverado Trail
29

Cakebread is noteworthy, however successful Robert Pepi may have been in the past.

Sangiovese, Italian Varieties and Rhone

Robert Pepi is the pioneer, with Sangiovese being produced in commercial quantities since 1990, and showing why there should be on-going interest in the variety. For its part, Swanson will be marketing a high class Syrah from its recently acquired old plantings of that variety.

ABOVE ~ *Oakville map.*

OPUS ONE

It is given to very few people to create something which they know, with absolute certainty, will be looked at with awe and admiration in 200 or 300 years' time. The cost of such rare creations is inevitably way beyond the norm, and the financial return will have neither prompted nor justified the investment. The major return is intangible: the knowledge that something so extraordinary has been created that neither time, technological advances or an inbuilt obsolescence factor will in any way diminish or shorten the life of the creation.

ABOVE ~ *Stanley Kubrick might well have been tempted to use the futuristic Opus One Winery as a film set.*

The belief that the Opus One winery is such a creation is the only possible justification for the Mondavi and Rothschild families' decision to invest around $20 million in a building with a production capacity of 20,000 cases. What is more, the construction of the winery commenced ten years after the first vintage of Opus One was made, and five years after its reputation as one of California's truly great Cabernets was indelibly etched in the minds of consumers around the world.

In the meantime, the wine had been made at the Robert Mondavi Winery, a drop (however important) in the ocean of the production of that winery. While the volume of Opus One has grown slowly from the initial production of 2,000 cases to around 12,000 cases of the most recent vintage released (as at 1992, the 1988), and while it will quite certainly grow to the planned 20,000 cases, there is no question the Mondavi Winery could have continued to produce wines of similar (if not better) quality.

In much the same vein, none of the wines made between 1979 and 1988 contained grapes grown on Opus One's own vineyards. All of the grapes came from Mondavi's vineyards, either owned or managed. Opus One — which, incidentally, is a 50-50 joint venture between the two families — does own 108 acres of its own vineyard land, which it commenced to plant in 1981, using ultra-close spacing (at 2,200 vines per acre, four times as dense as old-style California plantings) and a then uncommon high-walled vertical trellis system. Part of the plantings (established in 1984) can be seen on the left-hand side of the Oakville Crossroad as you travel east. But 40 of the 75 acres (being principally those in front of the winery on the St. Helena Highway, or Highway 29) were ripped up in 1990 before they had produced a commercial crop, thanks to the work of phylloxera.

As is so often the case, there was a silver lining. Experience with the initial close plantings showed an undesirable build-up of heat and humidity, and the row orientation of the new plantings has been changed so that the prevailing winds will blow up rather than across the vine rows.

The unforeseen cost of replanting so much densely spaced vineyard (at around $20,000 per acre), not to mention the opportunity loss of the estate-grown crop, pales into insignificance against the cost overruns on the winery. The fact (and the principal causes) of the overrun has been officially recognized by Opus One, but precise figures have not. What is known is that the original estimate was $10 million, and that the final cost (depending on who is doing the guesstimate and what is included) was between $15 million and $23 million.

Right from the outset, this was to be no ordinary winery. Despite its size (80,000 square feet in all, with a 15,000 square feet first year barrel cellar), it was, in the words of architect Scott Johnson, "more a landscape statement than an architectural statement." The concept was to create a perfect earth form, and to bury the winery in the center. So it is that the hemispheric shape of the winery (or that much of it as is above the normal ground level) is surrounded by an earth berm (or slope) planted with native California plants, grasses and wild flowers. Johnson explains, "We have preserved the natural view corridors along the valley floor. What we have created is a very quiet profile."

Well, that is no doubt true, but no one driving up Highway 29 or traveling along the Oakville Crossroad is going to miss seeing the quite striking building, which has had all sorts of descriptions, the most noteworthy being that appearing in the *San Francisco Chronicle* on October 13, 1991: "The winery seems half space station, half Aztec sacrificial site and all style." I would simply add it also looks like a futuristic mausoleum, albeit a very stylish one.

It was the underground design which gave rise to most of the cost overruns; immense engineering problems were encountered in dealing with the underground water table (partially anticipated) and in combating underground soil temperatures of 72°F caused by nearby geothermal springs. The ultimate solution was a unique radiant cooling system installed within the concrete floor of the building. Its special relevance is to the spectacular underground circular first year cellar, where 1,000 barrels are arranged with ultimate precision in circles one barrel high.

Here the barrels are topped twice-weekly (shades of Sonoma-Cutrer) and racked four times in the first year. It is an extraordinarily lavish use of space, repeated right throughout the winery. What it means, in practical terms, are working conditions which any winemaker in the world would acknowledge as perfect. It is no exaggeration to say that many of those winemakers would cheerfully work at Opus One without salary — which, I hasten to add, is not the way things are.

From the outset, the emphasis has been on the joint venture, and it is no secret that there was considerable and spirited discussion on virtually every aspect of the building, from the elegant, period French furnishings of the various reception salons upstairs through to the winemaking equipment. Thus the fermentation tanks, replete with the double-faced Opus One emblem (the profiles of Robert Mondavi and Baron Philippe de Rothschild pointing left and right respectively) engraved on their sides, were fabricated in France. The story is that the Rothschild technical team wanted oak fermentation tanks, the Mondavis stainless steel. The compromise was luxuriously equipped stainless steel tanks made in France, rather than locally.

The obvious questions are: how good are the Opus One wines released so far, and how good will the wines be in the future. The first question is easy to answer. Both numerous tastings over the years in various parts of the world (including the International Wine Challenge in London against a swag of 1986 and 1988 first growth reds) and a mini-vertical tasting (1984 to 1988 inclusive) at Opus One in 1992 have emphatically established the greatness of the wine.

The wines are rich, powerful and concentrated, yet have wonderful balance and complexity. They are such mouthfuls that one hesitates to use the word elegance, but they certainly have finesse and real style. There are also surprising differences from vintage to vintage without compromising the coherence of the style, with diverse fruit flavors shining through perfectly integrated oak.

Over the years the Cabernet Sauvignon component has varied between 80% and 95%, with Cabernet Franc the major blend component, and Merlot usually making only a token appearance of between 2% and 6%. These really are wines designed to age for a long time, although vintages such as the 1987 are so superbly structured they can be drunk with enjoyment when released at five years of age.

How much better the wines will be in the future is an open question. It is probable that the amazing winery will lead to a minor improvement in the quality, but it is impossible to quantify the likely degree. The more interesting issue is the impact of the estate plantings. One can only assume that Opus One has had the pick of some of Mondavi's best grapes, notably from that part of the To-Kalon vineyard on the Oakville bench. Opus One's own vineyards are on the perimeter of the bench, and they are planted at high density and will be managed with the utmost skill. The yield per vine will be much less than on conventional spacing, and the canopy will be manipulated so that the grapes will have the best possible chemical composition and maximum flavor.

The vineyards may provide the answer to the question posed elsewhere in this book. Can modern viticultural techniques cause "ordinary" Napa Valley land to produce grapes of equal or better quality than those produced (using conventional viticulture) from benchland?

The answer will lie in part in the natural vigor of the vines: close spacing is a logical solution in the poor soils of France, but what about the far richer soils of the Napa Valley, and the abundant sunshine? Will the vines compete with each other for nutrients so that vigor will be naturally controlled?

In one sense, it doesn't matter too much. If the grapes are not equal or superior to those obtainable elsewhere, they will not be used in Opus One. It has been very careful not to put a timetable on the incorporation of the estate grapes, and its otherwise voluminous background material is silent on the precise vineyard sources used to date. And when you have a 200-year future, why should there be any hurry?

ABOVE ~ *The circular underground barrel room at Opus One is as functional as it is beautiful.*

WINERIES *of* OAKVILLE

CAKEBREAD CELLARS 1973

A: 8300 St. Helena Highway, Rutherford, CA 9453 **T**: (707) 963 5221 **V**: 10–4 daily **P**: 55,000 **W**: Bruce Cakebread

The first Napa Valley red wine I tasted from barrel was at Cakebread Cellars in 1979: it was a young Howell Mountain Zinfandel, and the sheer unbridled power of the wine remains vividly in my memory. Jack Cakebread had founded the winery as a part-time weekend retreat six years earlier, after a career which included working in the family auto repair shop, flying B47 bombers, and commercial photography (inspired by Ansel Adams). It was indeed a photographic assignment which first took him to the Napa Valley and to winemaking.

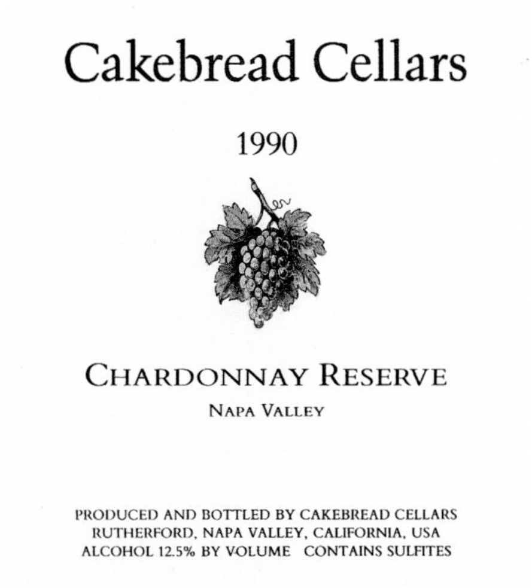
Cakebread Cellars
1990
CHARDONNAY RESERVE
NAPA VALLEY
PRODUCED AND BOTTLED BY CAKEBREAD CELLARS
RUTHERFORD, NAPA VALLEY, CALIFORNIA, USA
ALCOHOL 12.5% BY VOLUME CONTAINS SULFITES

The business has grown steadily: son Bruce graduated from U.C. Davis in 1978 and became winemaker, while brother Dennis is operations manager, and the estate vineyards now comprise 75 acres, albeit phylloxera-affected. Bruce sees this as a long-term benefit: he is moving the varietal plantings around to make better use of specific soil and site characteristics, and is in part replanting Cabernet Sauvignon with Sauvignon Blanc. "This is one of the best areas to grow Sauvignon Blanc in the whole of California," he enthuses, at the same time expressing concern that many Sauvignon Blanc plantings will disappear forever in the wave of phylloxera. (Cakebread Cellars purchases around 75% of its annual grape requirements.) He also sees the opportunity to use new trellis and canopy systems to grow better grapes overall, and hence make better wine.

Cakebread no longer makes Zinfandels, but it does produce a tough and sometimes bitter Cabernet Sauvignon which may or may not soften with age. The Sauvignon Blanc, by contrast, is quite delightful: crisp and tangy, with excellent mouthfeel. It is the latter characteristic which also distinguishes its nutty, textured Chardonnay, but overall I am entirely in accord with Bruce Cakebread's enthusiasm for his Sauvignon Blanc.

CAYMUS VINEYARDS 1971

A: 8700 Conn Creek Road, Rutherford, CA 94573 **T**: (707) 963 4204 **V**: 10–4 daily **P**: 50,000 **W**: Chuck Wagner

Being escorted as I was around Caymus by Charlie Wagner in 1992, I was left in no doubt that he was first and foremost a farmer, with a deep understanding of the soil, and of the reasons why some plants (and some varieties of plants) thrive, and others do not. For the famed Caymus Estate Vineyard had been purchased by Charles Wagner Snr. in 1906, and the family has been fruit growers since that time. Charlie Wagner, in his words, does not give a tinker's damn for subappellations, but he does know that the gravelly volcanic fans are infinitely superior to the deep alluvial loams when it comes to growing grapes, and to Cabernet Sauvignon in particular. He also stresses the importance of clonal selection: as the result of many decades of trial and error, the estate selection has become a source to many of the Napa Valley's finest vineyards.

In 1971 the family decided to keep some of the grapes it had been selling, and the following year produced its first Cabernet Sauvignon. Since that time it has barely missed a beat: whether Caymus made Randy Dunn's reputation or vice versa is a moot point (Dunn was winemaker between 1975 and 1979), but Caymus Cabernets are consistently superb. Indeed, so are all of the wines under the Caymus label, even if the Cabernets stand supreme. On reviewing my tasting notes, there is no other Napa Valley winery which scored such consistently high points for Cabernet Sauvignon, Zinfandel and Sauvignon Blanc (and the heavily oaked Conundrum). There are three Cabernets: the top of the line, strictly allocated, Special Selection (100% Cabernet Sauvignon and largely estate-grown); the Napa Valley (around 80% Cabernet Sauvignon, the balance Cabernet Franc, Merlot and Malbec); and the second label, Liberty School, made from Paso Robles grapes and made as an early (three to five year) drinking style. The Special Selection (30 months) and Regular (18 months)

ABOVE ~ *Dolores Cakebread with estate organically-grown produce for her winery cooking school.*

Cabernets are opulently oaked, the latter in American oak to produce a wine eerily reminiscent of some of the top Australian red wines made by Penfolds. The Special Selection — despite its longer barrel time — being driven by its luscious, sweet, ripe and concentrated fruit, miraculously avoids being heavy or jammy. The same balancing act is achieved with the Zinfandel, which is potent, opulent and layered, yet retains a touch of zesty spice — and can age superbly, as the 1980 demonstrated 12 years later. The Sauvignon Blanc and Conundrum (a complex proprietary blend) are also lavishly oaked in a highly sophisticated way: these are sensuous, seductive wines which will provoke an immediate reaction one way or the other.

CONN CREEK WINERY 1974

A: 8711 Silverado Trail, St. Helena, CA 94574 **T:** (707) 963 9100 **V:** 10–4 daily
P: 35,000 **W:** Jeff Booth

The fortunes of Conn Creek ebbed and flowed between the time it was founded by Bill and Kathy Collins in 1974 and its acquisition by Stimson Lane (the wine division of United States Tobacco Co.) in 1986. Given the dream start with its 1973 and 1974 Cabernet Sauvignons, and the later (if transient) involvement of the Woltner family of Chateau La Mission Haut Brion, one might have thought the Stimson Lane acquisition would have led to an ebb rather than, as has been the case, a beneficial transformation in the quality of the wines and the fortunes of Conn Creek generally.

EVENSEN VINEYARDS 1966

A: 8254 St. Helena Highway, Oakville, CA 94562 **T:** (707) 944 2396 **V:** By appointment
P: 1,000 **W:** Richard Evensen

Just why or how a former California Highway patrolman should have made an exceptionally Alsatian-like Gewurztraminer from a five-acre block on Highway 29 just across the road from Mondavi in the heart of Cabernet Sauvignon country might appear to be one of life's sweeter mysteries. It is partially explicable: way back in the late 1950s the Evensens had grown grapes near Yountville, but sold the property in the course of moving house. Evensen missed tending his vines, and in 1966 purchased a small vineyard and house where the family lives to this day. The vineyard was planted to Italian mixed black grapes, and Evensen knew he should replant, but to what? The choice fell on Gewurztraminer for three reasons: he liked the wine it made, it ripened before the duck season opened, and it is a particularly good match for wild duck. But it was not until 1979 that he took the plunge into winemaking, the winery financed by sale of part of the original property to neighbors Cakebread.

Since that first vintage (with some friendly hints from Stony Hill winemaker Mike Chelini) Evensen has made extraordinary Gewurztraminer, extraordinary for its bone-dry style and its longevity. In 1992 the 1985 was at the peak of its power, with mind-snapping lychee and spice flavours, the 1988 only just starting to open up. Evensen has a magician's touch in choosing the precise day on which to harvest his grapes, and in the winery in treading that ever-so-fine dividing line between a thin, faintly spicy, faintly sugary confection on the one hand and an oily, tannic and clumsy wine on the other. It is a sad reflection on the overall standing of the variety that the Evensens should have replaced some of their Gewurztraminer with Chardonnay, however well they have succeeded with the latter.

FAR NIENTE 1979

A: 1 Acacia Drive, Oakville, CA 94562
T: (707) 944 2862 **V:** By appointment
P: 36,000 **W:** Dirk Hampson

Far Niente is, in every sense, as flamboyant as it is enigmatic. It is housed in an 1885 vintage winery which went dormant at the outset of Prohibition and which was restored to life by Gil Nickel, a commercial nurseryman from Oklahoma with a passion for vintage sports cars and enough money not only to outbid Robert Mondavi when the property came on to the market but to restore it subsequently and have underground cellars made which Alf Burtleson (who has driven most of the Napa caves) describes as the most costly cave cellars he has ever completed. Having walked through them I can well believe it: recessed lighting, telecommunications, compressed gas, under barrel washing facilities, hot and cold water and heaven knows what else.

The gardens and landscaping are opulent; the extraordinary stone building, depicted on the most ornate and expensive gold leaf and gilt label imaginable, no less so, and the cars gleam in their own museum. Yet Far Niente is not open to the public; access through the electronic boom gates is granted only once your identity and prior appointment has been confirmed. Paradox one: the vineyards are established on the heart of the Oakville Bench adjacent to the famous Mondavi To-Kalon Vineyard, and long-serving winemaker Dirk Hampson (universally liked and respected) is denied nothing in his quest for wine of the highest quality. Paradox two: although the wines sell well enough at not inconsiderable prices, they are quite simply uninspiring. The Cabernet Sauvignons (12,000 cases) have been overly tannic (although the 1989, while in the same mold, was a relative success for the year), and the Chardonnays (24,000 cases) strong in toasty oak but relatively low in fruit, despite their role model of Louis Latour's Corton Charlemagne. But those at Far Niente acknowledge some of these shortcomings, and most observers (myself included) feel the best is yet to come from this magnificent obsession.

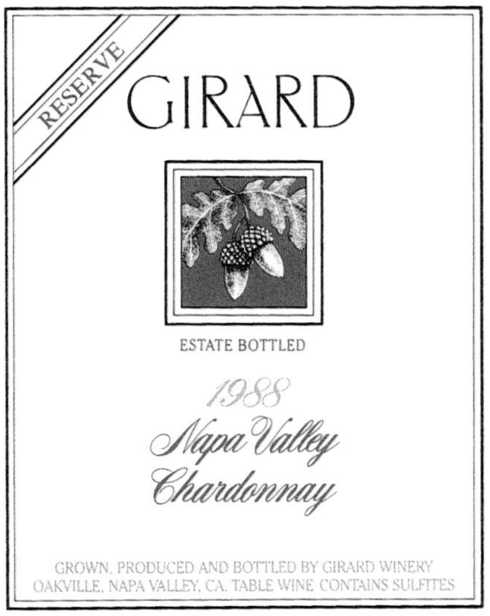
RESERVE
GIRARD
ESTATE BOTTLED
1988
Napa Valley
Chardonnay
GROWN, PRODUCED AND BOTTLED BY GIRARD WINERY
OAKVILLE, NAPA VALLEY, CA. TABLE WINE CONTAINS SULFITES

GIRARD WINERY 1980

A: 7717 Silverado Trail, Oakville, CA 94562
T: (707) 944 8577 **V:** 9–5 Mon–Fri
P: 20,000 **W:** Mark Smith

Girard draws its grapes from two estate vineyards in radically different locations: the first, purchased by ex-Kaiser Industries vice-president Stephen Girard in the 1970s, is on the Silverado Trail just north of the Oakville Crossroad and is also the site of the winery built in 1980. The second vineyard of 40 acres is part of a 400-acre property on the lower slopes of Mount Veeder behind Napanook purchased in 1982, and is situated in a hidden canyon. The Viridian vineyard, as it is called, is now usually the source of the Reserve Cabernet Sauvignon, the Estate Cabernet Sauvignon coming principally from the Silverado property. An Estate Chardonnay and an Estate Semillon are also produced, together with a Chenin Blanc from purchased fruit. The white wines are featureless if not downright bitter; the Cabernet Sauvignons are distinctly better, but neither seems to possess much vinosity, nor much fruit in the core of the flavor.

GOOSECROSS CELLARS 1985

A: 1119 State Lane, Yountville, CA 94599
T: (707) 944 1986 **V:** By appointment
P: 7,500 **W:** Geoff Gorusch

A Chardonnay specialist, initially selling the grapes from the 10-acre vineyard established in the early 1980s by father Ray Gorusch, then moving into winemaking in 1985 with son Geoff Gorusch at the helm. Then, Goosecross utilized only estate grapes; now — as demand has grown — it also offers a Napa Valley Chardonnay produced from grapes grown by three local growers. The 1989 version of this was rather mean, hard and green, but the 1989 Estate (which I did not taste) won a considerable number of medals in shows across the country.

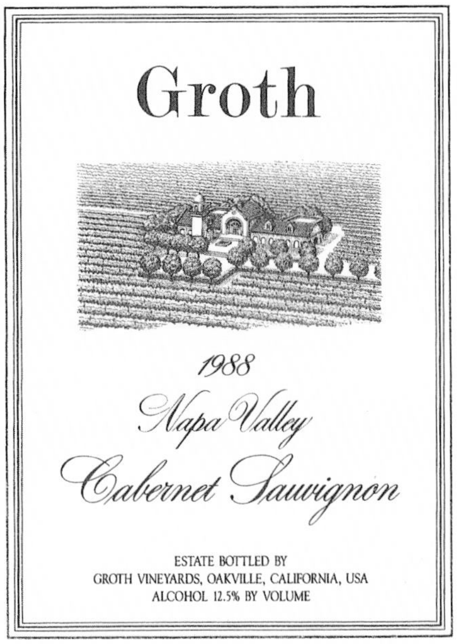
Groth
1988
Napa Valley
Cabernet Sauvignon
ESTATE BOTTLED BY
GROTH VINEYARDS, OAKVILLE, CALIFORNIA, USA
ALCOHOL 12.5% BY VOLUME

GROTH VINEYARDS & WINERY 1982

A: 750 Oakville Cross Road, Oakville, CA 94562 **T**: (707) 944 0290 **V**: By appointment **P**: 40,000 **W**: Nils Venge

After due consideration, I have come to the conclusion that, of all the edifices of the Napa Valley, Groth is the one I would least like to own. But for former Arthur Young & Co. partner and Atari executive (in its heyday) Dennis Groth and wife Judy, the May 1990 completion of the winery and associated administration and entertainment areas marked the realization of a lifelong dream, and already actively involves all three of their children. So my views are doubtless of supreme indifference to the Groths.

Under the direction of former Villa Mount Eden winemaker Nils Venge, five estate-grown wines are produced: Sauvignon Blanc, Chardonnay, Merlot, Cabernet Sauvignon and Reserve Cabernet. The Sauvignon Blanc and Merlot come from the 43-acre Hillview Vineyard at Yountville, the other wines chiefly from the 110-acre Oak Cross Vineyard at Oakville. The 1985 Reserve Cabernet was the first American wine to receive 100 points from the redoubtable Robert Parker in the *Wine Advocate*, ensuring lasting fame for the label. At the other end of the scale, as it were, the Cabernet Sauvignons also receive the seal of approval from Matt Kramer. The Chardonnays have been criticized for excessive oakiness — I could see no such fault with the apricot-tinged 1990 — but the 1990 Sauvignon Blanc was certainly flawed by raw, unintegrated oak.

JOHNSON TURNBULL VINEYARDS 1979

A: 8210 St. Helena Highway, St. Helena, CA 94562 **T**: (707) 963 5839 **V**: By appointment **P**: 5,000 **W**: Kristin Belair-Anderson

Local lawyer Reverdy Johnson is one of the central characters in James Conway's *Napa*, often looming larger than life — in much the same style as the super-minty Cabernet Sauvignons which have been produced from the property since 1979. In fact, when Reverdy Johnson and architect partner Bill Turnbull purchased a run-down vineyard (planted in 1967) and dilapidated farmhouse in 1977 they intended simply to sell the grapes and restore the house as a weekend holiday home. But a 1978 Cabernet Sauvignon made by Cakebread proved the grapes had remarkable qualities — in particular a minty flavor reminiscent of Martha's Vineyard, luring the partners into making their own wine in a tiny winery built little by little on the property.

From here the story becomes more complicated (and more fascinating). Five acres of the 1967 plantings remain, producing intensely minty wine; ten acres on the east side were replanted in 1982 and came into production in 1985 — but failed to produce any of the renowned minty character. Another two blocks, with two clones and on two rootstocks near the road, did produce minty wines. And now phylloxera (and viruses and other diseases) have intervened with an agenda of their own: all 35 acres were replanted at once after the 1992 vintage, and until they come back into production, the grapes will be purchased and the wine (temporarily) will cease to be estate. (Notwithstanding this hiatus, Chardonnay production from Turnbull's Teviot Springs Vineyard in the Knights Valley has been cut back from 2,000 to 250 cases.)

ABOVE ~ *The imposing Groth Winery, not everyone's cup of tea.*

Winemaker Kristin Belair-Anderson has, of course, heard all sides of the mint-eucalypt argument, and there are eucalypts on the property. She says the freshly crushed grapes do not show any minty character, and that it appears (if it is to appear) during fermentation. Up until the replanting, there were two Cabernets produced, one much mintier than the other. The expectation is that once the replanted vineyards come back into bearing, there will be only one Cabernet produced. The fascinating question is, will it be minty, or not? For the record, of the wines produced between 1986 and 1989, the 1986 and 1988 stood out in quality terms, the 1986 being the biggest and richest, the 1987 being least minty, and the 1989 being altogether too minty for the supporting fruit.

ROBERT MONDAVI WINERY 1966

A: 7801 St. Helena Highway, Oakville, CA 94562 **T**: (707) 963 9611 **V**: 9:30–4:30 daily **P**: 650,000 **W**: Tim Mondavi

Part of the history of the Robert Mondavi Winery appears earlier (pages 34-5), but it covers only part of the viticultural and enological achievements of this great winery. It is now able to draw upon 1,500 acres of vines, with 1,000 additional acres under its control, but it remains a major contract purchaser of grapes, which account for roughly half its total production.

The heart of its vineyard holdings is the To-Kalon Vineyard of almost 500 acres purchased by Robert Mondavi in 1965. Situated on prime benchland, it has been the major source of the Reserve Cabernet Sauvignon which is one of the hallmark wines, not just of the winery, but of the Napa Valley. It is invariably full of sweet berry fruit and soft, spicy oak, and the sometimes astringent finish of bygone vintages is now replaced by far more supple and fine grained tannins. The regular Cabernet Sauvignon is deliberately made in a lighter, simpler style without sacrificing varietal character.

Chardonnay accounts for 200,000 cases, twice the sales of Cabernet Sauvignon. Once again there is a stark contrast between the Reserve (produced in limited quantities) and the standard wine. The Reserve is primarily sourced from Mondavi's vineyards in the Stag's Leap district, and is marked by opulent barrel-ferment characters and luscious fruit — although there has been a deliberate downscaling in the overall richness in recent vintages in a quest for greater elegance and longevity. Carneros grapes will play a significant role in assisting this change of direction in future vintages, as may the Santa Barbara plantings. The standard wine is less voluptuous, but reflects all of the accumulated skills and knowledge of the Mondavi winemaking team in the use of barrel fermentation.

I have indirectly touched on the Fumé Blanc

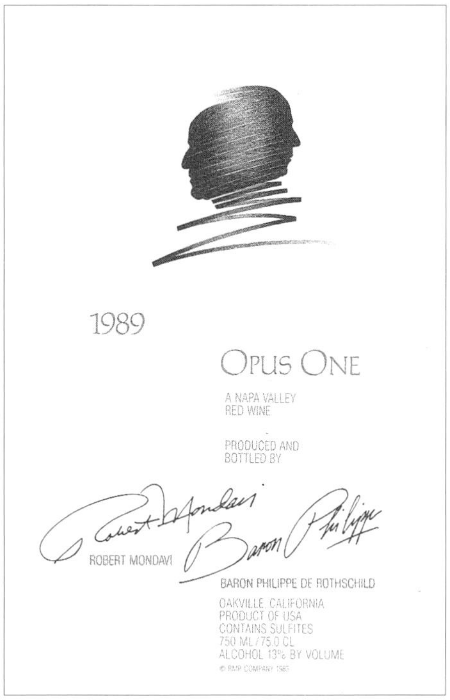
1989
OPUS ONE
A NAPA VALLEY RED WINE
PRODUCED AND BOTTLED BY
ROBERT MONDAVI
BARON PHILIPPE DE ROTHSCHILD
OAKVILLE CALIFORNIA
PRODUCT OF USA
CONTAINS SULFITES
750 ML / 75.0 CL
ALCOHOL 13% BY VOLUME

and Pinot Noir on pages 34-5, but not described the wines. The Reserve Fumé Blanc has exceptional varietal flavor, being tangy and classic in its green-tinged fruit, and with the oak influence kept under tight control. The standard wine is made for the mass market, softer and with less overt varietal character. The spicy, dark plum and cherry-filled Pinot Noir, with its velvety texture and immaculately handled oak, is quite outstanding in its Reserve mold, and more than useful in its standard form.

All in all, there is no other Napa Valley winery which is more reliable or more consistent in its quality, and its mid 1993 listing on the stock exchange should guarantee its future.

MUMM NAPA VALLEY 1984

A: 8445 Silverado Trail, Rutherford, CA 94573 **T**: (707) 963 1133 **V**: 11–6 daily **P**: 60,000 **W**: Greg Fowler

This is a large facility — capable of handling 150,000 cases a year, with up to three vintages on hand at any time —and as one drives along the Silverado Trail its long, green shingle roof and redwood walls cannot be missed. Yet it is built into the hillside on the lower side of the road, and in no way imposes on the landscape: both inside and out, it is a most beautiful (and functional) building. It also happens to have a particularly competent and acutely intelligent winemaker in Greg Fowler, and it is small wonder that the Mumm sparkling wines are among California's best. Like the other makers of the best sparkling wines, he has learnt that the flavor of the grapes is if anything more important than it is for conventional table wine. (Some growers are under the impression that grapes for sparkling wine can be heavily cropped and that, since they are picked at relatively high acid and low sugar levels, no one will notice or care about the fruit flavor.) He has also learnt the magical synergies of blending: 40% of Mumm's intake comes from Carneros, 40% from Yountville and South, and 20% from all over the place (Santa Maria, Sonoma and Mount Veeder amongst others). It grows 20% of its own grapes, and purchases the balance from 56 growers. At the end of vintage, Greg Fowler will have 95 tanks of different base wines with which to compose his Cuvees (or blends). And he does this without direction from France; quite specifically, he is not making Cordon Rouge. On the other hand, he does welcome visits from his Champagne counterparts: "They stop me falling in love with the defects," he says with a wry grin.

There are four wines: Brut Prestige, the volume leader, a 60% Pinot Noir, 35% Chardonnay and 5% Pinot Meuniere blend which typically spends 26 months on yeast lees; a Vintage Reserve (60% Pinot Noir, 40% Chardonnay) which spends 36 months on its lees; a non-vintage Blanc de Noirs (85% Pinot Noir, 15% Chardonnay); and a vintage-dated Winery Lake, made entirely from grapes grown in sister company Sterling's Carneros Vineyard, which is again a 60% Pinot Noir and 40% Chardonnay blend. These are splendid wines, all showing that hallmark of fine *methode champenoise*, length of palate and finish.

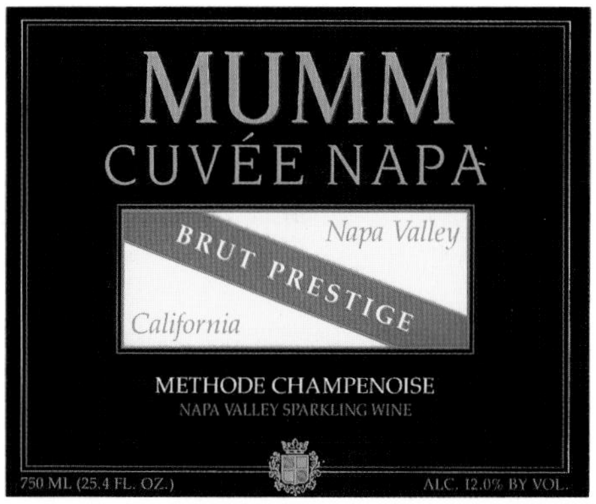
MUMM
CUVÉE NAPA
Napa Valley
BRUT PRESTIGE
California
METHODE CHAMPENOISE
NAPA VALLEY SPARKLING WINE
750 ML (25.4 FL. OZ.)
ALC. 12.0% BY VOL.

ROBERT PEPI WINERY 1981

A: 7585 St. Helena Highway, Oakville, CA 94562 **T**: (707) 944 2807 **V**: 10:30–4:30 daily **P**: 30,000 **W**: Jon Engelskierger

Robert Pepi was one of the early investors in the Napa Valley renaissance, acquiring a 70-acre property in 1966 which included 15 acres of Cabernet Sauvignon and a prominent rocky knoll on which a substantial stone winery was ultimately to be erected 15 years later. In the interim, grape growing and selling was an adjunct to his fur-dressing business in San Francisco, although he took the unusual step of removing the Cabernet Sauvignon and replacing it primarily with Sauvignon Blanc (his personal favorite), Semillon (to be blended with the Sauvignon Blanc) and Chardonnay. But by 1983 another fancy had taken hold: Sangiovese, of which seven acres were planted, leading to what is said to be the first commercial release of the variety, cheekily given the very Italian name of Colline de Sassi, beating Atlas Peak by a year. Phylloxera is now ringing further changes: more Sangiovese will be planted at the expense of Sauvignon Blanc, and new clones of Sauvignon Blanc will be introduced where that variety is replanted. Another change was the appointment of Jon Engelskierger, who had spent over seven years at Silverado Vineyards with Jack Stuart, as winemaker.

The current production mix is around 17,000 cases of a crisp, grassy, stylish Sauvignon Blanc (down from its high of 80%), 7,000 cases of Cabernet Sauvignon (purchased from Vine Hill Ranch), 5,000 cases of Chardonnay (part estate-grown, and part Carneros) and 2,500 cases of Sangiovese, which until 1991 always had 12–15% of Cabernet included, but which is now to be offered in two versions: 100% varietal, and a second wine with 20% Cabernet. The 1990 vintage shows Sangiovese to full advantage: strawberries, cherries and rose petals, crisp and light, with soft tannins, like a lightweight Zinfandel, and very much in the style which many astute makers see as a direction for the future.

ST. SUPERY WINERY 1987

A: 844 St. Helena Highway, Rutherford, CA 94573 **T**: (707) 963 4507 **V**: 9:30–4:30 daily **P**: 180,000 **W**: Bob Broman

The Skalli family of France do things both with a sense of style and on a grand scale; their French interests center on food, but with a very large and modern winery in the south of France which is aggressively marketing its products around the world with a distinctly California air to the packaging. St. Supery may sound like an outrageously French name for a California winery, but it is in fact the name of the French winemaker-owner, Edward St. Supery, who in 1899 acquired the site on which the present-day winery has been erected by Skalli.

The Skalli investment began in 1982 with the purchase of a 1,500-acre ranch in the Pope Valley, now the source for all of the winery's substantial production other than the Cabernet Sauvignon, which has been established on the 50-acre vineyard surrounding the winery and tourist center. That tourist center is an absolute must for anyone visiting the Napa Valley for the first time. The main reception area is a cross between what one normally finds in a winery, and what one might expect to find in a museum — simply because it was designed by a museum expert. It is brilliantly successful and has points of interest for novice and expert alike.

Under the principal label (St. Supery Dollarhide Ranch) four mainstream varietals are offered: Chardonnay, Sauvignon Blanc, Merlot and Cabernet Sauvignon. By virtue of their modest price and volume, these wines are aimed at the middle market, and are calculated not to offend. On the other hand, it cannot be said they set one's pulse racing.

SILVER OAK CELLARS 1972

A: 915 Oakville Crossroad, Oakville, CA 94562 **T**: (707) 944 8808 **V**: 9–4:30 Mon–Fri, 10–4:30 Sat **P**: 28,000 **W**: Justin Meyer

Nothing, so they say, succeeds like success, and viewed by almost any yardstick Silver Oak Cellars is one of the most successful (and, one suspects, profitable) wineries in California. The silent partner is Colorado oil man Ray Duncan, the very visible partner is former Christian Brothers priest and winemaker Justin Meyer. The unseen hand is former classmate of Justin Meyer and now general manager, Dave Cofran.

Silver Oak produces only one wine — Cabernet Sauvignon — but makes up for this in several intriguing ways. First of all, there are three separate vineyard sources — by far the largest being the Alexander Valley Vineyard, purchased in 1988, which provides well over two-thirds of the total production, the others

ABOVE ~ *The old water tower at Robert Pepi's vineyard is now used as a toolshed.*

TOP ~ *A quiet corner of the immaculately tended gardens of Far Niente.*

being a tiny bottling of Bonny's Vineyard (a four-acre planting around the Meyers' home), and a Napa Valley bottling made from grapes purchased from the Oakville area. Next, although each year's releases sell out in less than six months, there is a complicated Reserve and re-release program, which means that no wine is offered at less than five years of age, and that in 1992 one or another wine from every vintage since 1974 was available (at a suitably impressive price) ex-winery. Finally, just to make sure there really are enough options for the discriminating collector, many of these vintages are routinely available in magnums as well as bottles, while some of the older vintages are available in sizes ranging from double magnums to jeroboams.

The wine style itself is wholly distinctive. Meyer's philosophy is that a wine should be ready to drink when it is released, and that there is particular pleasure to be gained from mature Cabernet Sauvignon. This is achieved through the use of a rotofermenter (a type of fermenter very widely used in other parts of the world, and in particular Australia, but rarely seen in California) which — if properly used — extracts maximum fruit and color without excessive tannins; pressing the wine at dryness rather than extended maceration; and finally, lavish use of new American oak which has been specially coopered for the winery for many years now. Silver Oak jumped the field, it would seem, by a number of years in persuading its coopers that wine was an entirely different substance to bourbon, and that the barrels needed special treatment. To an Australian palate, many of the wines have a distinctly familiar feel about them, simply because of the softness and suppleness of the fruit, and that all-pervading perfumed American oak influence. The wines are wholly seductive, they command a fanatical following, they are distinctly different; whether they are great wines is a matter of opinion.

VICHON WINERY 1980

A: 1595 Oakville Grade, Oakville, CA 94562
T: (707) 944 2811 **V**: 10–5 daily **P**: 50,000
W: Michael Weis

You have well and truly commenced the ascent up the Oakville Grade (to the spectacular view of the Napa Valley which can be obtained from the top of this road) by the time you come to Vichon on the left. Nonetheless, it is treated as being in the Oakville region rather than the mountains, because the major part of the production comes from Mondavi-contracted or owned vineyards on the Napa Valley floor, and only a small part from the four acres of vines surrounding the winery.

The three founding partners of Vichon were more successful with their winemaking than their marketing, and after a few turbulent years Vichon was purchased by Robert Mondavi's three children (Michael, Timothy and Marcia). Tim Mondavi has assumed overall responsibility for Vichon and, by all accounts, has turned its substantial losses into significant profits.

One of the early specialties of the winery was a 50-50 blend of Semillon and Sauvignon Blanc called Chevrier; the wine continues but is now branded Chevrignon, and is a very well balanced and constructed wine which can be described as a food style in the positive sense, rather than (as is so often the case) as a disguised apology for the fact that it is devoid of character or flavor. This wine has both. The red wines are made in a no-compromise, give-them-the-lot style: I find them forbidding and somewhat overextracted, but would have to admit that they do have flavor and a legitimate place in the scheme of things in the Napa Valley.

VILLA MT. EDEN WINERY 1881

A: 20 Oakville Crossroad, Oakville, CA 94562 **T**: (707) 944 2414 **V**: 10–4 daily
P: 25,000 **W**: Michael McGrath

Now owned, like Conn Creek, by Stimson Lane (U.S. Tobacco Co.), Villa Mt. Eden nonetheless retains an intense sense of history, and — quite evidently — a desire to produce wines of the highest quality. In 1992 it acquired the services of Jed Steele as consultant winemaker, and left him in no doubt as to its lofty ambitions. Former owners James and Anne McWilliams purchased the property in 1969, and restored the 1880s winery in authentic style, hiring Nils Venge as their first winemaker, who was also charged with the task of reviving the old surrounding vineyard. When the McWilliams sold to Stimson Lane in 1986, they retained ownership of the surrounding vineyard, but it is now the principal source of grapes for Villa Mt. Eden.

Michael McGrath has been winemaker since 1982, and has done singularly well with the red wines. The Grand Reserve Cabernet Sauvignon is an outstanding wine with dark cherry/raspberry fruit with lots of flesh and soft tannins; the Cellar Select Cabernet Sauvignon is in the same attractively soft, plummy/berry fruit style, as is the Zinfandel, with a very strong family resemblance in terms of its structure and emphasis on soft, chewy accessible fruit rather than hard, abrasive tannins. If the red wines are consistently impressive, the Chardonnays are the reverse, with bitter, stony characters. The retention of Jed Steele as consultant should see the Chardonnays vault into the same league as the lovely red wines.

Z D WINES 1969

A: 8383 Silverado Trail, Napa, CA 94558
T: (707) 963 5188 **V**: 10–12, 1–4:30 Mon–Fri, 10–4:30 Weekends **P**: 18,000
W: Robert De Leuze

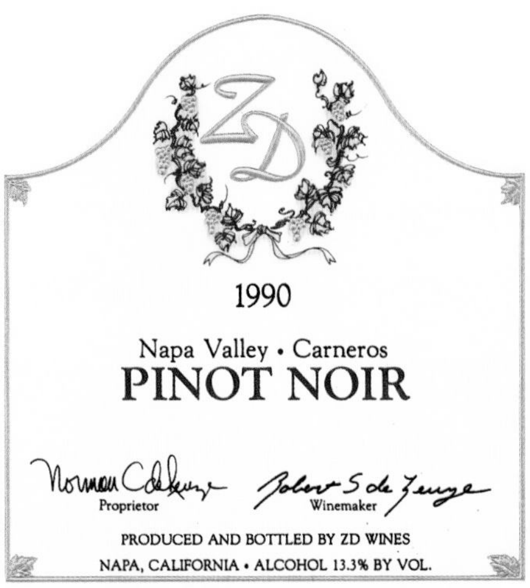
1990
Napa Valley • Carneros
PINOT NOIR
Proprietor
Winemaker
PRODUCED AND BOTTLED BY ZD WINES
NAPA, CALIFORNIA • ALCOHOL 13.3% BY VOL.

The ultra-economical name comes from the founders, the late Gino Zepponi and Norman De Leuze, aircraft engineers who started making small quantities of wine on a semi-commercial basis in a rented shed in Sonoma. The original simple plan of Chardonnay and Pinot Noir rapidly became more complicated; not only did the range of varietals increase sharply, but so did production, forcing a move to the present premises on Silverado Trail in 1979. In 1992 survey pegs were laid out to double the size of that facility, not, however, signifying an intention to double production, but simply to make exceedingly cramped winery conditions more tolerable.

I first came across Z D Pinot Noir in 1979, and well remember its strange opulence. But it was a 1983 Late Harvest Gewurztraminer which really made me an addict, and I still have bottles of this wine in quite remarkable condition. Yet for all that, it is the Chardonnay which presently gains much of the limelight for Z D. Curiously, it has a simple California Appellation, because it is a blend spanning Napa, Sonoma, Santa Barbara and Monterey. Brett De Leuze explains: "Z D has always run counter to everyone else. We started off with individually designated vineyard wines when no one else was doing so in the early 1970s. By the time other small wineries hopped on the bandwagon, we had become convinced about the synergies of blending." They had also become convinced about the synergy of American oak with Chardonnay, which certainly makes its presence felt in a wine which has undoubted complexity and balance — but frustratingly invites the question how much better might it be if the oak were French, not American.

OTHER WINERIES

DE MOOR 1975

A: 7481 St. Helena Highway, Oakville, CA 94562 **T**: (707) 944 2565 **W**: Aaron E. Mosley

SADDLEBACK 1983

A: 7802 Money Lane, Oakville, CA 94562
T: (707) 944 1305 **W**: Nils Venge

RUTHERFORD

While Rutherford and Oakville may be regarded as a pair of (non-identical) twins from the point of view of climate and *terroir*, Rutherford has an incomparably richer history, represented today by the names of Beaulieu and Inglenook and by the form of Niebaum-Coppola. It has also contributed most to the "bench" debate, for it was the Rutherford Bench which first came to be named and given international fame (or should I say notoriety).

The de Latour family had sufficient wealth to withstand Prohibition easily, and more particularly, to maintain the vineyards in good condition and — although Andre Tchelistcheff did not agree when he arrived to take over winemaking responsibilities in 1938 — the Beaulieu winery likewise. The first Georges de Latour Private Reserve Cabernet labeled as such was made in 1936, and ranks among the all-time California greats. Yet it was made in conditions so unsanitary and using equipment so antiquated as to defy the imagination of today's winemakers. Why, then, did it succeed? Because of the magic which lies in the Rutherford Bench.

The area covered in this chapter comprises approximately 6,650 acres, of which 2,880 acres are in the so-called Rutherford Bench, which runs from an ill-defined boundary several hundred yards east of Highway 29 west to the 500-foot contour line of the Mayacamas Range. The Rutherford Bench was shown in Jancis Robinson's *Wines Grapes and Vines* (published in 1986), and in the third edition of Hugh Johnson's *World Atlas of Wine* (Third Edition published by Mitchell Beazley in 1985). Johnson showed the eastern boundary as Highway 29, while Robinson showed it as being the Napa River (and incorporated the Oakville Bench to the south). The ill-fated (and abandoned) AVA application showed the eastern boundary of the benches as following the Napa River to a point just south of the town of Rutherford, then continuing parallel to Highway 29 until Bale Lane, where it crosses the highway to near the foothills before meeting Zinfandel Lane, thence proceeding west to the 500-foot contour line. Which definition is the most accurate is unlikely to ever be determined: the politics involved became too hot to handle, the geology too imprecise. What is certain is that this is prime viticultural land, which is almost entirely planted: a few houses and 31 bonded wineries take up all of the remaining space. Many of Napa's best known wineries are to be found here, including Beaulieu, Inglenook and Louis M. Martini.

ABOVE ~ *Jack Christianson, a 25-year veteran of Napa Valley viticulture, on the Beckstoffer verandah.*

OPPOSITE ~ *The imposing buildings housing the Beckstoffer Vineyard management group at Rutherford.*

THE REGION IN BRIEF

Climate, Soil and Viticulture

CLIMATE

Given the flat valley floor and the relatively small area covered, one might have thought there would be a uniform climate, but there are in fact differences grading both east to west, and from north to south. The vineyards in the extreme south-western corner of the Rutherford Bench, running up to the foothills of Bald Mountain and Mont St. John have a different and cooler climate from those on the north-eastern corner of Rutherford, on Zinfandel Lane. The east-west difference is due to the protection offered from the afternoon sun (so claim the vignerons concerned, in any event), while the south-north progression is simply that discussed at many points in this book (warmer in the north, cooler in the south). It is when one comes to individual vineyard measurements that the problems start: is this Region II as some have claimed, or is it in fact mid Region III (3,390 degree days)? The latter, at least, was the average for 1985 to 1988 inclusive. What matters is that climatically it is ideally suited to growing Cabernet Sauvignon, and that it is the morning fog intrusions followed by the afternoon breezes which provide the appropriate total heat summation. Rainfall is around 38–40 inches, falling almost entirely between October and March, thus conforming to the pattern for the valley as a whole.

VINTAGE CHART 1981-91
Rutherford

RED

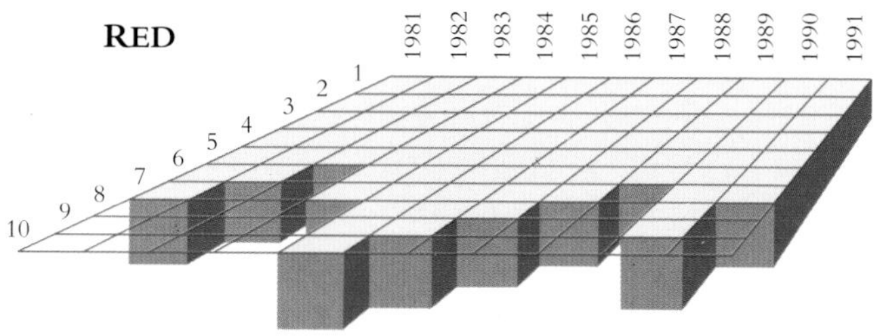
1981
1982
1983
1984
1985
1986
1987
1988
1989
1990
1991
1
2
3
4
5
6
7
8
9
10

WHITE

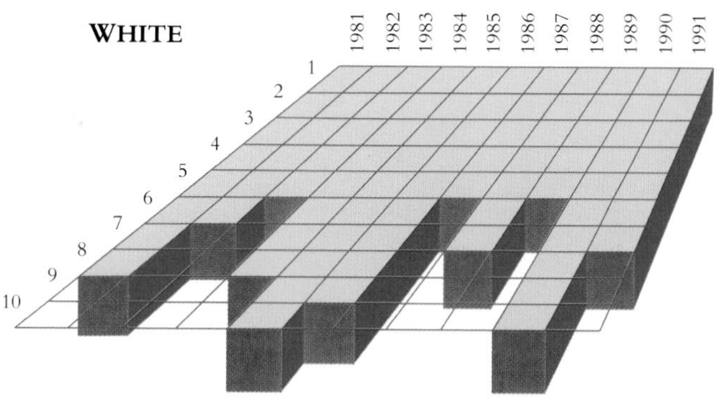
1981
1982
1983
1984
1985
1986
1987
1988
1989
1990
1991
1
2
3
4
5
6
7
8
9
10

SOIL

There are two major soil formations. First and foremost is that of the Rutherford Bench, which is a large alluvial fan composed of deep, gravelly, sandy clay from soils which, so we are told by Professor Deborah Elliot-Fisk, are derived from the marine sedimentary and slightly metamorphosed Franciscan Formation. What in practical terms this means is soils which have been brought down from the adjacent mountains by the Bear Canyon Creek, and which — while having good soil moisture retention capacity — are well above the Napa River water table, and are not especially fertile. Vines planted here have always tended to establish a natural balance between vegetation and crop load with minimal human intervention — a balance which in so much of the rest of the valley floor can only be achieved with much intelligent intervention.

On the eastern side of the Napa River the soils are primarily volcanic depositional soils of moderate to shallow depths over volcanic bedrock soils. Yet as any vigneron, whether on or off the bench, and whether in Rutherford or Oakville, will be quick to tell you, there can be such significant soil differences within a matter of hundreds of yards as to make generalizations hazardous in the extreme.

THE GROWING SEASON

This closely follows that of Oakville, with the same amelioration of the heat, and the same mid-season commencement of harvest, which runs through from the second half of August (for the early ripening varieties) to the first weeks of October (for Cabernet Sauvignon).

Contract Growers

Bella Oaks Vineyard Sixteen acres of famous Cabernet Sauvignon planted in 1971 on Bella Oaks Lane, and sold exclusively to Heitz for its Bella Oaks Cabernet Sauvignon.

Bosche Vineyard Twenty-one acres of outstanding Cabernet Sauvignon and Merlot, originally planted in 1964 and sold exclusively to Freemark Abbey for its Bosche label Cabernet Sauvignon.

Carpy Ranch Eighty-nine acres of Chardonnay on the Rutherford Cross Road established 1982 and sold exclusively by owner Charles Carpy to Freemark Abbey for its Carpy Ranch label.

Dickerson Vineyard Ten acres of Zinfandel which were planted in 1910 and are sold exclusively to Ravenswood for its famous Zinfandel of the same name.

Morisoli Vineyard Twenty-two acres of Cabernet Sauvignon planted 1980; Whitehall Lane is a purchaser. Also at Morisoli Ranch a two-acre block of mixed black varieties which were planted around 1900.

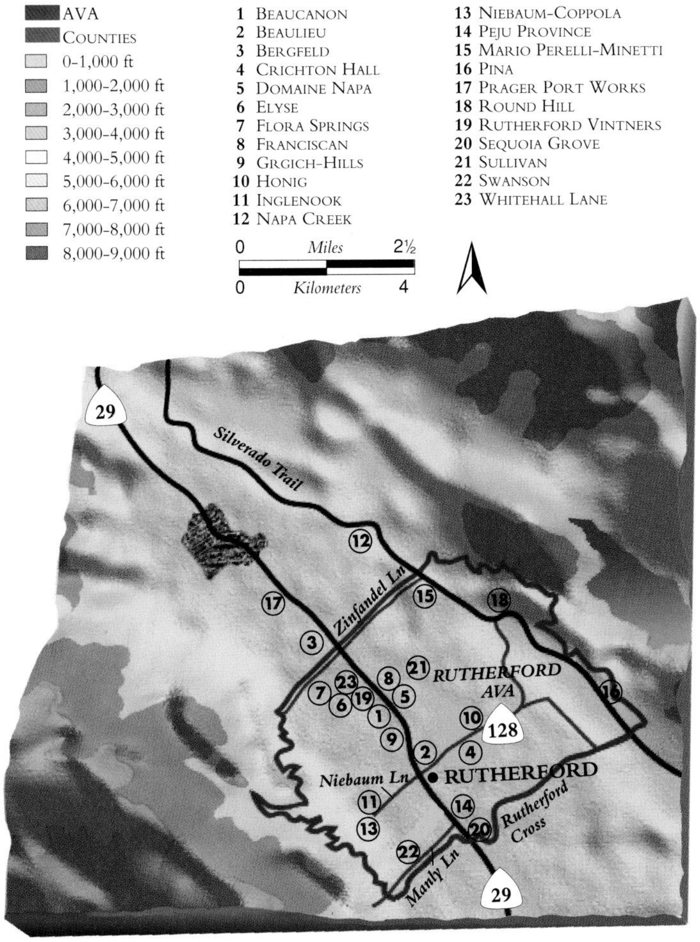
AVA
Counties
0-1,000 ft
1,000-2,000 ft
2,000-3,000 ft
3,000-4,000 ft
4,000-5,000 ft
5,000-6,000 ft
6,000-7,000 ft
7,000-8,000 ft
8,000-9,000 ft
1 Beaucanon
2 Beaulieu
3 Bergfeld
4 Crichton Hall
5 Domaine Napa
6 Elyse
7 Flora Springs
8 Franciscan
9 Grgich-Hills
10 Honig
11 Inglenook
12 Napa Creek
13 Niebaum-Coppola
14 Peju Province
15 Mario Perelli-Minetti
16 Pina
17 Prager Port Works
18 Round Hill
19 Rutherford Vintners
20 Sequoia Grove
21 Sullivan
22 Swanson
23 Whitehall Lane
0 Miles 2½
0 Kilometers 4
29
Silverado Trail
Zinfandel Ln
RUTHERFORD AVA
128
Niebaum Ln
RUTHERFORD
Rutherford Cross
Manly Ln
29

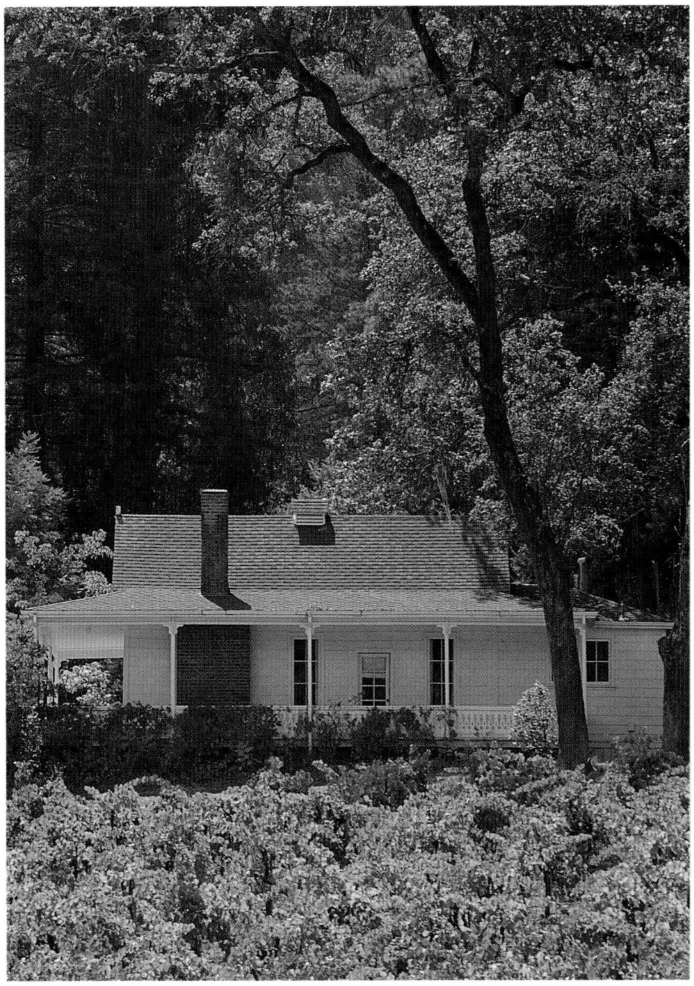

Preston Vineyard Twelve acres of Cabernet planted 1973 and sold exclusively to V. Sattui for its Preston Vineyard Cabernet Sauvignon.

Sycamore Vineyard Twenty-two acres of Cabernet Sauvignon, Cabernet Franc and Sauvignon Blanc planted in 1979 on Bella Oaks Lane, and sold to Freemark Abbey.

Principal Wine Styles

Cabernet Sauvignon

Andre Simon, the most prolific wine writer of the twentieth century, and founder of the International Wine and Food Society, was more familiar with the great Bordeaux reds of the last century than any other taster (with the exception of Michael Broadbent). When Simon tasted the 1887 Inglenook Cabernet Sauvignon in 1960, he described it as "every bit as fine as my favorite pre-phylloxera Clarets." More recent tastings of the 1892 and 1893 Inglenook wines demonstrate the same extraordinary quality and longevity, as have the vintages from 1933 onwards. With such age, these wines exhibit a distinctive "Rutherford Dust" character, an earthy, dusty note which has been described in young Rutherford Cabernets as a "rich, loamy, near spicy/rooty quality." My own reasonably extensive tasting notes show a remarkably consistent pattern: wines of depth, of dark berry fruit which has the concentration and flesh to carry the considerable tannins, and of perfectly balanced acidity. Beaulieu, Flora Springs, Heitz, Inglenook, Swanson and Round Hill consistently produce the finest Cabernets.

Red Meritage, Merlot and Others

I include "and others" in deference to the unusual varietal offerings of Cabernet Franc and of Malbec from Bergfeld, but the Meritage and Merlot-based wines are far more numerous (and significant). Niebaum-Coppola triumphantly leads the way with its Rubicon, a Meritage wine of exceptional power and depth, Flora Springs following a more restrained and elegant path with its Trilogy. Merlots of particular note have been made by Sullivan (superb in 1989), Swanson and Franciscan; more will join the list in the future.

Chardonnay

While not a major presence in terms of acres planted, Grgich Hills and Flora Springs alone make it an important wine. That of Grgich is 60% from Rutherford and 40% from Yountville, while Flora Springs is entirely estate-grown. Most of the other wineries have Chardonnays on their roster, much however coming from other parts of the Napa Valley (or even further afield). When the imprint of the winemaker's philosophy and technique is added, it is difficult to talk sensibly about Rutherford style or character, but Grgich Hills makes an emphatic statement about quality.

ABOVE ~ *Rutherford map.*

ABOVE ~ *Rose Cottage, the guest house on the Niebaum-Coppola estate.*

PHYLLOXERA

The cover of the *Wine Spectator* of August 31, 1992 was stark and arresting: an inset photograph of burning vines and the banner headline "California's Billion Dollar Nightmare." Its impact was every bit as dramatic as *60 Minutes'* piece on the French Paradox, which had gone to air earlier in the year and had led to a 40% increase in red wine sales as the health benefits of moderate consumption of wine were driven home.

Yet neither phylloxera nor the dramatic decrease in cardiovascular disease among regular wine drinkers were new discoveries. The link between prolonged life expectancy and moderate wine consumption had been suggested by serious medical studies (as opposed to some outrageous health claims made for wine in the days before Prohibition) as early as the 1920s, while it was America that exported phylloxera to Europe in the middle of the nineteenth century.

ABOVE ~ *The grim harvest of phylloxera: uprooted vines waiting to be burnt.*

Phylloxera was first discovered in California in 1873 at a vineyard near Sonoma. Its initial spread was typically slow, but thereafter its destruction gathered momentum as the phylloxera population multiplied by the billion. Between 1890 and 1892, 15,000 acres were destroyed in Napa County, and by 1900 only 3,000 acres were in production.

So what was the cause of the "Billion Dollar Nightmare" 90 years later? The answer lies in the incredibly complex life cycle of phylloxera, a microscopic louse which feeds on the roots of the vine, depriving it of the nourishment which would otherwise support the canopy and the crop in the growing season, and ultimately causing the vine to die, or to become so weak it is incapable of bearing fruit.

That life cycle may (but does not necessarily) go through 19 distinct phases in a full creative cycle — five underground and 14 above. The reproductive mechanisms which phylloxera has at its disposal are as bizarre and as difficult to grasp as Einstein's theory of relativity. Parthenogenesis — reproduction without mating — plays a major role; the life cycle moves in erratic and unpredictable ways; there are multiple egg and adult phases within a full cycle; there is a sexuparous (or hermaphroditic phase); at one stage a female may lay 500–600 eggs, at another (the last in the cycle) only a single egg — the "winter egg" — which is, however, potentially the forebear of 4,800 million females by mid summer.

Despite 120 years of research, there is no really effective chemical control; carbon disulfide injected into the ground will kill phylloxera, but is now regarded as an unacceptably toxic and dangerous gas, quite apart from the large cost of applying it and the need for on-going applications. Methyl bromide, widely used as a soil sterilant for nematodes, was banned at the end of 1992.

So the method of control remains as it always has been: grafting the desired variety (the scion) on to the American rootstock which had harbored the phylloxera in the first place and which over the centuries had become immune to its attack. These rootstock vines are natives of North America living east of the Rocky Mountains and fall into two families: *vitus rupestris* and *vitis riparia.*

After trying all manner of unsuccessful cures, it was the French who hit upon the idea of grafting on to resistant rootstocks, and by the early 1870s were experimenting with literally hundreds of different rootstocks, many bred by "crossing" various varieties. In 1876 Victor Ganzin crossed the *vitis vinifera* variety "Aramon" with *vitis rupestris*, producing a rootstock which will go down in history as AxR #1 (usually simply called AxR), and the cause of the nightmare.

For early on (back at the end of the last century) the French discarded AxR #1 as being insufficiently resistant to phylloxera. It has never been used there, and only a tiny amount was used in those parts of Australia which were affected by the original outbreak. But it was used in California, albeit sparingly; in 1958 Professor Lloyd Lider of U.C. Davis published a paper recommending AxR #1 as the best choice for coastal locations, notwithstanding knowledge that in other parts of the world it had failed to resist phylloxera. Indeed, all of the other rootstocks do not include *vinifera* in their parentage; they are either *rupestris*, *riparia* or a cross between the two.

AxR #1 was chosen because it was easy to graft, showed no incompatibility with any scion, and above all else produced big crops — a California dream. Up to that time a rootstock called St. George had been the near automatic choice, and it was not until the end of the 1960s that it was largely (though not entirely) replaced by AxR #1.

Ten years later the first inkling of trouble showed up: decline in the vine health and vigor in a vineyard just south of St. Helena. In 1983 the cause of the problem was identified: a form of phylloxera now known as Biotype B. It is somehow appropriate, however ironic, that by 1992, at least, the scientists at U.C. Davis had been unable to pinpoint any genetic difference between this form of phylloxera and that which had continued to live in Napa and Sonoma since the original outbreak 100 years earlier. The only observable distinction is that Biotype B breeds 40 times as fast as "normal" phylloxera.

There are those who see Biotype B — and the suggestion of some mutation — as mere face-saving by U.C. Davis. Whether this be an unduly cynical view or not, it is a fact that although by 1985 the shortcomings of AxR #1 were widely recognized, it was not until 1989 that Davis recanted and officially withdrew its recommendation.

So it was that between 1983 and 1992 Biotype B spread, slowly at first but then dramatically as the geometric rate of increase made its presence felt. The financial whistle was blown in July 1992 by the Napa-based firm of wine industry consultants and accountants, Motto, Krysla & Fisher, who calculated that 26,000 acres (of the total AxR #1 plantings of 43,000 acres in Napa and Sonoma) would have to be replanted due strictly to the effects of phylloxera. MKF assumed the balance would have been replanted in any event.

Even more frightening was the prediction that by 1997 the harvest in Napa and Sonoma would decline to 180,000 tons, compared to the 1991 harvest of 284,000 tons, and that the 1985 level would not be reached again until 2003, before climbing to 380,000 tons by 2006.

From this economic perspective, phylloxera can only be regarded as an unmitigated disaster. Yet vignerons are a resilient lot, as any farmers must be. Flood, fire and pestilence have been part of the landscape since humans began cultivating crops, and will remain so. Thus Bruce Cakebread encapsulated the views of many when he said to me, "If it were not for phylloxera, I would have been involved in two generations of vineyard replanting, the first in the 1970s and then 2010 — and by then I'd be 70. This drops in another generation, and hopefully that third generation of replanting will be perfect: this variety on this rootstock on this soil on this trellis."

In other words, phylloxera presents an otherwise unavailable opportunity to redress the legacy of the 1970s. Says Augustin Huneeus of Franciscan, "We had to renew the Napa Valley and Sonoma Valley vineyards because no consideration was given in the 1970s to proper varietal adaptation to climate and *terroir*, to trellis design and selection, or to planting density."

The payback is higher yields of better quality grapes. Yet Bruce Cakebread's words also carry a warning echoed by others. The sheer speed of replanting must mean new mistakes will be made: already several of the replacement rootstocks (3306) are showing signs of previously undetected viruses (a potentially appalling problem), while there has manifestly been insufficient research into the compatibility and matching of rootstock with scion and *terroir*. Likewise, New World viticulturists are on a wave of discovery with new trellis designs, but with insufficient practical knowledge of the way the widely varying designs will perform in a given location with a given variety.

Zelma Long of Simi sees yet another danger: that confronted with the inevitably severe economic pressures, growers will replace one small cross-section of varieties with an even smaller one — specifically that varieties such as Sauvignon Blanc, Johannisberg Riesling and Gewurztraminer will be replaced by yet more Chardonnay, Cabernet and Merlot.

Finally, there are those who see the scourge as likely to lead to the "corporatization" of the Napa and Sonoma Valleys. They argue that only the financially strong companies will come through intact, and that many of the small growers and not a few of the small wineries battling recession and phylloxera simultaneously will disappear. The consequence would be a change in the social fabric of the valleys that would be every bit as debilitating as phylloxera.

ABOVE ~ *Even from the air, the mounds of dead vines have a funereal air; the adjoining vineyards are sickening, too.*

WINERIES of RUTHERFORD

BEAUCANNON 1980

A: 1695 St. Helena Highway, St. Helena, CA 94574 **T**: (707) 967 3520 **V**: 10–5 daily **P**: 20,000 **W**: Jacques de Coninck

Owner Jacques de Coninck draws upon 375 acres of Napa vineyards planted progressively since 1980, and plans ultimately to lift production from its present level of 20,000 cases to around 70,000 cases in the bold new winery on the western side of the highway, roughly halfway between Rutherford and St. Helena. Three wines are produced: Chardonnay (50%), Cabernet Sauvignon (35%), and Merlot (15%), the first vintage for each being 1986.

The 1986 Cabernet Sauvignon (which contains 15% Merlot) has aged very gracefully, still retaining sweet fruit and well integrated tannins; like the 1990 Chardonnay, the wine shows more on the palate than the bouquet, the Chardonnay with pleasant citric/melon fruit, good length and acidity. Something of a dark horse, and something of a surprise: it will be interesting to see whether it aspires to a higher profile in the future.

BEAULIEU VINEYARDS 1900

A: 1960 St. Helena Highway, Rutherford, CA 94573 **T**: (707) 963 2411 **V**: 10–5 daily **P**: 450,000 **W**: Joel Aiken

Georges de Latour, the French-born chemist lured to California by the gold boom in 1883, founded Beaulieu in 1900 (although it was not his first venture into wine) and arguably did more than any other single person to make Napa Valley Cabernet Sauvignon famous around the world. In the twilight of his life, by which time much of the hard work had been done, he journeyed to Paris and hired a young Russian-born but French-trained wine technician, Andre Tchelistcheff, to become winemaker at Beaulieu — an investment in human resources as important as any de Latour made in land or buildings. The sale of Beaulieu to the Heublein Corporation in 1969 by Georges de Latour's aging daughter caused an emotional hue and cry of major proportions, but — until late 1992 — most critics believed that Heublein had preserved its fabulous inheritance well, the jewel in the crown being the Georges de Latour Private Reserve Cabernet Sauvignon.

These days the keeper of the faith is the wispy, blond-haired Joel Aiken, who is as firm as his predecessors in the view that Private Reserve has shown again and again how magnificently it matures in bottle, and there are no plans to change any of the winemaking techniques — including the use of American oak for maturation and the 100% use of Cabernet Sauvignon from the BV1 and BV2 vineyards.

But that does not mean sterility of thought or loss of that evergreen challenge to make better wine. Since 1981 Beaulieu has been engaged in an extensive clonal selection program, culminating in the 1989 planting on a fully commercial scale of the three best clones, clones with small berries producing wines of an extra dimension of color and flavor. A similar program for Pinot Noir and Chardonnay in the 350-acre Carneros vineyard is underway, and while the results of this may be a decade away, major changes in the making of Pinot Noir took place in 1992. To what extent these behind-the-scenes efforts to improve wine quality will be put in jeopardy by the major rearrangement of the Heublein wine interests (effectively merging the management of the great brands of Beaulieu and Inglenook with the lesser brands in the Heublein stable which took place in late 1992) remains to be seen.

In the meantime, I am one of those who does believe that the 1987 Georges de Latour is a worthy member of a great family of wines, with the sweet, fleshy fruit supported but not overwhelmed by coconut/vanillin oak. But a sentimental tasting of a 1947 Beaulieu Pinot Noir in 1992, courtesy of Darrell Corti, served to reinforce how far the Carneros Pinot Noirs and Chardonnays of 1989 and 1990 have to travel to recapture their former glory.

BERGFELD WINERY 1986

A: 401 St. Helena Highway South, St. Helena, CA 94574 **T**: (707) 963 8537 **V**: 10–4:30 daily **P**: 60,000 **W**: Rick Schultz

Bergfeld traces its history back to 1885, when the original winery — now incorporated into the main processing area — was built. Since 1934 it has operated as a co-operative, although it was not until 1986 that a decision was taken to establish its own brand, and hence The Napa Valley Co-operative Winery became Bergfeld, owned by over 100 Napa Valley growers. A tasting room and hospitality area, designed to recreate some of the feeling of the original winery, was opened to help lift awareness of the brand, and the winemaking facility modernized and upgraded. In 1990 Bergfeld also acquired ownership of the J. Wile & Sons brand from Hiram Walker, a logical enough move because Bergfeld had in fact made the J. Wile & Sons wines since 1986.

The J. Wile & Sons 1987 Cabernet Sauvignon shows what the winery is capable of achieving: clean and smooth redcurrant fruit aromas, with a smooth, long flavored palate, subtle oak and well-balanced tannins. The 1989 Bergfeld Cabernet Franc and 1989 Bergfeld

ABOVE ~ *Trellis modifications on Conn Creek Road look like birds taking flight.*

Malbec are of above average quality, offering varietal wines seldom encountered, and taking full advantage of the winery's ability to select special parcels from over 100 vineyards.

DOMAINE NAPA 1985

A: 1155 Mee Lane, St. Helena, CA 94574
T: (707) 963 1666 **V**: 10–5 daily **P**: 9,000
W: Grant Taylor

Owned by French-born Michael Perret, this curiously named winery (built in 1985) draws upon ten acres of estate-owned vines around the winery and 180 acres under management. The four principal wines produced are Sauvignon Blanc, Chardonnay, Merlot and Cabernet Sauvignon. Those tasted (covering the 1987, 1989 and 1990 vintages) were not exciting: those with adequate fruit flavor had rough edges; those without such fault tended to be rather thin and featureless.

ELYSE WINE CELLARS 1987

A: P.O. Box 83, Rutherford, CA 94573
T: (707) 963 5496 **V**: By appointment
P: 400 **W**: Raymond Coursen

Nancy and Ray Coursen make minuscule quantities of two wines: an immensely concentrated, muscular Zinfandel from the Morisoli Vineyard which was established in 1915, and (since 1990) Nero Misto, a neat name for an old Italian mixed block containing Petite Sirah, Zinfandel, Alicante Bouchet, Grande Noir, Grenache, Napa Gamay and Carignane. Both the 1987 and 1990 Zinfandel were very well made, as well as having that richness and power of old vines; I can but accept the Coursens' description of the Nero Misto as a deep, dark wine with the pepper and tannin of Petite Sirah and the fresh fruitiness of Zinfandel, as by 1992 their entire library stock consisted of six bottles!

FLORA SPRINGS 1978

A: 1978 West Zinfandel Lane, St. Helena, CA 94574 **T**: (707) 963 5711
V: By appointment **P**: 40,000 **W**: Ken Deis

Jerry Komes is yet another Bechtel Corporation retiree to enter the wine industry — but a very special one, which may help explain why Flora Springs has achieved so much in so short a time. For Jerry Komes was a self-made man, who worked his way up from the bottom to become the first president of Bechtel who was neither a member of the family nor had a college degree. The work ethic which led to this success has been passed on to his children, Julie and John, who play key roles in the running of Jerry and Flora Komes' "retirement" empire. Starting with the acquisition of an 1880s vintage winery (which had been used by Louis Martini during

ABOVE ~ *The much-loved car of a Flora Springs vineyard worker.*

the 1930s but had long since fallen into disrepair), the Komes family now owns 400 acres of vineyard in eight different locations. The centerpiece is the 110-acre Komes Ranch on the famed Rutherford Bench, planted to Cabernet Sauvignon, Merlot, Cabernet Franc, Petit Verdot and Sangiovese. Ignoring the short-term impact of phylloxera, 75–80% of the grape production is sold to other makers, allowing for tremendous flexibility in both selection and blending.

There are two brands: first, Flora Springs, which is reserved for 100% estate-grown wines and comprises Soliloquy (100% Sauvignon Blanc), Barrel Fermented Chardonnay, Reserve Cabernet Sauvignon and Trilogy (typically a blend of roughly equal proportions of Cabernet Sauvignon, Merlot and Cabernet Franc), with Sangiovese a future release. Second, there is the Floreal brand, which is not necessarily all estate-grown: for a variety of reasons (not just phylloxera) the family is content to find itself in the position of both selling and buying grapes, recognising the flexibility this approach allows. The Floreal wines are Sauvignon Blanc, Chardonnay, Merlot and Cabernet Sauvignon.

All of the wines have deservedly received high critical praise: James Laube rates the Flora Springs Chardonnay as first growth, the Cabernet Sauvignon/Trilogy reds as fifth growths. Without being too dogmatic, I would tend to reverse those rankings on the basis of the 1988 and 1990 vintages. Certainly, all of the wines have real character and distinct personalities, reflecting the on-going experimentation in both vineyard and winery.

FRANCISCAN VINEYARDS 1972

A: 1178 Galleron Road, Rutherford, CA 94573 **T**: (707) 963 711 **V**: 10–5 daily
P: 48,000 **W**: Peter Upton

The early years of Franciscan were, to put it mildly, tumultuous, passing through five owners until the present 50-50 partnership between the Eckes family of Germany and the Huneeus family of Chile was formed, since which time the Franciscan group has gone from strength to strength. It has five different estate operations: Franciscan itself, with 240 acres in the Rutherford-Oakville area, and called Franciscan Oakville Estate; an additional 280 acres in the heart of Rutherford, 170 acres of which has been planted to Cabernet Sauvignon, Merlot and Cabernet Franc, with the first release expected in 1997; Estancia Estate in the Alexander Valley; the Pinnacles Estate in Monterey; and Mount Veeder. (There are separate entries for each of Estancia, Pinnacles and Mount Veeder.)

The urbane Augustin Huneeus, who is president of the group, has a razor-sharp mind and heads a team of viticulturists and enologists which has led to a veritable flood of accolades — but with the vineyards (and the viticultural techniques) as the base for the quite remarkable achievements of the wines in the range.

None of my tastings were at odds with these paeans of praise and top rankings; wines to stand out on my scoresheets included the textured, toasty, honeyed 1990 Chardonnay Cuvee Sauvage, the more subtle and restrained melon flavors of the 1990 Oakville Reserve Chardonnay, and the elegantly framed but strongly varietal 1989 Oakville Merlot, with its slightly sappy, red berry fruit a triumph for a difficult vintage — but a dozen or so wines did not produce a single poor tasting note.

GRGICH HILLS 1987

A: 1829 St. Helena Highway, Rutherford, CA 94573 **T**: (707) 963 2784 **V**: 9:30–4:30 daily
P: 60,000 **W**: Mike Grgich

Having graduated from Zagreb University with a degree in wine science, Croatian-born Mike Grgich migrated to California in 1958 to escape the political turmoil which decades later was to explode into one of the most horrific events of the twentieth century. He promptly exhibited another aspect of his sixth sense, spending time with Lee Stewart at the old Souverain Cellars, Andre Tchelistcheff at Beaulieu and then Robert Mondavi. Small wonder that by the time he joined Chateau Montelena he was able to make the 1973 Chardonnay which stunned Paris in 1976, and by the time he established Grgich Hills in partnership with Austin Hills the following year he was able to produce a wine ranked first in a 220-wine tasting of Chardonnays from around the world organized in 1980. Or for that matter that James Laube, in

his book *California's Great Chardonnays*, says, "If I were forced to choose only one California Chardonnay to drink and cellar each year, it would probably be Grgich Hills," and inevitably accords Grgich first growth status.

The Chardonnay comes from four vineyards spanning Rutherford, Yountville and Carneros. Unusually for this part of the world, Grgich inhibits the malolactic fermentation in his Chardonnay, although he does employ the other usual methods of barrel fermentation and lees contact. I have long been an admirer of the Grgich Hills Chardonnays, but none more so than the absolutely stunning 1990, a wine of utterly exceptional length, complexity and character, the fruit easily swallowing up the significant oak contribution to the finished wine. Along with Kistler, surely the greatest Chardonnay from either the Napa or Sonoma Valleys. But Chardonnay is not the only wine in the Grgich armoury; Johannisberg Riesling was discontinued early in the piece, but he has always made Zinfandel (strong, well-ripened fruit in 1990, the 1985 aging as the 1990 promises to do), while Cabernet Sauvignon (firm and elegant) was introduced in 1980, and Fumé Blanc (ripe, complex and not grassy) in 1981 — and is the fastest growing wine in sales terms in the line-up.

HONIG CELLARS 1980

A: 850 Rutherford Road, Rutherford, CA 94573 **T**: (707) 963 5618 **V**: By appointment **P**: 11,000 **W**: James Hall

The Honig story started in 1966 when Louis Honig purchased a 67-acre property from Charlie Wagner of Caymus, and began reviving and extending that portion already planted to vines. By 1980 son Bill Honig — better known as California's former Superintendent of Public Instruction — started making a little wine, although then and now Honig remains primarily a grape-growing venture, with 29 acres of Sauvignon Blanc and 24 acres of Cabernet Sauvignon. In the wake of phylloxera the amount planted to Cabernet Sauvignon will increase and that planted to Sauvignon Blanc will decrease by about 15% — curious, given that Sauvignon Blanc is the winery speciality, both in terms of volume and quality.

The winery also has a thriving custom-crush and bottling business, which fully utilizes its 30,000 case capacity, and helps Honig even out the ebbs and flows in demand for its own products.

INGLENOOK 1879

A: 1991 St. Helena Highway, Rutherford, CA 94574 **T**: (707) 967 3110 **V**: 10–5 daily **P**: 150,000 **W**: Judy Matulich-Weitz

It is quite remarkable how much of the premium end of the California wine industry is English owned: quite apart from the rapidly expanding Hiram Walker Wine Alliance, there is Heublein Inc., ultimately owned by Grand Metropolitan PLC, with two of the greatest names in the valley in its portfolio: Inglenook and Beaulieu. One could write an entire book covering the history of Inglenook since Finnish fur trader Gustav Niebaum founded it in 1879 (once again, James Conway does an admirable job in his book *Napa*); earn a PhD tracing the reasons for the rise and fall and rise again in the quality of its leading wine, Reserve Cask; and

ABOVE ~ *The historic Inglenook Winery, color co-ordinated with spring blossoms.*

go quickly insane trying to determine whether Lewis Carroll or Edward Lear had the upper hand in the deliberations of the Heublein marketing geniuses as they added and subtracted from the range of wines incorporating the word Inglenook. That Inglenook Cask Reserve is of the quality it is and retains (in most, though not all, quarters) the reputation it deserves is nothing short of a miracle. As I have commented in the Beaulieu entry, it is to be devoutly hoped that the absorption of the Heublein fine wine group into the larger octopus of Heublein Inc. (it was the latter which gave birth to the horrendous Inglenook Navalle brand, having nothing whatsoever to do with the real Inglenook) does not bode further disasters.

The Cask Reserve series began in 1949; before that time the wine was simply labelled Cabernet Sauvignon, the 1941 vintage of which is said by James Laube to be "absolutely sensational and undoubtedly one of the greatest California Cabernets produced," although most of the wines made between 1933 and 1964 (when the property was sold) were of stellar quality. Production manager John Richburg — to whom Judy Matulich-Weitz and Joel Aiken of Beaulieu report — has recounted that it wasn't until 1972 (by which time Heublein had "inherited" Inglenook) that any money was spent in upgrading winemaking facilities and restoring the vineyards, and it wasn't until 1974 that Inglenook Cask Reserve began its comeback, a comeback of awesome proportions in the 1980s. The 1987 has a concentrated, powerful and textured bouquet, with blackcurrant fruit balanced by a whisker of astringency, while the palate delivers everything the bouquet promises: richly powerful and beautifully balanced, with dark berry/briary fruit and supple tannins — the sort of wine which should be sending wine writers into ecstasies in 50 years' time.

NIEBAUM-COPPOLA ESTATE 1978

A: 1460 Niebaum Lane, Rutherford, CA 94573 **T**: (707) 963 9435 **V**: By appointment
P: 4,000–5,000 **W**: Stephen Beresini

When a film-maker with a profile as high as that of Francis Ford Coppola purchases a house as famous as that built by Gustav Niebaum (together with 83 acres of prime Rutherford Bench vineyard which had been the heart of the Inglenook wines), one might have expected a publicity campaign of nuclear proportions. In fact the reverse occurred: Coppola purchased the house and land in 1975, but had no real understanding of wine, and even less about how it should be made and marketed. It took three years for the teething problems to be sorted out, and for Andre Tchelistcheff to be recruited as a consultant, setting the scene for what was to become the first vintage of Rubicon, made in 1978. Like all subsequent vintages, it spent almost three years in barrel, and around three years in bottle before release. Thus the first

Rubicon was not released until the spring of 1985, ten years after the Coppolas had purchased the property, while the 1986 was not released until September 1992.

Rubicon is the only wine produced for sale; it is a blend of between 60% and 70% Cabernet Sauvignon, with the balance comprising Cabernet Franc and Merlot. The substantial excess production is sold to other makers: in a nice twist of fate, 60% of the 1986 Inglenook Cask Reserve is said to be Niebaum-Coppola grapes. The 1978 and 1986 Rubicon, both tasted — nay, drunk — in 1992, were quite magnificent when consumed with food. Earlier, on the anonymity of the tasting bench, the tannins had fought with the fruit — and lost, but only just. The wines still scored gold medal points on the bench; with food they went off the scale. In his stylish but understated sales brochure Coppola says, "When I first considered how my wine would be made, I conceived of it as a claret blend of Cabernet Sauvignon, Cabernet Franc and Merlot, and asked that it be a full, rich wine that would live one hundred years." Well, his winemaking team has made a pretty useful start.

PEJU PROVINCE 1982

A: 8466 St. Helena Highway, Rutherford, CA 94573 **T**: (707) 963 3600 **V**: 10–6 daily
P: 5,000 **W**: Anthony Peju

Peju Province gained considerable notoriety during a two-year battle with the local planning authorities when it acquired the sobriquet of the Chain-Link Winery, its stainless steel tanks standing forlornly on a concrete pad. All that is now behind former Los Angeles nurseryman Anthony Peju and wife Herta, who moved into the now complete stone and masonry winery and tasting facility in September 1991, nine

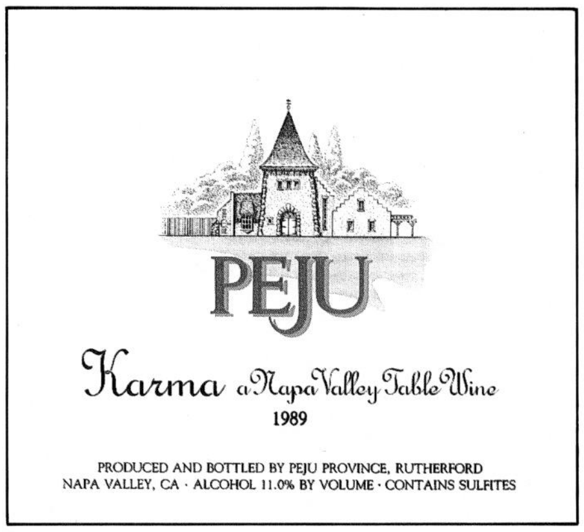
PEJU
Karma a Napa Valley Table Wine
1989
PRODUCED AND BOTTLED BY PEJU PROVINCE, RUTHERFORD
NAPA VALLEY, CA · ALCOHOL 11.0% BY VOLUME · CONTAINS SULFITES

years after making their first wine. The irony was that while the planning battle was raging, the 1986 Peju H B Vineyard Estate Cabernet Sauvignon was winning a double gold medal at the San Francisco National Wine Competition, a gold and Best of Region (Napa Valley) at the California State Fair and a 92 rating from the *Wine Spectator*.

The 30-acre vineyard is planted primarily to Cabernet Sauvignon with Chardonnay, Cabernet Franc and Petit Verdot added after the 1982 purchase. The first estate Chardonnay (rather tart and appley) was released in 1992; from time to time Peju has released late harvest Chardonnays, and in 1991 made an intensely botrytised Late Harvest Sauvignon Blanc. The Cabernet Sauvignons, either Napa or H B Vineyard, remain the winery forté, with the Napa Cabernet Sauvignon from 1989 showing masses of ripe fruit flavor and depth.

MARIO PERELLI-MINETTI WINERY 1988

A: 1443 Silverado Trail North, St. Helena, CA 94573 **T**: (707) 963 8762
V: By appointment **P**: 6,000
W: Kellie Carlin

Mario Perelli-Minetti
100%
1990
Napa Valley
CHARDONNAY
PRODUCED AND BOTTLED BY M.P.M. VINEYARDS,
RUTHERFORD, CA ALCOHOL 13.0% BY VOLUME

ABOVE ~ *The door to the Niebaum-Coppola barrel cellar exudes history.*

To say that Mario Perelli-Minetti was born into the wine industry is something of an understatement: the family name is over 800 years old, and the Perelli-Minettis have been making wine since the early sixteenth century, although the American involvement is rather more recent. Antonio Perelli-Minetti arrived in 1902, and built major wine businesses in both California's Central Valley and Mexico. The present winery is in the nature of a retirement hobby for Antonio's son Mario, producing only two wines, and in tiny quantities compared to the family's earlier wineries. The Chardonnay is a clean, direct wine with pleasant melon/grapefruit flavors, the Cabernet Sauvignon showing ripe fruit to the point of being overripe.

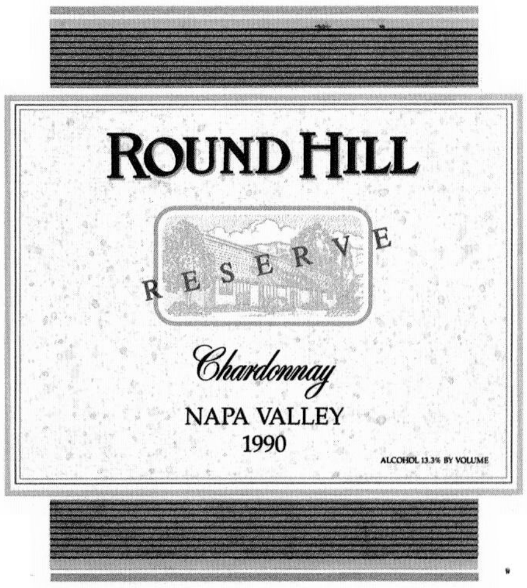
ROUND HILL
RESERVE
Chardonnay
NAPA VALLEY
1990
ALCOHOL 13.3% BY VOLUME

ROUND HILL WINERY 1977

A: 1680 Silverado Trail, St. Helena, CA 94574 **T**: (707) 963 5251 **V**: By appointment **P**: 315,000 **W**: Mark Swain

My background reading of the history of Round Hill made me regard my visit as a journeyman's one — and even after the visit I was impressed but not overwhelmed by a wholly functional winery with modest landscaping expenditure, and an intelligent but businesslike winemaker who had presided over much of the growth of the business from 30,000 cases in 1977 to its present level of over 300,000 cases. It was only after the blind tastings in which the Round Hill wines were placed that I sat bolt upright: Round Hill really does offer exceptional values with its wines. My initial ennui was prompted by the birth of the Round Hill label long before there was a winery, allowing highly successful retailer Ernie Van Asperen the opportunity of creating a house brand using wine made by others. He in fact briefly sold the label to Charlie Abela, allowing him (Van Asperen) to dispose of his retail shops and come back into the Round Hill Winery partnership (with 25 other stockholders), which moved into its present custom-built winery in 1987.

Production is divided into four lines: California's generics and varietals at the (very) bottom end of the market, including Cabernet, Chardonnay and White Zinfandel; then the vintage-dated Gold Label Napa varietals; next the Round Hill Reserve Range; and finally very limited production runs (500–2,000 cases of each) of Rutherford Ranch varietals, including a Merlot and a Cabernet Franc.

The 1990 Napa Zinfandel had a suggested retail price of $6 in 1992, and was utterly exceptional at the price, loaded with spicy fruit and oak, yet elegant and in no way showing its 14.3% alcohol. The 1990 Reserve Chardonnay and 1987 Reserve Cabernet Sauvignon (priced at $10.95) were no less impressive, the Chardonnay lively, fresh and citrus tinged, with subtle red berry fruit, again a touch of oak spice, and the sort of finish which leads to the second glass, and the third ... Surgeon General be damned.

SEQUOIA GROVE VINEYARDS 1980

A: 8338 St. Helena Highway, Napa, CA 94558 **T**: (707) 944 2945 **V**: 11–5 daily **P**: 25,000 **W**: Jim Allen and Michael Trujillo

Jim Allen, co-owner with brother Steve, writes, "My search for the perfect vineyard site for Cabernet Sauvignon ended in November 1978 when I bought 25 acres of prime vineyard land in the Rutherford area of the Napa Valley." It was a search which had its origins decades earlier while Allen was studying philosophy at the University of Innsbruck in Austria, where he first acquired an interest in wine (and an awareness of the importance of *terroir*). But having purchased the perfect Cabernet Sauvignon site (which, incidentally, was planted to everything but that variety) the Allens formed a limited partnership with others to purchase (in 1981) a 138-acre property in Carneros, which they planted to Pinot Noir, Chardonnay and a little Cabernet Sauvignon. This property subsequently became the site for the Taittinger Domaine Carneros development, leaving the Allens both with an interest in the Domaine Carneros partnership and a source for Carneros Chardonnay.

The winery produces two Chardonnays and two Cabernets: an Estate Chardonnay and Carneros Chardonnay (the latter close to being estate itself) and a Cabernet Sauvignon Estate and Napa. Production is roughly evenly split between the two varieties, but it is for the Cabernet Sauvignon that Sequoia Grove has a notable reputation. The Estate Cabernet, in particular, can show intriguing fruit characters, almost spicy/peppery. Winemakers Mike Trujillo and Jim Allen eschew malolactic fermentation in making their Chardonnays, and I applaud what I assume to be their desire to preserve fruit rather than concentrate solely on texture and structure. The problem is, it doesn't seem to work particularly well with either the Estate or Carneros Chardonnays, both of which tend to be somewhat anemic.

SULLIVAN VINEYARDS 1972

A: 1090 Galleron Road, Rutherford, CA 94573 **T**: (707) 963 9646 **V**: By appointment **P**: 3,000 **W**: Jim Sullivan

ABOVE ~ *Usibelli Ranch on Conn Creek Road, to the west of Rutherford.*

Erstwhile graphic designer Jim Sullivan made an early entry in the wine industry via home winemaking and home viticulture (all of 20 vines) in 1962. As so often happens, one thing led to another: extension courses at U.C. Davis; omnivorous reading of any book or article concerned with growing, making or drinking wine; and in 1972 to the establishment of a four-acre vineyard in Manley Lane. Along the way, he and wife JoAnn had produced five children — including three unnervingly beautiful daughters — who are all involved to a lesser or greater degree in the business.

The four acres of Cabernet Sauvignon at Manley Lane was a weekend occupation involving a weekly commute to Sullivan's Los Angeles business, but by 1978 he was ready to make the transition to full-time vigneron by purchasing 26 acres in Galleron Road, already planted to six acres of Chenin Blanc and now completed with Cabernet Sauvignon, Merlot and Chardonnay. Architect John Marsh Davies designed an inspired house which makes you feel you are on a hilltop cathedral, rather than the flat valley floor: it literally floats in space, being raised on a platform and giving floor to ceiling glass an entirely new meaning. A functional, small wooden winery sits next door where Jim Sullivan makes a dry Chenin Blanc, Cabernet Sauvignon, Coeur de Vignes (a proprietary Meritage blend) and Merlot (he sells his Chardonnay).

He developed a reputation for strongly flavored reds with increasing levels of volatile acidity: this is an insidious fault which can gradually permeate barrels and build in intensity without the winemaker realizing what is happening. In 1989 Sullivan broke free of the cycle by producing a rich, plump, juicy Merlot with the sort of flesh, soft tannins and sweet vanillin oak one expects from Silver Oak. The wine was rated at 92 by the *Wine Spectator* as one of the best reds from the 1989 vintage, and one can only hope it points the way for the future.

SWANSON VINEYARDS 1987

A: 1271 Manley Lane, Rutherford, CA 94573
T: (707) 944 0905 **V**: By appointment
P: 25,000 **W**: Marco Capelli

W. Clarke Swanson Jnr. inherited a great deal of money on the sale of the family's TV food business, but made his own career in communication and media industries (principally in Florida) and in banking, before selling those businesses and moving to the Napa Valley to become a major investor in the wine business. In so doing he has followed the old banking principle of only investing in the very best blue chip securities: on the famed Oakville Bench, he has a holding with Martha's Vineyard on one side and Inglenook on the other; he has most recently acquired the oldest planting of Syrah in the Napa Valley (a small vineyard immediately behind Mustards Restaurant); the Oakville Ranch looks across the Napa River on to Opus One; while the Silverado Vineyard has Groth, Caymus and Bonny's Vineyard as neighbors. If this were not enough, Swanson also has long term contracts with producers on Mt. Veeder, on Howell Mountain and in Carneros, giving winemaker Marco Capelli the ultimate choice in raw materials. By contrast, Swanson has not invested in a lavish winery or entertainment center. The relatively modest winery is an old construction (once the Cassayre-Forni Winery), which you can easily miss as you pass it on the northern side of the Mondavi Winery.

Swanson is an internationalist in outlook. One of his other significant wine-related investments was the acquisition of the famous English wine merchant, Averys of Bristol Limited, while winemaker Marco Capelli won a scholarship on graduating from U.C. Davis which allowed him to work one vintage at two of Tuscany's greatest estates. From there he went to Bordeaux to work a vintage in Sauternes, and in more recent years has formed a close working relationship with Australian winemaker Simon Adams of Yalumba. Not only that, Chris Anstee was, until 1992, president: Anstee's career started in South Africa, continuing in Germany, and thence to Australia where he had outstanding success in developing the export business of Lindemans before moving to Swanson. (He has since returned to Australia.)

While there has been a vigorous replanting program on the estate vineyard, which has limited production, only one-quarter of the annual crop is in fact made into wine for the Swanson label, the remainder of the grapes being sold. If the tough economic times of the 1990s allow Swanson to achieve its full potential, it could become one of the leading producers of the valley. Certainly the early wines were particularly impressive. The Chardonnays have typically creamy vanilla flavor and structure; the Merlots offer lush cassis berry fruit with plenty of supporting structure; the Cabernet Sauvignons are beautifully bred, with real elegance and mouthfeel, combining red berry and plum fruit flavors with soft tannins and a classically long finish. When some of the exotic varieties planted in the past few years come into bearing, and the first of the old Syrah becomes available, what is presently an interesting winery could easily become a superstar.

OTHER WINERIES

NAPA CREEK WINERY 1980
A: 1001 Silverado Trail, St. Helena, CA 94574
T: (707) 963 9456 **W**: Geoff Murray

PINA 1982
A: 8060 Silverado Trail, Rutherford, CA 94573
T: (707) 944 2229 **W**: Ken Robinson

PRAEGER PORT WORKS 1979
A: 1281 Levelling Lane, St. Helena, CA 94574
T: (707) 963 PORT **W**: James L. Praeger

RUTHERFORD VINTNERS 1976
A: 1673 St. Helena Highway, Rutherford, CA 94573 **T**: (707) 963 4117 **W**: Bernard L. Skoda

WHITEHALL LANE WINERY 1980
A: 1563 St. Helena Highway, St. Helena, CA 94574 **T**: (707) 963 9454
W: Ray Coursen

ABOVE ~ *The home built by Gustav Niebaum over 100 years ago now owned by movie director Francis Ford Coppola.*

St. Helena

The first vineyards were planted in St. Helena in 1846 by Florentine Kellogg (who came from Illinois) and by Reason P. Tucker — both names to conjure with, but who gave St. Helena the early start one would expect of a town which so proudly proclaims its nineteenth-century lineage.

Its main street is a delight: whether you are walking or caught in the perpetual traffic jam, there is always ample time to survey the handsome wooden (and occasional stone) buildings. If you enter the Napa Valley by Highway 29 — or, to give it its local name, the St. Helena Highway — this is the first (and only) town of any consequence you will pass through until you prepare to leave the valley at Calistoga — which is situated on a side street in any event.

Restaurants abound (Tra Vigne is the most famous), and there is the best wine merchant to be found between the Napa Valley and San Francisco. It is a tourist town, yet it is also a hub of business for the center of the valley, a place to which one gravitates without being conscious of having done so.

But it is dominated — in terms of history and of winemaking — by Jacob Beringer's Rhine House, which stands proudly amidst manicured gardens and huge trees on the northern side of the town. Beringer is big business, but it caters like few others for the tourist. Free wine tours are run daily between 9:30 A.M. and 4:30 P.M., starting at the bottom floor of the original (1877) gravity-fed winery built into the side of Spring Mountain, then moving into the hand-hewn caves built by Chinese laborers in the same decade, and still in use today. The tour ends 45 minutes later in the 1883 Rhine House with a wine tasting. The capacious parking lot bears testimony to the fact that, together with Mondavi, V. Sattui and Sterling, this is one of four tourist landmarks of the valley.

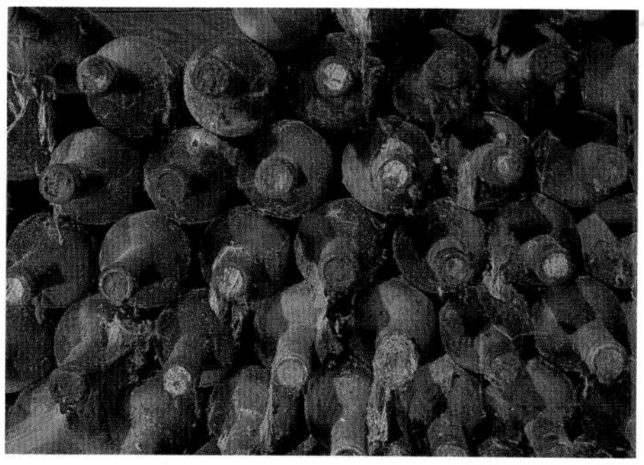

ABOVE ~ *The cobwebs and molds of museum cellars add to the atmosphere and in no way harm the wines.*

OPPOSITE ~ *The pastel pinks, greens, yellows and blues of spring at Charles Krug.*

THE REGION IN BRIEF

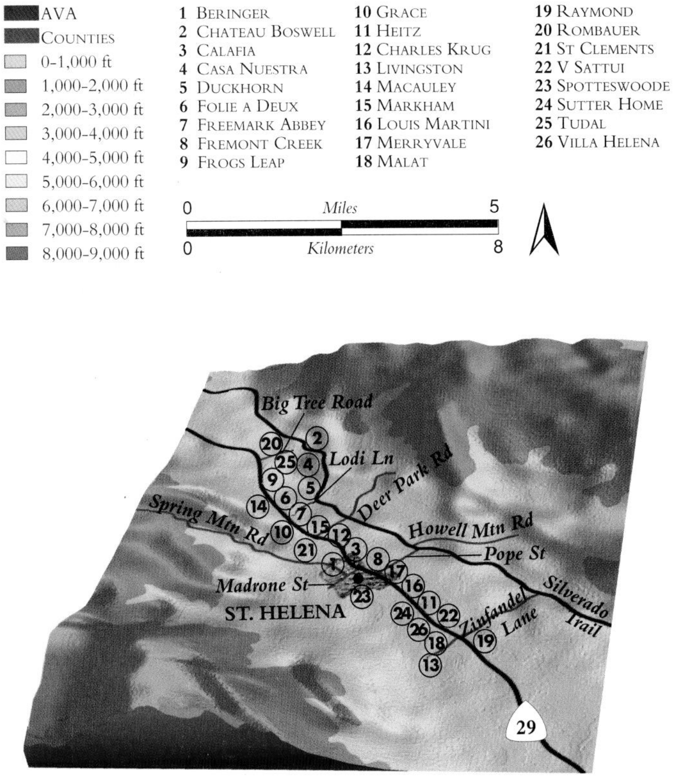
AVA
COUNTIES
0-1,000 ft
1,000-2,000 ft
2,000-3,000 ft
3,000-4,000 ft
4,000-5,000 ft
5,000-6,000 ft
6,000-7,000 ft
7,000-8,000 ft
8,000-9,000 ft
1 BERINGER
2 CHATEAU BOSWELL
3 CALAFIA
4 CASA NUESTRA
5 DUCKHORN
6 FOLIE A DEUX
7 FREEMARK ABBEY
8 FREMONT CREEK
9 FROGS LEAP
10 GRACE
11 HEITZ
12 CHARLES KRUG
13 LIVINGSTON
14 MACAULEY
15 MARKHAM
16 LOUIS MARTINI
17 MERRYVALE
18 MALAT
19 RAYMOND
20 ROMBAUER
21 ST CLEMENTS
22 V SATTUI
23 SPOTTESWOODE
24 SUTTER HOME
25 TUDAL
26 VILLA HELENA
0 Miles 5
0 Kilometers 8
Big Tree Road
Lodi Ln
Deer Park Rd
Spring Mtn Rd
Howell Mtn Rd
Pope St
Madrone St
ST. HELENA
Silverado Trail
Zinfandel Lane
29

VINTAGE CHART 1981-91
St. Helena

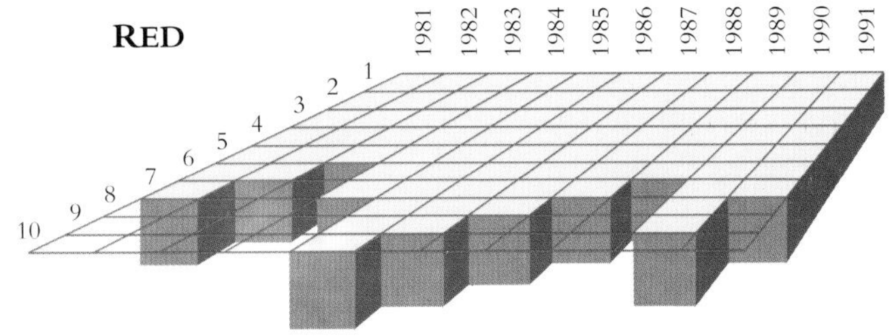
RED
1981
1982
1983
1984
1985
1986
1987
1988
1989
1990
1991
1
2
3
4
5
6
7
8
9
10

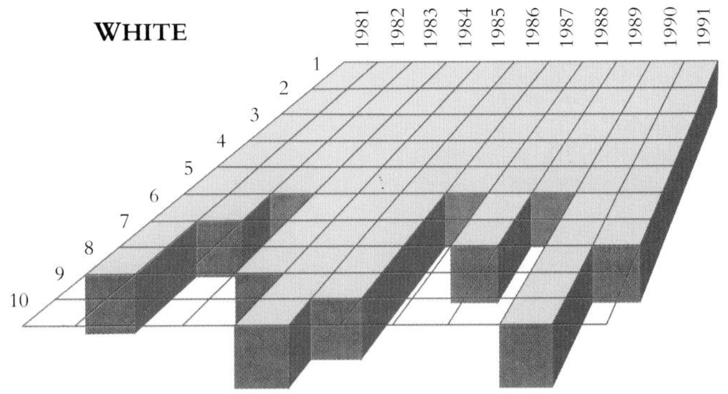
WHITE
1981
1982
1983
1984
1985
1986
1987
1988
1989
1990
1991
1
2
3
4
5
6
7
8
9
10

Climate, Soil and Viticulture

CLIMATE

There are those who aver that St. Helena is one of the warmest parts of the Napa Valley, but climatic data shows that Calistoga is indeed hotter. As ever, there is significant variation from one vintage to the next, and there is some disagreement about the long term average: one source puts it at 3,229 degree days (mid Region III), the other at 3,575 degree days (low Region IV). Small wonder, then, that by the time you reach St. Helena you are well and truly into red wine country. Rainfall varies around a long term average of 35–40 inches, significantly higher than the regions to the south. The risk of spring frosts is also higher, and all vineyards on the valley floor have one form of protection or another: smudge pots, wind machines or overhead sprinklers.

SOIL

The soils derive from the Sonoma Volcanics which rim the valley on both sides from St. Helena northwards. The deep, very gravelly sandy and sandy clay loams have low to moderate water-holding capacity, and vine vigor varies significantly according to the stone or gravel content, water retention and drainage. Technically, they fall variously within the Bale and Pleasanton series, with the richer, deeper (and more vigorous) soils adjacent to the Napa River.

THE GROWING SEASON

With the increased growing season warmth, vintage starts relatively early, Chardonnay and Sauvignon Blanc being picked from mid-August through to early September, and Merlot coming in soon thereafter, followed by Cabernet Sauvignon.

Contract Growers

Beckstoffer Vineyard Twenty-seven acres planted progressively between 1974 and 1989 on west side of Sulphur Creek Road, principally Cabernet Sauvignon with a little Merlot. Guenoc is a purchaser.

Carol's Vineyard Thirty-two acres of Cabernet Sauvignon planted in 1972 on the south side of Pratt Avenue; sold to J. Lohr.

Chabot Vineyard Thirty-five acres of historic vineyard, established in the nineteenth century, and now planted to Cabernet Sauvignon up to 40 years old. Sold exclusively to Beringer for its Chabot Vineyard Cabernet Sauvignon.

Collins Vineyard Another historic nineteenth-century vineyard of 54 acres, with Zinfandel dating back to 1920, and Cabernet Sauvignon, Cabernet Franc and Merlot planted between 1973 and 1987. Sold exclusively to Conn Creek.

ABOVE ~ *St. Helena map.*

SPOTTSWOODE
1401
PRIVATE
RESIDENCE
TRUCK ENTRANCE

Principal Wine Styles

CABERNET SAUVIGNON

The variety responds to the warmer climate in precisely the way one would expect, gaining a few pounds of weight around its girth like a well-fed big city lawyer, with the weight hidden by a perfectly tailored suit. The essence of St. Helena Cabernet is to be found in the wines of Grace Family and Spotteswoode. There is a luxuriance to the red and blackcurrant fruit which literally floods the mouth, yet the structure is disciplined to the point of firmness. The richness of the fruit provides a natural balance to the tannins, and one instinctively feels that these wines will age with grace (my apologies). The list of distinguished producers of Cabernet Sauvignon resident in the St. Helena district is a long one, although not all draw their grapes solely from within its boundaries. Beringer is the most noteworthy, but Duckhorn, Freemark Abbey, Frogs Leap, Heitz, Markham, Raymond, V. Sattui, Tudal and St. Clement are all producers of good to great Cabernets.

MERLOT AND RED MERITAGE

This is emphatically red wine country, and — particularly in the wake of phylloxera — there is certain to be a marked increase in the number of Merlots and Meritages coming from St. Helena. As with Cabernet Sauvignon, not all the Merlot comes from the region, but Duckhorn, the most famous producer, sources its Merlot from Sterling's Three Palms Vineyard, halfway between St. Helena and Calistoga. Other particularly noteworthy producers are Freemark Abbey, Markham and St. Clement.

ZINFANDEL

A variety which may find itself threatened in this ultra-premium region by the simple fact of economics, however well suited it is to the climate and soil. Frogs Leap Zinfandel, a blend of 55% St. Helena Valley floor grapes and 45% from the Rutherford Bench (the latter presumably an even more precarious source) has all the ingredients: cherry, plum and mint flavors backed by soft but ample tannins, and the depth to satisfy those who like the bigger style without becoming ponderous. Charles Krug and Beringer also provide Zinfandels with character, but with, I suspect, diverse sources.

CHARDONNAY AND SAUVIGNON BLANC

Unceremoniously lumped together simply because those relatively few wines made from grapes grown in the district lack distinction. Frogs Leap's Sauvignon Blanc is primarily sourced from Yountville, St. Clement's Chardonnay from Carneros, and Freemark Abbey's Chardonnay from all over.

ABOVE ~ *Spotteswoode is an unexpected inhabitant of the leafy back streets of St. Helena.*

V. Sattui and the Wine Tourist

Throughout the wine world, wine regions have a magnetic attraction for tourists whose interest in wine will range from negligible to an all-consuming passion. As the fame of the region grows, so does the number of tourists visiting it. And as the Napa Valley has so vividly demonstrated over the past 20 years, the balance between the supply of the basic tourist infrastructure, together with the range of attractions and opportunities offered by the wineries, and the demand for those services (in other words, the number of tourists visiting each day, week or year) is an exceedingly difficult balance to achieve.

If you visit Disneyland, part of the fun, the excitement, is the very mass of buzzing humanity. If you visit a wine region, you expect quiet, unspoilt beauty, and bitterly resent being caught in a traffic jam of tourists — conveniently forgetting you are yourself no less responsible for that jam than any other tourist. You want to have things to interest all members of the family, from grandmother to grandchild, yet you want to see vines and the occasional winery discreetly hidden by trees rather than semi-urban commercial ribbon development.

ABOVE ~ *The picnic grounds at V. Sattui welcome tens of thousands of visitors every summer.*

This irreconcilable tension worsens from the perspective of most of the permanent residents, and in particular the grape growers and those whose livelihood does not directly and immediately derive from the tourist trade. It does not help to point out that unless Napa wine was famous, there would be no market for the grapes in the first place. As I say many times in this book, James Conway's *Napa*, telling of the drama of the unfolding tensions of the last 20 years, is utterly compelling.

But when in 1974 Daryl Sattui conceived the idea of reviving his great-grandfather's wine business, which had lain dormant since Prohibition, the valley was a very different place. The majority of the wineries were relatively new, and barely a dozen had tasting facilities for the public. Mondavi, even then, was one of the more hospitable, and Mustards Restaurant — that unperishable and ever-popular symbol of Napa cuisine — was yet to open. If you wish to recreate the feeling of the Napa Valley of those days, drive down Charter Oak Street (which runs east from Highway 29 just south of St. Helena), and a short distance on your left you will find an old wooden building with a small sign announcing the presence of the Napa Valley Oil Manufacturing Co. A small door in the corner of the building is adjacent to a mini-park with four ancient tables and trestles; inside the building salamis hang from strings, today's bread is stacked endways in a basket on the floor, and there is a modest array of cheeses, olives and oils at extremely modest prices.

On a typical weekday you will find several of the tables occupied by a few locals (possibly Italian) paring salami and cheese with a penknife, and breaking chunks of sourdough bread, their sole audience being a couple of hopeful scrawny cats which materialize through a nearby fence.

So Daryl Sattui came up with the idea of opening a winery on Highway 29 which would offer simple food — then not so different from that of the Napa Valley Oil Manufacturing Co. — and modest but pleasant surroundings in which to eat it and enjoy a glass or two of Sattui wine while doing so.

The problem was that the family business had been located in the Mission district of San Francisco (so there was no winery or land) and Sattui had only $5,000. But then nobody told him you needed $1 million to start a Napa Valley winery either, and his idea appealed sufficiently to a group of friends and investors, who lent him $57,500. His greatest coup was to persuade a Napa Valley real estate agent to buy a four-acre block and erect a small winery building on it, leasing it to Sattui with an option to purchase.

Today V. Sattui Winery is a mecca: in 1991, 257,000 people entered the tasting room, purchased 370,000 bottles of Sattui wine, and spent very nearly as much in the Sattui delicatessen, which has an assortment of almost 200 domestic and imported cheeses, together with an array of carefully chosen salami, prosciutto, patés, and imaginative home-made salads, augmented by fresh tomatoes and fruits, and Acme bread which comes all the way from Berkeley. This is the exception to the other fresh daily foods, which are locally grown and chosen. There is a staff of 12 to run the tasting room, and even on weekdays they seldom have a moment's peace.

But, with a little patience and a little luck, the visitor can find peace in the two acres of grassed picnic grounds with tables and chairs spread under a giant oak tree or the walnut trees adjacent to Suzanne's Vineyard, all of which surround the now unrecognizable winery and sales complex (unrecognizable from the 1974 winery, that is). On a sunny day — and when is it not sunny in a Napa summer — it is an idyllic scene, and it is small wonder that Sattui is so popular.

In 1985 a 22,000 square foot, multi-story stone winery was built in nineteenth-century style, so successfully that the casual observer would have no idea it had not been there all along. Part functional winery and part marketing wizardry, it is the nerve center for the

10,000 people who buy at least a case a year, thereby staying on the mailing list and becoming members of the Cellar Club. There is a private tasting room, three wine caves, and two underground barrel cellars in which Cellar Club members can periodically attend barrel tastings (invaluable for the futures offerings, which are made from time to time in the newsletter) and which also house events such as the harvest ball and candle-lit banquets.

Yet if Daryl Sattui were to have the same idea today he wouldn't even be able to get it off the ground. In his first year of business he sold more food than wine: today his new winery would not be able to sell any food whatsoever, and he would only be able to build it subject to a host of regulations and requirements, none of which he would be able to satisfy.

For it has been agreed on all sides that the Napa Valley has reached saturation point, and that any further expansion of facilities will only worsen — not improve — the situation. A keen-eyed visitor to Sattui during a weekday (and not in the school holidays) will see the evidence: neatly stacked signs saying "Full House," "No Parking Available," "Please Call Back In Half An Hour," or words to that effect. It is a microcosm of the Napa Valley as a whole: the "Full house, no room, come back tomorrow" sign is as much a symbol of failure as it is of success.

ABOVE ~ *The stone winery and visitors buildings at Sattui seem much older than they in fact are.*

WINERIES *of* ST. HELENA

BERINGER VINEYARDS 1876

A: 2000 Main Street, St. Helena, CA 94574
T: (707) 963 7115 **V**: 9.30–5 daily (winter), 10–6 (summer) **P**: 1.3 million
W: Ed Sbragia

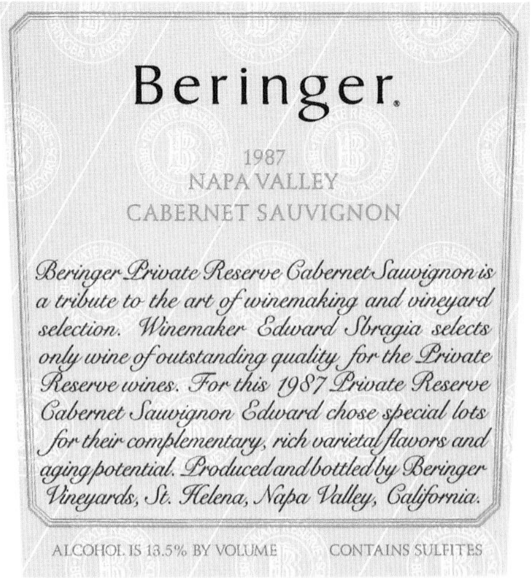
Beringer
1987
NAPA VALLEY
CABERNET SAUVIGNON
Beringer Private Reserve Cabernet Sauvignon is a tribute to the art of winemaking and vineyard selection. Winemaker Edward Sbragia selects only wine of outstanding quality for the Private Reserve wines. For this 1987 Private Reserve Cabernet Sauvignon Edward chose special lots for their complementary, rich varietal flavors and aging potential. Produced and bottled by Beringer Vineyards, St. Helena, Napa Valley, California.
ALCOHOL IS 13.5% BY VOLUME
CONTAINS SULFITES

The Beringer Rhine House, built in 1883, is one of the most prominent historic landmarks in the Napa Valley. The ornate Victorian mansion remained in the Beringer family until 1971, when the entire property (including 800 acres of vineyards) was purchased by Nestlé. By that time the once proud reputation of Beringer was at the lowest possible ebb, and Nestlé spent millions of dollars in renovating the Rhine House, building an entirely new production facility, renovating the vineyards and subsequently expanding those through additional purchases to 3,100 acres, 2,300 being in the Napa Valley, and the balance in the Knights Valley.

Nestlé, which also owns Chateau Souverain, Meridian, Napa Ridge and Los Hermanos, has proved to be a singularly beneficent owner, providing all of the capital necessary to build the business yet allowing local management a free hand in determining direction and style. This approach has paid big dividends: Beringer has managed to throw off its unenviable past reputation, surmount the lingering stigma which always attaches to conglomerate ownership, and successfully meet the quality challenges of a million-plus case production to the point where the 1986 Private Reserve Cabernet Sauvignon was rated the number one wine of the year in the *Wine Spectator* Top 100 in 1991. The 1987 Private Reserve Cabernet Sauvignon fared very nearly as well, topping a Vintner's Club tasting of what were expected to be the 12 best Cabernets from the 1987 vintage.

The Private Reserve Chardonnay and Private Reserve Cabernet Sauvignon head a very large list of wines covering virtually all of the principal varieties and styles. Some idea of the range (and the quality) can be gauged from the fact that at the 1992 Orange County Fair (one of the more important of the wine shows) Beringer's 1990 North Coast French Colombard, 1991 Gamay Beaujolais Premier Nouveau, 1991 North Coast White Zinfandel and 1987 Cabernet Sauvignon Port all won gold medals — yet these would come well down the theoretical pecking order of the Beringer portfolio. It is capable of producing absolutely delicious Fumé Blanc, with a Sancerre-like structure and delicacy, vibrantly fresh redcurrant and raspberry Zinfandel — and, of course, Cabernet Sauvignon equal to the best. In a range as wide as that of Beringer, not every wine is going to be great, but none are going to be bad.

CASA NUESTRA 1980

A: 3473 Silverado Trail, St. Helena, CA 94574 **T**: (707) 963 5783 **V**: 11–5 weekends and by appointment **P**: 1,500
W: Gene Kirkham

It took me almost 30 years to break free of the bonds of a large city law firm, but Gene Kirkham took no time at all, notwithstanding a Harvard education, a Fulbright scholarship to New Zealand and a promising career as a junior lawyer with a law firm in San Francisco. Kirkham says, "I was a flower child of the 1960s; I had a great job with a fine firm, and all it did was make me unhappy." In 1975 he and wife Cody were shown a house, a small shed, and eight acres of grapes on the western side of the Silverado Trail by a realtor who apologized for wasting their time, explaining he had not received a serious offer on it for about a year. Having very little money, the Kirkhams didn't make a serious offer either, but it was accepted. Within months he had given up his San Francisco job and joined a law firm in St. Helena, becoming a partner within a few years. Now he has weaned himself even of that necessity, happily crushing about 50 tons of grapes a year, selling half in bulk, and the rest through cellar door or by mailing list.

His specialities are Chenin Blanc (which he has a passionate attachment to, regarding it as a grossly underrated variety), and Cabernet Franc, coincidentally both natives of the Loire Valley. Coincidentally, because the Cabernet Franc came about as a result of the 1986 acquisition of six acres of Cabernet Franc next door which became available when the owners divorced. The Cabernet Francs are made in appropriately lean and austere style; after some deliberating, Kirkham has taken to incorporating 30% Merlot and 10% Cabernet Sauvignon, producing a home-spun version of Cheval Blanc, and the wines have been well reviewed by a number of critics. I would just like to see a little more fruit flesh, a slightly silkier texture.

DUCKHORN VINEYARDS 1976

A: 3027 Silverado Trail, St. Helena, CA 94574 **T**: (707) 963 7108 **V**: 9–5 daily
P: 25,000 **W**: Tom Rinaldi

DUCKHORN VINEYARDS
1989
NAPA VALLEY MERLOT
Three Palms Vineyard
Produced and bottled by Duckhorn Vineyards
3027 Silverado Trail, St. Helena, CA 94574 BWCA 4857
ALCOHOL 13.5% BY VOLUME

Dan Duckhorn is the eloquent, energetic and intelligent president of the ten-family company which owns and operates Duckhorn Vineyards. If David Graves of Saintsbury is California's Mr. Pinot Noir, Duckhorn is California's Mr. Merlot. Right from the initial crush of 28 tons in 1978, the accent has been on this variety. Duckhorn had been involved in the growing of grapes and grape plant propagation since 1971, and had become friends with Ric Forman at Sterling, and became fascinated with the potential of the variety. To this day, indeed, the principal Duckhorn Merlot is from the Three Palms Vineyard owned by Sterling.

Yet he is in some ways ambivalent about the grape. "I really don't like it on its own in most years; every now and then you get a vintage when it can perhaps account for 95% of the finished wine, but most years it needs more support — around 25%." As it is, the 1989 Three Palms Vineyard Merlot, for example, is precisely that: 75% Merlot, 10% Cabernet Sauvignon and 15% Cabernet Franc. This in turn reflects Duckhorn's view of red wines generally. He says that just as people like to talk dry and drink sweet, they talk smooth and elegant, but it is the big wines which make the impact on the public and the wine writers in particular. Well, Duckhorn acts as he speaks: tasted blind, my summary of the Three Palms Merlot was "big, brawny style, more power than fruit, and a touch of bitterness." On the other hand, the Cabernet Sauvignon drank superbly in a big style: strong, deep structure, with ripe fruit, good tannins, plenty of flavor and years of life in front of it. Dan Duckhorn may be a great spokesman for Merlot, but it seems to me he is like the father who secretly wishes his daughter were a son.

FOLIE A DEUX WINERY 1981

A: 3070 St. Helena Highway, St. Helena, CA 94574 **T**: (707) 963 1160 **V**: 11–5 daily **P**: 25,000 **W**: Rick Tracy

Folie a Deux — shared delusions of grandeur — is the project of two mental health and psychology professionals, Larry and Evie Dizmang. The name, the psychedelic label and its prominent position on St. Helena Highway gained immediate attention for the winery, and a subsequent professional scandal did nothing to keep the crowds away from cellar door.

Early vintages of the Chardonnay (particularly the 1983) received rave reviews, and continue to be highly regarded, accounting for more than half of total production. The other serious wine is the Cabernet Sauvignon: both are in mainstream Napa Valley style, but I have a preference for the concentrated, minty/plummy Cabernet Sauvignon, even if the tannins are fairly formidable.

FREEMARK ABBEY WINERY 1967

A: 3022 St. Helena Highway, St. Helena, CA 94574 **T**: (707) 963 9694 **V**: 10–4.30 daily **P**: 38,000 **W**: Ted Edwards

The seven partners who founded Freemark Abbey (effectively a sister winery of Rutherford Hill) have remained together since the beginning, welded together by the substantial figure of Charles Carpy, with the legendary Brad Webb in the background. At least in some quarters, there are suggestions that the quality of the wines over the years has been less stable: the initial vintages were received with enormous enthusiasm, and the winery had a reputation second to none. Yet other commentators still unhesitatingly put Freemark Abbey on the same pedestal it had in those early days, and few would seriously challenge the quality of the Cabernet Bosché, made since 1970 from the Bosché Vineyard and one of the first vineyard-designated Cabernets to be produced in California, ironically the only wine from Freemark Abbey not produced from partner-owned vineyards.

There are also suggestions that Freemark Abbey has not moved with the times. This seems as unreasonable as the suggestion that its quality has slipped. It has introduced a varietal Merlot, and also introduced the Carpy Ranch Chardonnay which is 100% barrel fermented and aged sur lees — in contrast to its standard Chardonnay, which is stainless steel fermented and sees relatively little oak. Every one of the wines I tasted, spanning the vintages 1988 to 1991, was good to outstanding. The Napa Valley Chardonnay is precisely what it is intended to be: attractively fresh and crisp, with apple/citric/passionfruit flavors and a long, clean finish; the Johannisberg Riesling is eerily like a first-class Riesling from Australia's Clare Valley; the Merlot shows excellent varietal character in a genuinely European style, neither excessively tannic nor excessively heavy; the Cabernet Sauvignon has fresh, soft, dark berry fruit and nicely balanced tannins. I cannot honestly say that the PR department left me overwhelmed, but with wines as good as these, who needs public relations anyway.

FROGS LEAP 1981

A: 3358 St. Helena Highway, St. Helena, CA 94574 **T**: (707) 963 4704 **V**: By appointment **P**: 35,000 **W**: John Williams

FROG'S LEAP
1990 ZINFANDEL
NAPA VALLEY
PRODUCED & BOTTLED BY FROG'S LEAP, ST. HELENA, CA
ALCOHOL 13.3% BY VOLUME CONTAINS SULFITES

The property on what passes for the Frogs Leap Winery (it is really a tank farm with most of the barrel storage in rented space elsewhere) was once a frog farm, and co-owners Larry Turley (a physician) and John Williams (whose first cellar job after graduating from U.C. Davis was at Stag's Leap Wine Cellars) came up with the name way back in 1977, when they were simply good friends with a penchant for puns. That penchant continues with the occasional release of Late Leap (a Late Harvest Sauvignon Blanc), and Clos De Toad waiting in the wings. Between the spawning of the tadpole in 1977, and 1981, John Williams spent three years as a winemaker in New York State, before moving back to become winemaker at Spring Mountain Vineyards, where he remained until 1988. The first Frogs Leap (700 cases) was made at Spring Mountain, and although production had risen to 6,000 cases by 1985, it nonetheless would sell out in about three weeks. So by 1988 it became perfectly clear that Williams had to choose between Frogs Leap and Spring Mountain, and it was not a hard choice.

One is used to the idea of tank farms and rudimentary winery facilities in other parts of California, and certainly in Australia, but Frogs Leap comes as something of a culture shock in the image-conscious Napa Valley. But once one tastes the wines, the reason for its continued success becomes obvious. It is hard to choose between the toasty, stylish, textured, barrel-fermented Carneros Chardonnay, the cherry and berry-filled Zinfandel, with its oriental five-spice overtones, and the beautifully structured and balanced fresh berry and soft tannin-clothed Cabernet Sauvignon. All of these wines scored very high points in the blind tastings for this book, the Sauvignon Blanc being an aberrational exception, and very possibly a faulty bottle.

GRACE FAMILY VINEYARDS 1976

A: 1210 Rockland Road, St. Helena, CA 94574 **T**: (707) 963 0808 **V**: By appointment **P**: 250 **W**: Gary Galleron

Salesman extraordinaire, fanatical, egotistical, philanthropist, money-tree man, strangely humble, blindingly efficient, disciplined, born-again ... Dick Grace is all these things to a degree I have never previously encountered. There are only three wines in the world which are as feverishly sought after as Grace Family Cabernet: Petrus, Romanée-Conti and Le Montrachet (of the Domaine de la Romanée-Conti). What they have in common is a very significant excess of demand over supply, both elevating the price and adding luster to ownership. But in the case of the latter three (but not Grace) there is sufficient supply for the wines to reasonably frequently be incorporated into blind tastings in various parts of the world. I am not for one moment suggesting that blind tasting is the only way of determining the quality of a wine; clearly, it is not. But when there is as much hype and peer group pressure (in the form of extravagant, glowing reviews) of a wine the identity of which is known, and which has the rarity of Grace, objectivity becomes extremely difficult.

I tasted both the 1990 and 1991 vintages from barrel. The 1990 was a beautifully made and balanced wine, as impeccable as any barrel sample I have ever tasted. Smooth, deep and with dark cherry and cassis fruits, there were no vegetable characters whatsoever, no excess tannins and — had I been the maker — I would have bottled the wine that very day. The 1991 had the same impeccable breeding, although it was a little shorter on the finish.

But are the Grace Family wines, as Matt Kramer says, "no snappier than any of a dozen other top rank valley floor Cabernets," or, as the *Underground Wine Journal* says, "gems which rank with 1941 Inglenook and 1947 Hallcrest, two of the finest California Cabernets ever produced?" I don't know the answer, and I suspect it simply doesn't matter. The facts are that these are beautifully made wines which are of the highest quality; that the 300 customers on the mailing list snap up their allocation (which varies between two and four bottles per customer), at $65 a bottle (1992 price), and that there are another 1,000 customers on the waiting list; that if Four Seasons or Roger Verge wishes to buy bottles, the price is the same; and that the Cellar Reserves (apart from outsize bottles which are never sold but only ever auctioned for charity) amount to one case of each wine.

The reasons for the quality are the oldest close-spaced vineyard in the valley, planted on a four feet by nine feet spacing, which commenced in 1976 (if you only have one acre, it does make sense to put the vines close together, although the plantings have since doubled to two acres), an absolutely open-ended budget, and infinite attention to detail. According to Dick Grace, 120 people came to help in the 1991 harvest; one has visions of each being given an allocation of four bunches to pick, then instructions to assess individually every single berry and discard any showing signs of physical or ideological unsoundness. The Cabernet itself is the small bunch, small berry Bosché clone, which yields only a little over two tons per acre, even on that close spacing, and there is then an open-ended budget with 100% new wood. The one extraordinary decision is to ship the wine to customers two weeks after bottling, when the wine will be showing its most profound bottle shock, it being perfectly certain that half the customers will immediately open at least one of their precious bottles.

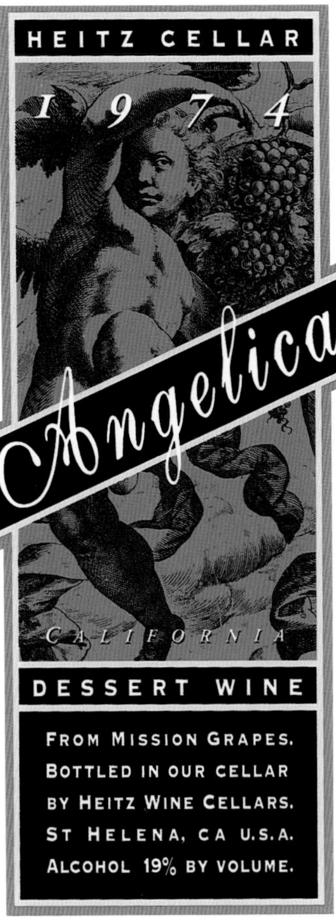
HEITZ CELLAR
1974
Angelica
CALIFORNIA
DESSERT WINE
FROM MISSION GRAPES.
BOTTLED IN OUR CELLAR
BY HEITZ WINE CELLARS.
ST HELENA, CA U.S.A.
ALCOHOL 19% BY VOLUME.

HEITZ WINE CELLARS 1961

A: 500 Taplin Road, St. Helena, CA 94574 **T**: (707) 963 3542 **V**: 11–4.30 daily at 463 St. Helena Highway **P**: 40,000 **W**: David Heitz

Joe Heitz is one of the greatest — some would say most formidable — characters in the California wine industry. I have met him on a number of occasions over the past 14 years, and have not noticed him taking so much as an inch backwards on any of the subjects discussed. His early achievements stand unchallenged and free from controversy: opulent Chardonnay from a vineyard on Zinfandel Lane (I still have some 1975 which is a superbly rich wine), Grignolino which Angelo Gaja imports into Italy because he thinks no one can make it as well there, and (commencing in 1966) Martha's Vineyard Cabernet Sauvignon, to which I return shortly. Dealing quickly with a few statistical matters, Heitz owns a substantial vineyard adjacent to the winery planted to Grignolino (1965) and Zinfandel (1980); two Chardonnay vineyards, one on Zinfandel Lane (replanted in 1979 after it had been destroyed by Pierce's Disease) and one south of St. Helena adjacent to the sales and tasting room (planted 1978); the 70-acre Trailside Vineyard on Silverado Trail, planted to both Cabernet Sauvignon and Chardonnay; and finally, an ambitious terraced hillside vineyard now being established on a 600-acre property on the lower slopes of Howell Mountain. While Heitz does not own its two most famous Cabernet vineyards — Martha's and Bella Oaks — the owners of those vineyards (the May and Rhodes families respectively) are shareholders in Heitz.

Martha's Vineyard Cabernet Sauvignon is widely regarded as one of the greatest California Cabernet Sauvignons, if not the greatest. Yet even here there are elements of controversy: in many vintages most tasters find a marked minty character accompanies the gamut of other deep fruit flavors which are the hallmark of this astonishingly long-lived wine. When it has been suggested this minty character might come from the nearby eucalypts, Joe Heitz has been known to storm from the room. Even on a peaceful day he will leave you in no doubt he views such suggestions as complete nonsense. But since 1987 an even more bitter row has erupted over suggestions that the Heitz Cabernets — Martha's Vineyard included — have the bacterial infection brettanomyces (called brett for short in the trade) or have been otherwise affected by mouldy barrels or corks. Sadly, I have to say that each of the three 1987 Cabernets — Martha's, Bella Oaks and Napa — showed bacterial/mold problems in blind tastings in San Francisco, although tasted over a subsequent lunch at the Heitz's home, the 1987 Napa was without flaw. It is the hope of everyone who understands the immensity of Joe Heitz's contribution to the California wine industry that this is a purely temporary phenomenon or — as Joe Heitz would no doubt have it — that we critics have lost our wits.

CHARLES KRUG WINERY 1861

A: 800 St. Helena Highway, St. Helena, CA 94574 **T**: (707) 963 2671 **V**: 10–4 daily **P**: 125,000 **W**: John Moynier

Richard Paul Hinkle eloquently summarized Charles Krug's contribution thus: "During the last century, Charles Krug was the bell-cow of Napa Valley's fledgling wine industry. Almost single-handedly he led wine from cottage commerce to major industry." After a circuitous entry into winemaking from his birthplace in Prussia in 1825, including time with Agoston Haraszthy, Charles Krug became seriously involved via his wife's dowry of a 540-acre property in St. Helena which is the core of the present-day operations. However, old age and phylloxera all but destroyed the once flourishing and very large business by the turn of the century, and it was not until a native-born Italian and Minnesotan iron miner, Cesare Mondavi, purchased Charles Krug from its bankers in 1943 that the restoration of its fortunes began. Between that time and the mid-1960s, the Mondavi family not only restored the reputation and fortunes of Charles Krug, but exceeded any of its prior achievements. A 1965 Chardonnay tasted in 1992 still showed surprising freshness and delicacy, with an intriguing touch of oak and real length to the palate. It must have been an extraordinary wine by the standards of its time. But a bitter falling out between brothers Peter and Robert Mondavi, and a long, well publicized and (for Robert) successful lawsuit diverted much of the resources (both in terms of time and money) of the remaining Mondavis from the business of Charles Krug, and it went into a period of marked decline.

Some see it as not having recovered, but others (myself included) are more sanguine. Krug pioneered the cold fermentation of Chenin Blanc (intriguingly, at precisely the same time and using much the same equipment as that being pioneered in Australia for the same purpose) in 1954, and Chenin Blanc still accounts for almost one-third of the Krug output; not surprising given that Krug has more acres of Chenin Blanc than any other single owner in the valley. It has 1,200 acres of vineyards throughout the valley, including two Carneros vineyards devoted to Chardonnay and Pinot Noir, and is developing 600 acres in Yolo County. Italian varieties are being planted, with plans to make 1,000–1,500 cases of Sangiovese, and possibly some Nebbiolo. Like many others, Marc Mondavi sees opportunities (as well as pain) coming from phylloxera, but in typical conservative Mondavi fashion believes there will be a 20 to 30 year learning curve, and that the forced replanting process will accelerate as many mistakes as successes.

That conservative attitude does show in the wines, but so does craft. The estate-bottled Vintage Select Cabernet Sauvignon is typically elegant, firm and discreet, rather than opulent and flashy — but so what. The Carneros Pinot Noir is seldom talked about, but in years such as 1989 shows some real style, with lively spicy cherry/strawberry fruit — almost daring to be flamboyant. The Zinfandel, too, while not a heavyweight, has very attractive and direct fresh red cherry aroma and flavor. At the price at which the wines are sold, there should be no cause for complaint.

MARKHAM VINEYARDS 1978

A: 2812 St. Helena Highway North, St. Helena, CA 94574 **T**: (707) 963 5292 **V**: 11–4 daily **P**: 110,000 **W**: Bob Foley

As 1992 drew to a close, the $14 million winery rebuilding program financed by Japanese owner Mercian (Japan's largest winemaker, formally called Sanraku) was finally finished, the chainlink fences and builders' rubble disappeared, and what might loosely be described as a rather more tasteful version of Clos Pegase presented a welcoming face to the public. When Mercian purchased the winery from founder Bruce Markham in 1988, production stood at 16,000 cases, and now it stands at 110,000. A significant portion of that is the second label, Glass Mountain, which grew from 4,000 to 40,000 case sales in the 12 months following its introduction in 1991.

The most remarkable thing about all of this is that while Mercian has unstintingly provided the money, everything else has been achieved by the two (still youthful) employees who started what was a makeshift winery in 1978: president Bryan Del Bondio and vice president and winemaker Bob Foley. Nor has the tremendous growth in production and sales been syphoned off to Japan; virtually none of the wine is sold there, a pattern repeated again and again with Japanese-owned wineries in California. It will be interesting to see what happens when, sooner or later, the floodgates open in Japan and wine becomes a social necessity.

Almost as remarkable is the quality of the wine, which has been maintained during this exponential growth. The 1989 Markham Chardonnay was rated by the *Wine Spectator as* the top wine in the vintage, while the Merlot

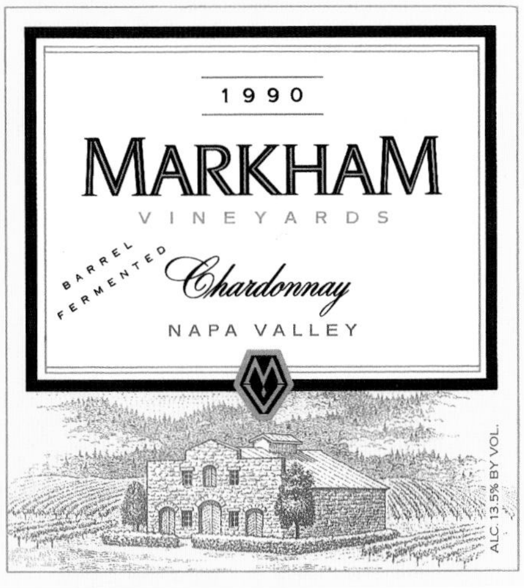
1990
MARKHAM
VINEYARDS
BARREL FERMENTED
Chardonnay
NAPA VALLEY
ALC 13.5% BY VOL.

receives consistently strong reviews. The answer lies partly in the self-evident brilliance of the Del Bondio/Foley team, but also in three immaculately placed vineyards which (between them) have 220 acres under vine. There is the Napa Ranch, just north of Napa and near Oak Knoll, in a Region I zone and planted to Chardonnay, Sauvignon Blanc and Semillon; the Yountville Ranch is on the Oakville Bench, just north of the Napanook Vineyard, and is planted to the red Bordeaux varieties, as is the Calistoga Ranch, occupying its own canyon at the headwaters of the Napa River on the base of Mount St. Helena.

The Markham label focuses on the classic varieties, while Glass Mountain ventures into the new wave, with a mixed black blend called Rubis du Val as well as Petite Sirah, Charbono, but also Cabernet Sauvignon and Chardonnay. Curiously, of all of the wines tasted, the Chardonnay (1990) was the least impressive: it was not that it was faulty, simply that it was rather plain and ordinary. By contrast, the flowery, fruity, scented, cedary Merlot and the stylish redcurrant-accented Cabernet were delicious, the Sauvignon Blanc full, soft, honeyed but with excellent gooseberry varietal flavor.

LOUIS M. MARTINI 1922

A: 254 St. Helena Highway, St. Helena, CA 94574 **T**: (707) 963 2736 **V**: 10–4.30 daily **P**: 225,000 **W**: Michael Martini

This, quite simply, is a great family company: it is extraordinary how many stories are told of acts of generosity (often advice or direct help) by members of the family to their fellow winemakers — who, after all, are their competitors. No less extraordinary was the foresight of Louis M. Martini in planning for the end of Prohibition and — even more — in purchasing the 250-acre Monte Rosso Vineyard in 1938 at an elevation of 900–1,200 feet on the western side of the Mayacamas Range, and following this in 1942 with the purchase of the 200-acre La Loma Vineyard in Carneros,

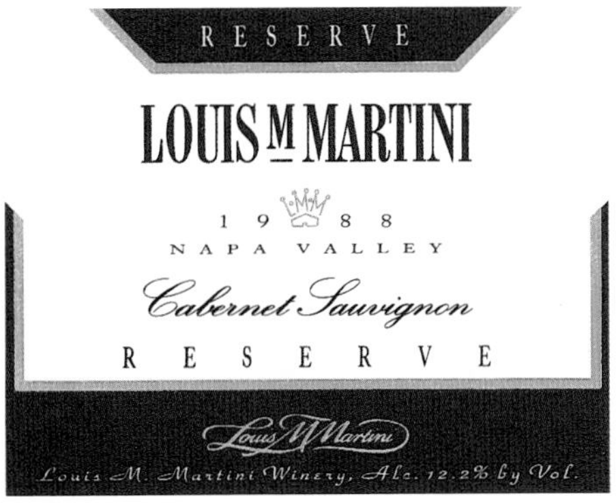
RESERVE
LOUIS M MARTINI
1988
NAPA VALLEY
Cabernet Sauvignon
RESERVE
Louis M. Martini Winery, Alc. 12.2% by Vol.

making the first varietal Pinot Noir from Carneros in 1952. Son Louis P. Martini added the 140-acre Las Amigas Carneros Vineyard between 1962 and 1972, and continued the pioneering spirit by establishing the Russian River vineyard Los Vinedos del Rio in 1962, and planting the vines which produced the first varietal Merlot in the United States at the end of the 1960s, as well as being a leader in clonal selection techniques and a pioneer of mechanical harvesting.

These cool climate vineyards (Regions I and II) account for a substantial part of the 1,000 acres of vines owned by the family; the 185-acre Glen Oaks vineyard in the Chiles Valley is also said to be Region II; and only the Perini Springs (in Lake County) and Pope Valley properties offer warmer sites. It is no doubt the preponderance of cool grown grapes and the "European" approach to winemaking which led to the Martini style: wines which appeared to be relatively light-bodied when young, yet comfortably outlive most of their heavyweight contemporaries. But as contemporary style diverged further with the ever-increasing use by others of new small oak (long resisted by the Martinis), so did the once very high reputation of the winery suffer. And whatever else, they were never wines of the style which would score 90-plus points from Robert Parker or the *Wine Spectator*.

The introduction of new oak through the 1980s and general winery refurbishment has made its mark: the 1987 Los Vinedos Merlot (cedary, almost citrussy and distinctly St. Emilion-like), both the Monte Rosso and Reserve Cabernets from 1988 (again showing a distinctly French touch, with marked length to the palate even if not so much weight) and a 1990 Sauvignon Blanc (direct, pungent and Sancerre-like) all scored high points in blind tastings, and are sufficient to persuade me that in the hands of third-generation winemaker Michael Martini all will be well.

MERRYVALE & SUNNY ST. HELENA 1983

A: 1000 Main Street, St. Helena, CA 94574 **T**: (707) 963 2225 **V**: 10–5.30 daily **P**: 25,000 **W**: Robert Levy

Merryvale and Sunny St. Helena are both owned by a partnership founded by William

MERRYVALE
VINEYARDS
1990
NAPA VALLEY
CHARDONNAY
STARMONT
PRODUCED AND BOTTLED BY MERRYVALE VINEYARDS,
ST. HELENA, CALIFORNIA, USA. ALCOHOL 13% BY VOLUME

Harlan, the late Peter Stocker, John Montgomery (these three having established the famed Meadowood Country Club) and Robin Lail, daughter of John Daniel Jnr. (of Inglenook fame). Merryvale is the brand on which the present (and future) rests; Sunny St. Helena is the name of the first winery built in the Napa Valley after the repeal of Prohibition. It sits prominently on the southern outskirts of St. Helena (on the left-hand side as you drive south with that great restaurant Tra Vigne situated conveniently next door) and was purchased in 1985 as a permanent home for Merryvale, having since been completely refurbished. The Sunny St. Helena label continues, but it would not surprise me if it quietly faded away.

The partnership is blatantly ambitious, and makes no secret of its desire for Merryvale to become one of the top names in the Napa Valley. The wines tasted from the 1987 and 1989 vintages did not seem likely to help that aim, but those from 1990 and 1991 were in a different class. The 1990 Reserve Chardonnay is a very complex wine, showing that bacony character one finds in barrels made by the French cooper Francois Freres, and with great feel and fruit-weight in the mouth; the 1991 Meritage (a Sauvignon Blanc/Semillon blend) also shows sophisticated use of oak, but is a wine of quite different flavor tones, in a spicy-lemony vanillin spectrum. A 1990 Merlot is an awesome wine, with tremendous power and extract — more akin to a full bodied Cabernet Sauvignon — but with the balance to soften and blossom for a decade or more.

RAYMOND VINEYARD 1971

A: 849 Zinfandel Lane, St. Helena, CA 94574 **T**: (707) 963 3141 **V**: 10–4 daily **P**: 120,000 **W**: Walter Raymond

Raymond Vineyard was established when Roy and Mary Jane Raymond (nee Beringer) sold Beringer Winery to Nestlé in 1970. The project started as an estate winery based on the 80 acres which surround the present much-expanded facility, but growth (and the impact of phylloxera on the estate vineyards) has meant that Raymond is now a major purchaser throughout the valley, buying from over 50 independent growers. Although the P.R. material handed out by the winery makes no mention of the fact, the Raymonds sold a majority interest in the venture to Kirin Brewing Inc. of Japan in 1989, but remain in control of management and production. That sale provided the capital for the immediate development of 300 additional acres of vineyards in 1989/90, with a further 170 acres now being established in the extreme south of the Napa Valley in Jamieson Canyon, above the Chardonnay Country Club. A major expansion of the winery facility was also scheduled to be completed by 1993.

Chardonnay accounts for 75% of the total production, Cabernet 20% and Sauvignon Blanc 5%, a shift in favor of Chardonnay and away from Cabernet Sauvignon which, given both the exigencies of the marketplace and (at least in my view) the quality of the wines, is quite surprising. The Raymonds are looking on with interest at the development of the Italian varieties, but have made no moves in that direction so far. On the other hand, both in the existing and the new vineyards, the evidence of modern viticultural techniques is everywhere to be seen; it is here, rather than in the winery, that dramatic changes and improvement are taking place.

The Cabernet Sauvignon is consistently impressive, with the Napa Valley version showing good, sweet fruit, with cedary/earthy overtones developing with age, and the tannins always under control. The Private Reserve is a much bigger and more powerful wine and, given the price differential, I would have little hesitation in opting for the Napa Valley version. But, as I say, both are impressive. The Reserve Chardonnay has slightly more fruit than the Napa Valley, but both wines (from the 1990 vintage) typified all that is ordinary and bland about Napa Chardonnay. It may well be that the development of the Jamieson Canyon Vineyard will see radical changes in the style of the Chardonnay, and wines with far greater definition and character.

ST. CLEMENT 1975

A: 2867 St. Helena Highway North, St. Helena, CA 94574 **T**: (707) 963 7221 **V**: 10–4 daily **P**: 14,000 **W**: Dennis Johns

The graceful wooden, gray-painted Victorian mansion which houses the visitors' center at St. Clement was built as a combined house and winery in 1878, but when it was purchased by Mike Robbins in the late 1960s and renamed Spring Mountain it had long since ceased production, and to this day has but one acre of estate vineyards. In 1975 Robbins sold the property to Dr. William Casey, retaining the name Spring Mountain and developing the winery now known by that name. Casey chose St. Clement as the name for his venture, and hired one of the rising superstars of the time, Charles Ortman, as winemaker. A modern winery was built behind the house in 1979, and in 1980 winemaking responsibilities passed to Dennis Johns. Yet a further change of ownership occurred in 1987 when Casey sold to Sapporo Limited of Japan, providing the funds to acquire a 20-acre Carneros vineyard which now gives its name to the St. Clements Abbotts Vineyard Chardonnay.

Self-taught Dennis Johns has very definite opinions about wine style, and Chardonnay in particular, which he expresses with appropriate elegance. He does not use malolactic fermentation, describing it as producing heavy hitting styles which override regional and varietal character, and simply provide a series "of carbon spit-outs." Warming to his subject he continues, "It is used by winemakers wanting to make a wine which looks five years old in six months; what you gain in texture, you lose in the fruit and in the finish." He also throws the rule book out when making his Cabernets, pressing before dryness, and likewise emphasising the fruit flavor rather than seeking extract and tannins. Which is not to say that either the St. Clement Cabernet Sauvignon or the St. Clement Merlot lack structure or concentration: these are stylish wines with all of the ingredients necessary for extended cellaring. And at 12 months of age, the 1991 Cabernet Sauvignon from barrel needs only a one-word description: luscious. The same applies to the Chardonnays: these are wonderfully subtle wines which develop intense, complex secondary aromas and flavors when given time in bottle. So many Napa Valley winemakers make the same claim of their own malolactic-dominated Chardonnays, yet they do not do so, while St. Clement does. It hardly needs be said that I wholeheartedly agree with Dennis Johns' philosophy and with his winemaking techniques.

V. SATTUI WINERY 1885

A: 111 White Lane (cnr. Hwy 29), St. Helena, CA 94574 **T**: (707) 963 7774 **V**: 10–5 daily **P**: 38,000 **W**: Rick Rosenbrand & Daryl Sattui

Part of the Sattui story is told on pages 96-7, but there I do not touch on the development of the winemaking (and grape growing) side of the business.

The first Sattui wines were bought in bulk, and sold at a suitably unpretentious price. Today, almost 50% of the Sattui grapes come from estate-owned or controlled vineyards: Rosenbrand, Preston, Suzanne's and Carsi (the last two owned by Sattui, the 30-acre Carsi vineyard south of Yountville purchased in 1989 for $1 million). And while all of the Sattui wine is made by Sattui at Sattui, President Tom Davies (very much a hands-on president) says, "We market to everyone who drives along Highway 29." He is referring to the product range, which extends from off-dry Johannisberg Riesling (still accounting for 25% of total sales) through blush wines (including a Gamay Rouge with 1.5% sweetness which was Sattui's single largest volume seller in 1991) and on to estate Chardonnays and Reserve Cabernet Sauvignons. The 1992 cellar door prices — and every single bottle is sold at these prices, 88% physically through the door, the remaining 12% by mail list — ranged from $7.50 to $20 for current release wines and up to $85 for museum stock (1980 Preston Vineyard Cabernet Sauvignon). Says Tom Davies, "We have no difficulty selling wines at $25–40 a bottle," a self-evident truth from the fact that sales are limited to between one and six bottles per customer, depending on the age.

Sattui has indeed developed a considerable reputation among the wine-knowledgeable for its Cabernet Sauvignons and for its Howell Mountain Zinfandels. This reputation is founded on more than the simple scarcity factor and the assiduously collected gold medals (some awarded, it must be said, in competitions which are less than household names). The reputation relies upon the consistency and quality of the wines right across the range: the Johannisberg Rieslings, for example, are reminiscent of good commercial Australian Rieslings (remembering just how major a category Riesling is in Australia), while the 1991 Carsi Vineyard Chardonnay shows deft handling of high quality oak as well as abundant Chardonnay fruit. One of the enduring advantages from a winemaking viewpoint is Sattui's ability to make and market small parcels of wine (500 cases or so) without running the wrath of national distributors, and constantly giving customers something new and different.

SPOTTESWOODE 1982

A: 1401 Hudson Avenue, St. Helena, CA 94574 **T**: (707) 963 0134 **V**: By appointment **P**: 6,500 **W**: Pam Starr

Visitors to Spotteswoode are infrequent, notwithstanding the fame of the wine. There are three principal reasons for this: Spotteswoode is hidden away in a side street well within the town of St. Helena, in the last place one would expect to find a vineyard; secondly, the wine is crushed and fermented elsewhere, and simply stored underneath what is the Novak family home; and thirdly there are no ex-winery sales, the wine all being sold on allocation through national and international distribution routes. For the few who are lucky enough to visit, it is not hard to see why general practitioner Jack Novak and wife Helen fell in love with the property and purchased it in 1972, with its gracious gardens and extremely attractive turn-of-the-century home. The one blot on the landscape is phylloxera, which is currently forcing the progressive replanting of the entire vineyard, which had been replanted between 1973 and 1975 to Cabernet Sauvignon and a lesser amount of Sauvignon Blanc.

The initial intention was both to grow grapes and to produce wine, but the premature death of Jack Novak in 1977, and the refusal of the St. Helena Council to allow an adjacent winery to be restored and used, put winemaking on hold until 1982. By that stage, purchasers of the Cabernet Sauvignon, including John Shafer and Dan Duckhorn, persuaded Mary Novak to venture into winemaking, arguing that the quality of the grapes demanded an estate label and identity. Tony Soter was hired as winemaker, and almost immediately Spotteswoode established its reputation as one of the greatest producers of California Cabernet Sauvignon. Soter has retired as executive winemaker, but continues as consultant, a critical role during the times of change confronting Spotteswoode. In 1990 the family purchased the old Kraft Winery diagonally opposite the north-east corner of Spotteswoode's vineyard, and are refurbishing it. Initially it will be used for barrel storage, but there are plans to construct a crushing and fermentation facility on the Kraft site, and also to establish the office administration center.

Because Spotteswoode has traditionally sold half its production, and because of a progressive replanting program, there is every reason to suppose that the style and quality of the wines will not be impaired — and indeed, may ultimately be enhanced. That, mind you, is an ambitious goal for a Cabernet which has so consistently stood out. Both the 1989 and 1990 vintages are superb wines, the 1989 concentrated and deep, with smooth red berry fruit, a hint of charred/toasty oak proclaiming both its past and its future, and putting the lie to any suggestion that great wines were not made in 1989. For the sake of completeness, it has to be said I do not find anything particularly exciting about the Sauvignon Blanc.

SUTTER HOME WINERY 1874

A: 277 St. Helena Highway South, St. Helena, CA 94574 **T**: (707) 963 3104 **V**: 9–5 daily **P**: 5 million **W**: Steve Bertolucci

That *eminence gris* of the California wine industry, Sacramento wine merchant Darrell Corti, appears behind the scene in the most unlikely places for, according to several reliable accounts, it was he who put the idea of White Zinfandel into Bob Trinchero's mind. The consequences were on one plane obvious, on another not so apparent.

Obviously, it transformed a small, relatively obscure family run and owned company. After 100 years of effort it was making some thousands of cases of wines of variable style and quality, by far the best of which was a red Zinfandel made from grapes grown on the Deaver Ranch in Amador County. In 1972 it made its first White Zinfandel, which attracted little attention, in 1975 adding a little sweetness, which attracted more. But even in 1980 its sales of White Zinfandel were only 25,000 cases: ten years later they were three million cases. Sutter Home had become a major force at the business end of the California wine industry.

The less obvious consequence was that the old plantings of Zinfandel (there being virtually no new plantings) were headed for extinction at the time the White Zinfandel boom took off. Some of us still cringe at the thought of 80- to 100-year-old vines producing grapes to be treated in this way — indeed some cringe at the very thought of White Zinfandel — but better this than no Zinfandel at all. It hardly needs be said that the public face of Sutter Home at Rutherford — the former bed-and-breakfast Victorian era house with its distinctive palm trees — is just that, and nothing to do with the inevitably massive process winery which receives grapes from all over California, and which is even less receptive to visitors than Gallo's Modesto plant. Whether the acquisition in late 1992 of the huge Heublein winemaking facility at Rutherford will make Sutter Home more accessible remains to be seen.

Sutter Home's White Zinfandel and California generics and varietals are no better (and no worse) than one would expect, but its Deaver Reserve Zinfandels (red, that is) are of the highest quality, invariably showing bright fresh spicy cherry/strawberry fruit with just a touch of tannin to give structure and authority to the wines.

OTHER WINERIES

CALAFIA CELLARS
A: 69 Fulton Lane, St. Helena, CA 94574
T: (707) 963 0114 **W**: Randle Johnson

CHATEAU BOSWELL 1982
A: 3468 Silverado Trail, St. Helena, CA 94574
T: (707) 963 5472 **W**: R. T. Boswell

LIVINGSTON 1987
A: 1895 Cabernet Lane, St. Helena, CA 94574
T: (707) 963 2120 **W**: Randy Dunn (Consultant)

MACAULEY VINEYARDS 1984
A: 3291 St. Helena Highway, St. Helena, CA 94574 **T**: (707) 963 1123 **W**: George Watson

MERLION 1985
A: 880 Vallejo Street, Napa, CA 94559
T: (707) 226 5568 **W**: John Mackay

MILAT VINEYARDS 1986
A: 1091 St. Helena Highway, St. Helena, CA 94574 **T**: (707) 963 0758 **W**: Mike Milat

ROMBAUER 1982
A: 3522 Silverado Trail, St. Helena, CA 94574
T: (707) 963 5170 **W**: Greg Graham

SPRING MOUNTAIN 1968
A: 2805 Spring Mountain Road, St. Helena, CA 94574 **T**: (707) 963 5233 **W**: Greg Vita

STREBLOW 1985
A: 2849 Spring Mountain Road, St. Helena, CA 94574 **T**: (707) 963 5892 **W**: Bruce Streblow

TUDAL 1979
A: 1015 Big Tree Road, St. Helena, CA 94574
T: (707) 963 3947 **W**: Arnold Tudal

VILLA HELENA WINERY 1984
A: 1455 Inglewood Avenue, St. Helena, CA 94574 **T**: (707) 963 4334 **W**: Don McGrath

STAGS LEAP

"The Stags Leap wine district begins seven miles north of the town of Napa, on the Silverado Trail. Its northern boundary is drawn by the Yountville Cross Road. Barely a mile wide and almost three miles long, the district is bounded by rocky hillsides to the east and the Napa River to the west." So run the calm words of an elegant brochure which gives no clue to the turbulent birth of this most famous of all the AVAs within the Napa Valley.

The origins of the much-disputed name go back to the nineteenth century, when in 1893 Horace B. Chase built a winery called Stags Leap — after the legend of a stag which eluded hunters with a prodigious leap across the towering palisades which today mark the eastern boundary of the region.

In 1972 two wineries were established: Stag's Leap Wine Cellars by Warren Winiarski, and Stags' Leap Winery Inc. by Carl Doumani. Over a decade of see-sawing and expensive litigation followed, which ultimately resulted in each producer being entitled to use the Stags name — but with the apostrophe placed differently.

Long before the conclusion of this litigation, Warren Winiarski was writing that, "Stags Leap is a regional designation which should in time become as familiar to wine buyers as certain domains in European wine-growing regions." So with the development of the AVA system, it was inevitable that an application would be made to the BATF, filed on August 22, 1985. Once again, disputes flared: the first and second were quickly resolved, moving the western boundary to coincide with the course of the Napa River, and the second to add the word "District" to the originally proposed Stags Leap. (At no time was it proposed that the regional name be graced with an apostrophe, a minute but very intentional subtlety.)

The third dispute concerned the northern boundary, originally proposed to lie along the ring of hills in the northern sector of the region. It was not until a lengthy public hearing had been held, reams of conflicting written expert evidence filed, 150 submissions received from wine lovers as far away as Sioux Falls, South Dakota (as well as from those more directly affected), and well over three years had passed, that on January 27, 1989 the BATF issued its painstakingly detailed final ruling which established the existence (and the boundaries) of the Stags Leap District as we know it today.

Anyone reading that testimony and the BATF ruling may well wonder how any Viticultural Area can be legitimately defined, and indeed how any atlas such as this can be logically justified. For the experts could agree neither on the climate nor the soils of this tiny area, and subsequent commentators and writers are unsure whether it is the climate or the soil (however each is defined) which makes the Stags Leap District such an exceptional — and distinctive — producer of Cabernet Sauvignon.

ABOVE ~ *Alfonso Zamora, vineyard foreman at Shafer Vineyards, watches over the harvest.*

OPPOSITE ~ *Looking south across the Napa Valley from Shafer Vineyards in Stags Leap.*

Yet all are agreed it *is* an exceptional area, and as you drive along the Silverado Trail between the northern and southern boundaries you will feel in your bones (as Bernard Portet of Clos du Val did so long ago, and Nathan Fay before him) that there is something unique about the feel of the district. The French, indeed, would have no difficulty, for they would use the word *terroir* in its fullest sense: that wonderful definition given by Bruno Prats, and quoted on page 130.

And it shows in the wine. Dick Steltzner expressed it as eloquently as anyone when he said to me, "Stags Leap's unique character has come to be recognized not as a result of promotional activity, but by virtue of repeated wine assessments and tastings by others sourcing the character back to the Stags Leap District."

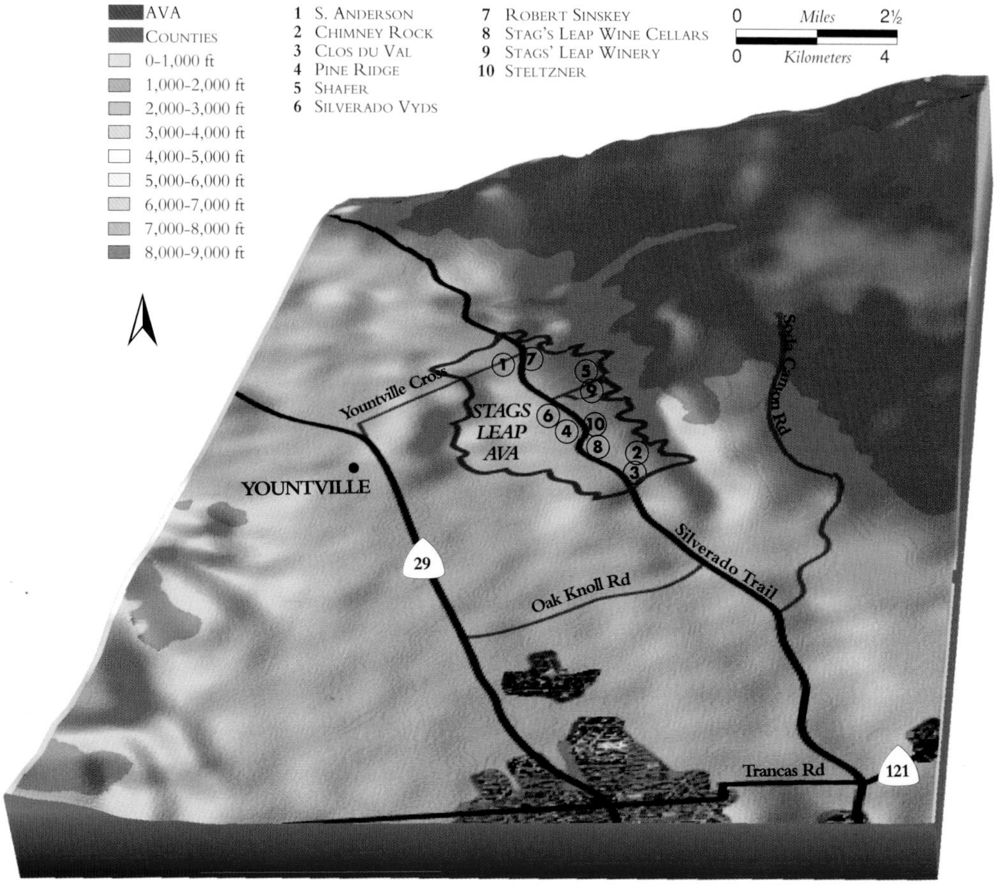
AVA
COUNTIES
0-1,000 ft
1,000-2,000 ft
2,000-3,000 ft
3,000-4,000 ft
4,000-5,000 ft
5,000-6,000 ft
6,000-7,000 ft
7,000-8,000 ft
8,000-9,000 ft
1 S. Anderson
2 Chimney Rock
3 Clos du Val
4 Pine Ridge
5 Shafer
6 Silverado Vyds
7 Robert Sinskey
8 Stag's Leap Wine Cellars
9 Stags' Leap Winery
10 Steltzner
0 Miles 2½
0 Kilometers 4
Yountville Cross
STAGS LEAP AVA
YOUNTVILLE
Soda Canyon Rd
Silverado Trail
Oak Knoll Rd
29
Trancas Rd
121

ABOVE ~ *Merlot vineyards in the Stags Leap district showing the moderate late season stress (of yellow leaves) which helps promote flavor ripeness.*

ABOVE ~ *Stags Leap map.*

TOP ~ *Vine-covered hills make for a picturesque landscape.*

ABOVE ~ *Checking on the condition of the grapes is an essential part of vintage, made all the more pleasurable when on horseback.*

THE REGION IN BRIEF

Climate, Soil and Viticulture

CLIMATE

The climate of the region is shaped by a complex series of countervailing influences. The relative importance of these in turn reflects the location of the vineyard: is it on a hillside; what is its aspect (i.e., north, south, east or west); if it is on flat land; in which direction is the nearest hill, and so forth. But in general terms what makes the climate unique is the wind funnel, which blows from south to north, but which eddies around the knolls and acts as a late afternoon air-conditioner to soften the heat which has built up earlier in the day from the mass of bare rocks which form the Palisades. Thus it is that Stags Leap District can record temperatures up to 10°F warmer than across the Napa River at Yountville, which is due west of the center of the district. So it is too that the heat summation is around 2,700 to 2,800 degree days, putting it comfortably in Region II. The rainfall averages around 30 inches, although years of drought (and floods such as that in 1986) make the same mockery of averages here as elsewhere.

SOIL

Having agonized endlessly over the borders of the district, the BATF came firmly to the view "that the soil (including the subsoil) is the primary geographical feature that distinguishes Stags Leap District from the surrounding areas." Professor Deborah Elliot-Fisk says that over 95% of the soils are derived from volcanic rocks; these are in turn chiefly gravelly floor soils of the Bale series, deposited by alluvial forces from parent materials from the Vaca Range which rises on the eastern rim of the Napa Valley. The soils are very well drained (and hence warm early in the growing season) but have only moderate water-holding capacity, and a harder clay-like bedrock subsoil at a depth of two to six feet, all of which means that vine vigor tends to be naturally controlled, although stress increases during periods of drought.

Stags Leap
VINTAGE CHART 1981-91

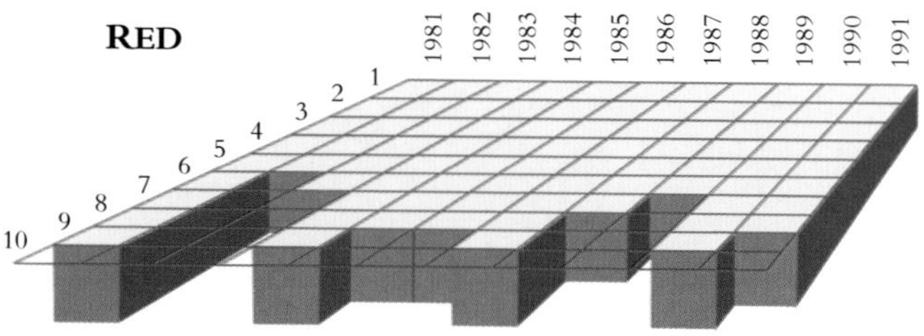
RED
1981
1982
1983
1984
1985
1986
1987
1988
1989
1990
1991
1
2
3
4
5
6
7
8
9
10

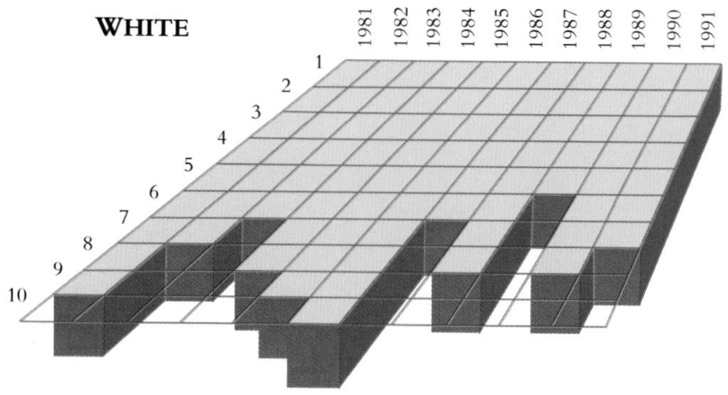
WHITE
1981
1982
1983
1984
1985
1986
1987
1988
1989
1990
1991
1
2
3
4
5
6
7
8
9
10

THE GROWING SEASON

The region has a distinctly longer season than other valley floor regions, with budbreak two weeks earlier but harvesting usually commencing mid to late season, resulting in a longer "hang-time" and greater physiological maturity. It is affected by the morning fogs, the noonday heat, those swirling afternoon winds and cool nights, all of which add up to a climate which draws out the ripening process. Chardonnay is typically harvested in the second half of August, Cabernet Sauvignon in the first half of September.

Contract Growers

The 2,700 acres within the boundaries are planted to approximately 1,500 acres of vines, much owned by the ten wineries in the region, and a great deal by Robert Mondavi, which is not in the region; Joseph Phelps, too, has holdings here. However, there are a number of independent growers including J. Abbruzzini, R. & V. Chambers, N. & J. DePuy, R. & R. Egan, F. S. Foote, E. Freethy, B. & J. Hartwell, E. Ilsey, D. Missimer, A. Regusci, N. & T. Robinson, F. Schweizer, M.J. Turnbull and D. Wilsey.

Principal Wine Styles

CABERNET SAUVIGNON

This is the undisputed prince of the district, and indeed there are those who, as a matter of personal preference, might place it first among all Napa Cabernets. Certainly, it can be no coincidence that in the Paris tasting of 1976 it was the 1973 Stag's Leap Wine Cellars which captured world headlines by being placed first, and that in the retasting ten years later the 1972 Clos du Val came first: this against the assembled might of France and the Napa Valley as a whole. The groundwork had been laid by Nathan Fay, who planted the first post-Prohibition Cabernet Sauvignon in the district in 1961, but some of the best viticulturists in the valley have followed in his wake. The style was once summarized by Warren Winiarski as "the iron fist in the velvet glove." The wines all have a suppleness, a fruity softness in the red berry spectrum which is prevented from becoming clumsy or too soft by the

persistent, fine-grained tannins. To single out producers for special mention barely seems necessary, but Stag's Leap Wine Cellars, Shafer, Silverado, Clos du Val and Steltzner are wineries which would always be on my personal shopping list.

Merlot

If Cabernet Sauvignon is the prince, Merlot is the princess, used in three ways: as a blend component in wines labeled Cabernet Sauvignon, in Meritage wines in which it plays a larger and sometimes dominant role, and as a varietal Merlot so-labeled. Clos du Val, Silverado, Shafer and Steltzner are among the leading producers; the admirable Sinskey Merlot is in fact sourced from its Carneros vineyards. In a region which is in any event noted for its supple wines, the naturally supple Merlot flourishes, producing soft, red berry fruited wines, sometimes with a hint of mint, which are very attractive. Clos du Val is one of those few producers content (as in 1989) to let Merlot make its own expression, and not blend in either Cabernet Sauvignon or Cabernet Franc.

Chardonnay

Once an obligatory part of the menu, Chardonnay is of rapidly declining importance in the wake of phylloxera. When one looks at what the players are doing, it seems a double-barreled recognition that this area *is* uniquely suited to the Cabernet family, and is *not* particularly well suited to Chardonnay (the Mondavi vineyard excepted). Thus Chimney Rock is phasing out its estate Chardonnay, looking to source its fruit from cooler regions; S. Anderson draws on 70 Carneros acres for its sparkling wine; Clos du Val has purchased Chardonnay specialist St. Andrews, well to the south on Silverado Trail; Pine Ridge sources almost half its grapes from two vineyards in the Oak Knoll district; Stag's Leap Wine Cellars and Sinskey use only Carneros grapes; Shafer pulled out ten acres of Chardonnay in 1992 and is now using Carneros and Oak Knoll grapes; Silverado has made no secret of the fact that it is cutting back on its Chardonnay production; and that wily bird Dick Steltzner didn't bother planting it in the first place, or making it in the second.

Other Varieties

Apart from the Bordeaux blend makes of Cabernet Franc, Malbec and Petit Verdot, there are only isolated patches of other grapes: Clos du Val has some Zinfandel and Pinot Noir (both uninspiring), while Stags' Leap Winery has an interesting patch of Petite Sirah, part dating back to the early 1900s.

ABOVE ~ *The replanting of vineyards goes on in Stags Leap as everywhere else, with ground sterilization under polythene the first step.*

Napa Valley Cabernet Sauvignon

It is a statement of the obvious to say that the Napa Valley is America's most famous wine region, with an international reputation which has penetrated the most parochial and conservative quarters of the great wine-producing countries of Europe. It is in turn quite certain that the valley owes this reputation to one grape and to one wine: Cabernet Sauvignon.

Given that when Andre Tchelistcheff arrived in the Napa Valley in 1937 there were less than 100 acres of Cabernet planted, and that even in the 1950s there were only two Napa Valley Cabernets of any quality (Beaulieu Vineyard Georges de Latour and Inglenook Cask), one is tempted to say that the reputation is essentially the creature of the 60s and 70s — and in particular the famed Stephen Spurrier tasting in Paris in 1976.

But the roots go back to the latter part of the nineteenth century with the establishment of Inglenook and Beaulieu on what is now known as the Oakville Rutherford Bench. For it is here that the fulcrum of Napa Valley Cabernet's greatness is to be found, and it is here that the validity of the French concept of *terroir* is so elegantly demonstrated.

ABOVE ~ *The refractometer allows the winemaker to instantly measure the sugar present in grapes or grape juice.*

The reason that Cabernet grown here has always been superb lies in the combination of climate and soil, which together have produced perfect yields of perfectly ripened grapes with a minimum of human intervention and manipulation. If there is a single key, it lies in the soil: two large alluvial fans with deep, gravelly sandy clay loams derived from Sandstone parent series. These soils are very well drained, of moderate fertility and excellent water-holding capacity, the type of conditions one encounters in the great estates of the Haut Medoc in Bordeaux (although the soils there, of course, are utterly different in source).

Thus even with the traditional, single-wire California trellis, or in its total absence, the vines established their own balance, neither over-vigorous, nor over-stressed in the dry summers, their roots foraging deep yet never finding easily come by water from a water table. The result was a canopy which was naturally open, remained viable right throughout the growing season although ceasing to grow actively at veraison, and a crop of around two tons to the acre.

Then there is the California climate: exceptionally sunny (once the morning fogs have dissipated) and — in this two-and-a-half mile stretch from south of Oakville to north of Rutherford — providing the perfect amount of heat for Cabernet to ripen into succulent opulence while still retaining that balancing cut of astringency from a touch of herbaceousness and appropriately firm tannins.

What happens either side of the fulcrum — and what may happen in the future — involves a complicated interplay between soil, climate and (wo)man. Let me touch briefly on soil, before coming to what I believe are the two most important facts: climate and human manipulation.

There are 32 different soil types within Napa County, and half of these are found within the Stags Leap District alone, a tiny area considered to be unique because of its soil. Within any given soil area as mapped by the authorities, there will almost always be small areas of other soils, often quite contrasting soils, which are called "inclusions." On an even smaller scale, any practicing vigneron will tell you that vine behavior can vary radically within a matter of yards, indicating differing soils and/or subsoil conditions. This will be so in flat country, but is even more marked on hillside terrain.

So in considering what most believe are the differing styles (and qualities) of Napa Valley Cabernets in the different subappellations, I doubt that too much importance should be placed on any particular soil type. (By this I do not mean the choice of exact site by the vigneron is unimportant – it clearly is.) But two aspects overall are very important: the soils should be well drained, and should not be too fertile. Thus the Rutherford Fan was formed 30 million years ago from the Mayacamas Range, and is radically different from the Bale series derived from the Vaca Mountains ten million years ago. But both soils have the appropriate structure to produce high quality grapes with minimum human manipulation.

As the fans give way to richer alluvials in the center of the valley, often very deep but with an underlying water table which — in parts at least — can be reached by the vine, the question of human intervention looms large. Even today you can see the old California sprawl viticulture alongside the new: it is a subject discussed and explained in greater detail elsewhere (pages 360–1). In short, however, with appropriate canopy management, clonal selection and rootstock selection, it may well be possible to close significantly the quality gap which once existed between the Rutherford Bench and the less highly regarded areas of the valley.

This leaves the question of climate, and the temperature gradient which I discuss on page 42. Does this, coupled with soil (or *terroir*) in its broader sense, give rise to distinctive styles of Cabernet in various parts of the valley? James Laube, who has spent more time thinking (and writing) about California Cabernet Sauvignon than most, throws down the challenge when he says,

California
1982–91 Acreage of Cabernet Sauvignon

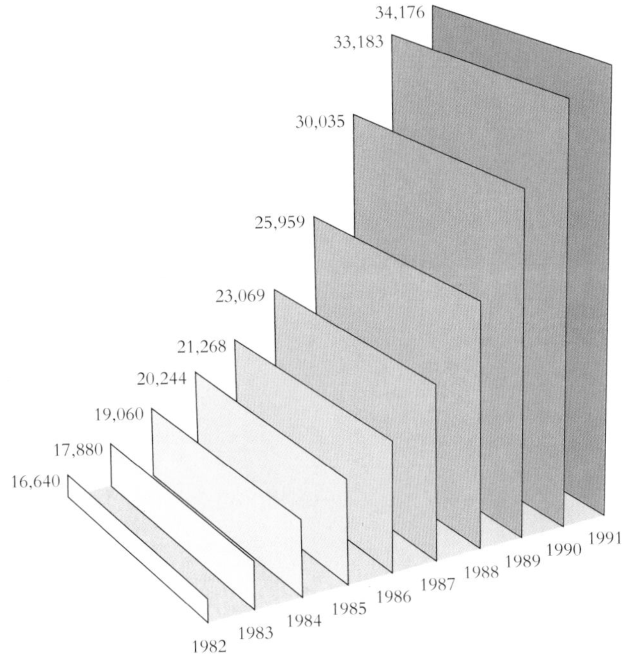
34,176
33,183
30,035
25,959
23,069
21,268
20,244
19,060
17,880
16,640
1982
1983
1984
1985
1986
1987
1988
1989
1990
1991

"The differences in styles among the subappellations are often significantly less apparent than some vintners, publicists or critics might preach." (*California's Great Cabernets*, page 38). Matt Kramer in his book *Making Sense of California Wine* takes a predictably opposing view, strongly arguing the link between place and style in wines of quality.

Perhaps the views are not so polarized, though, because there seems to be a broad measure of agreement between all the commentators when you get down to it. That agreement accords very much with the tastings of Cabernets I have conducted both over the years and specifically for this book. What is more, it accords with the performance of Cabernet Sauvignon in other comparable situations, and in particular Australia.

As one moves north along the valley floor from Napa to Calistoga the basic change is from an austere, very herbaceous wine to an intensely fat, rich and luscious Cabernet. Within that broad spectrum consistent descriptions are used: the firm, classic and slow developing wines of Yountville; the fine, supple, balanced plum, cherry and raspberry flavors and textures of Stags Leap; the aptly named mint belt around Oakville; the rich, black cherry and currant fruit of Rutherford with the Rutherford dust character; the effusive fruitiness, mint and spice of St. Helena; and finally, the earthy, dark chocolate, sweetly rich characters of Calistoga.

The mountain regions, too, have their own distinct personalities, although here the other aspect of human intervention comes into play: the tannin factor, which I discuss in the particular context of the mountain-grown grapes on page 120. In the broader context, the vast change (and improvement) in the quality of Napa Valley Cabernet which has occurred over the past 15 years has been brought about by the realization that more is not necessarily better. Levels of extract, and in particular levels of tannins, have been significantly reduced; for a wine to become great, it must be balanced right from the outset.

The changes have come from better vineyard management; from a far better understanding of the way tannins are extracted and how they may be softened; from more sophisticated use of French (and, increasingly, American) oak; and from the use of Merlot and Cabernet Franc to add both softness and complexity.

I have no doubt at all that those who wish to, and have the financial means to do so, will make better Cabernet Sauvignon in the future than has ever been made in the past. This will be an on-going achievement: while there will be individual wines hailed as supremely great, they will be part of a continuum. There is no magic wand to be waved in the winery; indeed, the trend is to use technology even more sparingly (and intelligently).

Likewise, the pace of viticultural change being imposed by phylloxera will inevitably breed a new generation of mistakes (as well as a rash of young vines). So little is really known about rootstocks, and rootstock/scion compatibility; so many clones remain to be explored. Then there is the move to organic viticulture, and within that move, the implications for genetic breeding and manipulation to produce disease-resistant wines.

But the bottom line will be Cabernets made in the 1990s which our grandchildren will regard with the same awe and reverence as that with which we regard the 1936 Beaulieu, or the great Inglenook, Martini and Georges de Latour wines of the 1940s and 1950s.

ABOVE ~ *Classic, loose-berried bunches of perfectly ripened Cabernet Sauvignon grown on the thin, mountain soils of Cain Vineyards.*

WINERIES *of* STAGS LEAP

S. ANDERSON 1979

A: 1473 Yountville Crossroad, Yountville, CA 94599 **T**: (707) 944 8542 **V**: By appointment **P**: 10,000 **W**: Carol Anderson and Gary Galleron

Dentist Stanley Anderson and dental hygienist wife Carol were lured into grape growing through home winemaking and friendship with the Chappellets and the Davies (of Schramsberg), purchasing a 50-acre property in 1971 in the Stags Leap district. Planting began in 1973, not to Cabernet Sauvignon, but to Chardonnay, setting S. Anderson on a course quite different from the standard pattern for Stags Leap, but which partially reverted to convention with the initial release of a 1989 Cabernet Sauvignon in 1992. But S. Anderson remains primarily a sparkling wine producer: the make-up is around 6,500 cases of sparkling wine and 2,500 of Chardonnay, with Cabernet (purchased from the Richard Chambers Vineyard on the east side of the Silverado Trail) edging up to 1,000 cases to meet the insatiable demand for the wine.

The move to sparkling wine came in five phases: initially the Andersons were simply grape growers, but during that time Carol Anderson studied enology at U.C. Davis; in 1979 the winery was bonded and production of Chardonnay (as a still table wine) commenced. The next phase was the move into making sparkling wine; next came the establishment of spectacular arched, cathedral-like underground caves in 1984 for storage of the 300,000 bottles of sparkling wine held at any one time; and finally in 1988 the Andersons purchased 70 acres of land in Carneros for a Chardonnay vineyard specifically dedicated to sparkling wine.

The Anderson sparkling wine style has relied upon prolonged yeast lees aging; the regular wines are left for five years on yeast lees before disgorgement, the Reserves for eight to ten years. The purchase of the Carneros property was prompted by two things: the early invasion of phylloxera on the original plantings, and (although the Andersons themselves do not say this) a recognition that perhaps the style of their sparkling wines was decidedly muscular and increasingly out of pace with the new direction of California sparkling wine.

The Carneros acquisition certainly indicates an intention to persevere with sparkling wine, but with the constantly reiterated intention of slow growth; until phylloxera hit, the Andersons were selling approximately 75% of the grapes they grew. Restricting the volume of the voluptuous Cabernet Sauvignon may likewise prove to be a very astute move: no doubt Gary Galleron (who also makes the Grace Family red wine) has had some words to say on this subject.

CHIMNEY ROCK 1980

A: 5350 Silverado Trail, Napa, CA 94558 **T**: (707) 257 2641 **V**: 10–4 daily **P**: 22,000 **W**: Doug Fletcher

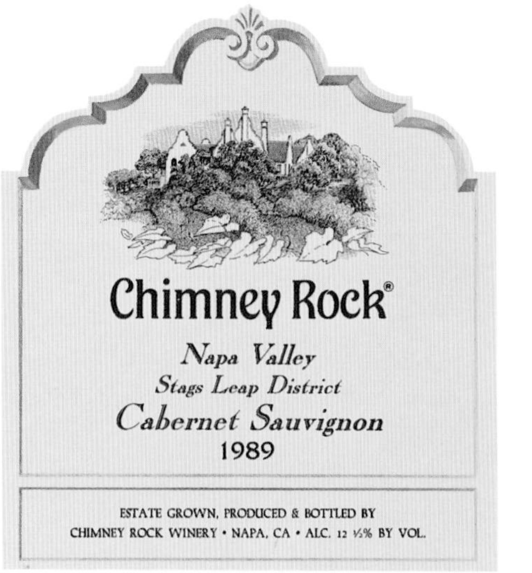
Chimney Rock®
Napa Valley
Stags Leap District
Cabernet Sauvignon
1989
ESTATE GROWN, PRODUCED & BOTTLED BY
CHIMNEY ROCK WINERY • NAPA, CA • ALC. 12 ½% BY VOL.

The Chimney Rock Cape Dutch architecture is an echo of the time that owners Hack and Stella Wilson spent in South Africa running Pepsi Cola. It was in fact only part of an incredibly successful career for Sheldon "Hack" Wilson, who as well as becoming the largest volume franchise Pepsi bottler in the world at one time with Los Angeles, Mexico and Puerto Rico under his control, became a major brewer in the 1960s. Then in the 1970s he moved into the hotel industry with partner William Zeckendorf, purchasing (amongst others) what is now the Ritz Carlton and the Mayfair Regent in New York. At the Mayfair, they introduced Le Cirque, acknowledged as one of the world's great restaurants.

Having flirted with the idea of purchasing a Bordeaux chateau, the Wilsons acquired the Chimney Rock golf course in 1980 and promptly bulldozed nine holes to create a 75-acre vineyard estate, building their house on the hill in 1983, completing the winery in 1989 and the lavish hospitality center in spring 1990.

Winemaker Doug Fletcher joined Chimney Rock in 1987, having been winemaker at Steltzner between 1982 and 1986, making the wines in rented space until the winery was completed prior to the 1989 vintage. Dick Steltzner is one of the Napa Valley's leading viticulturists, and (with the replanting necessitated by phylloxera) the Steltzner influence is to be seen in the new plantings, with the hillside vineyard close-planted to a vertical trellis, the more vigorous valley floor vineyards being established with open lyre trellises. The replanting will also accelerate the phasing out of Stags Leap Chardonnay and the development of Meritage style reds modeled upon those of St. Emilion: 40% Merlot, 40% Cabernet Franc and 20% Cabernet Sauvignon being one approach.

The Chimney Rock red wines released to date have been disappointing, even allowing for the deliberately downplayed style which Doug Fletcher favours. But barrel tastings from the 1991 vintage suggested much better — indeed great — things are in store. The Cabernet Sauvignon was an impeccably clean and beautifully balanced wine, while the St. Emilion-inspired Meritage blend showed strong red cherry fruit and positive but well-integrated new oak. The winery is immaculate, Doug Fletcher highly intelligent, and the new vineyards should surely produce grapes of the highest quality. I find it difficult to believe that the 1991 barrel tastings are anything other than a true portent of things to come.

CLOS DU VAL 1972

A: 5330 Silverado Trail, Napa, CA 94558 **T**: (707) 252 6711 **V**: 10–4 daily **P**: 60,000 **W**: Bernard Portet and Krimo Souilah

Clos du Val was bred in the purple. In 1970 John Goelet, a businessman whose family had had connections with the Bordeaux wine trade, decided he wished to invest in the winemaking business in a serious way, but without preconceived ideas as to where that investment might best be made. He hired Bernard Portet, elder son of Andre Portet, who was at that time technical director of Chateau Lafite. Bernard Portet himself had studied at the French winemaking schools of Toulouse and Montpellier, gaining advanced degrees in both agronomy and enology, so he was well equipped for the two-year search which followed, and which took him through France, South Africa, Australia, Argentina, Chile and the United States. France was ultimately rejected as being unrealistically expensive, and Bernard came up with two sites: one in Central Victoria, Australia, which was to become Taltarni, run by younger brother Dominique Portet; the other in the Stags Leap district of the Napa Valley, which was to become Clos du Val.

CLOS DU VAL
1989
ESTATE BOTTLED
MERLOT
STAGS LEAP DISTRICT
Napa Valley
Alcohol 13.2% by Volume

The stories vary as to precisely how and why Bernard Portet chose the Stags Leap property: one version has him driving a car down Silverado Trail, another riding a bicycle. The common link is that it was a hot summer's afternoon, and that as he traveled south past the distinctive knolls and hills which mark the northern end of the Stags Leap District, he noticed a substantial drop in the temperature. Having chosen the site, Bernard Portet wasted no time: winemaking (from purchased grapes, of course) got underway in 1972, and Portet immediately produced a Cabernet Sauvignon which became famous around the world as a result of a highly controversial tasting in Paris in 1976, repeated ten years later in 1986, pitting the might of Bordeaux against California, and on each occasion California wines emerging the victors — and in 1986 with the 1972 Clos du Val in first place.

These days, Clos du Val is a large and basically functional winery, with ivy softening the walls and no hint of an edifice complex anywhere to be seen. The vineyards now comprise 265 acres in three different areas of the Napa Valley: Stags Leap planted to Cabernet Sauvignon, Cabernet Franc, Merlot, Zinfandel and Semillon; Carneros to Chardonnay and Pinot Noir; and Yountville to Chardonnay. The primary focus is on Cabernet Sauvignon, Chardonnay and Merlot, with Pinot Noir, Zinfandel and Semillon rounding out the Clos du Val range. Next comes a range of premium wines under the Joli Val label made from grapes blended from Rutherford, St. Helena and Stags Leap districts, and finally there is the second label (and much cheaper) Le Clos Red and Le Clos White.

All of the wines are made with a distinctly French touch: all are made to age, and most do with considerable grace; all place as much importance on texture, balance and harmony as on power and primary fruit flavor. The citrussy/appley Carneros Chardonnay is notable for its length of flavor, the Cabernet Sauvignon for its balance, generous but not overstated fruit and soft oak; while the Merlot shows well above average varietal character, particularly if one accepts the wines of St. Emilion as providing the yardstick.

PINE RIDGE WINERY 1978

A: 5901 Silverado Trail, Napa, CA 94558
T: (707) 253 7500 **V**: 11–5 daily **P**: 72,000
W: Gary Andrus and Stacy Clark

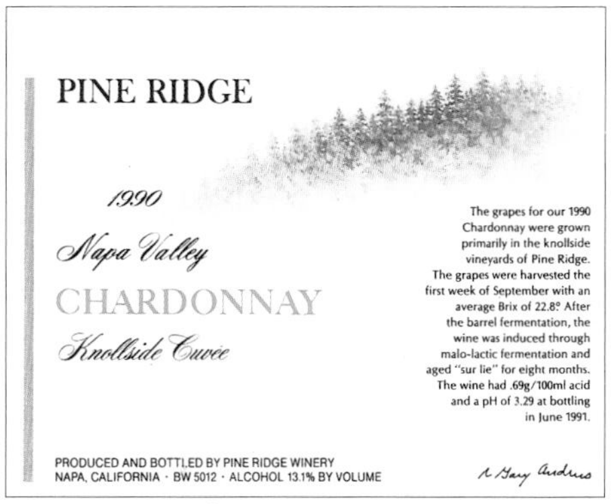
PINE RIDGE
1990
Napa Valley
CHARDONNAY
Knollside Cuvee
The grapes for our 1990 Chardonnay were grown primarily in the knollside vineyards of Pine Ridge. The grapes were harvested the first week of September with an average Brix of 22.8°. After the barrel fermentation, the wine was induced through malo-lactic fermentation and aged "sur lie" for eight months. The wine had .69g/100ml acid and a pH of 3.29 at bottling in June 1991.
PRODUCED AND BOTTLED BY PINE RIDGE WINERY
NAPA, CALIFORNIA · BW 5012 · ALCOHOL 13.1% BY VOLUME

Mormon-raised Gary Andrus first tasted wine as a member of the 1968 American Olympic skiing team in France, which is as circuitous an introduction to wine as one could wish for. Ten years later he purchased his Stags Leap estate property, upon which he constructed the winery (built around the shell of a long-defunct winery and now with underground caves for barrel storage), going on to accumulate a second vineyard at Silverado Trail, two vineyards at Oak Knoll, three vineyards in the Rutherford Bench area, another at Rutherford proper, and yet another in Carneros. In all, there are 145 acres under vine to the red Bordeaux varieties (all five), Chardonnay, and Chenin Blanc. Small wonder he and wife Nancy have invested over $2 million in the venture to date.

The emphasis is on vineyard-identified wines; if blending is to be done, it will be done through the varieties other than through vineyards or sub-regions. Andrus and winemaker Stacy Clark are fascinated by the differences in the wines produced using identical production techniques, differences which remain consistent from one year to the next and which they believe can only be ascribed to the interaction of *terroir* and climate. It is not hard to see why Andrus professes to be still strongly influenced by his original French exposure to wine, or why he was tempted to make a Cuvee Duet in 1985 in collaboration with Chateau Lynch-Bages.

The slightly sweet Chenin Blanc and the dusty/sawdusty Chardonnay quietly serve to focus attention on the various Cabernets, which are undoubtedly Pine Ridge's strength. There is a plethora of these made each year, some in tiny quantities, and at suitably impressive prices. The brand leader, as it were, is the 6,000 case Rutherford Cuvee, a red Meritage blend of Cabernet Sauvignon, Merlot and Cabernet Franc, and which in vintages such as 1987 shows why Pine Ridge is seen as one of the coming superstars. Unbelievably youthful, and with a deftly handled touch of charred oak, the wine will live for decades without the crutch of excess tannins to support it. The other wines deliberately reflect their varying origins, but do not shrink from the expansive use of oak.

SHAFER VINEYARDS 1979

A: 6154 Silverado Trail, Napa, CA 94558
T: (707) 944 2877 **V**: By appointment
P: 20,000 **W**: Doug Shafer

After 23 years in the Chicago publishing industry, John Shafer opted for a dramatic change of lifestyle for himself and his family with his 1972 acquisition of a 210-acre property in the north-eastern corner of the Stags Leap District. Says John Shafer, "It is my dumb luck story, because I was looking for a hillside vineyard, and in 1972 neither Clos du Val Wine Cellars nor Stag's Leap Wine Cellars had released their first wines, so no one really knew of the potential of the district." Dumb luck perhaps, but nor were the majority of aspiring vignerons looking for hillside vineyards back in 1972.

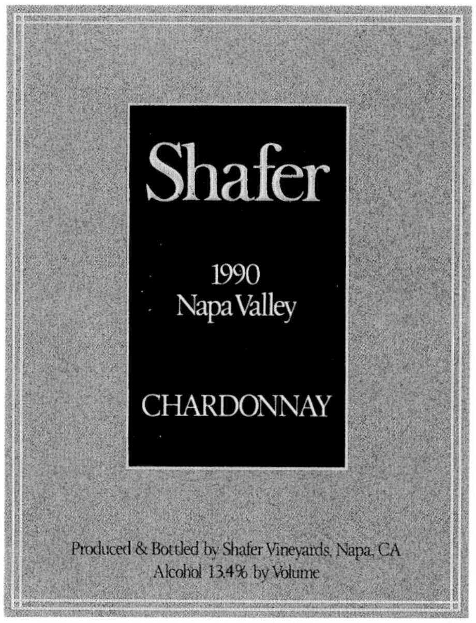
Shafer
1990
Napa Valley
CHARDONNAY
Produced & Bottled by Shafer Vineyards, Napa, CA
Alcohol 13.4% by Volume

Yet more dumb luck followed John Shafer when he decided to plant over 60% of the vineyards on St. George rootstock, and to concentrate on Cabernet Sauvignon and Merlot, rather than Chardonnay. Only eight acres were planted to Chardonnay at the bottom of the terraced hillsides, and in the aftermath of phylloxera (the Chardonnay was planted on AxR) this section of the vineyard is being replanted to Cabernet Sauvignon, Merlot and Cabernet Franc. Having completed the backbreaking task of recreating and reshaping the ancient terraces on which the estate hillside vineyards are planted, the Shafers successively purchased a 17-acre Chardonnay vineyard in the Oak Knoll region, and finally a 75-acre vineyard in Carneros planted to Chardonnay and Merlot.

Ultimately, the focus will be on the Stags Leap Cabernet Sauvignon (under two labels, Hillside Select and Stags Leap District), Merlot (again from Stags Leap) and Chardonnay (from Carneros), with the possibility of the development of a small volume of a high-priced Proprietary Red. The 1992 redevelopment and extension of the winery, first built in 1979, will see Shafer reach its ultimate production target of around 22,000–23,000 cases. The Shafers started off life as grape growers and sellers, and have every intention of continuing that role.

Son Doug Shafer became winemaker in 1980, having finished his degree at U.C. Davis and acquired practical experience working at Hanns Kornell and Robert Mondavi wineries. Since that time the Shafer portfolio has gained ever-increasing recognition and praise, all of which it richly deserves. The wines are models of consistency, and with a pleasing contrast between the Hillside Select and Stags Leap District Cabernets. Tasted blind, without knowing the identity of the winery and even less the identity of the vineyards concerned, the Hillside Select showed the dark chocolate fruit flavors typical (so the Shafers say) of the wine, while the Stags Leap District Cabernets showed the more classic, fresh red berry and cherry flavors of the region as a whole in a softer and more accessible mold than the tightly structured but very high quality Hillside wine. The Merlot is certainly made in a bold style, in some ways emulating that of Duckhorn; personally, I would rather see a little more fruit and a little less tannin, even if it meant a drop in total flavor and longevity. Finally, the Chardonnay shows the typical citrussy aromas and flavors of the southern end of the Valley, characters which will no doubt intensify as the Carneros component increases.

SILVERADO VINEYARDS 1981

A: 6121 Silverado Trail, Napa, CA 94558
T: (707) 257 1770 **V**: 11–4:30 daily
P: 100,000 **W**: Jack Stuart

Silverado Vineyards is owned by the widow and children of Walt Disney, and it is curious that — as so many people have observed — the whole development should have been created quietly and unobtrusively, without even the faintest echo of Disneyland anywhere to be seen. Indeed, even seeing the substantial stone winery is no mean feat, for despite its hilltop location, it is not visible from the Silverado Trail. The very entry into the business was no less unobtrusive; the Disneys first became grape sellers (when they purchased the then well-established Silverado Trail Vineyard in 1976); it was not until 1981 that the winery was built and winemaking commenced, with Jack

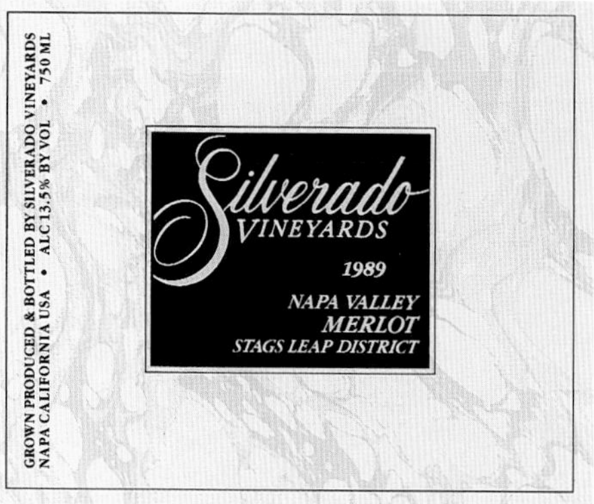
GROWN PRODUCED & BOTTLED BY SILVERADO VINEYARDS
NAPA CALIFORNIA USA • ALC 13.5% BY VOL • 750 ML
Silverado
VINEYARDS
1989
NAPA VALLEY
MERLOT
STAGS LEAP DISTRICT

Stuart at the helm right from the first day.

The same discipline has continued to pervade the business. The wines are very modestly priced — some would say underpriced — and when, after many years of hesitation, it was reluctantly agreed that certain outstanding parcels could be released as Reserve wines, Diane Disney-Miller insisted they be packaged in the same bottles, rather than exotic Italian bottles.

On the other hand, there is nothing static about the empire. Vineyard holdings now extend to over 300 acres, and while the core remains in the Stags Leap district for Cabernet Sauvignon and Merlot, a large Yountville vineyard provides Sauvignon Blanc; the Mount George Vineyard produces Cabernet Sauvignon, Cabernet Franc, Merlot and Chardonnay, but also Sangiovese which will come into production in 1993; while in 1991 yet another property was purchased on Soda Canyon Road which will be planted to Zinfandel and Sangiovese.

All of this will mean an increased emphasis on red wine production, and a decreased emphasis on Chardonnay, which at one time accounted for 50% of production. Rightly, Cabernet Sauvignon will remain the focal point. This is an absolutely delicious wine, which has always relied on supple fruit, silky texture and subtle oak rather than tannin and extract, and which has shown a quite unexpected ability to age well, notwithstanding its accessibility when young. Even in vintages such as 1989, Stuart managed to weave an outstanding wine, with luscious cassis fruit cut by just a touch of green olive character, an extremely supple mid palate and great length and flavor. The white wines are subtle and stylish, but simply not in the same class as the Cabernet Sauvignon or the Merlot, and it will be more than interesting to watch the emergence of the Italian varieties and Zinfandel.

ROBERT SINSKEY 1988

A: 6320 Silverado Trail, Napa, CA 94558
T: (707) 944 9090 **V**: 10–4.30 daily **P**: 8,000
W: Joe Cafaro and Jeff Vernig

Dr. Robert Sinskey is not only a famous eye surgeon, but a wealthy one, having successfully pioneered a now internationally used artificial lens. He had been one of Acacia's founding partners in 1980, but parted company in the mid 1980s when the winery was sold to Chalone, having already acquired a 35-acre property just up the road from Acacia which he had planted in 1983 to ten acres of Pinot Noir, 15 acres of Merlot and ten acres of Chardonnay. When the partnership broke up, and Acacia was sold to Chalone in the mid 1980s, Dr. Sinskey purchased the site on the Silverado Trail which had been earmarked for a second Acacia winery, and in 1987 began construction of the handsome stone and redwood winery which was completed for the 1988 vintage. In the same year he planted the surrounding five acres to four acres of Cabernet Sauvignon and half-an-acre each of Merlot and Cabernet Franc, a planting which should produce limited quantities of the first Stags Leap Cabernet Sauvignon by the time of publication of this book. In 1989 a further 50 acres of Carneros vineyard were established in Buhman Lane, planted to Pinot Noir, Merlot, Cabernet Franc and Cabernet Sauvignon: the climate here is unusually warm for Carneros, rated at Region II.

Winemaker Joe Cafaro has done wonders with the Carneros red wines. A Red Meritage, innocuously labeled Carneros Claret, is made from approximately 60% Merlot, 20% Cabernet Sauvignon and 20% Cabernet Franc. It has unexpected power, astringency and depth, with flavors running through the cedary and berry range rather than the vegetal. But it is with the Merlot that everything comes together: spotlessly clean, beautifully warm fruit and oak are woven together in the bouquet, leading on

1990
PINOT NOIR
ARIES
LOS CARNEROS

to a softly ripe, dark berried fruit with soft tannins running throughout the palate. Given the exceptional achievements of these two wines, the Pinot Noir comes as a minor disappointment: not that it is a bad wine, nor that it lacks varietal character, but somehow or other one expects rather more than the fairly obvious plum and cherry fruit of the 1990 vintage. Given that some of the controversial techniques developed by French consulting enologist Guy Accad have been used, and that three different clones are incorporated, not to mention the strong reviews given to earlier vintages, I can only imagine that the 1990 is atypical.

STAG'S LEAP WINE CELLARS 1972

A: 5766 Silverado Trail, Napa, CA 94558
T: (707) 944 2020 **V**: 10–4 daily **P**: 80,000
W: Warren Winiarski and John Gibson

When University of Chicago lecturer and amateur home winemaker Warren Winiarski quit academia in the late 1960s he did not leave behind one of the most enquiring and challenging minds I have encountered in any profession in any place in the world. His is the restless quest for perfection, whether it be his exquisitely beautiful hilltop-curved home, his twin white and red state-of-the-art wineries, or his near-obsessive viticultural work and experimentation. It is thus appropriate that the second wine which Warren Winiarski ever made — his 1973 Stag's Leap Cabernet Sauvignon — put not only Stag's Leap on the world wine map, but the whole of the Napa Valley when in 1976 it came first in a tasting organized in Paris by Stephen Spurrier and judged by leading French experts, beating (amongst other wines) 1970 Chateau Mouton-Rothschild and 1970 Chateau Haut Brion.

An intensely private and in many ways shy man, Winiarski has never been far from the headlines since. There was a lengthy legal battle with Stags' Leap Winery Inc., while the reputation for producing Cabernets of world class means that anything less is likely to create headlines of similar dimension. Thus in 1992 there was heated debate over the most recently released Cask 23 Cabernet Sauvignon, just at the time when praise was being showered from the skies for Stag's Leap 1990 Reserve Chardonnay, one of the best California Chardonnays I have tasted. (It is made primarily from Carneros grapes, with a little southern Napa Valley component.)

Cask 23 sits at the top of the red wine pyramid. Only 1,000 cases are made a year, and it comes as no surprise to find James Laube according it first growth status. Then come SLV (standing for Stag's Leap Vineyards) Cabernet Sauvignon and (since 1990) Fay Cabernet Sauvignon. In 1989 there was an SLV-Fay blend released as such. Chardonnay is released under both the Reserve and Napa Valley labels, while limited quantities of White Riesling (from the Wild Horse Valley) are also made. Then there is the Hawk Crest range, a brand which goes back to 1974, offering California Appellation Cabernet Sauvignon, Chardonnay and Sauvignon Blanc at a fraction of the price of the Stag's Leap Wines.

The enormous investment in time, money and intellect Winiarski has made in vineyard improvement, and in particular the Fay Vineyard purchased in 1986, will progressively benefit the Cabernet Sauvignons from 1990 and onwards. Wines which have been great in the past will become greater still, and of one thing you may be assured: Winiarski's drive for perfection will never cease.

STAGS' LEAP WINERY 1972

A: 6150 Silverado Trail, Napa, CA 94558
T: (707) 944 1303 **V**: By appointment
P: 25,000 **W**: Robert Brittan

While the address suggests Stags' Leap Winery is on the Silverado Trail, finding it is quite a feat. It is tucked away behind Shafer, up a long and imprecisely marked private road. It is part of an historic 240-acre estate, its antiquity immediately proclaimed by the ancient walnut, olive and palm trees, together with the giant prickly pears between which one drives to the old stone winery, dating from the last century, and which Carl Doumani slowly restored, crushing fruit for the first time there in 1979.

Initially the winery was best known for its Petite Sirah, made from a five-acre block of 100-year-old vines, but production is now driven principally by Cabernet Sauvignon (40 acres), Merlot (24 acres) and Cabernet Franc (four acres). The Petite Sirah has been expanded to 16 acres, and the leading varietal wines produced by the winery are Cabernet Sauvignon, Merlot and Petite Sirah. On the evidence of the 1989 Cabernet Sauvignon and the 1989 Merlot, it is not hard to see why Stags' Leap remains well and truly in the shade of its more illustrious near-namesake. The wines were pleasant, but light and unremarkable.

STELTZNER VINEYARDS 1977

A: 5998 Silverado Trail, Napa, CA 94558
T: (707) 252 7272 **V**: By appointment
P: 9,500 **W**: Dick Steltzner

Dick Steltzner has enormous experience as a viticulturist, having established his own vineyard at the base of the Stags Leap Palisades in 1966, having planted the Diamond Creek and Spring Mountain Vineyards, and having acted as vineyard manager for a number of major wineries. Listening to him talk, and looking at the practical results of his handiwork, one is reminded of Doug Meador of Ventana Vineyards. Both have embraced modern viticultural theories with fervor, and have played key roles in changing traditional attitudes to all aspects of grape production.

Having become a grape grower in 1966, Steltzner did not start making wine until 1977, between then and 1983 using rented facilities in other wineries. For that year he built a functional winery on his Stags Leap property, which had long burst at the seams by the time he constructed underground caves in the hillside immediately behind. These were completed in 1992, financed by the astute sale of the hillside land above the caves while retaining ownership of the underground portion.

Steltzner's grapes have provided some of California's great Stags Leap Cabernets, but have also provided some outstanding wines under his own label. The 1986 Cabernet Sauvignon is a wonderful wine, with big, ripe, dark fruit flavors, a touch of chocolate, and the tannins in balance; the 1988 Cabernet classic, complex and again with perfectly balanced soft tannins; the 1990 Merlot high-toned, high-flavored, with minty berry fruit and a lively, fresh and crisp aroma. The 1991 Sauvignon Blanc, drawn from a vineyard in the Oak Knoll region near Yountville of which Steltzner is a partner, was an exceptionally well-made wine: while the fruit was not particularly intense, suggesting a degree of over-cropping, the handling of oak and the general treatment of the wine was nothing short of brilliant. By 1993, when the temporary trailer offices and builders' rubble are but memories of the past, Dick Steltzner's long march from grape grower to winemaker (in the fullest sense of that term) will be complete.

ABOVE ~ *The modern winery makes quick work of receiving and crushing grapes.*

WEST MOUNTAINS

The Mayacamas Mountains start far to the north of Calistoga, running beyond Cloverdale at the northern end of Sonoma County's Alexander Valley. They dip down in two narrow saddles which mark either end of Knights Valley, and then rise again to provide the formidable bulwark which separates Napa County from Sonoma County. The county line carefully tracks the highest ridge line until it meets that of Lake County at the peak of Mount St. Helena. So it is that the West Mountains are (confusingly) the eastern side of the southern extremity of the Mayacamas Range, which commences to rise south of the city of Napa and continues up past (but only just past) Calistoga.

ABOVE ~ *Netting is the only sure protection against the birds which live in the forested hillsides.*

Within this area are three distinct regions: Diamond Mountain, Spring Mountain and Mount Veeder. As at 1992 only Mount Veeder was a recognised AVA, but it can only be a question of time before the other two request and receive similar recognition.

The wineries are congregated in two main groups. Mount Veeder hosts Chateau Potelle, Hess Collection, Jade Mountain, Mayacamas, Mount Veeder Winery and Sky. Then on Spring Mountain you will find Cain Cellars, Robert Keenan, Newton, Ritchie Creek, Smith-Madrone, Spring Mountain, Stony Hill and Philip Togni.

Diamond Mountain's most famous winery is Diamond Creek; Graeser is to the north of what may be its official boundary on Petrified Forest Road, while Sterling has one of its high quality vineyards on the mountain.

While there certainly are distinguishing characteristics of each district, they have far more in common with each other than the valley floor to the east of each. Elevation is, of course, the key, yet it would be idle to suggest that all are at the same elevation. The mountainside vegetation tells you much: at lower levels you find grasslands, oaks and occasional olive trees; at intermediate levels the density becomes greater, with a mixture of oaks, madrones and other shrubs; and finally redwoods, firs and some madrones at the highest levels.

The West Mountains boast spectacular scenery, heightened by those days on which fog enshrouds the valley floor, and by the changing colors of the seasons, reaching a peak with the gold and red hues of fall painting a vivid tapestry among the forests. For in these mountains, vineyards still have precarious toeholds. Life on the valley floor seems easy; that on the mountainside is as full of challenges as it is of rewards.

OPPOSITE ~ *Bob Travers, long-time owner and winemaker at Mayacamas, presides over an extended family including his assistant winemaker's son, Andy Stetler.*

The Region in Brief

Climate, Soil and Viticulture

Climate

In contrast to that of the valley floor, climate is much more affected by altitude than by the south to north thermal increase encountered at lower levels. The primary key is that of temperature inversion: in essence, this means warmer nights and cooler days than are encountered on the valley floor. The mechanism is simple enough. The warm air of the valley floor rises in the afternoon and evening, to be replaced by the marine fogs and the cooler air draining down from the mountainsides. In the early morning, most vineyards are situated above the fog line, warming far more quickly and receiving more sunshine hours. But later in the day the warming slows down: breezes, and the simple effect of the altitude, mean that on a typical summer's day the peak daytime temperature will be 10°–15°F lower than that of the adjacent valley floor.

Rainfall is also significantly higher: it may be as much as 65 inches compared to 25 to 30 inches on the valley floor, increasing progressively with greater altitude. The risk of frost is minimal, partly because of the inversion factor and partly because of natural cold air drainage down the slopes.

Defining the climate in terms of temperature summation is particularly hazardous, because of the importance not only of altitude, but aspect. To give but one example, Cain Cellars has plots facing north, south, west and east (the latter the most conventional on these mountains as a whole) at altitudes ranging from 1,400 to 2,100 feet. A given variety on one block may ripen three to four weeks later than the same variety on another block. But within that limitation, the climate ranges from high Region I to high Region II.

Soil

Mountain soils are typically thinner and more acidic (thanks to the effect of higher rainfall) than those of the valley floor, and the soils of this eastern slope of the Mayacamas Mountains are no exception. They are typical upland soils developed from the weathering of underlying sandstone and shale bedrocks. Textures range from loams and clay loams to gravelly or stony sandy loams; some are deep and permeable, others shallow with impermeable bedrock; the colors range from light gray to pale brown to red brown to dark brown. And if you want to see a full range of these soils standing in one spot, just make an appointment to visit Al Brounstein at Diamond Creek, or ask Jean-Noel Formeaux to show you the nine different soil types at Chateau Potelle. The unifying feature, partly through the higher acidity and partly through the generally shallower nature of the soils, is a self-limiting environment for the vine, resulting in naturally controlled canopies providing low to moderate yields.

The Growing Season

Budbreak varies according to site and soil-warming, but it is roughly in line with that of Carneros, perhaps a little later. Chardonnay blooms around May 1, Cabernet June 1, a time of year when wind and rain can (and frequently do) upset flowering, thus causing yields to vary wildly from year to year. Chardonnay is typically harvested in the first three weeks of September through to early October — picking dates which emphasize that while the mountains are cool, the long hours of sunshine more than compensate.

Contract Growers

Heinemann Vineyard Eight acres of Pinot Noir planted in 1971 at an elevation of 600 feet on the lower slopes of Spring Mountain, sold to Walter Schug.

Holbrook Mitchell Ranch Fourteen acres in Mayacamas foothills (100 to 350 feet) planted to Cabernet Sauvignon, Merlot, Cabernet Franc and Chardonnay.

Pershing Vineyard Twenty-five acres in Mayacamas Mountains (near Diamond Mountain) at 750 to 1,000 feet planted in 1970 to 1985 to Cabernet Franc, Cabernet Sauvignon and Merlot; sold to Stonegate.

Pickle Canyon Vineyard Twenty acres planted 1973 at 900 feet on Mount Veeder to Cabernet Sauvignon, Chardonnay, Merlot, Pinot Noir and Zinfandel.

Spaulding Vineyard Seventeen acres at 600 to 1,000 feet on Diamond Mountain planted 1971 to 1975 to Cabernet Sauvignon, Chardonnay and Merlot; sold to Stonegate.

Van Asperen/Corbett Vineyard Eighty acres at 500 to 1,600 feet south of Spring Mountain planted to Cabernet Sauvignon, Chardonnay and Napa Gamay; purchased by Round Hill, but also Corbett Vineyard (now owners of part of the vineyard).

York Creek Ranch Two hundred acres at 1,200 to 1,950 feet on Spring Mountain planted between the 1930s and 1977 to Cabernet Sauvignon, Merlot, Petite Sirah and Zinfandel; Ridge and Belvedere are significant purchasers. Owned by Fritz Maytag.

Principal Wine Styles

Cabernet Sauvignon

As the discussion of "Taming Mountain Fruit" (page 120–1) demonstrates, the style of mountain-grown Cabernet Sauvignon is fundamentally affected by the philosophy and winemaking practices of the winemaker receiving the fruit. At one extreme stand the wines of Mayacamas, Philip Togni and Diamond Creek, at the other those of Hess Collection and Ritchie Creek. Certainly, the underlying intensity and almost steely strength of

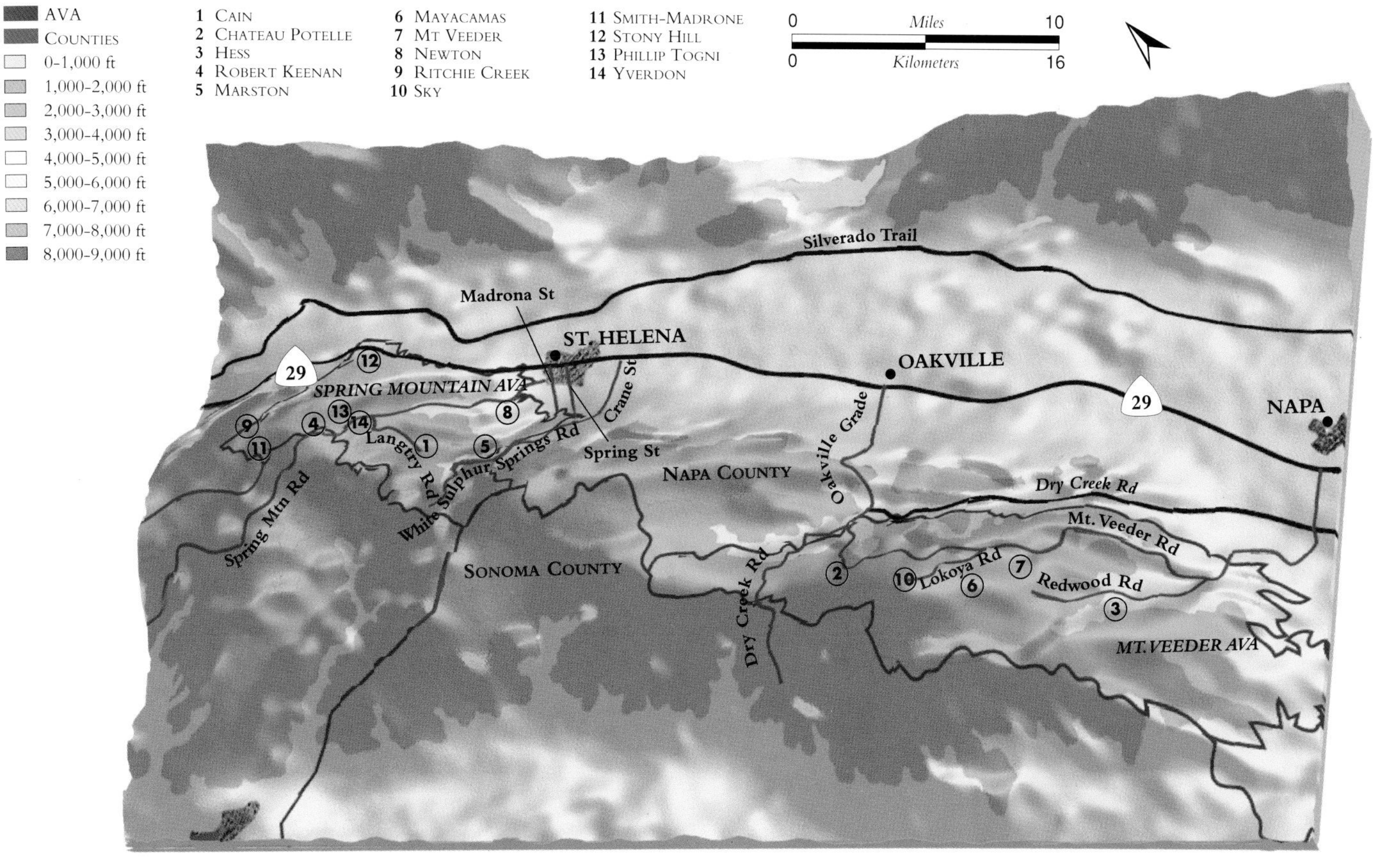
AVA
Counties
0-1,000 ft
1,000-2,000 ft
2,000-3,000 ft
3,000-4,000 ft
4,000-5,000 ft
5,000-6,000 ft
6,000-7,000 ft
7,000-8,000 ft
8,000-9,000 ft
1 Cain
2 Chateau Potelle
3 Hess
4 Robert Keenan
5 Marston
6 Mayacamas
7 Mt Veeder
8 Newton
9 Ritchie Creek
10 Sky
11 Smith-Madrone
12 Stony Hill
13 Phillip Togni
14 Yverdon
0 Miles 10
0 Kilometers 16
Silverado Trail
Madrona St
ST. HELENA
OAKVILLE
NAPA
29
SPRING MOUNTAIN AVA
Crane St
Oakville Grade
Langtry Rd
White Sulphur Springs Rd
Spring St
NAPA COUNTY
Dry Creek Rd
Mt. Veeder Rd
Spring Mtn Rd
SONOMA COUNTY
Lokoya Rd
Redwood Rd
MT. VEEDER AVA

mountain Cabernet comes through, but the way the fruit is textured and shaped determines whether the wine will be concentrated, tannic and unapproachable in its youth (and some would say in its old age) or whether it will be (relatively speaking) supple and graceful. The second major variable is that the wines of Spring Mountain — viewed as a whole — are softer and earlier developing than those of Mount Veeder. One reason is that the pH levels of the Spring Mountain Cabernets tend to be significantly higher than those of Mount Veeder. Whether improved canopy management will significantly alter fruit composition and flavor is another question which only time will answer.

Red Meritage Wines: Merlot, Cabernet Franc, Petit Verdot, Malbec

Little needs be said, other than that these are important varieties, usually blended with Cabernet Sauvignon, sometimes simply to soften the Cabernet Sauvignon a little, leaving its name intact, or increasingly to produce Meritage styles such as Cain Five and Mount Veeder's Meritage. Merlot is also making its presence felt in its own right, with Hess Selection and Newton among leading exponents. Finally, if I were growing grapes in these mountains, I would be tempted to plant Malbec rather than Petit Verdot.

Chardonnay

Whether it be Stony Hill, the maker of by far the most famous Chardonnay in this part of the world, or any of the other producers, there is a strong regional influence — one which is far more consistent than in the case of the Cabernet Sauvignons. The Chardonnays are all tight, reserved wines, built to age, and with minerally, stony, appley aspects rather than tropical, peach or apricot flavors. They benefit from long bottle-ageing, as the 20- to 30-year-old wines of Stony Hill so amply demonstrate.

Zinfandel

Zinfandel has been grown at various spots along the mountain range since the turn of the century, with Sky Vineyards, Chateau Potelle and York Creek Ranch (the latter simply as a grower) showing that these mountains can produce concentrated, dark fruited wines which can age superbly without compromising their appeal as young wines. The flavors have exotic overtones of cinnamon spice and pepper, which take on an attractive chocolate cast with age.

Rhone Varietals

Ritchie Creek with its Viognier and the nascent Jade Mountain with Syrah strongly suggest that these varieties may well come into their own over the next 20 years or so, providing wines which should show pronounced varietal character and the same longevity as the other principal wines.

Sauvignon Blanc

The wine is produced by a number of the producers, and performs in much the same way as does Chardonnay, producing a sinewy, powerful and concentrated wine.

ABOVE ~ *West Mountains map.*

TAMING MOUNTAIN FRUIT

There will be a substantial number of winemakers, critics and consumers who will scratch their heads and ask what this piece is all about. Indeed, they will see the questions it poses as falling in the "have you stopped beating your wife?" category. Foremost among such will be those who revere the wines of Mayacamas, Diamond Creek and Dunn.

So let me make one thing clear from the outset. There are no absolutes in this subject, no clearly demarcated rights and wrongs. Those who see the wines of Mayacamas as aging slowly, surely and majestically are entitled to their opinions. They include in their number some of the most respected and experienced palates in America.

ABOVE ~ *As vintage approaches, hours are spent collecting samples (of 200 to 300 individual berries) to accurately determine sugar levels.*

But there are those makers, critics and consumers who have come to the view that the Mayacamas wines will never come into balance; that the tannins will long outlive the fruit. To single out Mayacamas in this fashion may seem unfair, but its Cabernets do pose the question more clearly than any of the others. This is in no small measure due to the fact that it holds back 100 cases of its Cabernet for re-release when it is 12 years old, affording even the profligate the chance to taste the wines when (presumably) they are approaching their peak.

In some years, and in the hands of some makers, both sides will agree that magnificent wines can be made — Randy Dunn has succeeded more frequently than some. And no one decries the quality and individuality of mountain grapes, nor denies that truly ageworthy wines are entitled to their place at the top of the quality tree.

The questions are rather how does one extract the best, rather than the most, out of mountain *terroir* and climate, and how does one make wines which are balanced in their youth as well as in their maturity.

Three mountain winemakers who believe these are legitimate questions are Randle Johnson of The Hess Collection, Peter Franus of Mount Veeder and Chris Howell of Cain Cellars. By naming these three I am neither suggesting that they are critical of their fellow vignerons (they are not) nor that they are the only makers to be producing balanced wines from mountain grapes (there are others, and what is more, these three would be the last to suggest they have solved all the problems).

Each believes that mountain vineyards are, in one respect, no different from any others: great wine is made from great grapes, and unless the essential ingredients are there in the vineyard (and in appropriate balance), great wine will not be made.

Each knows, however, that mountain sites are so variable that each block, let alone each vineyard, has to be looked at separately.

Thus in selecting Merlot and Cabernet Franc for new plantings at Mount Veeder, Peter Franus and his viticultural team at Franciscan deliberately opted for big-berried clones, taking the opposite stance to the Franciscan valley floor plantings. For one of the features of mountain fruit is the small berry size, and the consequent high ratio of skins and pips to juice. To a certain degree, and in many vineyard situations, this is precisely what the quality-conscious vigneron will be seeking. But Franus wishes to balance his wine, and feels that some naturally softer and fruitier Merlot and Cabernet Franc will assist.

In the same way, Mount Veeder has installed drip irrigation in some of its blocks in an endeavor to increase berry size and thus naturally soften and reduce the amount of extract. At Hess, Randle Johnson is endeavoring to balance the vines at pruning, and to establish as large a root area per cluster as is possible. At Cain, Chris Howell is doubling the density of the plantings on existing terraces (by planting a second row), again aiming at producing fewer clusters per vine, and relying heavily on the concept of balanced stress.

Randle Johnson has introduced the most radical techniques in the winery, drawing upon the practical experience he gained during his earlier years at Mayacamas. The entire red wine fermentation cellar at Hess was designed with open-top tanks and a pneumatic plunger mounted on an overhead rail to allow punch down of whole berries. His belief — and surely it shows in the wines — is that this method extracts less tannins than standard pump-over techniques. The wines are then pressed at dryness and without extended maceration. Finally, fermentation temperatures are controlled to between 75° and 85°F.

He is also an advocate of the thin-staved chateau barrels which allow a small progressive oxygen transport through the wood into the wine. As well as helping soften the tannins in the wine, Johnson believes the action of the oxygen helps keep the wine alive and fresh.

Chris Howell at Cain uses a variety of techniques to control tannins and emphasize fruit. No one doubts that prolonged post-fermentation maceration will result in the tannins forming longer chains (or polymerizing) and hence softening. But Howell (amongst others) has observed that alcohol is a potent solvent and extractor of tannins, and that in the last stages of fermentation and in the first days of maceration tannin levels increase significantly. What is more, they are tough tannins. And the coup de grace is that just as you are polymerizing (or oxidizing) the tannins so are you oxidizing (and hence minimizing) the fruit.

So if you believe your mountain fruit has abundant tannins right from the outset, why not press the must before the end of the primary fermentation? This is one of the experiments Howell has in progress, and he is well pleased with the results.

From this point on, more conventional methods can be (and are) used. Deliberately oxidative rackings (a la Bordeaux) is one technique, while fining agents can reduce tannins levels very significantly.

The aim is to produce a wine which retains the intensity, the steely core and the longevity of mountain-sourced grapes, but which is balanced from the outset and which may be consumed without pain when it is four or five years old.

In a broader context, the response to mountain-grown grapes highlights the role of technique and technology for all types of winemaking and winestyle. As a new technique — or a new piece of equipment — is introduced with success in one part of the world, there is a tendency for winemakers everywhere to jump on the bandwagon. Thus some California winemakers appear to have adopted certain French techniques without stopping to consider whether their (California) grapes are different, and hence require a different approach. Surely this is true of mountain grapes.

West Mountains
VINTAGE CHART 1981-91

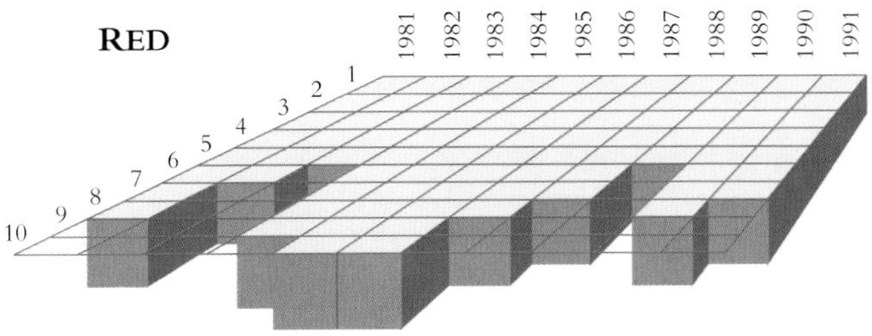
RED
1981
1982
1983
1984
1985
1986
1987
1988
1989
1990
1991
1
2
3
4
5
6
7
8
9
10

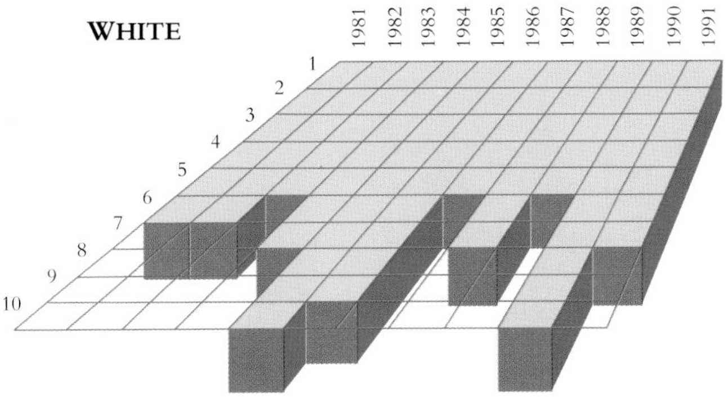
WHITE
1981
1982
1983
1984
1985
1986
1987
1988
1989
1990
1991
1
2
3
4
5
6
7
8
9
10

ABOVE ~ *Expensive contour planting and terracing was the solution of Cain Vineyards to the challenge of steep slopes.*

WINERIES *of* WEST MOUNTAINS

CAIN CELLARS 1982

A: 3800 Langtry Road, St. Helena, CA 94574
T: (707) 963 1616 **V**: By appointment
P: 5,000 **W**: Craig MacLean

1986
CAIN
Five
NAPA VALLEY
RED TABLE WINE
PRODUCED AND BOTTLED BY CAIN CELLARS
ST. HELENA, CALIFORNIA, BW 5135
CONTAINS SULFITES

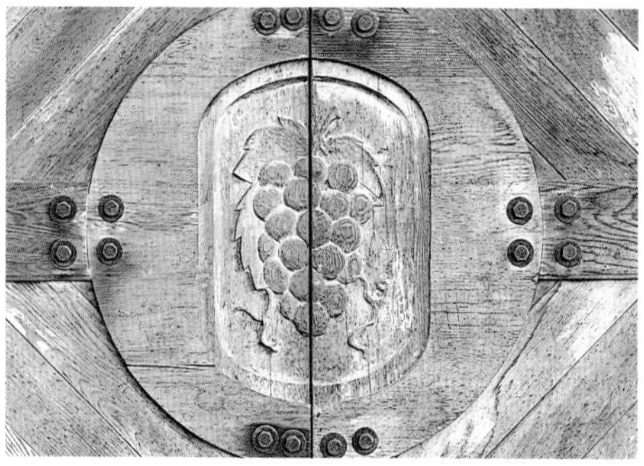

Every time I think of Cain Cellars, for some strange reason Samuel Taylor Coleridge's lines "In Xanadu did Kubla Khan/A stately pleasure-dome decree" come to mind. Perhaps it is the sheer immensity and improbability of the challenge, and of the size of the house, entertainment area and winery built by Jerry and Joyce Cain, which make the whole venture seem almost surreal. Without being unduly unkind, it can certainly be said to be a venture which proves the old adage about becoming a Napa Valley millionaire: start with $10 million. So it was that first Jim and Nancy Medlock became silent partners, and by the start of the 1990s had become sole owners, and one can only assume at a price rather less than the total investment to that time.

For these are some of the ultimate mountain vineyards, precariously established in small terraced patches at between 1,400 and 2,100 feet, inhibited by at times searing west winds and by the typically meager mountain soils. One hundred acres of Cabernet Sauvignon, Merlot, Cabernet Franc, Malbec and Petit Verdot have been established but are being reshaped under the direction of general manager Chris Howell, notably by selectively doubling the planting density through the simple expedient of planting a second row of vines on each terrace. Howell brings with him a deep understanding of both wine style and viticulture gained partially in Bordeaux and Montpellier in France.

The initial releases of Cain Five (which is necessarily at the higher end of the price range) were well enough received, but Howell is acutely aware of the delicate balancing act required to manage mountain tannins and extract. Over the past few years he has been experimenting with a number of options in both vineyard and winery, and the superb 1991 vintage tasted ex-barrel suggests that it is not beyond the realms of possibility that the enormous investment made will be justified — certainly in wine terms, even if not by strict financial criteria. A second label red, introduced on to the market from 1993, will also help economics, as to a lesser degree does the production of slightly fewer than 1,000 cases of Carneros Chardonnay and 600 cases of Sauvignon Blanc sold as Musque.

CHATEAU POTELLE 1983

A: 3875 Mt. Veeder Road, Napa, CA 94558
T: (707) 255 9440 **V**: 12–5 Thur–Mon
P: 25,000 **W**: Marketta Fourmeaux

Jean-Noël and Marketta Fourmeaux came to California in 1980 as emissaries of the French government to study first hand the California wine business; their own background lay in the wine industry of Bordeaux. They were sufficiently impressed to migrate to California in 1983, and begin an negociant business with the wines aged and bottled at Souverain. The next step was the acquisition of a 90-acre vineyard on the Silverado Trail, and later in the same year, the even more important purchase of a 270-acre vineyard and winery site on Mount Veeder, formerly known as Vose Vineyard. It is here that the future of Chateau Potelle lies, although the Formeauxs do intend to continue owning and farming the Silverado property. They see Mount Veeder as offering all of the advantages of the California sun (and the absence of disease) but yet providing a site where the poorness of the soil can naturally control the growth of the vine, and the cooler temperatures prolong the ripening season.

The Formeauxs admit they are going through a learning experience with the site, electing not to release the Chardonnay and Zinfandel made in either 1988 or 1989 from the Mount Veeder grapes. They were rewarded with a superb 1990 Zinfandel, showing all of the concentration of mountain-grown fruit but with sufficient sweetness to balance the tannin and extract, and with great varietal definition. The 1990 Chardonnay, too, is an elegantly fashioned wine with nicely weighted and balanced melon fruit flavors.

THE HESS COLLECTION 1978

A: 4411 Redwood Road, Napa, CA 94558
T: (707) 255 1144 **V**: 10–4 daily **P**: 25,000
W: Randle Johnson

How one avoids cliches and hyperbole in describing the creation of Donald Hess, I do not know. What I do know is that this extraordinary combination of art, museum and high-tech winery is as notable for its good taste (and brilliant design) as some of the other edifices of the Napa Valley are notable for their bad taste. Swiss-born and resident Donald Hess made a considerable fortune by diversifying his nine-generation family brewing business into mineral water, restaurant and other interests. It was indeed a search for suitable mineral water springs that brought him to the Napa Valley in 1978, and led to his first tasting of high quality California wines.

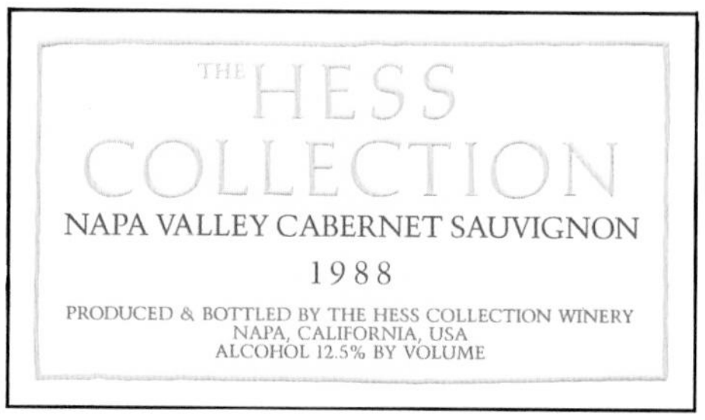
THE HESS
COLLECTION
NAPA VALLEY CABERNET SAUVIGNON
1988
PRODUCED & BOTTLED BY THE HESS COLLECTION WINERY
NAPA, CALIFORNIA, USA
ALCOHOL 12.5% BY VOLUME

With his Swiss background, it is hardly surprising that — having instantly decided he wished to invest in the California wine business — he should go to the steep slopes of Mount Veeder, purchasing a 550-acre property from William Hill in 1978. Over the ensuing years, 285 acres have been planted, divided into 95 blocks. Chardonnay and Cabernet Sauvignon lead the way, followed by Cabernet Franc and Merlot. The initial grape production was sold, but in 1983 Hess employed Randle Johnson as winemaker to make small quantities of wine from a small part of the total production. Johnson's career had taken him from Souverain

ABOVE ~ *The carved wooden door at Cain Cellars welcomes the visitor.*

to Mayacamas Vineyards and thence to Stag's Leap Wine Cellars, so his return to Mount Veeder in 1983 was to familiar territory.

But in a sense the story really begins in 1986, when the Christian Brothers Mount la Salle Winery, which had been built in 1903, was offered to Hess on a 50-year lease basis, together with the surrounding vineyard land. The vast stone winery was far larger than was needed for Hess's winemaking purposes, and his American-born wife Joanna suggested that he should use part of the space for his extraordinary collection of contemporary American art. Twenty-three million dollars later, the art collection is on display (though through unbelievable bureaucratic obfuscation, a planned display of statues outside is not), and a you-ask-for-it-and-you've-got-it winery in full operation. There is no point in endeavoring to describe further the Hess Collection; you must see it for yourself.

Randle Johnson's time at Mayacamas (between 1977 and 1980) taught him much about Mount Veeder fruit and, in particular, how essential it was to control the amount of extract. It was this which led to the installation of the large, open top fermenters with their pneumatic punch-down plates, allowing for a soft fermentation regime which in concept goes back to the dawn of time: foot stamping, or as the French call it, *pigeage*. Indeed, Johnson's whole attitude to winemaking (and in consequence, the style of the wines he makes) is a cross between the old world and the new. Says Johnson, "I have combined the French attitude that soil is the most important, with the California attitude that climate is the most important, seeking to establish as large a root area per cluster of vines as is possible, and to achieve vine balance during the winter pruning rather than by subsequent growing season manipulation." The winery manipulation is equally aimed at wines of subtlety and finesse, rather than raw, tannic power. The Chardonnay, Merlot and Cabernet Sauvignon all reflect this philosophy, and have been received with enthusiasm by the public and critics alike. There is also a second and significantly less expensive range under the Hess Select label, with a simple California Appellation, using Chardonnay and Cabernet Sauvignon sourced from across the state to produce a simpler, earlier-drinking style.

MAYACAMAS VINEYARDS 1889

A: 1155 Lokoya Road, Napa, CA 94558
T: (707) 224 4030 **V**: By appointment
P: 5,000 **W**: Robert Travers and Rick Stetler

If anyone wanted proof that those who own and operate a small winery are slightly mad (and remember that I am one of those), simply risk life and limb and drive (preferably in a rental car) to Mayacamas. What that trip must have been like when the stone winery and distillery were built in 1889, or even in 1941 when Shell Oil company executive Jack Taylor decided on a lifestyle change, is almost beyond imagination. Jack and Mary Taylor evidently found what they wanted, for it was not until 1968 that they sold Mayacamas to a syndicate headed by former stockbroker Robert Travers — and he too has found no need to change anything very much. Indeed, rather than purchase a piece of new equipment, he will spend twice as much in repairing that which has broken, otherwise abiding by the principle, "If it isn't broken, don't fix it, and most certainly don't replace it."

The same attitude applies to the shaping of these most formidable of all mountain wines — which, incidentally, only became estate-grown mountain wines after the Travers' purchase. Before that time much, if not all, of the fruit came from valley floor vineyards. So far, so good. It is in the perception and judgment of the style of the wines that opinions differ wildly. Both critics and supporters alike are agreed in one thing: do not drink them while they are young. And young, in this context, is a very relative thing, because the Cabernet is not released until it is five years old, and the Chardonnay three years old. One hundred cases of Cabernet Sauvignon are then reserved for re-release at 12 years of age, and 50 cases of Chardonnay when six years old.

James Laube rates the Cabernets as first growth, with AAA collectibility, and Matt Kramer is a strong supporter, believing the wines are worth the wait. Bob Thompson accords the wines three stars, but the *Connoisseurs Guide* is well and truly on the other foot, saying, "Sadly, the more recent efforts have lacked the fruit to bring the wine into focus, and, as a result, it has lost a good deal of standing among top producers." In other words, it is the classic argument: how much tannin are you prepared to accept, and will the tannins soften sufficiently before the fruit fades.

These are inevitably matters of personal judgment. All I can say is that, in 1992, I found the 1980 Cabernet to be soft, pleasantly aged in the bouquet with a touch of dark chocolate, and to show similar aged characters on the palate, but with the tannins still tough and hard. There is simply no way I could be persuaded that further time would improve the wine or bring it into better balance. The 1987 Cabernet was a surprisingly light and relatively astringent wine, showing no hint of future greatness. But then those with decades of experience of tasting Mayacamas wines will quickly point out that this is a classic error often made by the novice first approaching the wines. With age, the Chardonnay does develop distinct earthy notes, which are viewed enthusiastically by some as an indication of *terroir*; when young, they tend to show very tart, green appley flavors more akin to Sauvignon Blanc than Chardonnay. I guess that I must line up with the heretics and face damnation in purgatory.

MOUNT VEEDER WINERY 1972

A: 1999 Mt. Veeder Road, Napa, CA 94558
T: (707) 963 7111 **V**: By appointment
P: 12,000 **W**: Peter Franus

The first of the Mount Veeder wineries was planted by founders Mike and Arlene Bernstein in the mid 1960s, producing a range of legendary wines of extreme, and at times bizarre, style. In 1982 the property was sold to the Matheson family, who increased the plantings to 23 acres, and edged up production from 4,000 to 5,000 cases, but found it no more financially rewarding than had the previous owners. In 1989 it was acquired by Franciscan Vineyards, which provided the funds to plant an additional 17 acres, significantly expanding the Cabernet Franc and Merlot plantings.

Production should peak at 15,000 cases, being 10,000 of Cabernet Sauvignon and Meritage, and 5,000 cases of Chardonnay. The Meritage was made in the 1988 vintage, and will typically contain 40% Cabernet Sauvignon, 40% Merlot, 10% Cabernet Franc and 10% of Petit Verdot and Malbec — all estate-grown. That first vintage was an outstanding success: although the tannins are strong, and perhaps just a little too much so, the wine is very complex, with a rich fruit core and long flavor. The Chardonnay is made in a deliberately understated, discreet style: Franus simply does not like the cloying tutti-frutti versions of Chardonnay, and the mountain lends itself to his approach.

ABOVE ~ *Chardonnay sur lie (on the lees) at the Hess Collection in the hands of Randle Johnston.*

TOP LEFT ~ *Donald Hess, as creative as any of the artists he patronises.*

All in all, this is a winery to watch as the combined talents (and intelligence) of Peter Franus and the Franciscan team headed by Augustin Huneeus bear fruit.

NEWTON VINEYARD 1979

A: 2555 Madrona Avenue, St. Helena, CA 94574 **T**: (707) 963 9000 **V**: By appointment **P**: 27,000 **W**: John Konigsgaard

Following the acquisition of Sterling Vineyards by Coca-Cola in 1977, founding partner Peter Newton decided to start all over again, and to take winemaker Ric Forman into partnership. Both had no doubt about the quality potential of Diamond Mountain, and what is essentially a vertical two-mile strip of land was duly purchased, planting of what was to be 100 acres of vineyards commenced, an underground winery tunneled into the side of the hill, and an exquisitely landscaped reception and office area established. Local rumor has it that when Peter Newton's wife Su Hua decided to install a swimming pool above the cellar, Ric Forman decided his future lay elsewhere, and the winery, which was to have been named Forman, acquired its present name.

After flirting with Sauvignon Blanc for a period, the winery now concentrates on Chardonnay (produced from purchased grapes), an estate-grown Cabernet Sauvignon (also containing some Merlot), and Merlot. As from 1990, it was decided to leave the Chardonnay in barrel for an additional year, but I could find nothing much to like in either the old version (the 1989, bottled after one year) or the 1990 (bottled unfiltered and unfined after two years in barrel). There is a hard, green-apple character to these wines which does not appeal. The Merlot, too, seems to show some of the slightly sour notes evident in the Chardonnay, but I have no complaints at all about the Cabernet Sauvignon. Here is Cabernet with that slightly dusty aroma one finds in great Bordeaux, with ample redcurrant/raspberry fruit on the palate and nicely balanced tannins.

RITCHIE CREEK VINEYARD 1974

A: 4024 Spring Mountain Road, St. Helena, CA 94574 **T**: (707) 963 4661
V: By appointment **P**: 1,200 **W**: Pete Minor

In 1965 a young dentist from Santa Rosa called Pete Minor caught the wine bug and took an outrageously long shot by purchasing 50 acres of land at an elevation of 2,000 feet on Spring Mountain at a time when Napa Valley floor land was readily available and relatively inexpensive, and the whole of the Sonoma Valley was virtually there for the asking. He commenced the arduous business of clearing the land and planting vines in 1967, using an old, straggly, small-berried clone of Cabernet Sauvignon obtained from Charles Krug, a decision as instinctive as the acquisition of the land itself, but both deriving from his love of Bordeaux reds.

The winery was bonded in 1974, and Ritchie Creek Vineyards was in business. But although a still-sprightly Minor retired from dentistry in 1985, he has resisted the temptation to increase production. What he has not resisted was the temptation to try Viognier; here, too, he was one jump in front of the rest, and his 120 cases-per-year output is spoken for long before the grapes are crushed. Chardonnay, too, made its appearance in the early 1980s, and in volume terms is the winery leader, but for my money it is the Cabernet Sauvignon which has in some (but not all) years scaled the absolute heights. At its best, it has an elegance which is entirely akin to that of Bordeaux with an intriguing spiciness, and sweet fruit concentration which magically embodies a dash of herbaceousness without in any way detracting from the wine.

In May 1992 Pete Minor attended a vertical tasting of 18 vintages of his Cabernet Sauvignon (assembled by someone else) and modestly admitted that all the wines were holding up well, even the 1976 which he had never liked very much. Visiting Pete Minor in his idyllic mountain retreat, I would say he gives the impression that he is holding up even better than his Cabernets.

SKY VINEYARDS 1973

A: 1500 Lokoya Road, Napa, CA 94558
T: (707) 935 1391 **V**: By appointment
P: 1,500 **W**: Lore Olds

ABOVE ~ *Beautiful glades and creek beds abound on Spring Mountain.*

For reasons which are too complicated to explain, and which at the end of the day do not matter, I did not get to visit Sky Vineyards, but I did get to taste seven vintages of its only wine (Zinfandel) in 1992. And what a range of wines they are: only Storybook Mountain and Ridge could possibly challenge Sky for ability to age with grace. The 1975 was alive and vibrant with spicy, cigar-box notes; the 1981 had the color of a two- or three-year-old wine with concentrated, youthful fruit and aromas and tastes of dark chocolate; the 1982 slightly riper and more berry flavored, but again with that touch of chocolate; the 1985 being in relative terms the least of the line-up, but still fresh and crisp on the palate; the 1984 with exceptional freshness, crispness and elegance still; while the 1990 took me back to the 1975, with a strong, spicy aroma touched with cigar box leading on to a palate with an exotic combination of sweet cherry fruit, cinnamon and pepper. All in all, an outstanding demonstration of the capacity of selected Zinfandel to age magnificently, although I must for the record say that my highest points went to the 1990.

STONY HILL VINEYARD 1953

A: off Bale Grist Mill State Park Road (P.O. Box 308, St. Helena, CA 94574)
T: (707) 963 2636 **V**: By appointment
P: 4,000 **W**: Mike Chelini

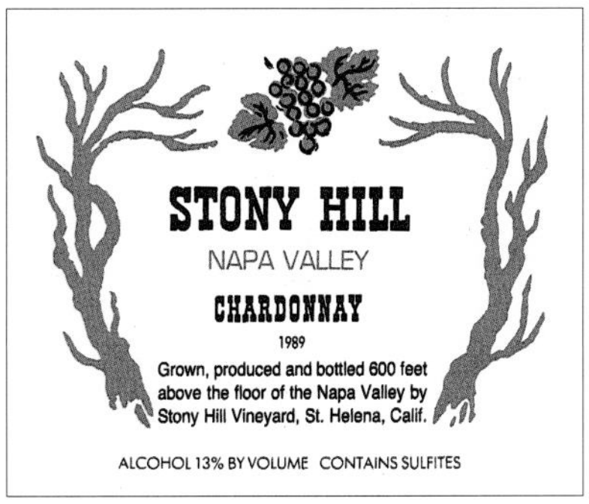
STONY HILL
NAPA VALLEY
CHARDONNAY
1989
Grown, produced and bottled 600 feet above the floor of the Napa Valley by Stony Hill Vineyard, St. Helena, Calif.
ALCOHOL 13% BY VOLUME CONTAINS SULFITES

Way back in 1943 Fred and Eleanor McCrea purchased a small estate on the lower slopes of Spring Mountain as a weekend and vacation retreat. They did so without any intention of planting vines, but as they became frequent visitors from their native San Francisco, their interest in wine grew, and in 1946 — purely on a hunch — they planted the then almost unheard of Chardonnay, including a few vines of Riesling and Pinot Blanc as insurance, and later adding Gewurztraminer and Semillon. They undertook winemaking courses at U.C. Davis, and learnt all they could from local winemakers, most notably Lee Stewart, who encouraged them to take the step from grape growing to winemaking.

The vineyard site is a rugged one — not for nothing did the McCreas name it "Stony Hill" — and the Wente clone of Chardonnay has always been noted for its quality rather than its quantity. The combination of soil, clone and a strictly non-interventionist winemaking approach by Fred McCrea resulted in tiny quantities of infinitely slow-maturing Chardonnay, which over the ensuing decades has gained for itself the reputation as one of California's greatest. In 1992 Darrell Corti served me a bottle of the 1965, enabling me to see for myself just why Stony Hill has the reputation it does. The wine showed absolutely no sign of decay, and as it sat in the glass throughout an evening punctuated with ten other wines of equal fame and in some cases even greater age, continued to develop, showing exquisite acidity and length to the flavor. One of the post-dinner curios was a 1976 Stony Hill Semillon de Soleil, made using the Vin de Paille technique — cutting the grapes and allowing them to dry in the sun, emphasizing that right throughout its fame as a Chardonnay producer, Stony Hill has continued to produce a surprising range of wines including Riesling, Gewurztraminer and Semillon.

First Fred and then Eleanor McCrea passed away, but Mike Chelini (appointed in 1974) continues to make the wine, and son Peter and wife Michelle McCrea continue to run the vineyard in much the same way as ever. However, Pierce's Disease, which is endemic on Spring Mountain, has taken its toll. Ironically, phylloxera has not, because the vines were all planted on St. George rootstock. But yields have declined, and the McCreas are being forced to replant vine by vine, simply because it would be impossible to rebuild the 1946 terraces.

During the ongoing replanting, Stony Hill has purchased Chardonnay from Howell Mountain, initially bottling it separately under the SHV label, but now incorporating it with the standard Stony Hill Chardonnay. Most observers feel that this has led to a change in style, and in particular to the wines becoming more accessible and fruity during their early years. Chelini keeps the McCrea candle alight by using few of today's winemaking tricks: there is no malolactic fermentation, new oak plays only a small part in shaping the wine, and only 70% is barrel fermented. If one were to taste the 1989 or 1990 vintages blind, I am fairly certain they would achieve very modest scores. But then that would be like judging a thoroughbred racehorse on the evidence of one training gallop around the track without knowing anything of its bloodlines.

PHILIP TOGNI VINEYARD 1985

A: 3780 Spring Mountain Road, St. Helena, CA 94574 **T**: (707) 963 3731
V: By appointment **P**: 2,500
W: Philip Togni

Notwithstanding 35 years in California, it is impossible to think that Philip Togni's manner or accent was any different 40 years ago as a member of the British army, in which he served briefly before studying geology at Imperial College, London, and journeying to Peru and Colombia for Shell to look successfully for oil. A period of leave in Spain introduced him to yet another world: that of wine. Patricio Gonzales advised him to talk to Maynard Amerine, then on sabbatical in Madrid, and Amerine told him to study either at U.C. Davis, Geisenheim, or Montpellier. The latter was closest, and Togni duly spent a year there before taking his new-found skills to Chile. He spoke Spanish, and felt that Chile had great potential, but found the feudalism all too much. From there he went to Algeria, only to be caught up in the civil war, being forced to flee to Bordeaux where he worked at Chateau Lascombes and took a degree in enology at the University of Bordeaux under Emile Peynaud. From thence he moved to Mayacamas, then Chalone and then (surely the most unpredictable move in a most unpredictable career) two years working for E. & J. Gallo in charge of varietal studies. Next came Chappellet and then Cuvaison before finally forging the chains which now bind him to the soil high on Spring Mountain. Here he makes Cabernet Sauvignon, Sauvignon Blanc, and a most curious wine called Ca'Togni made from Black Muscat of Alexandria in the same way that he believes the great South African sweet wine Constantia was fashioned in the eighteenth century.

Togni does not flinch from the consequences of growing mountain grapes, and is happy to be grouped with makers such as Mayacamas and Dunn. Not surprisingly, the massively flavored wines find great favor with critics such as Robert Parker, but I have to be honest and say that I find them altogether too much. On the other hand, Togni makes an excellent Sauvignon Blanc, full of all the bite and intensity one expects from the best Sancerre. And having just doubled the size of his winery in 1992, I would be most surprised if Philip Togni has not found his final resting place.

OTHER WINERIES

ARTISAN
A: 5335 Redwood Road, Napa, CA 94558
T: (707) 252 6666 **W**: Michael Fallow

CHATEAU CHEVALIER 1891
A: 3101 Spring Mountain Road, St. Helena, CA 94574 **T**: (707) 963 2342 **W**: Dirk Hampson

ROBERT KEENAN 1977
A: 3660 Spring Mountain Road, St. Helena, CA 94574 **T**: (707) 963 9177 **W**: Matt Cookson

MARSTON 1982
A: 3600 White Sulphur Springs Road, St. Helena, CA 94574 **T**: (707) 963 3069
W: Michael Marston

SMITH-MADRONE 1977
A: 4022 Spring Mountain Road, St. Helena, CA 94574 **T**: (707) 963 2283 **W**: Charles Smith

YVERDON 1970
A: 3787 Spring Mountain Road, St. Helena, CA 94574 **T**: (707) 963 4270 **W**: Fred J. Aves

YOUNTVILLE

Yountville takes its name from George Yount, who had the distinction of planting the first grapes in the Napa Valley at what was then called Caymus Rancho. George Pinney in *A History of Wine in America* records that Yount obtained his cuttings from General Vallejo in Sonoma, "A fact that will give pleasure to the partisans of Sonoma in the rivalry between California's two best known wine valleys."

It is the first wine region you will encounter as you enter the Napa Valley along Highway 29 from Vallejo. Only if you have a particularly observant eye will you have noticed the new vineyards planted to the east of the highway on some low rolling hills north of American Canyon Road (and well south of the city of Napa). And only if you are particularly well informed will you have detoured to the east of Napa city to visit the emerging Coombsville area, where you will find wineries such as Revere, Tulocay, Star Hill and Whitford Cellars, and which supplies Pahlmeyer (and Dunn) with outstanding Cabernet Sauvignon from the Caldwell Vineyard.

Coombsville is a hilly area, with the suburbs of Napa city reaching like fingers into the scattered vineyards. It reflects the uneasy balance of power between the pro-development southern extremity of the county and the anti-development center and north, although it is Yountville (rather than Napa city) which marks the invisible dividing line between the two camps and does so in an appropriately understated fashion.

For there really isn't much to see at this point. Certainly the mountains on either side of the valley stretch out in front of you, but the land is flat, the valley is at its widest, and landmarks few and far between. Domaine Chandon is discreetly hidden on the west side of the highway; the sign to the Yountville Veterans Home is far larger than that for Domaine Chandon. The town of Yountville — such as it is — is out of sight on the eastern side, while the other really large winery (Trefethen) is set a long way back from the highway amidst its sea of vines. The first landmark is Mustards Bar and Grill, that now legendary but ever popular restaurant, and immediately north of it the first winery you actually see — Cosentino, but situated on the wrong side of the road, as it were. For all that, you have indeed arrived in the Napa Valley.

ABOVE ~ *Roadside letterboxes near Trefethen, an everyday sight for Californians, but strange for visitors from overseas.*

OPPOSITE ~ *Vineyard off Yount Hill Road, which runs between Highway 128 and the Silverado Trail.*

THE REGION IN BRIEF

Climate, Soil and Viticulture

CLIMATE

This is by far the coolest part of the valley floor, most profoundly influenced by the night and morning fogs, and the afternoon sea breezes which come in from San Pablo Bay. The toes of the Mayacamas Range to the west do protect it from the howling winds which sweep across Carneros, and it has often been called "the point where the winds meet." Detailed weather data collected at Trefethen over 22 years shows a heat summation ranging from low Region I (2,150 degree days in 1975) to low Region III (3,233 degree days in 1985), with a 22-year average of 2,817 degree days, which is mid Region II. The rainfall has oscillated no less wildly, from 12.97 inches in 1976 to 60 inches in 1983, with a 32.43 average. 1989, the so-called vintage from hell, had only 22.78 inches, which simply goes to show it doesn't matter as much how much rain you have as when it falls. The figures also underline how broad are the generalizations which have to be made in any description or discussion of climate in a book such as this.

SOIL

The valley floor soils are predominantly comprised of the fine, gravelly silt loam and loam soils of the Cole series. These are well drained and moderately fertile, encouraging vine growth throughout the season. Next are smaller areas of Pleasanton gravelly fans issuing from streams in the Mayacamas Range. The outstanding Newlan Vineyard is on one such fan; there is an abundance of gravel and washed round stones with some clay, and the bedrock is Great Valley Sandstones. Here vigor is well controlled, and high quality grapes produced. The third major soil type on the plain is the younger Yolo loam in the flood plain of the Napa River. With high moisture retention levels, and higher percentages of organic matter, these soils tend to promote excessive vine vigor, making canopy management and control all-important.

THE GROWING SEASON

With a sharply reduced incidence of frost (compared to the upper end of the valley) the relatively early budbreak means an equivalently long growing season, with harvest dates not dissimilar to those of Carneros for both Coombsville and the valley floor. Both Pinot Noir and Chardonnay are typically harvested during the first two weeks of September (but with mid August and end September extremes), while Cabernet Sauvignon ripens in the last two weeks of September at some sites, early October in others.

Contract Growers

Caldwell Vineyard Twenty-five acres planted 1980–81 to Cabernet Sauvignon, Cabernet Franc, Malbec, Merlot, Petit Verdot and Chardonnay on terraced hillsides in the Coombsville region, co-owned by and used by Jason Pahlmeyer; also sold to Dunn.

Decelles Vineyard Five acres of Chardonnay planted 1980 on Big Ranch Road, and sold to Tulocay.

Haynes Vineyard Forty acres on Coombsville Road planted in 1968 to Pinot Noir and Chardonnay. Star Hill, Tulocay, Whitford Cellars and Stag's Leap Wine Cellars are purchasers.

George Hendry Vineyard Eighty acres planted 1972–74 to Cabernet Sauvignon, Chardonnay, Pinot Noir and Zinfandel; on Redwood Road, five miles west of Napa. Rosenblum is a purchaser.

Herrick Vineyard Three hundred and fifty acres south of Yountville, which are planted to Cabernet Sauvignon, Merlot, Sauvignon Blanc and Semillon. Purchased by Inglenook, used in Gustav Niebaum Collection.

Mast Vineyard Nineteen acres of Cabernet Sauvignon planted 1975 on western side of Valley between Napa and Yountville, purchased by Inglenook for Gustav Niebaum Collection.

Napanook Vineyard Forty-one acres of Cabernet Sauvignon, most of it replanted within the past 20 years, due west of Yountville. Dominus is entirely sourced from the grapes; a little is sold to Inglenook, and some is made into a second label by Dominus.

State Lane Vineyard Twenty-five acres planted 1971 to Cabernet Sauvignon near Yountville; sold to Beringer.

Vine Hill Ranch One hundred and thirty-five acres planted 1978–91 to Cabernet Sauvignon, Chardonnay, Merlot and Sauvignon Blanc; purchasers include Duckhorn and Robert Pepi.

Principal Wine Styles

CABERNET SAUVIGNON

The wine has a Jekyll and Hyde role, with soil, canopy management and aspect playing lead roles in determining whether or not the variety achieves satisfactory flavor ripeness. Monticello, on Big Ranch Road, says flatly the area is too cool for the variety, sourcing its grapes from various parts of the valley further north. On the other hand, Napanook, situated on the Dry Creek alluvial fan on the western side of the valley, has long been one of the Napa Valley's most famous Cabernet vineyards, these days going to produce Dominus. Bruce Newlan, on the same fan, also ripens Cabernet Sauvignon without difficulty while recognizing that this is the southern limit for the variety from a climatic viewpoint. Signorello, too, has made a fragrant, stylish Cabernet Sauvignon which has no excess herbaceousness, capsicum or green-olive characters. Finally, Trefethen has shown that Cabernet Sauvignon from its Hillside Vineyard can ripen readily, and on occasions exceptionally early — the1986 vintage harvest commenced on August 21, while the even warmer 1987 produced a wine with lots of ripe cassis and blackcurrant fruit.

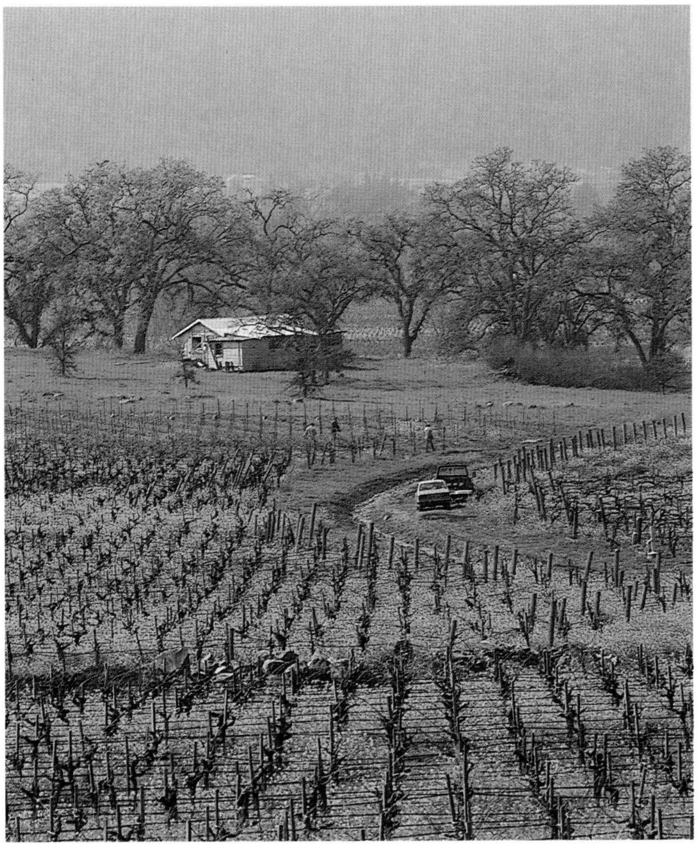

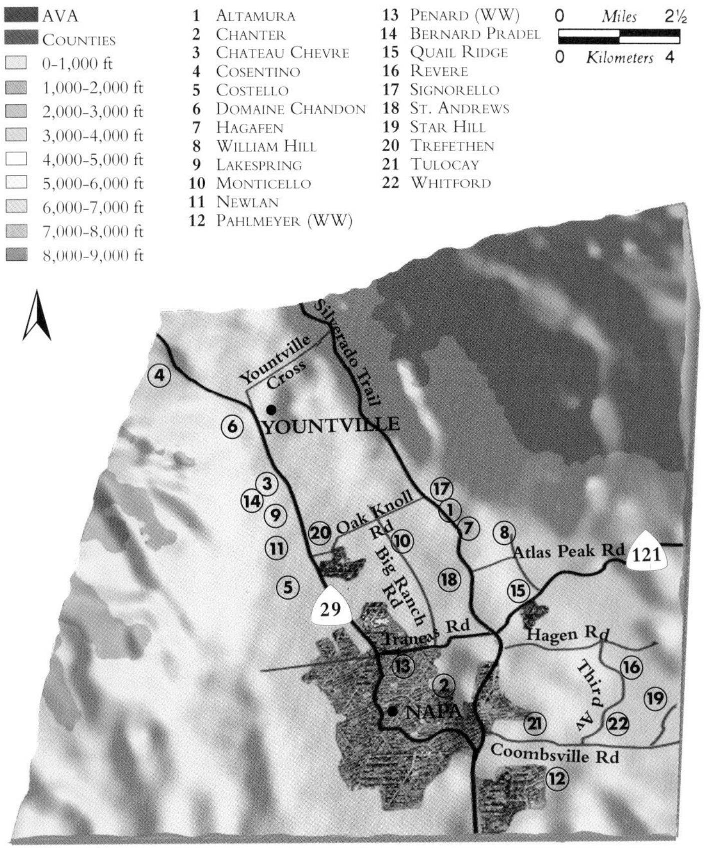
AVA
COUNTIES
0-1,000 ft
1,000-2,000 ft
2,000-3,000 ft
3,000-4,000 ft
4,000-5,000 ft
5,000-6,000 ft
6,000-7,000 ft
7,000-8,000 ft
8,000-9,000 ft
1 ALTAMURA
2 CHANTER
3 CHATEAU CHEVRE
4 COSENTINO
5 COSTELLO
6 DOMAINE CHANDON
7 HAGAFEN
8 WILLIAM HILL
9 LAKESPRING
10 MONTICELLO
11 NEWLAN
12 PAHLMEYER (WW)
13 PENARD (WW)
14 BERNARD PRADEL
15 QUAIL RIDGE
16 REVERE
17 SIGNORELLO
18 ST. ANDREWS
19 STAR HILL
20 TREFETHEN
21 TULOCAY
22 WHITFORD
0 Miles 2½
0 Kilometers 4
Yountville Cross
Silverado Trail
YOUNTVILLE
Oak Knoll Rd
Big Ranch Rd
Atlas Peak Rd
121
29
Trancas Rd
Hagen Rd
Third Av
NAPA
Coombsville Rd

CHARDONNAY

Logically, this is the end of the Napa Valley in which Chardonnay *should* be grown (and of course in Carneros). The cool climate produces wines which have finesse and length to the palate, but makers both within and without the Yountville/Coombsville area have shown it is also possible to create wine with textural richness and strength. Trefethen has long been a major producer, delivering deliberately understated wines; their Chardonnay plantings are in the middle of the Oak Knoll area, and clearly the Trefethen policy is to let the grapes (and time in bottle) do the work. At the other end of the style spectrum are Revere and Star Hill in Coombsville with highly idiosyncratic and complex wines. St. Andrews takes the mid-ground, producing barrel-fermented, lees-aged Chardonnays which still show their cool climate heritage in their graceful, lean lines.

PINOT NOIR

With the notable exception of Newlan, and the slightly eccentric Star Hill, little table wine of note has been made from this variety, much of the production going to sparkling wine. Overall, plantings are on the decline, and one assumes Trefethen will replace its substantial acreage with other varieties when the time comes.

SAUVIGNON BLANC

Like Pinot Noir, an underperformer, perhaps due in part to the American dislike for overly varietal, pungent, herbaceous styles — which is what one might expect to find from here. In fact the track record is inconsistent and spotty, but Frogs Leap is one well-known highly regarded producer to source its Sauvignon Blanc primarily from this region.

SPARKLING WINES

Domaine Chandon is, of course, the most important winery in the region, but the great majority of its grapes are grown in Carneros, and it is indeed in that chapter that California sparkling wine is examined in detail.

Yountville

VINTAGE CHART 1981-91

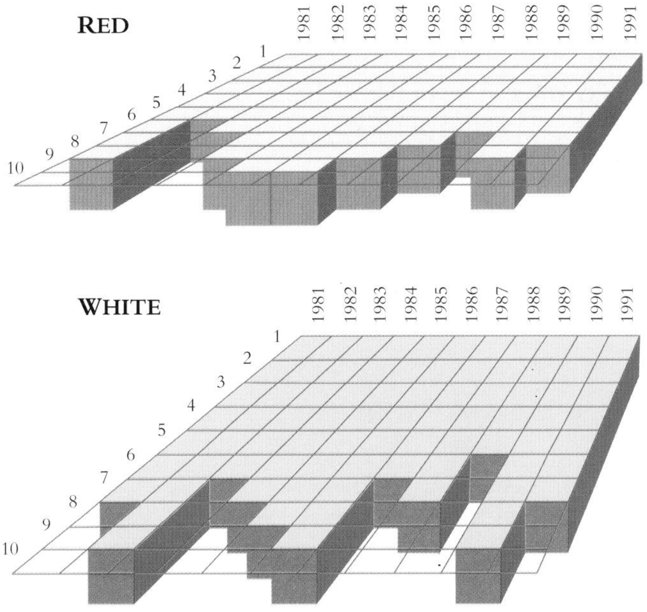
RED
1981
1982
1983
1984
1985
1986
1987
1988
1989
1990
1991
1 2 3 4 5 6 7 8 9 10
WHITE
1981
1982
1983
1984
1985
1986
1987
1988
1989
1990
1991
1 2 3 4 5 6 7 8 9 10

ABOVE ~ *View from Silverado Trail on a misty spring morning; as ever, vineyards create their own special beauty.*

ABOVE ~ *Yountville map.*

THE GREAT *TERROIR* DEBATE

What I term the great *terroir* debate first erupted between January and November 1983 in the columns of the English wine magazine *Decanter.* The chief protagonists were Bill Jekel (then owner of the Monterey vineyard and winery bearing his name) and Bruno Prats, owner of Chateau Cos-d'Estournel, the second-growth chateau in St. Estephe, Bordeaux.

ABOVE ~ *How long will it be before mechanical harvesters consign such sights to the history books?*

As I said on page 106, it is Prats who has given the most perfect definition of the word *terroir* one can imagine: "The very French notion of the *terroir* looks at all the natural conditions which influence the biology of the vinestock and thus the composition of the grape itself. The *terroir* is the coming together of the climate, the soil and the landscape. It is the combination of an infinite number of factors: temperatures by night and by day, rainfall distribution, hours of sunlight, soil acidity, presence of minerals, depth, water-retention, exposure to sunlight, slope and drainage, to name but a few. All these factors react with each other to form, in each part of the vineyard, what French wine growers call a *terroir.*"

Jekel was having none of this. "All too often, circular reasoning is used to explain the quality of wine, and its relation to the soil, as 'The wine from these soils is superior, hence these soils are superior ...' There is no component of any soil that has ever been demonstrated to contribute flavor to a wine, and there is no component in the soil of Bordeaux that does not exist in many other soils of the world."

On the latter point, he was (and is) correct; the distinguished Bordeaux soil scientist G. Seguin says, "As our knowledge stands at the moment, it is impossible to establish any correlation between the quality of wine and the soil content of any nutritive element, be it potassium, phosphorus or any other oligoelement. If there were such a correlation it would be easy, with the appropriate chemical additives, to produce great wine anywhere."

But when Jekel went on to suggest that "Declassification [of the 1855 division of the great Chateaux into growths] is a viable alternative that leaves the market place to adjust to the public perception of quality and value, without a system whose endorsement artificially inflates price," it is hard to believe he was serious.

Perhaps he sensed that the tide was turning against him, even in his native California. Professors Deborah Elliot-Fisk and Ann Noble have undertaken considerable research (which is on-going) which suggests there is an identifiable and repeatable link between the soils of the Napa Valley and the styles (and flavors) of the wines made from grapes grown on those soils. It must be said that as at 1992 the evidence for this proposition was far from compelling, but as methods of analysis of the sensory components of wine become ever more sophisticated, there is no logical limit to research of this kind. (Thus methoxypyrazines, which give Cabernet Sauvignon its distinctive taste, can be measured in levels of one part per trillion, equal to an ameba on the side of Mount Everest, or half-an-inch on the circumference of the earth.)

The Oregon-based author Matt Kramer is perhaps the most articulate terroirist. In his "Understanding" series of books, and most significantly in his most recent *Making Sense of California Wine,* he argues that all fine wines must exhibit a sense of place, a "feeling of somewhereness." It is when he dismisses a superbly made, flavorsome, perfectly balanced wine which nonetheless is not typical of its region that he starts to lose a percentage of his audience. Typicality, or *typicité,* as the French call it, is an admirable quality in the microscopic delineations of *terroir* found in the French appellations, but it is not the be-all and end-all. Should a Meursault be criticized because everyone picks it (blind) as a Le Montrachet?

Typicité, a sense of place, a feeling of somewhereness, also assume a certain static character which underpins grape growing and winemaking techniques. Does one argue that those Monterey Cabernet Sauvignons which have thrown off the excessively vegetal characters that so disfigured the first decade of production (thanks to improved canopy management and water-use practices) no longer have a sense of place? Or how does one deal with the hypothetical situation that Stony Hill or Hanzell should suddenly start using 100% barrel fermentation in new French oak, 100% malolactic and prolonged lees contact? The wines would be very different; some might prefer them more, others would vehemently disapprove. What I am prepared to wager is that the "sense of place" would disappear, simply because part of the existing sense of place in fact stems from the minimalist winemaking techniques employed.

Yet all of this said and done, I am in fundamental agreement with those who assert the importance of *terroir.* The problem is to determine how narrow or how wide one's perspective can (and should) be. Anyone who seeks to deny that Heitz Martha's Vineyard does not consistently and potently demonstrate a vivid sense of place should try their hand at music or concrete-laying — anything but wine. Likewise one cannot doubt Bruno Prats when he says:

> *It is easy to demonstrate that the terroir determines the quality of the wine. The best Bordeaux winemakers each work several chateaux. The same man, using the same varieties, the same equipment and the same procedures, will make at different places very different wines, and the same differences are found vintage after vintage.*

Within the same chateau, some plots give the best wine each year and have done so for more than 100 years. It is of course the terroir, and the terroir alone, which causes these differences.

To come back to California and to the Napa Valley, there is no question that the benchlands of Oakville and Rutherford would have been accorded first growth status had they been settled by French grape growers 500 years ago. Equally, the heavy, dark Yolo loams of the flood plain of the Napa River would have been consigned to the level of Crus Bourgeois and the Entre-Deux-Mers.

On an even smaller perspective, one of the silver linings to the phylloxera cloud has been the sudden opportunity (however forced and however costly) for grape growers with even relatively small vineyards to say, "This block is in fact better suited to Chardonnay than Cabernet, that block (100 yards away) is better suited to Cabernet than Chardonnay."

At the other end of the perspective scale, it has raised the question for many winemakers in the Napa Valley whether they should be growing Chardonnay at all. In terms of economics, the answer may be yes, but many have come to the conclusion that while it makes a perfectly adequate wine, their particular *terroir* will produce great Cabernet Sauvignon or great Merlot — not merely adequate. Earlier on, growers discovered the hard way that Pinot Noir was a perfectly miserable grape when planted in the wrong *terroir*, but Chardonnay is such an accommodating variety it papered over the cracks.

In all of this, it has to be remembered that to all intents and purposes the quality California wine industry as we know it today is barely 30 years old, and a real understanding of how and why vines grow (and how they should be manipulated) is still being acquired.

The challenge for California (and for all the New World) is to maximize the character and quality of the wine (or wines) of a given region without falling into the trap of stereotyping. The climate and absence of restrictive appellation laws present an abundance of choice: the right decisions will only be made if the character of the *terroir* is understood and respected.

ABOVE ~ *Looking west across Trefethen's plantings of Chardonnay towards Sugarloaf Range.*

WINERIES *of* YOUNTVILLE

COSENTINO WINERY 1982

A: 7415 St. Helena Highway, Yountville, CA 94599 **T**: (707) 944 1220 **V**: 10–5 daily **P**: 12,000 **W**: Mitch Cosentino

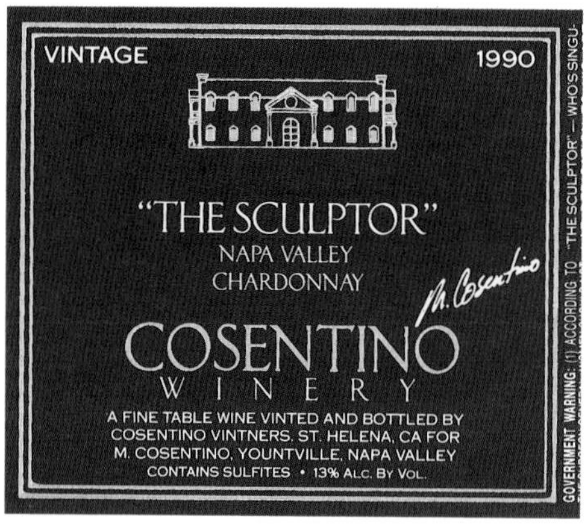
VINTAGE
1990
"THE SCULPTOR"
NAPA VALLEY
CHARDONNAY
COSENTINO
WINERY
A FINE TABLE WINE VINTED AND BOTTLED BY
COSENTINO VINTNERS, ST. HELENA, CA FOR
M. COSENTINO, YOUNTVILLE, NAPA VALLEY
CONTAINS SULFITES • 13% ALC. BY VOL.

They say that address is everything when it comes to selling real estate, and it is very nearly as important when it comes to selling wine. Cosentino may be on the wrong side of Highway 29, but it is the first winery you reach as you travel north (or the last as you travel homewards) and it is next to that epicurean magnet, Mustards. It is no coincidence, then, that former Central Valley wholesaler Mitch Cosentino found this tiny block upon which to erect his winery and plant four acres of grapes (Merlot) in 1990, having commenced winemaking a decade earlier in a rented corner of a Modesto warehouse. His initial wines were strictly Central Valley efforts, featuring such delicacies as Robin's Glow under the Crystal Valley Cellars label. But his first serious wine, a 1982 Reserve Cabernet Sauvignon, was a gold medal winner, and since that time Cosentino's wines have built up a formidable record of success in shows around the country and in critical reviews.

Cosentino concentrates on making wines in small batches (typically 1,000 to 1,500 case lots) and either giving them exotic brand names or pioneering varietals such as Cabernet Franc. Thus he offers The Sculptor, a Napa Valley Chardonnay so named because Cosentino sees it as a very precise and singular wine. Then there is The Poet, a Meritage blend named because it allows the free and fanciful use of ideas — thus the 1988 was a blend of Cabernet Sauvignon, Cabernet Franc and Merlot drawn from 13 different vineyards, aged in both French and American oak. Then there is Cos, a wine which incurred the legal wrath of Chateau Cos-d'Estournel, involving Cosentino in litigation running through 1992, a wine provocatively described as a special Paulliac (Bordeaux) style in the Cosentino newsletter. If all this is not enough there is The Zin (an unfined and unfiltered Sonoma County Zinfandel) and The Neb, a similarly treated Sonoma Valley Nebbiolo.

I tasted a wide range of the Cosentino wines and have to admit to a major sense of disappointment. Perhaps I was unlucky; for whatever reason I was unable to see the Cabernet Franc as the closest American wine to Chateau Cheval Blanc (Robert Parker's view) nor reconcile the Cabernet Franc with the 1986 vintage, which was the most awarded red wine in the United States of 1988, and so forth. At least Cosentino's location, friendly tasting room area and ready availability at the cellar door of a wide range of wines will allow you to make up your own mind.

DOMAINE CHANDON 1973

A: 1 California Drive, Yountville, CA 94599 **T**: (707) 944 8844 **V**: 11–6 daily May–Oct, 11–6 Wed–Sun Nov–Apr **P**: 450,000 **W**: Dawnine Dyer

RESERVE
NET CONTENTS
750 mL
ALCOHOL 12%
BY VOLUME
CHANDON
Réserve
PRODUCED AND
BOTTLED BY
DOMAINE
CHANDON
YOUNTVILLE, CA
NAPA VALLEY
SPARKLING WINE
METHODE
CHAMPENOISE

Domaine Chandon is one of the great and enduring institutions of the Napa Valley. It will be as much a landmark in the year 2077 as it was when completed in 1977, notwithstanding that it is one of the most self-effacing of all of the major wineries of the region, tucked into the gently folding hills behind the Yountville Veterans Home, invisible to passing traffic, and approached (for the last few hundred yards at least) by foot. It also symbolizes the long-term investment view shared by all of the great Champagne houses, and of the stability which that view engenders.

Curiously, it was conceived not by owners Moet et Chandon, but by management consultant John Wright, who persuaded employers Arthur D. Little that he should do an in-depth study of the investment opportunities in the Napa Valley in 1972. (Despite being a peripatetic would-be vigneron and unsuccessful home winemaker, Wright's business at that time was strictly that of management consultant, his tertiary qualifications a degree in chemistry.) Moet et Chandon read a summary of the three-volume report prepared by Wright, and within a year M. & H. Vineyards Inc was incorporated with John Wright as president — a position which he still retained 20 years later. Vice-president and winemaker Dawnine Dyer joined Domaine Chandon in 1976, and assumed her present position in 1981. She and John Wright have seen Domaine Chandon grow to the point where it is the largest Napa Valley producer of *methode champenoise* wines, reflecting the dominant position of its parent Moet et Chandon in Champagne.

Domaine Chandon has resolutely adhered to producing non-vintage wines, allowing the use of up to 30% of reserve wines from earlier vintages for the Brut, Cuvee and Blanc de Noir, and allowing a similar approach to the Chandon Reserve, which has the added complexity of prolonged aging on yeast lees before disgorgement. Indeed, one really wonders why the Reserve is not given vintage status: of the 11 Cuvees blended between 1975 and 1992, only four had been selected for the reserve program. But perhaps the ultimate in non-vintage blending comes in the form of Etoile, first released in 1992. This wine is a unique blend of wines made in 1984 and 1986: unique, not because of that particular blend, but because the blend was made after the wines were champagnized and after they had aged on lees in magnum. As at 1992 no other sparkling winemaker (Moet et Chandon itself included) had attempted, let alone achieved, such a blend. Along with the limited production Club Cuvee, disgorged after five years on yeast lees, Etoile shows just what can be achieved given the technology, the patience and the imagination of the winemaking team at Domaine Chandon.

The broad run of wines from the winery are solid, reliable and well priced. Since 1988 it has also been the owner of the Shadow Creek label, which passed through a number of hands before moving to Domaine Chandon, and utilizing grapes grown in the Mendocino, Sonoma, Santa Barbara and San Luis Obispo Counties. Once it fully settles into Domaine Chandon ownership, it should certainly produce a wine of distinctly different style, but with the same reliability and consistency of the wines of Domaine Chandon (reliability and consistency which its initial releases seemed to lack).

HAGAFEN CELLARS 1980

A: 4195 Silverado Trail, Napa, CA 94558
T: (707) 252 0781 **V**: By appointment
P: 3,000 **W**: Ernie Weir

The Hagafen wines are all made under the rules and direct supervision of an Orthodox Rabbinical Council, which means no work on holidays or the Sabbath and that all winemaking operations must be attended by a Mashgiach (a delegate of a Rabbi). Owner-winemaker Ernie Weir is Jewish, but non-orthodox, hence the requirement of the attendance of a Rabbi for up to 30 days each year to carry out key handling operations during the winemaking process. Despite all this, Hagafen's market is not aimed simply at Orthodox Jews, but seeks a broader base.

The offerings these days are a Chardonnay, a Chardonnay Reserve, a Pinot Noir Blanc and a non-vintage blended generic red. In earlier years, an Oak Knoll Cabernet Sauvignon, blended with estate Cabernet Franc, was particularly noteworthy. The wines are not exciting, but are certainly adequate, the much fruitier standard Chardonnay succeeding rather better than the clumsily oaked Reserve.

WILLIAM HILL WINERY 1976

A: 1761 Atlas Peak Road, Napa, CA 94558
T: (707) 224 4477 **V**: 10–5 daily **P**: 125,000
W: William H. Hill

William Hill has turned the development and sale of vineyards and wineries into a rarely encountered art form. It is also true to say that he has had a strong disposition to mountain vineyards, variously carving pieces out of Diamond Mountain, Mount Veeder and Atlas Peak. The only acceptable alternatives appear to have been cool climate regions, notably Carneros and, more recently, Oregon. In brief, the major vineyard developments he has commenced have been sold to Sterling Vineyards, The Hess Collection, and Atlas Peak Vineyards. However, he had retained control of his name until his 1990 decision to sell the large winery he had established on Atlas Peak Road (confusingly nothing to do with Atlas Peak Vineyards, which is on Soda Canyon Road) to the Wine Alliance, the wine division of Hiram Walker, which also owns Callaway and Clos du Bois. The William Hill range acquired by the Wine Alliance was a model of economy: a Reserve (or Gold Label) Chardonnay from estate-grown fruit and a Silver Label Chardonnay, part estate-grown and part from purchased grapes, with a matching pair of Cabernet Sauvignons. A Merlot and a Sauvignon Blanc-Semillon blend will be added to the range, most probably by the time of production of this book.

The Cabernet Sauvignon, in both the Reserve and standard guise, is an attractive wine with plenty of red berry fruit and vanillin oak; the Reserve has that extra dimension of structure and concentration, and needs more time in bottle. The Chardonnays are uniformly hard, thin and fruitless.

MONTICELLO CELLARS 1980

A: 4242 Big Ranch Road, Napa, CA 94558
T: (707) 253 2802 **V**: 10–4:30 daily
P: 25,000 **W**: Jim Kabacek

The casual visitor to Monticello Cellars might think they are in a time and place warp, which is exactly what founder and Jefferson-enthusiast Jay Corley intends, having built the hospitality center as an exact replica of Jefferson's Monticello home.

The vineyards were established in 1970, predominantly planted to Chardonnay and Pinot Noir. For a decade Corley was content to be a grape grower and seller, but the quality of the wines made from the grapes persuaded him that he should establish his own winery to vinify at least part of the crop. The original plan was for the Pinot Noir to be sold for sparkling winemaking, and for part of the Chardonnay to be vinified, but Cabernet Sauvignon (purchased from vineyards further up the valley in warmer sites, it being too cold for Cabernet Sauvignon on the Big Ranch Road site) snuck in the back door. As from 1990 it was joined by a Merlot, a wine which in 1991 had winemaker Jim Kabacek rubbing his hands with glee.

It is as well that the Cabernet got its start. Purchased from vineyards spanning Mount Veeder, Calistoga, Stags Leap and Rutherford, it produces two quite splendid wines: one called Corley Reserve, the other Jefferson Cuvee. I first tasted the 1987 Corley Reserve in a blind tasting of great Cabernets from around the world held in Australia in 1991, and was bowled over by its quality and by its elegance. It was no surprise, then, to find the 1989 Corley Reserve another wine of high caliber, although living up rather more to its reputation as a wine with pronounced oak, strong fruit, strong tannins and needing a long time in the cellar to give of its best. That it will do so I have every confidence. By contrast, the Pinot Noir was utterly unimpressive, the Corley Reserve Chardonnay dominated by cosmetic American oak, and an associated brand — Domaine Montreux — a slightly sweet but otherwise unmemorable sparkling Brut.

NEWLAN VINEYARDS AND WINERY 1981

A: 5225 St. Helena Highway, Napa, CA 94558 **T**: (707) 257 2399 **V**: By appointment
P: 6,000 **W**: Bruce Newlan

Former Lockheed Aerospace engineer Bruce Newlan explains his entry into the wine business this way: "As a home winemaker I was making so much Cabernet that I thought it would make sense to go professional." Together with partners, he purchased a block of land across the railroad track in a then thoroughly unfashionable area south of Yountville which had the redeeming feature of providing rocky, alluvial soil courtesy of the old flood plain of Dry Creek. Equally unfashionably, he planted it to Cabernet Sauvignon, defying conventional wisdom that it was too cool for the grape in that region. Four years later another 16-acre block was purchased adjacent to the original vineyard, and planted to Pinot Noir. The original partnership was dissolved in 1981, and Newlan Vineyards and Winery came into being. Three of Bruce and Jonette's sons have now joined the business, guaranteeing that Newlan will remain family owned and run for a long time to come.

Right from the outset his hunch that the alluvial fan soils, or benchland if you prefer, would produce high quality Cabernet Sauvignon was proved correct, and the grapes soon acquired a high reputation. Much the same applies to the Pinot Noir: Newlan has spent considerable time in evaluating Pinot Noir clones, following the same sort of track as Francis Mahoney at Carneros Creek, with whom he had many discussions. He eventually settled on five clones, but came to prefer one acquired through Joe Swan (allegedly sourced through Romanée Conti) above the others, and it is now the dominant (but not sole) clone. Etude and Robert Mondavi have been among the discriminating purchasers of Pinot Noir grapes excess to Newlan's production requirements.

Bruce Newlan is a quiet and unassuming man, and you have to piece together various bits of information to realize just how much he has thought about his viticulture and his winemaking. Happily, the rewards are there in the glass: the estate Pinot Noir (as in 1988) shows abundant flavor with strong, dark cherry fruit, while the Cabernet Sauvignon comprehensively gives lie to the idea that it will not ripen: chock-full of cassis, sweet berry fruit, if anything it strays to the overripe side. Newlan also makes a couple of fascinating oddities: between 700 and 1,000 cases annually of Century Selection, an old mixed-red Italian planting on Spring Mountain (Zinfandel, Petite Sirah, Carignane, Grand Noir and Alicante) and a minuscule quantity of Vieilles Vignes Pinot Noir from an ancient vineyard owned by John Gantner on Spring Mountain, the other half of which is sold by Gantner under his Schoolhouse label.

BERNARD PRADEL CELLARS 1984

A: 2100 Hoffman Lane, Napa, CA 94558
T: (707) 944 8720 **V**: By appointment
P: 2,500 **W**: Bernard Pradel

Bernard Pradel has family links with the wine trade in Chablis, but his first American venture was as a chef in Oregon. He is also something of an inventor, it seems, having patented a combined stainless steel and wooden barrel which, in times of a weak dollar and a strong

French franc, could have appeal to winemakers in both America and Australia. He has essentially taken a stainless steel drum and removed the steel ends, replacing them with oak header boards which can be reversed, reshaved, or replaced at will. With an indefinite lifespan and an initial cost no greater than a French barrel, and with shaving or reversing the wooden ends a near zero cost option, the barrel patent could prove a very valuable one.

In the meantime, Pradel makes Cabernet Sauvignon and a little Merlot in a primitive backyard winery, with much of the oak stored in a warehouse. The quality is variable: the 1987 Cabernet Sauvignon has various problems, showing both volatility and evidence of brettanomyces; the 1989 balanced fruit with attractive spicy characters; and the 1991 light and fragrant.

QUAIL RIDGE CELLARS AND VINEYARD 1978

A: 1055 Atlas Peak Road, Napa, CA 94558
T: (707) 257 1712 **V**: By appointment
P: 30,000 **W**: Elaine Wellesley

The Quail Ridge of today suffers from a case of extreme schizophrenia. It is nominally headquartered in the charming old stone building at Atlas Peak Road, and as a matter of courtesy as much as anything else, co-founder Elaine Wellesley continues as winemaker of record (with a degree from U.C. Davis and practical winemaking experience in Burgundy to her credit, it is true). She and her late husband had originally developed a ten-acre Chardonnay vineyard on Mount Veeder, specializing in the production of limited amounts of barrel-fermented estate Chardonnay, a Sonoma Chardonnay and a dry barrel-fermented French Colombard. But by 1988, and following various changes in direction, not to mention the death of Elaine Wellesley's husband, Quail Ridge was purchased by Christian Brothers and subsequently became part of the vast Heublein Fine Wine Group, where all winemaking now takes place. Chardonnay (17,000 cases), Sauvignon Blanc (5,000 cases), a Cabernet Sauvignon Meritage blend (5,000 cases) and a Merlot (3,000 cases) now constitute the range. All four wines are strictly conventional in character, all tending to show the plainer and more boring side of Napa Valley winemaking.

REVERE WINERY 1979

A: 2456 Third Avenue Napa, CA 94558
T: (707) 224 7620 **V**: By appointment
P: 1,000 **W**: John Kirlin

John Kirlin, a professor at the University of Southern California, and wife Anne, an attorney specializing in land use law, moved to their Coombsville property in 1979 with their two

C • H • A • R • D • O • N • N • A • Y
REVERE
CHARDONNAY
NAPA VALLEY 1988
ALCOHOL 13.5% BY VOLUME
PRODUCED AND BOTTLED BY REVERE WINERY
NAPA, CA 94558 CONTAINS SULFITES
R • E • V • E • R • E

daughters, building a singularly beautiful house, planting an 11-acre Chardonnay vineyard in five separate blocks, and building a small winery. John Kirlin's agricultural knowledge was gained while growing up on an Iowa farm, and his enological knowledge from a combination of extension courses at U.C. Davis, the Napa School of Cellaring, and the Napa Valley College, together with ten years of prior home winemaking experience.

Revere's 1988 Reserve Chardonnay was ranked by the *Wine Spectator* in its December 31, 1991 "Top 100 Wines of the Year" as the top-ranked Chardonnay tasted during the year, coming in 36th overall. Given 93 points, the *Spectator* commented, "It's a dead ringer for a Puligny-Montrachet." Earlier accolades included selection on two separate occasions among the Top Ten California Chardonnays by *Bon Appetit* magazine.

Well, on one issue I am in total accord. These wines show strong similarities to many French Burgundies I have tasted. Much as I wish I could say otherwise, they do not show strong similarities to the best French Burgundies I have tasted. Understanding the way the Revere Chardonnays are made, I am at a loss to understand why all this should be so, because while the winemaking techniques are — if you like — Burgundian, they are not excessively so. After pressing, the juice is allowed to settle in tank overnight, and it is then racked to a second tank where it is inoculated with cultured yeast. After fermentation has been initiated, the wine is then transferred to barrel, barrel fermented over a period of about 30 days, and then given lees contact. It is racked and bentonite-fined the following February, and then returned to barrel for further aging, with modest sulfur levels. Where the extreme, and to me bitter, French characters come from, I simply do not know.

SIGNORELLO VINEYARDS 1985

A: 4500 Silverado Trail, Napa, CA 94558
T: (415) 346 5515 **V**: By appointment
P: 3,500 **W**: Steve Devitt and Raymond Signorello Jr

The Signorello family, Raymond Sr. and Jr., have been highly visible and successful grape growers in the Oak Knoll area since the late 1970s. They have approximately 100 acres of vineyard, with only nine acres planted on AxR rootstock, which might either be described as good luck or good management. What is more, the varietal mix is a very interesting one; while dominated by Chardonnay with 25 acres, there are plantings of Viognier, Sauvignon Blanc, Semillon, Syrah, Cabernet Sauvignon, Merlot and Cabernet Franc, with two acres each of Zinfandel, Mourvedre, Nebbiolo and Sangiovese established in 1993.

Notwithstanding the erection of a new winery in 1992, and a 10,000 case permit, Signorello has no plans to alter its present arrangement which involves a sale of 80% of its grape production to Franciscan Vineyards. The remaining 20% goes to produce a limited range of Cabernet Sauvignon (until 1992 in fact made from purchased grapes), Pinot Noir, Semillon and Sauvignon Blanc. Of these, the Founders Reserve Cabernet Sauvignon stands out with its stylish, fragrant smooth red berry fruit flavors and neatly balanced tannins. A rare varietal Semillon also shows considerable character, although one would wish it had not spent 14 months on its lees in French oak, but something like half that time, for the oak really dominates the wine even if the honeyed, buttery texture and flavor are very seductive.

ST. ANDREWS VINEYARD 1980

A: 2921 Silverado Trail, Napa, CA 94558
T: (707) 252 6748 **V**: By appointment
P: 20,000 **W**: Daryl Eklund

St. Andrews, founded by Swiss-born Imre Vizkelety, but purchased by Clos du Val owner John Goelet in 1989, is a rare example of a California *monocru*. The 67-acre estate, at the extreme southern end of the Silverado Trail, originally planted in 1972 to a mixture of clones, is now planted exclusively to Chardonnay. Since its acquisition by Clos du Val it has ceased making Cabernet Sauvignon, the only

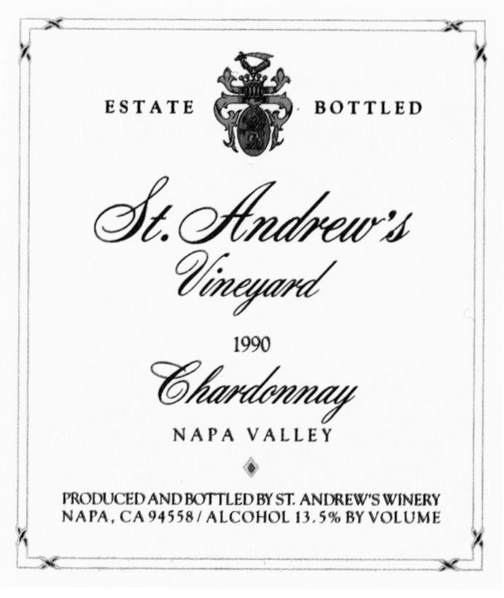
ESTATE BOTTLED
St. Andrew's
Vineyard
1990
Chardonnay
NAPA VALLEY
PRODUCED AND BOTTLED BY ST. ANDREW'S WINERY
NAPA, CA 94558 / ALCOHOL 13.5% BY VOLUME

variant to the Chardonnay being a limited quantity of Sauvignon Blanc made from purchased grapes and offering extraordinary value for money. Because of its extreme southerly location, it may well be that the *monocru* will change once replanting in the wake of phylloxera has been completed. Winemaker Daryl Eklund, with three years' experience at Trefethen and eight years at Conn Creek, is starting up a prototype Pinot Noir program, and has plans to plant a small amount of Pinot Noir — and strictly to limit the yield from those plantings.

In the meantime, the decision has been taken to produce a single wine: an estate-grown and bottled Chardonnay which offers fine value. The style is discreet and the fruit flavors restrained, perhaps reflecting the cool climate: one finds apple and citrus rather than peach, melon or apricot. As outstanding grape contracts (sale contracts, that is) run out, and the winery is expanded, production will peak at around 25,000 cases of estate wine, and with the added synergy of the Clos du Val production and marketing force, the accent should remain firmly fixed on value.

STAR HILL 1986

A: 1075 Shady Brook Lane, Napa, CA 94558
T: (707) 255 1957 **V**: By appointment
P: 2,000 **W**: Jacob Goldenberg

Jake Goldenberg is a specialist dentist by day in the city of Napa, and a winemaker by night and weekend (with some consulting help from outside). Just for good measure, he also runs the Pacific Star Winery way up north on the Mendocino coast.

Four acres of Chardonnay are planted adjacent to the winery in the Coombsville area, and are supplemented by grapes purchased from growers elsewhere in Coombsville and Carneros, although Jake Goldenberg is apt to make whatever takes his fancy, including such rarities as Charbono. He is also heavily into avant-garde winemaking techniques, reflected in the intense herbal/cassis/lantana 1991 Pinot Noir, using extended pre-fermentation maceration and wild yeasts, before being bottled unfined and unfiltered. The estate-grown Chardonnay, also barrel fermented, has considerable weight and individuality of style, while the Charbono has that typically soft, almost candy-like fruit which is extremely pleasant in flavor but is equally typically weak in structure.

TREFETHEN VINEYARDS 1973

A: 1160 Oak Knoll Avenue, Napa, CA 94558
T: (707) 255 7700 **V**: 10–4:30 daily
P: 80,000 **W**: David Whitehouse

The massive 1886 vintage wooden winery, built by Hamden McIntyre (who also built Greystone, Far Niente and Chateau Montelena)

Trefethen
VINEYARDS
ESTATE BOTTLED
NAPA VALLEY 1990
CHARDONNAY
ESTATE GROWN, PRODUCED & BOTTLED BY
TREFETHEN VINEYARDS NAPA, CA U.S.A.
ALCOHOL 13% BY VOLUME

is in proportion to the equally massive 600-acre vineyards which surround it at the southern end of the Napa Valley. It was purchased in 1968 by former Kaiser Industries president Gene Trefethen and wife Katie, and it is these days run by son John and daughter-in-law Janet Trefethen. The winery, which remained continuously in use, has been immaculately restored and is one of the Napa Valley landmarks. Only part of the massive estate production is vinified, the remainder being sold to other winemakers.

Chardonnay is the mainstay of the production, the ultimate exercise in enological minimalism. It is entirely fermented in stainless steel; no malolactic fermentation is used; no lees contact is used, and only half the wine is put into oak, virtually none of which is new, and which has only six months to impart any impact on flavor and texture before the wine is bottled in July of the year following vintage. There is no question that there is a place for such wines, and equally no doubt that a style such as this usually benefits from bottle age. It is this which leads the Trefethens to hold back a percentage of each vintage for release seven or eight years later as a library selection: thus the 1985 was on sale in 1992. It was not a bad wine, but age had certainly not transformed a sow's ear into a silk purse. There was some gentle bottle-developed aroma, a touch of honeyed fruit on the aroma, some vague camphor notes on the palate, but my tasting note read "from a varietal viewpoint, necrophilia." The then current 1990 release was firm, crisp with green mint characters and a rather hard finish, which is more or less what one should expect from cool grown, simply vinified Chardonnay — almost a cross between a dry Riesling and Chardonnay in terms of its structure.

By contrast, the 1987 Cabernet Sauvignon had surprisingly ripe fruit flavors with tastes and aromas of cassis, blackcurrant and spice, an unexpected role reversal. A White Riesling (most unattractive) and two proprietary blends, Eshcol White and Eshcol Red, make up the portfolio.

TULOCAY WINERY 1975

A: 1426 Coombsville, Napa, CA 94558
T: (707) 255 4064 **V**: By appointment
P: 2,000 **W**: Bill Cadman

Bill Cadman, in his own words, used to be "a chalky at the Stock Exchange" before deciding on a less stressful lifestyle and purchasing a house in the Coombsville area, where he constructed a small winery. He learnt his winemaking the practical way, working in the cellars of Charles Krug, Heitz, Carneros Creek and Clos du Val, before joining Robert Mondavi Winery where he conducts winery tours.

He makes Chardonnay, Pinot Noir and Cabernet Sauvignon purchased from a variety of vineyards basically situated at the southern end of the Napa Valley, the Pinot Noir from a Coombsville vineyard owned by Duncan and Pat Haynes (who also make and sell their own wine under the Whitford Cellars label). Bill Cadman is a delightful, gentle person, but desperately needs technical or consulting help in cleaning up his wines before they go into bottle.

OTHER WINERIES

ALTAMURA 1985
A: 4240 Silverado Trail, Napa, CA 94558
T: (707) 253 2000 **W**: Frank C. Altamura

CHANTER WINERY 1984
A: 2411 Third Avenue, Napa, CA 94558
T: (707) 252 7362 **W**: Bob Rogers

CHATEAU CHEVRE 1979
A: 2030 Hoffman Lane, Yountville, CA 94599
T: (707) 944 2184 **W**: G. P. Hazen

COSTELLO VINEYARDS
A: P.O. Box 2996, Napa, CA 94558
T: (707) 252 8483 **W**: John and Mieke Costello

LAKESPRING WINERY 1980
A: 2055 Hoffman Lane, Napa, CA 94558
T: (707) 944 2475 **W**: Randy W. C. Mason

PLAM VINEYARDS & WINERY 1984
A: 6200 Washington St, Yountville, CA 94559
T: (707) 944 1102 **W**: Nikolaus Koengeter

SILVERADO HILL CELLARS 1979
A: 3103 Silverado Trail, Napa, CA 94558
T: (707) 253 9306 **W**: Dr John D Nemeth

WHITFORD CELLARS 1983
A: 4047 E Third Avenue, Napa, CA 94558
T: (707) 257 7065 **W**: Duncan Haynes

ABOVE ~ *The remarkable wooden winery of Trefethen built by Hamden McIntyre in 1886.*

SONOMA COUNTY

Talking to the vignerons of Sonoma County leaves one in no doubt that they genuinely believe they are the custodians of a viticultural Garden of Eden. There is no question they prefer to be where they are and, specifically, do not wish to be in the Napa Valley. The cynical will no doubt think this is just sour grapes, but I am not so sure. Indeed, their conviction that Sonoma is the finest place on God's earth in which to grow grapes and make wine is as absolute as that of the most parochial Burgundians, Bordelaise or Champenoise.

Manifestly, they are proud of the history of viticulture in the Sonoma Valley, which predates that of the Napa Valley, and began with the Sonoma Mission, which was secularized by General M.G. Vallejo in 1835. It must be said that Thomas Pinney in *A History of Wine in America* puts the scope of this particular enterprise into perspective by recording that in 1841 the vineyard comprised 300 square feet, yielding 450 gallons of wine.

If this was a modest start, that of Agoston Haraszthy was not. He founded Buena Vista on 560 acres of land in 1856, and as well as establishing 300 acres of vineyards of his own, planted extensively for other landowners including Gundlach Bundschu and Krug. By the beginning of the 1860s he claimed to have the largest vineyard in the state, sometimes (with a typical Hungarian touch of exaggeration) describing it as the largest in the world.

This make-believe count-colonel (he was neither) was a man of prodigious energy who achieved much for the California wine industry, but when he left Sonoma in 1866 under extreme financial pressure, the early momentum of the Sonoma Valley faltered, and it was to be the Napa Valley which became (and remains) the symbol of quality California wine.

The flip side of the coin is that Sonoma County has by and large remained free of the development pressures which have so benighted the Napa Valley. Given that Sonoma County is twice as large as Napa County, this is not altogether surprising. Mind you, those living or seeking to live in Santa Rosa or anywhere adjacent to Highway 101 may have a different view of things, but this really has to be seen as the exception which proves the rule.

This absence of pressure is one of the factors which so pleases the average Sonoman. The Mayacamas Mountains may provide a physical barrier between the two valleys, but there is an equally impenetrable mental barrier. Thus it must secretly irk the Sonoma vigneron to be reminded that the southern end of the Napa Valley is climatically very similar to that of southern Sonoma (and I am not just thinking of Carneros, which spans the two regions).

Likewise, as one travels north (though not west) one moves into steadily warmer regions. At this point Sonoma County, however, starts exerting its own diverse personality. While Napa County has the Coombsville, Wild Horse, Chiles and Pope Valleys — not to mention the East and West Mountains — it does not provide such a range of *terroir,* climate and viticultural alternatives that Sonoma does. The future of the Napa Valley is already largely determined and circumscribed. That of Sonoma is as unlimited as it is exciting.

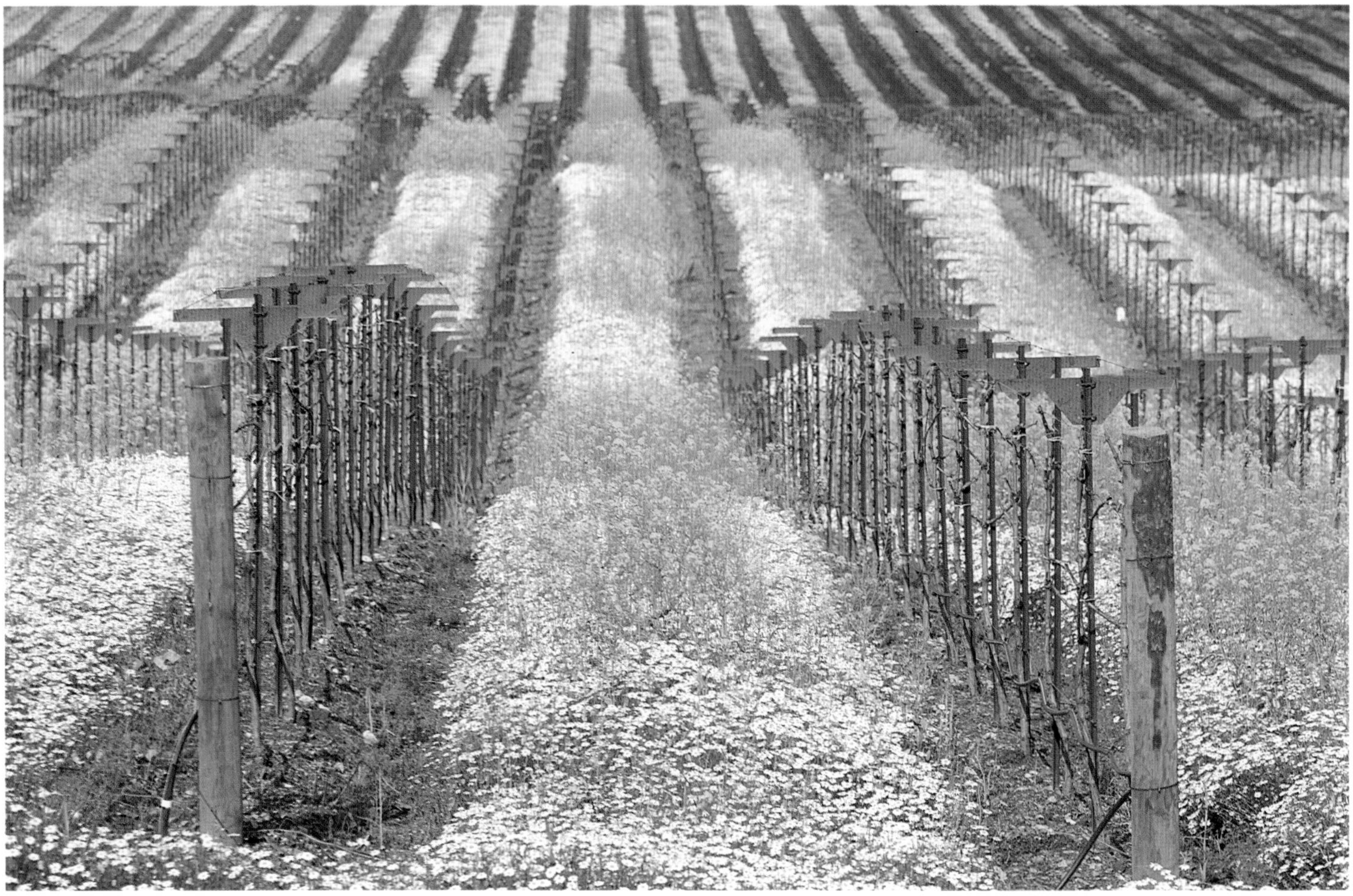

PREVIOUS PAGE ~ *The Rites of Spring in the Chalk Hill region of Sonoma Valley.*

ABOVE ~ *Vineyard architecture and spring flowers in the Alexander Valley create a picture of rare beauty.*

ABOVE ~ *Ground fumigation under massive polythene sheets prior to planting may soon be banned.*

GALLO

Anyone wishing to gain a glimpse of the future of Sonoma needed only to drive up Highway 101 to Asti at any time during 1992. Immediately adjacent to the western side of the highway was a scene straight from a science fiction blockbuster. Dozens upon dozens of vast pieces of earthmoving equipment were literally moving mountains, turning steep hills into gentle slopes, filling in valleys and gullies, creating giant-sized plough patterns, and encasing the newly formed slopes in billowing plastic. Unless one knew better, one might think it was the work of a crazy Japanese developer seeking to build the biggest golf course in the world, with Christo playing the opening round.

ABOVE ~ *Shovelling pomace is still part of the routine, even at the high-tech Gallo Sonoma winery.*

In fact it was the Gallo brothers at play, using the knowledge gained during a smaller scale development at the Frei Vineyard in Dry Creek, and the equipment they purchased *en bloc* when the Alaskan Pipe Laying Authority had finished its work. You scrape off thousands of tons of topsoil, push the mountain tops into the gullies, replace the topsoil, and mulch it into the subsoil, thereby creating an environment in which mountainside vines will grow evenly and predictably.

For Gallo, the largest wine company in the world, sees its future as lying in Sonoma, however much its past may remain rooted in the Central Valley. The size of those roots are prodigious. Gallo sells $1 billion of wine a year, with sales of around 70 million cases. It has 2,000 employees, with 500 at the Modesto headquarters. Here a 45-acre air-conditioned warehouse can and does accommodate an entire train; a glass works produces hundreds of millions of bottles annually, the furnaces glowing 365 days a year; it makes its own caps and closures (and sells to others); at any one time there will be 12 million cases of fully packaged wine on hand; the laboratories carry out analysis and research on a scale unimaginable anywhere but Gallo; and yet not a drop of wine is made at Modesto (most is made at a huge processing plant some miles away at Livingstone, although the seven million gallon Dry Creek plant is vast by any normal standard, and the fortified wine facility at Fresno likewise).

In this perspective the 2,000 acres of Sonoma Valley vineyards owned by Gallo pale into statistical insignificance, as they are capable of producing little more than 1% of the company's annual output. But they are of tremendous symbolic importance.

For a start, Gallo does not own any vineyards in Napa or Mendocino Counties, and so far as one can tell, does not plan to do so. Divining Gallo's intentions is never easy: Ernest Gallo gave his first ever in-depth press interview in 1991, aged 82 and in his 58th year at the helm of Gallo, while the group's official public relations spokesperson is the affable Dan "No Comment" Solomon. Having visited the Modesto headquarters (and been driven around and through it in a minibus) I can vouch for the fact that there are no signs pointing the way to it or telling you that you have indeed arrived.

But E. & J. Gallo has not grown from a standing start in 1933 to where it is today without being one jump ahead of the competition, without being sensitive to those winds of change which it has not created itself. Gallo was the catalyst in the move away from generics (such as its famous hearty Burgundy) in the mass market, offering growers all manner of inducements to change from the second-class grapes (Mission, Flame Tokay, Carignane and Thompsons Seedless) which dominated the industry until the end of the 1960s.

It introduced its varietal wines in 1974, featuring Peter Ustinov in nationwide television. (Gallo may not be particularly communicative in its dealings with the press, but its annual advertising budget is as awesome as Ernest Gallo's ruthless handling of the passing parade of advertising agencies which have held the account.) It boasts that it has not used Thompsons Seedless in any of its table wines since 1972/3, and that at one time 40% of all the grapes grown in Sonoma and 20% of all those grown in Napa went to Gallo.

There are those who sneer at Gallo's claim to be the leader in the premium varietal cork-finished wine market, suggesting that this is a gross distortion of the word premium. But the fact is that it is the leader, and that notwithstanding the extraordinary growth of Glen Ellen, Kendall-Jackson, Fetzer, Sutter Home and Mondavi Woodbridge in the 1980s, it will remain the leader.

And here, once again, we come back to its Sonoma County vineyards. These run from the 360-acre Laguna Ranch vineyard in the Russian River Valley (planted exclusively to Chardonnay), the Frei Ranch (625 acres) and Canyon Creek Vineyards (200 acres) in the Dry Creek Valley (planted to Cabernet Sauvignon, Chardonnay, Zinfandel, Merlot and Cabernet Franc), thence to the Alexander Valley vineyards of Lyeth (100 acres), Chiotti (100 acres) and Asti (600 acres).

The last two are still in the course of development, with plantings which commenced in 1991, continuing through 1992, and into at least 1993. While the primary focus remains on the same varieties as those in the Dry Creek vineyards, there is experimentation (on the typical Gallo scale) with Italian and Rhone varieties at Asti — particularly appropriate, given the historical links with the Italian-Swiss colony.

Without fanfare, but once again pointing to the future, Gallo has been farming its Sonoma vineyards using integrated pest management techniques for over five years. The aim has been to reduce as many chemical inputs as possible, practicing what is best described as sustainable viticulture (but which is often called organic viticulture). Deodorant soap bars hung around the periphery of the vineyards to repel deer, predatory mites to control red spider mites, biodegradable wood pulp road surfaces, soap sprays to kill leaf hopper nymphs, and allelopathic cover crops (plants with natural weed suppression abilities) are among the many tools being evaluated by Gallo viticulturists.

It is sharing the results of these trials freely with all of its contract growers, and actively encouraging them to move to sustainable viticulture. Other major companies are doing the same thing, of course, but receive considerably more publicity for so doing. At the same time Gallo is experimenting with as much enthusiasm as Fetzer, Mondavi or any other major quality winemaker with planting densities, canopy management, rootstock trials (16 different trials underway in 1991), and clonal trials (14 Chardonnay and nine Cabernet Sauvignon clones). During 1991, more than 150 experimental wines from these trials were made in the research-oriented micro-winery established at Modesto — in 1947!

It is at the Frei Ranch that Gallo plans to build its answer to Opus One, a 10,000 case-winery purpose-built to make the $30 Chardonnay and $60 Cabernet Sauvignon which Ernest Gallo unveiled in his September 1991 interview, and which represent the last mountain for E. & J. Gallo to climb. By the end of 1992 those wines were still to actually make an appearance; when they will do so was simply not known, but they will sooner or later.

Likewise, an oak and madrone covered knoll on a hillside above the Frei Ranch has been selected as the site for the first-ever visitors' center for Gallo. It is not planned to open it to the public, but it will be used for trade and media entertainment. And the intrepid will make their way up a steep mountain behind to the platform — rather like an inland jetty — which commands an eagle's view of the Frei Ranch and a sizeable chunk of the Dry Creek Valley behind it. Of one thing you may be sure: if Gallo decides to put itself on display, there will be no half measures.

TOP SEVEN CALIFORNIA WINERIES
1991 Production in Gallons

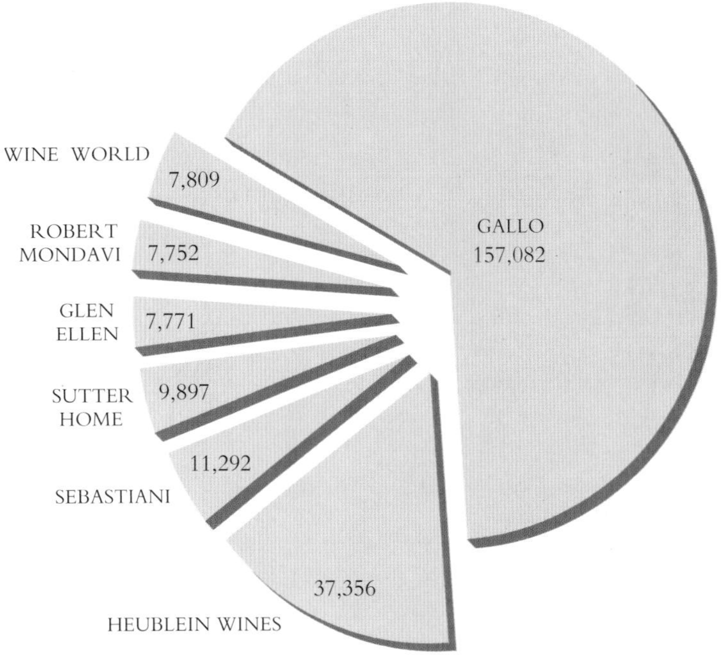
WINE WORLD
7,809
ROBERT MONDAVI
7,752
GLEN ELLEN
7,771
SUTTER HOME
9,897
11,292
SEBASTIANI
37,356
HEUBLEIN WINES
GALLO
157,082

ABOVE ~ *Gallo fundamentally alters the shape of the landscape as it creates new vineyards.*

ALEXANDER VALLEY

If Cyrus Alexander, the Rocky Mountains fur-trapper who arrived in Healdsburg in 1840 to manage the vast Sotoyme land grant for San Diego magnate Captain Henry Fitch, were to revisit the Alexander Valley of today, he would have no difficulty recognizing it. The air is as clean, the Russian River very nearly so, the soils as rich and fertile, and the skies as open and blue as they were 150 years ago. If you *really* want to escape to the country, the Alexander Valley is the place to go.

For while there was substantial development within the region following 1959, when Russell Green (a Los Angeles oilman) planted his first 50 acres of grapes, that development seems to have been swallowed up by the 50,000 acres of valley floor and mountainsides which since 1990 have been officially included within the Alexander Valley AVA. Russell Green, incidentally, subsequently purchased Simi Winery, the region's only surviving winery from the nineteenth century, owning it briefly during the mid 1970s.

The valley floor now has a number of big name wineries to keep Simi company: Chateau Souverain, Clos du Bois, Geyser Peak and Jordan, with Alexander Valley Vineyards and Gauer Estate also adding weight to the identity of the region. But for all that, a not-inconsiderable part of the production from the 6,500 acres of vineyard goes to wineries in other parts of Sonoma and further afield.

The list of independent contract growers is awesome, attesting to the ease with which everything (and certainly vines) grows in this modern day Garden of Eden. Indeed, its serpent has been excessive vigor: while the yields have been generous (often too generous), vine canopies were positively gargantuan. The on-going change in emphasis from Chardonnay to Cabernet Sauvignon — and the concomitant increase in wine quality — has come in the wake of the adoption of modern viticultural techniques, with Simi Winery one of the leading innovators. Even if many vineyards still need to be retrellised (in the wake of phylloxera), leaf pulling and shoot thinning are now orthodox practice, yet unheard of a decade ago and a novelty five years ago.

Thus the initial reputation of Alexander Valley Cabernet Sauvignon was for thin, vegetal wines, notwithstanding the warm climate. The reason was the excessive uncontrolled vigor (and hence shading of the grapes). The radical improvement in viticultural techniques has led to Cabernet Sauvignon taking its rightful place, and has lifted grape and wine quality across the board.

ABOVE ~ *Viruses cause the vine's leaves to turn red, making opportunities for photographers but inhibiting photosynthesis.*

OPPOSITE ~ *Iron T-trellises undulate across the ground like giant caterpillars.*

THE REGION IN BRIEF

Climate, Soil and Viticulture

CLIMATE

This is a warm grape-growing region, comfortably falling within Region III. While it is only 18 miles to the Pacific Ocean, and the coastal influence via the Russian River undoubtedly affects the climate, it does so to a minor degree. In the evidence submitted to the original BATF hearing in 1984, two experts testified (in the words of the BATF) "that fog intrusions have a minimal effect on growing conditions within the valley due to the fact that the breakpoint for significant amounts of fog is outside the valley to the south of Healdsburg." This, it would seem, is disputed by some vignerons (and official area literature), and it is certain that there is a gradual but marked increase in warmth from the south-eastern corner to the north-western tip of the valley — a distance of some 20 miles. Taking some kind of average, the rainfall is given as 40 inches (with a seasonal range of 25 to 50 inches) with Cloverdale at the northern end having a mean July temperature of 72.9°F, Healdsburg at the southern end 69.4°F (bracketing, for purposes of comparison, St. Helena at 70.8°F). Curiously, there is said to be relatively little difference in the climate on the high mountain sides on which Gauer Ranch sits; specifically, these too have a region III summation.

SOIL

The valley floor soils are a mixture of loam, gravelly loam and gravelly sandy clay loam. Technically, they belong to the series and phases comprising the soil association known as Yolo–Cortina–Pleasanton. In less technical terms, they are relatively rich, well-drained deep alluvials in which an iron bar will grow leaves and bear fruit. In the eastern foothills and mountainsides are uplands range loams, but these are typically diverse.

THE GROWING SEASON

With a frost-free season of between 240 and 270 days, relatively early soil warming and budbreak, and a relatively low marine fog influence, virtually any variety can be (and is) ripened with ease. Chardonnay is typically harvested from the end of August through to the second week of September; Zinfandel towards the end of September; and Cabernet Sauvignon in early October.

CONTRACT GROWERS

There are so many independent growers supplying grapes to others it is not possible to give full details. The principal vignerons (and acreages) are as follows: Belle Terre Vineyard (100 acres), Black Mountain Vineyard (115 acres), Canepa Vineyard (15 acres), Cramer Ridge Vineyard (15 acres), Douglas Hill Vineyard (40 acres), Gauer Ranch (550 acres), Gravel Bar Vineyard (10 acres), Hafner Vineyard (95 acres), Jimtown Ranch (200 acres), Laurelwood Vineyard (15 acres), River Lane Vineyard (20 acres), Stuhlmuller Vineyard (200 acres), Trentadue Vineyard (160 acres), Robert Young Vineyard (425 acres).

Principal Wine Styles

CHARDONNAY

Belle Terre Vineyard, Robert Young Vineyard of Chateau St. Jean, Calcaire Vineyard of Clos du Bois, Clos du Bois Winemakers Reserve, Ferrari-Carano, Simi and Jordan alone suffice to place Chardonnay as Alexander Valley's leading wine style in the mind of the consumer, and these labels are but the tip of the iceberg. Alexander Valley Chardonnays range from fleshy, warm, tropical fruited, creamy wines (which are exactly what one might expect) through to the lean, appley, austere slow-developing style which makes Simi Reserve famous and the Alexander Valley Vineyards less so. As ever, the range from black to white (with every shade in between) is in part a function of yield and viticultural practice, in part climate, and in part winemaking philosophy and technique. If there is an overall criticism, it is a lack of intensity and length of flavor of the less successful wines.

CABERNET SAUVIGNON

As viticultural techniques have improved, so have the essential sweetness and softness of the Alexander Valley Cabernet Sauvignon emerged. Because of the exceptionally easy growing conditions — both in terms of soil and climate — the tannins are both softer and riper, and wines which have been variously described as charming and supple are the result. Silver Oak and

Alexander Valley
VINTAGE CHART 1981–1991

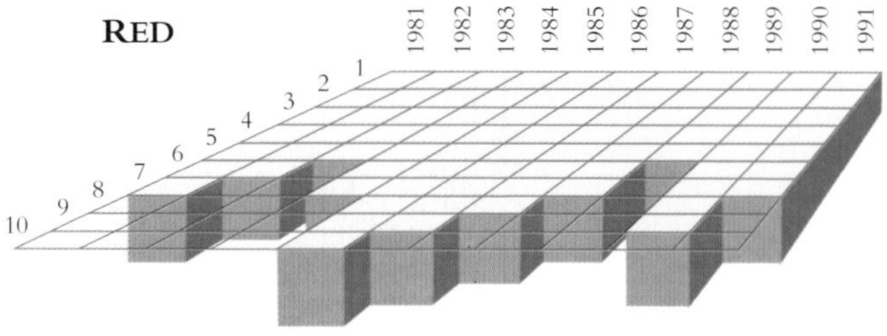
RED
1981
1982
1983
1984
1985
1986
1987
1988
1989
1990
1991
1
2
3
4
5
6
7
8
9
10

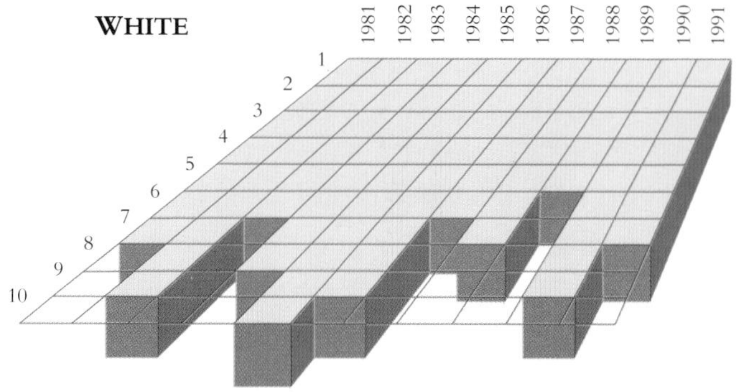
WHITE
1981
1982
1983
1984
1985
1986
1987
1988
1989
1990
1991
1
2
3
4
5
6
7
8
9
10

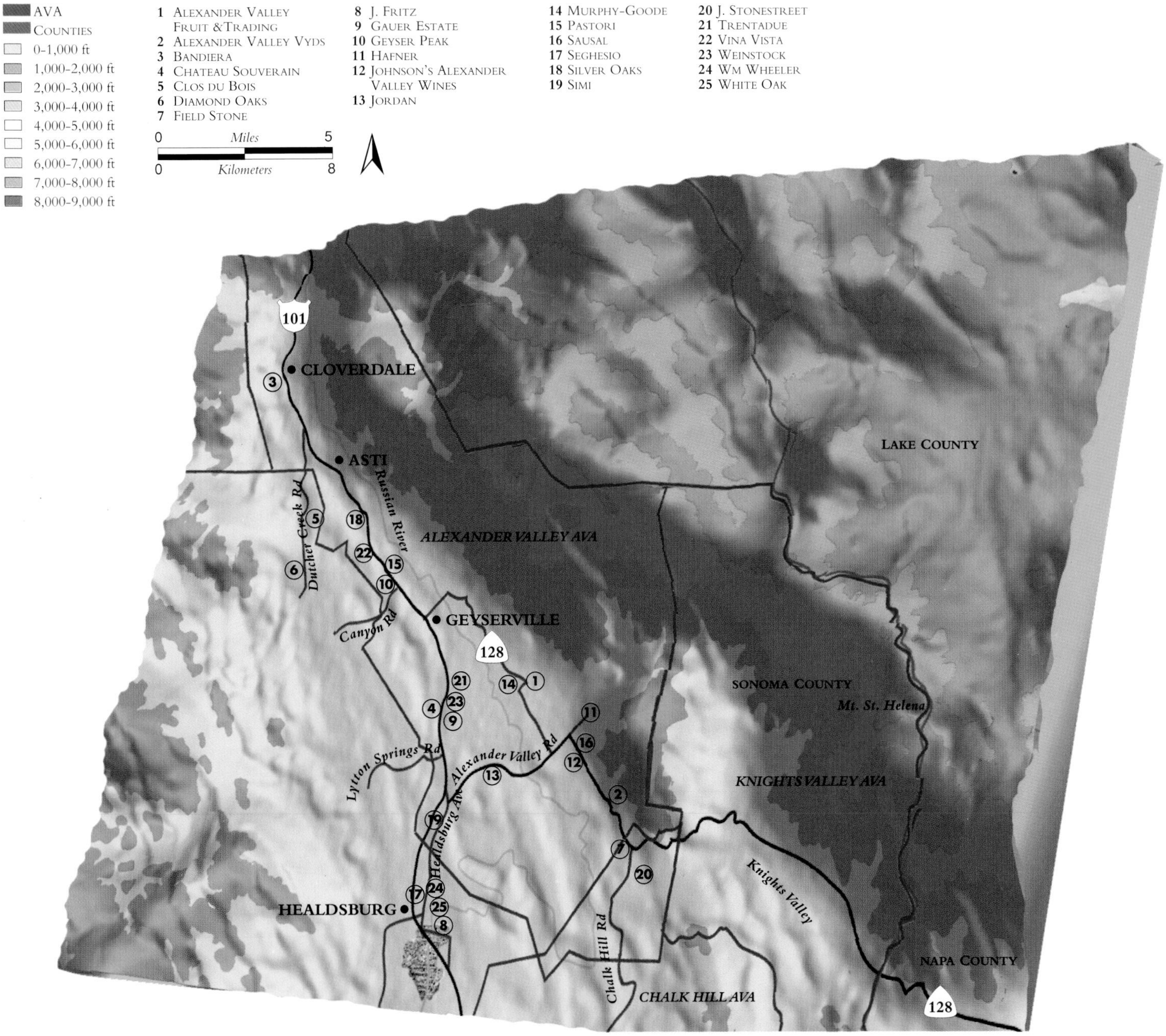
AVA
Counties
0-1,000 ft
1,000-2,000 ft
2,000-3,000 ft
3,000-4,000 ft
4,000-5,000 ft
5,000-6,000 ft
6,000-7,000 ft
7,000-8,000 ft
8,000-9,000 ft
1 Alexander Valley Fruit & Trading
2 Alexander Valley Vyds
3 Bandiera
4 Chateau Souverain
5 Clos du Bois
6 Diamond Oaks
7 Field Stone
8 J. Fritz
9 Gauer Estate
10 Geyser Peak
11 Hafner
12 Johnson's Alexander Valley Wines
13 Jordan
14 Murphy-Goode
15 Pastori
16 Sausal
17 Seghesio
18 Silver Oaks
19 Simi
20 J. Stonestreet
21 Trentadue
22 Vina Vista
23 Weinstock
24 Wm Wheeler
25 White Oak
0 Miles 5
0 Kilometers 8
101
CLOVERDALE
ASTI
Russian River
Dutcher Creek Rd
ALEXANDER VALLEY AVA
GEYSERVILLE
Canyon Rd
128
LAKE COUNTY
SONOMA COUNTY
Mt. St. Helena
Lytton Springs Rd
Alexander Valley Rd
Healdsburg Ave
KNIGHTS VALLEY AVA
Knights Valley
HEALDSBURG
Chalk Hill Rd
CHALK HILL AVA
NAPA COUNTY

Simi have both shown that the valley can produce ageworthy Cabernets, and Jordan certainly believes it is doing so. But all of these wines are as delicious when young as they are with bottle age: certainly they change, but I am not sure they improve. Chateau Souverain, Geyser Peak, Gauer Ranch and Simi are among my personal favorites, with Clos du Bois, Jordan and Murphy-Goode in the second rank.

Zinfandel

Zinfandel ought to produce wines of distinction in this climate, and Ridge Geyserville and Sausal Reserve prove it can do so. But overall there is a slightly amorphous character to the wines: they lack the sparkle of the Russian River, the intensity of Dry Creek. Instead of having the best of all worlds, they end up as some kind of common denominator. This may seem a harsh judgment, particularly granted that — if pressed — I would say it applies right across the board. But in commercial terms, the common denominator is precisely that which many winemakers seek to find.

Sauvignon Blanc

A vexing variety is Sauvignon Blanc. By rights the climate should be too soft, too warm to produce wines with any particular varietal character. But a surprising number of wines with good structure and flavor are at least partially sourced from the Alexander Valley — with help from Dry Creek and the Russian River.

Aromatic White Wines

Alexander Valley Vineyards does the seemingly impossible with Riesling and Gewurztraminer; Chenin Blanc produces a wine which is as undistinguished as its pedigree suggests it should be.

ABOVE ~ *Alexander Valley map.*

MOUNTAIN VITICULTURE

I should start this piece with a disclosure of interest: my own vineyards are steep hillside, with gradients of 25 degrees in part. I took the decision to buy the land, and was physically involved in the planting. Indeed, one horrendous spring I knelt before almost every one of the 30,000 newly planted vines on one block, pulling away weeds by hand — the pre-emergent herbicides had failed to work, and the weeds were too strong, the vines too small to allow the use of weed eaters (or whipper snippers, as they are called in some parts of the world). In other words, I have the same love-hate relationship which most hillside or mountain viticulturists have with their vines.

ABOVE ~ *Prime Sauvignon Blanc awaiting collection at Gauer Estate.*

I use the phrases interchangeably, not because they necessarily denote the same thing (one can have flat vineyards on a mountain plateau, and hillsides at low elevations which are not part of what one would normally call a mountain) but because of the fundamental differences from traditional valley floor vineyards. So henceforth I shall use the term mountain viticulture, having recognized it can mean different things in different situations.

The common feature of mountain vineyards worldwide is the higher cost of production per ton of grapes than that of valley vineyards. This is caused by two factors: lower yields and higher labor costs. The irony is that in some instances (witness many of the mountainside vineyards rimming the Napa Valley) the decision to buy land and plant the vineyard was due to the lower initial land cost; in others, such as the Santa Cruz mountains in the last century, it was due to security of land tenure, which was not available in the plains.

Yields are lower because mountain soils are typically thinner, rockier and more acidic than alluvials, and because so many mountain vineyards are dry-farmed. They are dry-farmed in part because the rainfall tends to be higher, and because of the absence of aquifers or conveniently accessible water sources during the summer months. (To save an endless litany of qualifications, I am now talking of California mountain vineyards, and I am necessarily making some sweeping generalizations). Costs are higher because mechanization is less easy, all of the vineyard processes are slower, and because of the typically fragmented nature of the plantings, with short row lengths a major factor.

The obvious questions are whether mountain-grown grapes are better, and, if so, why are they better? Or if not better, are they different, and if so, why? Until relatively recent times it would have been possible to give a global yes to the first limb of those two questions — in other words, to say mountain grapes were both better and different. There was a simple reason: the grapes are produced from vines which typically have a naturally balanced canopy and which withstand late season stress very well.

Mountain vineyards have not lost these advantages; what is changing is our understanding of the importance of the balance between the growth of the vine and the crop which it bears. In so doing, viticulturists are learning to transport mountain virtues down to valley floors, and to have the best of both worlds. In a similar vein, the natural advantages of the Oakville and Rutherford Benches may well be minimized as viticultural techniques across the valley floor improve.

The concept of expressing yield in tons per acre has come in for increasing criticism in the wake of our greater knowledge of vine training, particularly with the realization that in many high vigor valley floor situations involving widely spaced vines it is almost certain that higher yields of better quality grapes can be obtained by converting the traditional single wire trellis to (say) a quadrilateral cordon.

In this circumstance, it is said, yield should be expressed in terms of ounces per inch of fruiting cane or square inches of active foliage. In close-spaced, high density vineyard plantings growers tend to talk of yield in terms of pounds per vine.

Yet regardless of the complexity of the trellis system and the density of the plantings, experience worldwide suggests that the highest quality grapes are obtained from vines which (without intervention such as crop thinning, and on the other hand, without undue stress or disease, viral or fungal) produce between two and a half and three tons to the acre.

It just so happens that most mountain vineyards produce at or below this level. It also happens that crop thinning is (or was) unheard of, and that simple trellises were the order of the day. These trellises could be employed because of the self-limiting nature of the growth of the canopy: the canes had sufficient leaves to ripen the crop, yet not so many as to excessively shade either the bunches of grapes or next year's buds.

The reason why it has been possible to improve both yield and quality on valley floor vines all stems from the role of sunlight — and the concept of the vine in balance. The vine's very name gives part of the clue, and its woodland ancestry the other part. It grew in the forest, using trees as its trellis. It knew that sunlight was essential for its growth, so for as long as it remained in shade in the lower and middle heights of the forest, it focused all of its energy on vegetative growth. Only once it had reached the roof of the forest and come out into the sunlight did it permit the production of grape bunches.

But, as a perennial, it also needed an early warning system. Thus it is that the buds which will produce next year's growth are formed this year, and their fruitfulness will be determined between March and June this year, even though the bunches will not appear until almost a year later. The degree of fruitfulness will be profoundly influenced by the amount of sunlight falling on the bud: the more sun, the more fruitful; the less sun, the less fruitful.

Thus the old valley floor vines, growing in rich soil, but confined to a grossly inadequate trellis, gave themselves confusing signals. The canopy became so dense that inadequate sunlight fell on the buds, reducing the crop and leading to a vicious cycle of excessive vegetative growth and to those triffid-like objects, reaching across eleven-foot rows in an impassable jungle.

No such fate befell mountain vines; what is more, we now understand that dappled sunlight on the bunches themselves enhances flavor and color development, although all of the mechanisms for this remain to be fully understood. So by virtue of the way the vines grew, they naturally produced grapes with intense flavor and (in the case of red varieties) intense color.

The other major advantage enjoyed by mountain vineyards is a typically more moderate climate, with warmer nights and cooler days than the adjacent valley floor. The cold air sinks down the hillsides, and the warmer valley floor rises, causing what is known technically as an inversion layer. The cold air drainage also reduces the risk of frost on the mountains (and increases it in the valleys below). If marine fog invades the valley, the inversion effect is accentuated.

In the mornings, mountain vineyards will typically be bathed in early morning sunshine, and may well accumulate much of their biologically effective heat before lunchtime in precisely the conditions which most favor the grapes. Yet, their peak daytime temperatures tend to be 10°F (or more) lower than those of the adjacent valley — a figure which will, of course, vary with altitude. Greater air movement is one reason, and less heat reflection another. And if there is a breeze to be found, you may be sure the mountainside will get it first.

ABOVE ~ *The vineyards at Gauer Estate thread their way past rocky outcrops and gullies, creating a patchwork quilt on the mountainside.*

WINERIES *of* ALEXANDER VALLEY

ALEXANDER VALLEY VINEYARDS 1964

A: 8644 Highway 128, Healdsburg, CA 95448 **T**: (707) 433 7209 **V**: 10–5 daily **P**: 45,000 **W**: Hank Wetzel

WETZEL FAMILY ESTATE
ALEXANDER VALLEY
CABERNET SAUVIGNON
ESTATE BOTTLED
1989
ALEXANDER VALLEY
VINEYARDS

Anyone fortunate enough to stay in the Alexander Valley School House, built by Cyrus Alexander in 1868, cannot help but have both a feeling of affection for Alexander Valley Vineyards (and for that matter, the Alexander Valley as a whole) and a sense of its fascinating history. Future generations will owe much to Harry Wetzel and his entire family, who purchased the property in 1962 and who had the financial resources (and the time) to restore all of the buildings on the property, including the stately Victorian home in which the Wetzels now live. The setting on the front porch of the School House, both early in the morning and late in the evening of a perfect California summer's day, is not something I shall quickly forget.

The estate is planted to Cabernet Sauvignon (42 acres), Merlot (31.5 acres) and Chardonnay (30 acres), with approximately five acres each of Pinot Noir, Zinfandel, Chenin Blanc, Johannisberg Riesling and Gewurztraminer. This leads logically enough into the production pattern, which is dominated by 10,000 cases each of Cabernet Sauvignon (with 10% Merlot), Chardonnay and Merlot (the latter including 20% Cabernet Sauvignon, and a rising star in terms of production, first made in any significant quantities in 1989).

The winery, built in time for the 1975 crush, is appropriately functional, as are the wine styles. Alexander Valley Vineyards' initial reputation was founded on its Chardonnay, but these days is centered upon the Cabernet Sauvignon (and the Merlot), made in the typically soft style of the region. In fact, I found some of the lesser wines, admittedly made in a straightforward commercial style, to be particularly pleasant, notably the Chenin Blanc, White Riesling and Gewurztraminer.

CHATEAU SOUVERAIN 1973

A: 400 Souverain Road, Geyserville, CA 95441 **T**: (707) 433 8281 **V**: 10:30–5 Tues–Sun **P**: 120,000 **W**: Thomas Peterson

The history of Chateau Souverain between 1973 and 1986 is a litany of disaster, interesting only for those who wish to learn how not to lose tens of millions of dollars in quick-fire time. Its 1986 acquisition by Nestlé arm Wineworld Inc. saw a complete role reversal from the very bad to the very good. Nestlé's track record is impeccable: it first of all provided the millions of dollars needed to upgrade the facility, but then left the winemaking and production team to get on with its job of producing wines which would obliterate the unhappy memories of prior ownerships, and the marketing team with the job of establishing a brand identity for a winery name which had had more twists and turns than an Agatha Christie novel.

In many ways, the most remarkable aspect of the renaissance has been the patient way in which the revitalization task has been approached, and the long-term strategic planning which lies behind it. By 1992 it was paying rich dividends: an exceptionally impressive array of Sonoma County-sourced wines was on offer, coming from the Alexander Valley, Dry Creek Valley, Sonoma Valley, Russian River Valley, with a Carneros Chardonnay thrown in for good measure.

The Cabernet Sauvignon and Merlot are primarily sourced from Alexander Valley hillside vineyards, with wines such as the 1990 Merlot and 1988 Cabernet Sauvignon coming as close to benchmarks for the region as anyone could reasonably expect. Zinfandel from the Dry Creek Valley has been consistently excellent, Chardonnays from the Russian River Valley and Carneros likewise.

The initial acquisition by Nestlé did not include vineyards, but Chateau Souverain has acquired 500 acres in the Asti area, of which 200 are planted, with another 50 to go. Here Syrah and Petit Verdot will be established in commercial quantities, while the first Pinot Noir was produced ex-Carneros in the 1990 vintage. For the time being, the focus will remain on the present varietal range of Chardonnay, Sauvignon Blanc, Cabernet Sauvignon, Zinfandel and Merlot as production grows to 140,000 cases, but with estate-produced wines and some more exotic varieties (in limited quantities) a distinct possibility. And if you are planning on visiting Chateau Souverain, do not forget it has a superb restaurant, open from noon to 9 P.M. Wednesday to Sunday.

CLOS DU BOIS 1976

A: 5 Fitch Street, Healdsburg, CA 95448 **T**: (707) 433 5576 **V**: 10–5 daily **P**: 350,000 **W**: Margaret Davenport

Clos du Bois is in many ways the mirror image of Chateau Souverain. When it was purchased by Hiram Walker's Wine Alliance in 1988 it had no winery, but had a well-regarded brand and 590 acres of prime Alexander Valley and Dry Creek vineyards. Chateau Souverain had a very large and expensive winery, no vineyards, and no brand reputation. Yet both have gone from strength to strength, producing wines of absolutely admirable quality given the scale of production.

The focus of Clos du Bois is on Chardonnay, with production moving from 200,000 to 300,000 cases, all of it of unimpeachable quality within its volume and price range. By far the largest quantity is of the Alexander Valley Barrel-fermented Chardonnay, typically with sweet peachy fruit and soft, simple, easily accessible flavor. Then there is Calcaire Chardonnay from the Alexander Valley, and Flintwood from the Dry Creek Valley, made in much smaller quantities, and 100% barrel fermented in a high percentage of new oak. The 1990 vintage of each was of exceptional quality, the Calcaire with gently spicy oak, and melon/peach fruit; the Flintwood with lively, fresh grapefruit and citric flavors, and yet made supple with beautifully balanced spicy oak. The Meritage blend of around 60% Cabernet Sauvignon, 35% Merlot and 5% Malbec marketed under the Marlstone brand (and also

1987
CLOS DU BOIS
MERLOT
SONOMA COUNTY
77% Merlot
23% Cabernet Sauvignon
ALCOHOL 13.6% BY VOLUME

sourced from the Alexander Valley) is a soft, fruity and supple wine which, once again, shows archetypal Alexander Valley style, surpassing itself in 1989. Merlot, too, is very much on the future agenda.

By the time the new facility is completed in the mid 1990s, Clos du Bois's presently fragmented winemaking operations will have been amalgamated with its marketing division, and all should be well with the world. The address given, incidentally, is that of its tasting room, which was the only facility open to the public in 1992.

FIELD STONE WINERY 1977

A: 10075 Highway 128, Healdsburg, CA 95448 **T**: (707) 433 7266 **V**: 10–5 daily **P**: 11,000 **W**: Michael Duffy

Field Stone was founded by mechanical engineer Wallace Johnson, responsible for many inventions but best known in the wine industry as the inventor and manufacturer of the UpRight Mechanical Grape Harvester. The vineyards were established in the 1960s, but it was not until 1977 that a winery was dug into the side of an oak-covered knoll and completed with a front wall made of the stones which gives the winery its name. Two years later Johnson died suddenly, and management of the vineyard and winery passed to daughter Katrina and her husband John Staten. Dr. John Staten was (and is) a highly distinguished theologian and author, and remains actively involved in theological teaching as well as running Field Stone Winery.

The winery has its own 50-acre estate planted to Cabernet and Petite Sirah (the latter partially dating from 1894), receives grapes from the family's adjacent vineyards, and since 1987 has purchased Chardonnay from Alexander Valley, Carneros and Russian River growers. In nett terms the enterprise is a major grape seller: in all, the family vineyard holdings amount to 175 acres. A significant portion of the relatively modest production is sold through a sophisticated mailing list program and through the cellar door. The most striking wine is, without doubt, the Petite Sirah, massively concentrated and astringent in youth, a vivid testament to the old vines which produce it.

Some years ago, a patch of Viognier was planted, and the first 300-case release of this wine was made in late 1992. Part of the Viognier will also be used to lighten the Petite Sirah, in a quasi-Rhone blend. New plantings of Cabernet Sauvignon and Merlot in 1991 will also extend the estate range. The less said of the Sauvignon Blanc, blended with 10% Symphony, the better.

GAUER ESTATE 1985

A: 18700 Geyserville Avenue, Geyserville, CA 95441 **T**: (707) 433 4402 **V**: By appointment **P**: 10,000 **W**: Kerry Damskey

Ed Gauer purchased 5,000 acres of mountainside ranch on the eastern side of the Alexander Valley in the early 1970s. He was the owner of the Roos-Atkins chain of clothing stores, which he subsequently sold for $16 million, and was thus in a position to undertake the arduous and extremely expensive business of establishing a series of vineyards running up the mountainside at elevations of 400 to 2,400 feet. Most of the initial plantings were in 1972 and 1973, as bad luck would have it, not on the traditional mountain rootstock of St. George but AxR. There was another burst of planting between 1978 and 1982, and again between 1987 and 1992, lifting total acreage to 557 spread over nine completely separate sites.

ABOVE ~ *Vineyard workers picking Sauvignon Blanc at Gauer Estate.*

Originally content to sell his grapes (and by then in his 80s), Gauer subsequently decided he wanted to establish his own winery and label, and in 1986 retained Allan Hemphill to advise him. Hemphill dissuaded him from building a winery, and instead convinced him to purchase the very large custom-crush facility known as Vinwood and situated on Geyserville Road. The first wine under the Gauer Estate Vineyard label was made at Vinwood in 1987, and the quality of that wine and the wines made in 1988 were such that Gauer felt he had achieved his ambition, and without an heir wishing to continue the business, sold it to Huntington Beach Associates, the property division of Chevron Corporation.

A drive to the top of Gauer Estate is a breathtaking experience, and a picnic lunch on the slab trestles and tables overlooking the cascading vineyards and ultimately the valley floor is no less so. In best mountain tradition, the majority of the vineyards are well above the fog line, benefiting from cooler daytime temperatures and more sunlight and suffering no threat from frost. Notwithstanding that, yields are very low (averaging two to three tons per acre) and vintage is two to four weeks later than the valley floor, although the gap does narrow as the season progresses.

One of several mysteries is why Ed Gauer would have thought that his ranch was included in the Alexander Valley viticultural area when it was first promulgated, and, having found that it was not, sought to have it included. Having initially sharply differentiated the valley floor from the mountains, both in terms of climate and soil, the BATF proved once again it was nothing if not acquiescent when confronted with a me-too application, and Gauer Ranch is now part of the Alexander Valley in the eyes of the BATF, at least. One can only suppose it is because Gauer Estate remains first and foremost a grape seller, and a separate appellation might have made its grapes less useful to some of its purchasers. On the other hand, it is hard to see why the lowest common denominator factor should apply: these grapes are far more expensive to produce than valley floor grapes and are distinctively different. The Chardonnay is fine, discrete and long flavored in the mouth, the Cabernet Sauvignon (from 1988) an absolutely lovely wine, fine, elegant and with beautifully articulated dark cherry, cassis and spice varietal character.

A yet further mystery is the modest pricing of these wines: if they are intended as a showcase for the estate, and are produced in such limited quantities, one would have thought it would make sense to price them higher, and to use the extra dollars in promotion. Yet another twist to the tale emerged in December 1992. Owner Chevron Corporation rejected a management buyout bid from Allan Hemphill, and sold Vinwood to the omnivorous Kendall-Jackson. Some vineyards were included, but details were sketchy. The belief was that it was the valley floor, rather than the mountain, vineyards which were acquired.

GEYSER PEAK WINERY 1880

A: 22281 Chianti Road, Geyserville, CA 95441 **T**: (707) 857 9463 **V**: 10–5 daily **P**: 600,000 **W**: Daryl Groom

Geyser Peak Winery proudly displays the year of its establishment on the winery wall, but the fact is that for the first 109 years of its life, it had what might kindly be described as a checkered existence. The potential for change began in 1982, when local businessman Tony Trione purchased the winery, giving it access to more than 1,000 acres of prime vineyard land the Trione family had already acquired in the Alexander and Russian River Valleys. But the real turning point came in 1989, when Australian industry leader Penfolds acquired a 50% interest in the winery, although ownership of the vineyards remained with the Trione family. Part of the deal was that Penfolds should supply one of its brightest young winemakers, Daryl Groom, who for the previous five years had had executive responsibility for Penfolds' world-famous flagship red, Grange Hermitage.

Groom's arrival resulted in a dramatic change in wine style and quality. Whether judged by the quality of the wine in the glass, or the 1991/92 show results (but not necessarily all critical reviews), Geyser Peak is making some of the most deliciously flavored and accessible wines in California today.

In 1991 Penfolds, having itself been acquired by an even larger Australian company, sold back its interest in Geyser Peak to the Trione family, and sought to lure Daryl Groom back to Australia. A tug-of-war ensued, and for a while it appeared Geyser Peak might become well and truly fragmented, with the vineyards staying with the Triones, the brand being sold in one direction, and the winery itself in yet another (Kendall-Jackson was rumored to have a keen interest in purchasing it), with Daryl Groom returning to Australia. In the outcome, none of those things occurred, but it is anyone's guess where the key players will be in five years' time.

It is, I suppose, inevitable that I should react favorably to the Groom Geyser Peak style. But, as I say, the wines have had phenomenal success in California wine shows, so it is not all parochial bias. The Semchard (a proprietary brand of 75% Livermore Valley Semillon and 25% Sonoma County Chardonnay) is quintessentially Australian, both in terms of the blending of these varieties and in terms of the sophisticated oak handling, which adds a rarely seen dimension to the wine. In blind tastings, the 1989 Cabernet Sauvignon and 1989 Merlot both scored very high points, the latter in particular showing spotlessly clean, fresh red berry fruit, with excellent weight, hints of spice and leafy varietal character, and a long finish. Tastings of the younger red wines (not blind) suggested even better things are in store, particularly with the proprietary Meritage blend Reserve Alexandre. All in all, a winery to watch, in more ways than one.

ABOVE ~ *A scene reminiscent of the Douro in Portugal, but in fact Gauer Estate.*

ABOVE ~ *The interplay of mountains, valleys and fog seen from the top of Gauer Estate.*

HAFNER VINEYARD 1967

A: 4280 Pine Flat Road, Healdsburg, CA 95448 **T**: (707) 433 4675 **V**: By appointment **P**: 11,700 **W**: Parke Hafner

Dick Hafner purchased a prune and pear ranch in 1967, and began the conversion to a vineyard in 1969 with Cabernet Sauvignon, continuing in 1973 with Chardonnay and Gewurztraminer. In all there are 98.7 acres of vines, and Hafner remains primarily a grape grower and seller. However, in 1982 an elegant wooden winery was constructed, which I first visited shortly after it was commissioned. Not too many people get to see Hafner, because it has no cellar door sales nor conventional distribution. It is very much a family business: Dick and wife Mary are managing partners; Parke is winemaker; Scott is in charge of marketing; while design work is done by Sarah Clifford-Hafner.

Ninety per cent of the wine is sold by mailing list, the remaining 10% direct to restaurants. Seventy-five per cent of the production is of Chardonnay (in two guises, standard and Reserve), the remainder being Cabernet Sauvignon with an occasional Late Harvest Johannisberg Riesling. The Hafners use a very interesting pricing strategy for their mailing list, giving sharply reduced prices for multiple case buyers, an incentive system which seems to have the desired effect.

The Reserve Chardonnay, entirely barrel fermented, lees contacted, and spending 15 months in French oak before being given two years' cork age, is by far the best wine in the portfolio, even though its price is not dramatically higher than the standard Chardonnay. It ages well, has good complexity and a distinctive honeyed/nutty texture. The Cabernet Sauvignon, by contrast, is rather lean and astringent, at odds with the reputation of the valley for soft, subtle wines.

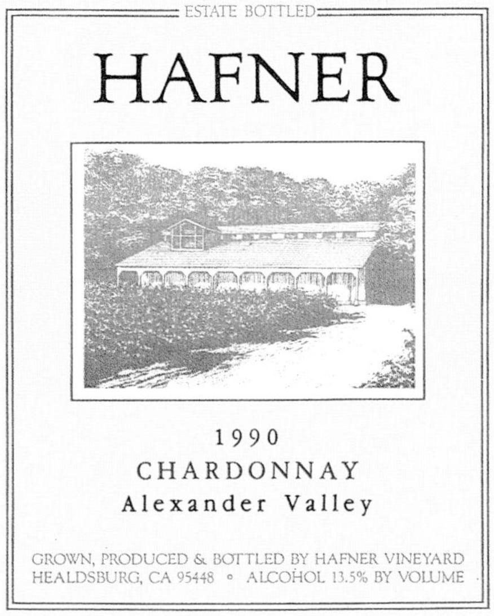
ESTATE BOTTLED
HAFNER
1990
CHARDONNAY
Alexander Valley
GROWN, PRODUCED & BOTTLED BY HAFNER VINEYARD
HEALDSBURG, CA 95448 • ALCOHOL 13.5% BY VOLUME

ABOVE ~ *The massive trunks and arms of fast-growing Cabernet Sauvignon in the de Lorimer vineyard.*

JORDAN VINEYARD & WINERY 1972

A: 1474 Alexander Valley Road, Healdsburg, CA 95448 **T**: (707) 431 5250 **V**: By appointment **P**: 60,000 **W**: Rob Davis

Founding and ultimately selling an extremely successful oil and gas exploration company gave Tom Jordan the financial resources to build one of the landmark wineries of the Alexander Valley on a 1,500-acre estate, 240 acres of which are devoted to vineyards, and 1,000 acres as a game reserve for migratory birds (and no doubt other forms of wildlife). The first vines were planted in 1973, and the first vintage made in 1976 from purchased grapes. I visited the winery in 1979, not long before that first vintage was due to be released, and remember vividly the impression the winery left on me — it seemed like a cross between Chateau Lafite and Schloss Vollrads — and the extraordinary marketing hype which had been built up around the wine. No one, but no one, was allowed to taste it until its release, and it was in fact some years later before I finally had my first experience of Jordan Cabernet.

It was somehow appropriate that in 1992 I should drink a bottle of the 1978 Cabernet Sauvignon, the first produced from estate-grown grapes and, in the view of some, now past its prime. I found it totally enjoyable, and while not suggesting for one moment that it has further improvement in store, could not see any signs of decay. The 1981, it is true, showed some aged leafy/tobacco characters on the palate, but was still reasonably fresh on the bouquet, while the 1988 showed the soft, sweet redcurrant fruit and texture which is the hallmark of the Alexander Valley. In common with many observers, I find the Chardonnay uninteresting when young, and equally uninteresting with bottle age. It comes as no surprise to find that Chardonnay production has been progressively decreased from 25,000 cases down to 15,000 cases.

Alexander Valley Cabernets as a whole have a reputation as being quick maturing, and it is ironic that winemaker Rob Davis wishes to extend the present four-year gap between vintage and release to five years. Despite the lukewarm acceptance of Jordan Cabernets in some quarters, the present level of sales (and the enforced replanting of the vineyards in stages in the wake of phylloxera) mean that the extra year in bottle is still some way off.

If the original venture was ambitious and marked by a level of marketing and promotional expenditure unusual even by the standards of the Napa Valley, that of the 1986 departure into sparkling wine via the Jordan Sparkling Wine Company (an undertaking of Tom and daughter Judy Jordan) took packaging (and marketing) on to a hitherto unexplored plane. Land was purchased on Eastside Road in the Russian River region, and planted to Pinot Noir and Chardonnay. It is seen as a quite separate operation, and a sparkling wine facility has been established there, but curiously the Cocquard press (only the second installed outside France) resides at Chateau Jordan. The first winemaker employed was the late Claude Thibault; he has been succeeded by Oded Shakked, who in fact assisted Thibault with the first two vintages, 1987 and 1988. The specially designed bottle with the single bold yellow letter "J" emblazoned on its side, and the two-piece capsule of unique design, should not disguise the fact that both the 1987 and 1988 J (like Dom, get it?) are very nice wines. Both are stylish, with complex, sweet, creamy fruit, good body and the Pinot Noir component melding perfectly with the Chardonnay. Some see the wines as a little sweet; I suspect this has as much to do with fruit as sugar sweetness.

MURPHY-GOODE ESTATE WINERY 1985

A: 4001 Highway 128, Geyserville, CA 95441
T: (707) 431 7644 **V**: 10:30–4:30 daily
P: 45,000 **W**: Christina Benz

Murphy-Goode is a partnership of three: Dale Goode, Tim Murphy, and Dave Ready. Both Goode and Murphy had been grape growers in the Alexander Valley for more than a decade when they formed the vineyard partnership in 1980, and were joined by Dave Ready, a marketing and sales specialist, in 1985 when a depressed grape market persuaded the two founding partners it was time to get into the winemaking business. Naturally, the partners chose the variety they were having the most difficulty selling as grapes, and with Merry Edwards as consultant, made 7,000 cases of Fumé Blanc at the Rodney Strong Winery. They priced the wine at the low end of the market, and with Rick Theis (briefly but no longer a member of the partnership), worked coast to coast, selling the wine in six months and setting Murphy-Goode on a success path it does not look like leaving.

In 1987 Christina Benz, a one-time medical school student with a master's degree from U.C. Davis and practical experience at Roudon Smith in the Santa Cruz Mountains, Joseph Phelps and Schug in the Napa Valley, and Lindemans Wines in Coonawarra, South Australia, joined as winemaker. By 1988 the winery was completed, and by 1992 was bursting at the seams with production at 45,000 cases. By then it was planned to double the size of the winery in 1993, allowing production ultimately to reach 80,000 cases and fully utilize the partnership's vineyard resources.

If the expansion occurs, it will be with the Fumé Blancs, one tank-fermented but barrel-aged to give a fruity, easy-drinking style, the other barrel-fermented in new oak and partially MLF; and with the varietal Merlot, phenomenally successful but still in relatively limited production. Another innovation will be the production of a Pinot Blanc (or Melon), which started with a few hundred cases in 1990 and which will go over 2,000 cases by 1992. Christina Benz is full of pithy one-liners about the difficulties of marketing Chardonnay, but while it will decrease as a percentage of the total make it will still be an important line. The Cabernet Sauvignon is likely to diminish on both scores.

All of the wines are well made in that typical, easy-going Alexander Valley style. If there is a fault it seems to lie in the vineyard, because there is a lack of concentration, a certain diluteness, which seems suggestive of high crop levels.

SAUSAL WINERY 1973

A: 7370 Highway 128, Healdsburg, CA 95448
T: (707) 433 2285 **V**: 10–4 daily **P**: 15,000
W: David Demostene

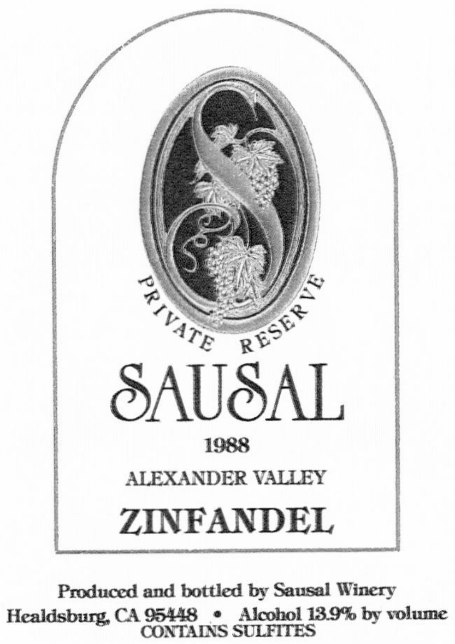
PRIVATE RESERVE
SAUSAL
1988
ALEXANDER VALLEY
ZINFANDEL
Produced and bottled by Sausal Winery
Healdsburg, CA 95448 • Alcohol 13.9% by volume
CONTAINS SULFITES

Leo Demostene was born into a winemaking family, and had worked as a winemaker for many years at other wineries before purchasing Sausal Ranch in 1955, removing the prune and apple trees and planting vines to accompany an existing vineyard on part of the property dating from 1925. In 1973 Leo Demostene died, having just commenced the task of converting an old prune dehydrater into what is now a (much expanded) winery, and David Demostene was responsible for the first vintage in 1974.

Throughout much of the 1970s most of the wine (Napa Gamay and Petite Sirah) was sold in bulk, with the prized Zinfandel grapes being sold to Grgich Hills, Phelps and other luminaries. Gradually, however, the Demostene family (and many members are involved) have built up their own label, and in so doing established a foremost reputation as a producer of exceptionally rich, big and fleshy Zinfandel which, as the 1980 vintage tasted in 1992 demonstrated, can age superbly, still having rich chocolatey-edged fruit and nicely balanced tannins. Some bitter, tarry notes have intruded from time to time in some of the Zinfandels, but by and large it is not hard to see where the reputation comes from. The white wines are decidedly less attractive; but just to confuse the issue further, Sausal's 1991 White Zinfandel achieved the impossible. I actually liked the wine, and in no way regretted seeing prime Zinfandel grapes handled in this way. It is as good as they come, with light, spicy cherry aromas, fresh fruit, and length without relying on sweetness.

SEGHESIO WINERY 1902

A: 14730 Grove Street, Healdsburg, CA 95448 **T**: (707) 433 3579 **V**: By appointment
P: 100,000 **W**: Ted Seghesio

For 80 years Seghesio was purely a bulk winery, selling finished wine to others, made from 320 acres of estate vineyards in the Alexander Valley, Dry Creek Valley and Russian River Valley regions. The Seghesio house specialty is called Chianti Station, a blend of 85% Sangiovese with the remaining portion coming from an old Italian mixed black planting. It is by no means the most important wine in terms of volume; here the leaders are Cabernet Sauvignon, Zinfandel and White Zinfandel, with new plantings of Sangiovese pointing the way for the future. The Zinfandel, in particular, stands out on a value for money basis. At two or three years of age, it shows clean, fragrant cherry and strawberry fruit aromas and flavors, with a touch of spice and appropriately gentle tannins. There are no tricks to the making, and there are no tricks to the wine.

SIMI WINERY 1876

A: 16275 Healdsburg Avenue, Healdsburg, CA 95448 **T**: (707) 433 9681
V: 10–4:30 daily **P**: 150,000
W: Zelma Long and Nick Goldschmidt

Simi has a rich, if not downright exotic, history, impossible to tell in so short a space, but encapsulated by the death of the founding brothers Guiseppe and Pietro Simi in August 1904, right at the time an already large winery was in the middle of an ambitious expansion program. Ownership and management passed to Guiseppe's daughter Isabel; she had had two years' practical experience in the winery but was exactly 14 years old. She not only weathered that experience, but also the 1906 earthquake and Prohibition and comfortably outlived her husband and (tragically) her daughter, eventually being forced by arthritis and old age (she was nearly 80) to sell in 1969. After several interim ownerships, Moet Hennessy purchased Simi in 1981, and in so doing acquired the services of Zelma Long, who had left Robert Mondavi to become Simi winemaker two years earlier.

Zelma Long is one of the most intelligent, articulate and innovative winemakers to be found anywhere in the world. Although she has some time since been elevated to president, and although peripatetic New Zealander Nick Goldschmidt has for some years been winemaker, I could not resist showing both as winemakers, for Zelma Long remains intimately involved in the never-ending quest at Simi to grow better grapes and make better wine.

She sees the challenge of the 1990s as being to integrate finally the vineyard and winery. "There should be a winegrowing team: the people who are responsible for the vineyards think about the wine (rather than the grapes) as their end product, and regard every manipulation in the vineyard as directed to a specific wine goal; the people who work in the winery are thinking about the grapes in the vineyard as the start of the cycle, rather the grapes in the picking bins as they reach the winery." The extension of this philosophy is, again to quote Zelma Long, "Rather than say we are making Chardonnay using malolactic fermentation, barrel fermentation, lees contact and so forth, we should say we are making Chardonnay from this site or that site, and this is our response to the particular attributes and demands of that site." In other words, the marriage is between winery and specific site, rather than between winery and grape or winery and region.

Thus it is that Simi has 35 sections in its 175 acres of Alexander Valley vineyards (and another 100 acres in the Russian River planted to Chardonnay) and the wines from those 35 sections are all kept separate until the end of the year, with the aim of improving each lot the following year.

In the mid 1980s Zelma Long pioneered oxidative juice handling of Chardonnay, with the aim of producing subtle wines with secondary, stony/minerally/gravelly fruit flavors, texture, length and longevity, rather than primary-fruited Chardonnay which would flower briefly and then fade. Some see the resulting wine style as boring and bland, others as ultimately sophisticated and seamless, perfect in every respect. To be honest, I respect the Simi Chardonnay style greatly, but it is not my personal choice. On the other hand, the Sauvignon Blanc is absolutely delicious in its crisp, fragrant, direct fruit style, while the improvements made in the Cabernet Sauvignon in the latter part of the 1980s leave me in no doubt that Simi makes the best Cabernet Sauvignon to be found in the entire Alexander Valley. It is chock full of sweet, blackcurrant, red berry, blackberry and chocolate flavors, soft and voluptuous, yet supported by lingering tannins. It is everything that Alexander Valley Cabernet Sauvignon is reputed to be, but so often is not.

J. STONESTREET 1983

A: 4611 Thomas Road, Healdsburg, CA 95448 **T**: (707) 433 9000 **V**: By appointment **P**: 40,000 **W**: Steve Teat

J. Stonestreet is yet another winery (and separate brand) under Kendall-Jackson ownership. The winery was built in 1973 by Stephen Zellerbach, who leased the facility and the label to William Baccala in 1986. There was an attached purchase option, which Kendall-Jackson acquired from Baccala in 1988, having been associated with the vineyard and winery since 1983. From that time Kendall-Jackson purchased grapes from the 83 acres of planted vineyard, using the Merlot and Cabernet in some of its top-rated wines, including the 1985 Cardinale.

Stonestreet is now producing estate-grown Cabernet Sauvignon and Merlot, with a Red Meritage wine in the course of production and quite possibly released by the time of publication. Chardonnay and Pinot Noir are also produced, made from grapes purchased from various locations in Sonoma County.

WILLIAM WHEELER WINERY 1980

A: 130 Plaza Street, Healdsburg, CA 95448 **T**: (707) 433 8786 **V**: 11–4 daily **P**: 23,500 **W**: Julia Iantosca

William and Ingrid Wheeler purchased a 175-acre property in the Dry Creek Valley in 1970, planting Zinfandel and Cabernet Sauvignon on some of the steeper slopes. Another to mix town and country, they established a crushing and fermenting facility in the Dry Creek Valley, followed by a barrel-aging and tasting room complex in Plaza Street, Healdsburg. The brand succeeded, with Chardonnay (made from grapes purchased in Carneros, the Russian River, Dry Creek and Alexander Valleys), Sauvignon Blanc (from various vineyards in the Dry Creek Valley), and Cabernet Sauvignon (largely estate-grown but fleshed out with 15% Merlot and 10% Cabernet Franc) leading the way. In 1989 French investment bank Paribas (owner of Chateau la Lagune and Champagne Ayala) acquired a majority interest, but left the Wheelers in charge, and winemaker Julia Iantosca in place. A Rhone red is in the pipeline, and with the finance provided by Paribas, so is the expansion of the winemaking facilities. In the meantime, well-made wines are the order of the day: a crisp, clean Sauvignon Blanc showing nicely balanced herbal and gooseberry flavors with a hint of spice coming from the 50% of the wine which was barrel fermented, and a smooth, ultra-commercial toasty oak and sweet-fruited Chardonnay.

WHITE OAK VINEYARDS 1981

A: 208 Haydon Street, Healdsburg, CA 95448 **T**: (707) 433 8429 **V**: 10–4 Fri–Sun **P**: 12,000 **W**: Paul Brasset

Town and country meet at the White Oak Vineyards winery in downtown Healdsburg. It was built in 1980 by owner Bill Myers, who has a small six-acre Alexander Valley vineyard planted to Chardonnay and Cabernet Sauvignon. The remainder of the grapes are purchased from growers in the Alexander and Russian River Valleys to produce a varietal range comprising Chenin Blanc, Sauvignon Blanc, two Chardonnays and a Cabernet Sauvignon. The Sauvignon Blanc is an excellent example of Russian River-grown fruit, with crisp, clean lively varietal flavor exhibiting a citric accent and good acidity; the Limited Reserve Chardonnay (principally grown on Bill Myers' own vineyard) is an elegant, underplayed and subtle wine, the epitome of the food style that so many seek but fail to achieve; and the Cabernet Sauvignon an excellent regional example with soft, red berry and cherry flavors and tannins which are easy on one's tongue.

Other Wineries

ALEXANDER VALLEY FRUIT & TRADING CO. 1987
A: 5110 Highway 128, Geyserville, CA 95441
T: (800) 433 1944

BANDIERA WINERY 1937
A: 155 Cherry Creek Road, Cloverdale, CA 95425 **T**: (707) 894 4295

CHARIS VINEYARDS
A: P.O. Box 697, Geyserville, CA 95441
T: (707) 433 3533

DIAMOND OAKS VINEYARD 1972
A: 26900 Dutcher Creek Road, Cloverdale, CA 95425 **T**: (707) 894 3191
W: Ronald C. Brown

J. FRITZ WINERY 1979
A: 24691 Dutcher Creek Road, Cloverdale, CA 95425 **T**: (415) 771 1900
W: David W. Hastings

JOHNSON'S ALEXANDER VALLEY WINES 1975
A: 8333 Highway 128, Healdsburg, CA 95448
T: (707) 433 2319 **W**: Ellen Johnson

LYETH VINEYARDS 1981
A: 24625 Chianti Road, Geyserville, CA 95441
T: (707) 857 3562 **W**: Robert Hunter

PASTORI WINERY 1914
A: 23189 Geyserville Avenue, Cloverdale, CA 95425 **T**: (707) 857 3418 **W**: Frank Pastori

PAT PAULSEN VINEYARDS 1980
A: 25510 River Road, Cloverdale, CA 95425
T: (707) 894 3197 **W**: Monty Paulsen

TRENTADUE WINERY 1969
A: 19170 Geyserville Avenue, Geyserville, CA 95441 **T**: (707) 433 3104
W: Leo Trentadue

VINA VISTA WINERY 1971
A: P.O. Box 47, Chianti Road, Geyserville, CA 95441 **T**: (707) 857 3722
W: William R. Hunter

128
EAST
Geyserville
Calistoga
GAS FOOD

ABOVE ~ *Road signs at the northern end of the Alexander Valley, strangely compelling graffiti.*

ABOVE ~ *The house at Alexander Valley Vineyards was built by Cyrus Alexander in 1860.*

DRY CREEK VALLEY

Doug Nalle makes great Zinfandel. Why? Dry Creek. "Simple," says Nalle, "If I lived in Carneros I might well be making Pinot Noir instead." In other words, the horse in Nalle's life is Dry Creek, the cart is Zinfandel. And it is not the least bit hard to understand why Nalle and the other two dozen winemakers (and many more growers) enjoy every aspect of life in the Dry Creek Valley. There is a quiet intimacy about the valley, with no two views the same, every twist in West Dry Creek Road opening up another vista. The pace of life is slower; there is a feeling of contentment. Traffic is minimal, so much so that for 20 minutes I successfully drove along Upper West Dry Creek Road thinking I was in Australia — negotiating numerous blind corners on the wrong side of the road.

The Dry Creek AVA is a valley arm 16 miles long and two miles wide at its widest point with approximately 20,500 acres on the valley floor, and 60,000 acres on the hillsides which enclose the valley on all sides other than its south-eastern corner, where Dry Creek joins Russian River. Six and a half thousand acres of vineyards have been established, principally on benchlands and hillsides, rather than the narrow valley floor.

A significant proportion of those vineyards were established up to a century ago by Italian families, who, naturally enough, favored Zinfandel and Italian mixed black plantings. Zinfandel has never lost its grip, but it is somehow appropriate that Italian (and Rhone) red varieties should be attracting much interest these days. That interest is particularly evident at the northern end of the valley, with highly-regarded grower Lou Preston engaged in much replanting as he matches varieties with specific site conditions.

And even though the valley is much cooler at its southern end, where it receives the maximum influence from the Russian River (and abuts the Russian River AVA), Dry Creek Valley is more red wine country than white.

Having said that, consider the varieties to be found on Lou Preston's 125 acres: Sauvignon Blanc, Chenin Blanc, Semillon, Muscat Canelli, Viognier, Marsanne, Zinfandel, Cabernet Sauvignon, Merlot, Syrah, Petite Sirah, Mourvedre, Carignane, Cinsault, Grenache and Barbera. If there is a pattern to be found through the valley at large, it is that the red grapes are grown on the hillsides and benchlands, the white grapes on the valley floor, with a preponderance of the latter at the southern end.

ABOVE ~ *An old vine or a Chinese Dragon in a shadow play?*

OPPOSITE ~ *Many of the best vineyards of Dry Creek are on the gentle slopes and the benchlands above the alluvial plain.*

THE REGION IN BRIEF

Climate, Soil and Viticulture

CLIMATE

Because it is so tightly pocketed by mountains on all sides, the climate is quite different from the Alexander Valley (which runs parallel to it, only a few miles to the east) and likewise different from that of the Russian River to the south. It does experience fog intrusions from the Russian River pattern, but these seldom enter before nightfall, and are less dense. What is more, the fog influence steadily diminishes, and the heat degree days steadily increase, as you move north. Somewhat surprisingly, it has a significantly higher rainfall than the Russian River. Not surprisingly, it is much warmer; Healdsburg, at its southern end, has a mean July temperature of 69.4°F. By the time you reach Yoakim Bridge Road heat summations are in the high Region II to low Region III levels, with temperatures regularly reaching the mid 80s°F during July, August and September. One notable feature of the climate is the absence of winds — again a consequence of the one-way nature of the valley.

SOIL

The hillside or benchland soils are composed of a geologically unique, gravelly material known as Dry Creek Conglomerate which is found nowhere else in Sonoma County. These distinctive red-colored rocky soils are frequently mixed (through on-going erosion) with the geologically younger alluvial material of the valley floor. Thus even on dead-flat valley floor vineyards such as those of Lou Preston, specific soil and subsoil characteristics differ markedly within short distances. What they do share are good drainage characteristics, but water-retentive subsoils. Combined with generous rainfall, the region thus lent itself to the dry farming techniques of a century ago, producing good yields of high quality grapes.

Dry Creek Valley
VINTAGE CHART 1981-1991

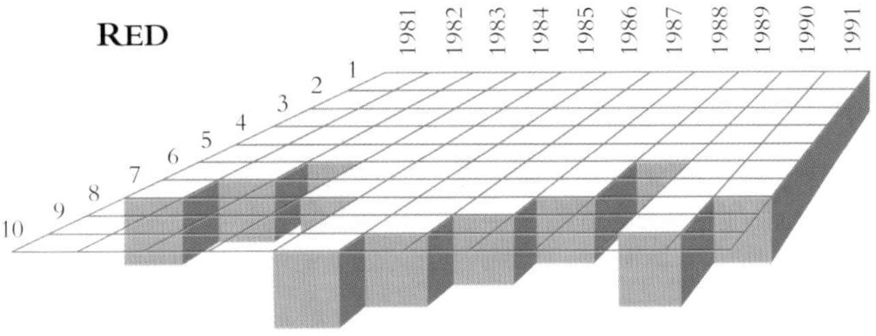
RED
1981
1982
1983
1984
1985
1986
1987
1988
1989
1990
1991
1
2
3
4
5
6
7
8
9
10

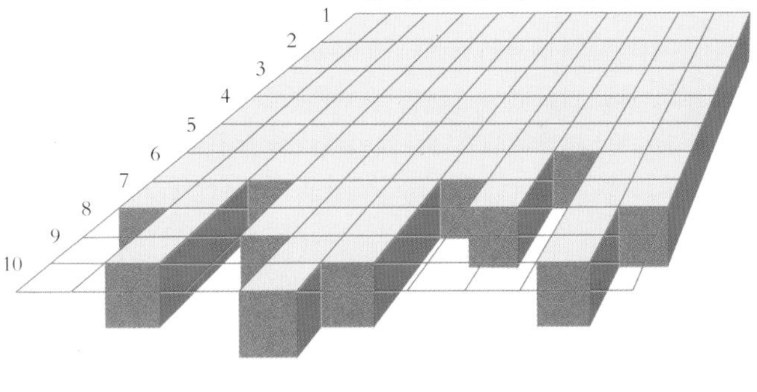
WHITE
1981
1982
1983
1984
1985
1986
1987
1988
1989
1990
1991
1
2
3
4
5
6
7
8
9
10

THE GROWING SEASON

Because of the relative absence of wind, and the warming effect of the hillsides reflecting (respectively) morning and afternoon sun, the ground warms early in the season, producing early budbreak and thus lengthening the growing season — although claims to have a longer growing season than the Russian River AVA seem dubious. Harvest time is as much dependent on site and yield as on the south to north heat progression, and the numerous varieties ripen in seemingly random fashion, with vintage a frantic scramble through September in normal years, intensified for those who grow Zinfandel by the incredibly narrow time-windows in which the grape must be picked if it is to give of its best.

Principal Wine Styles

ZINFANDEL

Zinfandel was first planted in the valley in the 1880s, and vineyards dating from that time onwards miraculously survived the dark ages before the Zinfandel renaissance (which I discuss at length on pages 160–1). If the fluid, ever-moving, ever-changing chameleon personality of the grape and its wine has a stable centerpoint, it must be the Dry Creek Valley. The wines are neither as spicy nor vibrant as those of the Russian River, as dense as those of Howell Mountain, nor as sensuously sweet as those of Amador County. They have a concentration and a structure which demands that you treat them as serious wines, yet the demand is delivered *sotto voce*. Nalle makes peerless Zinfandel, but Ridge's Lytton Springs Vineyard and Rafanelli have done more than their fair share in establishing Dry Creek's great reputation, while Dry Creek Vineyard, Preston and Quivira are all top-flight producers.

CABERNET SAUVIGNON AND RED MERITAGE

Charles Richard of Bellerose, at the southern end of the valley, frankly acknowledges that the climate there is at the cool edge for properly ripening Cabernet Sauvignon in many years. The further north, the lesser the problem, although most makers these days are using Cabernet as a major part of Meritage blends. Thus it is that Dry Creek Vineyard's excellent Meritages and Merlots have Dry Creek appellations, but its Cabernet Sauvignon (while partly Dry Creek sourced) has a Sonoma County appellation, while Ferrari-

Carano sources its seductive Cabernet Sauvignon from the Alexander Valley, Mazzocco Vineyards likewise. But wines such as Quivira's Cabernet Cuvee (with 73% of Cabernet Sauvignon) show why Cabernet plantings throughout the valley are increasing, sometimes at the expense of even Zinfandel.

Sauvignon Blanc, Fume Blanc and White Meritage

David Stare, of Dry Creek Vineyards, has been described by Bob Thompson as the father of Sonoma Sauvignon Blanc, introducing his first highly successful wine in 1972 and in many ways setting the pace ever since. If you like crisp, faintly herbal (or grassy, it is all a matter of linguistics) Sauvignon Blancs, those of the Dry Creek Valley will appeal to you as much as they do to me. Good producers include Alderbrook (a touch of asparagus, but a nice touch), Bellerose (in a powerful Meritage blend which oscillates between honeyed and pungently grassy), Dry Creek Vineyards (both Sonoma County Fumé and Dry Creek Reserve), and Preston (classic, elegant, smoky/grassy and long).

Sonoma County
1971 and 1991 Acreage/Grape Varieties

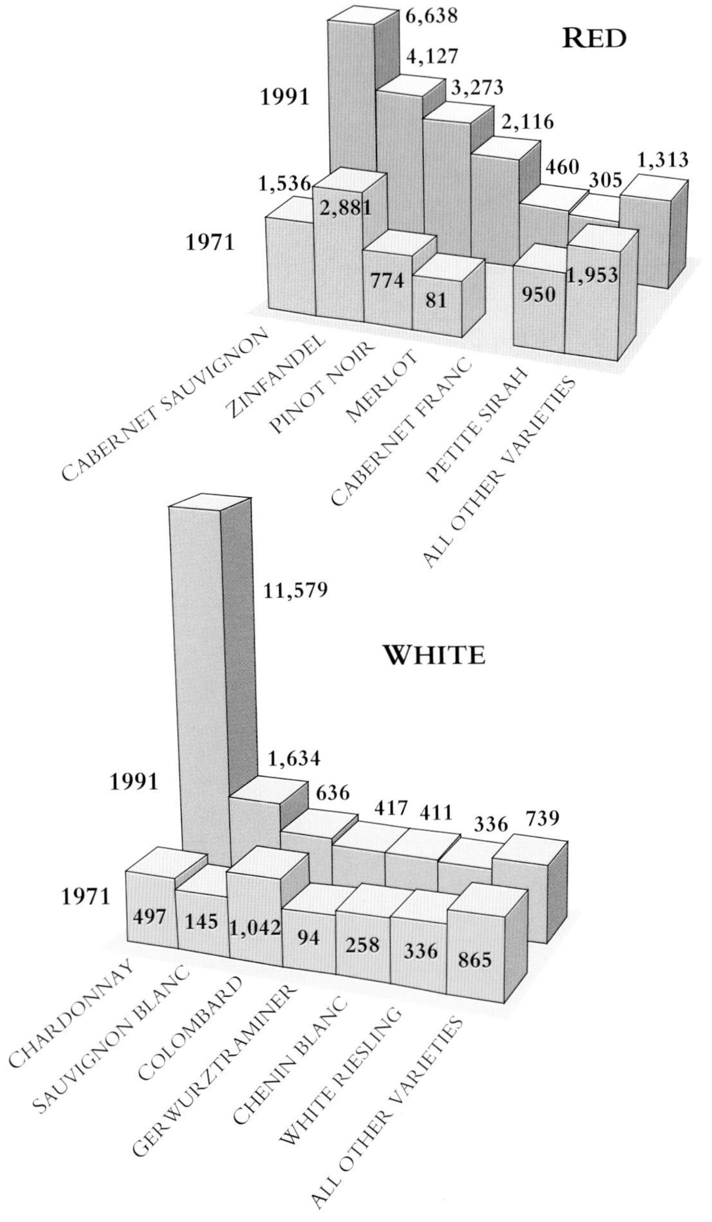
RED
1991
1971
6,638
4,127
3,273
2,116
460
305
1,313
1,536
2,881
774
81
950
1,953
CABERNET SAUVIGNON
ZINFANDEL
PINOT NOIR
MERLOT
CABERNET FRANC
PETITE SIRAH
ALL OTHER VARIETIES
WHITE
1991
1971
11,579
1,634
636
417
411
336
739
497
145
1,042
94
258
336
865
CHARDONNAY
SAUVIGNON BLANC
COLOMBARD
GERWURZTRAMINER
CHENIN BLANC
WHITE RIESLING
ALL OTHER VARIETIES

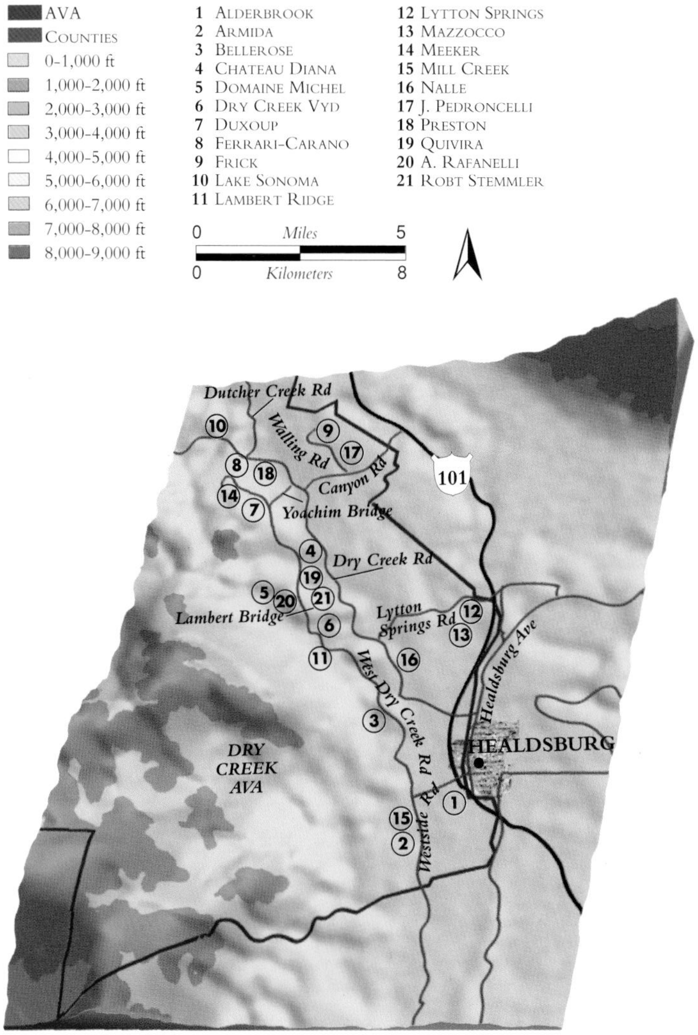
AVA
Counties
0-1,000 ft
1,000-2,000 ft
2,000-3,000 ft
3,000-4,000 ft
4,000-5,000 ft
5,000-6,000 ft
6,000-7,000 ft
7,000-8,000 ft
8,000-9,000 ft
1 Alderbrook
2 Armida
3 Bellerose
4 Chateau Diana
5 Domaine Michel
6 Dry Creek Vyd
7 Duxoup
8 Ferrari-Carano
9 Frick
10 Lake Sonoma
11 Lambert Ridge
12 Lytton Springs
13 Mazzocco
14 Meeker
15 Mill Creek
16 Nalle
17 J. Pedroncelli
18 Preston
19 Quivira
20 A. Rafanelli
21 Robt Stemmler
0 Miles 5
0 Kilometers 8
Dutcher Creek Rd
Walling Rd
Canyon Rd
Yoachim Bridge
101
Dry Creek Rd
Lambert Bridge
Lytton Springs Rd
Healdsburg Ave
West Dry Creek Rd
HEALDSBURG
DRY CREEK AVA
Westside Rd

ABOVE ~ *Dry Creek Valley map.*

Chardonnay

While a considerable number of the Dry Creek wineries have a Chardonnay on their roster, the majority are blended with wines from other AVAs (notably the Alexander Valley, but also the Russian River), Alderbrook and Domaine Michel being the more notable exceptions. It is ironic that the best example, Clos du Bois Flintwood (these days a brand name, made however from the Flintwood and Rued Vineyards), should be made outside the valley, a wine of outstanding subtlety and length of flavor.

Rhone Varietals

The foremost exponents — experimenters, if you prefer — are Preston and Quivira, with the relatively newly-arrived (and much smaller) Frick poised to add its contribution. There is no doubting that winemakers Kevin Hamel and Grady Wann are genuinely excited about the potential, while Bill Frick has certainly voted with his feet (and his money). To date, it is Preston which has turned promise into reality.

ZINFANDEL

It is entirely appropriate for the chameleon-like Zinfandel that no one should be sure what its genetic ancestry is or precisely when, how and by whom it was introduced into California. As to the former, it is generally accepted — though seemingly without much conviction — that it is a clone of the Italian variety Primitivo. As to the latter, credit was for long given to Agoston Haraszthy, apparently fostered in part by the mistaken belief that it was a Hungarian variety. Ironically, this belief was supported by William Robert Price; he grew it in his greenhouses on Long Island, New York as early as 1830, and supplied many of the cuttings used in California in the mid nineteenth century.

ABOVE ~ *Fully ripe Zinfandel, with some shrivelling starting to show, from the Madrona Vineyard in El Dorado.*

However that may be, Zinfandel has found a home for itself in California as nowhere else in the world. Like Shiraz in Australia, its familiarity bred contempt as it spread everywhere and was used to make oceans of wine which varied between alcoholic and inflammable. Much beloved of the innumerable Italian immigrants who derived part or all of their income from grape growing, it had the particular advantage of growing well if head-pruned — in other words, if grown without the aid of a trellis — and if frosted early in the season, it would produce a second crop nearly as large as a normal first crop.

The statistics and brief outline of the variety given earlier (on page 25) emphasize just how widely distributed the grape is throughout California. Yet the precious (and still expensive to maintain) plantings of very old vines might have passed into the pages of the history books were it not for a chance discussion between Sacramento wine merchant Darrell Corti and Bob Trinchero in 1972. From this grew the first White Zinfandel, and the at first feeble beginnings of one of the most remarkable marketing stories of all time as Sutter Home and blush wines soared from obscurity to national prominence. In doing so, Sutter Home joined the likes of Gallo in introducing millions of American men and women to the taste of wine. Mind you, it was not the taste of wine that most readers of this book would particularly enjoy: slightly pink, slightly sweet, slightly chalky and distinctly bland, yet clearly suited to the average untrained American palate.

Coincidentally, a few years earlier Ridge Vineyards had begun to release vineyard-designated Zinfandels (in dry table wine format) starting with Trentadue in 1966, and — even more coincidentally — Lytton Springs in 1972. And, having acknowledged the role played (and still being played) by White Zinfandel, it is on this genre of high quality red table wines that the focus of this chapter rests.

Yet even here controversy still abounds. Putting to one side the excessively alcoholic, jammy quasi-ports (the unfortified ones, that is) of bygone days, what is the style of Zinfandel which winemakers should aim for? More specifically, should they be making a wine which is at its best within three or four years of vintage or one which can age in the fashion of a Cabernet Sauvignon?

Having participated in a 1992 tasting of 130 or so Zinfandels organized for Robert Parker, comparing (for each participating winery) its 1990 wine with its 1985 (or older) wine, I have no doubt that as a general rule Zinfandel is most enjoyable while young. Having propounded that rule, let me immediately prove it by instancing some notable exceptions which emerged from the tasting, arranged alphabetically rather than order of merit: Burgess 1978, Caymus 1980, Deer Park 1982, Dry Creek 1984, Mark West Robert Rue 1984 and 1985, Quivira 1985, Sausal 1980, Shenandoah Vineyards 1982, Sky 1975, 1981, 1982, 1984, and Storybook Mountain 1980, 1984, 1985.

Indeed, it is a happy chance that the list should finish with Storybook Mountain, because here is a winery which does two remarkable things. Not only does winemaker/owner Jerry Seps prove that it is possible to make Zinfandel which is equally delicious at two, five or ten years of age, but he does so consistently. And when I say delicious in speaking of his older wines, I am pointing to wines which have retained distinctive varietal character and fruit freshness (a characteristic shared by the other wines I singled out above).

For the problem which most Zinfandels suffer with age is a loss of identity, even if they retain vinosity and a certain warmth. Doug Nalle told me a sweet/sour story of going to a Great-Wines-of-the-World tasting with some friends, with each member of the group providing a bottle and all wines being tasted blind. He took an old Zinfandel but did not divulge its variety because he was sure it would be automatically downgraded. It rated very highly in the group, opinions being divided as to whether it was an old California Cabernet or an old Australian red of some note. Matt Kramer likes wines to have a sense of place; I like them to have a sense of variety (or varietal style, if blended).

Surely the outstanding feature of Zinfandel is its brightness, its freshness, its silky/satiny texture, and its array of fruit flavors running the gamut from strawberry through red cherry to black cherry. In some respects, at least, it is like Pinot Noir. While usually quite high in alcohol in even its most civilized forms, it is not tannic. It is a wine driven by its exotic perfume and the sheer exuberance of its fruit (which is one of the main reasons why few makers waste too much money on new oak with the wine).

What is to be gained by cellaring such a wine? In most instances the loss of fruit freshness and personality will not be compensated for by a gain in complexity (and softening of tannins), simply because neither the tannins nor the latent complexity are there in the first place.

Yet this is a reality which many of the top makers deny in public, however much they may agree in private. For they and their growers are between the proverbial rock and a hard place. Almost without exception, the greatest Zinfandels are made from very old, low yielding vines — in other words, very expensive grapes to produce. Yet there is no way the public is prepared to pay the same price for a Zinfandel as for a Cabernet Sauvignon of similar quality.

The idea that a wine has to be capable of aging (and improving) for decades before it can be considered serious is deeply ingrained in the average American consumer's mind. It is an affliction which affects Pinot Noir as well as Zinfandel, and is in part a legacy of those tannic monsters of the 1970s and early 1980s. Can I simply say that young(ish) California Zinfandel is one of the world's most enjoyable red wine styles, a wine of individuality, of rare grace and of great quality. Which, I suppose, leads to the vexed question of which areas suit it best. Its statistical stronghold still remains the San Joaquin Valley, and there are those — such as Robert Mondavi Vineyard manager Dave Lucas — who swear blind that Lodi produces some of the best Zinfandel in California (he has his own little winery there which produces Zinfandel and nothing else). Lodi, it must be said, is one of the coolest parts of the San Joaquin/Central Valley, but it is still very warm.

California
ACREAGE OF ZINFANDEL
1982–1991

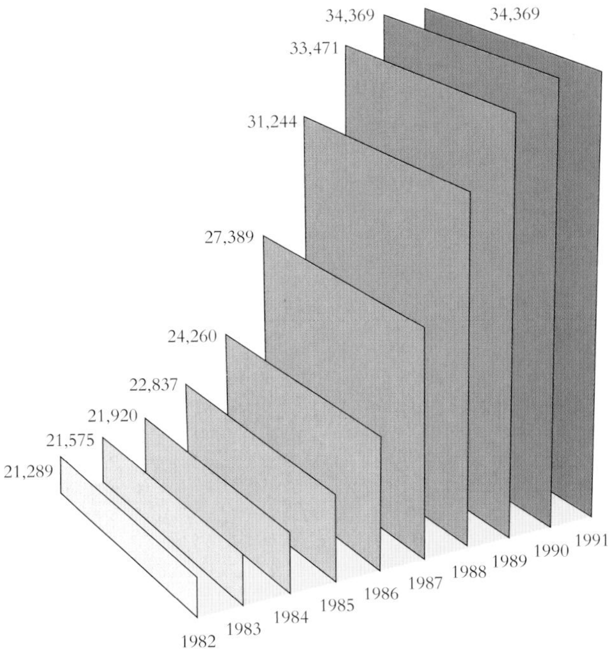
21,289
21,575
21,920
22,837
24,260
27,389
31,244
33,471
34,369
34,369
1982
1983
1984
1985
1986
1987
1988
1989
1990
1991

Then there are those who believe that Amador and El Dorado in the Sierra Foothills produce some of the most distinctive (and best) of all Zinfandels. It was where Sutter Home started (with its red Zinfandels), and the flame burns brightly today with its Deaver Vineyard Reserve. I must say I find the flavors tend to be just a little too cooked, a little too jammy, a little too minerally — a view with which Bruce Cass enthusiastically disagrees.

The Zinfandels of Paso Robles (and that little pocket at the furthest inland reach of the Arroyo Grande AVA, Saucelito Canyon) are also in a generous warm mold, but rather more to my liking. Indeed some superb wines have come from here, with Peachy Canyon, Arciero, Eberle and Castoro Cellars to the fore, but by no means alone in making sensuous, raspberry/redcurrant-accented wines.

The Napa Valley — and in particular its hillside subappellations — needs no particular herald: many outstanding wines come from there, with Lamborn, Sky, Green and Red, Chateau Potelle and Summit Lake being random selections.

But it is in Sonoma County that I would grow Zinfandel if given the chance, yet would fight to have a vineyard in each of the Russian River Valley, Sonoma Valley, Sonoma Mountain and Dry Creek Valley AVAs. If forced to chose between these, I would take either a very carefully chosen site in the Russian River or anywhere on the Dry Creek benchlands. Or come to think of it, I might prefer to copy (exactly) what Joel Peterson has done at Ravenswood or Kent Rosenblum at Rosenblum Cellars, by standing in one spot and casting a dry fly with infinite precision into the most propitious corners and eddies of the stream passing by — purchasing small parcels of old-vine Zinfandel from little vineyards spread across the state.

ABOVE ~ *Gerry Carreras in his vineyard, which supplies high quality Zinfandel to Doug Nalle.*

WINERIES *of* DRY CREEK VALLEY

ALDERBROOK VINEYARDS 1981

A: 2306 Magnolia Drive, Healdsburg, CA 95448 **T**: (707) 433 9154 **V**: 10–5 daily **P**: 30,000 **W**: Philip Staley

The simple design of the classic white and grey ranch-style tasting room gives no clue to the complicated, but very successful, Alderbrook partnership. Suffice it to say that Mark Rafanelli, a cousin of David Rafanelli of A. Rafanelli Winery, owns the 55 acre vineyards; partner John Grace is vineyard manager, while former dentist Philip Staley is winemaker. Ownership of the brand rests with the partners, but the title to the vineyards and the tasting room building lies with Rafanelli.

Alderbrook is situated at the extreme southern end of the Dry Creek Valley, the vineyards having much more in common with those of Russian River in terms of climate, and it was for this reason that the partnership has confined its attention to three white wines: Chardonnay, Sauvignon Blanc and Semillon. The original intention was to grow slowly and thus remain debt free, but the quality (and the value) offered by the wines has driven sales to 30,000 cases. Both the Chardonnay and the Sauvignon Blanc are clean, well made wines, with clear varietal definition and good intensity.

BELLEROSE VINEYARD 1979

A: 435 West Dry Creek Road, Healdsburg, CA 95448 **T**: (707) 433 1637 **V**: 10–5 daily **P**: 6,000 **W**: Charles Richard

While former classic guitarist Charles Richard would categorically deny copying Coulée de Serrant (the tiny Loire Valley producer which has taken organic farming to its ultimate extremes) he certainly would not object to comparisons, and in particular to mention of the fact that both use Belgian draft horses in cultivating the vineyard – Coulée de Serrant exclusively, Charles Richard for part of the vineyard work. And while Richard was one of the pioneers of the concept of sustainable viticulture and basic adherence to organic methods, he says "I don't wear my heart on my sleeve when it comes to organic farming, and if the need arose, I would not hesitate to use disease or pest control methods not permitted by the organic code." Much the same approach is taken in the winery: filtration and fining are kept to a minimum, as is the addition of sulfur dioxide — but not forbidden.

Charles and Nancy Richard came into the business circuitously; Charles Richard established a vineyard in Mendocino while completing his Master's degree in music and aesthetics, but it was the 1978 acquisition of the Bellerose Vineyard, already planted to 20 acres of Cabernet Sauvignon and Merlot respectively, which marked the full transition from music to wine. Richard was one of the first in California to conceive of the idea of a red blended wine based on the full complement of Bordeaux varieties, and established half an acre of Malbec and one and a half acres of Petit Verdot to accompany the Cabernet Sauvignon, Cabernet Franc and Merlot, also adding four acres of Sauvignon Blanc and half an acre of Semillon.

Cuvee Bellerose, as the Bordeaux blend is called, remains the principal wine, but a Reserve Merlot was added in 1983, and a Reserve White Meritage based on the Sauvignon Blanc is also produced.

The red wines are all formidable in their extract and tannin, and one wonders whether they will ever come into balance. The Sauvignon Blanc-Semillon blend, however, is a quite lovely wine exhibiting herbal/grassy characters in the cooler years and richer, lemony/honeysuckle fruit in the riper years, but invariably showing skilled barrel fermentation and oak handling.

DOMAINE MICHEL 1987

A: 4155 Wine Creek Road, Healdsburg, CA 95448 **T**: (707) 433 7427 **V**: By appointment **P**: 25,000 **W**: Fred Payne

Swiss-born investment banker and lawyer Jean-Jacques Michel has built a dream house and winery on the 100-acre site he purchased in 1979 and receives visitors and guests with ultimate charm and hospitality. Indeed, stories are still told of the party held to celebrate the completion of the house and winery in 1986, with some of the guests flown in from Geneva, and the creme de la creme of the California wine society present. In between time, Michel had planted 25 acres of Chardonnay, 14 acres of Cabernet Sauvignon, eight acres of Merlot and four acres of Cabernet Franc, with the first harvest in 1983 (and those ensuing until 1986) being processed at Jordan Winery (Tom Jordan being a close friend of Jean-Jacques Michel).

Domaine Michel is hidden from the road, and entrance is gained via electronic, voice-controlled gates, in part reflecting county restrictions on public visits (there are none) and no doubt in part by the Michels' understandable desire for privacy. Notwithstanding the superbly equipped winery, and the absolute commitment to quality (a number of the wines made have been relegated to second label or sold in bulk), critical reception and sales have remained cool. The Cabernet Sauvignon has been by far the most consistent performer, in 1987 and 1988 showing cherry and chocolate fruit flavors, but tannins which tremble on the brink, as it were. Winemaker Fred Payne joined the team in 1989, and it may be that better things are in store, although I cannot in all honesty say that I was much taken by the 1989 Chardonnay, which seemed hard and alcoholic.

DRY CREEK VINEYARDS 1972

A: 3770 Lambert Ridge Road, Healdsburg, CA 95448 **T**: (707) 433 1000 **V**: 10:30–4:30 daily **P**: 115,000 **W**: Larry Levin

David Stare, former engineer and inveterate sailor, is credited with establishing the first premium quality winery in the Dry Creek area after Prohibition, and of championing the Loire Valley white varieties which he believed would be particularly suited to the climate — Chenin Blanc and Sauvignon Blanc. The irony is that much of the initial Chenin Blanc came from the Delta area, although these days it is entirely sourced from vineyards in the Dry Creek region. After an initial period of growth, Dry Creek's momentum faltered, but it has once again picked up momentum under the guidance of Stare's daughter, Kim Stare-Wallace. As production has broken first through the 75,000 case barrier, then 100,000 cases, and now 115,000 cases, so has the proportion of purchased grapes necessarily increased. Dry Creek Vineyards has 100 acres of its own vineyards, 70 in the Dry Creek Valley planted to Sauvignon Blanc, Chardonnay, Cabernet Sauvignon, Merlot and Cabernet Franc and 32 in the Alexander Valley planted

PRODUCED & BOTTLED BY DRY CREEK VINEYARD, INC, HEALDSBURG, SONOMA COUNTY, CA USA • ALC 13.3% BY VOL
1987
meritage
DRY CREEK VINEYARD
DRY CREEK VALLEY
RED TABLE WINE

to Sauvignon Blanc and Chardonnay.

To my mind, the red wines of Dry Creek are as exciting as its white wines are boring (with one notable exception, the standard Fumé Blanc being splendidly crisp, clean and direct in style). The Red Meritage from 1987 and 1988, the Cabernet Sauvignon from 1989, the Merlot from 1989 and the Zinfandel from 1990 (and for that matter from 1984) are all beautifully made and balanced wines, showing stylish use of oak, perfectly balanced tannins and positive fruit flavors in the redcurrant/dark cherry/raspberry spectrum. The Zinfandel, of course, marches to its own tune, being unmistakably Dry Creek in style.

DUXOUP WINE WORKS 1981

A: 9611 West Dry Creek Road, Healdsburg, CA 95448 **T**: (707) 433 5195 **V**: By appointment **P**: 2,000 **W**: Debra Cutter

Andy and Debra Cutter named their winery after the Marx Brothers' movie *Duck Soup*, but there is nothing slapstick about the way they have organized their business. Right from the outset they decided on two things: they did not wish to grow the grapes, and they did not wish to be involved in hand-selling the wines. Thus there are no cellar door sales, and there is no mailing list; yet on the other hand, their tiny production goes as far afield as London, Hong Kong, Switzerland and 20 States. The winemaking shows the same almost monastic simplicity: it is entirely run on gravity flow, with not a pump in the place, wine movements from barrel to barrel or to bottling being pushed by gas. The wines are fermented in open fermenters, and all are bottled within 12 months of harvest.

Duxoup started with Zinfandel from the Alexander Valley, Napa Gamay from Dry Creek and Syrah from the Preston Vineyard, making its first experimental wine in 1979 and the first commercial wine in 1981. Charbono and Pinot Noir (from the Hudson Vineyard in Carneros) have since been added to the register, and the Zinfandel discontinued after 1990. The Calistoga-sourced Charbono has a most attractive blackberry/earthy/scented fruit, with that slightly hollow structure which seems to haunt the variety, but is an interesting wine nonetheless. All of the wines show full, strong fruit flavor, in part reflecting their relatively early bottling.

FERRARI-CARANO 1981

A: 8761 Dry Creek Road, Healdsburg, CA 95448 **T**: (707) 433 6700 **V**: 10–5 daily **P**: 50,000 **W**: George Bursick

The Ferrari-Carano winery and the Ferrari-Carano label make the precise statement one would expect from a highly successful second generation Italian–American, Reno-born and raised lawyer-turned-hotelier Don Carano. His wife Rhonda was also raised in Reno and is a second generation Italian–American. By the time Villa Fiore, the planned culinary and hospitality center, is surrounded by five acres of landscaped theme gardens, the statement will be even more emphatic. But before I go any further, I should make it clear that I am singularly impressed by the Farrari-Carano wines, and necessarily the viticultural and winemaking skills which have been employed in their production. For this is a very serious enterprise, and one which seems bound to succeed handsomely. Five hundred acres of vineyards on 12 different vineyard sites spread from the Alexander Valley to Carneros, and from hillsides to valley benchlands, provide a richly diverse source of grapes. The winery is of particular interest to an Australian observer, because it is one of the few to use rotofermenters. Indeed, the whole approach of winemaker George Bursick has a distinctly Australian feel to it, not the least being the generous and largely very successful use of new oak.

The red wines are soft, seductive and very fruity, always round and mouthfilling, and never tannic, the Merlot coming from Sonoma County and the Cabernet Sauvignon from Alexander Valley. The Alexander Valley Chardonnay and Sonoma County Fumé Blanc show spicy/toasty barrel ferment characters with lots of rich, tropical fruit flavors. Only the Reserve Chardonnay seem to go over the top with its oak. I can imagine, however, that the overall style of these wines will not necessarily please American palates accustomed to less fruit and more tannin in their wines.

FRICK WINERY 1972

A: 23072 Walling Road, Geyserville, CA 95441 **T**: (707) 857 3806 **V**: By appointment **P**: 1,500 **W**: Bill Frick

This is the "been everywhere, done everything" winery, starting life in an abandoned gas station in Bonny Doon, then moving to a warehouse in Potrero Street, Santa Cruz (now known as Storrs), and finally making the quite dramatic move to Dry Creek in 1988.

ABOVE ~ *West Dry Creek Road at times takes on the feel of an English country lane.*

Here the Fricks have established a hillside vineyard on slopes worthy of the Santa Cruz mountains, even if on a much smaller scale, having inherited a small mixed black planting dating back to 1946 of Napa Gamay, Petite Sirah and Zinfandel. The new plantings, which run straight up and down the steep but short slopes, are very close planted in full-blown European style, and will ultimately be trained in a thin, vertical trellis with movable catch wires. The emphasis is on what are very loosely called the Rhone varieties, with a Syrah Viognier blend projected for the future, together with Cinsault, Zinfandel, Petite Sirah and (to break up the pattern) a Pinot Noir.

Bill Frick uses open fermenters and believes in letting the grapes express themselves to the fullest. The Gamay, Petite Sirah and Zinfandel are all full-blown, full-bodied wines, as bold as the labels which grace them.

LAKE SONOMA WINERY 1977

A: 9990 Dry Creek Road, Geyserville, CA 95441 **T**: (707) 431 1550 **V**: 10–5 daily
P: 4,500 **W**: Donald Polsen

Another peripatetic venture, with its origins as Diablo Vista Vineyards in Contra Costa County, purchased by the Polsen family in 1982, who already owned vineyards in the Dry Creek Valley. Until 1986 the wines were made at Benicia in Contra Costa, but between 1986 and 1990 the present Lake Sonoma Winery was progressively built, and all winemaking now takes place there. The principal wines are Zinfandel, Sauvignon Blanc and Merlot, the Zinfandel being simple and unpretentious, but showing attractive strawberry fruit in the sort of medium to full-bodied style that one comes to expect from Dry Creek.

LYTTON SPRINGS WINERY 1975

A: 650 Lytton Springs Road, Healdsburg, CA 95448 **T**: (707) 433 7721 **V**: 10–4 daily
P: 7,000 **W**: Paul Draper

The acquisition of Lytton Springs Winery by Ridge Vineyards in 1991 was as inevitable as Desert Storm. Back in 1972 Paul Draper discovered the 50 acres of Zinfandel planted in the early 1900s which formed part of the 150 acre Lytton Springs Vineyard (then owned by Ridge Vineyards), and made one of the seminal vineyard-designated Ridge Zinfandels from it. But Lytton Springs Vineyard had nothing to do with Lytton Springs Winery, which could not resist the temptation to jump on the bandwagon. It commenced winemaking operations of its own in 1977, producing a series of unfiltered, unfined wines which varied from undrinkable to magnificent according to the whims of the bacteria which invaded them, and to no less a degree how ripe (or overripe depending on one's view) the grapes were permitted to get.

Palette
Red Table Wine • Produced and Bottled by
Lytton Springs Winery • Healdsburg, Ca • Contains Sulfites

It remains to be seen where Ridge will take Lytton Springs Winery in the years to come, but one thing is perfectly certain: wine quality will become much less variable. One of the curious mementos of the previous ownership is a non-vintage proprietary blend called Palette, which is composed of 60% Zinfandel and 40% Merlot, which must go close to taking the palm for the most bizarre red wine combination imaginable. For all that, it was a soft, slightly spicy, quite velvety textured wine which had obvious commercial appeal. But, as I say, "Quo vadis."

MAZZOCCO VINEYARDS 1985

A: 1400 Lytton Springs Road, Healdsburg, CA 95448 **T**: (707) 433 9035 **V**: 10–4 daily
P: 15,000 **W**: Nancy Steele

Like Dr. Robert Sinskey, Dr. Thomas Mazzocco is an eye surgeon who could not resist the idea of establishing his own winery, acquiring an 18-acre Chardonnay vineyard in the Alexander Valley and a 13-acre Cabernet Sauvignon-dominant vineyard in Dry Creek, acquisitions which have subsequently been expanded to 45 acres in total, although Mazzocco continues to buy Zinfandel and Cabernet Sauvignon from other growers. The winery was one of those to achieve national prominence in the most unfortunate fashion when it became embroiled in the Vintech disaster, and ownership has now reverted to Dr. Mazzocco, the only legacy of the Vintech interregnum being a second Europress, which allows hard working winemaker Nancy Steele to make 15,000 cases with the help of only one other assistant during crush, who in 1991 happened to be another female.

The maturing wine is stored partly at Mazzocco and partly at Vinwood, an arrangement which never seems to work particularly well because of the difficulties of monitoring progress in barrel, handling and so forth. I suspect it is as much a combination of that factor and the trauma of the Vintech years which produced a string of fairly ordinary wines between 1988 and 1990, and hopefully there are distinctly better things in store.

NALLE WINERY 1984

A: 2383 Dry Creek Road, Healdsburg, CA 95488 **T**: (707) 433 1040 **V**: By appointment
P: 2,700 **W**: Doug Nalle

I am quite sure that there are certain California winemakers who have dispensed with blood in their veins, and have had a transfusion of Zinfandel in its place. There is a passionate fire that burns from within; if in 1992 either Jerry Seps or Doug Nalle had been a presidential contender on the Zinfandel ticket, there might have been a great deal more excitement. Doug Nalle is the ultimate perfectionist: he says to his growers and pickers, "If you don't want to eat it, I don't want to crush it." On the other hand, he is almost fatalistic about his obsession: "I love living in Dry Creek, and because I live here, Zinfandel is the only possible grape. If I lived in Carneros, it might well be Pinot Noir." Nalle's career has taken him from Souverain to Jordan, thence Arroyo Seco, Balverne and finally Quivira from 1986 to 1989. But in 1984 he had started his own label on the side, and by 1989 felt the time had come to devote his full time to the Nalle brand. Two and a half thousand cases of that production is of Zinfandel, principally sourced from plantings dating back to the period 1880–1910, but he does blend in a touch of Petite Sirah to fill out the mid palate and give structure. Two hundred cases of Cabernet Sauvignon are a concession to convention, but little more. For my money, Nalle makes one of the great classic Zinfandels, exemplified by the 1990, wonderfully concentrated, rich and deep, with superb structure, soft tannins and perfectly balanced fruit ripeness.

J. PEDRONCELLI WINERY 1904

A: 1220 Canyon Road, Geyserville, CA 95441 **T**: (707) 857 3531 **V**: 10–5 daily **P**: 130,000 **W**: John Pedroncelli

The Pedroncelli family purchased what was then a 90 acre vineyard and winery from wholesale grocer John Canata in 1927, a brave decision given that the ending of Prohibition was still some time in the future. Since that time, the business has remained unequivocally family-owned and run, initially selling in bulk, but starting to develop its own label in the 1950s, with management passing to sons John and Jim in 1963. Walking through the sprawling building complex, one is struck by the immaculately clean and ordered facility which, given its age and the fact that it has clearly grown like Topsy over the last 65 years, might be expected to have a quite different air.

The mixture of old and new, of conservatism and what borders on radicalism, is evident in the range of wines on offer and, more particularly, in the avant-garde packaging and labeling introduced at the end of the 1980s. Yet underneath, the winemaking philosophy is salt of the earth stuff. "When it comes to winemaking," says John, "we're definitely non-procedure types. Every time you put a wine through a procedure, you take something out of it. Jim and I refer to it as non-winemaking. We tend wine more than we make it, but we try to tend it quite elegantly. I like to think we treat our wines like people are supposed to treat each other, with delicacy and kindness." How one could be critical of the Pedroncelli wines given that statement of philosophy, I do not know.

PRESTON VINEYARDS 1975

A: 9282 West Dry Creek Road, Healdsburg, CA 95448 **T**: (707) 433 3372 **V**: 12–4 Mon–Fri, 11–4 weekends **P**: 30,000 **W**: Kevin Hamel

Lou Preston just happens to have an M.B.A. from Stanford University and a year studying viticulture and enology at U.C. Davis under his belt. But degrees do not grow great grapes, even if they do help an enquiring and never-satisfied mind. When Lou and Susan Preston purchased an old prune and pear ranch in Dry Creek Valley in 1973 with the intention of becoming grape growers (and not winemakers) they purchased a remarkable property, the full potential of which is still to be realized. As at 1992, the 125-acre vineyard was planted to Sauvignon Blanc, Chenin Blanc, Semillon, Muscat Canelli, Viognier, Marsanne, Zinfandel, Cabernet Sauvignon, Merlot, Syrah, Petite Sirah, Mourvedre, Carignane, Cinsault, Grenache and Barbera. Missed anything out? Most certainly: Sangiovese, for one, is on the list to be planted, and very possibly Nebbiolo. If this were not enough, the Prestons commenced organic farming in 1989, and have come firmly to the conclusion that, while the original focus on Rhone varietals may have been correct, much of the specific matching of variety and *terroir* was wrong. A vigorous grafting and replanting program is underway, and the emphasis on Rhone varietals will increase rather than decrease. It hardly needs be said that Chardonnay will remain conspicuous by its absence.

It seems strange that winemaker Kevin Hamel should have joined the team as recently as 1989, for his background is as iconoclastic as that of the vineyard. He studied under

ABOVE ~ *Doug Nalle inspecting the Zinfandel in one of his contract grower's vineyards.*

Australian Professor Roger Boulton at U.C. Davis, before going to work for Darrell Corti, moving to Cockburn in Portugal for a year, and then coming back to work for Darrell Corti for six years, before becoming assistant winemaker at Santino Winery (in Amador County) where he was dealing with many of the same varieties as those at Preston.

The 1990 red wines, and the 1991s tasted from barrel, are absolutely delicious. 1990 saw the introduction of Faux-Castel Rouge, a southern Rhône blend of Carignane, Mourvedre, Zinfandel, Petite Sirah, Syrah and Grenache, enough to keep the owners of Beaucastel happy with its luscious, sweet red cherry to dark cherry Zinfandel-like flavors and strong tannins, in sharp contrast to the much more polished, lighter and gentler Barbera (still, however, with a sweet fruit heart) and the lush dark cherry and chocolate Zinfandel, rounded off by soft tannins. Perhaps the most elegant of all of the wines is the Sauvignon Blanc, crisp, faintly herbal, with a touch of smoky oak and a long, lingering, elegant palate. Even the Chenin Blanc, one of my least favorite varieties, shows excellent crisp fruit salad flavor.

It's quite a drive in to Preston (and to its most attractive gray wooden winery) but once there you will find some of the most unusual (and the best) wines in the whole of Sonoma County.

QUIVIRA VINEYARDS 1981

A: 4900 West Dry Creek Road, Healdsburg, CA 95448 **T**: (707) 431 8333 **V**: 10–4:30 daily **P**: 20,000 **W**: Grady Wann

Quivira is the retreat of SmithKline Beecham Chairman Henry Wendt and wife Holly. With 55,000 employees in 102 countries, and a $7 billion turnover, SmithKline Beecham is one of the pharmaceutical giants of the world. Small wonder that Wendt has guided Quivira's progress with a great deal more precision and success than the navigators who spent 200 years searching for a place born in the imagination of an Indian endeavoring to lead a Spanish Conquistador away from his homeland. Wendt's principle is effective delegation: choose the right people, and let them get on with their job. So it was that he chose Doug Nalle as his first winemaker, resulting in the production of a string of absolutely outstanding Zinfandels. When Doug Nalle retired to his own business, Grady Wann, boasting a PhD in organic chemistry and six years experience as winemaker under Bill Bonetti at Sonoma-Cutrer, was his replacement. Grady Wann is as articulate as he is intelligent, and the quality of the 1989, 1990 and 1991 red wines leaves no doubt that Nalle's inheritance is in good hands, and that Wendt's judgment is not in question.

I will pass over the Sauvignon Blanc, simply because I can only assume I tasted an unrepresentative wine. But the Zinfandel (1985, 1990 and 1991) is right at the top echelon of Dry Creek winestyle, with exceptionally concentrated dark berry fruits, fully ripe — yet not jammy or porty — flavor, and the structure to carry the wine for five to seven years with ease. Even more impressive is the Cabernet Cuvee, a blend of Cabernet Sauvignon (around 75%), Cabernet Franc and Merlot, with the Merlot content increasing progressively over the years 1989 to 1991. In the pipeline is Dry Creek Cuvee, a Rhone mix of 60% Grenache, 23% Mourvedre and 17% Syrah planted in 1989. While those varieties were coming into bearing, Grady Wann was busy experimenting with small lots purchased in the region, including a strawberry-flavored Grenache made from 50-year-old vines.

A. RAFANELLI WINERY 1972

A: 4685 West Dry Creek Road, Healdsburg, CA 95448 **T**: (707) 433 1385 **V**: By appointment **P**: 6,000 **W**: Dave Rafanelli

A. Rafanelli was Americo, but was always called Am, just as his father Alberto was called Al. It was these two who purchased 100 acres of land on West Dry Creek Road in 1954, planting Zinfandel, Gamay Beaujolais, Early Burgundy and French Colombard. Twenty years later Am ventured into winemaking, selling Cabernet Sauvignon, Zinfandel and Gamay Beaujolais. By the end of the 1970s, Rafanelli had started to establish a reputation of some note, and by the time David Rafanelli took over following the death of his father in 1987, the name was well and truly established.

The business now draws its grapes from 50 acres of vineyards, including 15 acres of Zinfandel, 12 of Cabernet Sauvignon and two of Merlot. Only two wines are made: Zinfandel and Cabernet Sauvignon, each crafted in a spotlessly clean wooden winery which in some ways reminds one of an outsized doll's house.

The wines are neither fined nor filtered, and the whole making methods are directed to placing the focus on the fruit — and the whole focus of the vineyard is in gaining maximum flavor and extract in the grapes. The result is wines of at times formidable flavour, structure and depth, which have a quite fanatical following.

ROBERT STEMMLER WINERY 1977

A: 3805 Lambert Bridge Road, Healdsburg, CA 95448 **T**: (707) 252 7117 **V**: 10–5 daily **P**: 2,500 **W**: Robert Stemmler

Carrying on a conversation with Robert Stemmler is an almost surreal experience; one does not have the faintest idea where his mind will dart next, and least of all whether the topic of discussion will be in any way wine-related. Perhaps it is part a reflection of an extraordinary career, which started in Bad Kreuznach in Germany in 1952, continued in 1961 at Charles Krug in the Napa Valley when he was hired (from Germany) to develop a sterile filtration

ROBERT
STEMMLER
WINERY
1988
SONOMA COUNTY
PINOT NOIR
PRODUCED AND BOTTLED BY
ROBERT STEMMLER WINERY
HEALDSBURG, CA U.S.A.
ALCOHOL 12.5% BY VOLUME

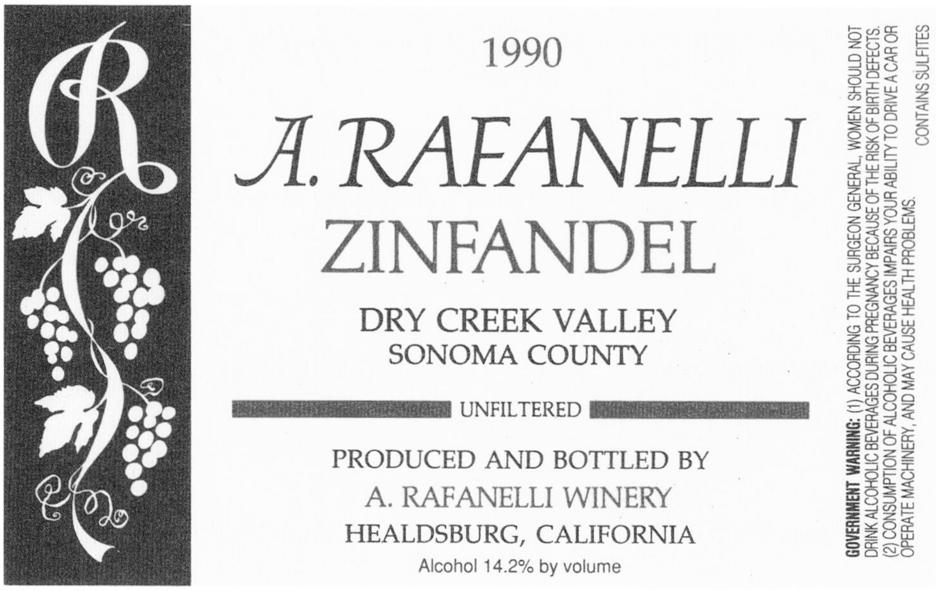
1990
A. RAFANELLI
ZINFANDEL
DRY CREEK VALLEY
SONOMA COUNTY
UNFILTERED
PRODUCED AND BOTTLED BY
A. RAFANELLI WINERY
HEALDSBURG, CALIFORNIA
Alcohol 14.2% by volume
GOVERNMENT WARNING: (1) ACCORDING TO THE SURGEON GENERAL, WOMEN SHOULD NOT DRINK ALCOHOLIC BEVERAGES DURING PREGNANCY BECAUSE OF THE RISK OF BIRTH DEFECTS. (2) CONSUMPTION OF ALCOHOLIC BEVERAGES IMPAIRS YOUR ABILITY TO DRIVE A CAR OR OPERATE MACHINERY, AND MAY CAUSE HEALTH PROBLEMS.
CONTAINS SULFITES

system to deal with the problem of a sweet Chenin Blanc which had a nasty habit of re-fermenting in the bottle, a project which was intended to take months, but which led to his staying at Krug for six and a half years before he was hired as winemaker at Inglenook. He stayed there until 1970 before joining Simi, where he worked for three years.

Then followed a period of consultancy in Argentina, Chile and California, and it was not until 1977 that he decided to establish his own small winery on Lambert Bridge Road. He did so without any thought of making Pinot Noir, and the initial vintages did not feature it. But in 1982 Simi decided it was no longer going to make Pinot Noir, and a parcel of unwanted grapes landed in Stemmler's lap. By 1988 he was making 8,000 cases of Pinot Noir, and in a most unusual deal, Racke U.S.A. (owners of Buena Vista) purchased the Stemmler Pinot Noir label and of course the marketing rights. The Pinot Noir is now made at Buena Vista under Stemmler's direction, while the Dry Creek Winery is as much a cellar door sales facility as anything else these days. I can only hope that the move to Buena Vista leads to an improvement in wine quality, because all of the Stemmler Pinot Noirs I have tasted up to and including 1988 seemed to be deficient in what I, at least, regard as varietal Pinot Noir flavor or style.

Other Wineries

Armida Winery 1990
A: 2201 Westside Road, Healdsburg, CA 95448
T: (707) 433 2222 **W**: Frank Churchill

Chateau Diana 1987
A: 6195 Dry Creek Road, Healdsburg, CA 95448 **T**: (707) 433 6992
W: Craig T. Manning

Lambert Bridge 1975
A: 4085 West Dry Creek Road, Healdsburg, CA 95448 **T**: (707) 433 5855 **W**: Ed Killan

The Meeker Vineyard 1984
A: 9711 West Dry Creek Road, Healdsburg, CA 95448 **T**: (707) 431 2148
W: Michael Loykasek

Mill Creek 1976
A: P.O. Box 758, Healdsburg, CA 95448
T: (707) 433 5098 **W**: Dennis Hill

ABOVE ~ *Rows of Zinfandel vines at Quivira Vineyard.*

TOP ~ *Gallo's James R. Gowan watching Chardonnay fall from his truck into the crusher.*

RUSSIAN RIVER VALLEY

I have explained elsewhere (on page 19) the utterly bewildering and schizophrenic nature of the AVA system, citing the Russian River Valley as one of the prime examples of the schizophrenia. In a way this is unfair to the valley, for with the qualified exception of the Chalk Hill AVA (which, as I explain, forms part of the Russian River Valley along with the Green Valley AVA) this region makes sense, tied together by the umbilical cord of the Russian River which flows through it and which has such a profound effect on its climate.

When, in the middle of its feeding frenzy, the BATF created these three AVAs (between November and December 1983) it noted of the Russian River Valley that it covered 150 square miles, and that the name "is now used by four wineries in the viticultural area." Less than ten years later there were 45 wineries within its compass (not all using the Russian River name, it is true) and it had over 9,000 acres of vineyards.

It has a long viticultural history, enshrined in the Korbel Champagne (sic) cellars, built in 1886 and today the foremost vinous tourist destination in the Russian River Valley. Korbel is at the western edge of the AVA, only two miles east of Guerneville in a steep, narrow redwood-clad valley carved by the Russian River.

Much of the western side of the area is very beautiful, whether one is exploring the wineries around Forestville, those grouped along Westside Road, or the hills around Iron Horse in the Green Valley. As the Green Valley Creek joins the Russian River, and you follow the latter upstream towards Healdsburg where it enters the Alexander Valley — which the Russian River also beautifies — the countryside opens up on to the Santa Rosa Plain, before once again merging with the foothills of the Mayacamas Mountains, most notably in the Chalk Hill area.

But there is something about the air, solitude, and vegetation which, apart from its Region I climate, tells you this is a great area for Pinot Noir, for Chardonnay and for sparkling wines made from those varieties, and why Joseph Swan chose to come here. Matt Kramer puts it quite beautifully: "Over time, Russian River Valley producers will put down a Pinot Noir vineyard here and there, persistently feeling about the landscape, like a contact-lens wearer on hands and knees searching for a missing lens."

Some have already searched (not only for Pinot) with notable success: Dutton Ranch, Rochioli, Davis Bynum, Howard Allen (for Williams Selyem) and Iron Horse, to name a few. In this ever-changing landscape, more will succeed in the future.

ABOVE ~ *The cool climate of the Russian River is reflected in all its trees and vegetation.*

OPPOSITE ~ *Ocean fogs and mists regularly penetrate the Russian River Valley at the Korbel Winery and vineyards.*

The Region in Brief

Climate, Soil and Viticulture

Climate

The climate is profoundly maritime-influenced through the dual agency of the Russian River as it makes its mercifully unspoilt way to the ocean, and by the winds sweeping in from Bodega Bay, through the Petaluma Gap and turning north. So it is that, viewed at large, this is a Region I climate. In the Green Valley AVA it is at the lower end — in some seasons as little as 2,000 degree days — while in the Chalk Hill AVA it varies between 2,500 and 3,000 degree days (in other words, Region II).

The morning fog and afternoon sea breeze pattern reflects the maritime influence, of course. But the mean temperature of July of around 66°F (at Graton it is 65.8°F) is low, and varies little throughout the growing season, providing a slow but even accumulation of heat. Frost, too, by and large poses a lesser threat than it does in the Napa Valley, notwithstanding the cooler growing season climate.

Soil

In general terms, the soils are of the same Franciscan series as one finds on the western side of the Napa Valley, i.e. west of the Napa River. Chalk Hill does have its particular white soils which give the area its name: these are sandy to silt loam, clay and quartzite soils which are high in volcanic ash deposited (according to some) as a result of the volcanic activity of nearby Mount St. Helena. Likewise, the soils of the Green Valley AVA are distinguished from their neighbors by being Goldridge fine sandy loam. As one comes out on to the Santa Rosa plain on the north-eastern corner of the region, the soils thicken with a greater clay content; these highly water-retentive soils are more suited to white varieties than reds. But the majority of the soils of the region are well drained, thanks to the high percentage of degraded sandstone and shale in their make up, aided in many instances by the alluvial gravels and boulders deposited by the Russian River and its tributaries in the course of their wanderings.

The Growing Season

The season is a long one, up to 115 days between fruit set and picking. Thus even the early ripening Pinot Noir is not picked until early to mid-September for table wines in "normal" growing years like 1990, while in late years such as 1991 Iron Horse did not commence picking for its sparkling wines until September, de Loach leaving its Gewurztraminer until September 30 in that year. Chardonnay is typically harvested in the second half of September and Sauvignon Blanc in early October, followed by Zinfandel in mid month and Cabernet Sauvignon through to the end of the month. Interestingly, the harvest dates for Chalk Hill are not much different, running from mid September for Chardonnay and Cabernet Sauvignon from late September to early October.

Contract Growers

Allen Vineyard Fifty-eight acres of high quality Chardonnay and Pinot Noir planted in 1973 on benchland hillside above the Russian River; sold to Williams & Selyem and Gary Farrell among others.

Aquarius Ranch/McIlroy Vineyard Forty-three acres on Westside Road north of Forestville planted to Chardonnay, Gewurztraminer and Pinot Noir between 1973 and 1992.

Bacigalupi Vineyard Another important Westside Road vineyard planted to 60 acres of Chardonnay and Pinot Noir, with Belvedere and Gary Farrell being purchasers.

Dutton Ranch The Green Valley Chardonnay vineyard made famous by Kistler.

Olivet Lane Vineyard Eighty acres of Chardonnay and 20 acres of Pinot Noir planted in 1976, supplying Pinot Noir to Williams & Selyem and also the owner's brand (Pellegrini).

Rochioli Vineyard As well as providing grapes for its own label, this 100 acre vineyard planted to Pinot Noir, Chardonnay, Zinfandel, Cabernet Sauvignon, Sauvignon Blanc and Colombard sells to others including Williams & Selyem and Gary Farrell.

Principal Wine Styles

Pinot Noir

While Carneros and the Edna, Santa Maria and Santa Ynez Valleys all have claims to be recognized as the preeminent Pinot Noir regions (not forgetting San Benito), so does the Russian River Valley. This is in no small measure due to two vineyards more or less opposite each other — Rochioli and Allen — and to the skills of four winemakers: Gary Farrell, Tom Rochioli, Burt Williams and Ed Selyem. The synergy of vineyard and winemaker has produced some exquisite Pinot Noirs, combining elegance with intensity, varietal clarity with complexity. These have all the tightness of Carneros Pinots, yet have an extra dimension, a touch of wildness which Carneros all but misses. At the other end of the scale, Dehlinger produces opulent, rich Pinot of structure and longevity, the sort of wine of which one imagines the late Joseph Swan would have thoroughly approved.

Zinfandel

Calling the varietal shots in this area is not easy, but I have to put Zinfandel next, simply because of the many outstanding wines I have tasted from here. Given that Zinfandel is more commonly encountered in Region II and III climates, and that Dry Creek, Lodi, Amador County, Calistoga and so forth each lay claim to producing the greatest Zinfandels, my choice may seem all the more quirky. Why such wonderfully balanced, concentrated and deeply fruited wines should abound I do not know. The flavors range from vibrant, spicy cherry (what one might expect from a cool growing region) through to unctuous, almost briary, blackcurrant and strawberry. Some are made to be drunk young, others (the

Russian River Valley
VINTAGE CHART 1981-1991

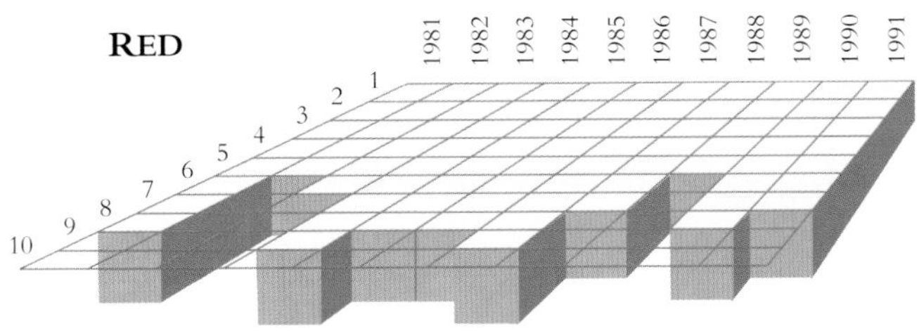
RED
1981
1982
1983
1984
1985
1986
1987
1988
1989
1990
1991
1
2
3
4
5
6
7
8
9
10

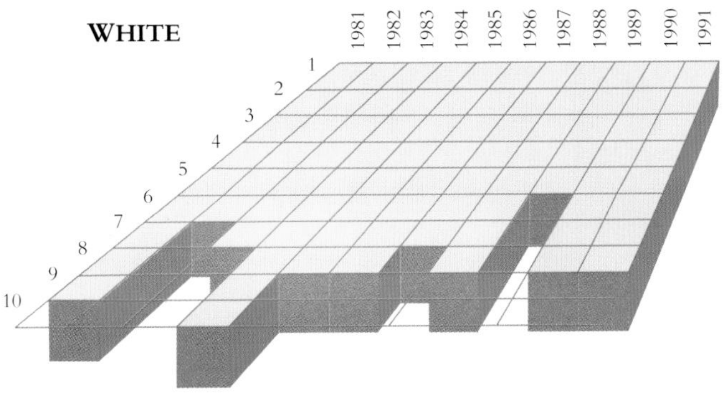
WHITE
1981
1982
1983
1984
1985
1986
1987
1988
1989
1990
1991
1
2
3
4
5
6
7
8
9
10

de Loach single vineyard wines, Mark West Robert Rue Vineyard and Hop Kiln) will age wonderfully well if that is what you wish. Davis Bynum and Rodney Strong are other outstanding producers.

CHARDONNAY

The towering presence of Kistler makes the relegation of Chardonnay to third place an act of blasphemy even before one turns to Sonoma-Cutrer. It is perhaps justified in part by the extreme range of style: what do the wines of Iron Horse, Kistler, Sonoma-Cutrer, Dehlinger, Chalk Hill and Rochioli have in common? Apart from "Chardonnay" on the label, nothing, with Iron Horse and Kistler Dutton Ranch being polar opposites in terms of style, yet both coming from the Green Valley AVA. One thing is certain: somewhere you will find a Russian River Chardonnay which will suit your palate to perfection, and there is no question about the legitimacy of its place in this part of the world.

SAUVIGNON BLANC

If you are not afraid of the true flavor of Sauvignon Blanc, then some of California's greatest wines of this much-mistreated and maligned variety come from the Russian River, led by Rochioli's intense gooseberry and passionfruit wines — wines of startling flavor, length and style. At the other end of the spectrum comes the Graves-like, powerful wine of Chalk Hill. By rights, we should see and hear more about this variety from here, but the Ides of March may tell against it.

MERLOT

As the Laurels Vineyard Merlot of Davis Bynum shows, this must be a variety for the future given the enormous interest in it. And given David Ramey's presence at Chalk Hill Winery, which arguably has the best location of all for its production, Merlot may well be a superstar of the future.

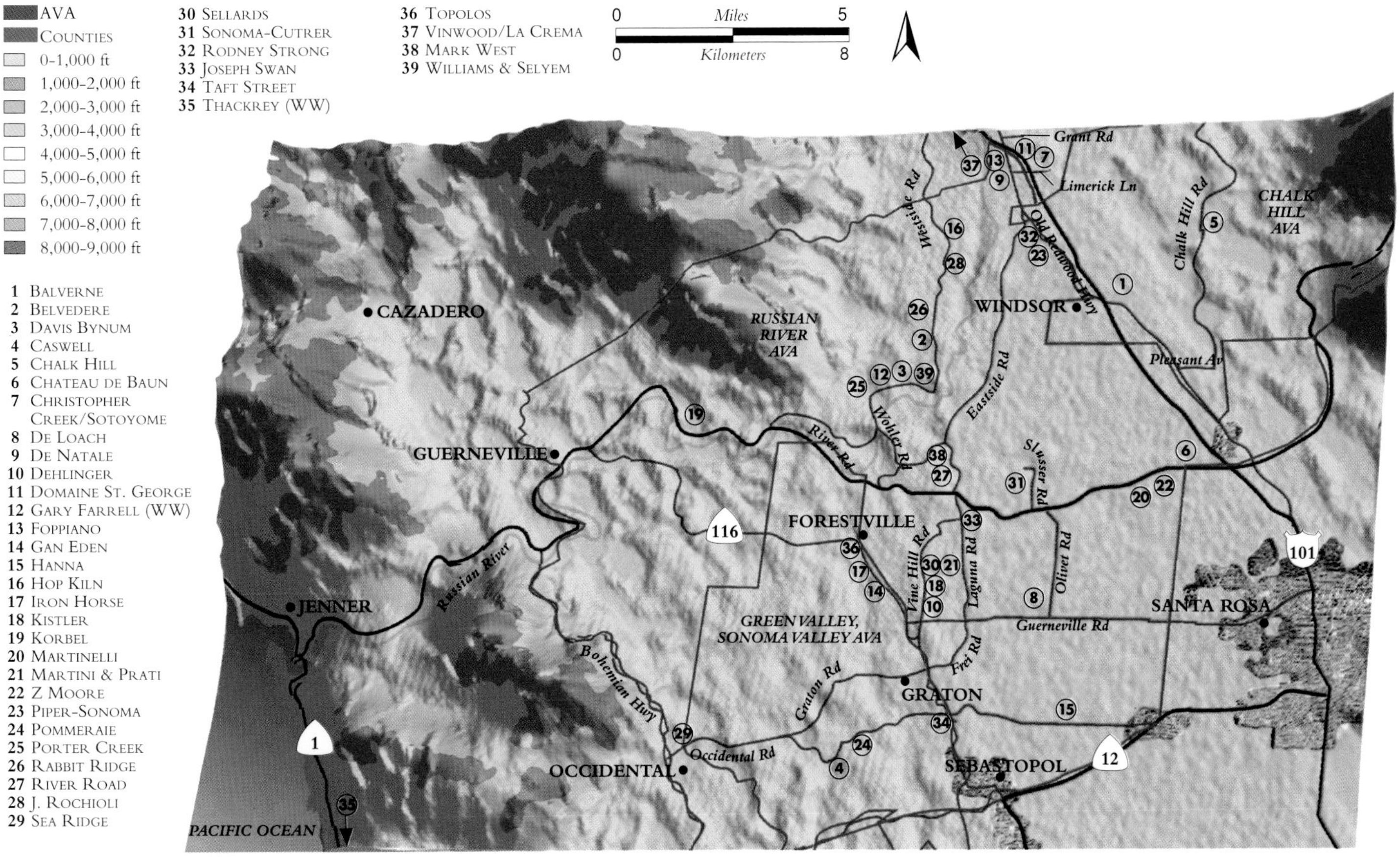
AVA
COUNTIES
0-1,000 ft
1,000-2,000 ft
2,000-3,000 ft
3,000-4,000 ft
4,000-5,000 ft
5,000-6,000 ft
6,000-7,000 ft
7,000-8,000 ft
8,000-9,000 ft
1 BALVERNE
2 BELVEDERE
3 DAVIS BYNUM
4 CASWELL
5 CHALK HILL
6 CHATEAU DE BAUN
7 CHRISTOPHER CREEK/SOTOYOME
8 DE LOACH
9 DE NATALE
10 DEHLINGER
11 DOMAINE ST. GEORGE
12 GARY FARRELL (WW)
13 FOPPIANO
14 GAN EDEN
15 HANNA
16 HOP KILN
17 IRON HORSE
18 KISTLER
19 KORBEL
20 MARTINELLI
21 MARTINI & PRATI
22 Z MOORE
23 PIPER-SONOMA
24 POMMERAIE
25 PORTER CREEK
26 RABBIT RIDGE
27 RIVER ROAD
28 J. ROCHIOLI
29 SEA RIDGE
30 SELLARDS
31 SONOMA-CUTRER
32 RODNEY STRONG
33 JOSEPH SWAN
34 TAFT STREET
35 THACKREY (WW)
36 TOPOLOS
37 VINWOOD/LA CREMA
38 MARK WEST
39 WILLIAMS & SELYEM
0 Miles 5
0 Kilometers 8
Grant Rd
Limerick Ln
Westside Rd
Old Redwood Hwy
Chalk Hill Rd
CHALK HILL AVA
WINDSOR
CAZADERO
RUSSIAN RIVER AVA
Eastside Rd
Pleasant Av
Wohler Rd
River Rd
GUERNEVILLE
Slusser Rd
FORESTVILLE
116
Vine Hill Rd
Laguna Rd
Olivet Rd
101
JENNER
Russian River
GREEN VALLEY, SONOMA VALLEY AVA
Guerneville Rd
SANTA ROSA
Bohemian Hwy
Frei Rd
Graton Rd
GRATON
Occidental Rd
OCCIDENTAL
SEBASTOPOL
12
1
PACIFIC OCEAN

ABOVE ~ *Russian River Valley map.*

SONOMA-CUTRER

The approach of this atlas follows that of an earlier work on Australia and New Zealand. Thus it was preordained that each chapter would contain a feature on a major subject directly or indirectly arising from the region. Quite early in the piece I was asked to decide what the features would be: the first visit by photographer Oliver Strewe was months in advance of my first research trip, and not unreasonably he was seeking some guidance as to what he should photograph.

ABOVE ~ *Chardonnay grape bunches provide a temporary home to spiders, which help control insect pests.*

I remained resolutely uncooperative. I felt that not until I had reached the end of the research road could I sensibly start to sort out the pieces of the jigsaw puzzle, and decide on the features — which are a deliberately idiosyncratic assemblage of places, people, grapes, practices and philosophies. But had I been honest I would have admitted that one or two articles were pre-ordained, and that Sonoma-Cutrer was one of them.

Without ever having visited it, I was utterly fascinated by everything it stood for, everything it had done. I had been absorbed by the proceedings of its two symposia on Chardonnay, the first staged at Sonoma-Cutrer in 1986, the second in Burgundy in 1990. One of the cellar rats for the 1992 vintage at my winery had done a vintage at Sonoma-Cutrer. I had tasted its wines more than once in international blind tastings of some significance. And of course I had read (or heard) about its unique production techniques, its relentless quest for perfection.

Yet the fates nearly conspired against me. The visit was scheduled 3 P.M. on Friday May 29, the ninth of 13 wineries I was meant to visit that day, starting with Adler Fels at 8 A.M., then Golden Creek, then Matanzas Creek before I even entered the Russian River.

I never suffer jet lag, and in any event I had arrived the previous Sunday, spending three days tasting in San Francisco, before embarking on the Thursday on my 10,000 mile odyssey driving on the wrong side of the road. That Thursday night I did suffer jet lag: at no stage did I even remotely look like going to sleep. Early the following morning I left the motel, thinking I would at least enjoy the early morning scenery and arrive a little early at Adler Fels. Alas, my map showed Corrick Lane running directly off Highway 12, and in the ensuing hour I learnt that asking directions from locals in California is even more pointless than doing so in France. It was a nightmare start to the day, but by a miracle I arrived at Sonoma-Cutrer more or less on time for my appointment, only to find that Chief Executive Brice Jones was unaware of the arrangement, and had certainly never heard of me.

But he was there, and — for heaven knows what reason — agreed to see me, and, equally importantly, arranged for me to see the winery and ask whatever questions I wished. I wonder whether I would have done the same, had the roles been reversed. Somehow I doubt it. But then that is why Sonoma-Cutrer is what it is; why I was drawn to it like a magnet; and why I am writing about it.

Just how and when the investors who banded together in January 1973 to back Brice Jones expect to receive a return on their investment, I do not know. The exceedingly generous California tax laws of the early 1970s no doubt played a role in the vineyard establishment phase, but the rules had changed substantially by 1981 when the winery was commenced and the former Air Force pilot and Harvard Business School graduate embarked on the second phase of his vision splendid.

One could write an entire book about Sonoma-Cutrer, so extraordinary — and at times bizarre — is the whole venture. More money must have been spent on marketing and image-building than most wineries would spend in a lifetime on winery equipment. There is not one international-standard croquet lawn at the front of the winery, but two. The attention to detail in the making of the wine can only be described as fanatical: there is the unbelievably rigorous selection process of the grapes involving sorting tables and the discarding of any disfigured grape (and I mean grape) before the clusters pass through the chilling tunnel and thence direct to the press; the near-hospital sterility of the winery; the twice-weekly topping of barrels; the special machine which dusts each cork before it is inserted in the bottle ... the list goes on and on.

The first winemaker was the legendary Bill Bonetti. Brice Jones would settle for no one less, and ran prominent advertisements, throwing resumés away without even reading them until finally Bonetti applied for the job. After ten years he has retired to take up the position of Emeritus Winemaker, leaving assistant Terry Adams in charge. It is not likely that the style of the wines will change. That style is dictated by the combination of climate and *terroir,* and by the understandable designation of the Chardonnays into three distinctly different vineyards: Les Pierres, Cutrer Vineyard and Russian River Ranches.

It is here, indeed, that the plot thickens. The observant will know that all of the Sonoma-Cutrer wines carry the Sonoma Coast appellation. This is because its premier vineyard — Les Pierres — in fact lies outside the Russian River AVA, although the other two (and the winery itself) are within it. Few other wineries have the need to acknowledge the existence of the sprawling Sonoma Coast AVA, but for Sonoma-Cutrer it is an essential link in the vital estate bottle image. Indeed, it would be the final travesty of justice (and common sense) if the winery were to be denied it.

Les Pierres covers 100 acres of cobblestone soil, producing 11,000 cases a year of the finest, longest-lived of all the Sonoma-Cutrer wines. Among its many admirers is James Laube who, in *California's Great Chardonnays,* places it as one of the 11 First Growth Chardonnays of California. It is a measure of the process of selection that so few cases are produced under this label. At a yield of (say) 2.5 tons per acre (low even by the standards of the great domaines of Burgundy), 100 acres should produce over 16,000 cases.

Much the same pattern appears with the Cutrer Vineyard; it also covers 100 acres, and provides only 10,000 cases a year. While the mesoclimate is slightly cooler, the soil produces a marginally softer wine, with faintly buttery characters edging through.

It is not until the Russian River Ranches label makes its appearance that production figures start to return to normal. The Ranches, which in fact comprise three vineyards, cover 210 acres, and around 50,000 cases a year are made under this label. This is the most accessible of the three wines in its youth, with crisp citric/melon fruit and impeccable mouthfeel.

The reason for the distortion in the figures is threefold. First, all of the Sonoma-Cutrer wines are made from what is virtually free run juice. Once the press reaches half a bar, the juice is "cut off" as is done in Champagne. The pressings are sold in the bulk market, where one imagines they bring a tidy sum. Second, the part of Les Pierres and Cutrer's wine which doesn't perform precisely as anticipated is likely to end up as a component of Russian River Ranches. Thirdly, Sonoma-Cutrer is engaged in its never-ending quest for perfection in the vineyard as much as the winery. Thus all manner of viticultural trials are constantly being evaluated, with particular emphasis on vine spacing and canopy management in the wake of its 1990 "Focus on Chardonnay" seminar in Burgundy.

The overall style of Sonoma-Cutrer is as consistently flawless as one would expect. Because nothing is left to chance, nothing surprising happens. They are wines which appeal to the intellect rather than the gut, and they demand time in bottle if they are to come into full flower.

Paradoxically, they are the product of a philosophy which, while exceptionally disciplined, is essentially non-interventionist. Bill Bonetti puts it this way: "A winemaker needs to let a wine talk to the consumer about its origins, its soil, its climate, its vintage. In order for a wine to express its heritage, the winemaker cannot allow himself to intervene." It is a remarkable statement from a man who over 30 years did so much to create the greatest California Chardonnays.

LA

ABOVE ~ *Croquet American style, at Sonoma Cutrer: the legs belong to C.B. Smith, winner of that year's American Croquet Association's Annual Open.*

WINERIES *of* RUSSIAN RIVER VALLEY

BELVEDERE WINERY 1979

A: 4035 Westside Road, Healdsburg, CA 95448 **T**: (707) 433 8236 **V**: 10–4:30 daily **P**: 65,000 **W**: Erich Russell

Belvedere was founded in 1979 by two partners with remarkable industry knowledge and contacts: Peter Friedman, who started Sonoma Vineyards with Rodney Strong, and Bill Hambrecht, a partner of Hambrecht & Quist, investment bankers with a worldwide portfolio of wine and winery clients, and who floated Chalone Inc. to the public. The partnership was built around an idea: it had neither vineyards, winery nor winemaker. The idea was to produce two lines of wine: one which offered exceptional value for money, the other higher-priced vineyard designated wines of consistent quality. The winery was duly built and a winemaker (Don Frazer) installed, with Paul Draper as consultant. The value for money wines were styled "The Discovery" series, virtually all purchased on the bulk market; the vineyard designated wines were called "The Grapemaker" series, and featured the name of the producer so prominently that many consumers failed to make the connection with Belvedere. Nonetheless, both lines were tremendously successful, and sales soared to the extent that "The Discovery" series had to be blended and stored elsewhere.

What goes up, must come down. By 1989 shortages on the bulk wine market had hit "The Discovery" series, and sales of "The Grapemaker" wines slumped. Belvedere made a U-turn, focusing its attention on just two lines, both under the Belvedere label, and with a heavy emphasis on barrel-fermented Chardonnay. By far the largest production is the Alexander Valley Chardonnay, selling for $9 in 1992, with 15,000 cases of Russian River Valley Chardonnay selling for $13. The base commercial portfolio is filled out with a Dry Creek Zinfandel, a Dry Creek Merlot, and an Alexander Valley Muscat Canelli. The reformulation was a huge success, with Belvedere quadrupling its sales in a market which was in overall decline. New winemaker Erich Russell has also been able to introduce small quantities of ultra-premium, preferred stock, fully barrel-fermented Chardonnay which is on strict allocation. Most remarkably of all, Belvedere has been able to sell 75% of its wine to restaurants.

The Alexander Valley Chardonnay is a plain, rather featureless wine which is more or less what you would expect given the price and the provenance. The Russian River Chardonnay is a very distinct cut above, discrete, but with some attractive barrel-ferment characters augmenting

ABOVE ~ *One of the tasks of winter and early spring: tying down the vines on their trellis.*

the tightly structured fruit. The Merlot, from Dry Creek, can be outstanding at the price, with lots of sweet fruit, generous tannins (almost a little too generous) and far more character and style than one would anticipate.

DAVIS BYNUM WINERY 1965

A: 8075 Westside Road, Healdsburg, CA 95448 **T**: (707) 433 5852 **V**: 10–5 daily **P**: 22,000 **W**: Gary Farrell

The amazing collection of buildings and winemaking equipment huddled together at the top of the steep drive, centered around a 1950s hop kiln which seems much older, is wholly appropriate given the charmingly idiosyncratic history of the Davis Bynum Winery. It started in 1951 when young newspaper reporter Davis Bynum bought 50 pounds of Petite Sirah from Robert Mondavi to make three and half gallons of not very distinguished but quickly consumed wine. His interest had been sparked by his father, Lindley Bynum, himself a wine judge and occasional wine writer. Fourteen years of home winemaking later, Davis — urged on by his father — opened a small winery in the rear of a small plumbing supply warehouse near the University of California at Berkeley. Attesting to the primitive winemaking techniques employed during his amateur days, Davis Bynum had jokingly labeled some of his wine "Barefoot Bynum" (and privately referred to it as Chateau la Feet). By the time the brand was sold in 1986, 20,000 cases of wine were being sold under it in the fighting varietal market.

In the interim, the Bynums had long since outgrown the Berkeley facility, and in 1973 (after flirting with the Napa Valley) purchased the 83-acre River Bend Ranch in the Russian River Valley, where the winery and 12-acre hillside vineyard planted to Pinot Noir (five different clones) and Merlot are presently situated. The following year Gary Farrell joined Davis Bynum as winery worker, becoming winemaker in 1978 and being named Winemaker of the Year for 1991 by the *Los Angeles Times*.

A year before Farrell's arrival, Davis Bynum had produced and marketed the first Pinot Noir made exclusively from Russian River Valley grapes, and it is to premium varietal wines that the winery has returned after the sale of the Barefoot Bynum label. The range covers three whites (Chardonnay, Fumé Blanc and Gewurztraminer) and four reds (Pinot Noir, Cabernet Sauvignon, Merlot and Zinfandel). Most are good, some serendipitous, exemplified by the absolutely glorious limited release Sonoma County Merlot from 1989 and the Russian River Zinfandel of 1990, wines of exceptional fruit, quality, intensity, style and balance. It would be unreasonable to expect all of the wines to reach the same level of quality, but they do share a common thread of elegance and finesse, particularly the finely sculpted Pinot Noirs.

CHALK HILL 1974

A: 10300 Chalk Hill Road, Healdsburg, CA 95448 **T**: (707) 838 4306 **V**: By appointment **P**: 65,000 **W**: David Ramey

San Francisco anti-trust and class action lawyer Fred Furth is a self-made man who defied the odds by becoming a lawyer, and perhaps even greater odds by being a particularly successful one. The same relentless drive has transformed what was meant to be a healthy distraction from the pressures of legal practice into a magnificently appointed and very large winery on a showcase estate, with 1,100 acres planted to 278 acres of hillside vineyards.

Those vineyards are not planted on the contour, but straight up and down the hills, utilizing sod culture between the rows in a manner identical to my own vineyards. Regrettably (from my viewpoint) that is where the similarity ends. For Furth has been able to invest literally millions of dollars in the estate, employing unimaginable numbers of people and (by way of random example) establishing a maintenance shop which services 40 vehicles and all the winery equipemnt. Oh, and he has also established 30 miles of roads within the property, while burying all power and phone lines to preserve the natural beauty.

For all that, there is general agreement that until David Ramey joined as winemaker in 1990 the Chalk Hill wines were decidedly unexciting. Ramey, who has two vintages at Chateau Petrus under his belt, a vintage in Australia, four years as assistant winemaker at Simi, and five as senior winemaker at Matanzas Creek, is without question one of the brightest talents in California. Ramey's arrival marked an immediate transformation in the style and quality of the wines, with richly flavored, tropical fruit and hazelnut Chardonnay, and complex and mouthfilling Sauvignon Blanc. As at 1992, the Ramey-made Cabernet Sauvignon (the third of the three principal estate wines) had not been released, but by the time of publication will have reached the market, and almost certainly received the type of adulatory reviews his Matanzas Creek wines were accorded. And just to keep everyone interested, Chalk Hill is also making limited quantites of a Pinot Gris which — if for no other reason than scarcity — will be sought in much the same fashion as its occasional Late Harvest Semillon.

CHATEAU DE BAUN 1986

A: 5007 Fulton Road, Fulton, CA 95439 **T**: (707) 571 7500 **V**: 10–5 daily **P**: 30,000 **W**: Jamie Meves

The hospitality center of Chateau de Baun established in the middle of the 105-acre estate may not be in harmony with the landscape, but is certainly in tune with engineer–inventor Ken de Baun's iconoclastic view of wine and wine styles. Although he traces his lineage back to the city of Beaune (hence the family name), he acquired the first 20 acres of vineyard more or less accidentally, in what he describes as a "property-tax swap." The following year he, and wife Grace, purchased an adjoining 40-acre parcel of land, at that stage unplanted, and in the spring of 1982 planted ten acres of Pinot Noir, ten acres of Chardonnay and ten acres of Symphony, a patented cross developed by Professor Harold Olmo by crossing Muscat of Alexandria with Grenache Gris.

The decision to plant Symphony (and to continue planting it to the point where at one stage Chateau de Baun had more Symphony under cultivation than any other winery in California) was purely and simply due to the inventor make-up of de Baun's mentality; he had to find a variety that no one else was growing. The 42 acres of Symphony have since been fashioned into a dry varietal table wine called Overture, an off-dry cocktail wine called Prelude, a sweet light dessert wine called Theme, and a late harvest called Finale; it has been blended with 40% Chardonnay to produce Chateau Blanc, a proprietary generic; it has been blended with 10% Pinot Noir to produce Rhapsody, a Brut Rosé sparkling wine, and to make Romance, a 100% Symphony-based sparkling wine. The long-suffering Pinot Noir from the estate plantings is blended with 15% Petite Sirah from Clarksburg to produce Chateau Rouge.

BARREL FERMENTED
CHÂTEAU
DE BAUN
1990
Chateau Blanc
RESERVE WHITE TABLE WINE
RUSSIAN RIVER VALLEY
ALC 13% BY VOL

The wines are as strange and baroque as the mock French chateau which constitutes the hospitality center. The Muscat component of Symphony overwhelms everything it comes into contact with, in particular the inherently delicate and elegant Russian River Pinot Noir and Chardonnay grapes. By far the best wine is the late harvest Finale, intensely grapey and muscaty, but well balanced by firm acidity. But then the tune of Chateau de Baun is essentially different from that of any other Russian River winery, and successfully demands a different audience.

DE LOACH VINEYARDS 1975

A: 1791 Olivet Road, Santa Rosa, CA 95401
T: (707) 526 9111 **V**: 10–4:30 daily
P: 110,000 **W**: Cecil de Loach and Randy Ullom

© 1987 Navajo Snow by Sally Baker
DE LOACH VINEYARDS®
ESTATE BOTTLED • RUSSIAN RIVER VALLEY
1989 PINOT NOIR O.F.S.®
PRODUCED & BOTTLED BY DE LOACH VINEYARDS, INC.
SANTA ROSA, SONOMA COUNTY, CALIFORNIA, USA
ALC. 13.0% BY VOL. • CONTAINS SULFITES

Quietly-spoken Cecil de Loach is a quite extraordinary man. After leaving school in 1956 he did a stint in the marine corps and, after a brief career as a race-track photographer, joined the San Francisco fire department in 1964 and is more than content that he should simply be known as a fireman (not as a fire chief) who worked for the department for the next 16 years and was able to scrape together a few dollars on the side to grow grapes in a small way (and to grow from there). But in fact, he simultaneously put himself through San Francisco State University, graduating with honors in physical anthropology, and doing research in urban anthropology under a grant from the National Institute of Mental Health in his spare time. No, Cecil de Loach was not your everyday fireman.

In 1969 he and his wife Christine found a 24-acre property on Olivet Road owned by Lewis Barbieri, whose father had planted Zinfandel on the property between 1905 and 1927. Barbieri was passionately attached to his vines, and could not bear the thought of the land being sub-divided, and the de Loachs persuaded him they would preserve the property and its vines. A deal was struck: Barbieri sold the property on favorable terms, and agreed to live in the farmhouse for a year and teach the de Loach family how to tend vines and grow grapes. Cecil lived in a small trailer on the ranch, where he spent every hour while not on duty in San Francisco.

In 1971 Barbieri moved out, and the de Loachs moved in, scraping together enough money to buy another 28-acre parcel on Olivet Road the following year, on which site the winery now stands. Initially the grapes were sold to the Sonoma County Co-operative Winery in Windsor; in typical de Loach fashion, he first served on the board of directors of the winery (in 1972) and in 1973 was elected president. In between those duties, growing grapes, and answering fire calls, he took extension courses in enology and wine chemistry from U.C. Davis, and by 1975 was ready to venture into winemaking, making his first Zinfandel in a small unit in a Santa Rosa industrial park, with a total investment of $4,500.

In 1979 he began the first phase of construction of the winery (right from the outset, it was planned to build it progressively with the aid of his two sons), and the following year quit the fire department. From that point on, it has been one continuous success story, first with White Zinfandel, then voluptuous Chardonnays, and now some of California's finest Zinfandels (all of which lines, together with a highly regarded Gewurztraminer and an excellent Healdsburg-sourced Cabernet Sauvignon continue in production).

In all, de Loach has 200 acres of estate vines, with a further 75 acres held on long-term lease. The top varietal wines have always been released under the OFS signature, nominally standing for "our finest selection," but apparently other versions of the meaning do exist. But in 1990 de Loach extended his range of (red) Zinfandels to five: the standard Estate Bottled, the Estate Bottle OFS, and three vineyard designated Estate Bottled wines (Barbieri Ranch, Papera Ranch and Pelletti Ranch). The latter four are made in strictly limited production — the standard Zinfandel which in fact comes from the same vineyard sources accounts for 6,000 cases, but the others are produced in only 500 case lots. The standard wine is exemplary, with fragrant, fresh red berry fruit in an early-drinking style, the other Zinfandels showing far more concentration and complexity, yet having distinctly individual personalities.

DEHLINGER WINERY 1976

A: 6300 Guerneville Road, Sebastopol, CA 95472 **T**: (707) 823 2378 **V**: 10–5 daily
P: 8,000 **W**: Tom Dehlinger

The 50-acre estate vineyards are a viticultural showcase, a unique blend of Old World and New World philosophy and practice. In the manner of a Burgundian tending his one- or two-acre plot, Dehlinger has come to know every vine as an individual and to understand the influence of *terroir* which has shaped the individuality of that vine. If anyone thinks this is an exaggeration, a quick walk through the vineyard will convince them otherwise: each vine is color coded into one of four categories, basically reflecting the vigor of the vine. The New World is represented by the response to the varying levels of vigor, with the vineyard architecture being radically transformed in the early 1990s, allowing for different trellising and training techniques according to vigor.

Even by the time (1985) that Tom Dehlinger made the decision to cease buying grapes from outside growers, and to produce only estate-made wine, Dehlinger had established itself as one of the leading producers of Pinot Noir in California, and as a very fine producer of Chardonnay. (These two varieties account for 35 acres, the remaining 15 acres being divided between Cabernet Sauvignon, Merlot and Cabernet Franc.) The Dehlinger Pinot Noirs were (and remain) extremely rich, voluptuous, almost chewy Pinot Noirs, as far removed from (say) those of Rochioli or Williams-Selyem as one could imagine. It is fascinating to speculate how the style of the Dehlinger Pinot Noirs of the 1990s will evolve: it is difficult to conceive of them becoming richer still, but the theoretical consequence of the changes in viticultural technique is that they should do so. Apart from a preference for the use of puncheons (barrels twice the size of the more usually encountered barrique) there is nothing unusual in the way the Pinots are made, although increasing use of whole bunches in the ferment may add another dimension of finesse and complexity.

FOPPIANO VINEYARDS 1896

A: 12707 Old Redwood Highway, Healdsburg, CA 95448 **T**: (707) 433 7272
V: 10–4:30 daily **P**: 185,000 **W**: Bill Regan

Lou Foppiano (the third generation chief executive by that name) is nobody's fool. In July 1992 he had just returned from a trip to Burgundy, and was busy extracting details of his visits from his laptop computer. He is familiar with the whole world of wine; John Buck of Te Mata Estate in the Hawke's Bay region of New Zealand (and maker of New Zealand's best Cabernet-based wines) is a friend. Yet unless you look closely, you might think that this is just another old fashioned producer of Italianate jug wines. In fact the winery has been progressively, and very skillfully modernized, with an unseen but extensive use of computerization to keep track of every barrel and every parcel of wine in the winery.

The winery produces three brands, drawing in part on 160 acres of estate vineyards, and in part on purchased grapes, and endeavoring to keep the identity of those three brands as separate as possible. At the top of the range is the very limited production Fox Mountain Reserve Cabernet Sauvignon and Reserve Chardonnay, each consisting of only 2,000 cases. Next come the Foppiano Vineyards varietals of Chardonnay, Sauvignon Blanc, Petite Sirah and Cabernet Sauvignon, totalling 30,000 cases or thereabouts. Finally there is the Riverside Farm range, 150,000 cases of low-priced varietals (Chardonnay, Zinfandel and Cabernet Sauvignon) and white and red generics. As the 1988 Riverside Farm Zinfandel and the 1990 Foppiano Petite Sirah handsomely demonstrate, Foppiano can give you rather more than you either expect or pay for, although it must be said that overall the wines do not rise above their station in life.

GAN EDEN 1985

A: 4950 Ross Road, Sebastopol, CA 95472
T: (707) 829 5686 **V**: By appointment
P: 30,000 **W**: Craig Winchell

Craig Winchell was born Jewish, but of a non-practicing family; his father, a doctor, had a fine cellar of imported wines, giving Craig a taste for wine long before he acquired a taste for Judaism. For all that, his entry into wine was circuitous, his first college work relating to research in nuclear medicine, before managing a wine shop in Greenwich Village, and finally undertaking the fermentation science degree from U.C. Davis which he completed in 1981. He then worked for several wineries, and met his wife Jennifer in so doing. Her conversion to Judaism turned Winchell from non-observant to Sabbath observant, or Orthodox, which meant that he could only drink kosher wine from that point onwards. This in turn left him with only one choice: to start his own winery and to make fully certified kosher wine.

Gan Eden (Garden of Eden in Hebrew) is the result, and with it what must surely be the producer of the finest kosher wines in the world. The 1986 Cabernet Sauvignon won several competitions as the best Cabernet Sauvignon produced in America that year, while the 1987 and 1988 wines (the latter particularly) are both of high quality. The 1988 has masses of sweet fruit, cassis and chocolate, and is a triumph for what was a fairly mediocre vintage overall. The 1987 is no slouch either, having been awarded 90 points by the *Wine Spectator*. The main problem has been some variation in style, as Gan Eden has no vineyards of its own, and its vineyard sources tend to switch from year to year. The Chardonnay (and the other white wines in the portfolio) are less exciting, but you can't have everything. Since only Sabbath-observant people are involved in making the wine, it is the only fully kosher winery in America, and is not subject to the usual restrictions. Heart bypass surgery did cause Winchell to slow down, however, there is much pressure is on to expand the Cabernet and Chardonnay production in the warehouse-type winery he has built just down the road from La Crema.

HOP KILN 1975

A: 6050 Westside Road, Healdsburg, CA 95448 **T**: (707) 433 6491 **V**: 10–5 daily
P: 9,000 **W**: Steve Strobl

The Hop Kiln Winery must be the most-photographed winery in the whole of Sonoma, if not California — quite apart from anything else, four movies have been made there. But it was sheer luck that it was Dr. Marty Griffin, and not someone else, who purchased the 240-acre ranch with its 1905 vintage hop kiln. For Dr. Griffin has had a long and distinguished career in medicine, public health and a wide range of conservation issues; it was the conservationist in him which led him and two friends to embark upon the seemingly impossible task of restoring the building, which had not been used since the 1940s and which was in imminent danger of collapse. It was also fortuitous that this former teetotaller from Utah had spent a year in Italy, there gaining the interest in wine which led to his expanding the vineyard from the few acres of very old Petite Sirah and Zinfandel growing there to the 65 acres of today.

Restoration of the building was completed in 1974, and Dr. Marty Griffin made his first

THE
HOP KILN
WINERY

ABOVE ~ *One of the landmarks of the Russian River region, painstakingly restored by owner Dr. Marty Griffin.*

two wines in that year: a Petite Sirah and a Johannisberg Riesling. He continued as winemaker until 1984, when increasing production led to the appointment of Steve Strobl as executive winemaker. An exotic range of wines is produced in this exceptionally exotic winery: a non-vintage generic white romantically called "A Thousand Flowers," Gewurztraminer, Johannisberg Riesling, Valdiguie (formerly labeled Napa Gamay), Marty Griffin's Big Red (a Zinfandel-based blend along with lesser quantities of Cabernet Sauvignon, Petite Sirah and Valdiguie which once beat Opus One and Phelps Insignia at the Orange County Fair), Zinfandel, Primitivo Zinfandel (Dr. Griffin has registered the name Primitivo, but others do appear to be using it in contravention of the registration), Cabernet Sauvignon and Verveux (the last a sparkling wine made from Johannisberg Riesling). Without question, Zinfandel is the star performer, both in its standard and Primitivo guises. Wines such as the 1985 Primitivo tasted in 1992 show why some regard the Hop Kiln wines as being over the top, but the two 1990 wines are simply glorious: the standard with tingling, vibrant, cherry, strawberry, pepper and spice flavors; the Primitivo with concentrated dark berry fruit, hints of blackcurrant and appropriate tannins. Even if the wines do not approach this quality every year, no one should go to the Russian River without visiting Hop Kiln.

IRON HORSE VINEYARDS 1976

A: 9786 Ross Station Road, Sebastopol, CA 95472 **T**: (707) 887 1507 **V**: By appointment **P**: 45,000 **W**: Forrest Tancer

The Iron Horse Vineyard site was originally selected by Rodney Strong in 1971 and the then youthful Forrest Tancer hired to commence the development work. The waning of the Rodney Strong financial fortunes and several changes of ownership meant that by the time the property was purchased by Barry and Audrey Sterling in 1976, only part of Tancer's original plan had been carried out, with trellising incomplete, no frost protection and one third of the vines in need of replanting. Tancer was reinstated as vineyard manager, and in 1979 formed a partnership to build a winery, becoming winemaker and also supplying grapes from the Tancer family estate in the Alexander Valley.

The 55 acres each of Pinot Noir and Chardonnay at Iron Horse produce 20,000 cases of sparkling wine and 25,000 cases of table wine, with an Estate Chardonnay and an Alexander Valley Cabernet leading the way, and with lesser quantities of Fumé Blanc (declining through the ravages of phylloxera) and intermittent releases of Pinot Noir (often downgraded to the second label, Tin Pony).

The Iron Horse Cabernet is uncharacteristically thin and hard, given its Alexander Valley provenance, but it comes as no surprise to find the Iron Horse Chardonnay extremely austere, flinty and Chablis-like, given Barry Sterling's assertion that this the coolest vineyard in California (a claim hotly disputed by Doug Meador of Ventana Vineyards, among others). Be that as it may, this is in low Region I category, and it certainly shows in this ultra-reserved, chalky and austere style.

As one would predict, it is the sparkling wines which have done particularly well: while the fruit base (properly) reflects the climate, the wines are constructed with great style, with a neatly judged dosage to provide enough sweetness to balance the citric flavors underneath. Nor is it surprising to find that in 1990 the Iron Horse partners announced a joint venture with Laurent-Perrier of Champagne to develop an entirely new vineyard and produce a sparkling wine planned for release in mid 1999.

ABOVE ~ *The ever-beautiful Westside Road, as its name implies, runs along the west side of the Russian River.*

KISTLER 1979

A: 4707 Vine Hill Road, Sebastopol, CA 95472 **T**: (707) 823 5603 **V**: By appointment **P**: 16,000 **W**: Steve Kistler and Mark Bixler

How can one improve on perfection, and add complexity to the already impossibly complex? Perhaps one can't, but the completion of the state-of-the-art, luxuriously appointed new winery which partners Steve Kistler and Mark Bixler have erected on the Vine Hill Road Vineyard they purchased in 1986 may allow them to do so. In some ways it seems an inappropriate home for the Kistler wines, simply because right from the word go, Kistler (a former English major and creative writer) and Bixler (a former chemistry professor) have deliberately pushed the making of their Chardonnay to the very edge of the unknown and the unknowable, succeeding brilliantly with their first vintage in 1979 and failing dismally with their second in 1980 — taking years to recover from the trauma, and from the lurid stories of winery representatives traveling around retailers armed with a hypodermic syringe to inject copper into the bottles through the cork to deal with the offending sulfides.

All of that is behind them now, for since the mid 1980s Kistler has produced a celestial range of five vineyard-designated Chardonnays. Only the best Au Bon Climat Reserve Chardonnay can seriously challenge these wines for the opulence, complexity and sheer hedonistic satisfaction they impart. Heated arguments are likely to break out when the question of longevity comes up: it is a largely academic debate, partly because almost all of the wine is drunk within weeks or months of its release, and secondly because, in my view at least, the wines simply do not need to be cellared.

The edge to which the Chardonnays are still pushed is a highly stressed, very slow fermentation in a nutrient-deficient must, counterbalanced by a precisely controlled percentage of solids (the heavy particles normally allowed to settle before fermentation commences), and the deliberate encouragement of what Steve Kistler refers to as the development of "nice sulfides" part way through the fermentation.

The other ingredient is the very specific choice of vineyards with low yielding clones, and in particular clones with the irregular berry size and loose set — known in France and elsewhere as "hen and chicken" — and the rejection of the muscat-type clones, and of course, the dreadful high-yielding heat-treated Davis selections which so bedevil the Napa Valley and elsewhere.

The new cellar has five separate barrel fermentation rooms, so that each of the Kistler Estate, Durrell Vineyard, McCrea Vineyard, Vine Hill Road Vineyard and Dutton Ranch Vineyard Chardonnays can be dealt with separately, for each inevitably demands separate treatment. In every way, Kistler's approach is that of the Burgundian, his role models — which he emulates with spectacular success — being the greatest white Burgundies. Of the five 1990 Chardonnays, the Kistler Estate stood apart even in that exalted company simply because of the extraordinary intensity and length of its flavor. Next came Vine Hill Road, hotly pursued by Dutton Ranch, McCrea Vineyard and Durrell Vineyard, but I would have no problem with those who sought to place them in a different order. I do know that they were a landmark in the weeks of bench tastings in San Francisco, at once exhilarating and depressing: exhilarating because they demonstrated how great California Chardonnay can be, and depressing because they also demonstrated just how banal much of it in fact is.

ABOVE ~ *The Spanish Moss which festoons oak trees in winter is, amazingly, a relative of the pineapple.*

KORBEL CHAMPAGNE CELLARS 1862

A: 13250 River Road, Guerneville, CA 95446 **T**: (707) 887 2294 **V**: 9–5 daily **P**: 1,450,000 **W**: Robert Stashack and Greg Gessner

Korbel is the wine tourist's paradise. Its publicity simply says that it is open "year round," and I would not be surprised if one of these days it emulated the department stores by remaining open 24 hours a day. The landscaped gardens, the immaculately maintained and restored buildings dating back to 1880, the nearby Russian River, the redwoods, and ever-so-slick tours and sales and tastings areas are of world class if looked at from the perspective of the general tourist. The scale of production, too, is world class: 1.1 million cases of sparkling wine, and a staggering 350,000 cases of California brandy (the latter produced in the Central Valley). If wine quality is modest — which it is — it is exceedingly unlikely that anyone is going to be heard to complain. And, indeed, the Sparkling Brut and Sparkling Blanc de Blancs Masters Reserve probably deserve rather more than the faint praise of being "modest." What is more, conscious of the fact that the overall quality of California sparkling wine has changed and improved out of all recognition over the last decade, Korbel is moving to produce a Premium Cuvee for release in 1994, made from a blend of 75% Pinot Noir and 25% Chardonnay, following the classic variety, classic method formula and utilizing a brand new Bucher tank press installed in 1991 specifically for the purpose.

LA CREMA 1979

A: 4940 Ross Road, Sebastopol, CA 95472 **T**: (707) 829 2609 **V**: By appointment **P**: 100,000 **W**: Dan Goldfield

It is ironic that the exotically named La Crema Vinera (Cream of the Vintner) should have started life in one dreary warehouse in Petaluma and moved to another equally utilitarian and spartan facility at the end of an obscure gravel road in the Russian River Valley. In the meantime it experienced wild swings of fortune and wine quality under its original owners and winemaker (the latter, Rod Berglund, now of Joseph Swan), before settling down to orthodoxy and rapidly escalating sales following its purchase by Long Island rare wine merchant Jason Korman in 1985 (Korman being head of a syndicate).

While the Russian River winery has 70 acres planted to Pinot Noir and Chardonnay, La Crema draws additional Chardonnay from Santa Barbara, Monterey and the Potter Valley, and Pinot Noir from Santa Clara and the Anderson Valley. Thus even though the two winery specialties — Pinot Noir and Chardonnay — are offered under a standard and Reserve label, all are simply "California Appellation." The same applies to its volume-driven and much cheaper white generic Creme de Tete, a blend of Chenin Blanc, Semillon and Chardonnay.

Winemaker Dan Goldfield has an extraordinarily exotic technical background, with double majors in philosophy and chemistry from Brandeis University, and having spent years doing underwater research at Woods Hole, energy research at Berkeley, and toxicology research at the U.C. Medical Centre in San Francisco, all the while drinking French Burgundies, before finally succumbing and doing his master's degree at U.C. Davis. Not surprisingly, his first love is Pinot Noir, and it is this that the winery does best. Goldfield did not arrive at the winery until May 1990, and one suspects there are still residual problems with older oak barrels to be sorted out, but given his technical background and four years working at Robert Mondavi and Schramsberg prior to joining La Crema, he should do just that.

PIPER-SONOMA 1980

A: 1147 Old Redwood Highway, Healdsberg, CA 95448 **T**: (707) 433 8843 **V**: 10–5 daily **P**: 150,000 **W**: Chris Markell

When Piper-Heidsieck came to California in 1980 to form a joint venture with Sonoma Vineyards (now Rodney Strong Vineyards) and Renfield Corporation (Sonoma Vineyards' distributor) it was the second Champagne house to make the move across the Atlantic. While Piper-Heidsieck now owns 100% of the operation, its proximity to the Rodney Strong Winery goes back to those joint venture origins. It is a large operation, and one of the few French-controlled houses to undertake substantial contract making for other producers and labels.

Piper-Sonoma's own range consists of four wines: Brut (a Pinot Noir-dominant blend which includes Chardonnay, Pinot Blanc and — since 1987 — Pinot Meuniere, with the component of the latter increasing rather than decreasing); a Blanc de Noir, made from Pinot Noir and Pinot Meuniere (and once again with an increasing component from the Meuniere, a variety much favored by winemaker Chris Markell); a Brut Reserve; and top-of-the-line Tete de Cuvee (each containing roughly equal proportions of Chardonnay and Pinot Noir). The Tete de Cuvee is very late disgorged, spending seven years on yeast lees before release.

The other unusual feature of Piper-Sonoma is that it owns only 40 acres of grapes, being heavily reliant on long-term grower contracts, allowing maximum flexibility (and complexity) in the blending process.

PORTER CREEK VINEYARD 1982

A: 8735 Westside Road, Healdsburg, CA 95448 **T**: (707) 433 6321 **V**: 10:30–4:30 Sat–Sun **P**: 3,000 **W**: George Davis

George Davis, who has suffered more than the occasional outrageous arrow of misfortune, has now found peace in a quiet corner of the Russian River Valley, making small quantities of Pinot Noir and Chardonnay from the 21-acre vineyard established in the early 1980s. The winemaking facility is tiny and basic, but George Davis showed his talent with his first vintage of 1987 Pinot Noir, a fragrant and scented wine with almost essency cherry and strawberry fruit allied with a touch of vanilla and cinnamon, followed by a less flamboyant, but nicely balanced, 1988. One of those tiny wineries for Pinot Noir aficionados to follow and watch.

J. ROCHIOLI VINEYARDS 1982

A: 6192 Westside Road, Healdsburg, CA 95448 **T**: (707) 433 2305 **V**: 10–5 daily **P**: 6,000 **W**: Tom Rochioli

Rochioli is one of the superstars of the future, and a not too distant future at that. Mind you, it has been well and truly established as a superstar in the minds of a number of astute vignerons who have been queuing up to pay top prices for the Rochioli grapes, and in particular its Pinot Noir, for more than a decade. The property had been acquired by the Rochioli family in 1938, planted to hops on the river flats and vines on the hillsides. In 1959 the hops went, and Cabernet Sauvignon and Sauvignon Blanc planted in their place, but before long Joe Rochioli became convinced that this was the place for Pinot Noir, and established the famous Allen Vineyard across the road for owner Howard Allen. Needless to say, Joe Rochioli also planted Pinot Noir on his own property, and today there are 95 acres under vine, with Zinfandel and Cabernet Sauvignon planted on the highest slopes; Cabernet and Pinot Noir on the middle slopes; and Pinot Noir, Chardonnay and Sauvignon Blanc on the river flats.

The basic framework for the winery was established in 1976, with Joe Rochioli making little bits and pieces of Pinot Noir for fun. The first commercial release was from the 1982 vintage, and son Tom (now winemaker) joined in 1983, obtaining consultancy advice from Gary Farrell in 1985 which launched Rochioli into full scale commercial winemaking.

Joe Rochioli is a master vigneron, one of the very best, and Tom would no doubt be the first to admit the quality of the fruit he is presented with. But I believe his achievements in the winery have been grossly underrated: the 1991 Sauvignon Blanc, in both standard and Reserve modes, is the best Sauvignon Blanc I have ever tasted from California. The Chardonnays, again coming both in standard and Reserve, are immaculately made, subtle, but long and satisfying in the mouth; while the 1990 Reserve Pinot Noir (tasted blind from bottle) and the 1991 Reserve (tasted from cask) are absolutely outstanding. The standard Pinot Noir has been criticized (or, if not criticized, not appreciated) in some quarters because it is somewhat simple and direct, but it shows exemplary varietal character and considerable finesse.

As I have said elsewhere, the Russian River was one of the great discoveries for me, and Rochioli one of the jewels in that voyage of discovery.

SEA RIDGE 1980

A: 13404 Dupont Road, Occidental, CA 95465 **T**: (707) 875 3329 **V**: 9–5 summer weekends; other times by appointment **P**: 2,000 **W**: Dan Wickham

Sea Ridge was originally located near the town of Cazadero, an ultra-cool region only three miles inland from the Pacific. Co-owner and founder Dan Wickham also happened to be a marine biologist of considerable distinction, so the name Sea Ridge (and the striking label) came easily. That partnership was in fact dissolved in 1989, with Dan Wickham retaining the brand and moving to an old winery near Occidental, which had been built in 1903, and which had remained in production until 1960. Dan Wickham and wife Dee now lease the facility, buying Zinfandel locally from old vineyards and Pinot Noir from the Hirsch Vineyards, situated near the original winery site at an elevation of 1,500 feet, and overlooking the ocean.

The Hirsch Vineyard Pinot Noir proclaims its ultra-cool origins with strong, spicy overtones to both aroma and palate, characters which are by no means classic but equally by no means unpleasant. The 1991 Occidental Zinfandel is loaded with cassis and blackcurrant fruit along with more conventional flavors, a wine of above-average complexity and concentration. The ultra-cool grown Chardonnay (in 1991 picked at the end of October at 21° Brix) produces a wine which is very hard in its youth, but which could conceivably soften with time.

SONOMA-CUTRER 1973

A: 4401 Slusser Road, Windsor, CA 95492
T: (707) 528 1181 **V**: By appointment
P: 70,000 **W**: Terry Adams

I describe this remarkable producer and its wines in the introduction to this chapter on pages 172–3.

RODNEY STRONG VINEYARDS 1961

A: 11455 Old Redwood Highway, Healdsburg, CA 95448 **T**: (707) 433 6511
V: 10–5 daily **P**: 525,000 **W**: Rod Strong and Rick Sayre

If former dancer/choreographer Rodney Strong were to turn the story of his life into a ballet, it would contain as much drama as any of the masterpieces, old or modern. The only problem would be finding space for all of the actors on the stage, and limiting the length of the performance to something less than Wagner's *Ring Cycle*.

Suffice it to say that in March 1989 ownership of Rodney Strong Vineyards changed (once again) to Klein Foods in a deal said to be worth $40 million. The long-serving and long-suffering Rodney Strong was in fact the underbidder, but has elected to stay on and continue to provide a (very) human face to what (for all its vicissitudes) is a very substantial business. Around 425,000 cases a year are sold through the direct mail operation of Windsor Vineyards, which statistics show to be the winner of the greatest number of medals of any brand in the United States. Without wishing to decry the Windsor label unduly, that seems to me to be a statistic deriving more from the number of shows it enters than anything else, for the wines are not the stuff of which dreams are made.

On the other hand, the portfolio of vineyards (totalling 1,200 acres) gives the Rodney Strong label access to some marvelous material, and produce the vineyard-designated wines Alexander's Crown Vineyard Cabernet

RODNEY STRONG
1990
Chalk Hill Vineyard
Chardonnay
CHALK HILL, SONOMA COUNTY

Sauvignon, Chalk Hill Vineyards Chardonnay, Charlotte's Home Vineyard Sauvignon Blanc, River East Vineyard Pinot Noir and Old Vines River West Vineyard Zinfandel. With the solitary exception of a somewhat pepperminty Alexander's Crown Vineyard Cabernet Sauvignon, all of these wines are of exemplary quality and character, with the Zinfandel and Pinot Noir outstanding.

JOSEPH SWAN VINEYARDS 1969

A: 2916 Laguna Road, Forestville, CA 95436
T: (707) 573 3747 **V**: By appointment
P: 4,000 **W**: Rod Berglund

When former commercial airline pilot Joe Swan died from cancer in 1988, he had the comfort of knowing that over the prior 19 years he had made a series of wines which would live in the memories of connoisseurs for decades to come. He had the further comfort of knowing that his son-in-law, Rod Berglund, would take over winemaking, having been well and truly indoctrinated into the Joseph Swan philosophy in the years prior to Swan's death, and before that having had the practical experience of being winemaker at La Crema Vinera for a number of years.

Joe Swan started making wine for his own pleasure and for consumption by his family, only selling that portion surplus to his own capacity. Rod Berglund keeps that tradition alive, too, in a fashion. For although he makes 4,000 cases in all, almost all of the wines are made in minute quantities. In any one year, he is likely to be selling up to 15 different wines. Thus Zinfandel, the early 1970s vintages of which ensured Swan's immortality, accounts for 50% of production. But it is made and marketed in the most complicated fashion imaginable: three to five separate vineyard bottlings are offered as futures, and once all the orders are in, precisely the amount of each wine ordered is bottled, and what is left is blended into a single Zinfandel which is then sold in the conventional manner as a bottled wine. The 13-acre estate vineyards are planted to Chardonnay and Pinot Noir, the latter Joe Swan's personal passion, and these two account for the next 40% of production. From this point on the wines are made in tiny quantities: a Steiner Cabernet Sauvignon, a Wolfspierre Chardonnay and a Semillon-Sauvignon Blanc from Sonoma Mountain, while 275 cases of a Rhone-style wine from a 70-year-old mixed vineyard were introduced in 1990.

Wine quality may be variable, as may style, but there is no shortage of character.

TOPOLOS AT RUSSIAN RIVER 1963

A: 5700 Gravenstein Highway North, Forestville, CA 95436 **T**: (707) 887 1575
V: May 1–October 31, 11–5.30 daily; Nov 1–April 30, 11–5 Wed–Sun **P**: 7,500
W: Michael Topolos

The Topolos winery looks like an old hop kiln building, which is precisely what Fred and Helene Riebli intended when they built it in 1969 to handle the grapes from the vines they had established five years earlier. Rapid ownership changes in the mid 1970s caused both excitement and confusion, but little else. So when the Topolos family assumed control in 1979, they created one of the longest winery names I have ever encountered. They also inherited a restaurant which had been created in an 1879 manor house; initially franchised, the Topolos family took control of it, too, in 1983. The two businesses run together, manned by the entire family, and with typical Greek verve.

Topolos is a red wine specialist, making Zinfandel, Petite Sirah, Alicante Bouschet, most purchased from the organically grown dry

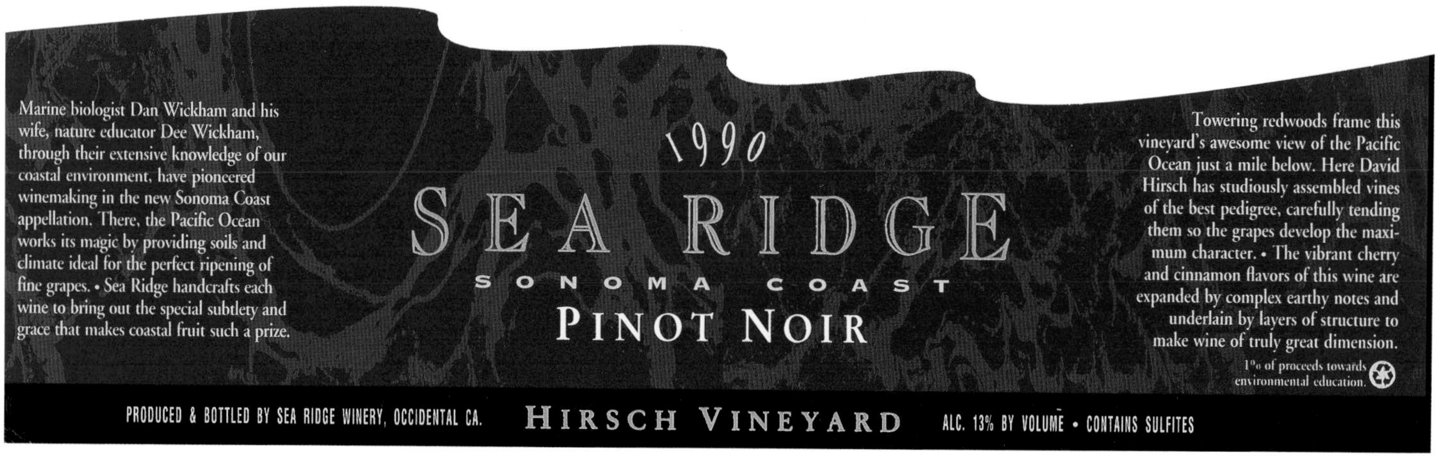
Marine biologist Dan Wickham and his wife, nature educator Dee Wickham, through their extensive knowledge of our coastal environment, have pioneered winemaking in the new Sonoma Coast appellation. There, the Pacific Ocean works its magic by providing soils and climate ideal for the perfect ripening of fine grapes. • Sea Ridge handcrafts each wine to bring out the special subtlety and grace that makes coastal fruit such a prize.
1990
SEA RIDGE
SONOMA COAST
PINOT NOIR
Towering redwoods frame this vineyard's awesome view of the Pacific Ocean just a mile below. Here David Hirsch has studiously assembled vines of the best pedigree, carefully tending them so the grapes develop the maximum character. • The vibrant cherry and cinnamon flavors of this wine are expanded by complex earthy notes and underlain by layers of structure to make wine of truly great dimension.
PRODUCED & BOTTLED BY SEA RIDGE WINERY, OCCIDENTAL CA.
HIRSCH VINEYARD
ALC. 13% BY VOLUME • CONTAINS SULFITES

TOPOLOS
AT RUSSIAN RIVER VINEYARDS
SONOMA COUNTY
ZINFANDEL
PRODUCED AND BOTTLED BY TOPOLOS AT RUSSIAN RIVER VINEYARDS, FORESTVILLE, CA, USA.
ALCOHOL 12% BY VOL. CONTAINS SULFITES.

farmed Rossi Ranch established off Warm Springs Road near Kenwood in 1910. Winemaker Michael Topolos gives this formidable material free reign, producing massive wines, extremely concentrated and extractive. Technically, they have a range of problems, but in many instances the sheer force of the fruit at least partially obscures those problems. All in all, wines for the strong of heart.

MARK WEST VINEYARDS 1976

A: 7000 Trenton-Healdsburg Road, Forestville, CA 95436 **T**: (707) 544 4813
V: 10–5 daily **P**: 30,000 **W**: David Hapkins

Mark West Vineyards was in a state of transition in 1992, having just been acquired by a partnership comprising marketer Dennis Marion (who brought with him his own pre-existing Marion brand), Ed Natarius, former Kendall-Jackson honcho, and OCVC, a Canadian stock exchange-listed venture capital company specializing in vineyard and real estate investments. The partnership plan is to establish various brand identities, each with specific target markets. Mark West Estate will be retained, aimed at the upper end and concentrating on Pinot Noir and Chardonnay in two tiers: Reserve and Russian River. The Marion label will be developed for the middle market fighting varietal sector; while a Sports Series is to be sourced from the bulk market and sold under labels exclusive to the users, such as major hotel chains, sports resorts, and so forth. The idea here is to supply the wine at a relatively low price, allowing the user considerable latitude on price margin without coming under competitive price pressure.

One suspects that what has happened in the past will be very much a matter of the past, but for the record the 1984, 1985, 1987, and 1989 Robert Rue Vineyard Zinfandels tasted in 1992 were all of wonderful quality, none more so than the lively, spicy, bright and zippy 1987, looking more like a one-year-old than a five-year-old wine, and proving once again the extraordinary quality of old (1906-planted) Russian River Zinfandel.

WILLIAMS SELYEM WINERY 1981

A: 6575 Westside Road, Healdsburg, CA 95448 **T**: (707) 433 6425
V: By appointment **P**: 4,000
W: Burt Williams and Ed Selyem

ABOVE ~ *The alluvial river that is carved by the Russian River can produce grapes of exceptional quality.*

The world of wine is a strange place, full of surprises, full of wonderful characters, full of contradictions and paradoxes. How paradoxical, then, that Sonoma-Cutrer should spend untold millions of dollars in a tightly focused, highly disciplined pursuit of greatness (and in my view not yet have achieved it) with Chardonnay, that most malleable and amiable of all grapes; and that a few miles away two technically unqualified, visibly under-financed knockabout characters should achieve greatness with that most difficult of all grapes, Pinot Noir. I remain to be convinced these are the greatest Pinot Noirs made in California, but they are certainly among the top three or four, wines of extreme finesse and style, even in their lesser manifestations.

How a San Francisco typesetter (Burt Williams) and local wine buyer (Ed Selyem) have come to make such great wine reads like an improbable fairy story. Between 1983 and 1989 their "winery" was a small garage on River Road in Fulton, their fermentation tanks, then and now, converted dairy vats. In 1990 they moved into a rented winery built for them by Howard Allen, from whom they purchase the grapes for their top-ranked Pinot Noir, Allen Vineyard. It is followed by Rochioli Vineyard, and then Olivet Lane. Summa Vineyard features in the register but is usually consigned to their Russian River "volume" brand, simply to give it more body and character. In 1991 the partners took the decision to keep a single barrel of Summa Vineyard separate: they had paid the equivalent of $6,000 a tonne for the half ton of grapes that came off Summa Vineyard in that year, and it is hard to imagine how they will fail to make more enemies than friends when it comes to rationing out the wine. Much is sold by mailing list: in 1992 they returned $50,000 to would-be purchasers who had ordered far beyond the winery's capacity to supply. Another example of the extraordinary demand for the wine is the wine list at Healdsburg's superb Tre Scalini restaurant: in 1992 it offered the Williams Selyem Allen Vineyard Pinot at $65 per bottle, but with a limit of one bottle per table.

Having spent more than my fair share of dollars on Williams Selyem wines in restaurants at every opportunity, and having tasted my way through the barrels in 1992, it is certain that these are some of the most beautifully crafted wines imaginable, made with ultimate precision and sensitivity. Williams Selyem may put on farm boy airs, but they know precisely what they are doing. Perhaps the ultimate recognition of that is the fact that Burgundy courtier Becky Wasserman actually imports their wines into the heartland which first inspired them to seek (and achieve) the holy grail of great Pinot Noir.

Other Wineries

BALVERNE 1980
A: 10810 Hillview Road, Windsor, CA 95492
T: (707) 433 6913 **W**: Mitchell Firestone-Gillis

CASWELL 1982
A: 13207 Dupont Road, Sebastopol, CA 95472
T: (707) 874 2517 **W**: Dwight Caswell Jnr.

CHRISTOPHER CREEK 1974
A: 641 Limerick Lane, Healdsburg, CA 95448
T: (707) 433 2001 **W**: Paul Brasset

DE NATALE 1985
A: 11020 Eastside Road, Healdsburg, CA 95448
T: (707) 431 8460

DOMAINE ST. GEORGE 1934
A: P.O. Box 548, 1141 Grant Avenue, Healdsburg, CA 95448 **T**: (707) 433 5508
W: Bob Fredson

HANNA 1985
A: 5345 Occidental Road, Santa Rosa, CA 95401
T: (707) 575 3330 **W**: Dean Cox

MARTINELLI 1987
A: 3360 River Road, Windsor, CA 95492
T: (707) 525 0570 **W**: Daniel Moore

MARTINI & PRATI 1951
A: 2191 Laguna Road, Santa Rosa, CA 95401
T: (707) 823 2404 **W**: Frank Vannucci

Z. MOORE 1987
A: 3364 River Road, Windsor, CA 95492
T: (707) 544 3555 **W**: Daniel Zuccarelli-Moore

POMMERAIE 1979
A: 10541 Cherry Ridge Road, Sebastopol, CA 95472 **T**: (707) 823-WINE **W**: Curtis Younts

RABBIT RIDGE 1985
A: 3291 Westside Road, Healdsburg, CA 95448
T: (707) 431 7128 **W**: Erich Russell

RIVER ROAD VINEYARDS 1979
A: 7145 River Road, Forestville, CA 95436
T: (707) 887 7890 **W**: Gary Mills

SELLARDS 1980
A: 6400 Sequoia Circle, Sebastopol, CA 95472
T: (707) 823 8293 **W**: Thomas Sellards

TAFT STREET WINERY 1982
A: M/A 2030 Barlow Lane, Sebastopol, CA 95472 **T**: (707) 823 2049 **W**: John Tierney

ABOVE ~ *A newly established vineyard in the Russian River Valley forsakes the river flats.*

RAIDERS

SONOMA VALLEY AND MOUNTAIN

The very title to this chapter pays further tribute to the tortured minds of the denizens of the BATF who have conspired to so baffle those seeking to understand the Sonoma Valley. For as anyone who has driven across from Oakville to Glen Ellen or driven up Moon Mountain Drive to Carmenet will testify, the eastern side of the Sonoma Valley is most certainly not a valley, but wild and precipitous hills. But if you then travel west, and ascend Sonoma Mountain Road to visit Dave Steiner's vineyard or Laurel Glen, you will see that the kidney-shaped Sonoma Mountain AVA is most certainly not surrounded by a valley on its northern or western sides: it sits suspended in its mountain fastness, its boundary the 1,100-foot contour line, with the 2,000-foot line still beckoning, yet deemed to be part of the Sonoma Valley.

But this is being churlish to what is a quite exceptionally beautiful region, with no small part of that beauty stemming from its diverse topography. It is appropriate too, that it should have been called the Valley of the Moon by its original inhabitants, and that Agoston Haraszthy should have succeeded here (after earlier failures elsewhere) in 1857 in establishing the first major vineyard of European grape varieties (adjacent to the present-day Hacienda Winery).

The Sonoma Valley AVA in 1992 had 33 wineries, 188 growers and 6,500 acres of vineyards — remembering, however, that its southern end includes the Sonoma side of Carneros, which I have treated separately. The Sonoma Mountain AVA is of course, much smaller, with no wineries other than Glen Ellen normally open to the public, but with some extremely important vineyards in its 600 acres, notably Laurel Glen, Jack London Ranch, Martini's Monte Rosso Vineyard and the Steiner Vineyard.

The town of Sonoma has the historic Buena Vista cellars and tasting room, Gundlach Bundschu, Sebastiani and Hacienda all virtually within walking distance, and all attesting to its exceptionally rich viticultural history. As you drive north up Highway 12, the Mayacamas Mountains loom high on your right hand side, Sonoma Mountain on the other, and the valley has a feeling of intimacy which reminds me forcibly of Australia's Clare Valley. It is not until one reaches the extreme northern end of the Sonoma AVA (past Kenwood) that it opens out, and then only marginally. It is, in every way, a fitting entry-point for the whole of Sonoma County.

ABOVE ~ *Sonoma Mountain Road: fogs, mists and winter rain create a fantasyland.*

OPPOSITE ~ *Vineyard crew working on old bush-pruned vines in the Pagani Vineyards on the valley floor.*

The Region in Brief

Climate, Soil and Viticulture

Climate

As one moves north from Sonoma town, ultimately reaching the southern outskirts of Santa Rosa (which mark the northern limit of Sonoma Valley AVA), the temperature gradually increases, although not as dramatically as it does in the Napa Valley, and cooling again as one reaches Santa Rosa. Sonoma town is tucked in between the southern end of the two mountain ranges, and does not experience the westerly winds which sweep across Carneros; indeed its mean July temperature of 69°F is significantly higher than that of Santa Rosa at 66.8°F. This is due to the fact that the valley is subject to two cooling influences: one from San Pablo Bay, the other through the Petaluma Gap. The meeting of the two wind currents is one of the reasons why Sonoma Valley has a rainfall of 20 inches, making it one of the driest regions in the county. And it also explains why the fog intrusions are less persistent around Kenwood than they are further south and north, and why the pattern of grape plantings (and wine styles) changes as one moves north from Glen Ellen.

Sonoma Mountain receives 30% more rain, is basically above the fogline, and experiences lower diurnal temperature fluctuations. Its vineyards mostly face east, which is one major point of differentiation from most the the hillside vineyards on the opposite Mayacamas Range.

Soil

The valley floor soils are the typical melange spewed by the intense geological activity which makes the past, present and future of California. Technically known as the Franciscan Melange, they are composed of a mixture of sandstone and shale, pieces of oceanic crust, blocks of oceanic sediment, and sand and gravel eroded from the mountain sides. They are well drained, deep and frequently quite fertile, capable of producing large yields and requiring disciplined viticulture if quality is to be maintained. The mountainside soils are quite different; on Sonoma Mountain they are a mixture of volcanic tuffs (or ash) and metamorphic igneous rock mixed with churned gravelly river sediments during the upwelling which gave rise to the mountains. Depth and fertility tends to be lower, even though tremendous variations

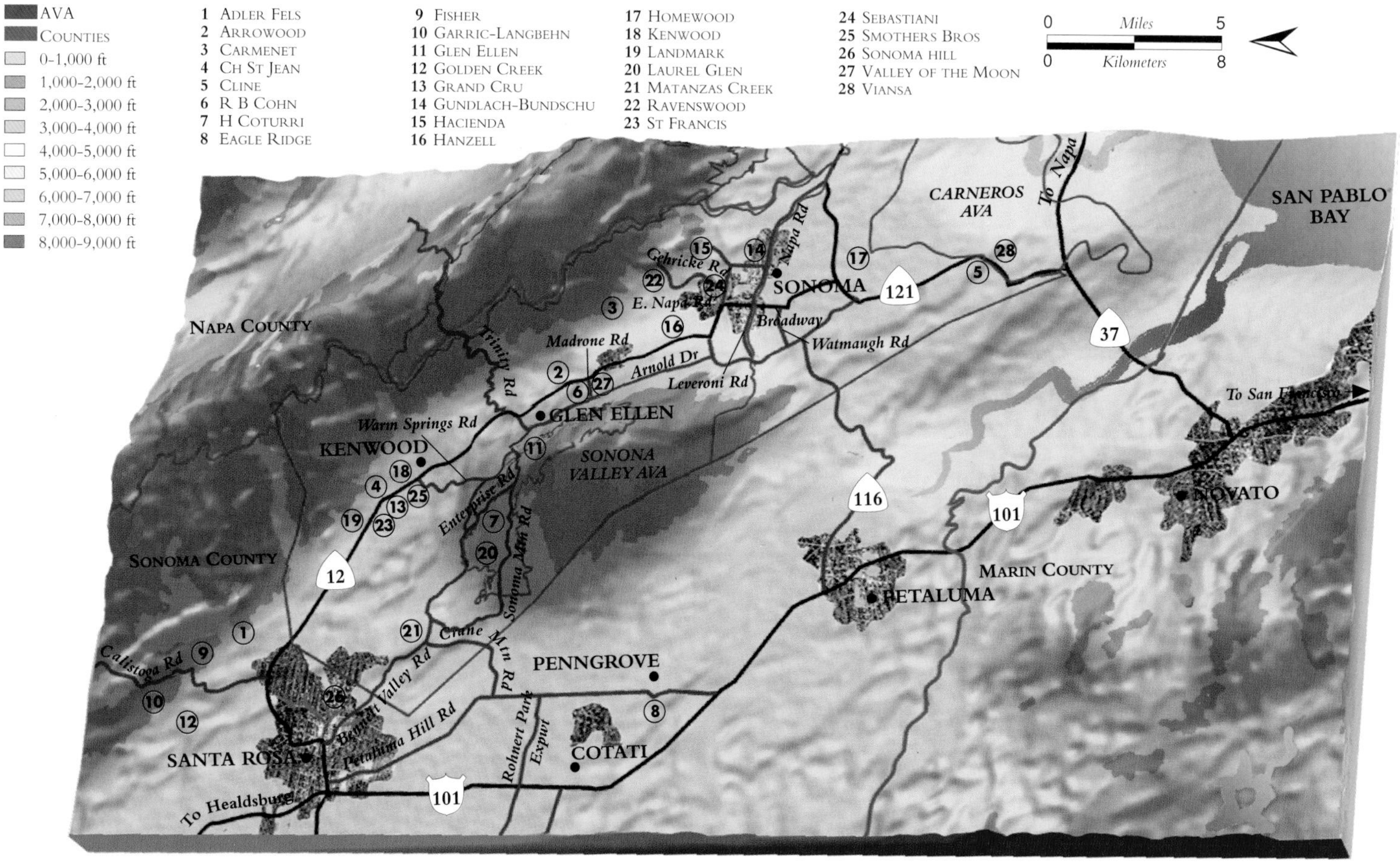
AVA
Counties
0-1,000 ft
1,000-2,000 ft
2,000-3,000 ft
3,000-4,000 ft
4,000-5,000 ft
5,000-6,000 ft
6,000-7,000 ft
7,000-8,000 ft
8,000-9,000 ft
1 Adler Fels
2 Arrowood
3 Carmenet
4 Ch St Jean
5 Cline
6 R B Cohn
7 H Coturri
8 Eagle Ridge
9 Fisher
10 Garric-Langbehn
11 Glen Ellen
12 Golden Creek
13 Grand Cru
14 Gundlach-Bundschu
15 Hacienda
16 Hanzell
17 Homewood
18 Kenwood
19 Landmark
20 Laurel Glen
21 Matanzas Creek
22 Ravenswood
23 St Francis
24 Sebastiani
25 Smothers Bros
26 Sonoma hill
27 Valley of the Moon
28 Viansa
0 Miles 5
0 Kilometers 8
CARNEROS AVA
To Napa
SAN PABLO BAY
Napa Rd
SONOMA
121
E. Napa Rd
Broadway
Watmaugh Rd
37
NAPA COUNTY
Madrone Rd
Arnold Dr
Leveroni Rd
Trinity Rd
GLEN ELLEN
To San Francisco
Warm Springs Rd
KENWOOD
SONONA VALLEY AVA
Enterprise Rd
116
101
NOVATO
SONOMA COUNTY
12
MARIN COUNTY
PETALUMA
Calistoga Rd
Crane
Sonoma Mtn Rd
PENNGROVE
Bennett Valley Rd
Petaluma Hill Rd
Rohnert Park Expwy
COTATI
SANTA ROSA
To Healdsburg
101

ABOVE ~ *Sonoma Valley map.*

Sonoma Valley and Mountain
VINTAGE CHART 1981-91

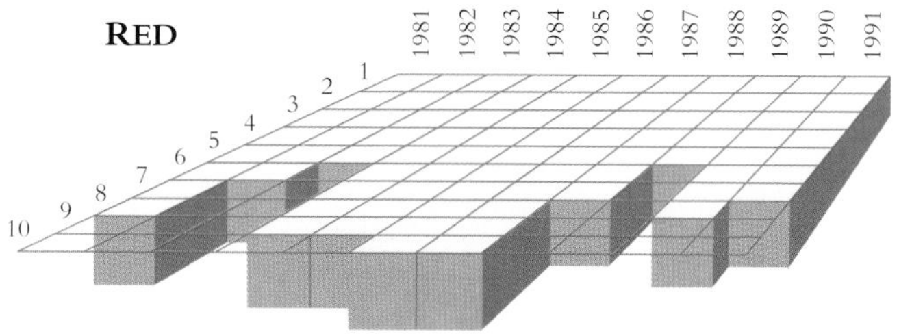
RED
1981
1982
1983
1984
1985
1986
1987
1988
1989
1990
1991
1
2
3
4
5
6
7
8
9
10

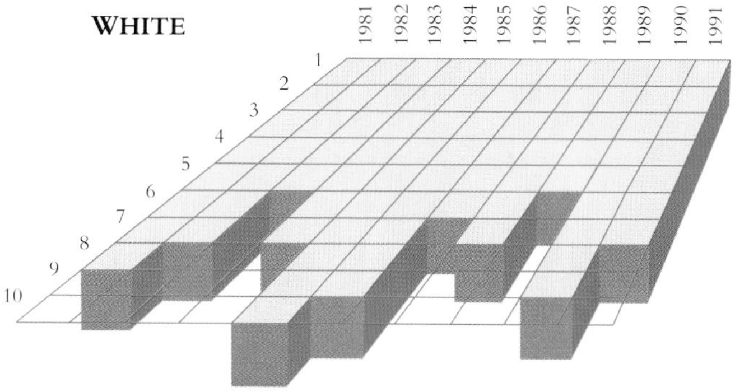
WHITE
1981
1982
1983
1984
1985
1986
1987
1988
1989
1990
1991
1
2
3
4
5
6
7
8
9
10

occur in the tightly folded hillocks and gullies which are part and parcel of mountain-side farming.

The Growing Season

The mixture of high Region I and low to mid Region II climates produces a mild and relatively long growing season, with frosts posing no threat on the mountainsides and seldom causing damage on the valley floor. The winds are moderate and fog makes a variable impact. Merlot is typically picked in the first half of September, but as late as October 10; Chardonnay is a little earlier, particularly at the southern end of the valley; Cabernet ripens throughout October, depending on the site and season.

Contract Growers

Beltane Ranch 80 acres planted to Chardonnay, Sauvignon Blanc, Zinfandel, Cabernet Sauvignon and Merlot, all sold to Kenwood.
Durrell Vineyard Planted primarily to Chardonnay and Pinot Noir, but also with the Bordeaux varieties, Syrah and Zinfandel; 155 acres in total. Kistler and Kendall-Jackson are principal users.
Francisco's Vineyard Thirty-four acres at Kenwood planted with old Zinfandel and (1976–81) Chardonnay and Pinot Noir.
Jessandra Vineyard 50 acres of Cabernet Sauvignon and a little Sangiovese; sells to H. Coturri and others.
Jack London Vineyard Planted 1972 on Sonoma Mountain to 124 acres Chardonnay, Pinot Noir, Merlot, Cabernet Franc, Cabernet Sauvignon and Zinfandel; supplied exclusively to Kenwood.
McCrea Vineyard Thirty acres of Chardonnay planted 1970 near Jack London Park sold exclusively to Kistler.
Old Hill Vineyard Eighteen acres Zinfandel planted in the 1890s three miles north of Sonoma. Sold to Ravenswood and Topolos
Pickberry Vineyard Sonoma Mountain vineyard supplying Ravenswood with Cabernet Sauvignon and Merlot.
Steiner Vineyard Sonoma Mountain, planted 1973 to 1979 with Cabernet Sauvignon (25 acres), Cabernet Franc (1.5 acres) and Pinot Noir (four acres). Users include Joseph Swan and Kenwood.

Principal Wine Styles

Cabernet Sauvignon

Cabernet Sauvignon grown on the Sonoma and Mayacamas mountainsides produces superb wines, those from Sonoma Mountain tending to be slightly more fragrant and supple, those from the Mayacamas side having a touch more sinew and muscle, but on both sides producing wines of impeccable varietal character, concentration and balance. These are not the spectacular wines of the Rutherford Bench; their closest counterparts in the Napa Valley are those of the Stags Leap area. Outstanding producers from mountainside vineyards included Laurel Glen, Kenwood, Martini Monte Rosso, Carmenet and Ravenswood. B.R. Cohn does well with its valley floor Cabernet Sauvignon, while Buena Vista and Gundlach Bundschu at the cooler, still extreme, southern end produce wines of elegance and finesse, but which lack the richness of those mountainside wines.

Merlot

There are some spectacular Merlots produced at the far northern end of the valley, with Matanzas Creek leading the way, hotly pursued by St. Francis and then Golden Creek. But it does well all over the place, both on the mountains and — as one might expect — in the far south, although it is more frequently used in Meritage blends than in its own right as a varietal. Here Carmenet and Kistler (Pickberry Vineyard) are prime examples.

Chardonnay

With names such as Kistler (Dutton Ranch, MacRea Vineyard), Sonoma-Cutrer (Les Pierres Vineyard), Hanzell, Chateau St. Jean, Kenwood and Benziger of Glen Ellen drawing upon Chardonnay grown in the two AVAs, plantings are under no threat from other varieties in the wake of phylloxera. If there is a common thread, it is the intensity of the flavor; what varies is the structure sought by the winemaker, and this varies greatly — from the equivalent of Chablis to that of Montrachet.

Pinot Noir

Once one steps north of the Carneros portion of the Sonoma Valley, the Pinot Noirs — Hanzell's being by far the most famous, but with Hacienda and Kistler in there too — seem to double in weight whether they are grown on the valley floor or on either mountainside. It is a style which is distinctive, and has appeal to those who enjoy the heartier style of French Burgundy.

Zinfandel

Wines of great distinction and power are made by producers within the region — Ravenswood being the most obvious — but using grape sources both within and without. But vineyard-identified wines such as Jack London, Barricia (both from Kenwood) and Ravenswood Old Hill show that, given half a chance, and better still half a century, Sonoma Valley and Mountains can produce wines equal to the very best.

HANZELL

The story of Hanzell reads like a modern-day fairytale, with plenty of twists of fate, mysterious undertones and, one might imagine, a not entirely certain future.

James D. Zellerbach was born into wealth and into all the privileges which go with it. Leon Adams (*The Wines of America*) recounts with a perfectly straight face that "while living in Europe during the 1940s Zellerbach had developed a liking for Montrachet and Romanée-Conti...." His Europeanization was strengthened by serving as U.S. Ambassador to Italy during the Eisenhower administration, and no doubt his taste for the finer things of life which both his ambassadorship and chairmanship of the vast Crown Zellerbach paper company gave him access to.

ABOVE ~ *Bob Sessions, the long-serving and gently self-effacing winemaker at Hanzell.*

Thus when he decided to establish a vineyard and winery on his 200-acre property high on a hillside overlooking the Sonoma Valley just to the north of Sonoma town, there were no half measures. If it were possible to make Montrachet and Romanée-Conti in Sonoma, he would do so, regardless of the cost.

So in 1952 he caused 20 acres of terraced hillside vineyard to be planted to the then all but unheard of Chardonnay and the (slightly) better known Pinot Noir. To make the vines feel at home, he proceeded to have built a winery which was a doll's house replica of Clos de Vougeot. At least, an external replica, for the winemaking equipment installed inside was unlike anything to be found in either France or California at that time. To this day, indeed, many of its features remain unique. The feel is that of a timeless piece of Georg Jensen design, an illusion no doubt triggered by the beautifully crafted and polished stainless steel mini fermentation vats.

Indeed, in many ways Hanzell seems suspended in a time warp, not a situation which is at peace with either the go-go 1980s or the recession-ravaged 1990s. But I digress: how did this come about? Well, Zellerbach simply went to U.C. Davis and to André Tschelestcheff and said, "Tell me how to design and equip what you would regard as the perfect winery, regardless of cost."

The result was the installation of a winery in which stainless steel was used throughout, and in a wholly innovative way. There is a connected bank of square, gleaming open-topped stainless steel fermentation vats for the Pinot Noir, each of which holds a ton or thereabouts of grapes. The first temperature-controlled stainless steel fermentation tanks in California were installed for the Chardonnay. Even more remarkably, what is believed to be the first stainless steel grape crush in the world was built by Valley Foundry; the basket press was likewise made entirely of stainless steel.

But when it came to the stainless steel holding tanks, Zellerbach excelled himself. In those days no one was sure about the implications of storing Chardonnay in stainless steel, so the tanks were glass-lined. The heat process darkened the exterior, so Zellerbach promptly ordered that they be sand-blasted and painted grey. To this day they remain the only glass-lined, painted stainless steel tanks in the world.

The other inspirational moves were more to do with J.D. Zellerbach than with U.C. Davis. First, he decided he wished to use the identical barrels to those which were used in Burgundy, and imported the first Sirugue chateau barrels to be used in California. (Some say Martin Ray was the first, others that he was simply the first to use barrel fermentation.)

Second, he employed Ralph Bradford Webb as his winemaker: Brad Webb was to become a legend in his lifetime, and is universally respected as one of the great California winemakers. (He is a partner in and still consults to Rutherford Hill.)

A demijohn of Chardonnay was made in 1956 and sufficient in 1957 to slake the thirsts of Ambassador Zellerbach and his friends. James Laube (in *California's Great Chardonnays*) tells of tasting it in January 1990 as part of a vertical tasting of every Hanzell Chardonnay made from that time, describing it as having "an amazing amount of fruit for a wine of this age ... with honey, butter and custard flavors that are still well defined and long on the finish," rating the wine at ninety.

Despite the fact that Brad Webb did much pioneering research into malolactic fermentation, these early Hanzell Chardonnays did not undergo this (nor were they barrel fermented). It has been suggested by several acute American writers that this may be one of the reasons for the extraordinary longevity of these wines and the similarly-handled Stony Hill Chardonnays. If that does not give some of the present generation makers of Napa Valley (and Sonoma) Chardonnay food for thought, I don't know what will.

The first period of Hanzell came to an abrupt end in 1963 with the death of James Zellerbach. His wife Hana (whose name inspired that of the winery) evidently had some scores to settle with her late husband, for she promptly auctioned the entire museum bottled stock of Hanzell wines together with the two vintages then in barrel. Barney Rhodes and Fred Holmes purchased the barreled wines in a joint venture with Joe Heitz, under whose label they were ultimately bottled and sold.

No wine was made in 1963 or 1964, but making recommenced in 1965 under new owners Douglas and Mary Day, who retained

it until 1975. It was then purchased by Barbara de Brye, an Australian-born ex-Cambridge archaeology student who had once planted a vineyard in England (so great was her interest in wine) and had married Count Jacques de Brye, a Parisian banker. Two years earlier Bob Sessions had become winemaker while Brad Webb continued to act as consultant (as he had since 1965), ensuring a winemaking continuum to this day.

In 1991 Barbara de Brye died suddenly, but her son Alexander has indicated his desire that the estate (but a small portion of the de Brye family wealth) be retained in its present form. The question must be, will it?

One legacy of Barbara de Brye was the establishment of four acres of Cabernet Sauvignon (she was a claret drinker, it seems) which some critics have suggested is far more suited to the sun-drenched slopes than Pinot Noir or Chardonnay. Bob Sessions believes there has indeed been a climate change (specifically, a warming) since the 1950s, but does not agree for one moment that Cabernet Sauvignon (or Zinfandel) are better choices.

But the grim reality is that whereas once the Hanzell wines were all sold on strict allocation at (relatively) high prices which reflected their high cost of production, and rarely — if ever — appeared in retail shops, today Hanzell is being forced to actively seek markets.

It would also be dishonest to say that its wines are today seen as the California equivalents of Montrachet or Romanée-Conti, although the Chardonnay has its fierce supporters: James Laube rates it as a first growth, and Matt Kramer says, "They retain a distinction of place that renders them among California's most singular wines."

The thoughtful and gentle winemaker Bob Sessions does not have too many worries about the Chardonnay, even if its 10% barrel fermentation and 25% malolactic component mean that (for all its ripeness and strong peachy fruit) it is bred to stay, rather than dazzle from the day it is released.

It is the Pinot Noir that Bob Sessions has had to come to terms with. Bob Thompson in *Notes on a Californian Cellar Book* puts it ever so evocatively when he writes, "Hugh Johnson puzzled over the Hanzell 1965 — the first one from estate-grown grapes — for a long time one autumn evening in 1978 before he finally made up his mind. 'First it makes me think of Pinot Noir,' he said, 'then port, then Pinot Noir, and port again. May I have some more?' That has been the story in most if not all of the vintages since."

Having tasted five vintages from the 1980s I can only concur, despite the on-going efforts of Bob Sessions to tame the tannins and extract while investing the wine with varietal character and intensity. Since 1985 he has been experimenting with whole clusters, but has had to abandon returning stems because of the tannins they impart. Having attended the winemaker's Pinot Noir Conference at Steamboat in Oregon in 1992 he went away inspired to try several more techniques. If one of these days he turns up with a great Pinot Noir, I shall not be surprised, and I shall be very pleased.

ABOVE ~ *Hanzell Vineyard, with the Clos Vougeot-inspired winery in the background.*

WINERIES *of* SONOMA VALLEY AND MOUNTAINS

ADLER FELS 1980

A: 5325 Corrick Lane, Sonoma Valley, Santa Rosa, CA 95409 **T**: (707) 539 3123 **V**: 9–5 daily by appointment **P**: 15,000 **W**: David Coleman

1990
ADLER FELS
E·S·T·A·T·E
SONOMA COUNTY
FUMÉ BLANC
(DRY SAUVIGNON BLANC)

Whether one looks at the Coleman-designed labels for Far Niente, Arrowood, or most of the other 60 winery labels he has created, or at the Tudor-style house perched incongruously (and precariously) on the edge of a cliff high above the Sonoma Valley, it is easy to understand that here is a flamboyant, free spirit. Thus when in 1980, a year after his marriage to Ayn Ryan whose family had founded Chateau St. Jean, David Coleman decided to build a winery and make wine, his lack of formal training or experience did not worry him one iota. The same free spirit led to him installing a golf tee above the ravine below the winery, so that he and Ayn could practice their driving and later engage in some fairly serious exercise in what must at times be a fruitless search for the golf balls. No less consistent has been his periodic battles with planning authorities, nor his 1991 installation of an underground bunker warehouse storage area further up a steep (one in three) hillside road, enough to make the most experienced forklift driver tremble in fear. Finally, he claims to have invented the variable capacity wine tank, a device now widely used throughout the world and the subject of various patents (not all, I fancy, held by Coleman).

Adler Fels owns no vineyards, and produces only white wines: Fumé Blanc, Chardonnay, Gewurztraminer and a sparkling wine made from a blend of Johannisberg Riesling and Gewurztraminer called Melange a Deux. Coleman sources his Sauvignon Blanc from the Russian River, and does not back away from uncompromising varietal character, an attitude with which I agree wholeheartedly. It is an excellent wine, not the least bit mean or herbal, but with intense gooseberry fruit, rather like a nicely ripened Sancerre from a good vintage. The Gewurztraminer is made off-dry, and shows good varietal character in an unashamedly commercial mold.

ARROWOOD VINEYARDS & WINERY 1987

A: 14347 Sonoma Highway, Glen Ellen, CA 95442 **T**: (707) 938 5170 **V**: 10–4:30 daily **P**: 20,000 **W**: Richard Arrowood

Dick Arrowood is one of the best known winemakers in California, following his 16 years (1974–90) at Chateau St. Jean, although he had originally entered the wine industry way back in 1965 at Korbel Champagne Cellars. His fame rested upon the development of vineyard-designated Chardonnays in the mid 1970s, wines which were as striking for their depth of flavor as their labeling. Within a few short years, the Belle Terre and Robert Young Vineyards, both in the Alexander Valley, had become household names, and those vineyards retain a preeminent reputation to this day. He also made some quite extraordinary late harvest, heavily botrytised Riesling and Gewurztraminer; those wines from the latter part of the 1970s have turned dark brown in colour, but still retain exceptional intensity of flavor.

In 1984 Chateau St. Jean was purchased by Suntory, and both for this and other reasons, Arrowood realized that sooner or later he would wish to leave and establish his own winery. In 1987 that winery became a reality, although Arrowood remained as winemaker and vice president of Chateau St. Jean until 1990. Since that time he has devoted his whole effort to Arrowood.

The approach at Arrowood is as far removed from that of Chateau St. Jean as one could possibly imagine. The two principal wines are Chardonnay and Cabernet Sauvignon; the Cabernet Sauvignon is blended from 13 different vineyard lots, and includes a percentage of Merlot, Cabernet Franc, Malbec and Petit Verdot grown on the four acres in front of the winery (which in fact are the only vineyards owned by Arrowood). The Chardonnay is made from two Alexander Valley vineyards, three Russian River vineyards, and one Sonoma Valley vineyard; the Chateau St. Jean wines were noted for their opulence, deriving in part from extended skin contact, whereas the Arrowood Chardonnay is positively austere. The Cabernet Sauvignon, by contrast, is a rich and complex wine, with sweet cassis and spice fruit, strong tannins and noticeable oak, a nice contrast to the crisp, youthful, almost glittering red berry Merlot which made its first appearance in 1988. After a long hiatus, a Late Harvest Riesling (from the 1991 vintage) was released in 1992, showing wonderful lime juice intensity and a lovely finish. I suspect Dick Arrowood is a happy man; his winery may be functional, but it lacks for nothing, and it is small wonder that his wines are receiving constant critical acclaim.

CARMENET VINEYARD 1982

A: 1700 Moon Mountain Drive, Sonoma, CA 95476 **T**: (707) 996 5870 **V**: By appointment **P**: 30,000 **W**: Jeffrey Baker

Carmenet is one of those vineyards and wineries which make you wonder whether one ought to pay for the privilege of working there, rather than be paid. Its spectacular mountainside location, its rippling, undulating hillside vineyards, the precisely designed and engineered circular winery, and the underground barrel caves are all stuff of which dreams are made. Certainly Jeff Baker, who first worked at Mayacamas seems content with his lot, even if the quest for greater wine quality continues unabated in both vineyard and winery. Carmenet, incidentally, is the Cabernet arm of the Chalone group, Carmenet being one of the old Bordelaise terms for Cabernet Sauvignon.

The vineyards are established between 1,150 and 1,650 feet, mainly on the south-facing slopes of the south-western side of Mount Veeder. Cabernet Sauvignon is the predominant variety, with 15% Cabernet Franc, 6% Merlot and a little Petit Verdot. Much work has been going on in the vineyard over the past few years, basically designed to establish thin-walled vertical trellises in the less vigorous areas, and divided canopies on the more vigorous sites. In common with so many growers, common sense farming — in other words, a basic organic approach — is also the order of the day.

The Meritage blend, with its very precise label disclosing its cepage (which varies slightly from year to year but which is based around 80–85% Cabernet Sauvignon) is the *raison d'être* of the winery. These are always tightly structured wines of finesse, and barrel tastings suggest the future releases of Carmenet Cabernet are going to make headlines: they were truly sensational. Carmenet also makes a Sauvignon Blanc-Semillon blend; after some prevarication, it has now been settled that this will be sourced solely from sister winery Edna Valley Vineyards.

Finally, for some strange reason, Carmenet makes small quantities of a barrel-fermented French Colombard from old Napa Valley vines, a wine capable neither of offending nor pleasing.

CHATEAU ST. JEAN 1973

A: 8555 Sonoma Highway, Kenwood, CA 95452 **T**: (707) 833 4134 **V**: 10–4:30 daily **P**: 175,000 **W**: Don Van Staaveren

Ninety thousand visitors a year walk through the immaculately maintained gardens of Chateau St. Jean to visit its no less immaculate colonnaded buildings and tasting/reception facilities. Somehow or other it seems right that Chateau St. Jean should be in Japanese ownership, having been purchased by Suntory in 1984, by which time it was one of the showplaces of the Sonoma Valley, and for that matter, one of the foremost names in the California industry. Yet, as with the vast majority of the other Japanese-owned California wineries, Suntory is basically content to let Chateau St. Jean get on with its business, and in particular to market its wines in the United States and what other export markets it can find, but not Japan. All quite strange.

Chateau St. Jean is carrying on in the wake of the departure of Dick Arrowood, who guided its fortunes from day one through to 1990. Chardonnay still remains the backbone of the Chateau St. Jean production, accounting for 120,000 cases a year. The Belle Terre Vineyard and Robert Young Vineyard still supply vineyard-designated wines, complemented by a Chateau St. Jean Estate Selection. Clearly, the marketplace enjoys these wines, but I cannot get the least bit excited about them. Much the same applies to the White Riesling, Sauvignon Blanc, Gewurztraminer and the generic Vin Blanc.

On the credit side of the ledger is a fleshy, sweet-fruited and vanillin-oaked Cabernet Sauvignon, an excellent Late Harvest Gewurztraminer showing strong apricot botrytis characters and harking back to the golden Arrowood days, and an outstanding 1982 sparkling wine which is made at a separate facility at Graton, which also custom makes sparkling wines for other wineries.

But Chateau St. Jean is far from ossifying. Management has been charged with coming up with one new wine a year, initially in a 500-case volume, with the idea it will be expanded to 2–3,000 cases a year if it works. The primary focus will still remain on Chardonnay and Cabernet, but there will be greater diversity. Thus the winemaking team has been experimenting with various red Rhone blends, an estate-grown Viognier, and more latterly with Nebbiolo and Sangiovese, plantings which produced their first grapes in 1991. A white fermentation room has been converted to handle red wines in open tanks with punch-down techniques, and it would not surprise me to find some very interesting red wines emerging from Chateau St. Jean.

CLINE CELLARS 1982

A: 27437 Arnold Drive, Sonoma, CA 95476 **T**: (707) 935 4310 **V**: 10–6 daily **P**: 25,000 **W**: Matt Cline

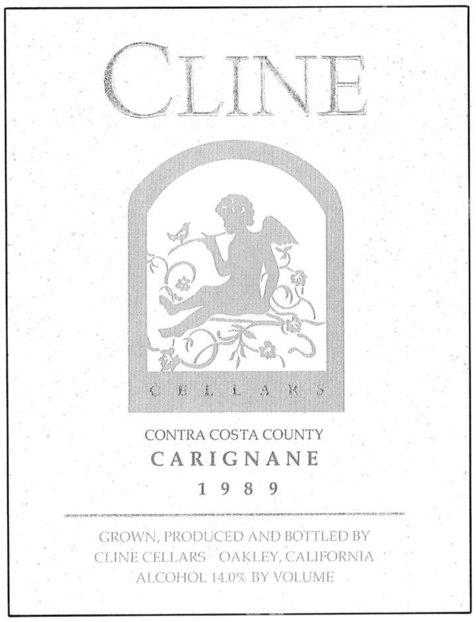
CLINE
CELLARS
CONTRA COSTA COUNTY
CARIGNANE
1989
GROWN, PRODUCED AND BOTTLED BY
CLINE CELLARS OAKLEY, CALIFORNIA
ALCOHOL 14.0% BY VOLUME

Fred and brother Matt Cline are grandsons of Valeriano Jacuzzi, inventor of the device which bears his name. One might have thought that when Fred Cline decided to go into winemaking in 1982, he did so with a silver spoon in his mouth. In fact, he did invest his share of the $70 million sale price of the Jacuzzi business; the trouble was, his share amounted to only $12,000. On the credit side, Valeriano Jacuzzi had established vineyards at Oakley in Contra Costa County, planted to those ever-popular Mediterranean varieties Zinfandel, Barbera, Carignane and Mourvedre. Fred Cline used to spend his summers on his grandfather's ranch, learning viticulture the practical way, but was later to supplement that by taking a degree in agriculture science and management from U.C. Davis.

Throughout the 1980s Fred Cline managed a substantial farming and vineyard enterprise, but grape prices were low, and the market for the wines he was making all but non-existent. When the surge of interest in Rhone varietals began, Bonny Doon, Edmunds St. John and others started bidding for the grapes and pushing the prices up, and (to cap it all off) Robert Parker gave his seal of approval to the Cline wines.

The turnaround was dramatic, sufficiently so for the Cline family (as a whole) to raise funds to purchase a 350-acre horse ranch on Arnold Drive at the southern end of the Sonoma Valley, to which Cline Cellars moved in 1991. The winery is situated in a vast renovated horse barn, and 20 acres of close-planted Syrah, together with seven acres each of Marsanne and Viognier and a little Roussanne, have been established on the hillsides behind the winery. The trellis design is extremely unusual for California, being taken directly from the Australian approach, which involves the use of wooden posts every four or five vines, and with a thin high-wall vertical trellis system.

In the meantime, Cline Cellars continues to produce its Contra Costa Rhone styles led by Oakley Cuvee (a Mourvedre, Carignane and Zinfandel blend), Cotes d'Oakley (a Carignane, Mourvedre blend with a little Cabernet Sauvignon and Zinfandel included), varietal Mourvedre, Zinfandel, Late Harvest Zinfandel, Semillon and Angel Rosé (a Rhone-blended Rosé). The 1989 Oakley Cuvée was one of a large tasting of Cline wines which shows why they have such a strong hold on the market, with lavish dark cherry and berry fruit, and real overtones of the Rhone Valley in terms of style and structure. When the estate vineyards around the winery come into production, many options will open up: varietal blending, regional blending of the same variety or single variety/single region wines. One thing is for sure: Cline Cellars is on the march.

B.R. COHN WINERY 1984

A: 15140 Sonoma Highway, Glen Ellen, CA 95442 **T**: (707) 938 4064 **V**: By appointment **P**: 14,000 **W**: John Speed

Bruce Cohn, a long time Sonoma resident, made his fortune as manager of the Doobie Brothers, providing him with the income which led to his 1974 purchase of a 46-acre ranch (subsequently extended to 65 acres) which he named Olive Hill Vineyard, after the grove of huge old olive trees on the knoll on which the winery, house and tasting area nestle so comfortably. Initially he planted Cabernet Sauvignon, being content to sell it to others, but proved that the site was exceptionally well suited to the variety, even if fashion also dictated the planting of Chardonnay. An old dairy barn was converted into an unpretentious winery in 1984, and B.R. Cohn Winery was duly bonded.

The subsequent arrival of phylloxera has at least given the opportunity to replant entirely to Cabernet Sauvignon and Merlot, to which the

B.R. COHN
1989 SONOMA VALLEY
CABERNET SAUVIGNON
Olive Hill Vineyard
PRODUCED AND BOTTLED BY B.R. COHN
GLEN ELLEN, CALIFORNIA • ALCOHOL 13.2% BY VOLUME

estate is clearly most suited. It has also led to the development of the Gold label (estate) and Silver label (made from purchased grapes) wines, the latter at a lower price point.

For the time being the Gold label is restricted to the estate Cabernet Sauvignon, but will ultimately expand to include a Merlot; the Silver label will include these two varieties and Chardonnay. The Cabernets are rich, full-bodied and noticeably oak-influenced, and have earned high praise.

H. COTURRI & SONS 1979

A: 6725 Enterprise Road, Glen Ellen, CA 95442 **T**: (707) 996 6247 **V**: By appointment **P**: 3,000 **W**: Tony Coturri

The Coturri family — father Harry, winemaker son Tony and vineyardist Phil — together with partner Dan Parun, have taken organic viticulture and winemaking to its ultimate extreme. They have applied no sprays of any description in their ten-acre estate vineyard for the last four years, not even the elemental sulfur permitted under the most strict organic code. They do use organic fertilizers, and disc in peas planted between the rows; their other allies are predators of insects which might otherwise attack the vines, and somewhat controversially, a belief in microbes which attack mildew spores. "In any event," says Tony Coturri "Zinfandel is not susceptible to mildew." They also manage several other vineyards which supply grapes to the winery using the same strict organic principles.

In the winery, it is more of the same. Appropriately, it looks like a relic of a bygone century, and winemaker Tony uses wild yeasts, does not filter his wine, does not fine it, and does not use any sulfur. Zinfandel and Cabernet Sauvignon are the principal wines, with lesser quantities of Chardonnay and Sauvignon Blanc produced from time to time. They sell to a niche market which is apparently prepared to accept the high levels of aldehydes present in all of the wines.

EAGLE RIDGE WINERY 1986

A: 111 Goodwin Avenue, Penngrove, CA 94951 **T**: (707) 664 9463 **V**: 11–4 daily **P**: 5,500 **W**: Kevin McGuire

Eagle Ridge gives its address as 111 GoodWine Avenue; it lists its phone number as 664-WINE, its fax number as 795-VINE; its brands include Eagle Ridge, Quail Creek, A Class Act and Cardinal Zin. It is advertised as the largest winery in Penngrove, which it is simply because it is the only one, established by owner Barry Lawrence in an 1880s dairy once owned by his grandfather. Lawrence's interest in wine, having been born of a 1978 course at the German Wine Academy, led him to plant his three-and-a-half-acre vineyard to Ehrenfelser, which some might have thought needed a far cooler climate. He makes a Rosé called Cotes de Penngrove Aigle d'Or, and has probably trade marked those names by now, too. Yes, Lawrence is heavily into marketing, his only real concession to convention being the purchase of Zinfandel from the Grandpere Vineyard in Amador County, sharing, in a small way, its output with Santino Winery and Amador Foothill Winery. The wine is big, rich and plummy with some meaty characters and soft tannins. The remaining wines, including a Late Harvest Zinfandel, are not aimed at a critical audience.

FISHER VINEYARDS 1979

A: 6200 St. Helena Road, Santa Rosa, CA 95404 **T**: (707) 539 7511 **V**: By appointment **P**: 8,000 **W**: Max Gasiewicz

Fred Fisher (of the Body by Fisher family) and wife Juelle first planted vines in their eagle's nest on the spine of the range which separates the Sonoma and Napa Valleys back in 1973. When the time came to build a winery, the Fishers hired Bill Turnbull, of Johnson & Turnbull, to design the award-winning winery built from redwoods cut and milled on the property, taken from a spot where vines now stand. In 1975 the Fishers purchased two vineyards totaling 50 acres, off the Silverado Trail in the Napa Valley, placing Fisher in a unique position. Even though all of their grapes are sourced from their own vineyards and are made and bottled at the winery, they cannot be called "estate bottled" because they are grown in two counties.

A Super-Reserve Chardonnay is kept exclusively for mail list customers, the two wines distributed conventionally being the Coach Insignia label (the Reserve equivalent) and the other under the standard Napa/Sonoma label. Fisher and his winemaking team have been constantly involved in research, in particular into the action of wild yeasts, which are used for both the white and red wines. Part of the aim is to break down the "candy" fruit flavors of Chardonnay and to substitute subtlety and complexity in its place. The result will please some, but not others. The Coach Insignia Cabernet Sauvignon, with its strong fruit and high tannins, is likewise masculine in its structure, and not for the faint hearted.

GARRIC-LANGBEHN WINERY 1987

A: 5400 Alpine Road, Santa Rosa, CA 95404 **T**: (707) 539 2078 **V**: By appointment **P**: 1,000 **W**: Larry Langbehn

There is absolutely no chance of a visitor arriving without an appointment at Garric-Langbehn, unless they have become hopelessly lost in remote mountain country and taken the apparently suicidal course of driving across an ancient wooden bridge which will surely collapse under the weight of the next passing car. And if they do, they will have to open the door of a small shed to find the casks and thus recognize that they have indeed found a tiny winery. Most of the year there will be no winemaking equipment, as it is all used on a communal basis by others — unless perchance,

1 9 8 9
Garric-Langbehn
SONOMA COUNTY
CHARDONNAY
PRODUCED AND BOTTLED BY GARRIC•LANGBEHN WINERY, SANTA ROSA, CA • ALC. 13.2% BY VOL.

Larry Langbehn is tinkering with some of it in an endeavor to make it work. Yet this tiny winery, with a present production of 1,000 cases and aspirations to reach 3,000, is the home of Larry Langbehn who was winemaker at Freemark Abbey from 1976 to 1985, and who had previously spent five years working in the chemistry department of U.C. Davis after receiving his degree in chemistry (following it ultimately with a degree in enology). In other words, both technically and practically, Larry Langbehn is a highly qualified winemaker.

It is indeed these qualifications which these days provide a substantial part of his income as a technical consultant for international wine import companies. This business takes him frequently to eastern Europe, Russia, and China, and he finds himself on the horns of a dilemma: should he increase his consulting activities and give away the idea of the winery, or vice versa? On the evidence of his 1990 Chardonnay, a blend of Alexander Valley and Carneros grapes, it would be a great pity if he opted solely for consulting. It is a lovely wine, with pointed fruit flavor in a grapefruit melon spectrum, and a nice hint of spicy oak adding complexity.

GLEN ELLEN VINEYARDS AND WINERY 1980

A: 1883 London Ranch Road, Glen Ellen, CA 95442 **T**: (707) 935 3000 **V**: 10–4:30 daily **P**: 3,500,000 **W**: Bruce Rector

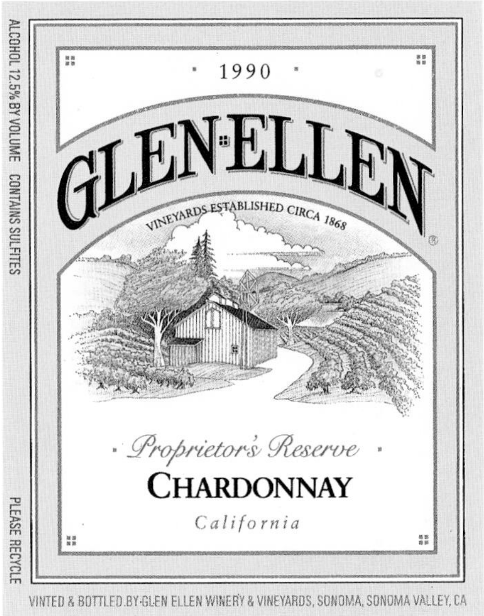
ALCOHOL 12.5% BY VOLUME CONTAINS SULFITES
1990
GLEN ELLEN
VINEYARDS ESTABLISHED CIRCA 1868
Proprietor's Reserve
CHARDONNAY
California
PLEASE RECYCLE
VINTED & BOTTLED BY GLEN ELLEN WINERY & VINEYARDS, SONOMA, SONOMA VALLEY, CA

Endeavoring to explain the extraordinary phenomenon of Glen Ellen — or, if you prefer, Benziger of Glen Ellen — in a few paragraphs is a daunting task. Suffice it say that from a cold start in 1980, by 1992 the group was selling three million cases a year under the Glen Ellen label, 400,000 cases under the Vallejo label and 100,000 cases under the Benziger label. The latter is made at their Glen Ellen winery (and for those who do not know, the town of Glen Ellen actually exists, and has the unreal, manicured beauty of a film set), while the Glen Ellen and Vallejo wines are made at 13 contract wineries spread across California.

If there be a secret to Glen Ellen's success, it is that — like Gallo — it was market-driven. Founder Bruno Benziger had a simple philosophy: sell, sell, sell. And in the first three years of phenomenal growth, Glen Ellen was able to tap the then flush bulk market. Joe Benziger looks back and marvels that they were basically allowed to build their very substantial place in the sun without interference during those first two to three years.

When the bulk market dried up, the Benzigers realized they had to establish long-term grower contracts, and currently only source between ten and 20% of their requirements from the bulk market, and then only to even out irregularities between projected and actual demand. Early on they established a 70-acre experimental vineyard at the London Ranch winery, split into 22 different blocks, the grapes of which are fermented separately. Twenty cases of wine from each block are bottled separately to monitor the ongoing development of what is essentially a giant field laboratory. They apply the same principles to their growers: one winemaker is employed solely to carry out micro-vinification of separate lots, making 600 different wines in 1991 — wines which were then shown to the growers concerned. Glen Ellen has gone so far as to trademark the phrase "farming for flavours," constantly reiterating the link between vineyard and wine quality.

Fifteen wines under the three labels spread through a series of blind bench tastings produced utterly consistent results: the Glen Ellen and M.G. Valejo labels gained the commercial points one would expect, exhibiting precisely the kind of soft, fairly neutral flavors appropriate to that sector of the market. On the other hand, with the exception of a somewhat bitter Merlot, the Benziger wines were excellent, the 1990 Fumé Blanc outstanding, and the 1989 Cabernet Sauvignon showing super-sophisticated use of spicy oak together with gentle fruit.

Where now? "Oh," says Joe Benziger, "I guess we would be happy with sales of between five to six million cases by the latter part of the 1990s."

GOLDEN CREEK VINEYARD 1983

A: 4480 Wallace Road, Santa Rosa, CA 95404 **T**: (707) 538 2350 **V**: By appointment **P**: 1,000 **W**: Ladi Danielik

Czechoslovakian-born Ladi Danielik escaped from Czechoslovakia during the brief Dubcek inter-regnum, obtaining permission for himself and his wife to visit friends in Austria over Easter. A dental laboratory technician by training, he successfully applied for permanent U.S. residency, moving to New Jersey. But he had been brought up in a vineyard area, and he and his father had made wine in their cellar from his grandfather's vineyard. So he migrated for a second time: from New Jersey to the Sonoma Valley, where in 1977 he purchased 75 acres of rolling hillside five miles east of Santa Rosa. Twelve acres are now planted; in 1988 he grafted over the smaller patches of Gewurztraminer and Sauvignon Blanc to Cabernet Sauvignon and Merlot, and these varieties are now the only two grown.

The quality of the grapes is very high, and he could sell them many times over. But he does make around 1,000 cases a year of Cabernet Sauvignon and Merlot, both of which are quite lovely wines. The Cabernet typically shows perfectly ripened fruit flavors, gentle tannins and an intriguing touch of spice — intriguing because it does not come from oak, which Danielik does not like. The Merlot is warm, fleshy and generously proportioned. The wines deserve a wide audience, but then I am not too sure that Danielik really wishes this. Like so many of his European counterparts, he is most content in the vineyard, moderately happy in the winery, and not the least bit interested in the nasty commercial business of actually selling the wine.

GUNDLACH BUNDSCHU WINERY 1858

A: 2000 Denmark Street, Sonoma, CA 95476 **T**: (707) 938 5277 **V**: 11–4:30 daily **P**: 40,000 **W**: Linda Trotta

Five generations of Gundlachs and Bundschus have grown grapes continuously on the 375-acre Rhinefarm Vineyard planted by Jacob Gundlach, who took Charles Bundschu into partnership in 1862 when the latter married Gundlach's daughter. Within a relatively short period of time, the partners had established a 150,000-gallon stone winery, and a large cellar and offices in San Francisco. The business survived phylloxera, and by 1906 their San Francisco warehouse covered an entire city block — and was completely destroyed in the earthquake of that year. But it was rebuilt, and winemaking continued until Prohibition. Even then, the grape growing business was maintained. One of the curiosities of Prohibition was that the price of grapes actually went up rather than down, partly due to the enormous upsurge in home winemaking. As Prohibition ended, the Rhinefarm began supplying large quantities of grapes to the major wineries of the day, and it was not until 1969 that Jim Bundschu decided the time had come to once again make wine on the Rhinefarm. Only three walls remained of the original winery, and the restoration process took three years, producing the first vintage in 1973.

Since that time, Gundlach Bundschu has established itself as a maker of a substantial

VINTAGE RESERVE
GUNDLACH BUNDSCHU
CABERNET SAUVIGNON
SONOMA VALLEY
ALCOHOL 13.0% BY VOLUME CONTAINS SULFITES

range of wines which are honest, elegant and fairly priced. No small part of its success has been due to the at time outrageous humor of the Gunny-Bunny team: Jim Bundschu, consultant winemaker Lance Cutler, and marketer Jim McCullough. One of their more celebrated exploits was to hijack the Napa Valley Wine Train, masked and guns drawn, forcing the startled but eventually totally co-operative passengers to drink Gundlach Bundschu wines.

Apart from the vivid murals which now adorn sections of the winery, perhaps the best-known advertising gimmick is the Napa Valley Sobriety Test No. 1, showing a highway patrolman interviewing Jim Bundschu's mother at the wheel of her ancient car with the caption, "If you can't say Gundlach Bundschu Gewurztraminer, you shouldn't be driving."

This is a very cool corner of the Sonoma Valley, and the white wines in particular reflect the climate: the often-praised Gewurztraminer is crisp and appropriately spice- and lychee-accented; the Chardonnay (purchased from the nearby Sangiacomo Vineyard, and the only wine to be non estate-grown) light and crisp, and it is left to Zinfandel to prove once again what an extraordinary variety it is. While criticized from time to time as being overripe, when it hits the nail on the head as it did in 1990, it literally bursts with essency strawberry fruit and spice. Lance Cutler and successor Linda Trotta have worked hard with Cabernet Sauvignon and Meritage blends, but I suspect more work will have to be done in the vineyard if these are to succeed consistently. The investment has certainly been made in the winery, with the recent opening of lavish underground caves for barrel storage, an investment on a scale which shows that Jim Bundschu can be serious when he so wishes.

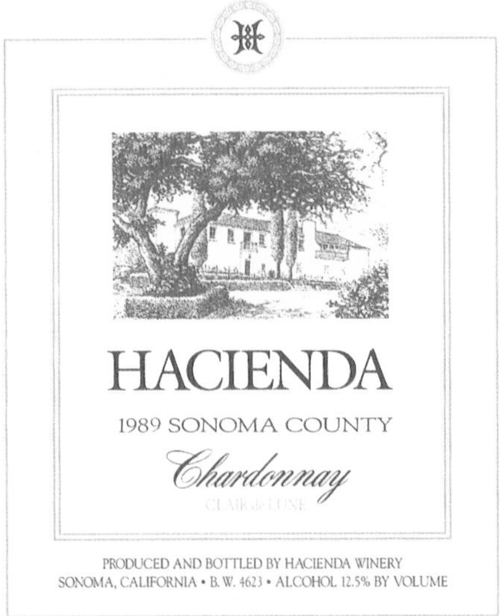
HACIENDA
1989 SONOMA COUNTY
Chardonnay
PRODUCED AND BOTTLED BY HACIENDA WINERY
SONOMA, CALIFORNIA • B.W. 4623 • ALCOHOL 12.5% BY VOLUME

HACIENDA WINERY 1973

A: 1000 Vineyard Lane, Sonoma, CA 95476
T: (707) 938 3220 **V**: 10–5 daily **P**: 30,000
W: Eric Laumann

Notwithstanding that Hacienda was not established until 1973, and only by the conversion of the former Sonoma Valley District Hospital into a winery by the then-owner, the late Frank Bartholomew, Hacienda has much history attached to it. The vineyards in front of the winery are established on the site first planted by Agoston Haraszthy in 1857, and were part of the Buena Vista holdings acquired by Bartholomew in 1941. When he sold Buena Vista in 1968, he retained ownership of this 50-acre vineyard (which has 14 acres of Chardonnay, 13 acres of Cabernet and six acres of Pinot Noir), providing the original grape source for Hacienda. The Haraszthy connection — and the obvious sense of history — was then heightened by the recreation of the elaborate Pompeiian villa which Haraszthy had constructed on the site in 1857.

By the end of the 1970s, Hacienda had been purchased by Crawford Cooley (assisted by his son Robert) who continues to run the winery to this day. Cooley was a founding partner of the first venture capital business in California, a highly successful foray which provided him with a capital base not only to acquire Hacienda, but to continue as an active private investor in the venture capital field.

The wine portfolio of Hacienda has been trimmed down somewhat in recent years. The focus is on Chardonnay (around 10,000 cases), Chenin Blanc (8,000 cases, the 1991 vintage a triple gold medal winner, and as ever, sourced from Clarksburg), Cabernet Sauvignon (with a little Cabernet Franc), Antares (a 500-case Meritage selection of the very best wines) and Pinot Noir (700 cases). The Pinot Noir is distinctly old style, with minimal varietal character; the Chardonnay (called Clair de Lune) surprisingly simple and direct in its citrus/melon fruit (surprising given that it is 100% barrel-fermented and 100% MLF). Appropriately enough, the wine which shines brightly is Antares, which, while on the slightly lean side, is well made with some real pretensions to Bordeaux style.

In December 1992 Hacienda — though not the Cooley family vineyards — was purchased by J.F.J. Bronco, the vast San Joaquin Valley winery. Where Hacienda heads from here remains to be seen.

HANZELL VINEYARDS 1956

A: 18596 Lomita Avenue, Sonoma, CA 95476
T: (707) 996 3860 **V**: By appointment
P: 3,000 **W**: Bob Sessions

The story of Hanzell is told on pages 188–9.

KENWOOD VINEYARDS 1906

A: 9592 Sonoma Highway, Kenwood, CA 95452 **T**: (707) 833 5891 **V**: 10–4:30 daily
P: 175,000 **W**: Mike Lee

When the Lee family combined their life savings to purchase the old Pagani Winery, producer of Italian-style jug red since 1906, even the most optimistic business plan they might have had could not have foreseen the rise to fame (and fortune) which Kenwood Vineyards has enjoyed. Yet — with one exception — that fame has come through the sheer quality of the wines, rather than through lavish expenditure on edifices or promotional ventures and material. Even the one exception was in a sense fortuitous. Vice president and marketing manager Marty Lee was, and remains, an art collector, and had the bright

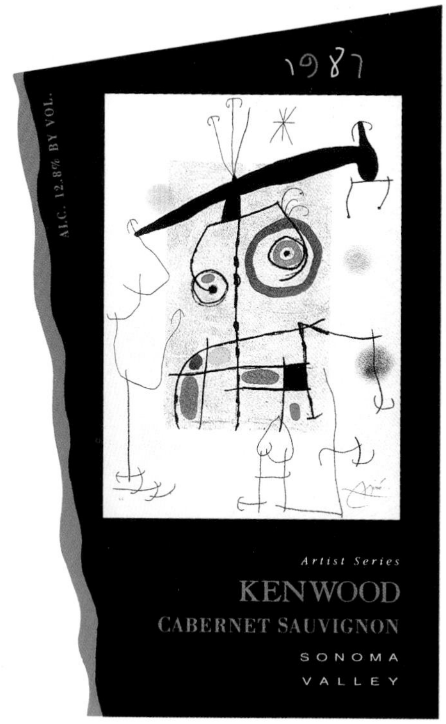
1987
ALC. 12.8% BY VOL.
Artist Series
KENWOOD
CABERNET SAUVIGNON
SONOMA
VALLEY

idea of commissioning leading artists to design a label for each vintage in the manner of Mouton-Rothschild. The first artist he chose was David Goyins, whose works are included in the Museum of Modern Art, the Smithsonian and the Louvre. As has been told in practically every book written on California wine, the BATF excelled even its own fine standards when it rejected the label because it showed a (very small) nude lady reclining on a hillside. Goyins, unperturbed, redrew the label, this time with a skeleton. Once again, the BATF rejected the label, displaying all of the logic of the Mad Hatter and the March Hare in citing "current opinion on the fetal alcohol syndrome and alcoholism." The label was finally approved sans nude and sans skeleton, and today the Artist Series Cabernet Sauvignon is regarded as one of the foremost Sonoma Cabernets. In fact the Sonoma Valley Cabernet can be just as good at half the price, showing luxuriant ripe fruit, obvious but not overwhelming tannins and tremendous depth and texture — as it did, for example, in 1987.

Although Kenwood itself is situated on the valley floor, between 80 and 90% of its grapes come from mountain vineyards. Right from the word go, it has enjoyed exclusive rights to the Jack London Vineyard (situated near Patrick Campbell's Laurel Glen) providing it with the distinctively labeled Jack London Zinfandel and a goodly part of its best Cabernet. But it has also established 135 acres of its own estate vineyards, and continues to purchase special parcels of high quality fruit. Thus in 1990 it released its first Barricia Vineyard Zinfandel, from a 60-year-old vineyard on the outskirts of Agua Caliente, a wholly seductive wine with masses of spicy fruit, beautifully balanced tannins and a nice touch of oak. Yet if all the discussion is about the Kenwood red wines, sales are driven by its Chardonnay (Sonoma Valley, Yulpa Vineyard and Beltane Ranch being three manifestations) and its ripe, full-bodied Sauvignon Blanc.

Winemaker Mike Lee was coming up to his 23rd harvest when I visited the Kenwood facility in 1992. As others have said, Kenwood is a very slick operation in which actions speak louder than words, and with modesty and gentle humor the order of the day.

LANDMARK VINEYARDS 1974

A: 101 Adobe Canyon Road, Kenwood, CA 95452 **T**: (707) 833 0053 **V**: 10–4:30 daily **P**: 20,000 **W**: William R. Mabry III

If Kenwood has gone about its business one way, Landmark has taken the precisely opposite course. It moved to its present site in 1990, and became solely owned by Damaris Deere Wyman Etheridge when suburban encroachment forced the closure of the original facility at Windsor and the dissolution of the founding partnership (no doubt with a handsome financial return to all concerned). John Deere descendant Damaris Etheridge had been one of the partners, as had the Mabry family, but it suited all concerned for Damaris Etheridge to become proprietor and Bill Mabry to continue as managing partner and winemaker of the lavish new facility erected on the outskirts of the hamlet of Kenwood. The bold new label, the lavish entertainment and reception area (especially built to accommodate functions and weddings, and extensively used for that very purpose) and the incredible array of objects on sale in the visitors' center all make the same statement.

On the enological front, Landmark has set itself up as a Chardonnay specialist, offering three Chardonnays: Landmark, Two Williams and Damaris Reserve. Fifty per cent of the crush comes from Landmark's vineyards in the Sonoma Valley and Alexander Valley, and the balance is purchased. Landmark also purchases sparkling wine and red wines for use in the function room and sale from the tasting room, but not for national distribution. The top of the line Damaris Reserve, from the Alexander Valley, is the richest of the three wines, followed by the Two Williams, which shows some nice barrel fermented characters but is a little light on so far as fruit concentration is concerned, and the Sonoma County Chardonnay being of modest proportions.

LAUREL GLEN VINEYARD 1977

A: 6611 Sonoma Mountain Road, Glen Ellen, CA 95442 **T**: (707) 526 3914 **V**: By appointment **P**: 5,000 **W**: Patrick Campbell

Let there be no bones about it: Patrick Campbell is, and has for long been, one of my heroes. He has a formidable intellect (indicated, if it is not immediately evident in talking to him, by his master's degree in the Philosophy of Religion from Harvard's Divinity School following an English major), and a serene refusal to let the fact that childhood poliomyelitis effectively deprived him of the use of his legs stand in the way of his chosen career as a viticulturist (first and foremost) and a winemaker (second). I well remember first meeting Patrick Campbell over ten years ago as he skipped nimbly through the vineyard, airily dismissing "all that janitor stuff" as he waved towards the winery.

Together with his wife and three children, he has carved out a piece of heaven on the high Sonoma hillside vineyard he purchased in 1977. He now has 40 acres under vine, principally to Cabernet Sauvignon, with a little Cabernet Franc and Merlot for blending, and a few test plots of Syrah, Tempranillo and Mourvedre. At a vertical tasting of all of the Laurel Glen wines made since 1978 (but also including the 1977 made by Chateau St. Jean) demonstrated, Patrick Campbell knows a great deal about "that janitor stuff."

The 1978 vintage, homemade, is a glorious wine, with abundant sweet fruit, soft tannins and great length to the palate, proving that first class California Cabernet can indeed age majestically. Other wines to stand out in a class field were the 1981, 1985, 1986 and 1990. Some see the Laurel Glen wines as strong and robust; I see them as elegant and subtle, which all goes to show why wine provokes such debate among those supposed to know all the answers.

MATANZAS CREEK WINERY 1978

A: 6907 Bennett Valley Road, Santa Rosa, CA 95404 **T**: (707) 528 6464 **V**: 10–4 Mon–Sat; 12–4 Sun **P**: 30,000 **W**: Susan Reed and Bill Parker

After due consideration, I have come to the conclusion that one of the people in the wine industry I would least like to cross is Matanzas Creek co-owner and founder, Sandra MacIver. Happily, I see no reason why I should do so, because I have only praise for the vineyard, the functional but aesthetically pleasing winery and surrounds, and above all else, the wines. I simply detect an extraordinary will and determination to succeed in the self-professed aim to create one of the finest wine estates in the world. "A lofty goal," acknowledges MacIver, but one she has not deviated from. This has meant a number of tough decisions along the way, but the wines (drawn largely from the 45-acre vineyard estate) seem to get better and better.

Quite apart from dispensing with the services first of Merry Edwards and then of David Ramey as winemaker, one of the tough decisions was to drop a highly acclaimed Cabernet Sauvignon and to put all of the effort into a varietal Merlot. If there was a better Merlot made in 1989 in California, I have not seen it: the wine has wonderful varietal character and mouthfeel, with red berry fruit tinged by a touch of Merlot sappiness, appropriate in every way in weight, style and texture, and with perfectly integrated oak. The Chardonnay, with grapefruit/citrus/melon flavors and tremendous length on the palate, is of the highest quality, while it is not hard to see why the Sauvignon Blanc, reserved but intensely powerful, has also received consistent praise — and why the winery has decided to concentrate on these three varieties.

RAVENSWOOD 1976

A: 18701 Gehricke Road, Sonoma, CA 95476
T: (707) 938 1690 **V**: 10–5 daily **P**: 40,000
W: Joel Peterson

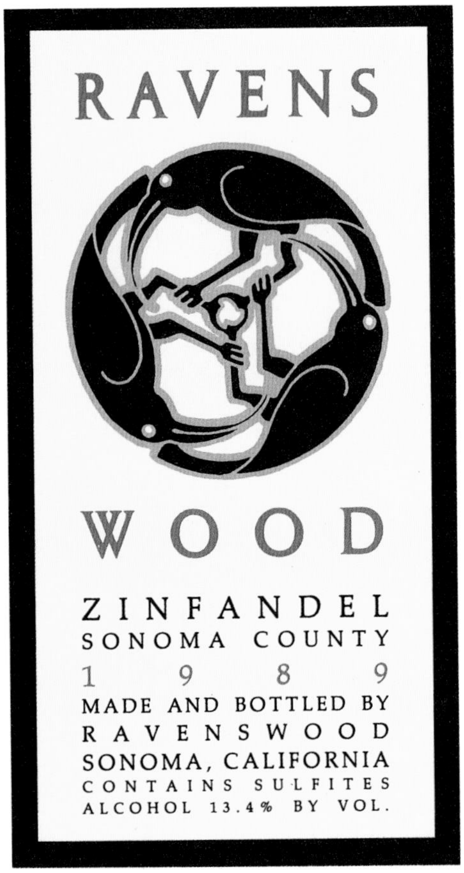
RAVENS
WOOD
ZINFANDEL
SONOMA COUNTY
1989
MADE AND BOTTLED BY
RAVENSWOOD
SONOMA, CALIFORNIA
CONTAINS SULFITES
ALCOHOL 13.4% BY VOL.

A barrel tasting at Ravenswood is a thoroughly unnerving experience. The first red offered by winemaker Joel Peterson seems so superbly flavored, concentrated and balanced that one instinctively feels the next will have to be something of an anti-climax. Instead, each wine tastes better than the one before, and you start wondering whether you are under some form of magic spell, induced perhaps by the hypnotic and somehow disturbing label. Peterson and partner W. Reed Foster have come a long way since Peterson (with a biochemistry degree and several years of cancer research) apprenticed himself to Joseph Swan in the early 1970s and made his first 327 cases of Zinfandel in 1976 in a rented corner of Swan's winery. Released in 1979, it was an instant success, and in 1981 Ravenswood moved into its own facility just south of the town of Sonoma. Ten years later, with production at 40,000 cases, it had grown out of that facility, and in early 1991 moved into the former Haywood Winery on Gehricke Road.

Right from the outset, Peterson's attitude to winemaking has been heavily influenced by the beliefs (and practices) of Joseph Swan. Notwithstanding his degree in biochemistry, he relies on wild yeasts, and has never bothered to employ a microscope to monitor their progress. In the same way, he adopts a minimal intervention approach right through the winemaking process: "I rely primarily on my nose and my palate; when they tell me I need to refer to my science, I do so." Consistent with this, the wines are gently fined, but filters and centrifuges used as little as possible.

Ravenswood has never owned a vineyard; instead, Peterson has hunted out old, dry-farmed, low-yielding and often virus-infected vineyards to give him the raw material to fashion his extraordinary wines. Seventy-five per cent of the production is of Zinfandel, and of that the major part is the Vintners Blend, deliberately made in a style which encourages those who purchase it to drink it immediately. Then there are the exceptional single vineyard Zinfandels: Dickerson, Old Hill Ranch and Cooke Vineyard, amongst others. The 1990s each scored stellar points in the blind tastings, but each was utterly different to the other: the Dickerson with lifted mint and cherry aromas and flavors; the Old Hill Ranch with strong cherry fruit and tannins; the Cooke Vineyard with briary, dark cherry and chocolate flavors melding into a wine of extraordinary intensity. Then there is the supremely elegant Pickberry Vineyard Meritage blend of approximately one-third Cabernet Sauvignon, one third Cabernet Franc and one third Merlot, with its dancing fruit flavors, deftly handled charred oak, and fine-grained tannins.

ST. FRANCIS VINEYARDS & WINERY 1979

A: 8450 Sonoma Highway, Kenwood, CA 94452 **T**: (707) 833 4666 **V**: 10–4:30 daily
P: 40,000 **W**: Tom Mackey

Former furniture store business owner Joseph T. Martin opted for a lifestyle change in 1971, selling his share in that business and purchasing a 100-acre walnut and prune orchard at Kenwood. In place of walnuts and prunes he planted Merlot, Chardonnay, Riesling, Gewurztraminer and Pinot Noir, establishing 90 acres of vineyard in all. In 1979 he took the next step of establishing the large, functional winery which is kept spic and span by winemaker Tom Mackey, who joined the following year.

Right from the outset St. Francis produced a varietal Merlot, being one of the earliest exponents of the variety. Right from the outset, too, Tom Mackey decided that Merlot should stand on its own two feet, and chose not to blend in Cabernet Sauvignon or Cabernet Franc. "I am not trying to make a light Cabernet, but a Merlot. Why should I try to hide it, dilute it or strengthen it?" From time to time he and owner Martin have agonized over this decision, because the wines have not always fared well in the show ring, but their final answer was to bud over all of the Johannisberg Riesling, Gewurztraminer and Pinot Noir to Merlot after the 1988 harvest, so that the vineyard now comprises 68 acres of Merlot and 22 acres of Chardonnay.

Small amounts of Cabernet Sauvignon, Gewurztraminer and Zinfandel are purchased from other growers (St. Francis is in fact a net seller), but the primary focus — obviously enough — is on Chardonnay and Merlot. And it is indeed with these two varieties that the winery excels. The Chardonnay is smoky, stylish and crisp, striking a nice balance between austerity and opulence. To my mind, both the standard and Reserve Merlot (it is made in both guises) are outstanding, showing some of the most intense varietal flavor I have seen anywhere outside of Bordeaux. The overtones of tobacco and that faint stemminess which (to me) is the hallmark of Merlot may not appeal to everyone, but the Reserve Merlot surely shows wonderfully intense fruit, style and length.

SEBASTIANI VINEYARDS 1904

A: 389 Fourth Street East, Sonoma, CA 95476 **T**: (707) 938 5532 **V**: 10–5 daily
P: 4 ,000,000 **W**: Doug Davis

When Sam Sebastiani took over management of the vast Sebastiani wine empire following his father's death in 1980, he saw the need for profound change if Sebastiani were to maintain its position as one of the foremost wineries in the country. He dramatically trimmed the number of wines being produced, started to promote varietal rather than generic labels, upgraded and focused the sources of supply, and started to replace old redwood tanks with new French barrels. In an eerie replay of the Krug-Mondavi saga 20 years earlier, Sam was voted out in a very public family brawl which erupted in 1986, and brother Don put in his place. Sam went down the road to start Viansa, and a thoroughly shaken and uncertain Sebastiani Vineyards was left to decide what in fact should be its future direction.

The irony is that many of the changes which Sam Sebastiani initiated have been continued, and there can be no question that Sebastiani these days is making far better wines than it was 20 years ago. Smart new labels have been designed, and a range of wines headed by the Sonoma Series (in both standard and Reserve release form), with next the August Sebastiani Country Wines, then August Sebastiani

Proprietors Wines, then The Eye of The Swan (with Pinot Noir and Chardonnay joining the original blush-style Pinot Noir Blanc), and finally Vendange (Chardonnay, Cabernet Sauvignon and White Zinfandel) at the bottom of the range.

The Sonoma Valley wines are more than decent, the Barbera and Cabernet Sauvignon being well made and quite well structured, even if not especially fruity, while the Chardonnays rise above their station, with the Reserve (in 1990) being precisely the sort of wine which Sam Sebastiani envisaged would restore the fortunes of the group.

VIANSA WINERY 1987

A: 25200 Arnold Drive, Sonoma, CA 94576
T: (707) 935 4700 **V**: 10–5 daily **P**: 3,000
W : Sam Sebastiani

At least to this point, Sam Sebastiani does not seem to have made the same impression as did Robert Mondavi when he walked out of Charles Krug to establish Robert Mondavi Wines. If anything, Viansa is seeking to emulate V. Sattui: its pink, Italianate villa, set atop a hill, and the first winery one reaches on the way to Sonoma, has a delicatessen to end all delicatessens, a gift shop of monumental proportions, and a vast (and not unattractive) tiled sales and reception area. Sebastiani's professed aim is to plant 25 acres of Sangiovese and ultimately to become a winery devoted exclusively to estate-grown Sangiovese. The first vines are in the ground in evidence of that aim. In the meantime a full complement of wines is being released, including some very high-priced items packed in ritzy Italian glass, headed by 1987 Obsidian, which in 1992 was selling for $65 a bottle, or $14 a glass at the winery. It is not Tuscan, nor even Italian, being a blend of 58% Cabernet Franc and 42% Cabernet Sauvignon. Indeed, if one excludes some dessert wine offerings of Muscat Canelli, all of the wines were from the stand-bys of Sauvignon Blanc, Chardonnay and the Cabernet family, unless one includes a Barbera Blanc.

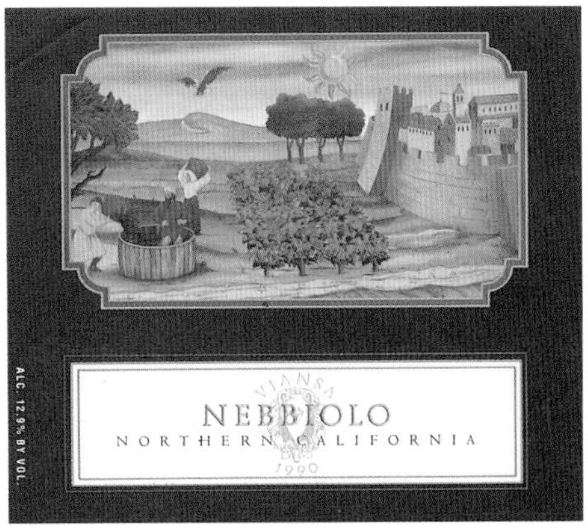
VIANSA
NEBBIOLO
NORTHERN CALIFORNIA
1990
ALC. 12.9% BY VOL.

OTHER WINERIES

GRAND CRU VINEYARDS 1970
A: 1 Vintage Lane, Glen Ellen, DA 95442
T: (707) 996 8100 **W**: Barbara Lindblom

HOMEWOOD WINERY 1988
A: 23120 Burndale Road, Sonoma, CA
T: (707) 996 6353 **W**: David Homewood

SMOTHERS BROTHERS 1977
A: 9575 Highway 12, Kenwood, CA 94542
T: (707) 833 1010 **W**: T. B. Smothers III

SONOMA HILLS
A: 4850 Peracca Road, Santa Rosa, CA 95407
T: (707) 523 3415

VALLEY OF THE MOON WINERY 1939
A: 777 Madrone Road, Glen Ellen, CA 95442
T: (707) 996 6941 **W**: Harry Parducci Jr.

ABOVE ~ *Pickberry Vineyard sells grapes to makers as disparate as Glen Ellen and Ravenswood.*

MENDOCINO AND LAKE COUNTIES

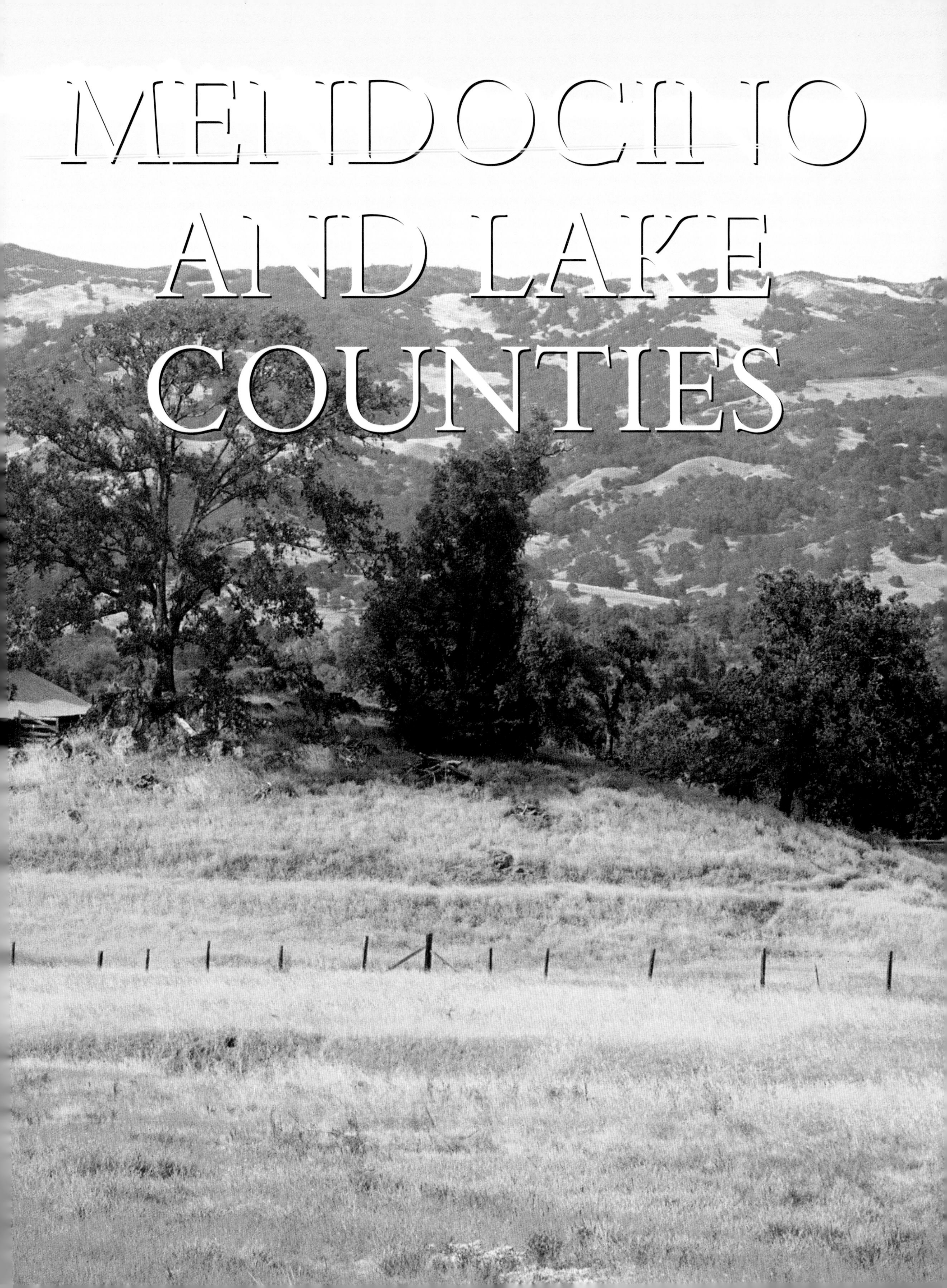

Mendocino and Lake rolls off the tongue so easily it is not hard to understand why these two adjacent counties have been traditionally grouped together. Indeed, they have a number of things in common: a substantial history of viticulture and winemaking in the late nineteenth and early twentieth centuries, followed by a long period of inactivity; a spread of AVAs which confuse more than they inform; and a range of climates profoundly influenced by the mountain ranges which occupy so much of each county and which corral the vineyards into the little valleys gouged by the rivers (or in the case of Lake County, onto the shores and foothills surrounding Clear Lake).

While the Mendocino AVA is confined to the southernmost third of the county, it encompasses 430 square miles (or 275,000 acres) of country as climatically diverse as that of San Luis Obispo. The two northward-pointing fingers of Mendocino take in the Anderson Valley AVA in the western finger and the Potter Valley and McDowell Valley AVAs in the eastern one — together with the Redwood Valley and Talmage, which are often treated as having AVA status but do not.

Mendocino and Lake Counties
1971 AND 1991 ACREAGE/GRAPE VARIETIES

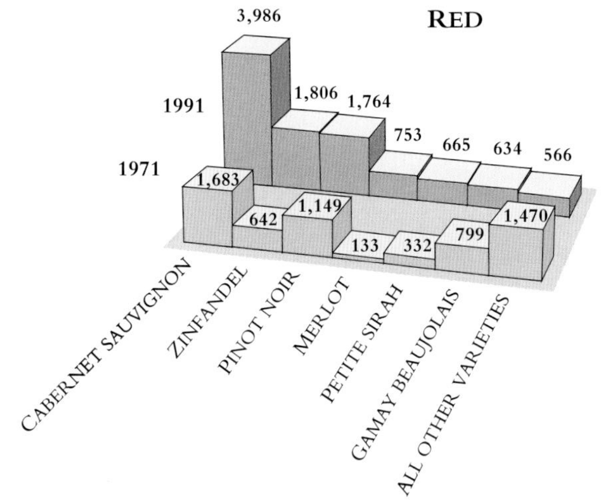
RED
1991
1971
3,986
1,806
1,764
753
665
634
566
1,683
642
1,149
133
332
799
1,470
CABERNET SAUVIGNON
ZINFANDEL
PINOT NOIR
MERLOT
PETITE SIRAH
GAMAY BEAUJOLAIS
ALL OTHER VARIETIES

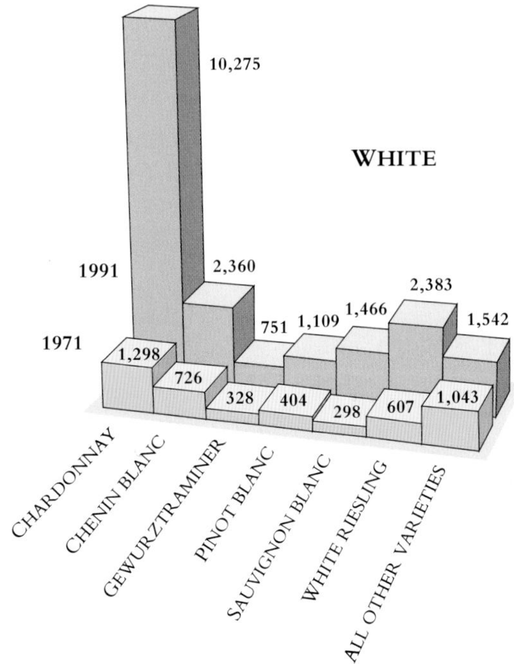
WHITE
1991
1971
10,275
2,360
751
1,109
1,466
2,383
1,542
1,298
726
328
404
298
607
1,043
CHARDONNAY
CHENIN BLANC
GEWURZTRAMINER
PINOT BLANC
SAUVIGNON BLANC
WHITE RIESLING
ALL OTHER VARIETIES

The Anderson Valley is so distinct, both in terms of its cool climate (Region I to Region II) and its geographical separation, that I have elected to treat it separately. The remaining subdistricts (whether or not with AVA status) are strung together by the mighty Russian River, which rises just to the north of the border of the Mendocino AVA.

While vines were grown in the Anderson Valley in the late nineteenth century, the main center of activity was to the east along the Russian River. Plantings commenced in the 1860s, and by 1910, 5,800 acres of grapes and nine wineries were producing 90,000 gallons of wine a year. One of these was the French American Wine Company, which survived — and indeed prospered — during Prohibition by selling a grape concentrate called Caligrapo to home winemakers. After the repeal of Prohibition it made and marketed Victor Mendocino Zinfandel, but production waned during the 1950s and the abandoned winery was destroyed by fire in the 1970s.

Indeed, in 1967 the only operating winery in Mendocino County was Parducci; Fetzer was bonded the following year, and the boom was underway. In 1992 there were 12,364 acres under vine and over 20 bonded wineries in operation.

The history of Lake County followed a similar path. By 1884, 600 acres of grapes were planted, and in the early years of this century 36 wineries were operating. All disappeared during Prohibition, with pear and walnut orchards replacing almost all of the vineyards. Today there are five producers in the Clear Lake AVA, one in the Guenoc Valley AVA, Channing Rudd on its own near Middletown, and that most obscure of AVAs, the Benmore Valley, sitting in splendid isolation in the southwest corner of the county (and boasting no winery of its own). Three thousand four hundred acres of vines are in production, and Kendall-Jackson is the county's flagbearer as Fetzer is for Mendocino.

PREVIOUS PAGE ~ *Hopland, the essence of Mendocino County, made famous as the base of Fetzer, one of California's most successful wineries.*

ABOVE LEFT ~ *Visitors to the tasting room at Kendall Jackson's Clear Lake Winery enjoy an idyllic view of the estate's Sauvignon Blanc.*

ABOVE ~ *The cold waters of the Mendocino coastline have a profound influence on the climate of the Anderson Valley.*

FETZER AND ORGANIC VITICULTURE

The winery which left the deepest impression on me following my first wine-specific visit to California in 1979 was Fetzer. I came back to Australia to write a glowing article for the *National Times* about a family-owned and run winery making 100,000 cases a year, and I still have vivid memories of breakfast with Barney and Kathleen Fetzer (and various of their children) in their Redwood Valley home next to the winery complex.

I kept track of the Fetzer wines — and of the amazing growth of the business over the ensuing years — and nothing I read or tasted caused me to downgrade my opinion. So it was that I returned to Fetzer in June 1992 while researching this book and spent an afternoon and evening with the Fetzer family, first at Hopland and thereafter at the Big Dog Saloon at the Redwood Valley Winery, as famous (some might say infamous) as the hospitality center at Hopland.

ABOVE ~ *As well as grapes, fruit and vegetables are organically farmed here.*

There was no hint of the pending sale to Brown Forman, which was announced little over a month later, and which was one of the best kept secrets in an industry known for the effectiveness of its own information grapevine. There is always a sadness when a thriving family business passes into corporate ownership and a concern that its personality will be lost — but it is hard to imagine that this will happen to Fetzer, at least in the short to medium term.

For the Fetzers have always had a remarkable approach to the business of grape growing, winemaking and wine marketing, managing to integrate and personalize all three. This no doubt stemmed from the fact that 11 of Barney Fetzer's children ran the business with their mother Kathleen, and one of them (Diana) married Fetzer's chief winemaker, Paul Dolan.

All the way from the vineyard to the market, the accent was (and is) on personal communication. Fetzer has the largest certified organic vineyard holdings in California, and is at the forefront of viticultural research. It enjoys an exceptionally close relationship with the growers, akin to that of Mondavi, ever encouraging them to grow better grapes more economically and with respect for the environment.

At the other end of the scale, Fetzer's proud boast was that it did not spend a dollar on advertising — in sharp contrast to Gallo, Glen Ellen, et al. Instead, it spent an equivalent amount on educating (in a thoroughly entertaining fashion) the legion of distributors and retailers who handled its products across the United States.

The center stage for this program has been the Valley Oaks Wine and Food Center at Hopland, with its five acres of surrounding organically farmed fruit and vegetable gardens started in 1986 and producing over 1,000 varieties of edible products. Here noted restaurateur John Ash, together with an endless stream of visiting celebrity chefs, holds cooking schools using produce from the garden and — of course — emphasizing the marriage of wine and food.

The very large open-plan kitchen with its ceiling mirror reflecting the work bench capable of handling 40 plates at a time gives the audience the feeling of direct participation, which is so much the Fetzer hallmark.

Weekend seminars are held throughout the summer and autumn which are open to the public, with lodging on the Valley Oaks Estate included. As one might imagine, demand is heavy.

The Big Dog Bar and Saloon was built by the Fetzer children in the style of the gold rush days in a compound at the Redwood Valley Ranch. When it burnt to the ground in 1991, the entire local community turned out and rebuilt it over two weekends. Big Dog turns on a riotous barbecue and dance evening at least twice a week during the summer months, easily swallowing up 100 guests if called upon to do so.

Members of the Fetzer family will be present to play host, sometimes most of them. The one concession to the demands of the following day is that the Saloon closes at 10 P.M. sharp. The Saloon, incidentally, is not open to the public, although Valley Oaks is open for self-guided tours of the organic gardens during weekends and for guided tours of the full facility (by prior appointment) during the week. The tasting room, in the town of Hopland, is open seven days a week from 9 A.M. to 5 P.M.

Quite apart from having built a business worth over $100 million, the most enduring and important contribution of Fetzer has been the development of organic viticulture on a large scale. For long regarded as a quirky pastime of social dropouts, organic farming is now a major item on the social and economic agenda. By some estimates, 8 to 9% of U.S. farm production will be organically grown by 1995.

The implications for California viticulture are immense: when companies as powerful as Gallo, Fetzer and Buena Vista formally endorse and commit themselves to organic growing, the long-term outcome is certain. Their motives are a potent mixture of altruism, opportunism, economic rationalism and fatalism, each sufficient on its own account to drive the program forward.

Concern for the environment, sustainable development and so forth will be the battle cries of the last decade of this century.

How much they are founded on emotion rather than any deep understanding of the incredibly complex scientific and economic issues is beside the point: it is the way of the future.

It is here that California is uniquely well placed among the leading wine producing regions of the world. Its climate, and the happy coincidence that downy mildew (the principal scourge of Europe and Australia) is unknown, make organic viticulture entirely feasible in both functional and economic terms. The generally cold winters, the lack of summer rainfall, the relatively low humidity and high daytime temperature peaks and (in many regions) the wind coalesce to provide an inhospitable climate for the various mildews and molds (including botrytis) which so bedevil other parts of the world.

No less importantly, a close examination of the laws — essentially based on French legislation introduced in 1981 and adopted by the European Community in 1991 — might lead the cynical observer to say that all organic farming requires is that its practitioners adopt the practices of their fathers and grandfathers. In other words, the vast proportion of the chemically synthesized sprays (usually systemic in their action) have been developed since the Second World War, frequently as by-products of the petroleum industry.

On the other side of the ledger, pyrethrin-based products, soaps and other organically derived substances are being rapidly developed. Thus while it is rare to encounter a major grape grower today who is not already committed to the principles of sustainable viticulture, and to most of its practices, growers are watching this development of alternative treatments. Many are not yet prepared to commit to organic certification, simply because they can neither afford to nor wish to see a crop destroyed or severely damaged by disease or insects which can only be controlled by chemical sprays forbidden by the organic code.

But the day is not far away — in California at least — when that constraint will no longer exist. Then the only barriers will be the greater discipline and the initially higher cost of organic viticulture, barriers which peer group pressure or government legislation (or both) will dismount. And when this happens Fetzer will, once again, be one jump in front of the field.

TOP ~ *The oak trees which give Fetzer's Valley Oaks property its name.*

ABOVE ~ *Organic viticulture at Fetzer has many facets, including soil enrichment through inter-row cover crops.*

ANDERSON VALLEY

More than one commentator has pointed to the similarities between the Anderson Valley and the Russian River AVAs, and in particular the western portion of the latter. Most obvious are the rivers which have formed the shape of the valleys and which draw in the cold marine air which so profoundly affects the climate in each region. In the Anderson Valley it is the Navarro River — still unspoilt and still receiving its annual run of steelhead trout and salmon — while the Russian River gives that appellation its name.

At first blush, the Anderson Valley AVA is a true appellation: the area is so concise, the valley so narrow and so clearly defined, barely a mile wide, and sandwiched between Greenwood Ridge on the western side and the Whipple Ridge on the inland or eastern side. But it is these ridges — and in particular Greenwood Ridge — which primarily destroy the illusion of a climatically and topographically cohesive AVA; the bisection of the valley floor into two distinctive climate zones completes the task.

ABOVE ~ *Night-harvesting by hand at Navarro Vineyards ensures the grapes reach the winery in the best possible condition.*

For the Greenwood Ridge area (which gives its name to one of the wineries in the district) was the site of some of the earliest plantings by Italian immigrants who arrived in the 1890s. At an elevation of 1,200 to 1,400 feet, this strikingly beautiful countryside, with its soaring stands of redwoods and firs, is utterly different from the valley floor. It is above the fog line, and receives far more sunshine hours.

Thus it is that the 15-acre DuPratt Vineyard was planted to Zinfandel in 1916, and has supplied Kendall-Jackson with the grapes to make one of its finest vineyard-designated Zinfandels. Likewise, Greenwood Ridge Vineyard successfully ripens Cabernet Sauvignon and Merlot, unthinkable on the valley floor.

The first post-Prohibition attempt to grow grapes on the valley floor was in 1946, when the Italian-Swiss colony planted 200 acres, a costly project abandoned in the early 1950s because the grapes (of unspecified varieties) failed to ripen adequately. The next attempt was made in the 1960s when Dr. Donald Edmeades planted 24 acres of Chardonnay, Gewurztraminer, French Colombard and Cabernet Sauvignon. This succeeded: following his father's death, son Deron established Edmeades Winery in 1972.

In all, the AVA covers 57,600 acres of wonderfully wild and unspoilt countryside. The 1,000 acres of vineyard now established are predominantly of Chardonnay and Pinot Noir, with Roederer by far the largest vineyard holder, and — together with Scharffenberger — setting the agenda for the future of the valley.

OPPOSITE ~ *The magnificent redwoods of the Anderson Valley line the road to the coastline.*

The Region in Brief

Climate, Soil and Viticulture

Climate

Notwithstanding its relatively small and compact area, the Anderson Valley has three distinct climatic zones. The valley floor is bisected by a line just south of Philo: the northwestern section of the valley is a Region I climate, becoming progressively cooler as the valley approaches the coast. Here late evening and morning fogs are a daily occurrence throughout the growing season and the rainfall is higher. South of Philo the level of the valley floor rises from 200 feet to 600 feet above sea level, the marine influence is moderated, the winters become colder, and the summers warmer with a Region II heat summation. Then there is the mountainside (or mountaintop) climate of the Greenwood Ridge; fog seldom reaches up here, and the long hours of sunshine provide a low Region II climate which is very different from that around Boonville. Rainfall varies according to elevation (and of course on a year-by-year basis) but averages 40 inches between November and March.

Soil

The soil along the river terraces on the valley floor shows typical alluvial mixes of clay and gravel. While they are not especially rich, the climate is conducive to vigorous growth early in the season, making sophisticated trellis and canopy management essential for properly balanced and ripened grapes. The hillside soils are thinner and more acidic, inhibiting growth and making management fractionally easier.

The Growing Season

The growing season is extremely long, with Chardonnay's budbreak in late February, but not being picked until early September for sparkling wine and, in years such as 1983 and 1991, not being picked for this purpose until late in the month. Even an early-ripening variety such as Gewurztraminer is sometimes not picked until October 1, and there is no question the slow, late-ripening conditions are critical in shaping the quality of the grapes. The principal problems encountered in the season are frosts (protection is essential) and botrytis, the latter encouraged by the frequent fogs and by the regular occurrence of at least some rain during vintage.

Contract Growers

The most famous is the DuPratt Vineyard, planted to 15 acres of Zinfandel (from 1916) and Chardonnay (1980) on the Greenwood Ridge hills. Other vineyards include Eaglehearth, Ferrington, La Tourette Bagnall, Mendocino Hills, Misty Hills, Nova and Valley Foothill Vineyards.

Anderson Valley
Vintage Chart 1981–91

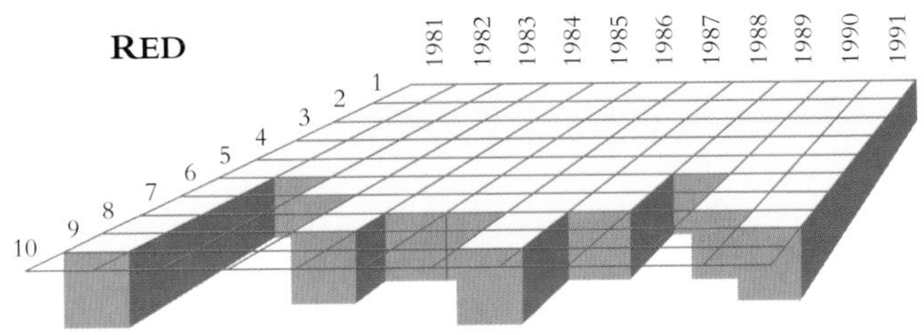
RED
1981
1982
1983
1984
1985
1986
1987
1988
1989
1990
1991
1
2
3
4
5
6
7
8
9
10

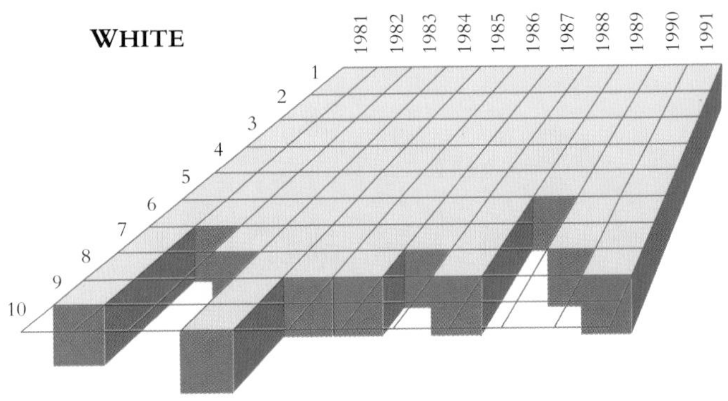
WHITE
1981
1982
1983
1984
1985
1986
1987
1988
1989
1990
1991
1
2
3
4
5
6
7
8
9
10

Principal Wine Styles

Sparkling

The wines of Roederer and Scharffenberger confirm what the statistics suggest: this is an absolutely first class area for sparkling wines made from the classic varieties of Chardonnay and Pinot Noir. The accumulation of heat is slow and even in the north-western half of the valley, with 90°F days rare, and 100°F days all but unheard of. There is a corresponding delicacy and fineness to the structure of the wines without any sacrifice of fruit flavor, and it is no wonder that Michel Salgues of Roederer looks so disdainfully upon Pinot Meuniere (and even more on Pinot Blanc). These, he says, are insurance grapes, and there is no need of insurance here. So far Roederer has contented itself with the classic blend of Chardonnay and Pinot Noir, leaving the Blanc de Blanc (100% Chardonnay) and Brut Rosé (100% Pinot Noir) to Scharffenberger. Handley Cellars, incidentally, also makes a stylish sparkling wine with a distinctly French accent.

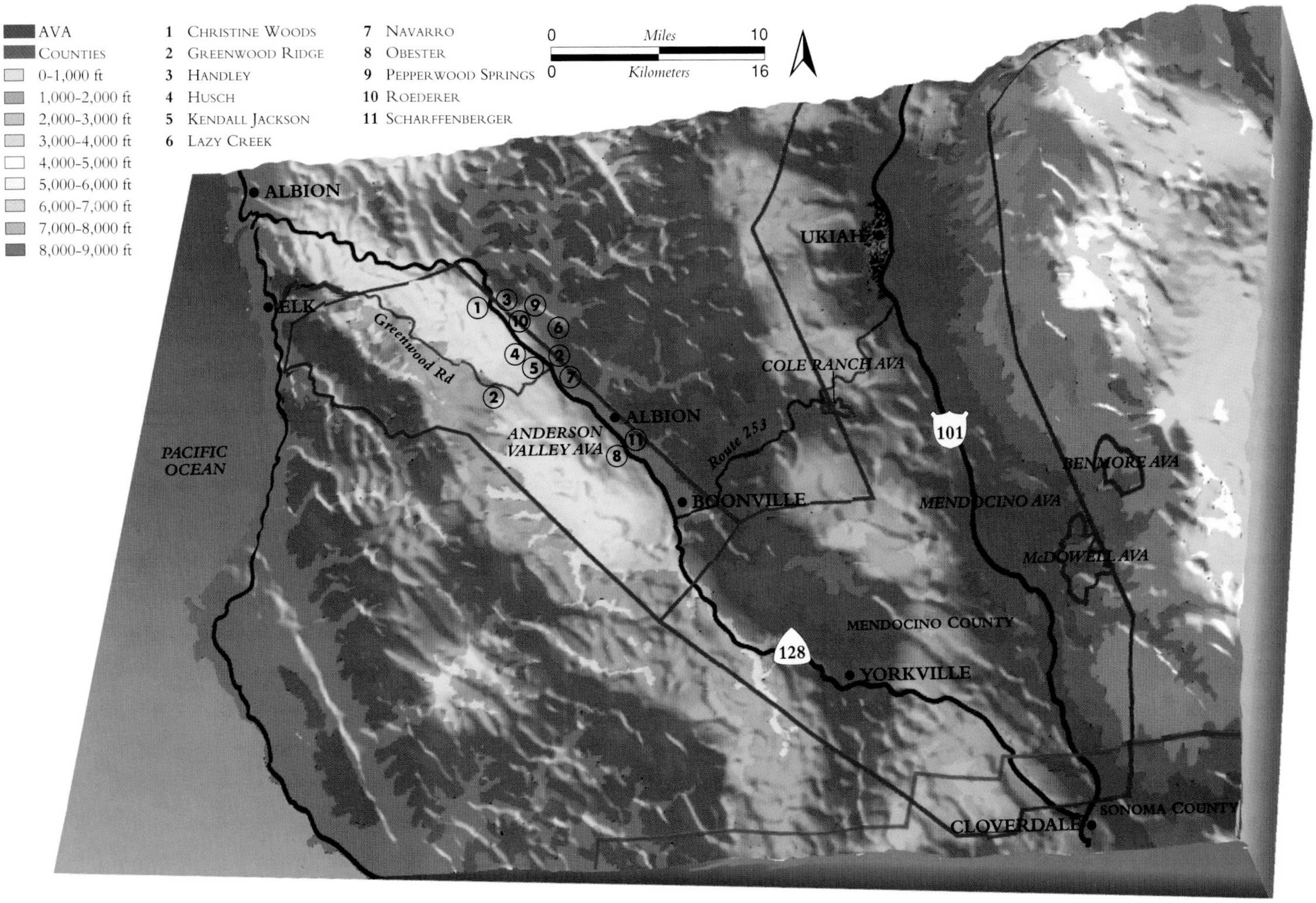
AVA
Counties
0-1,000 ft
1,000-2,000 ft
2,000-3,000 ft
3,000-4,000 ft
4,000-5,000 ft
5,000-6,000 ft
6,000-7,000 ft
7,000-8,000 ft
8,000-9,000 ft
1 Christine Woods
2 Greenwood Ridge
3 Handley
4 Husch
5 Kendall Jackson
6 Lazy Creek
7 Navarro
8 Obester
9 Pepperwood Springs
10 Roederer
11 Scharffenberger
0 Miles 10
0 Kilometers 16
ALBION
ELK
Greenwood Rd
UKIAH
COLE RANCH AVA
ALBION
ANDERSON VALLEY AVA
Route 253
101
PACIFIC OCEAN
BOONVILLE
BENMORE AVA
MENDOCINO AVA
McDOWELL AVA
MENDOCINO COUNTY
128
YORKVILLE
CLOVERDALE
SONOMA COUNTY

Riesling

With more than 110 acres planted, Riesling just shades Gewurztraminer as the most important still table wine grape. It is made into delicate, citrus and lime dry wines and — particularly in years such as 1989 and 1990 — into intense, botrytis-influenced late harvest styles. Handley Cellars wines in this style are outstanding, those of Greenwood Ridge and Navarro good.

Gewurztraminer

Like Riesling, the 105 acres of Gewurztraminer are fashioned into both dry and late harvest styles, and it is arguable that this is *the* variety for the region. The wines are notably crisp and delicate, with clear varietal character; it is perhaps the sheer delicacy which prompts leading makers such as Navarro to leave a little residual sugar in the wine and Lazy Creek to barrel ferment a small portion of the blend.

Chardonnay

As one might expect, the Chardonnays are crisp, apple and pear dominated wines; Handley, Husch and Navarro (sometimes) have all come to the conclusion that the best wine will be made from a blend of Anderson Valley and warmer region grapes.

Pinot Noir

For whatever reason, Pinot Noir has failed to produce table wines of distinction. There is a cosmetic, jammy taste common to all the Pinots, curiously at odds with the climate. The finger of suspicion must point at the clones planted, for the making techniques used are wholly appropriate.

Cabernet Sauvignon, Merlot and Zinfandel

These are grown principally on the mountains, with lesser plantings on the valley floor around Boonville. The DuPratt Zinfandel of Kendall-Jackson has been superb, while Greenwood Ridge is the leading exponent of Cabernet Sauvignon and of Merlot, both in a leafy/cherry mold.

ABOVE ~ *The characteristic pink and bronze tints of bunches of Gewurztraminer.*
TOP ~ *Anderson Valley map.*

NAVARRO AND DIRECT MARKETING

Navarro Vineyards and Alexander Valley's Hafner Vineyards have both met the problems of isolation and an increasingly competitive retail market by deliberately developing direct sales through mail order. It is a technique which is systematically used by surprisingly few wineries: the major exceptions are the Windsor label of Rodney Strong and V. Sattui of the Napa Valley. No doubt the difficulty and expense of shipping wine out of California has held back the development of this method, but even within the state (and now the cooperating states of Oregon, Colorado and New Mexico) there is a very substantial market for those who seek it.

ABOVE ~ *Navarro Vineyards is an acknowledged specialist in the making of high class Gewurztraminer, sparing no trouble or expense in so doing.*

The Navarro newsletters are object lessons in how to communicate to a market spanning all degrees of wine knowledge and interest. In a stapled, paperback-sized format, each 12-page booklet makes extensive use of photographs to simultaneously break up and illustrate the text. The newsletters cover a wide range of subjects, cleverly making highly technical matters seem simple. The approach is always breezy and friendly, yet not dismissive. The reader is taken into the winery and made to feel as if he or she was actually present as the winemakers agonized over vintage conditions, picking decisions, blending combinations and so forth.

It all seems disarmingly simple, but clearly an enormous amount of thought and planning goes into each newsletter. There will be several wines offered on a pre-release basis; a core of wines which are simultaneously on offer at the cellar door; and a few older vintages. Then, occasionally, there will be special offers of very limited quantities of old or experimental wines which can only be ordered via a toll-free phone call, and are typically subject to a bottle limit.

Precise analytical details are given in tabular form for each wine: harvest dates, picking sugar, bottling date, cases produced, alcohol, acidity and pH. Then there is a chatty but always informative background to the wine, often picking up a point of particular interest. Thus 70% of the 1990 Premier Reserve Chardonnay was fermented in new barrels from the French cooper Radoux: nothing new about that, except these barrels had toasted ends (or heads) as well as toasted staves — which is unusual. So the reader is given photographs of the toasting process (a small fire is lit in a container and the barrel, without ends and with the staves only partially bent is placed over it), together with a short explanation of the flavor changes which result from the toasting.

The newsletters are judiciously sprinkled with favorable critical reviews and wine show results, without dwelling too much on such matters. At the other end of the spectrum, mistakes are admitted with disarming freshness, following the old adage, "If you've got a problem, feature it."

So it was that the March 1992 newsletter introduced a new second label, Indian Creek, with Chardonnay at $5 a bottle and Gewurztraminer at $4. The Chardonnay was not good enough for the top labels; the Gewurztraminer was the result of a miscalculation about likely yields from Navarro's own plantings (extra grapes were purchased and then not needed). "Rather than sell it to a negotiant for blending we decided to offer it to you at a negotiant price," read the newsletter. Within three months, the remaining newsletters were overprinted "sold out."

In similar vein, the 1989 vintage earned the headline, "1989 Gewurztraminers: A Perfectly Rotten Vintage," a neat way of introducing a year which provided an abundance of high quality botrytised Rieslings and Gewurztraminers, and a not unwarranted dig at the French. "Perhaps we've gotten used to inclement weather, since there has been only one vintage in the last 15 when it didn't rain during harvest in Alexander Valley. But it rains all summer in France, and when the sun comes out for more than a week, they dictate 'a Vintage of the Century' ... so here's to Navarro's Vintage of the Century (according to the French tradition we are limited to one per decade)."

The wines are all given sub-names which are at once descriptive and imaginative, helping to extend an otherwise slightly limited portfolio. Thus there is Pinot Noir Nouveau and Pinot Noir Methode Ancienne; Chardonnay Premier Reserve and Chardonnay Mendocino; Sauvignon Blanc Cuvee 128 (from three vineyards along Highway 128); Gewurztraminer Dry Cuvee Traditional and Gewurztraminer Late Harvest; White Riesling Semisweet and White Riesling Cluster Select Late Harvest — and so forth.

Partners Ted Bennett and Deborah Cahn always personalize the newsletters, and always manage to come up with a new angle. No wonder they enjoy a loyal clientele.

ABOVE ~ *Even under the distortion of night floodlights, the distinctive pink skins of Gewurztraminer cannot be mistaken.*

WINERIES *of* ANDERSON VALLEY

GREENWOOD RIDGE VINEYARDS 1973

A: 24555 Greenwood Road, Philo, CA 95466 **T**: (707) 877 3262 **V**: 10–5 daily (5501 Highway 128, Philo) **P**: 3,000 **W**: Van Williamson

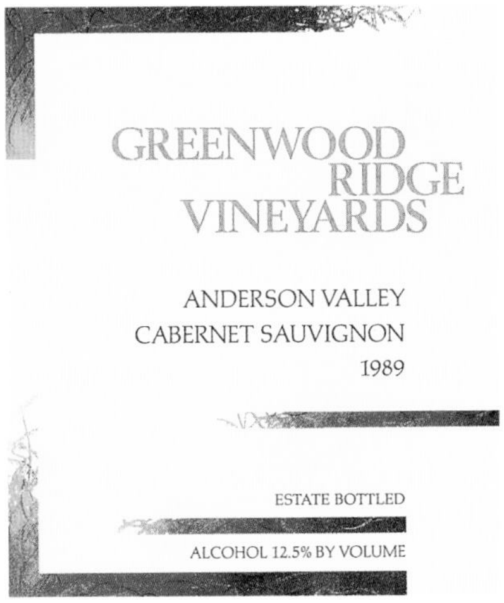
GREENWOOD RIDGE VINEYARDS
ANDERSON VALLEY
CABERNET SAUVIGNON
1989
ESTATE BOTTLED
ALCOHOL 12.5% BY VOLUME

When in 1971 the family of graphic designer Allan Green purchased a 700-acre sheep ranch at an elevation of 1,200 feet on the mountain from which it takes its name, Green immediately knew where his future lay. Anyone who visits the vineyard and winery will know why: after driving for what seems an eternity through the towering redwoods and Douglas firs which cover much of the property, you emerge on the mountain rooftop to be greeted by views of exquisite beauty. The following year Tony Husch planted eight acres of vines on an adjoining property, establishing four acres each of Merlot and Cabernet Sauvignon which he knew would never ripen in the fog-shrouded valley below. The following year (1973) Allan Green persuaded Husch to sell the then-infantile vineyard to him, and in 1976 moved to the property full time, continuing his graphic design business by remote control.

In 1978 and 1979, Allan Green followed the home winemaking path, experimenting with the small amounts of grapes coming from the vineyard which was expanded to 12 acres with the addition of four acres of White Riesling. The first commercial wines were produced in 1980, and in 1985 Green hired his first winemaker, a position filled since 1988 by Van Williamson.

At this elevation fog rarely interrupts the growing season, but it has been a long struggle to persuade the Cabernet Sauvignon and Merlot to throw off leafy/herbal characters. Changes in canopy management have done much to achieve this goal, with wines such as the 1988 Merlot receiving international recognition. Both the Dry and Late Harvest White Riesling are of consistently high quality, as is the Zinfandel (purchased from the Scherrer Vineyard in the Alexander Valley). Indeed, the 1989, 1990 and 1991 Zinfandels were all absolutely delicious, to my mind the best of a portfolio which also includes Anderson Valley Sauvignon Blanc and Pinot Noir, and a Chardonnay from the Anderson and Redwood Valleys.

HANDLEY CELLARS 1982

A: 3151 Highway 128, Philo, CA 95446 **T**: (707) 895 2190 **V**: 11–6 daily **P**: 15,000 **W**: Milla Handley

Milla Handley initially studied art at U.C. Davis, a background which is immediately obvious as you enter the tasting room with its extraordinary array of eastern artifacts. But this great-granddaughter of Henry Weinhard (of brewing fame) found herself increasingly attracted to wine, and completed her degree in fermentation science from U.C. Davis in 1975. Then followed three years as assistant winemaker to Dick Arrowood at St. Jean, followed by three years at Edmeades Winery under Jed Steele.

In 1982 Handley Cellars was bonded in the garage underneath Milla and husband Rex McClelland's home. The first wine she made, a 1982 Chardonnay, was sourced from her parents' 20-acre vineyard in Dry Creek. The wine won a gold medal at the Orange County Fair, and Handley Cellars has not looked back since. The 15,000-case portfolio now comes from the Dry Creek vineyard and from 20 acres of vines surrounding the winery in the Anderson Valley. All except the Dry Creek Chardonnay and Sauvignon Blanc are Anderson Valley-sourced, comprising a second Chardonnay, a Gewurztraminer and two vintage sparkling wines, Brut and Brut Rosé.

Milla Handley has learnt her craft well, but is still striving to improve canopy management in the vineyard and continuing to search for extra dimensions in her wines. The thoroughly French-accented sparkling Brut, the splendidly crisp clean and delicately oaked Sauvignon Blanc, and the opulent apricot/lime botrytised Late Harvest White Riesling show she is equally at home with a very wide range of wine styles.

HUSCH VINEYARDS 1971

A: 4400 Highway 128, Philo, CA 95466 **T**: (707) 895 3216 **V**: 10–6 Summer, 10–5 Winter **P**: 30,000 **W**: Mark Theis

Tony Husch established the first winery in the Anderson Valley after Prohibition when he opened for business in 1971, but in 1979 he sold out to the Oswald family, which has retained the Husch name. The Oswalds had been grape growers for three generations, owning the 110-acre La Ribera Vineyards on the Russian River in the Ukiah Valley. They have also established a 42-acre vineyard across the road from the original Husch planting (21 acres), lifting their Anderson Valley plantings to 63 acres of Pinot Noir, Gewurztraminer and Chardonnay. Cabernet Sauvignon, Sauvignon Blanc, Chenin Blanc and some Chardonnay come from La Ribera, and all of the wines are estate-grown and bottled. This in fact requires the maintenance of two facilities, one at Ukiah (where the white wines are handled), and the other in the Anderson Valley (dedicated to red wines and the smaller amounts of Gewurztraminer and Chenin Blanc which are produced). All of this keeps winemaker Mark Theis fully occupied during vintage, although he can usually count on finishing things at Ukiah before the Anderson Valley vintage gets underway.

The Anderson Valley Pinot Noir shows the rather simple, slightly confectionery cherry/strawberry fruit characters which, for whatever reason, seem to be the hallmark of Anderson Valley Pinot. But while it is the white wines which have won most critical praise, I found the Cabernet Sauvignon (and in particular the North Field Select version) particularly attractive. The latter is an elegant, fresh, fruit-driven wine with discrete oak and nicely balanced tannins. For all that, a Special Reserve Chardonnay, involving a higher component of Anderson Valley material, more malolactic fermentation and more new oak, may well prove to be a star of the future.

ABOVE ~ *Milla Handley, winemaker-owner at Handley Cellars.*

KENDALL-JACKSON VINEYARDS 1988

A: 5500 Highway 128, Philo, CA 95466
T: (707) 263 9333 **V**: By appointment
P: Nil as yet **W**: John Hawley

In September 1988 Kendall-Jackson purchased the Edmeades Vineyard & Winery (the second to be bonded in the Anderson Valley) together with its 11 acres of vineyard. An additional 100 acres of vineyards are to be planted, and a major sparkling wine production facility is planned for the site.

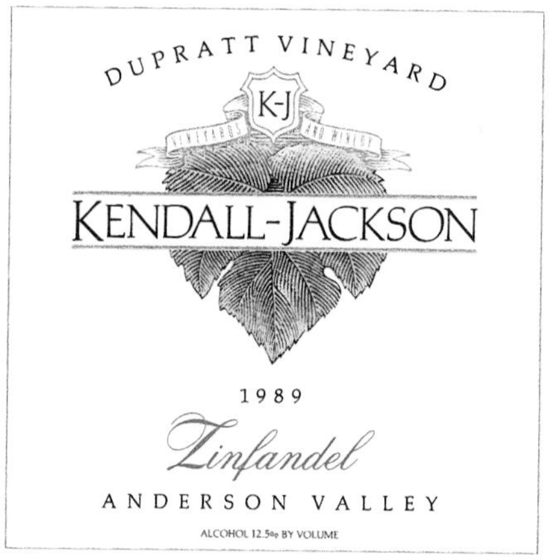
DUPRATT VINEYARD
K-J
KENDALL-JACKSON
1989
Zinfandel
ANDERSON VALLEY

LAZY CREEK VINEYARD 1973

A: 4610 Highway 128, Philo, CA 95466
T: (707) 895 3623 **V**: By appointment
P: 4,000 **W**: Hans Kobler

Lazy Creek does not advertise its presence; only the eagle-eyed will spot the minuscule sign and take the tiny little dirt road across two wooden bridges above tree fern-lined gullies which leads to the small and crowded winery established by former restaurateur Hans Kobler and his wife Theresa. Son Norman Kobler tends the 20 acres of vines, having learnt a great deal about cool climate viticulture while working in Swiss vineyards.

Lazy Creek is justly renowned for its Gewurztraminer, packed with limey/citrussy flavors, and with remarkable textural richness, perhaps deriving in part from the small portion which is barrel fermented. By comparison, the Chardonnay and Pinot Noir are no more than adequate, the latter once again raising the question of why it is not performing better in this region.

NAVARRO VINEYARDS 1975

A: 5601 Highway 128, Philo, CA 95466
T: (707) 895 3686 **V**: 10–6 daily **P**: 20,000
W: Ted Bennett

When Ted Bennett and Deborah Cahn purchased a 900-acre grazing ranch in the Anderson Valley in 1974, it would have been hard not to find a beautiful spot for the winery and sales and tasting area which they planned. However, it did not necessarily have to be adjacent to the highway: as it turns out, the superbly sited and landscaped complex is so situated, which perhaps is a partial explanation for the tremendous success Navarro has had in the direct marketing of its wines. I look at the other reasons on page 208.

The 50 acres of terraced vineyards planted to Gewurztraminer, Chardonnay and Pinot Noir supply part of the production, but many of the, at times, dazzling array of wines on offer carry the Mendocino appellation, attesting to the purchase of additional grapes from throughout Mendocino County, and necessarily from warmer regions. Ted and Deborah selected the site in the first place because they wished to grow and make Gewurztraminer, and this remains the wine on which Navarro's reputation is founded. When, as in 1989, botrytis strikes hard, some spectacular late harvest wines are made — three years' supply, says Ted Bennett somewhat wryly. The 1989 Cluster Select Late Harvest Gewurztraminer was harvested at 39.3° Brix, and has 21% residual sugar. If one accepts the level of volatile acidity (always a component of such wines, and a necessary one at that), this is a truly extraordinary wine.

ROEDERER ESTATE 1982

A: 4501 Highway 128, Philo, CA 95466
T: (510) 652 4900 **V**: 11–4 Mon–Fri
P: 40,000 **W**: Michel Salgues

Roederer has certainly done things in style since Jean-Claude Rouzaud and uncle André Rouzaud selected a 580-acre property in the Anderson Valley after a two-year search throughout California. It was on this piece of land, situated at the northwest end of the valley, that the 48,000 square foot redwood winery, designed and located with extraordinary sensitivity by architect Jacques Ullman, was built. Seventy-seven acres of grapes had already been planted at the time of purchase, and a further 86 acres were planted between 1985 and 1987, bringing the total on this ranch to 125 acres.

Long before the first wines were made, the Roederer team had recognized the temperature gradation within the Anderson Valley, acquiring 274 acres in the Philo district, and establishing 160 acres of vines, principally between 1983 and 1984. Finally, 181 acres were purchased in the Boonville district, 80 acres having been established at the time of acquisition, and a further 37 acres being planted in 1985 and 1986. This impressive array of vineyards signifies three things: firstly, that Roederer Estate is the only French-based California sparkling wine producer to grow all of its own grapes; secondly, that through the diversity of *terroir* and climate it can achieve the blending complexities so essential to great sparkling wine; and thirdly, it has the ultimate luxury of producing 140% of its annual requirements.

For as sales have increased, so has production, rising from 180 tons in 1985 to 1,450 tons in 1990. It is also a quite remarkable

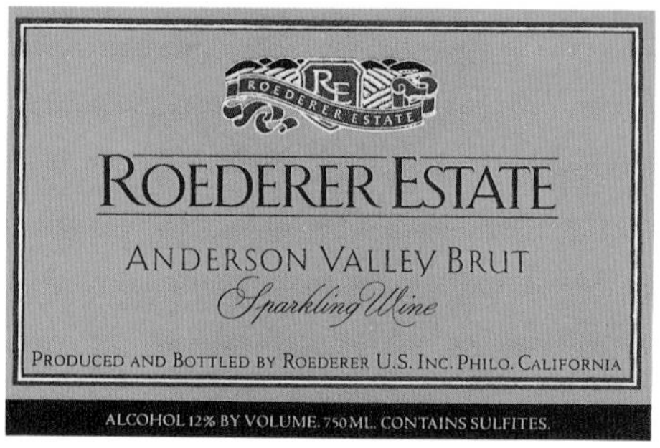
ROEDERER ESTATE
ROEDERER ESTATE
ANDERSON VALLEY BRUT
Sparkling Wine
PRODUCED AND BOTTLED BY ROEDERER U.S. INC. PHILO, CALIFORNIA
ALCOHOL 12% BY VOLUME. 750ML. CONTAINS SULFITES.

ABOVE ~ *This superb home is situated next door to Roederer Estate.*

fact that Roederer Estate has the largest plantings of the Carbonneau open-lyre system in the world, with 175 acres utilizing this system. The open lyre, incidentally, consists of two posts driven diagonally into the ground, effectively creating two canopies from a single vine, producing higher than normal yields of grapes of higher than normal quality (within any given situation), but extremely expensive to maintain.

There are other trellising systems in use (notably the thin-wall vertical) and, as one might expect, there are on-going trials with new clones of Chardonnay and Pinot Noir. But when you ask Michel Salgues which clone, which trellis system, and above all else, which of the three vineyard areas are the most promising, he will simply shrug his shoulders and smile, saying, "I will tell you the answer to that if you come back in ten years' time."

Salgues, with a PhD in enology from the University of Montpellier and a professorship at the Institut de la Recherche Agronomique (INRA), has guided Roederer through its establishment years. He is totally familiar with the Roederer sparkling wine operation in Tasmania, Australia, and is very much a citizen of the wine world. He says, "I go every year to France to participate in the blending there to refresh my palate. It is all too easy to be influenced by local tastes, and to lose one's perspective."

The initial release of Roederer (a non-vintage wine) caused a fair degree of discussion, chiefly because of the evident oak influence in the wine. The second non-vintage release was absolutely exemplary, an exceedingly complex and stylish wine, with great structure, character and length — in every way, a complete sparkling wine. Interestingly, it is 75% Chardonnay and 25% Pinot Noir, the reverse of the usual Californian pattern. In 1992 a Tete de Cuvee 1989 vintage wine was in the course of preparation, due to be released in a special bottle. Amounting to a mere 3% of the total production, it has my tongue hanging out.

SCHARFFENBERGER CELLARS 1981

A: 8501 Highway 128, Philo, CA 95466
T: (707) 895 2065 **V**: 11–5 daily **P**: 25,000
W: Tex Sawyer and John Scharffenberger

John Scharffenberger followed a circuitous and lengthy path to the Anderson Valley, acquiring his taste for things agricultural as a ten year old arriving at one of the last large undeveloped ranches in the Los Angeles basin. His tertiary training came through a dual major in biogeography and land use management at the University of California at Berkeley, augmented by studies in biodynamic farming under horticultural visionary Allan Chadwick at Santa Cruz. From there he progressed to Stony Hill Vineyards in the Napa Valley, and also worked under Bill Bonetti for a time. In 1973 he purchased 2,000 acres of grazing land near

BLANC DE BLANCS
1988
Scharffenberger
ALCOHOL 12% BY VOLUME
MENDOCINO COUNTY SPARKLING WINE

Ukiah for his father, planting 70 acres of terraced Zinfandel and Petite Sirah, and installed what is said to be the first large-scale drip irrigation system in California.

From there he moved to his own 50-acre farm in nearby Talmage, growing grapes, strawberries and lawn turf. In 1981 (encouraged, he says, by his bank) he sold out at a handsome profit, giving him the capital to establish Scharffenberger Cellars in the Anderson Valley. Quite how he was able to release the first Scharffenberger sparkling wine in the same year I do not know, but he did so. Slowly but steadily, both output and reputation increased, rising to 25,000 cases by 1985, and by 1989 enticing Pommery, the French Champagne house, to make an offer which he was unable to refuse (although he remains a minority partner and president of the American corporation).

The dramatic infusion of capital by Pommery resulted in the building of a state-of-the-art winery (designed by Jacques Ullman, albeit in radically different but equally great taste from that of Roederer), and the acquisition of a 680-acre site upon which an additional 180 acres of vines are being developed, while preserving a 1,000-year-old redwood grove. The new winery was completed just in time for the 1991 vintage, but has been designed on a modular basis so that at some far distant point in the future, production could in fact reach 200,000 cases, although 50,000 cases are the projected maximum for the end of this decade.

Four wines are produced: a vintage Blanc de Blancs, a non-vintage Brut, a non-vintage Brut Rosé, and a non-vintage Cremant. The Brut and the Cremant are blended from 70% Pinot Noir and 30% Chardonnay, the Blanc de Blancs from 100% Chardonnay, and the Rosé from 100% Pinot Noir. The wines have great character and individuality; some show a certain degree of no doubt deliberately induced and controlled aldehydes, others are crisp, clean, direct and totally commercial. Curiously, with the exception of the Cremant, I liked them all; never a fan of Rosé, and least of all sparkling wines made entirely from Pinot Noir, I cannot help but like the punch and vivacity of the Rosé, while I have always been an easy touch when it comes to a well made Blanc de Blancs (even if it does have a touch of aldehyde).

OTHER WINERIES

OBESTER 1977
A: 9200 Highway 128, Philo, CA 94566
T: (707) 895 3814 **W**: Bruce Regalia

PEPPERWOOD SPRINGS 1981
A: 1200 Holmes Ranch Road, Philo, CA 95466
T: (707) 895 2920 **W**: Gary and Phyllis Kaliher

CHRISTINE WOODS 1982
A: 3155 Highway 128, Philo, CA 95466
T: (707) 895 2115 **W**: Vernon J. Rose

ABOVE ~ *The town of Mendocino is on the coast, and is some distance away from the vineyards bearing its name.*

EAST MENDOCINO, CLEAR LAKE & GUENOC

EAST MENDOCINO

The Potter Valley AVA is the northernmost extension of the eastern fork of Mendocino. It is an entirely enclosed valley of substantial size, and differs from the rest of Mendocino in that its climate is seldom influenced by maritime intrusions. Once a major producer of hops and prunes, it is now given over to pears and grapes but, not having a winery of its own, suffers from a lack of identity. One of the important growers in the region is Skip Lovin of B.J.L. Vineyards, who makes a strong claim (repeated by many in other districts) that the Potter Valley produces the best Sauvignon Blanc in California.

Certainly Sauvignon Blanc, Semillon and Riesling do well here, the latter producing high quality botrytised grapes for a largely uninterested market. Chardonnay and Pinot Noir are also grown, and all well enough, but are of less distinction. Spring frosts and phylloxera are the major hazards: most of the vineyards were established on their own roots, and the "normal" (not Biotype B) phylloxera is hard at work.

The Redwood Valley is a geographically distinct area running north from Lake Mendocino. Its major claim to fame is being home to the original Fetzer Winery, situated in an idyllic arm of the valley under the lee of Black Hill, replete with the redwoods which give the area its name. This was also the site of the first Fetzer estate vineyards, and remained the administrative headquarters up to 1992.

As you travel south out of the Redwood Valley, the hills close in as you pass through Calpella, opening up again opposite the southern end of Lake Mendocino at the approach to Ukiah, and extending all the way south to Hopland (where the massive new winery facilities and hospitality center of Fetzer are located). To the west of Ukiah, nestling in the foothills of the extreme northern end of the Mayacamas Mountains, is Talmage, which gives its name to the northern end of what is a more or less continuous grape growing area south to Hopland.

ABOVE ~ *The driver's view as he reverses his truck to position the grape bins, ready for the crusher.*

OPPOSITE ~ *Mount Konocti towers above Clear Lake, giving its name to one of the wineries of the region.*

Cole Ranch AVA is in the eastern foothills (on Highway 253) situated in a tiny 150-acre, elevated valley (1,400 feet) with 61 acres of Cabernet Sauvignon, Riesling and Chardonnay, most of which are sold to Fetzer. McDowell Valley AVA is on the opposite side and further south, situated on Highway 175 before it begins to ascend the Mayacamas Range (on its way across to Clear Lake).

Clear Lake

The drive across the Mayacamas Mountains from Hopland to Lakeport affords vistas as spectacular as those of the Santa Cruz Mountains. So swift is the ascent (and the descent) it is easy to lose sight of the fact that Ukiah is at an elevation of 600 feet, and Clear Lake at 1,350 feet.

As with the Potter Valley, Clear Lake differs from Mendocino in that its climate is in barely affected by maritime influences — unless one takes into account the considerable cooling effect of Clear Lake itself, which is the largest body of fresh water found entirely in the state of California (Lake Tahoe is partially in Nevada).

While there are some similarities in the growing conditions (and the consequent wine styles) of Clear Lake and East Mendocino, there are also critical differences and factors peculiar to Clear Lake. Thus it was that the original recommendations from U.C. Davis were that the red varieties should be planted on the lower plains around the lake, and to the south (in Region III summations), and the white varieties on the cooler (Region II) hillsides. Experience has shown those recommendations to be entirely wrong, largely because of soil conditions but also because of inadequacies in the heat summation method. The silver lining of the phylloxera invasion is that the growers are being given the opportunity to rectify matters, and to plant the Rhone and Italian varieties to which the hillsides are (arguably) best suited.

Guenoc Valley and Benmore Valley

Little need be said of the Benmore Valley AVA, except to note that, at an elevation of 2,400 feet, it has a low Region I summation of less than 2,000 degree days and is presently devoted exclusively to the growing of 125 acres of Chardonnay.

It is in stark contrast to the Guenoc Valley AVA, the latter being in the far south of the county and climatically having more in common with the Chiles and Pope Valleys of Napa County. Indeed, Guenoc Estate (the only winery in the AVA) extends from the Guenoc Valley into Napa County.

East Mendocino, Clear Lake & Guenoc
VINTAGE CHART
1981–91

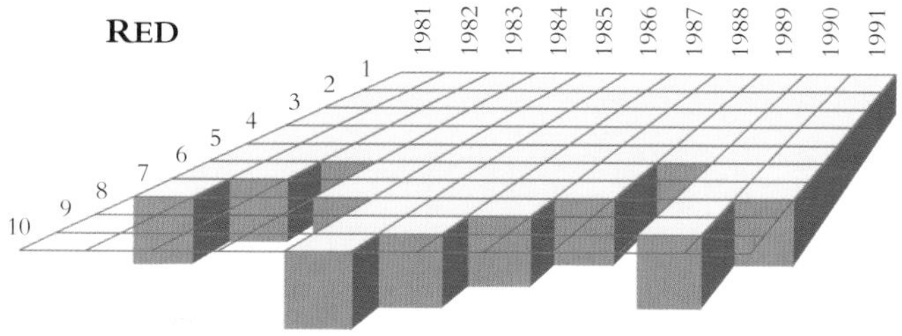
RED
1981
1982
1983
1984
1985
1986
1987
1988
1989
1990
1991
1
2
3
4
5
6
7
8
9
10

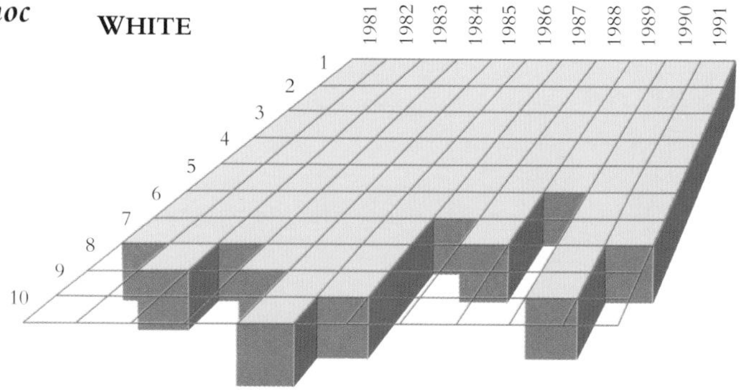
WHITE
1981
1982
1983
1984
1985
1986
1987
1988
1989
1990
1991
1
2
3
4
5
6
7
8
9
10

ABOVE ~ *The house built by Lillie Langtry is now part of the impressive Guenoc Winery enterprise of Orville T. Magoon.*

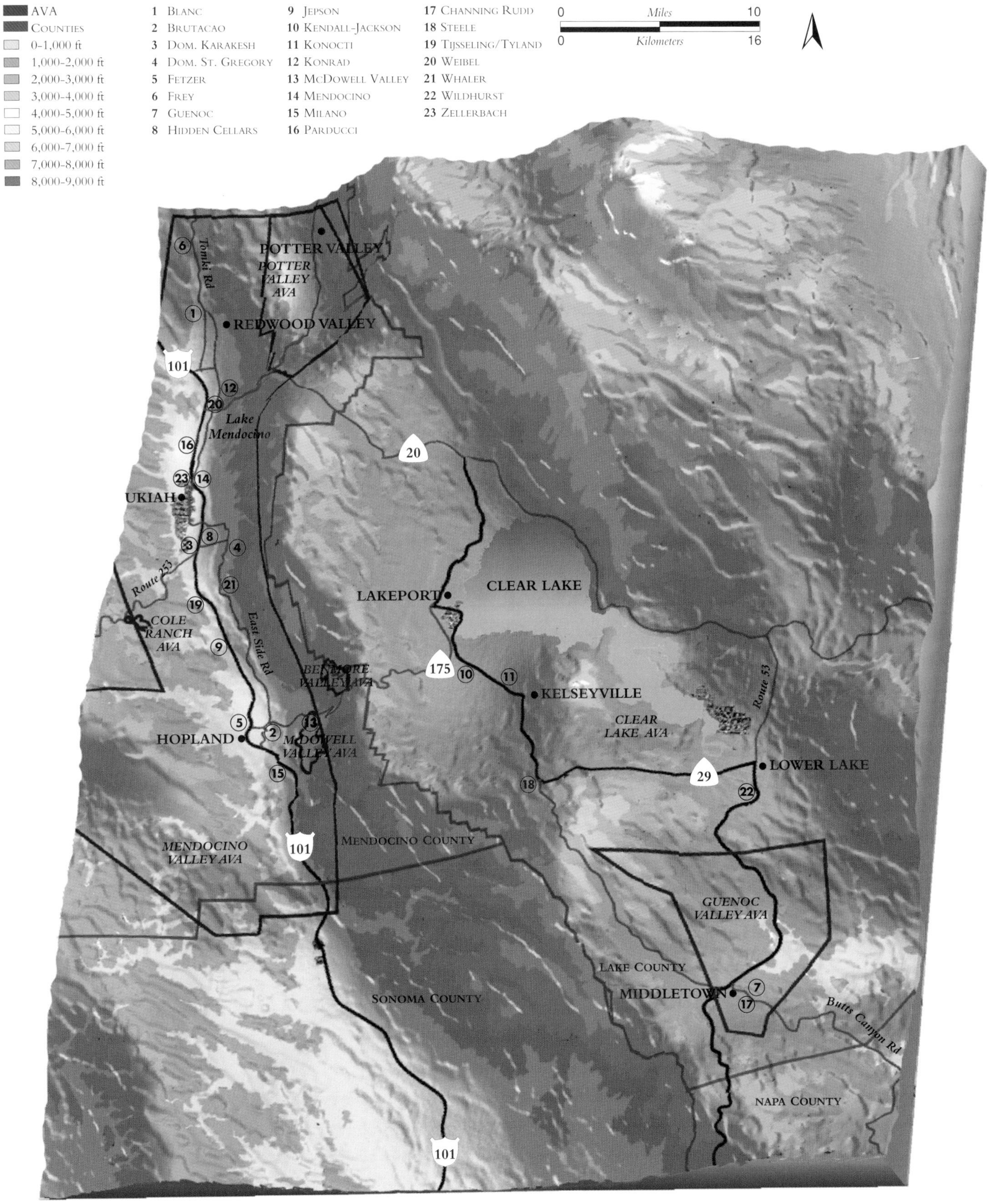
AVA
Counties
0–1,000 ft
1,000–2,000 ft
2,000–3,000 ft
3,000–4,000 ft
4,000–5,000 ft
5,000–6,000 ft
6,000–7,000 ft
7,000–8,000 ft
8,000–9,000 ft
1 Blanc
2 Brutacao
3 Dom. Karakesh
4 Dom. St. Gregory
5 Fetzer
6 Frey
7 Guenoc
8 Hidden Cellars
9 Jepson
10 Kendall-Jackson
11 Konocti
12 Konrad
13 McDowell Valley
14 Mendocino
15 Milano
16 Parducci
17 Channing Rudd
18 Steele
19 Tijsseling/Tyland
20 Weibel
21 Whaler
22 Wildhurst
23 Zellerbach
0 Miles 10
0 Kilometers 16
POTTER VALLEY
POTTER VALLEY AVA
Tomki Rd
REDWOOD VALLEY
101
Lake Mendocino
20
UKIAH
Route 253
COLE RANCH AVA
East Side Rd
BENMORE VALLEY AVA
175
LAKEPORT
CLEAR LAKE
KELSEYVILLE
CLEAR LAKE AVA
Route 53
LOWER LAKE
29
HOPLAND
McDOWELL VALLEY AVA
MENDOCINO COUNTY
MENDOCINO VALLEY AVA
GUENOC VALLEY AVA
LAKE COUNTY
MIDDLETOWN
Butts Canyon Rd
SONOMA COUNTY
NAPA COUNTY

ABOVE ~ *Mendocino and Lake County map.*

ORGANIC WINEMAKING

"O what a tangled web we weave,/When first we practice to deceive," and never more so than with organic winemaking. Only in California has there been any attempt to define what is and is not permitted in organic wine, and then only as recently as 1990. Elsewhere in the world, and before that time in California, chaos and uncertainty reign supreme.

This situation is in curious contrast to organic grape growing, which — as I have explained on pages 202–3 — has been legislatively defined in France since 1981, legislation since adopted by the EC.

So an initial distinction must be drawn between wine made from organically grown grapes, and organically made wine (which in a real world will certainly be made from organically grown grapes, but I fancy as a matter of strict logic does not have to be so made).

ABOVE ~ *Petite Sirah, correctly named Durif, makes massive red wines, and is a variety well suited to organic winemaking.*

While there are commonly agreed international standards for organic growing, there is a substantial difference (in legislative terms) between certified organic grapes, and organically grown grapes. The latter will have been produced by a grower who espouses all of the principles and practices of the certified organic grower, but for any number of reasons has not submitted himself or herself to the official inspection procedures, to the period of "transition," and to the absolute obligation to refrain from using synthetic chemicals in the vineyard.

The first stirrings in California came in the early 1980s in legislation which focused on food products (which, as in much of the Western world, include wine), but largely neglected processing. This was left to be regulated by standards known as GMPs, or "good manufacturing processes."

In this period, there were two camps. On the one hand stood OGWA, the Organic Grapes into Wine Alliance, with French-born Veronique Raskin as its secretary. OGWA recommended the use of California-certified organically grown grapes, but tolerated organically grown but uncertified grapes. No problems there, although some of the recommended practices for handling grapes might be thought to have precious little to do with anything.

When it came to winemaking, and to the key issue of the use of sulfur dioxide, OGWA decreed, "SO_2 levels in California Organic Wines shall be no more than 100 parts per million total and 30 parts per million free SO_2 at the time the wine is released."

This is a watered down version of the stance of one of the two opposing camps in France, which has proposed sulfur dioxide limits ranging between 110 parts per million and 320 parts per million (the latter for sweet white wines). On the other side of the fence, the French DGCCRF (the Department for the Repression of Frauds, which enforces appellation laws) has proposed that sulfur dioxide may not be used in the making of organic wine.

Back in California, this was in fact the stance adopted by the overwhelming majority of makers who claimed to be making organic wine — including Frey, Coturri, Organic Wine Works and Orleans Hill. In 1990 their stand was enshrined in the Organic Food Act passed by the legislature in that year, the key provision of which was that it outlawed the addition of sulfur dioxide.

The obvious questions are, firstly, what is the function of sulfur dioxide, and secondly, what is its effect on those who drink wine containing it? Its function is a dual one: it is a bactericide, and it is a preservative (or anti-oxidant). All wines contain bacteria unless they have been pasteurized or sterile filtered at bottling. These bacteria can adversely affect the taste of the wine, but — unlike those bacteria in other foodstuffs, such as salmonella — are not toxic to humans.

The low pH of wine (normally less than 4, compared to neutral pH of 7, with the scale being a logarithmic one), and its alcoholic strength combine to prevent the development of pathogens which can be detrimental to your health. So the bacterial action is, if you like, cosmetic: perhaps one of the better known consequences of inadequate protection can be the development of brettanomyces (although it by no means automatically follows) that gives a distinctive gamey taste to the wine, which at high levels is generally regarded as very unpleasant. Scrupulously clean winery practices and appropriate temperature control can eliminate or reduce bacterial action to an acceptable level; so from this aspect sulfur dioxide cannot be said to be essential.

The preservative role is more critical, particularly so for white wines. The problem here is oxidation, both before and after bottling. Oxidized wines lose their fruit aroma and flavor, becoming dull and bitter — and ultimately undrinkable. Red wine is less prone to oxidation because of the anthocyanins and tannins it contains, both of which are natural preservatives.

A wine which has become oxidized before it is bottled is called aldehydic: once recognized, the combination of bitterness and loss of fruit flavor is not forgotten. Every winemaker knows that even a small amount of sulfur dioxide will magically remove what is a thoroughly obnoxious character.

Oxidation after bottling is a more insidious process: a wine bottled with aldehydes will retain them, but purely bottle-developed oxidation is a more subtle process. What it can do is make a two-year-old white wine appear 20 years old, and a two-year-old red wine appear ten years old — and as if it had been stored in hot conditions in the meantime.

The second question relates to the health implications of sulfur dioxide. I assiduously read all of the international papers and reports on this type of question (those written in English) and I have never seen it suggested that sulfur dioxide in wine has caused the death of any allergic person. However, the World Health Organization has calculated that the safe daily intake of sulfur dioxide is 0.35 milligrams per kilogram of bodyweight. This means that a 154-pound person can safely drink three-quarters of a bottle of wine a day provided it contains no more than 50 parts per million of sulfur dioxide.

Whether or not that intake is exceeded, the fact is some consumers suffer a reaction to wine or food which contains sulfur dioxide. In hyper-sensitive people, the reaction may be extreme, but they will inevitably be under strict medical supervision. For the majority of those affected, the reaction may be no more than a hangover, and may well be caused by histamines or even simply the alcohol. But whether real or imagined, their response to preservative-free food and wine is quite different.

For such people, and for those with extreme environmental convictions, organically made wine is the answer, whatever its deficiencies in taste may be. For the intelligent winemaker, the challenge is to reduce levels of sulfur dioxide across the board, and routinely to produce wines with as little as 10 parts per million free and 15 parts per million total sulfur. Typical levels have already come down by more than half compared with those of 20 years ago, and better wines are the result.

But unless there is a major technological breakthrough, sulfur dioxide-free wines will remain a specialty product aimed at a niche market. And by way of a parting remark, some sulfur dioxide is naturally formed by the yeasts during fermentation, so strictly speaking one should differentiate between "contains sulfur dioxide" and "contains added sulfur dioxide."

ABOVE ~ *The youngest generation of the Frey family, happily eating organically-grown apples.*

WINERIES *of* MENDOCINO

BRUTACAO CELLARS 1986

A: 2,300 Highway 175, Hopland, CA 95449
T: (707) 744 1320 **V**: By appointment
P: 2,000 **W**: Nancy Walker

When long-term local grape grower Leonard Brutacao decided to branch into winemaking, he took all of the right decisions. He erected a totally functional gray Butler shed, purchased the press second-hand from Mondavi, the bottling machine second-hand from Ridge, and the corker from somewhere else. And rather than try to make the wine himself, he spent the money he had saved on the winery and equipment on hiring Nancy Walker, a trained and experienced winemaker. The venture will grow as time goes by; for the time being, only part of the available grape production is vinified. Whether Nancy Walker will be able to fashion a good Chardonnay from this area remains to be seen; initial efforts were unconvincing, although showing remarkably little development after three years in bottle. On the other side of the fence, the Cabernet Sauvignon and Merlot are exotically, indeed excessively ripe, suggesting that — if picked a little earlier — some striking wines could be made. A Semillon-Sauvignon Blanc blend is on the boards and, given the overall performance of the district, should do well.

DOMAINE ST. GREGORY 1988

A: 4921 Eastside Road, Ukiah, CA 95482
T: (707) 463 1532 **V**: By appointment
P: 2,000 **W**: Greg Graziano

Domaine St. Gregory produces an eclectic range of wines, drawing upon the full gamut of climatic regions within Mendocino. Monte Volpe Moscato de Mendocino (in fact a second label) is made in the traditional Italian fashion in honor of winemaker/owner Greg Graziano's grandfather, Vincenzo Graziano. Bottled with a slight effervescence, and with a touch of residual sugar, this Knights Valley-grown wine has extremely attractive citric fruit flavors which neatly balance that touch of acidity. Cold fermentation for three weeks at 45°F has been used to full effect. Next on the roster is a Mendocino Pinot Noir, one-third coming from the Dennison Vineyard in the Anderson Valley, and two-thirds from the Mid-Mountain Vineyard in the Potter Valley. Here again, classic Pinot Noir methods (one-third whole bunches in open fermenters with punchdown) are used and a very useful Pinot Noir is the result, in which the cool, stemmy characters of the Anderson Valley fruit cut back the ripe flavors of the Potter Valley component.

FETZER VINEYARDS 1968

A: 13500 F. Highway 101, Hopland, CA 95449 **T**: (707) 744 1737 **V**: 8:30–5 daily
P: 200,000 **W**: Paul Dolan

One can only assume that Brown Forman, owners of Fetzer since 1992, see virtually unlimited growth opportunities for brands such as Fetzer's Sundial Chardonnay, and the Bel Arbors range including White Zinfandel and Merlot. With appropriate management, there is no reason why Brown Forman's hopes should not be realized. Those with a knowledge of history, and imbued with a little cynicism, will sound a cautionary note. The track record of the distillers and breweries around the world which have invested in the wine industry has been less than impressive, not infrequently ending in abject defeat.

This, however, is not the place for a homily to the Brown Forman management. The fact is that Fetzer has built an absolutely first-class portfolio of brands, and has achieved that which Gallo still seeks: recognition for the quality of its top end wines. The Reserve Chardonnay and Reserve Cabernet Sauvignon, selling for over $20 a bottle in 1992, are worth every cent, and are handsomely backed up by the premium priced Barrel Select range at around $12. In terms of volume, these wines are not so significant, but in terms of image they are.

It will be fascinating to see what happens to Fetzer over the next decade. Will history repeat itself or will it be rewritten?

FREY VINEYARDS 1980

A: 14000 Tomki Road, Redwood Valley, CA 95470 **T**: (707) 485 5177 **V**: By appointment
P: 15,000 **W**: Jonathon Frey

The extensive Frey family, headed by former Mendocino physician Dr. Paul Frey, wandered into grape growing and ultimately organic winemaking without any burning ambition or missionary zeal. The property was purchased in 1961, and it was not until 1965 that the need for a tax shelter led to the establishment of vineyards, and to the casual advice from a friend that "perhaps you should try this new-fangled Cabernet Sauvignon." The stimulus which led to the move to certified organic farming came from eldest son Jonathon, who learnt his organic winemaking from the famous British organic horticulturist Allan Chadwick in Santa Cruz. Having taken this step, it was inevitable that when the children decided to venture into winemaking in 1980, the winery should produce

wine using strict organic methods — and in particular no sulfur. The winery has been aptly described as a scene from *Deliverance;* it was built out of second-hand wood salvaged from the old Gareth Winery in Ukiah, while the winemaking equipment is similarly salvaged, patched together and improvised — the one exception being the conventional Howard press. Eight of the Frey children are now involved in the business, which has grown steadily in response to the ever-increasing interest in organic wines. But Jonathon Frey is far from the burning zealot one might expect. He receives thousands of calls a year from interested people, many of whom end up buying the Frey wines, but he says matter of factly, "Is it in their head or in their body? I don't know."

The wines are marketed in a variety of ways: by mail order from the winery, through health food shops and through conventional distribution methods. As Jonathan Frey himself is quick to acknowledge, he has been much more successful with the red wines than the white wines. To be frank, one would need to be wholly committed through health reasons or philosophical conviction to organic wines to wish to drink the whites. The reds are in a different category, as robust and rustic as one would expect, but having undoubted character. Zinfandel, Syrah, Petite Sirah and Cabernet Sauvignon are the pick of the extensive range on offer, with Petite Sirah capable of showing superb, voluptuous fruit, and massive extract.

ABOVE ~ *Jonathon Frey, with help from son Tommy, assessing the flavor of his Cabernet Sauvignon.*

HIDDEN CELLARS 1981

A: 1500 Ruddick-Cunningham Road, Ukiah, CA 95482 **T**: (707) 462 0301
V: 10–4 weekdays **P**: 15,000
W: Dennis Patton

Dennis Patton started Hidden Cellars on a shoestring in 1981 in an obscure East Canyon location. In 1983 he acquired a partner and the financial ability to construct the present substantial but functional winery; in time-honored tradition, the winery was built while the 1983 vintage was in full swing. Since that time Hidden Cellars has in fact carried on two very successful businesses: its own production, now around 15,000 cases, and far larger custom crush work, amounting to 40,000 cases in 1991.

Highly articulate and intelligent, Dennis Patton shares with Jed Steele (several of whose clients use the custom crush facilities) a love of Mendocino and Lake County grapes. Not surprisingly, the grapes most favored by Patton are Semillon and Sauvignon Blanc, blended together to produce a Meritage wine styled Alchemy, which is priced at the top end of the Hidden Cellars range and which invariably sells out prior to the next release. Other winery specialties are a Botrytis Riesling sourced from the Potter Valley, with strong lime fruit; a Late Harvest Semillon called Chanson d'Or, replete with intense mandarin and cumquat botrytis aromas and flavors; and — best of all — Pacini Vineyard Zinfandel, made from 50- to 80-year-old vines grown on benchland in the southeast corner of the Ukiah Valley. As one would expect, this is a wine with cherry fruit and tannins in abundance, made for cellaring.

JEPSON VINEYARDS 1986

A: 10400 S. Highway 101, Ukiah, CA 95482
T: (707) 468 8936 **V**: 10–5 daily **P**: 18,000
W: Kurt Lorenzi

The former William Baccala Estate was purchased by banker Robert Jepson in 1986; he acquired a modern and functional winery with a capacity of 30,000 cases, 110 acres of vineyard, and an Alembic still. That still, coupled with ten acres of estate Colombard, produces between 500 and 1,000 of one of California's best brandies. While production levels are necessarily modest, this gives Jepson an identity and presence in the marketplace which it might otherwise not have.

The winery mainstays are Chardonnay (both standard and Estate Reserve), Sauvignon Blanc and a Blanc de Blanc Methode Champenoise made entirely from Chardonnay, which is partially barrel fermented. Winemaker Kurt Lorenzi graduated from the Meridian/Estrella River finishing school, and spent several years on the Central Coast as a viticultural consultant. He sees Sauvignon Blanc as better suited to the climate than Chardonnay, a judgment which others would share. The Chardonnay is made in a down-played style, lean and is (for want of a better expression) Chablis-like. The Sauvignon Blanc is similarly quiet, a wine which no doubt is commercially acceptable, but does not set the pulse racing.

MCDOWELL VALLEY VINEYARDS 1978

A: 3811 Highway 175, Hopland, CA 95449
T: (707) 744 1053 **V**: 10–5 daily (Hopland tasting room) **P**: 115,000
W: John Buechsenstein

Replete with its own AVA (granted in 1982), McDowell Valley Vineyards is a very substantial operation. Owned by the Keehn family and William Crawford, it draws upon 375 acres of estate vineyards (supplemented by some outside grape purchases). When the Keehns purchased the first ranch in 1970, included in the plantings were 36 acres of what was then thought to be old Petite Sirah, but which was subsequently identified as true Syrah. The majority of the pre-existing vines were, however, of less exalted varieties, and progressive land acquisitions, replanting and new vineyard planting have resulted in the present 375 acres of vineyards equally split between white and red varieties, with Chardonnay and Cabernet Sauvignon initially taking center stage both in the vineyard and in the winery.

While these two wines remain very important commercial lines for McDowell Valley Vineyards, increasing emphasis has been placed on the Rhone varietals. The initial 36

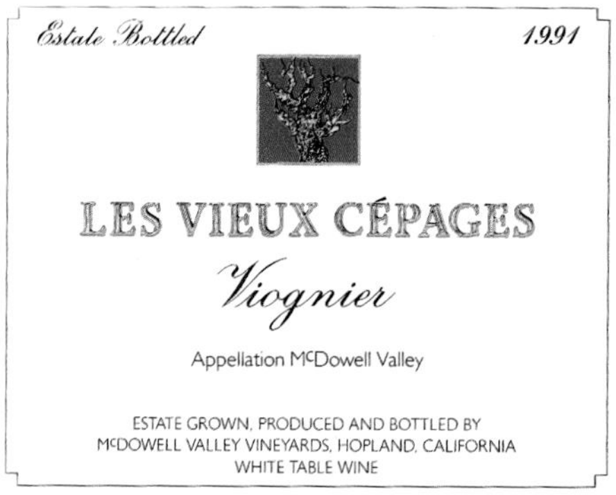
Estate Bottled
1991
LES VIEUX CÉPAGES
Viognier
Appellation McDowell Valley
ESTATE GROWN, PRODUCED AND BOTTLED BY
McDOWELL VALLEY VINEYARDS, HOPLAND, CALIFORNIA
WHITE TABLE WINE

acres of old Syrah (identified in 1981) has been joined by a further 30 acres of newer plantings, together with 19 acres of Zinfandel, 17 acres of Petite Sirah, 14 acres of Grenache, 11 acres of Mourvedre, 5 acres of Cinsault, and 5.3 precious acres of Viognier. It was these varieties which led to the 1989 introduction of the Les Vieux Cepages range of Syrah, Viognier and Grenache Reserve. While in current production terms only the Syrah is significant (there was a mere 250 cases of the 1991 Viognier), one is tempted to say that for both the McDowell Valley Vineyards and Mendocino as a whole the varieties may point the way for the future.

The Viognier is of particular interest, with exotic fruit pastille, peach and passionfruit flavors; the Grenache (of an earlier vintage) was hailed by Robert Parker as one of the three great Rosés of the world, which may be a bit extreme, but which is nonetheless a clean, well made wine with some style; while the Syrah has been described with marvelous economy and precision as "jammeaty" by winemaker John

ABOVE ~ *Old Cabernet Sauvignon vines near Ukiah in East Mendocino cohabit with a saw mill.*

Buechsenstein. Buechsenstein sees these gamey/jammy/minty characters as very much a part of the varietal character, and it certainly produces a wine which is very distinctive. For the sake of completeness, the Sauvignon Blanc and Cabernet Sauvignon are competently made wines with direct fruit flavors, although somewhat lacking in concentration.

Finally, a word on the winery. It is not, as some would have it, solar powered: however, solar power is integrated into the system, and does provide the copious quantities of hot water used in any winery. More importantly, it is a model of efficiency and practicality, and in John Buechsenstein has a highly perceptive and intelligent winemaker.

PARDUCCI WINE CELLARS 1932

A: 501 Parducci Road, Ukiah, CA 95482
T: (707) 462 3828 **V**: 10–5 daily **P**: 400,000
W: Tom Monostori

From 1932 until 1973 Parducci was the only winery of any consequence in Mendocino County. In that year ownership passed to a teachers' retirement fund investment vehicle, but the Parducci family remains visibly in control of operations. It started as a typical Italian-owned bulk wine producer of traditional Italian-accented grape varieties; as the wave of new varietals came on the scene, it progressively adapted itself to the production of those varieties, but eschewing the use of any new oak, and concentrating on providing low-priced wines. As the market became more sophisticated and demanded more, the old redwood tanks were partially replaced by new oak barrels; then in 1987 an entirely new fermentation cellar was constructed, equipped with two 50-ton Bucher presses (the Rolls Royce of presses) and a vast array of stainless steel, temperature controlled fermentation tanks.

With a capacity of 750,000 gallons, the cellar represented a major investment by the owners, as well as an emphatic statement in the belief of the Parducci brand, which had stayed stationary (in terms of sales) while neighbor Fetzer had grown from less than 100,000 cases to over 2 million cases.

The grapes come in part from the 375 acres of estate vineyards, but are also purchased from Ukiah, Talmage, Lake County and (to a minor degree) Anderson Valley growers. Winemaker Tom Monostori has a simple rule in vintage: the day starts at 7 A.M., and finishes when the last grapes are crushed or pressed (as the case may be). Specifically, he does not believe in two shifts, simply because this results in split responsibility. He and John Parducci are also firm believers in the importance of post-fermentation blending, not surprising given the diversity of fruit sources at their disposal.

The wines, headed by Cellarmaster Chardonnay, Sauvignon Blanc, Cabernet Sauvignon, Cabernet Merlot, Petite Sirah, Zinfandel and Merlot (there is in fact a vast range of Parducci wines) are sound, well-constructed wines, made without any particular artifice, but none the worse for that.

WEIBEL VINEYARDS 1939

A: 7051 N. State Street, Redwood Valley, CA 95470 **T**: (707) 485 0321 **V**: 10–5 daily (also at 1250 Stanford Avenue, Mission San Jose, CA 94539 10–5 daily) **P**: 900,000
W: Richard T. Casquerio

Rudolph Weibel arrived from Switzerland in 1936 to start a new life; after a brief foray in northwest Oregon, he moved to San Francisco with his son Fred and quickly built up a prosperous business. By 1945 he was able to purchase the then abandoned but historic Leland Stanford Winery at Warm Springs, near San Jose, reviving the vineyards and setting a course which was to make Weibel one of the largest family-owned wineries in California. From that day to this, much of the production has been of wines for other vintners — using that term in the classic sense. In other words, providing other brand or own-brand labels, with an amazing portfolio of between four and five hundred different labels (for others) at any one time. In turn, the business concentrated on sparkling wines (produced by the Charmat process) and established the only complete Solera system still existing in California for sherry. As urban pressures grew, and as the market changed and became more sophisticated, the family started looking for alternative vineyard sources, and purchased land in Mendocino's Redwood Valley in the early 1960s. It is here that the varietal table wines (now accounting for more than 50% of total production) are made, drawing upon 1,100 acres of estate vineyards.

The Mendocino venture flourished, driven by roaring sales of the white varietal Green Hungarian, made with 2.5 to 3% residual sugar. Inevitably, with the passage of time, Green Hungarian has ceased to be a major weapon in the Weibel armoury, although sales still amount to a healthy 45,000 cases. To keep pace with changing market demands, there has been much replanting of the Mendocino vineyards over the last 15 years, with the white grape varieties being planted on alluvial river soils, and red grapes on the upper benchlands.

The wines are direct, simple and unpretentious, appropriately priced and skillfully distributed and marketed.

WHALER VINEYARD 1981

A: 2600 Eastside Road, Ukiah, CA 95482
T: (707) 462 6355 **V**: By appointment
P: 1,000 **W**: Ann Nyborg (Consultant Jed Steele)

Russ and Ann Nyborg had a 24-acre Zinfandel vineyard planted in 1972, providing Russ Nyborg with a challenge during his spells ashore from his occupation as a San Francisco Bay sea captain and pilot. That career was also the inspiration for the name, and for the strikingly designed label, featuring an old wooden whaling boat.

For a while the Nyborgs made a White Zinfandel, but these days concentrate on a single red version, and (with Jed Steele's help) are doing so with considerable success, even if they are content to sell most of the grapes from the vineyard. The Zinfandel is intensely fragrant, with wonderfully sweet dark cherry fruit, pleasantly supporting tannins and a very long, lingering finish. It is packed with flavor, without being jammy, and is one of those Zinfandels which can be cellared, however attractive it is in its youth.

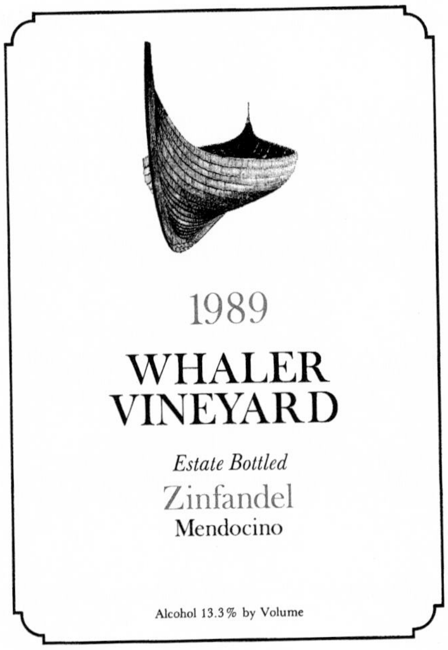
1989
WHALER VINEYARD
Estate Bottled
Zinfandel
Mendocino
Alcohol 13.3% by Volume

OTHER WINERIES

BLANC VINEYARDS
A: 10200 West Road, Redwood Valley, CA 95470 **T**: (707) 485 7352 **W**: Robert Blanc

DOMAINE KARAKESH
A: 4001 Spring Mountain Road, St. Helena, CA 94574 **T**: (707) 963 9327
W: Miles Karakasevic

KONRAD ESTATE
A: 3620 Road B., Redwood Valley, CA 95470
T: (707) 485 0323
W: Kevin Robinson

MENDOCINO VINEYARDS
A: 2399 N. State Street, Ukiah, CA 95482
T: (707) 462 2985 **W**: George Phelan

MILANO 1977
A: 14594 S. Highway 101, Hopland, CA 95449
T: (707) 744 1396 **W**: James A. Milone

TIJSSELING–TYLAND 1981
A: 2150 McNab Ranch Road, Ukiah, CA 95482
T: (707) 462 1810 **W**: Fred Nickel

WINERIES *of* LAKE COUNTY

GUENOC WINERY 1981

A: 21000 Butts Canyon Road, Middletown, CA 95461 **T**: (707) 987 2385 **V**: 10.30–4.30 Thur–Sun **P**: 110,000 **W**: Derek Holstein

It seems wholly fitting that a house and property purchased by Lillie Langtry in 1888 with the intention of making "the greatest Claret in the country" should end up in the ownership of Orville T. Magoon, a descendant of Hawaiian royalty and of Chinese ancestry, who became the (involuntary) owner of 23,000 acres of Lake County real estate when 23 acres of prime Hawaiian land was compulsorily acquired by the government for the University of Hawaii. Orville Magoon, with a masters degree in civil engineering from Stanford University, spent 30 years with the U.S. Army Corps of Engineers, retiring as chief of the coastal engineering branch of the planning division of the army in July 1983. Confronted with a 30-square-mile property which in fact straddles the Lake County and Napa County borders, Magoon has put his engineering skills to work in creating a major vineyard and associated development project, simultaneously displaying sophisticated marketing skills.

Thus a 1,200-acre portion of the estate, including the Langtry home, became the first single-proprietor AVA in the United States in 1981. The Guenoc label features a painting of Lillie Langtry (who, incidentally, took her winemaking venture seriously, producing and marketing wines with her "likeness" on the bottle before returning to France in 1906), and developing an evocative Le Breton second label. Guenoc is also unique in that, as well as having its own AVA for part of the vineyard (within Lake County), it has established significant plantings within Napa County adjacent to a very large lake engineered by Magoon and constructed as part of a youth training program.

Winemaker Derek Holstein, too, has an exotic background, majoring in music and psychology before spending three years as a pre-med student, eventually transferring to U.C. Davis to complete his Bachelor of Science degree in fermentation science. After graduation he spent six years with Christian Brothers, and was primarily responsible for the development of computer software programming to control winery operations, yet another of his interests and talents. He then moved to Domaine Chandon to organise its winemaking and computer programming, before joining Guenoc in 1987. Here he presides over precisely the sort of winery one would expect to be built by a senior construction engineer, functional down to the last screw — and of course fully computerized.

After initial peregrinations in style, the Guenoc wines have become prolific gold medal winners in shows, and it is not hard to see why. The White Meritage and the Red Meritage

ABOVE ~ *The Guenoc vineyards and grounds create patterns of appropriately military precision.*

under the Langtry label are both outstanding wines, showing particularly skilled use of oak. The White Meritage has pronounced spicy barrel ferment characters, but has the fruit to carry the oak; the Red Meritage is beautifully constructed and balanced, with dark fruits, judicious tannins and perfectly integrated and balanced oak. The Petite Sirah shows another aspect of the oak handling, this time with strong vanillin American notes which harmonize well with the fruit. The second label Le Breton wines are clean, well made, not particularly intense, but provide excellent value. The 1990 Chardonnays, under various labels, are outstanding; they show highly skilled use of barrel fermentation and wonderful fruit.

KENDALL-JACKSON VINEYARDS 1982

A: 600 Matthews Road, Lakeport, CA 95453
T: (707) 263 9333 **V**: 11–5 Wed–Sun
P: 600,000 **W**: John Hawley

What started as a holiday retreat and a bit of fun for San Francisco lawyer Jess Jackson has

PROPRIETOR'S GRAND RESERVE
KENDALL-JACKSON
1989
Chardonnay
CALIFORNIA

become one of the great success stories of the last ten years, and the much-publicized departure of Jed Steele in 1991 (and the subsequent no-less publicized litigation) has failed to slow its momentum. Jackson purchased the Lake County property way back in 1974, intending simply to grow and sell grapes. By 1981 his plans had changed, and in 1982 (with consultancy help from Ric Forman) the first Vintners Reserve Chardonnay was produced, blended from Santa Barbara, Monterey, Sonoma and Lake County grapes, going on to win the first ever platinum award from the American Wine Competition. What Forman started, winemaker Jed Steele (who arrived in in 1983) built on, producing multi-region blended Chardonnays of extraordinary quality, consistency and style. By 1990 the Vintners Reserve Chardonnay was made up of fruit from 30 different vineyards in five counties, much of it barrel fermented. Indeed, Kendall-Jackson has 16,500 barrels of Chardonnay fermenting each year, 9,500 at the Lake County Winery, and another 7,500 at the Cambria Winery in the Santa Maria Valley.

By 1986 Jed Steele was receiving Winemaker of the Year awards, and the winery the Winery of the Year awards. With sales skyrocketing, Jackson acquired 1,000 acres of vineyards in the Santa Maria Valley (the major part of the famed Tepusquet Vineyards) and established the Cambria brand. The following year he acquired the then-defunct Edmeades Winery in the Anderson Valley, together with 120 acres (Jed Steele having been winemaker at Edmeades before joining Kendall-Jackson); in 1989 he acquired the Stephen Zellerbach Winery in the Alexander Valley (together with 160 acres of vineyards), now renamed J. Stonestreet & Sons; and in 1991 added a

ABOVE ~ *Lillie Langtry determined in her words, "to make the greatest Claret in the country."*

further 1,300 acres of Monterey County vineyards, with a further 1,200 acres secured under long-term lease.

The winemaker and winery of the year awards continued to flow, and according to independent analysis by Varietal Fair, Kendall-Jackson was among the top six gold medal winners (and also the top six overall medal winners) in major wine competitions in every year from 1985 through 1991, continuing its winning way as the Golden Winery Award winner at the 1992 California State Fair.

Chardonnay has been the driving force for this extraordinary success. One of the more interesting aspects of the court proceedings was the use of a little sweet Gewurztraminer (or Gewurztraminer muté) to fill out the finish of the Chardonnays, investing them with a honeyed softness which clearly had enormous market appeal. It is agreed on all sides that Steele's mastery of blending so many different components was also critical.

Steele's replacement, John Hawley, joined Kendall-Jackson after nine years at Clos du Bois, during which time he established his own credentials in the handling of barrel-fermented Chardonnay and Sauvignon Blanc. Steele's shoes will be difficult to fill, but if anyone can do it, John Hawley can.

It hardly needs be said that wine quality is exemplary and utterly reliable. While aimed at the upper end of the market, the Kendall-Jackson wines are made to be drunk, rather than cellared or talked about in great detail. They are, in many ways, distinctly Australian in style, making a direct appeal to the heart rather than to the intellect. But to cater for all tastes, Kendall-Jackson does produce limited quantities of single vineyard, single varietal wines, exemplified by an outstanding array of Zinfandels. Jackson has always believed in giving his winemakers latitude, and some of their hobby wines are bottled in lots as small as 200 cases. It is a very clever way of satisfying the creative urge which exists within the breast of most winemakers, and which is not always satisfied in the large winery context.

KONOCTI WINERY 1974

A: Thomas Drive at Highway 29, Kelseyville, CA 95451 **T**: (707) 279 8861
V: 10–5 daily **P**: 50,000
W: David Hansmith

Konocti was founded as a cooperative venture by local growers who owned 500 acres of Lake County grapes. Initially the wines were custom crushed, but in 1979 the Konocti Winery was built and bonded. As so many cooperatives have found, turning grapes into wine may solve the short-term problem of what to do with the grapes, but there is still the necessity of then selling the wine. This realization, coupled with the always greater-than-anticipated costs, led to the Parducci family acquiring a 50% interest in 1983, and then a further 25% being sold subsequently to outside investors.

Konocti mirrors the learning curve which the whole of Lake County has undergone since the early 1970s. As well as establishing the red grape vineyards in the appropriate locations, the Konocti philosophy is now to let the natural expression of Cabernet Sauvignon and Cabernet Franc grown in the area have free reign: in other words, instead of trying to fill the wines with tannin and pump them up into junior copies of Napa Valley wines, the accent is on softness and fresh fruit flavors. The red wines, now being bottled within a year of vintage, represent an exciting new direction for California wine. It is no coincidence that Jed Steele is consultant winemaker, and that his former employer, Jess Jackson, sees lighter-bodied, fruity red wines as a major growth market. The varietal Cabernet Franc, Cabernet Sauvignon and Merlot from Konocti are all totally delicious wines.

But it is with Sauvignon Blanc (marketed as Fumé Blanc) and with the Sauvignon Blanc-Semillon White Meritage that Konocti really moves into top gear. Even in an indifferent vintage such as 1989, the White Meritage was quite outstanding, with classic style and length to the flavor, and a harmonious blend of herbal and riper peach and melon fruit flavors. The Sauvignon Blanc has all of the intensity and power one could hope for, and it is not surprising that new winemaker David Hansmith (English-born, and spent four years with Darrell Corti) is excited about the challenge and opportunities which Lake County fruit offers.

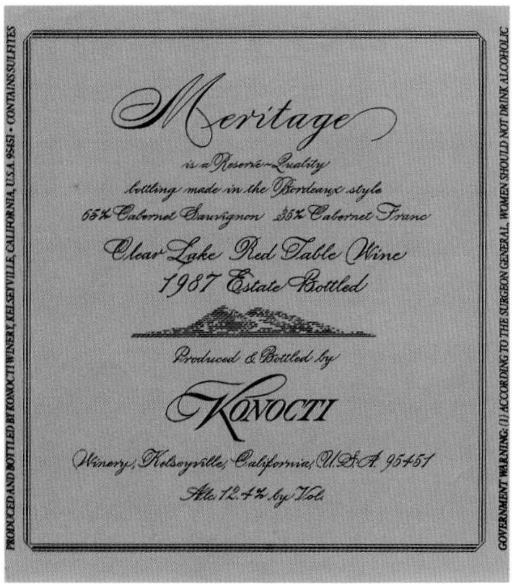
PRODUCED AND BOTTLED BY KONOCTI WINERY, KELSEYVILLE, CALIFORNIA, U.S.A. 95451 • CONTAINS SULFITES
Meritage
is a Reserve Quality
bottling made in the Bordeaux style
65% Cabernet Sauvignon 35% Cabernet Franc
Clear Lake Red Table Wine
1987 Estate Bottled
Produced & Bottled by
KONOCTI
Winery, Kelseyville, California, U.S.A. 95451
Alc. 12.4% by Vol.
GOVERNMENT WARNING: (1) ACCORDING TO THE SURGEON GENERAL, WOMEN SHOULD NOT DRINK ALCOHOLIC

ABOVE ~ *Trees and vines alike await the coming of spring at Guenoc.*

CHANNING RUDD CELLARS 1976

A: 21960 St. Helena Creek Road, Middletown, CA 95461 **T**: (707) 987 2209
V: By appointment **P**: 1,000
W: Channing Rudd

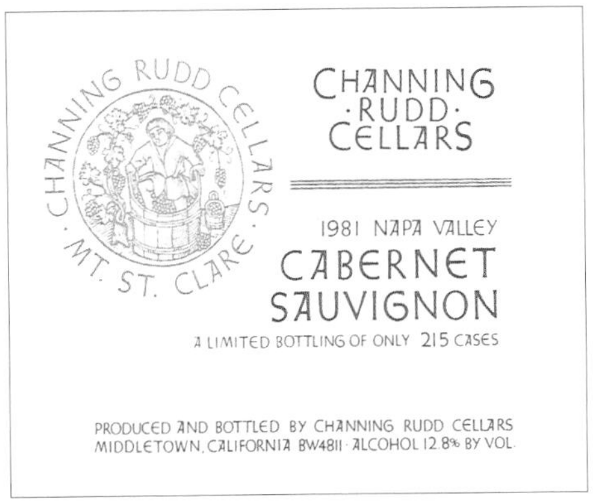
CHANNING RUDD CELLARS
MT. ST. CLARE
CHANNING ·RUDD· CELLARS
1981 NAPA VALLEY
CABERNET SAUVIGNON
A LIMITED BOTTLING OF ONLY 215 CASES
PRODUCED AND BOTTLED BY CHANNING RUDD CELLARS
MIDDLETOWN, CALIFORNIA BW4811 · ALCOHOL 12.8% BY VOL

Grape growing and winemaking are still essentially diversions for graphic designer and commercial artist Channing Rudd, and his wife Mary. The former Seagram and Paul Masson Vineyards art director Channing moved from Connecticut (where his family has lived since 1639) to California in 1965, and almost immediately became involved in home winemaking. In 1977 he turned professional, making wine in the bonded area underneath his Alameda home. Five years later he moved to Lake County, and has established an 8.5-acre vineyard at an elevation of between 1,400 and 1,600 feet planted to Chardonnay, Cabernet Sauvignon, Cabernet Franc, Merlot and Malbec. The property comprises 55 acres in all, and it is not surprising that Channing Rudd (for the time being, at least) has contented himself with a little under ten acres of vineyard; sitting on a wooden pallet dragged behind a tractor driven by wife Mary does not seem the easiest way of leveling land before planting.

Channing Rudd's winemaking has been influenced by the late Joe Swan (who was Channing Rudd's personal hero), and John Thacher of Cuvaison, with the wines of Silver Oak made in the style which brought Rudd much fame during the period he was able to buy the second crop of Cabernet Sauvignon from Bella Oaks Vineyard. When the wine he made was rated higher than the Heitz Bella Oaks, Joe Heitz decided enough was enough, and that wine is no more.

As the estate vineyards come into production, and the wines are released, production will rise to 2,000 cases, even then leaving plenty of scope for Channing Rudd to continue his striking labeling and packaging design business from the studio of his newly built house.

STEELE WINES 1991

A: 4793 Cole Creek Road, Kelseyville, CA 95451 **T**: (707) 279 0213 **V**: By appointment
P: 5,000 **W**: Jed Steele

STEELE
1991
CLEAR LAKE
ZINFANDEL
Catfish Vineyard

As a matter of strict logic, Steele Wines should really be found in the chapter entitled "Warehouse Wineries" (page 380). However, Jed Steele has such a high profile by virtue of his long tenure at the helm of Kendall-Jackson that his on-going intense commitment to Clear Lake really demands that his winery (which does not in fact yet exist) be listed here.

Steele freely says that he has absolutely no ambitions to create a business to rival that of his former employer. His main activity these days is as wine consultant (to Wildhurst and Konocti within the Clear Valley, and to others outside, including Villa Mt. Eden), and he is making limited quantities of wine at the urging of his wife, who was for years involved in the marketing of Kendall-Jackson wines. While the initial production was sold before it was even made, Steele does not see rapid growth for the label, and is content that initially it be limited to two Chardonnays and a Clear Lake Zinfandel. As one would expect, the 1991 Chardonnays were immaculately crafted wines, with lush fruit, sophisticated oak and a creamy, lingering finish. A second label, Shooting Star, was added in late 1992.

OTHER WINERIES

WILDHURST

A: 11171 Highway 29, Lower Lake, CA
T: (707) 994 6525
W: Kathy Redmond

ABOVE ~ *Although machine harvesters were first developed in California, much of the crop is still hand-picked.*

ABOVE ~ *Clear Lake occupies half the surface area of Lake County.*

SAN FRANCISCO BAY

PREVIOUS PAGE ~ *Evening light adds to the science fiction feeling of the Livermore Valley wind machines.*

ABOVE ~ *The Altamont Pass above the Livermore Valley, simultaneously creating and using energy.*

San Francisco Bay
1971 and 1991 Acreage/Grape Varieties

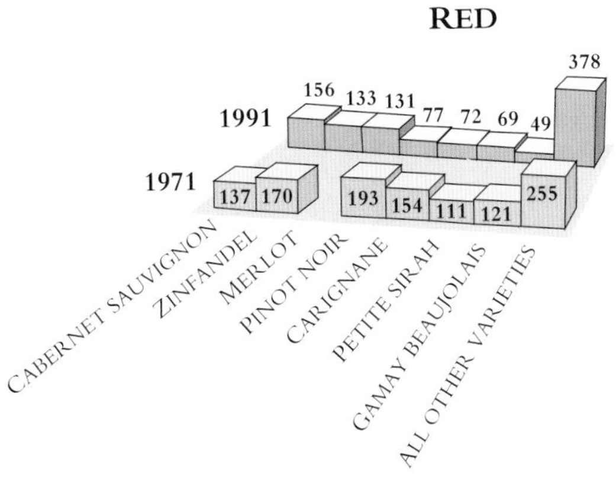
RED
1991
156
133
131
77
72
69
49
378
1971
137
170
193
154
111
121
255
CABERNET SAUVIGNON
ZINFANDEL
MERLOT
PINOT NOIR
CARIGNANE
PETITE SIRAH
GAMAY BEAUJOLAIS
ALL OTHER VARIETIES

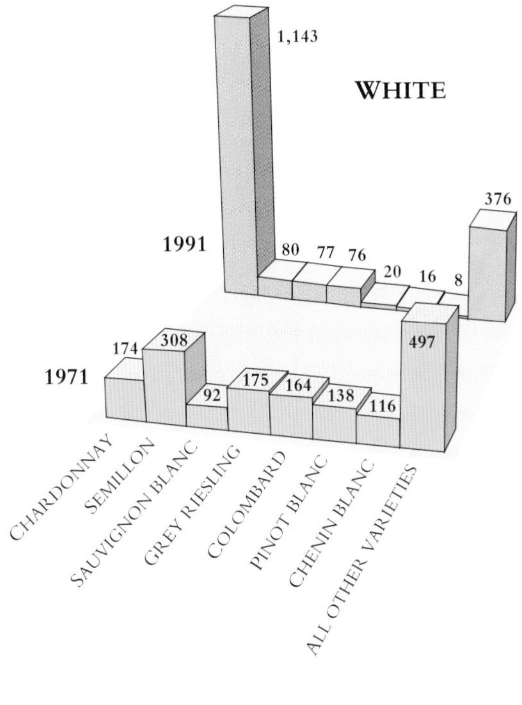
WHITE
1,143
1991
80
77
76
20
16
8
376
1971
174
308
92
175
164
138
116
497
CHARDONNAY
SEMILLON
SAUVIGNON BLANC
GREY RIESLING
COLOMBARD
PINOT BLANC
CHENIN BLANC
ALL OTHER VARIETIES

The long southern tip of the San Francisco Bay announces the valley which stretches from Oakland to San Jose and thence to Hollister, starting in Santa Clara County and finishing in San Benito County. This valley encompasses the Santa Clara AVA in its northern reach, skirts the Pacheco Pass (which straddles the border between the two counties) and then takes in the turkey's nest of AVAs south of Hollister as it runs into the Gabilan Range.

On the western side the Santa Cruz Mountains rise precipitously from the ocean floor, descending equally precipitously into the Santa Clara Valley. To the northeast, and running at right angles, is the diminutive Livermore Valley, only 14 miles long and magically fighting a rearguard action against the urban pressures reaching south from Palo Alto and San Jose. For, as almost any schoolchild anywhere in the Western world knows, this is Silicon Valley, the birthplace of the computer industry.

That urban pressure diminishes as you pass Gilroy, the garlic capital of the world and purveyor of garlic wine (a truly ghastly thought), and that pressure cannot reach into the heights of the Santa Cruz Mountains, although it eats away at foothills and valleys such as the beautiful Hecker Pass area.

Wente is staging a heroic fight against urbanization in the Livermore Valley, recently joined by an unlikely ally in the form of Jack Nicklaus, the figurehead for a golf course and residential development which will actually see 500 acres of vineyards added to (rather than taken away from) plantings in the region.

The Santa Cruz Mountains are, and always have been, a law unto themselves, as remote from the normal commercial constraints of the twentieth century as they were during the nineteenth century.

ABOVE ~ *Hand-harvesting is slow and expensive, but is essential for whole-bunch pressing.*

LIVERMORE AND SANTA CLARA

LIVERMORE VALLEY

The Livermore Valley takes its name from the English sailor who established a ranch in the valley in 1844, planting vines and making wine for his own consumption. However, it was not until the entrepreneur Charles Wetmore invested in Livermore in 1882 and began to trumpet its virtues in inimitable Wetmore style that viticulture really took hold. The 1870s plantings of 40 acres soared to over 4,000 acres by 1884; one of those to listen to Wetmore's oratory was Carl Wente, who acquired his first 50 acres in 1883. So did a series of wealthy families, establishing wineries glorying in such names as Chateau Bellevue, Olivina, Chauche and Bon, Mont Rouge, Ravenswood and La Bocage.

Wente, Wetmore, Semillon and Sauvignon Blanc provide the continuity between the nineteenth century and the 1990s. Charles Wetmore established Cresta Blanca on the 480-acre property he purchased in 1882, and armed with a letter of introduction from neighbor Louis Mel, went to Chateau d'Yquem to obtain cuttings of Semillon, Sauvignon Blanc and Muscadelle. Returning triumphant, he divided the spoils between himself and Louis Mel, whose vineyard was ultimately acquired by Wente, as was the Cresta Blanca Winery.

It was at Cresta Blanca that the famous winemaker Myron Nightingale (with help from U.C. Davis enologists) produced the first botrytised Sauternes-style wine made in California. The grapes were harvested at normal maturity, placed on trays and then sprayed with an innoculum of *Botrytis cinerea*, the mold which produces the great sweet wines of Sauternes and of Germany. By controlling the temperature and the humidity, the growth of the mold can be controlled; it is a technique which has also been used in Australia, although it is relatively expensive and time consuming.

So it has been the Wente family which has guided the fortunes of the Livermore Valley, and will take it as a thriving viticultural region into the next century — and will do so with style.

ABOVE ~ *Old oak barrels, some made from native timbers, are fast-disappearing from the scene.*

OPPOSITE ~ *The hands of the grape picker, and the hook knife which is so much faster than secateurs.*

SANTA CLARA

Notwithstanding the substantial presence of the Mirassou and J. Lohr Wineries in the suburbs of San Jose, Santa Clara is but a shadow of its former self, with vineyards in fast retreat from urban sprawl until one reaches Gilroy in the south. Yet it once stood proud among the hierarchy of California wine regions, and has a history second to none. Grape vines were planted as early as 1780 at the Mission Santa Clara de Asis, 40 years earlier than the first plantings north of the Bay. By the middle of the nineteenth century there were six commercial wineries in operation; as with the Livermore Valley, many of the vignerons were French, and led the way in importing superior vitis vinifera varieties. Despite the invasion of phylloxera in the 1890s, at the turn of the century Santa Clara County had over 100 wineries and 8,500 acres of vines, more than the Napa Valley.

Nor did Prohibition take undue toll: 8,000 acres of vines remained in production in 1933, and 64 wineries reopened for business in the region which Burgundian-born Paul Masson made so famous and which became his domain for so long. It is as much an indictment of corporate owners (successively Seagram and Vintners International) as of local authorities hungry for development and the concomitant rate income that Masson is no more (in Santa Clara), and viticulture north of the Hecker Pass nearly gone also.

The statistics suggest there may still be a flicker of life: from a low point of 588 acres in 1982, plantings have recovered to 860 acres in bearing and 141 still to come into bearing (as at 1991) for a total of 1,001 acres.

Much of this life is likely to come from the eastern slopes of the Santa Cruz Mountains which flow into Santa Clara County, the vineyards of which are caught in the statistical net of the County even though they are within the Santa Cruz Mountains AVA. Well-known names with this dual citizenship include Ridge Vineyards and Mount Eden Vineyards. But once one leaves the protection of the mountains, urban and commercial pressures will increase rather than diminish, and the Santa Clara viticultural scene of the twenty-first century will bear no relationship to that of the nineteenth, or even the first half of the twentieth century.

Livermore Valley and Santa Clara
VINTAGE CHART 1981-1991

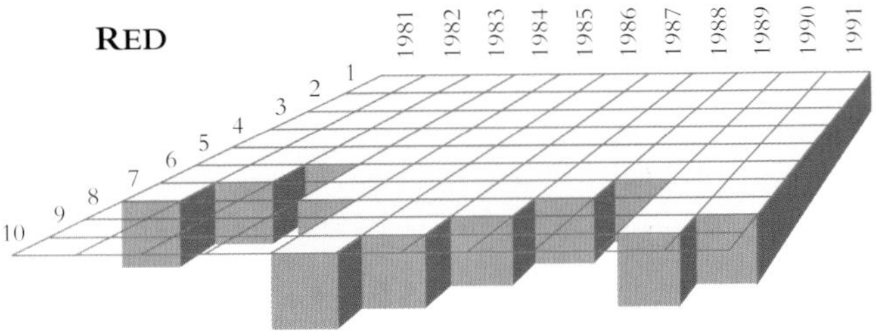
RED
1981
1982
1983
1984
1985
1986
1987
1988
1989
1990
1991
1
2
3
4
5
6
7
8
9
10

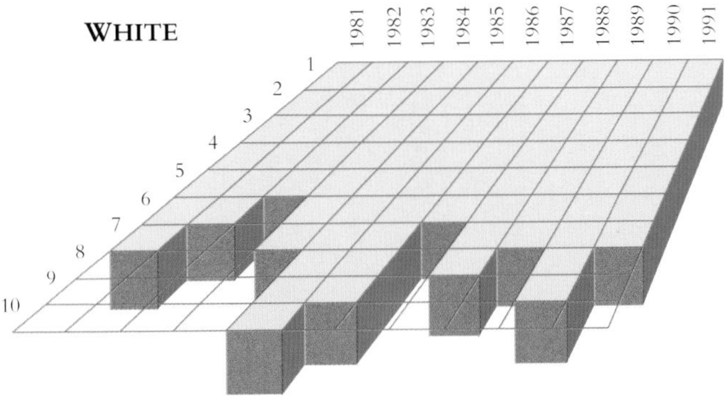
WHITE
1981
1982
1983
1984
1985
1986
1987
1988
1989
1990
1991
1
2
3
4
5
6
7
8
9
10

ABOVE ~ *Gino Fortino, family and friends upholding the traditional way of life in the Hecker Pass.*

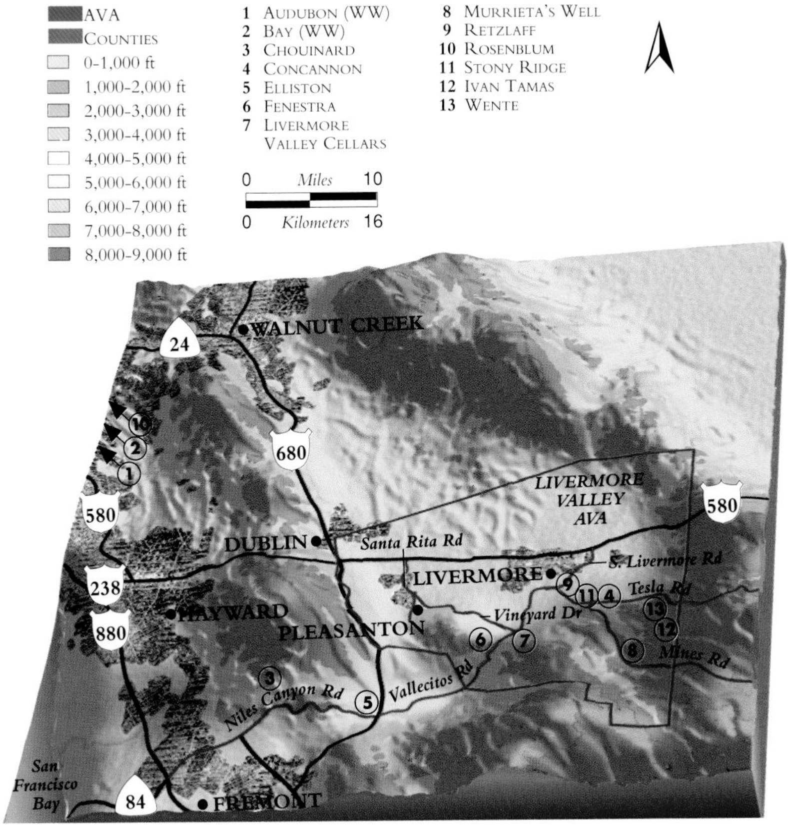
AVA
Counties
0-1,000 ft
1,000-2,000 ft
2,000-3,000 ft
3,000-4,000 ft
4,000-5,000 ft
5,000-6,000 ft
6,000-7,000 ft
7,000-8,000 ft
8,000-9,000 ft
1 Audubon (WW)
2 Bay (WW)
3 Chouinard
4 Concannon
5 Elliston
6 Fenestra
7 Livermore Valley Cellars
8 Murrieta's Well
9 Retzlaff
10 Rosenblum
11 Stony Ridge
12 Ivan Tamas
13 Wente
0 Miles 10
0 Kilometers 16
WALNUT CREEK
24
680
580
LIVERMORE VALLEY AVA
DUBLIN
Santa Rita Rd
S. Livermore Rd
LIVERMORE
Tesla Rd
238
HAYWARD
PLEASANTON
Vineyard Dr
880
Mines Rd
Niles Canyon Rd
Vallecitos Rd
San Francisco Bay
84
FREMONT

Livermore Valley and Santa Clara 1971 and 1991 Acreage/ Grape Varieties

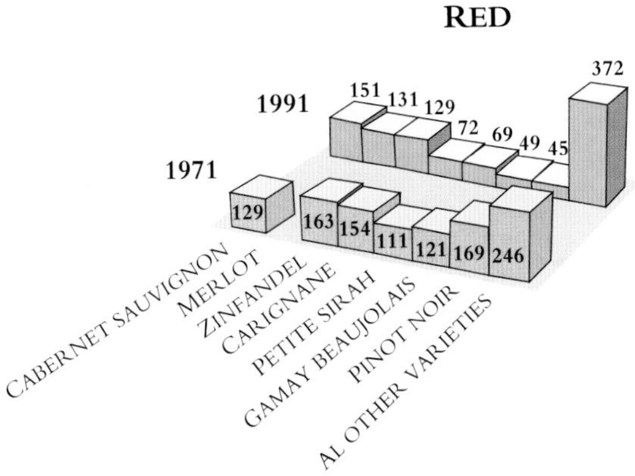
RED
1991
1971
151
131
129
72
69
49
45
372
129
163
154
111
121
169
246
CABERNET SAUVIGNON
MERLOT
ZINFANDEL
CARIGNANE
PETITE SIRAH
GAMAY BEAUJOLAIS
PINOT NOIR
AL OTHER VARIETIES

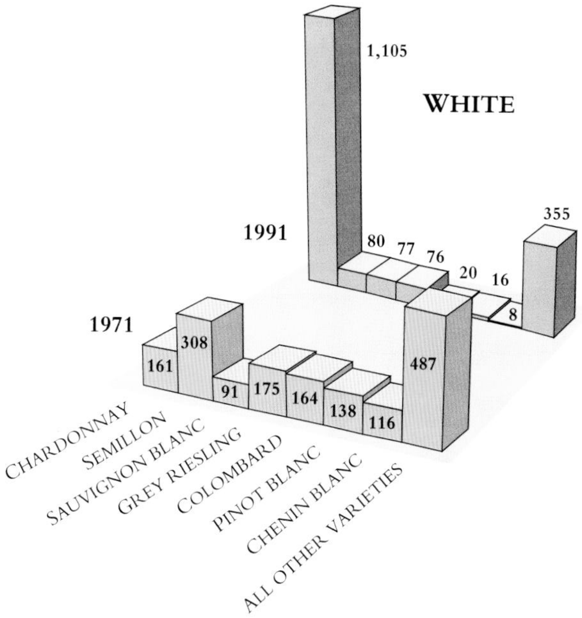
WHITE
1991
1971
1,105
80
77
76
20
16
8
355
161
308
91
175
164
138
116
487
CHARDONNAY
SEMILLON
SAUVIGNON BLANC
GREY RIESLING
COLOMBARD
PINOT BLANC
CHENIN BLANC
ALL OTHER VARIETIES

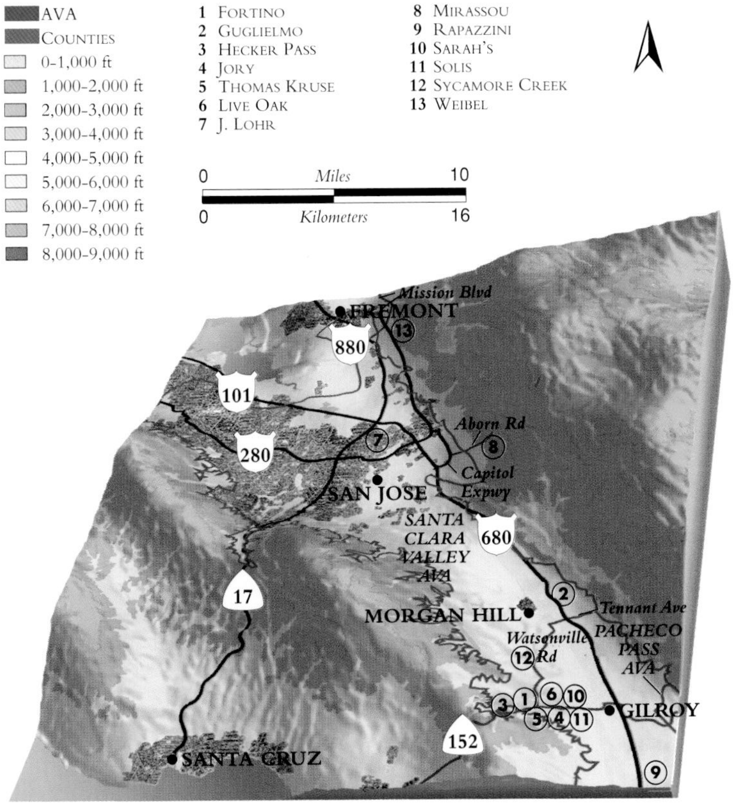
AVA
Counties
0-1,000 ft
1,000-2,000 ft
2,000-3,000 ft
3,000-4,000 ft
4,000-5,000 ft
5,000-6,000 ft
6,000-7,000 ft
7,000-8,000 ft
8,000-9,000 ft
1 Fortino
2 Guglielmo
3 Hecker Pass
4 Jory
5 Thomas Kruse
6 Live Oak
7 J. Lohr
8 Mirassou
9 Rapazzini
10 Sarah's
11 Solis
12 Sycamore Creek
13 Weibel
0 Miles 10
0 Kilometers 16
Mission Blvd
FREMONT
880
101
Aborn Rd
280
Capitol Expwy
SAN JOSE
SANTA CLARA VALLEY AVA
680
17
MORGAN HILL
Tennant Ave
PACHECO PASS AVA
Watsonville Rd
GILROY
152
SANTA CRUZ

ABOVE ~ *Santa Clara map.*
TOP ~ *Livermore Valley map.*

The Region in Brief

Climate, Soil and Viticulture

Livermore Valley

Climate

The 15 miles long and ten miles wide Livermore Valley AVA is confined to a lesser or greater degree on all sides by mountains which partially inhibit the extent of the maritime cooling which might otherwise be expected from San Francisco Bay. But sea breezes can and do make their presence felt. If you leave the Livermore Valley in the direction of the San Joaquin Valley, you will see one of the strangest of all sights: hundreds of wind-driven electricity-generating machines, a surreal scene which would have sent Salvador Dali reaching for his brushes.

The moderation of the coastal influence within the valley results in a Region III climate, much warmer that that of its neighbors. Only in a few spots does the heat summation drop to high Region II. Rainfall is 14 to 15 inches, falling — as ever — in winter and spring. The early vineyards survived (and flourished) because of the high under-ground water table which the vine roots were able to reach. Urbanization caused the water table to drop alarmingly, and the Del Valle Dam and Reservoir mean that the Arroyo Mocho and Arroyo del Valle Rivers are now assured of year-round flow for irrigation, supplemented by the South Bay Aqueduct, completed in 1967.

Soil

Well-drained gravelly to very gravelly soils predominate through the valley, particularly in the south. Charles Wetmore, presumably by good management rather than good luck, established his vineyard on a unique chalk and loam alluvial fan washed down from the hillsides and spread by the wanderings of the Arroyo del Valle River over the millennia.

The Growing Season

The growing season runs from March through to early November for the late-ripening varieties, with a length of 254 days. Bursts of high temperatures (over 100°F) do occur, but rarely last more than a few days before the marine air asserts its normal pattern.

Contract Growers

Raboli Vineyard Ninety-eight acres planted 1922 on Mines Road to Sauvignon Blanc, Semillon, Alicante Bouschet, Carignane, Mourvedre, Petite Sirah and Zinfandel. Sold to Wente.

ABOVE ~ *It is all done with mirrors: a disembodied vineyard worker at Wente Bros.*

Santa Clara Valley

Climate

The broad southwards sweep of the valley is strongly influenced by marine cooling from San Francisco Bay to which it opens directly. The length of travel, for one thing, moderates the influence somewhat, and overall the valley has a summation of 2,700 degree days, or mid Region II. Most of the days are sunny, although in summer a high fog hangs over the valley in the morning hours before it is replaced by the prevailing northwest winds of the afternoons. Rainfall is 16 to 20 inches, 80% falling between November and March.

Two southerly regions — one with its own AVA and the other, on a matter of strict logic, deserving it — have distinct mesoclimates. The San Ysidro District AVA is situated in Gilroy on the eastern side of the valley tucked into the Diablo Range at the foot of the Pajaro Gap and Chittenden Pass which act as a passage for cool maritime air into the San Joaquin Valley. As a consequence of more intense fogs and stronger afternoon breezes, San Ysidro has a dramatically lower heat summation of 2,085 degree days (low Region I), compared to that of nearby Gilroy with 2,630 degree days.

The Hecker Pass, on the other side of the valley, suffers from a degree of schizophrenia, being incorporated within both the Santa Clara Valley and Santa Cruz Mountains AVAs, yet not having its own AVA. It is physically dominated by the Santa Cruz Mountains, but the vineyards are all on the valley floor or gentle knolls; it, too, is a passage for cold air drawn in from the ocean.

Soil

The soil associations are dominated by very deep soils on alluvial plains, fans, stream benches and terraces, differentiated from those of the Livermore Valley by the absence of gravels. The overall fertility is high; it is not for want of good agricultural land that plantings have decreased so dramatically. In San Ysidro, the clay and gravel component increases somewhat, offering slightly better water-holding capacity.

The Growing Season

Heavy frosts do not occur in the growing season, which can be as long as 300 days. Summer temperatures can briefly rise above 100°F, but seldom persist for long. Harvest commences in early September with Chardonnay, and continues through mid to late October, although exceptional years such as 1991 can delay the commencement until the last week of September.

Contract Growers

Elizabeth Garbett Vineyard One and a half acres of Chardonnay on Page Mill Road in Los Altos Hills, which is sold exclusively to Page Mill Winery.

Mistral Vineyard Two hundred acres adjacent to San Ysidro Vineyard east of Gilroy planted, since 1960, to Chardonnay, Pinot Blanc, Pinot Noir, Merlot and Sauvignon Blanc and sold exclusively to Concannon.

San Ysidro Vineyard One hundred and fifty acres planted early 1960s to 1980s to Chardonnay, Pinot Noir and Merlot sold to Jory, Storrs and Sunrise.

Principal Wine Styles

Livermore Valley

Semillon, Sauvignon Blanc and White Meritage

Notwithstanding the long history of Semillon, which under the Wente Dry Semillon label became famous in the 1940s, the variety is of less importance these days. Wente's plantings of 87 acres are still significant, although less than its 123 acres of Sauvignon Blanc. The pattern is for Sauvignon Blanc to incorporate a percentage of Semillon (but to be labelled Sauvignon Blanc) or for a Meritage-style proprietary wine to be made. Fenestra is one of those which continues to produce a noteworthy Semillon, and of course Wente does likewise, while Kalin Cellars produces some voluptuously rich and textured wines which age beautifully. The Wente Sauvignon Blanc is soft, full and fleshy, usually supported by generous amounts of oak.

Chardonnay

The ubiquitous Chardonnay accounts for almost half the plantings in the valley, and virtually all the wineries dutifully make a Chardonnay. The Herman Wente Vineyard Estate Reserve leads the way, lush and smooth with the ripe, creamy fruit one would expect from the warm climate. It would be hard to suggest, however, that the wines are particularly distinctive — which the Semillons and Sauvignon Blancs are.

Cabernet Sauvignon and Merlot

These are the other important varieties in the Livermore Valley, producing generously flavored wines which run through blackberry, currant, plum and dark chocolate. The wines are seldom excessively tannic, although tannins are certainly present. Rather like Chardonnay, the wines are amiable and pleasant.

Principal Wine Styles

Santa Clara Valley

Chardonnay

The only white variety to trouble the statisticians, representing almost 80% of the white plantings. Even then it is not easy to make profound statements about its style: the two largest makers (Lohr and Mirassou) are absentee growers, relying on other regions (essentially Monterey) for their wines. Sarah's Vineyard makes distinctive, if oaky, Chardonnay from its Hecker Pass estate plantings, while Page Mill makes an absolutely splendid wine from the small Elizabeth Garbett vineyard which was planted specifically for Page Mill. The San Ysidro region also produces distinctive Chardonnay (and Pinot Noir, which it supplies to Page Mill).

Cabernet Sauvignon and Merlot

The two most important red varieties, with Cabernet Sauvignon leading the way. It is a moot point whether Fellom Ranch should be regarded as being in the Santa Cruz Mountains or the Santa Clara Valley: either way it produces small quantities of striking Cabernet Sauvignon from its hillside vineyard, while Fortino in the Hecker Pass region produces massive but soft Italianate Cabernet Sauvignon. Jory weighs in with a good Merlot from the San Ysidro Vineyard.

The Wente Bros: The Response to Urban Pressures

Carl Heinrich Wente emigrated from Hanover in 1880, and spent three years learning winemaking California-style with Charles Krug in the Napa Valley. In 1883 he purchased a 50-acre vineyard which had been established four years earlier in the Livermore Valley by Dr. George Bernard, quickly expanding his holdings to 300 acres. Leon Adams in the *Wines of America* records that Carl advised his eldest son Carl F. Wente to learn bookkeeping: he did so, getting a job as a bank messenger and becoming President of the Bank of America 45 years later.

The other two sons stayed in the fold, Ernest attending the College of Agriculture at U.C. Davis, and youngest son Herman studying enology at the University of Berkeley, becoming one of the finest winemakers of his generation. Indeed, both of the brothers showed the same sort of vision and ability which propelled Carl F. Wente to the top of the Bank of America. While studying at Davis, Ernest became interested in Chardonnay: he acquired one clone from the Gier Vineyard in Pleasanton, but sourced the other from the Montpellier Nursery in the south of France, managed by the brother of one of his college professors, Leon Bonnet.

ABOVE ~ *Chardonnay bins are sprinkled with sulfur dioxide prior to crushing.*

Wente Bros. — as it had become in 1918 — sold its wine in bulk before and during Prohibition, but immediately on its repeal launched into bottled wines under the Valle de Oro label, releasing the first American wine ever to be varietally labelled Chardonnay in 1936. In 1960, there were only 230 acres of Chardonnay in production in California, and the Wente 1959 Chardonnay is recognized as one of the all-time classics. In the ensuing decades Wente became the source, directly or indirectly, for many of the most famous Chardonnay plantings: the Wente clone is to be found everywhere, either under that name or under the heat-treated identification of Davis Clone #4.

Its exploits with Sauvignon Blanc and Semillon — in many ways the symbol of the Livermore Valley — are no less impressive. When Wente acquired Louis Mel's El Mocho vineyard in the 1920s, Ernest took selections which have been as influential as those of the Chardonnay. The Wente Sauvignon Blanc clone became Davis Heat-treated Clone #1; the Wente records show that 15 of the 29 California counties have Sauvignon Blanc which is directly descended from the Louis Mel plantings.

Wente released varietally labelled Semillon in the mid 1930s (and has also been credited with the first Sauvignon Blanc, although it makes no claim to this effect) and hosted a visit by the Marquis de Lur Saluces of Chateau d'Yquem in 1938. The marquis's father had tasted Livermore Valley wines at the 1889 Paris International Exhibition where a Cresta Blanca wine made by Charles Wetmore won a Grand Prix, a feat repeated by Wente's Sauvignon Blanc at the Paris Exhibition of 1937 — and which prompted the visit of the marquis in the following year.

The Wente star rose even further the following year when the Valle de Oro Sauvignon Blanc won the Grand Prize for White Wines at the 1939 San Francisco Golden Gate Exposition. This led Frank Schoonmaker to select and nationally sell Wente Sauvignon Blanc, Semillon, Grey Riesling, Pinot Blanc and Ugni Blanc under the Frank Schoonmaker Selection label, but with Wente Bros. shown as winemakers.

In 1949 Karl Wente, Ernest's son, joined the business which he guided until his premature death in 1977. In the mid 1960s he made two key decisions: to invest in vineyard land in the Monterey Valley, but (in 1968) to retain the base in the Livermore Valley by taking advantage of the then newly introduced Williamson Act (which allows California farmers to ensure their properties are valued for rating purposes as agricultural land regardless of their potential residential or industrial value).

Indeed, in addition to their 1,190 acres of Livermore Valley vineyards, the Wentes have a 2,000-acre cattle ranch, with both vineyards and cattle under the direction of fourth generation Philip Wente who says, "I'm just as proud of my estate-grown beef as I am of my estate-bottled wines," a sentiment which winemaker brother Eric might not entirely agree with.

But, as they say, it's all happening at Wente. In 1981 the family purchased the long-abandoned Cresta Blanca Winery site and surrounding land, replanting what is now called the Charles Wetmore Vineyard between 1984 and 1986 to Merlot, Cabernet Sauvignon, Chardonnay, Sauvignon Blanc and Semillon. The winery and 650 feet of sandstone caves were restored, and a large Spanish-accented white stucco walled and red shingle roof restaurant and hospitality center were built.

In February 1992 Philip Wente joined forces with former Concannon winemaker Sergio Traverso to create Murrieta's Well, using the 115-year-old Louis Mel Winery. Two super-premium Meritage wines, one white and one red, are being sold under the Vendimia label: one a blend of Sauvignon Blanc and Semillon, the other a blend of Cabernet Sauvignon, Cabernet Franc and Merlot. These will be nationally distributed; other wines exclusive to the cellar door are also available.

This venture pales into insignificance against the other moves by Wente. In April 1992 it led a syndicate which purchased the Concannon Winery. The winery had changed hands five times in seven years, and had totally lost direction. Precisely how Concannon will be re-positioned remains to be seen, but it will surely be for the better: all that was said in 1992 was that the varietal wines of Petite Sirah, Chardonnay, Cabernet Sauvignon and Sauvignon Blanc will continue to be made.

The Wente family is also involved in the very large golf course and residential development headed by Jack Nicklaus. Earlier proposals had foundered in the face of local opposition, but all sides are happy with the Nicklaus proposal, which was inspired by the South Livermore Valley Study. This will involve 20-acre lots (as opposed to the existing 100-acre minimum subdivision) with a house and vineyard, with 500 acres of vines in all to be established. The developers will also restore the historic Ruby Hill Winery built in the 1880s and which made wine on and off for the next 100 years; $500,000 is being spent in refurbishing the splendid brick and stone winery.

Fenestra is one winery which will benefit from the vineyards to be established around it, but the hope of the developers (including Wente) is that some of the purchasers will establish their own small wineries.

Indeed, the whole approach of Eric, Philip and Carolyn Wente is as intelligent as it is refreshing. The front page of one of the 1992 Wente newsletters featured the Ivan Tamas Winery, founded in 1984 by Hungarian-born Ivan Tamas and Steve Mirassou (who left his family's business to help establish Ivan Tamas). Given the massive urban populations within an easy drive of the Livermore Valley, Wente no doubt realize the benefit to be gained from an industry seen to have a fresh impetus and new face. It is a tide which all too often runs in the opposite direction.

ABOVE ~ *Wente Bros. own much of the historic vineyards of the Livermore Valley.*

WINERIES *of* LIVERMORE VALLEY

CONCANNON VINEYARD 1883

A: 4590 Tesla Road, Livermore, CA 94550 **T**: (510) 447 3760 **V**: 10–4 Mon–Sat, Sun 11–4:30 **P**: 65,000 **W**: Mari Kirrane

Concannon was founded by Irish entrepreneur James Concannon, who emigrated from Ireland in 1865 at the age of 18, engaging in all manner of money-making schemes, from selling rubber stamps before the invention of the typewriter through to street-cleaning systems for Mexico City. When he purchased his Livermore Valley property in 1883, his intention was to make wine for the Catholic church, albeit using the new importations of *vitis vinifera* from France. Altar wine became the mainstay of the business, a fortuitous decision which kept Concannon in good health throughout Prohibition. As a mark of respect and gratitude, James Concannon's son, Joseph Concannon, sent a barrel of his finest Muscat de Fontignan to the Pope every five years through the rest of his (Joseph's) life. By the early 1960s, however, attention was focused on the production of Petite Sirah and Cabernet Sauvignon. Aging facilities caused the once proud winery to slip in the 1970s, and at the end of the decade it was sold to Distillers Company, which on-sold it to a partnership headed by then-winemaker Sergio Traverso and Deinhard of Germany in 1988. Deinhard then briefly became sole owner before selling Concannon to Wente in April 1992.

The 180 acres of estate vineyards are planted to Sauvignon Blanc, Semillon, Cabernet Sauvignon and Petite Sirah; Chardonnay is purchased from San Luis Obispo and Santa Barbara County vineyards. The wines are rich and full flavored, particularly the Sauvignon Blanc and Petite Sirah; the 1990 Petite Syrah is an outstanding wine crammed with juicy red cherry fruit.

FENESTRA WINERY 1976

A: 83 East Vallecitos Road, Livermore, CA 94550 **T**: (510) 862 2292 **V**: 12–5 Sat–Sun **P**: 4,000 **W**: Lanny Replogle

Dr. Lanny Replogle was, until 1992, a chemistry professor at San Jose State University, who just happened to find winemaking rather more interesting than chemistry, and who followed the time-honored path from home winemaker to professional producer in his spare time. Following his 1992 retirement, he is now able to devote the whole of his attention to Fenestra. The winemaking business has had a peripatetic existence, moving from the Stony Ridge Winery to the old three-story Ruby Hill Winery, before moving on to the equally historic winery which had been built by George True in 1889. The True Winery remained in production until around 1960, but by the time the Replogle family moved there in 1980, it had been entirely abandoned and dilapidated, having been used by cows as a convenient shelter. Tons of rubble and dirt were removed from the floors, and a new roof installed, resulting in the handsome winery of today. Outside, winemaking equipment installed in the 1940s provides a living museum.

For a relatively small winery, Fenestra produces a remarkably wide range of wines, all except one of the Cabernet Sauvignons (purchased from Smith & Hook) of Livermore Valley origin. The roster includes Chardonnay, Sauvignon Blanc, Semillon, Pinot Blanc, White Zinfandel, Late Harvest Riesling or Late Harvest Semillon, Cabernet Sauvignon, Merlot and Zinfandel. Just for good measure, an El Dorado Barbera is also added to the list from time to time. The Livermore Valley Semillon shows all of the varietal character one would expect from this famous region, with the structure to reward prolonged cellaring. The rich Livermore Cabernet Sauvignon has abundant plummy fruit together with tastes of dark, bitter chocolate which are both striking and attractive; the Merlot, again from the Livermore Valley, has similar ripe plummy fruit, strong tannins and masses of weight.

RETZLAFF VINEYARDS 1986

A: 1356 South Livermore Avenue, Livermore, CA 94550 **T**: (510) 447 8941 **V**: 12–2 Mon–Fri, 12–5 Sat–Sun **P**: 3,000 **W**: Robert Taylor and Dan Gehrs (Consultant)

A small, family-owned winery, with production centered around its 14 acres of vineyards, producing Grey Riesling, Sauvignon Blanc, Chardonnay, Cabernet Sauvignon, Merlot, a Cabernet Merlot-Meritage blend, and Reserve Cabernet Sauvignon. The latter was one of the nine double-gold medal winners at the 1991 California State Fair, and inevitably focused considerable attention on this hitherto little-known winery.

WENTE BROS. 1883

A: 5565 Tesla Road, Livermore, CA 94550 **T**: (510) 447 3603 **V**: 10–4.30 daily **P**: 600,000 **W**: William Joslin

The remarkable story of the Wente family has been told on pages 238–9. It is wholly appropriate that its Chardonnays, both Estate Reserve

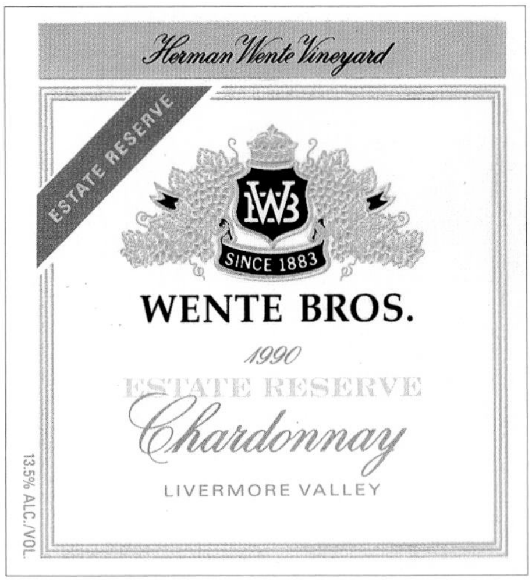
Herman Wente Vineyard
ESTATE RESERVE
WB
SINCE 1883
WENTE BROS.
1990
ESTATE RESERVE
Chardonnay
LIVERMORE VALLEY
13.5% ALC./VOL.

and Central Coast (the latter from the Arroyo Seco in Monterey) should be its flagbearers. In their respective price brackets, the wines can only be described as excellent, the Livermore Valley Reserve wine being extremely rich, full-bodied and toasty, the Central Coast version with a combination of more tropical fruit, but greater acidity, and oak playing only a minor role.

The Late Harvest Rieslings from Arroyo Seco develop great character with a few years in bottle, showing an intense botrytis influence. The range of *methode champenoise* sparkling wines produced at the restored Cresta Blanca facility, and comprising a Blanc de Blancs, Blanc de Noir and Reserve Brut, are all reliable, if slightly stolid, wines.

OTHER WINERIES

CHOUINARD VINEYARDS 1985
A: 33853 Palomares Road, Castro Valley, CA 94552 **T**: (510) 582 9900
W: Damian Chouinard

ELLISTON VINEYARDS 1983
A: 463 Kilkare Road, Sunol, CA 94586
T: (510) 862 2377 **W**: Dan Gehrs

LIVERMORE VALLEY CELLARS 1978
A: 1508 Wetmore Road, Livermore, CA 94550
T: (510) 447 1751 **W**: Chris Lagiss

MURRIETA'S WELL 1991
A: Louis Mel Winery, Mines Road, Livermore, CA 94550 **W**: Sergio Traverso **T**: (510) 449 9229

STONY RIDGE WINERY 1991
A: 4948 Tesla Road, Livermore, CA 94550
T: (510) 449 0458

IVAN TAMAS WINERY 1984
A: 5565 Tesla Road, Livermore, CA 94550
T: (510) 447 3663 **W**: Ivan Tamas and Steve Mirassou

WINERIES *of* SANTA CLARA

FORTINO WINERY 1948

A: 4525 Hecker Pass Highway, Gilroy, CA 95020 **T**: (408) 842 3305 **V**: 9–5 daily **P**: 25,000 **W**: Gino Fortino

Founder Ernest Fortino learnt winemaking and grape growing in his native Calabria, where his family operated a winery. In 1959 he moved to California and, after working with a number of wineries in northern California for the next ten years, purchased what is now known as Fortino in 1970. The 52 acres of estate vineyards produce a range of traditional wines: Chardonnay, Chablis, White Burgundy, White Zinfandel, Johannisberg Riesling, Chenin Blanc, Carignane, Pinot Noir, Reserve Burgundy, Zinfandel, Ruby Cabernet, Petite Sirah, Charbono and Cabernet Sauvignon, the majority of which are offered in non-vintage form. The wines are made in the old Italian style; in 1992 the 1984 Cabernet Sauvignon had just been bottled (as had the 1987, but only because it was unusually soft and forward in style). The 1983 Cabernet Sauvignon was still being sold from the tasting room, a massive wine, with formidable tannin but with its fair share of rich fruit. Fortino is particularly interesting because it is typical of the numerous Italian-owned wineries which once flourished in the Santa Clara region but which by and large have passed into the mists of time.

JORY WINERY 1986

A: 3920 Hecker Pass Highway, Gilroy, CA 95020 **T**: (408) 847 6306 **V**: 11–5 Wed–Sun **P**: 5,000 **W**: Corey Wilson

Jory was founded in 1984; in that vintage it rented space in a winery to fashion a couple of wines for restaurants, but in 1986 officially entered business as Jory, moving to the Novitiate Winery above Los Gatos. There founder Stillman Brown met winemaker Corey Wilson, and when Wilson moved to the old Bertero Winery west of Gilroy, Jory followed suit.

Conversation with Stillman Brown will quickly reveal a highly articulate and amusing character, who quite evidently cannot make up his mind whether he wishes to enrage Randall Grahm or Robert Parker the most: the Black Zeppelin and Red Zeppelin labels are certainly aimed in the direction of Randall Grahm, Old Barrister at both men. Red Zeppelin is a blend of Zinfandel, Carignane and Cabernet Franc, Black Zeppelin a blend of Mourvedre and Syrah. Stillman Brown also advocates blending Mourvedre and Merlot, Sauvignon Blanc with Pinot Blanc and Chardonnay, arguing, "It is the synergy of the blend that matters, and not the historical or regional associations of the two." Bowing to convention, as it were, Jory does also make small quantities of varietally labeled Merlot, Pinot Noir and Chardonnay bearing the Santa Clara County appellation; the Zeppelin wines are simply California.

The wines in bottle from the 1988 and 1989 vintages are erratic, an essency blackcurrant Merlot being the best. The Red Zeppelin from barrel was utterly delicious, bursting with cherry and jam fruit flavors, with appropriate fine-grained tannins. The Black Zeppelin is strangely eucalypt mint-accented, but with soft, accessible fruit. Says Stillman Brown, "So far, the number of legal threats against Jory has been exceeded by the number of medals won in competition by the Red Zeppelin." Whether that will remain the case after the introduction of the Old Barrister Claret or the White Zeppelin Blimp de Blanc remains to be seen.

J. LOHR WINERY 1974

A: 1000 Lenzen Avenue, San Jose, CA 95126 **T**: (408) 288 5057 **V**: 10–5 daily **P**: 250,000 **W**: Geoff Runquist

Jerry Lohr had been in the construction and development business all his life, and it was this business which financed the acquisition of a 280-acre vineyard site near Greenfield in Monterey which was planted in the early 1970s. With this coming into bearing, he and his then-partner purchased an old brewery site in the industrial section of San Jose, in which the principal operating winery is now established. How long it remains there depends on the ever-increasing value of the land: it can only be a question of time before it moves, and there are plenty of options open. For over the years Lohr has also established vineyards in the Napa Valley (55 acres of Cabernet Sauvignon known as Carroll's Vineyard, presently being replanted to Merlot as leaf-roll virus and phylloxera take their hold); in the Delta region (225 acres principally planted to Chenin Blanc, Chardonnay and Johannisberg Riesling, largely sold to Gallo); and the Seven Oaks Vineyard in Paso Robles (planted principally to Cabernet Sauvignon, Merlot and Cabernet Franc). The Paso Robles vineyard has its own substantial winery, and only juice is moved to San Jose from any of the vineyards, with all the crushing and pressing carried out in the region.

After an initial spotty reputation, J. Lohr has settled down to producing consistently good to very good wines from the 1,200 acres of vineyards under its control. The Wild Flower Gamay, grown on its Greenfield Vineyard in Monterey, is absolutely delicious, fresh and bright, with sparkling red cherry fruit and faultless style. The Bay Mist White Rieslings from the same source, made both dry and late harvest, are of high quality, with powerful lime flavor and, in the case of the late harvest, with strong botrytis influence. The Paso Robles Cabernets, released under the Seven Oaks label, deliberately feature the soft Paso Robles fruit. Says winemaker Geoff Runquist, "When people taste the wine, they always want to know how much Merlot is in it. When I tell them none, they are astonished. The whole point is that we are not going to try to Napify a Paso Robles Cabernet." I must say the wines do have substantial oak input, which at times tends to obscure the very attractive sweet red cherry fruit, but a few years in bottle may well see the wine come back into better balance. The role of oak is also quite evident in the Riverstone Chardonnay, along with complexing malolactic-derived characters. The California-designated second label Cypress range is as it should be.

MIRASSOU VINEYARDS 1854

A: 3000 Aborn Road, San Jose, CA 95135 **T**: (408) 274 4000 **V**: 10–5 Mon–Sat, Sun 12–4 **P**: 300,000 **W**: Tom Stutz

Mirassou bills itself as America's oldest winemaking family, and offers its Monterey-based wines under the snappy new label design as "Fifth Generation Family Selection." Louis Pellier established the Pellier Gardens nursery in San Jose in 1850, and arranged for brother Pierre to bring vine cuttings from France in 1853. Pierre returned to France for yet more cuttings, and history relates that the base of each cutting was implanted in a potato to

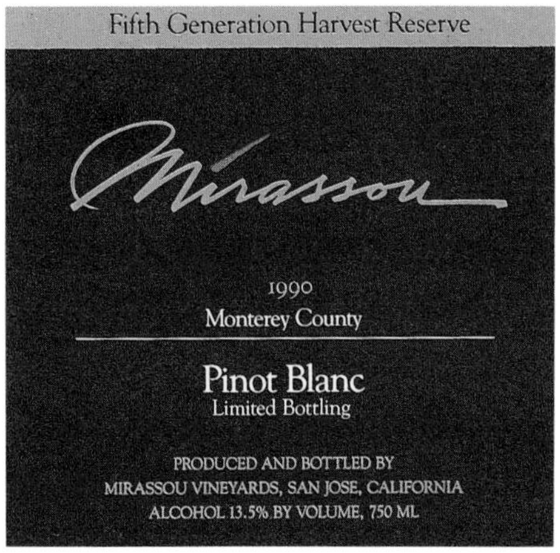
Fifth Generation Harvest Reserve
Mirassou
1990
Monterey County
Pinot Blanc
Limited Bottling
PRODUCED AND BOTTLED BY
MIRASSOU VINEYARDS, SAN JOSE, CALIFORNIA
ALCOHOL 13.5% BY VOLUME, 750 ML

75-YARDS
WINE TASTIN
OPEN TODAY
WINE
VINEGAR
MADE-SOLD
HERE

protect it on the long journey out from France. In 1859 he planted the vineyard and established the site upon which son-in-law Pierre Mirassou (and the subsequent generations of Mirassous) built their business in the Evergreen district on the slope of Mount Hamilton. But it was not until the 1940s that Mirassou started to develop its own brand identity; prior to that time it had sold wine in bulk to others. While growth through the 1960s and early 1970s was substantial, it was not without difficulty. In 1966 the fifth generation took over management of the business, and (forced out of Santa Clara County by urbanization and rising land values), rapidly expanded their Monterey County intake. Right throughout the 1970s, Mirassou became notorious for the vegetal character of the red wines it produced from that region. Both vineyard and winemaking (and labeling) rationalization has done much to redress the situation.

At the head of the Mirassou range are four Limited Bottling Monterey County-designated varietals: Chardonnay, Pinot Blanc, Pinot Noir and Cabernet Sauvignon under the Fifth Generation Harvest Reserve banner. Then under the Fifth Generation Family Selection umbrella come a California appellation Cabernet Sauvignon (utilizing Cabernet from areas such as the Napa Valley to add flesh and ripeness) and Monterey County Chardonnay, White Burgundy (made from Pinot Blanc), Pinot Noir, Petite Sirah, Riesling, Chenin Blanc and Gamay Beaujolais. A separate facility produces the *methode champenoise* range of vintage-dated Brut, Blanc de Noirs, Brut Reserve and Au Naturel.

Wines such as the White Burgundy Pinot Blanc can rise above their station, with crisp stone fruit flavors, excellent acidity and length, showing more attractive flavors than the more complex Limited Bottling Pinot Blanc, with its honeyed overtones. The Blanc de Noirs has also excelled, with structure, length and style, and certainly suggesting that there is one very good use to which Monterey Pinot Noir can be put. The Limited Bottling Pinot Noir and Chardonnay are, by contrast, somewhat disappointing, being rather dilute and washed out.

SARAH'S VINEYARD 1978

A: 4005 Hecker Pass Highway, Gilroy, CA 95020 **T**: (408) 842 4278 **V**: By appointment **P**: 2,000 **W**: Marilyn Otteman

Sarah's Vineyard is located on the side of a small ridge, the immaculately tended vineyards running up to the winery on one side, descending briefly on the other before acres of commercial flower gardens stretch away. On either side, the steep mountains which girdle the Hecker Pass provide a spectacular backdrop. It is not hard to see why it was love at first sight for Marilyn Otteman when she and husband John purchased the ten-acre property in 1977, subsequently establishing the seven acres of Chardonnay which provide part of the winery's production. The name Sarah's Vineyard comes from Marilyn Otteman's alter ego, Sarah; one is never sure in talking to Otteman whether she is being serious or outrageous, mystic or practical joker. Certainly it is as well that she is a female; in all other circumstances her pronouncements about her wines would be regarded as outrageously sexist. All of her wines are female: one was described as "Five feet nine inches and very aggressive. Show her off at elegant functions." Another as being "More adaptable. She's not as tall and has Greek eyes. She is the type you marry to be with every day." Pinot Noir "Is the redhead to me; there are a few good ones, but most are also-rans." Her Mexican vineyard crew, being exhorted to treat the vines gently, are told, "Each plant is like a lady; she is unique and individual. If you don't pay attention to her, she won't go out with you."

Otteman is a self-taught winemaker; she spent some years working in a home winemaking store, went to night school at Napa and worked in other wineries. Her own winery is small, functional and immaculately equipped and maintained. The labels are without question the most expensive imaginable: the dye for the intricate embossed design was sculpted by an engraver from Smith & Wesson, and the labels are printed by Jeffries Bank Note Company on woven paper normally reserved for wedding invitations, or on heavy gold paper. The tasting room, open by invitation, has to be seen to be believed: it is replete with bottles offered in velvet-lined boxes, crystal glasses, flowers and the whole works.

Sarah's Vineyard offers two Chardonnays (one from the estate, and one from Ventana Vineyard), a Merlot and a *methode champenoise*. The latter is called "Au Natural," subtitled "Enchanté." Says Otteman, "To embrace Enchanté is to embrace one's very being — radiant, full and evolving. Pale golden in hue with a sleek chiffon finish, this enchanting beauty reflects the care and nurturing shared by her winemaker." Somehow or other, I never got to taste the wines.

SOLIS WINERY 1989

A: 3920 Hecker Pass Road, Gilroy, CA 95020 **T**: (408) 847 6306 **V**: 11–5 Wed–Sun **P**: 5,000 **W**: Corey Wilson

Solis is owned by David Vanni and family, which owns and operates a cut-flower nursery in

Solis
WINERY
BARREL FERMENTED
1990
SANTA CLARA COUNTY
CHARDONNAY
PRODUCED AND BOTTLED BY SOLIS WINERY. BW. 1625
GILROY, CALIFORNIA U.S.A. ALC. 12% BY VOLUME

ABOVE ~ *Santa Clara roadside signs, an unconscious contribution to the cause of pop-art.*

nearby Watsonville. In 1980 the family purchased ten acres of vineyard which had been planted in the 1890s and which was adjacent to the Bertero Winery built in 1917. In 1988 the five-acre block on which the winery stood was also acquired by the Vannis, and the building was restored and opened in time for the 1989 vintage. The old vines on the original ten-acre block had been replanted by the Vannis in the mid 1980s to Chardonnay and Merlot, and it is these plantings which provide the core of the estate production. The Bertero Winery block is being replanted to additional Merlot, Sangiovese and Cabernet Sauvignon, but in the meantime the crush is supplemented by Merlot, Riesling and Pinot Noir purchased from Central Coast vineyards.

Wine style and, it must be said, wine quality are somewhat erratic. There is great promise from the wines in barrel, but not all safely make the transition to bottle.

Other Wineries

Emilio Guglielmo Winery 1925
A: 1480 E. Main Avenue, Morgan Hill, CA 95037 **T**: (408) 779 2145
W: George E. Guglielmo

Hecker Pass Winery 1972
A: 4605 Hecker Pass Highway, Gilroy, CA 95020 **T**: (408) 842 8755 **W**: Mario Fortino

Thomas Kruse Winery 1971
A: 4390 Hecker Pass Road, Gilroy, CA 95020
T: (408) 842 7016 **W**: Thomas Kruse

Live Oaks Winery 1912
A: 3875 Hecker Pass Highway, Gilroy, CA 95020 **T**: (408) 842 2401 **W**: M. Takemoto

Rapazzini Winery 1962
A: 4350 Monterey Highway, Gilroy, CA 95020
T: (408) 842 5649 **W**: Jon Rapazzini

Sycamore Creek Vineyards 1976
A: 12775 Uvas Road, Morgan Hill, CA 95037
T: (408) 779 4738 **W**: Make Yamaki

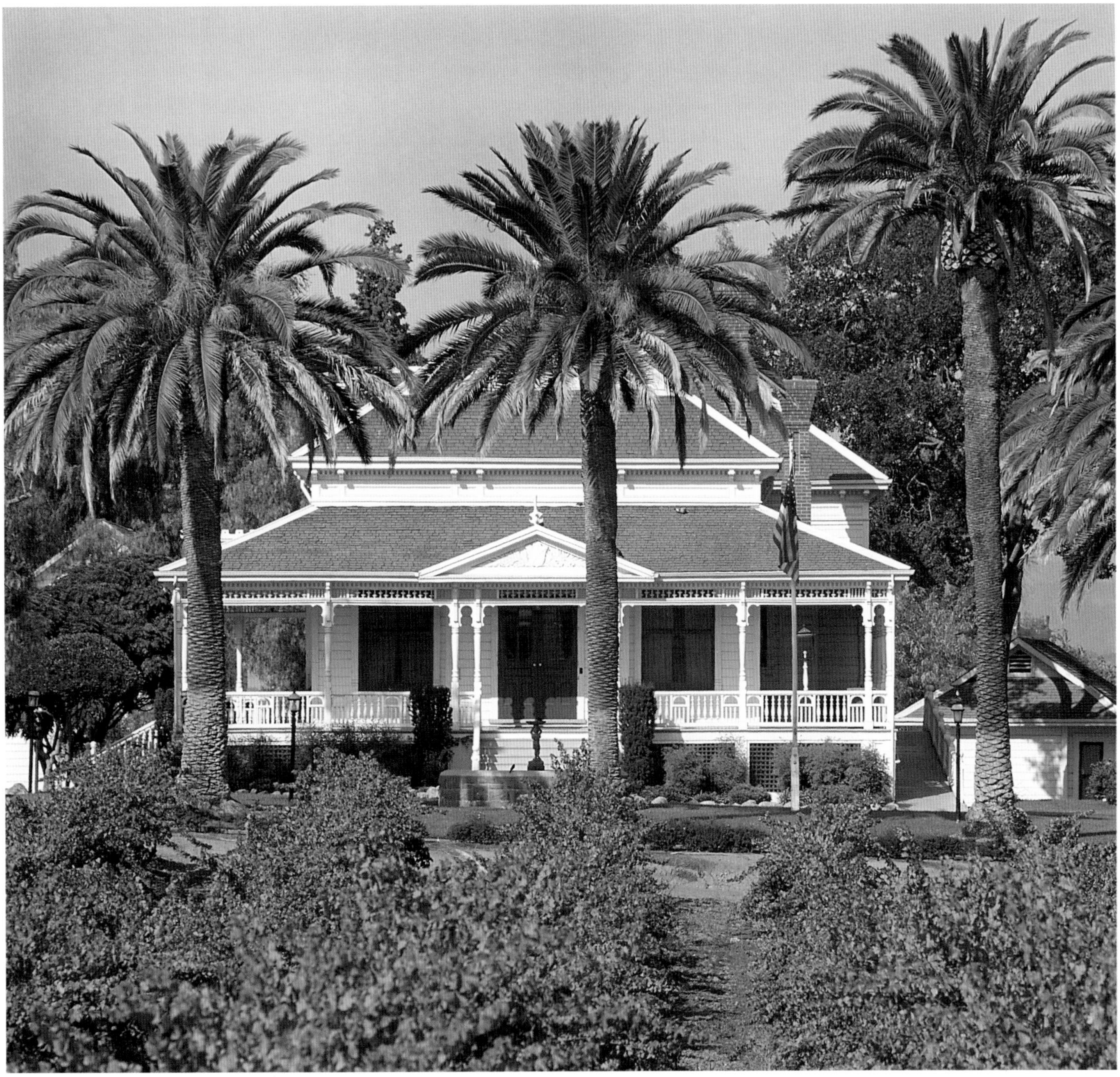

ABOVE ~ *Christopher Buckley, known as the Blind White Devil, mixed 1880s politics and winemaking at Ravenswood, which is now state-owned.*

SANTA CRUZ MOUNTAINS

No other winegrowing region of California left a greater impression on me than did the Santa Cruz Mountains: perhaps it was partly due to the ferocity of the schedule which led to my crisscrossing the mountains several times in a two-day period in June (with a return visit in August). Perhaps it was the subliminal knowledge that the San Andreas fault sheers through the mountains, leaving that dizzy gap which opens up beneath Ridge's Montebello Vineyard. In any event, the remoteness, the improbability, the noble grandeur of these mountains left an indelible imprint on my consciousness.

It also raised a major question: why on earth were vineyards established in these inhospitable and unlikely surroundings in the nineteenth century when there was a seeming abundance of suitable valley land? The answer is twofold. After the first exhilarating decade of the goldrush, the suddenly swollen population of California started to look for other forms of wealth. The massive ancient redwood forests of the Santa Cruz Mountains provided one such source, and were ruthlessly clear felled.

This left open hillside country, well serviced by the network of roads and railroads established to move out the logs. Land speculators and agents then swarmed in, creating small farms and even housing blocks. The land was cheap, and it offered guaranteed legal title, something not assured in the lowlands where Spanish land grants left a legacy of uncertainty in the wake of the establishment of the American rule of law.

So it was that the Jarvises, themselves land developers, planted vines in the Vine Hill region in 1869, about the same time as John Burns named Ben Lomond Mountains (recently given its own AVA) and began agricultural development in the Bonny Doon area. Wines from the Ben Lomond Wine Company were described as being "comparable to any made in Europe" by the Royal German Viticultural Commission in the 1890s.

In 1883 Emmet Rexford planted Cabernet Sauvignon at his La Questa Vineyard near Woodside; it was to produce some of California's most famous Cabernets, and one precious acre remains in production. Around the same time the Novitiate Winery was established in the hills behind Los Gatos. The Novitiate vineyards, too, remain in (somewhat diminished) production to this day.

By 1890 there were 800 acres of grapes around Woodside, and 2,100 acres in Santa Cruz County. In 1892 Dr. Osea Perrone established his Montebello Vineyard, while in 1896 the Pichetti Winery was built further down the Montebello Ridge, the same

ABOVE ~ *The precious bunches of Marsanne of Bonny Doon are protected from hungry birds by netting.*

OPPOSITE ~ *The white swans on the lake at Thomas Fogarty welcome the wedding parties which frequently use the winery's reception facility.*

year as Paul Masson purchased the land upon which he established his famous sparkling wine cellars.

Even though there were 1,600 acres of vines and 39 wineries in the Santa Cruz Mountains at the onset of Prohibition, little survived at Repeal. The chronically low-yielding vineyards, the remoteness, and a market which was primarily concerned with cheap fortified wine all conspired against the Santa Cruz Mountains.

One of the survivors was the extraordinary Paul Masson, who obtained the only licence in the United States for the production of "Medicinal Champagne" during Prohibition, which was sold through drug stores on doctors' prescriptions. Masson's enterprise was, however, matched by that of a gang of robbers who, posing as Federal Prohibition agents, raided the winery and largely emptied it by taking away four truckloads of wine.

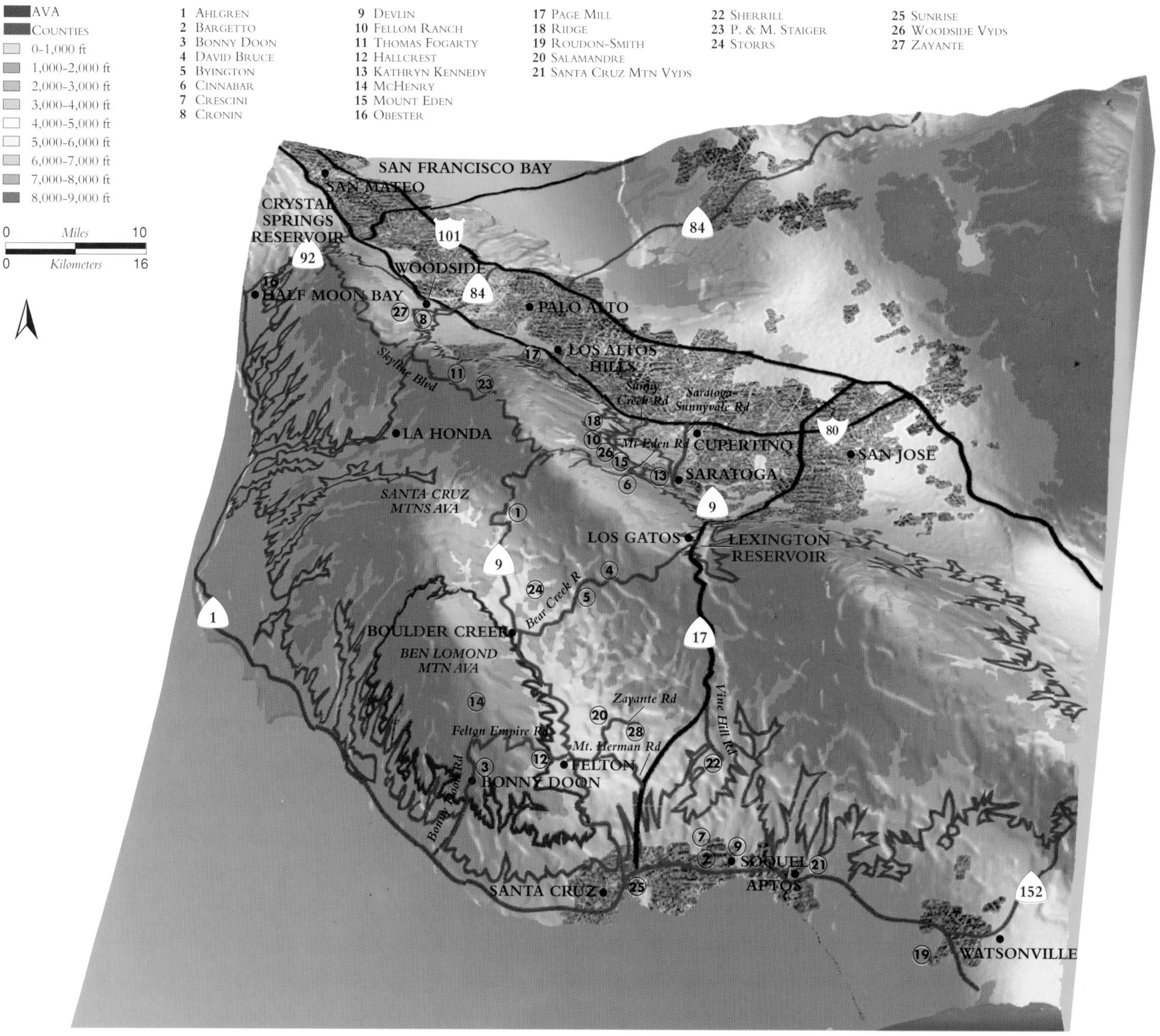
AVA
Counties
0-1,000 ft
1,000-2,000 ft
2,000-3,000 ft
3,000-4,000 ft
4,000-5,000 ft
5,000-6,000 ft
6,000-7,000 ft
7,000-8,000 ft
8,000-9,000 ft
0 Miles 10
0 Kilometers 16
1 Ahlgren
2 Bargetto
3 Bonny Doon
4 David Bruce
5 Byington
6 Cinnabar
7 Crescini
8 Cronin
9 Devlin
10 Fellom Ranch
11 Thomas Fogarty
12 Hallcrest
13 Kathryn Kennedy
14 McHenry
15 Mount Eden
16 Obester
17 Page Mill
18 Ridge
19 Roudon-Smith
20 Salamandre
21 Santa Cruz Mtn Vyds
22 Sherrill
23 P. & M. Staiger
24 Storrs
25 Sunrise
26 Woodside Vyds
27 Zayante
SAN FRANCISCO BAY
SAN MATEO
CRYSTAL SPRINGS RESERVOIR
101
84
92
WOODSIDE
HALF MOON BAY
PALO ALTO
LOS ALTOS HILLS
Skyline Blvd
Sunny Creek Rd
Saratoga-Sunnyvale Rd
LA HONDA
Mt Eden Rd
CUPERTINO
80
SAN JOSE
SARATOGA
SANTA CRUZ MTNS AVA
9
LOS GATOS
LEXINGTON RESERVOIR
1
Bear Creek R
BOULDER CREEK
17
BEN LOMOND MTN AVA
Zayante Rd
Vine Hill Rd
Felton Empire Rd
Mt. Herman Rd
FELTON
BONNY DOON
Bonny Doon Rd
SOQUEL
APTOS
SANTA CRUZ
152
WATSONVILLE

ABOVE ~ *Santa Cruz Mountains map.*

Two notable figures arrived on the scene shortly after Prohibition: former stockbroker-turned-realtor Martin Ray purchased Paul Masson's mountain vineyard and winery, which he sold to Joseph Seagram in 1942, thereafter establishing his vineyards on Table Mountain. He was joined by lawyer Chaffee Hall, who planted Cabernet Sauvignon at his Hallcrest Vineyard near Felton.

Martin Ray guaranteed that the Santa Cruz Mountains were not forgotten. He produced tiny quantities of Pinot Noir, Chardonnay and (from the mid 1950s) Cabernet Sauvignon of extraordinary concentration, longevity and unpredictability, typically putting the Chardonnay and Pinot Noir in Champagne bottles and securing the corks with agrafes. Extremely high prices for the small quantities of wine he deigned to sell, coupled with on-going transfusions of capital from an ever-expanding group of investors whom Ray inveigled into his web, kept Martin Ray in business until 1972. However, his legendary disdain for the hands that fed him finally led to his eviction from the property in that year and to the change of name from Martin Ray Vineyard to Mount Eden Vineyards.

The next two notable arrivals were David Bennion (and partners) in 1959 and David Bruce (who trained at Martin Ray's feet) in 1961. Bennion established Ridge Vineyards, and David Bruce the winery which bears his name. But still the Santa Cruz Mountains remained locked in on themselves: by the mid 1970s Leon Adams was recording that "less than 100 acres (of vines) were left; many old vineyards had been replanted with Christmas trees, which in this mountainous region are easier to cultivate than vines." (As at 1992, official records show only 106 acres in Santa Cruz County, 43 acres in San Mateo County. How much of the Santa Cruz Mountains AVAs' plantings fall in Santa Clara I do not know. Local vignerons suggest there were between 400 and 500 acres of grapes in the mountains in 1992.)

In the same breath, Leon Adams went on to describe the first stirrings of the renaissance which has taken place over the last 20 years. But viticulture in the Santa Cruz Mountains will never be easy: terraces have to be painfully established or reclaimed on the precipitous hillsides, or little patches of level land found on knolls or in small valleys. It is as well the rainfall is as high as it is, for most of the vineyards are necessarily dry-farmed and are, by and large, pitifully low yielding.

The compensations are the quality and the individuality of the wines, and the sheer physical beauty of the ever-changing and breathtakingly grand scenery. It is impossible to say whether the vistas from Santa Cruz Mountains Vineyard, Cinnabar, Ridge or Mount Eden are the most compellingly spectacular — or which of the four winery approaches is the most daunting.

The sense of history, too, is palpable, nowhere more so than at Ridge, Hallcrest, Sunrise and Zayante. Finally, there are the personalities, ranging from the flamboyant Randall Grahm of Bonny Doon to the accumulated wisdom of consultant Dan Gehrs, to the intense, focused discipline of Paul Draper at Ridge, with every shade of gray in between.

As the departure of the Paul Masson empire so long ago, and the recent failure of the Congress Springs Winery show, this is a region for the passionate amateur and not the large corporate players. The winemakers of Santa Cruz may be singularly contented with their lot, but it is unlikely that fortune will accompany fame.

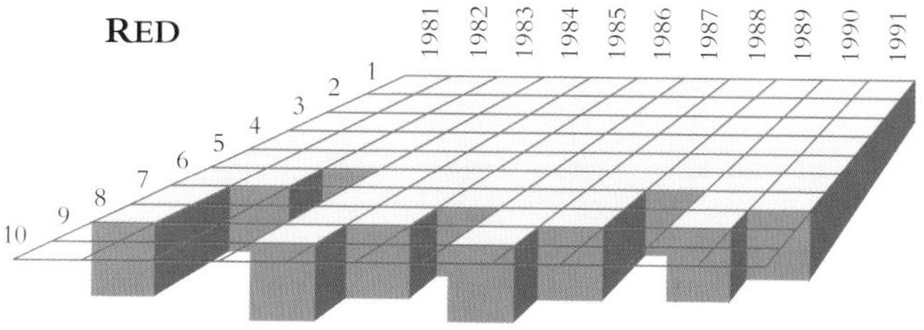
RED
1981
1982
1983
1984
1985
1986
1987
1988
1989
1990
1991
1
2
3
4
5
6
7
8
9
10

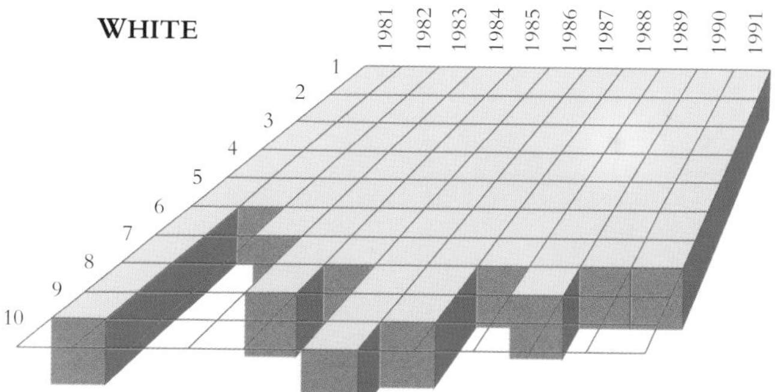
WHITE
1981
1982
1983
1984
1985
1986
1987
1988
1989
1990
1991
1
2
3
4
5
6
7
8
9
10

ABOVE ~ *Hand-making Chardonnay takes on another dimension at Mount Eden through an ancient but gentle destemmer gravity feeding to the tiny press.*

THE REGION IN BRIEF

Climate, Soil and Viticulture

CLIMATE

Any complex mountain district will provide a multiplicity of mesoclimates: the angle of the slope, the direction in which it faces, its position on the mountainside and its elevation will all operate to influence the growing and ripening conditions. When the mountain range is as substantial as that of Santa Cruz, and when one side plunges into the Pacific Ocean, the other side into an inland valley, the climatic pattern becomes even more complex. For all that, the major part of the AVA has a Region I climate: Bonny Doon (2,140 degree days), Woodside (2,320), Santa Cruz town (2,320) and Ben Lomond (2,390) are all solidly within the range. But some sites are distinctly warmer, moving into Region II. The rainfall, too, increases significantly at higher elevations in the southern portion, grading from less than 30 inches at Woodside to 60 inches above Ben Lomond. The other major distinction is between the vineyards which fall on the inland side of the mountains, facing east and southeast, some at lower elevations (in particular around Woodside), and those on the ridge tops and western slopes which are directly influenced by the Pacific Ocean. The east facing vineyards were called the Chaine d'Or (the golden chain) by the San Francisco wine merchants of the nineteenth century, and are by and large much warmer.

SOIL

The soils are in the Franciscan shale family, which are unique to the region. They are basically residual material from the decomposition of bedrock, with the particular soil type depending on the underlying bedrock. These residual soils are typically thin and stony, a mountain characteristic exacerbated in the Santa Cruz region by surface erosion. Rainfall over the millennia has impoverished the soil, and the free drainage means that vines grow slowly and sparingly, producing very small crops.

ABOVE ~ *Rick Anzalone checking sugar levels in the Mariani Vineyards Chardonnay: the grapes were picked the next day.*

THE GROWING SEASON

All except the lowest vineyards are above the fog line; this, coupled with the temperature inversion, produces very long hours of relatively cool sunshine in a growing season which is in excess of 300 days — frost being all but unknown on the hillsides. Early morning temperatures are typically 6° to 8°F warmer than those of the Santa Clara Valley. Seasonal (and site) variation results in the Chardonnay harvest commencing any time between August 31 and October 1, Cabernet Sauvignon starting two weeks later.

Contract Vineyards

Bates Ranch Twenty-four acres planted 1975 at 600 to 800 feet on old Redwood Retreat Road to Cabernet Sauvignon and Merlot; sold to Ahlgren, Bargetto and Santa Cruz Mountains Vineyard.

Beauregard Ranch Ten historic acres originally planted nineteenth century, replanted around 1970 at 1,600 feet near Bonny Doon; Cabernet Sauvignon, Chardonnay and Zinfandel sold to Ahlgren, Devlin, Hallcrest and Storrs.

Jimsomare Ranch Forty acres at 1,300 to 2,000 feet planted to Cabernet Sauvignon (30 acres) and Chardonnay; near Ridge, to which it is sold exclusively.

Matteson Vineyard Fourteen acres planted 1980 on terraced vineyards at 500 to 800 feet northeast of Watsonville to Chardonnay and Pinot Noir; sold to Salamandre and Santa Cruz Mountain Vineyard.

Meyley Vineyard Seven acres planted 1984 at 1,600 to 1,700 feet to Chardonnay; sold to Devlin, Hallcrest and Storrs.

Peter Martin Ray Vineyard Fifteen acres planted 1961, replanted 1982, at 1,800 feet above Mount Eden Road to Cabernet Sauvignon, Pinot Noir and Chardonnay; sold to Cronin.

St. Charles Vineyard Thirty-two acres planted 1938, 1955 and 1985 at 1,500 feet on Bear Creek Mountain Road to Sauvignon Blanc, Semillon, Chenin Blanc, Pinot Blanc and Pinot Noir and sold to Ahlgren.

Vanumanutagi Vineyard Ten acres on site originally owned by Robert Louis Stevenson's wife, in four blocks called Jekyll, Hyde, Treasure Island and Kidnap at 600 to 900 feet near Watsonville planted to Chardonnay; sold to Cronin and Storrs.

Principal Wine Styles

CHARDONNAY

The wines have all the distinction, concentration and style promised by the low yielding, thrifty vines and the cool but unexpectedly temperate climate. The intensity of the base wine allows the makers a wide range of latitude in the making of the wine and in the use of oak: the imprint of the *terroir* is most unlikely to be obliterated by that of the winemaker's thumbprint. Many exceptional Chardonnays are made given the paucity of the total plantings, for this is liquid gold. In alphabetical order Bargetto's, Cinnabar, Cronin, David Bruce (on his day), Mount Eden, Page Mill (true, from Santa Clara), Ridge, Storrs and Woodside all excel; a personal top three would be Mount Eden, Ridge and Page Mill, with Bargetto's in hot pursuit.

CABERNET SAUVIGNON

A variety which attests to the very particular attributes of the region, for it achieves far greater ripeness, concentration and flavor than in any other Region I/low Region II area in California. Part of the explanation lies in the low yield and sparse canopy providing excellent exposure. The other part derives from the long hours of sunshine at typically moderate temperatures, which effectively provide more growing season heat than the summation would suggest. Indeed, the problem lies more with too much flavor and extraction than too little, with a number of producers still needing to pull back in their making. Bargetto's, Cronin, Kathryn Kennedy, Ridge and Woodside have mastered the art, although these are certainly not wines for the faint-hearted or impatient.

PINOT NOIR

These are wines which simply serve to underline emphatically the lessons of the Cabernet Sauvignon: that this is a warmer area than it appears at face value, and that it produces extremely concentrated grapes. Santa Cruz Mountain Vineyard's struggle to tame and control its fruit says it all, a struggle echoed, incidentally, at Thomas Fogarty. Over the years David Bruce and Mount Eden have produced some striking and voluptuous wines, but the seasonal conditions clearly play a deciding role in determining style for these two makers.

ZINFANDEL AND SYRAH

These are grown in tiny quantities, the latter in particular, but Dan Gehrs, who knows the mountains like the back of his hand, avers there are some great sites for Syrah (Randall Grahm concurs), while Zinfandel has proved its worth for a century. One might expect it to produce massive wines, but in fact it does not necessarily do so: some are downright elegant and spicy, as the ill-fated Congress Springs Winery demonstrated. Bonny Doon is the producer to watch.

MARSANNE AND ROUSSANNE

Acknowledged in deference to Bonny Doon's estate plantings, which give rise to Le Sophiste.

ABOVE ~ *Chardonnay "cake" at Mount Eden after the horizontal plate press has done its work.*

Randall Grahm: Rhone or Italy or ...

Anyone who has read and understood all of the literary creations and allusions in the Bonny Doon newsletters of the past five years either has or is entitled to a Master of Arts degree in English Literature, majoring in satire. James Joyce, T.S. Eliot, Proust, Mozart and Umberto Eco are among those who have inspired Randall Grahm's pen; the *Wine Spectator*, Robert Parker (in particular) and the Burro de Firecrackers, Alcoholico y Tabac — or BFAT — have all felt its lash. Like fellow philosopher Patrick Campbell of Laurel Glen, Randall Grahm is none too keen on points scores for wines, and even less tolerant of fools and bureaucrats.

He can also be disarmingly introspective. In "Don Giovese in Bakersfield," an *opera giacosa*, Lebrunello sings to Giovese (alias Grahm):

At the risk of being too bold
I've remarked a tendenza in you and I don't
mean to scold
Filosofos might call it a tragic flaw.
You don't like any grape, you seem to love them all.
At least for a season or two, until they no longer enthuse you
But by then you've found a new vitacious musa to amuse you.
Your grape inconstanza just makes my head spin.

Ca'del Solo
Big House Red

ABOVE ~ *The labels — and the names — conjured up by Randall Grahm for his Rhone-inspired wines are known the world over.*

Lebrunello expands on this theme at great length in a later aria, referring to the 35-acre vineyard which Grahm has planted near Soledad to a range of Italian varieties ranging from the well known to the exceedingly obscure. As at 1992 this venture was the official (if there be such a thing in the evanescent world of Bonny Doon) new direction for Grahm, but rumors abounded that he was already laying plans for the planting of equally obscure German varieties, while Lebrunello sings of Romanian and Albanian grapes which Giovese had discarded.

The Rhone Rangers, of which Randall Grahm was Crown Prince, are thoroughly upset at this lack of constancy, but in truth they have little cause for complaint. For it was the creation of the 1984 Le Cigare Volant which simultaneously brought Bonny Doon and the Rhone varietals on to center stage. As many know, the flying cigar label was prompted by a regulation passed by the town council of Chateauneuf-du-Pape in the 1950s which prohibited UFOs from landing in the region.

Le Cigare Volant remains the most important red wine in the Bonny Doon range, a varying blend of Grenache, Mourvedre and Syrah primarily sourced from Contra Costa but carrying a California appellation. I have seen the wine criticized (or damned by faint praise) and am unable to understand why: it is hard to imagine a more supple, fruity and immediately enjoyable red wine. The fact that it is wholly evocative of the wines of the southern Rhone Valley is beside the point, and it is not for this reason that I praise it. There are spices, redcurrant fruits and silky tannins in abundance, and it is equally irrelevant that the wine may benefit from some years in the cellar.

The red (and pink) Rhone wines are completed, for the time being at least, by Old Telegram, Clos de Gilroy, Vin Gris de Cigare, Grahm Crew Vin Rouge and Ca' Del Solo Big House Red. Old Telegram is a powerful, concentrated and (inevitably) slightly tough wine made from 100% Mourvedre, and will satisfy those who have a compulsion to put wine in their cellar rather than their mouth.

Clos de Gilroy is at the opposite end of the spectrum, a partial carbonic maceration wine made from Grenache, beefed up by a portion of conventionally made Grenache, but not so much as to alter its nouveau style. The other wines are house blends made up of bits and pieces left over, and are priced accordingly.

Le Sophiste (introduced from 1989) is the estate-grown Rhone White, made from 80% Marsanne and 20% Roussanne, a wine which is feverishly sought after simply because there is so little of it, and because (in California terms at least) it is so unusual. The fact that it is an exceptionally good wine is as like as not to go unremarked, as is its potential to evolve wonderfully with five or more years' bottle age.

As if responding to Lebrunello's strictures, Grahm admitted in his Fall 1990 newsletter:

It's Rhonely at the Top. The Italian obsession is a souffle du coeur (I am writing Miss Rhonely-hearts for advice on this matter) ... And at long last we are releasing Le Sophiste ... and our first Estate Syrah (both barrels) and the potential for this varietal in Bonny Doon knows no limit. We have acquired some additional acreage further up Ben Lomond Mountain and are hoping to see the law firm of Marsanne, Roussanne, Viognier and Syrah expand its practice.

So there is no question — for the time being — about Grahm's commitment to the Rhone varieties, but it is another matter whether this is simply due to the quixotic nature of his personality (and his marketing genius) or to a genuine belief in the quality of the wines. Whatever a truth drug might reveal, there are a considerable number of respected vignerons across the state who see a real future for the varieties.

Cline Cellars, recently established at the southern end of the Sonoma Valley, remains in control of much of the Contra Costa plantings used by Bonny Doon (and others). In Dry Creek, Preston Vineyards is one of the pacemakers; McDowell Valley Vineyards performs the role in Mendocino; Qupe in Santa Barbara County and Ojai in Ventura County are small but impressive makers; while the Phelps Vin du Mistral range is flagbearer in the Napa Valley.

The problem is putting the achievements of these and other makers into some kind of present and future perspective. There was a total of 310 acres of Mourvedre and 413 acres of Syrah as at 1991; only Grenache and Carignane are statistically important, and no one looks like taking up the cause of the latter as a grape of undiscovered quality. The white varieties of Roussanne, Marsanne and Viognier are not separately recorded in the California Agricultural Statistics Service, so small are the plantings.

Yet Viognier perfectly illustrates the fallibility of statistics: the November 30, 1992 issue of the *Wine Spectator*'s Buying Guide casually reviewed Viogniers from La Jota, Joseph Phelps, McDowell Valley, Alban, Preston and R.H. Phillips; Ritchie Creek, Field Stone and Qupe leap to mind as other producers, and there were yet more as at 1992, with many more in the pipeline.

Now I have some doubt about Viognier's adaptability to the wide range of climate and *terroir* in which it is being grown, and cannot help but observe how tiny its hold is in the viticultural regions of the world. But I have no doubt at all about the class and the adaptability of Syrah, which by any logic should become the cornerstone of the Rhone Rangers' burgeoning empire.

Grown in cool climates, it produces elegant, fragrant and spicy wines which neither need or deserve blending. In warmer regions it produces softer, fleshier wines which may well be advantaged by blending with Grenache and Mourvedre.

Grenache and Petite Sirah (the cross-bred grape which is in fact Durif and which I have not mentioned) also respond to the climate and *terroir* in which they are grown. If encouraged to crop heavily (which it certainly will) Grenache makes an ordinary, plain jug wine. If treated with respect it can produce wines which mirror Syrah, ranging from spicy and elegant to full blooded and fleshy.

ABOVE ~ *A grove of redwoods make an imposing portal to the Bonny Doon plantings.*

ABOVE ~ *Bird netting protecting Marsanne, Roussane, Viognier and Syrah in the Bonny Doon Vineyard.*

WINERIES *of* SANTA CRUZ MOUNTAINS

AHLGREN VINEYARD 1976

A: 20320 Highway 9, Boulder Creek, CA 95006 **T**: (408) 338 6071 **V**: By appointment **P**: 2,500 **W**: Dexter Ahlgren

Former engineer Dexter Ahlgren became interested in winemaking when his wife Val started making mead and elderberry wine. The latter in particular caused Dexter to become involved, and by 1972 he was crushing two tons of Zinfandel in the driveway of their suburban Sunnyvale home, the garage being converted to a wine cellar and the cars being left outside. In that same year the Ahlgrens purchased their Santa Cruz Mountains property on which the vineyard, house and winery are now situated, with the house so designed as to accommodate the winery underneath. The site is extremely steep, and only ten acres out of the 26 will be plantable; experimental work with rootstocks and clonal selections has confirmed the choice of Semillon, which will be progressively established. In the meantime Ahlgren sources Pinot Noir, Sauvignon Blanc and Chenin Blanc (planted in the early 1940s) and Semillon (planted in 1955) from the old Novitiate Vineyard, and Cabernet Sauvignon from the Bates Vineyard and Chardonnay from the Meyers Vineyard. Zinfandel is also due to return to the roster, having disappeared off the list for some time.

Barrel-fermented Chardonnay is the winery's forte, and can be outstanding, even if the choice of American oak for Chardonnay does not appeal to my palate; it may appeal to others more. The Cabernet Sauvignon is typical Santa Cruz Mountains stuff: immensely concentrated and tannic, and requiring both patience and faith.

BARGETTO'S SANTA CRUZ WINERY 1933

A: 3535 North Main Street, Soquel, CA 95073 **T**: (408) 475 2258 **V**: 10–5 daily **P**: 35,000 **W**: Paul Wofford

Bargetto's may be the oldest winery in the region, but it is certainly moving with the times. Situated in downtown Soquel, but backing on to a tree and fern-lined creek, it purchases all of its grapes, partly from the Santa Cruz Mountains, and partly throughout the Central Coast. It also purchases a variety of fruits to make astonishingly good fruit wines, vibrantly faithful and pure renditions of the base material, and by far the best I have tasted from any maker anywhere in the world. (From my early days as a judge, I speak with some authority in the matter, having judged all types of such wines, including such oddities as wines made from grass.)

The immaculately equipped winery now produces Dry Gewurztraminer, Sauvignon Blanc, a Central Coast Chardonnay, Santa Cruz Mountains Chardonnay, White Zinfandel and Gewurztraminer made medium dry, Pinot Noir, and four Cabernet Sauvignons — California, Cypress, Komes Ranch and Santa Cruz Mountains. The fruit wines are sold under the Chaucers label offering Plum, Raspberry, Olallieberry, Apricot and Mead. The Santa Cruz Mountains Chardonnay and Cabernet Sauvignon are absolutely exemplary examples. The Chardonnay is tightly structured, but elegant and intense, with very well-handled and subtly integrated oak. The Cabernet Sauvignon promises exceedingly long life, yet is neither tannic nor extractive: fresh dark berry fruits dominate both the bouquet and palate, and the tannins are in balance. If Bargetto's were more fashionable, it is quite certain that its wines would receive greater critical praise.

BONNY DOON VINEYARD 1983

A: 10 Pine Flat Road, Santa Cruz, CA 95060 **T**: (408) 425 3625 **V**: 12–5 Wed–Mon **P**: 20,000 **W**: Randall Grahm

The Catalyst
RED TABLE WINE
CALIFORNIA

ABOVE ~ *Sculpture à la Bonny Doon — by Skip Wagner.*

It is hard to tell at times whether Randall Grahm has really given up his former avocation of philosophy lecturer in the wake of establishing his vineyard in 1981. Initially, he intended to specialize in Pinot Noir and Chardonnay; Pinot Noir was eliminated first (although up to 1990 he flirted with Oregon Pinot Noir before announcing no more — or at least until he changes his mind), while Chardonnay (both estate-grown and purchased from Monterey) lived on death row for years, with innumerable last minute stays of execution, but was seemingly executed in 1992.

As I have recounted earlier, Grahm's attention over the second half of the 1980s was fixed on an array of Rhone Valley wines: the white Le Sophiste, a couple of blush or light reds, and then the big three reds of Clos de Gilroy, Old Telegram and the band and brand leader Le Cigare Volant. Some truly superb Eau de Vies (Cerise, Poire and Prunus), showing startlingly pure fruit flavors and technically perfect, are also part of the roster (until Grahm tires of them, which hopefully he will never do). The anchor at the end is the Vin de Glaciere, made from freeze-concentrated juice of Muscat Canelli, a totally delicious wine.

Other wines come and go; there is a quasi second label range of Ca' Del Solo, signalling the next direction, which is Italy. One can only hope that Grahm's business and bank managers remind him that the public has had the perception to recognize the quality of his Rhone Range, and that he will not forsake it.

DAVID BRUCE WINERY 1964

A: 21439 Bear Creek Road, Los Gatos, CA 95030 **T**: (408) 354 4214 **V**: 12–5 Thur–Sun **P**: 30,000 **W**: David Bruce

Dermatologist David Bruce fell in love with wine when he drank a bottle of 1954 Domaine de la Romanée-Conti Richebourg in the mid 1950s. This led directly to his becoming acquainted with Martin Ray, and to serving an apprenticeship with him. Small wonder, then, that David Bruce is regarded by all and sundry as having inherited the mantle of Martin Ray, and that many of his winemaking methods were

(and are) similar to those of Ray. Having graduated from medical school, and set up his dermatology practice in San Jose, David Bruce purchased his property on Bear Creek Road in the early 1960s, and planted 25 acres of vines, now extended to 30 acres. In the late 1950s and 1960s he was essentially a home winemaker, but in 1964 commenced the construction of the disconnected gaggle of buildings which now constitute the winery.

Over the next 13 years the fame of his wines reached as far afield as Australia, with bottles turning up in the most unlikely places, and opening majestically or dreadfully. Notwithstanding the fact that he retired for a time from active winemaking (he is now very much back in command), David Bruce is unwilling to admit that there has been any change in either his winemaking philosophy or in the wines themselves. He has no doubt that it is simply the media which has gone off at tangents of its own, and continues to do so. It seems to me that it has always been a dangerous practice to make generalized statements about the David Bruce wines, and that it remains dangerous to this day. Given his minimal handling philosophy, reliance on lees contact rather than sulfur dioxide to protect the wines pre-bottling, not to mention a disposition which encourages the wine to show its own personality, it is not surprising that style (and quality) should be variable.

At their best, the wines are powerful, complex and emphatic in their statement. The Pinots can range from earthy to sappy, from vegetal bitterness through to ripe, concentrated sweet plummy fruit. The Chardonnays can show somewhat flabby canned pineapple flavor or marvelously complex and concentrated toasty/nutty aromas and flavors. The Zinfandels run from being stemmy and green, through to elegant wines with delicious cigar box and spice aromas and flavors. Whatever else, life is never dull with David Bruce wines; I suspect his one-time mentor Martin Ray would approve.

BYINGTON WINERY & VINEYARDS 1990

A: 21850 Bear Creek Road, Los Gatos, CA 95030 **T**: (408) 354 1111 **V**: 11–5 daily **P**: 12,000 **W**: Greg Bruni

The opulent Byington Winery-cum-sales area-cum-wedding reception facility is spectacularly sited over the eight acres of terraced estate Pinot Noir vineyards (producing their first commercial harvest in 1993), thence out over a redwood forest to Monterey Bay. Bill Byington runs Byington Steel, so the 25,000-case capacity winery lacks for nothing.

Winemaker Greg Bruni's family owned the once very large San Martin Winery, where Bruni worked in his teens before graduating from U.C. Davis and then working at Bandiera and Arciero Wineries, until he joined Byington in 1988. Between that year and 1990 the wines were produced under custom crush arrangements, but are now made at the Italianate Byington chateau. Even when the estate plantings of Pinot Noir come into production (together with a tiny plot of Syrah which will be sold exclusively at cellar door), the accent will be on grapes purchased elsewhere.

The range comprises of Chardonnay and Cabernet Sauvignon from the Napa Valley, Sauvignon Blanc variously described as coming from the Livermore Valley and from the Ventana Vineyard in Monterey, and a California appellation Pinot Noir made from Santa Barbara, Monterey and Napa Valley grapes. All of the initial releases were dull, many showing evidence of oxidation. One can only assume that better things are in store for the future.

ABOVE ~ *The Santa Cruz coastline, as imposing as the mountains themselves.*

CINNABAR VINEYARD & WINERY 1983

A: 23000 Congress Springs Road, Saratoga, CA 95071 **T**: (408) 741 5858
V: By appointment **P**: 5,000 **W**: Tom Mudd

Even by the exceptional standards of the Santa Cruz Mountains, Cinnabar is a spectacular vineyard and winery. Tom Mudd found the property by locating it from a helicopter, not surprising if you have driven up the extraordinarily long private access road to the 1,650 feet ridgetop site. The former Stanford PhD research engineer gave up laser spectroscopy in 1982 to develop Cinnabar, and together with his wife, Melissa Frank, supervised the clearing, terracing and planting of 24 acres of Chardonnay and Cabernet Sauvignon on the mountainside property. The Chardonnay came from Mount Eden, and is said to be the Corton Charlemagne clone; the Cabernet Sauvignon had its ancestry at La Questa and, before that, Chateau Margaux. A state-of-the-art winery was completed in 1987, the product of visiting more than 50 wineries specifically to look at design and function, and also from first-hand experience gained in working at several local wineries. An external crush pad at the highest level feeds in to seven fermentation tanks arranged in a circle on the second level, with the barrel storage down at the third (and lowest) level. Mudd chose the Cinnabar name because, he says, "I, as a winemaker, think of myself as an alchemist," referring to the blood red ore called cinnabar, from which comes mercury.

The Cabernet Sauvignon has an almost Chinon-like feel and weight, being distinctly herbal but possessing elegance. The Chardonnay is very good, much weightier and more complex, with nutty flavors and a fleshy, creamy texture.

CRONIN VINEYARDS 1980

A: 11 Old La Honda Road, Woodside, CA 94062 **T**: (415) 851 1452 **V**: By appointment
P: 2,000 **W**: Roger Givens

Former Silicon Valley computer executive Duane Cronin finally made his mistress his wife when he retired from the computer industry in 1992, and winemaking became his sole business. With county ordinances restricting him to his present production level of 2,000 cases, and with the huge and unsatisfied demand for his Chardonnays, it will be interesting to see whether he is content with his basement winery. The demand stems from two factors: he makes up to four Chardonnays and two Cabernets each year, with a maximum of 400 cases of any one wine. Then there is the extraordinary reputation that the wines have garnered for themselves. Duane Cronin is unashamedly Burgundian in his approach, and is very much the self-taught winemaker, having graduated from home winemaking via extension courses conducted by Bruce Rector (now chief winemaker at Glen Ellen).

He buys Chardonnay from the Alexander Valley, from Monterey (Ventana Vineyards) and from the Napa Valley, and makes each of these separately. He also buys grapes from Santa Cruz Mountains; in most years the production from the one acre of estate vines in front of the house goes into the Santa Cruz Mountains wine, but occasionally it is released as a separate estate wine. Cronin does not greatly modify his handling techniques for each region, although he uses less malolactic fermentation with the Ventana fruit than with the Alexander Valley fruit (the reverse of what one might expect, but it does make sense) and, where he "likes the taste of the dirt," will only roughly settle the wine after pressing — this for the Santa Cruz Mountains wine.

The Chardonnays are complex, rich and full flavored, showing obvious ambient barrel ferment temperature characteristics and, to a lesser degree, the influence of the low-vigor yeast used in their making. The Santa Cruz Mountains Cabernet Sauvignon can be every bit as good, if not better: it has dark berry and dark chocolate fruit flavors, abundantly sweet and with perfectly balanced tannins.

THOMAS FOGARTY WINERY 1982

A: 19501 Skyline Boulevard, Woodside, CA 94062 **T**: (415) 851 1946 **V**: By appointment
P: 7,500 **W**: Michael Martella

Cardiovascular surgeon and inventor Dr. Thomas Fogarty purchased a 300-acre property at a 2,000-feet elevation above the Portola Valley in 1968, but did not start to establish the vineyards until 1978, when he began the development of 18 acres of Chardonnay and seven acres of Pinot Noir. The winery was built in time for the 1981 vintage, but both then and now buys the major part of its annual crush from vineyards from within and without the Santa Cruz Mountains appellation. Like Byington, the spectacularly situated facility specializes in wedding receptions and high-flying parties, which has led to the production of some rather indifferent sparkling wine to complement the table wine range.

Three Chardonnays (from Monterey Ventana, Edna Valley and Santa Cruz Mountains), a Gewurztraminer from Monterey's Ventana Vineyards, an estate Pinot Noir and a Napa Valley (Steltzner Vineyard) Cabernet Sauvignon are regularly offered. The one consistently outstanding wine in the line-up is the Gewurztraminer, which wins sweepstakes and gold medal awards with monotonous regularity, the lychee-accented 1991 being no exception. The estate Pinot Noirs are very firm and surprisingly closed, lacking the fragrance and delicacy which by rights ought to be the hallmark of the variety. There are some dark cherry fruit flavors there, and it was planned to release a Reserve Pinot Noir from the 1991 vintage. Tasted from barrel, that wine was certainly impressive in its power, but needed a lot of work to bring out its fruit.

HALLCREST VINEYARDS 1987

A: 379 Felton Empire Road, Felton, CA 95018 **T**: (408) 335 4441 **V**: 11–5.30 daily
P: 17,000 **W**: John Schumacher

The original Hallcrest Vineyard was established by lawyer Chaffee Hall in the 1940s; its

ABOVE ~ *The tally clerk keeps track of the number of buckets each vineyard worker picks.*

reputation for Cabernet Sauvignon in particular was outstanding. In 1992 a bottle of 1964 Cabernet still showed exceptionally youthful, sweet fruit, with a fine, delicate and lingering finish, giving every indication it would handle the next 25 years as easily as it had handled the first. Hall closed the winery before his death in 1969, and the estate-grown Riesling and Cabernet grapes were sold to Concannon until the vineyard was leased by a partnership in 1976, and reopened as Felton-Empire Vineyards. Felton-Empire initially picked up where Hallcrest had left off, being particularly noted for its Rieslings, both dry and botrytised. But by the mid 1980s financial and other problems began to set in, and in 1988 the remaining 4.7 acres of Riesling and the winery were purchased by the Schumacher family. John Schumacher had previously made wine under the Davis Wine Cellars and Shumacher Cellars labels in the garage of his house at Davis, which had been bonded in 1984. When he arrived at Santa Cruz, the Hall family gave him permission to revive the Hallcrest label, thus (more or less) completing the circle.

Schumacher is one of those quicksilver characters, a disposition evident as he trots around the winery with baby daughter strapped to his back, and in the range of conventional and organic wines and grape juices constantly on offer. The 1992 production of 17,000 cases will be made up from 17 different wines. The organic wines are released under the Organic Wine Works label, and are what they claim: in other words, made from organically grown grapes without the use of sulfur in the making process. Together with Frey, they are the only organic wines nationally distributed (as at 1992). The range is exceptionally wide, comprising a Fumé Blanc and a Semillon from the Napa Valley, a Chardonnay from Sonoma (claimed to be the first organic Chardonnay produced in California), Pinot Noir from Sonoma, Merlot from the Napa Valley and Barbera and Zinfandel from Amador County, together with a proprietary red called "A Notre Terre." Viewed as a range, the wines are of better quality than those of Frey, even if they do show some evidence of oxidation. Certainly, they should be consumed promptly after purchase, and under no circumstances should they be cellared.

The conventionally made wines are likewise adequate, the most interesting being the estate-grown Riesling, with its exceptionally powerful flavor and structure deriving from the very low yielding, old, dry-farmed vines.

KATHRYN KENNEDY WINERY 1979

A: 13180 Pierce Road, Saratoga, CA 95070
T: (408) 867 4170 **V**: By appointment
P: 1,000 **W**: Martin Mathis

This, surely, is one of the most remarkable of all California wineries. The vineyard was established in 1973 by Kathryn Kennedy with the aim of discouraging real estate development, occupying land which even then had a very high value, let alone now. But she took her task seriously, attending viticulture courses at U.C. Davis and deciding to plant Cabernet Sauvignon only after extensive consultation on the most appropriate variety. The original eight-acre planting was in fact extended with another one-and-a-half acres being planted in 1988.

In 1980 younger son Martin Mathis constructed the tiny insulated wooden shed which constitutes the micro-winery. From then until 1988 annual production varied between a low of 150 cases and a maximum of 600 cases, dipping to 200 cases in 1988 and to 150 cases in 1990. The 1988 crop led to the introduction of a second wine called Lateral, a Bordeaux blend of Merlot and Cabernet Franc which deliberately carries a simple California appellation, as Mathis wishes to have complete freedom to vary his vineyard sources from year to year (and the blend too).

At its low elevation, the Cabernet vineyard is the warmest site in the Santa Cruz Mountains, and this reflects in the exceptionally rich and concentrated style of the wine. Mathis says he is trying to make the most intense, gutsy and old-fashioned style possible, believing that refinement and elegance will come during bottle development rather than through the winemaking process. I think Mathis downplays his role: the 1991 wine tasted ex-barrel was a quite lovely wine, generously proportioned, to be sure, but lacking nothing in refinement.

At this scale it is "a very difficult business to make a living out of," observes Mathis in a masterly understatement. The Kathryn Kennedy wine retails for $45 a bottle (as at 1992), Lateral at $16.50. Even at those prices, this is a labor of love.

MOUNT EDEN VINEYARDS 1972

A: 22020 Mount Eden Road, Saratoga, CA 95070 **T**: (408) 867 5832 **V**: By appointment
P: 7,500 **W**: Jeffrey Patterson

The establishment date of 1972 in fact marks the end of a celebrated and protracted court battle which saw Mount Eden Vineyards purchase the top half of the mountainside property established in the early 1940s by Martin Ray, and Martin Ray retreating to the bottom half with the Martin Ray Vineyard name under which he had previously traded (and in fact continued to trade until 1983, shortly prior to his death). The vineyard acquired a legendary reputation during the Martin Ray days, a reputation justified by the several bottles of very old Martin Ray wines I have been privileged to drink.

After a period of uncertainty, the Mount Eden Chardonnays, in particular, have returned to the illustrious heights of bygone days. Production from the old estate plantings of Pinot Noir and Chardonnay, going back to 1943, are minuscule. Pinot Noir averages 200 cases a year, Chardonnay 800, and the wines are sold on

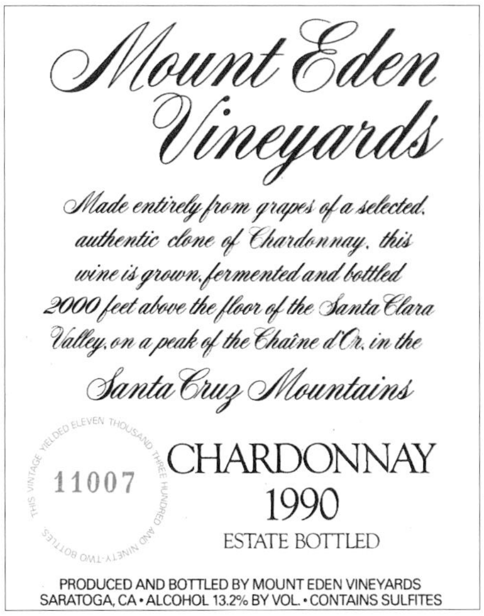
Mount Eden Vineyards
Made entirely from grapes of a selected, authentic clone of Chardonnay, this wine is grown, fermented and bottled 2000 feet above the floor of the Santa Clara Valley, on a peak of the Chaîne d'Or, in the Santa Cruz Mountains
11007
CHARDONNAY
1990
ESTATE BOTTLED
PRODUCED AND BOTTLED BY MOUNT EDEN VINEYARDS
SARATOGA, CA • ALCOHOL 13.2% BY VOL. • CONTAINS SULFITES

strict allocation even through the mailing list. The estate-grown Cabernets are released in two versions: Lathweisen Ridge from plantings at the 1,400 foot level (the Chardonnay and Pinot at 1,800 to 2,000 feet) established at the end of the 1970s, and the Estate Cabernet Sauvignon (simply so labeled) from the Cabernet planted in the 1950s. Around 600 cases of each of these two wines are also released, again on allocation. The volume comes from 4,000 cases of non-estate Chardonnay, formerly purchased from the MacGregor Vineyard in the Edna Valley, but in 1990 coming from the Sierra Madre and Cottonwood Canyon vineyards. This is augmented by small releases of non-estate Pinot Noir.

The Estate Chardonnay is a glorious wine, with freakish concentration and richness, yet avoiding heaviness. The Santa Barbara County version suffers in comparison to the Estate wine, but not in comparison to any other Chardonnays. The Cabernet Sauvignon, too, is exceedingly stylish, with a touch of briary, stemmy character offset by deep, redcurrant fruit: these briary touches are wholly desirable, I should add. I find the Pinot Noir to be (in relative terms) the least of the three wines, but still of well above average quality: certainly, it lacks nothing in intensity and power.

PAGE MILL WINERY 1976

A: 13686 Page Mill Road, Los Altos Hills, CA 94022 **T**: (415) 948 0958 **V**: By appointment
P: 2,000 **W**: Dick Stark

Dick Stark turned home-hobby winemaking into a business when he excavated a large cellar under the family home in the foothills behind Stanford University in 1976. It is a winery without vineyards of its own, focusing instead on a simple philosophy: purchase each grape variety from a vineyard and region which you feel can provide the best possible wine. Thus it is that two Chardonnays are made, one from the

Elizabeth Garbett Vineyard in Santa Clara, and one from the Bien Nacido Vineyard in Santa Barbara; the Sauvignon Blanc comes from French Camp Vineyard in San Luis Obispo; Zinfandel and Cabernet Sauvignon from Volker Eisele's Vineyard in the Chiles Valley; and Pinot Noir from the Bien Nacido Vineyard in Santa Barbara.

I cannot speak too highly of the overall quality of the Page Mill wines. Dick Stark is an exceptionally talented winemaker, treating all of his varieties with sensitivity and skill. The oak handling throughout is subtle but positive; the wines are invariably elegant, and not overworked or overextracted; and varietal fruit expression is given free play, without compromising complexity. Outstanding amongst a range of consistently good wines are the Elizabeth Garbett Chardonnay, the Bien Nacido Pinot Noir and the French Camp Sauvignon Blanc — but I would cheerfully have any of the wines on my table at any time.

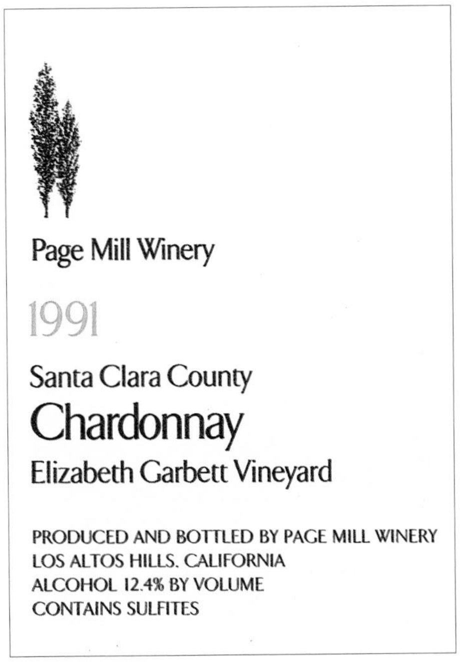
Page Mill Winery
1991
Santa Clara County
Chardonnay
Elizabeth Garbett Vineyard
PRODUCED AND BOTTLED BY PAGE MILL WINERY
LOS ALTOS HILLS, CALIFORNIA
ALCOHOL 12.4% BY VOLUME
CONTAINS SULFITES

RIDGE VINEYARDS 1962

A: 17100 Monte Bello Road, Cupertino, CA 95015 **T**: (408) 867 3233 **V**: 10–3 daily **P**: 40,000 **W**: Paul Draper

Ridge's standing as one of the top half dozen California wineries is, in bank parlance, undoubted. It draws upon a fabulous history, great vineyard sources, and the genius of chief executive and chief winemaker Paul Draper. That history goes back to 1885 when Osea Perrone purchased 180 acres near the top of Monte Bello Ridge, terracing the slopes, planting the vineyard and constructing the Monte Bello Winery using limestone quarried nearby. It is this cellar, built into the mountainside on three levels at an elevation of 2,600 feet, which now serves as the Ridge production facility. The next strand of history was woven in 1949, when theologian William Short purchased the Torre Winery and Vineyard just below the Monte Bello Winery, replanting the vineyard to Cabernet Sauvignon. It was this property which three Stanford Research Institute engineers (together with their families) purchased in 1959, making ten gallons of estate Cabernet in that year.

The venture grew steadily but slowly, with the Monte Bello Winery being rebonded in time for the 1962 vintage, which produced the famed Monte Bello Cabernet Sauvignon of that year: it was one of an array of extraordinary bottles Darrell Corti served me in 1992, still resplendent with its dark chocolate and mint fruit flavors and aromas. In 1964 the first Ridge Zinfandel was made from vines planted in the nineteenth century on the neighboring Pichetti Ranch, followed in 1966 by the first Geyserville Zinfandel. During the first half of the 1960s, the founding families spent all of their weekends and holidays reclaiming the Monte Bello terraces, increasing the vineyard size from 15 to 45 acres, and of course making the wines.

But even by 1967, when Ridge Vineyards was incorporated, and Dave Bennion gave up his job at the Research Institute to become president, production was still less than 3,000 cases a year. From that point on, however, output was to increase rapidly, as Ridge established its pattern of purchasing Zinfandel from Lytton Springs Vineyard in Dry Creek, from Geyserville, from Howell Mountain and from York Creek and Paso Robles; Cabernet Sauvignon from Jimsomare and York Creek; Merlot from Bradford Mountain; Chardonnay from Howell Mountain; and Petite Sirah from York Creek. The production mix is now 40% Cabernet Sauvignon and Merlot, 40% Zinfandel, 15% Chardonnay and 5% Petite Sirah.

Of equal importance was the arrival of Paul Draper in 1969, who has since been instrumental in shaping the direction of the winery (it is in fact now Japanese-owned), and the style of the wines. To say that quality is exemplary is to very nearly damn the wines by faint praise, although it is a difficult task to decide which are the most outstanding. On its day, the Chardonnay can outpoint them all, with super-sophisticated barrel ferment oak handling and voluptuous fruit, however much the traditionalists might support the dark, textured classic Zinfandel from Lytton Springs (which as a matter of interest has 10% Petite Sirah, 6% Carignane and 4% Grenache incorporated for extra complexity), or however highly the Monte Bello Cabernet Sauvignon, with its powerful, clean blackcurrant cassis fruit augmented by charred oak might rate. The Geyserville Red Rhone, made up of 64% Zinfandel, 18% Petite Sirah and 18% Carignane, is in fact in the same Olympian class, gloriously fruity and voluptuous, with intense, ripe blackcurrant and dark cherry fruit oozing out of every pore.

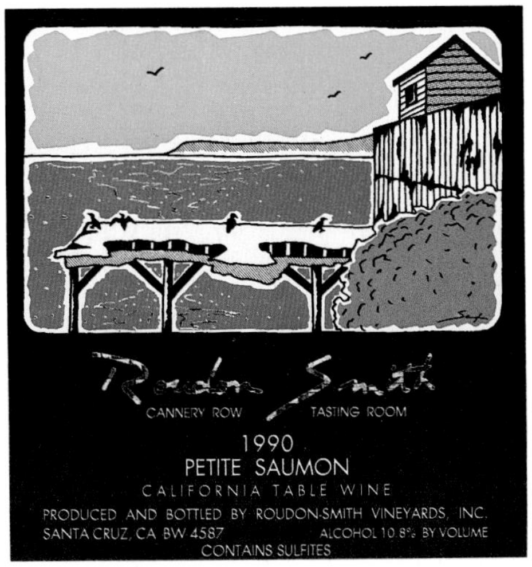
CANNERY ROW TASTING ROOM
1990
PETITE SAUMON
CALIFORNIA TABLE WINE
PRODUCED AND BOTTLED BY ROUDON-SMITH VINEYARDS, INC.
SANTA CRUZ, CA BW 4587 ALCOHOL 10.8% BY VOLUME
CONTAINS SULFITES

ROUDON-SMITH VINEYARDS 1972

A: 2364 Bean Creek Road, Scotts Valley, CA 95066 **T**: (408) 438 1244 **V**: 11–4:30 Sat–Sun at winery; daily except Tues at 807 Cannery Row, Monterey **P**: 6,000 **W**: Bob Roudon

Bob Roudon and Jim Smith were electrical engineers working for Amdahl in its heyday. Bob was an amateur winemaker, and as the value of Amdahl stock which the two received as part of their salary package rose, so did their thoughts of establishing their own vineyard and winery. In 1972 Bob Roudon quit, and the partners acquired their remote but beautiful winery and vineyard site deep in the redwood-clad Scotts Valley. The following year Jim Smith retired, and the two built the wooden winery which was completed by 1978.

The roster of wines, and the quantity produced, has varied somewhat from year to year, but is anchored in five acres of estate Chardonnay featured on the somewhat alarming labels, with their vivid purple border surrounding the photograph of the very green vineyards. Cabernet is purchased from the Cienega Valley, Zinfandel from west Paso Robles, Petite Sirah likewise; Pinot Noir formerly came from the Cox Vineyard in Santa Cruz Mountains, but Pierce's Disease has now eliminated that source. Overall, wine quality is solid, without setting the pulse racing. The Estate Chardonnay, with its apple, camphor and mint flavors is the best bet.

SANTA CRUZ MOUNTAIN VINEYARD 1974

A: 2300 Jarvis Road, Santa Cruz, CA 95065 **T**: (408) 426 6209 **V**: By appointment **P**: 3,500 **W**: Ken Burnap and Jeff Emery

The Santa Cruz Mountains madness so vividly described by Matt Kramer in *Making Sense of California Wine* is nowhere more evident than at Santa Cruz Mountain. How anyone could have found their way to this wild, remote and craggy spot in 1853 to plant vines is as incomprehensible as Ken Burnap's decision to purchase the property in the late 1960s and painstakingly establish 13 acres of Pinot Noir and one acre of Chardonnay, clinging to the dry-farmed mountainside. The most the vines have ever yielded is 1.2 tons to the acre in the boom vintage of 1980; a normal yield is half a ton to the acre.

Cabernet Sauvignon of similar dimension is purchased from the Bates Ranch in the Santa Cruz Mountains; Merlot has from time to time been acquired from Central Coast appellations; while the first Cabernet Franc was made (in tiny quantities) in the 1991 vintage. Matt Kramer has written that Santa Cruz Mountain Vineyard underwent a change in 1985, when Ken Burnap decided to lighten the style; I simply cannot imagine what it must have been like before that point. The hillside winery relies on gravity, and the grapes are fed direct to the open six-ton fermenters. Forty per cent whole clusters are now added in an endeavor to control the tannins, and the wines are pressed at dryness after being punched down six times a day. (Extended maceration during the 1970s failed to polymerize the tannins, instead magnifying them.) Throughout the accent is on minimal handling, with extended barrel age (14 months for the Pinot Noir and 26 months for the Cabernet Sauvignon), followed by two years in bottle intended to partially tame and soften the wines prior to their release.

Notwithstanding this, the wines are of heroic dimensions, and inevitably will polarize opinion. They cannot be judged by normal standards, and must be absolutely respected for their authenticity.

STORRS WINERY 1988

A: 303 Portero Street, #35, Santa Cruz, CA 95060 **T**: (408) 458 5030 **V**: 12–5 Mon–Fri **P**: 3,000 **W**: Stephen and Pamela Storrs

By strict logic, Storrs should be included in the chapter on warehouse wineries, for it is a warehouse (no more no less) that it inhabits, and which was indeed the original Frick Winery. I include it here in the Santa Cruz section for two reasons: firstly, it is situated within Santa Cruz, and secondly, the Storrs are fanatic advocates of the Santa Cruz Mountains region, sourcing all three of their Chardonnays (which constitute the major part of the output) from Santa Cruz Mountains vineyards. Husband and wife Stephen and Pamela share the winemaking responsibilities: both are graduates of U.C. Davis, and both worked at Felton-Empire (now Hallcrest) before starting their own venture out of the old Frick warehouse. Says Stephen Storr emphatically, "Santa Cruz Mountains is the best region for Chardonnay in the State," pointing to the southwest corner of the area as providing wines with backbone, acidity and longevity from the Region I climate. They purchase their grapes from vineyards owned by the wife of Robert Louis Stevenson at the turn of the century, rejoicing under the names of Vanumanutagi, Treasure Island, Jekyll, Hyde, and Kidnapped. In fact, their label uses the unpronouncable Vanumanutagi, together with the Meyley Vineyard from Bonny Doon and the Gaspar Vineyard overlooking the village of Saratoga. These three are released as single-vineyard wines, with the Santa Cruz Mountains Chardonnay being a blend of the three, and made in the greatest volume.

The wines are given the full treatment: barrel fermentation in a high percentage of new French oak, 100% malolactic fermentation, and prolonged lees contact. The result is extremely rich, concentrated and stylish wines, with pronounced nutty/bready/yeasty characters from the malolactic fermentation. But just to prove they are not simply Chardonnay makers, their 1990 Merlot from the San Ysidro Vineyard in Santa Clara County was ajudged the Best Wine from the Greater Bay Appellation Region at the 1992 California State Fair, winning a gold medal along the way. A Ventana Vineyard White Riesling (also a gold medal winner) and Monterey County Gewurztraminer and a Beauregard Vineyard Zinfandel round off a portfolio of classy wines.

SUNRISE WINERY 1976

A: 1300 Monte Bello Road, Cupertino, CA 95014 **T**: (408) 741 1310 **V**: 11–3 Fri–Sun **P**: 2,000 **W**: Rolayne Stortz

Sunrise had its origins in a different location and with a rather larger partnership: Rolayne and Ron Stortz now own the business, and in 1983 acquired the historic Picchetti Ranch, from which Ridge had made its first Zinfandel. This 95-year-old three-acre planting provides Sunrise with its precious Zinfandel; a four-acre Cabernet Sauvignon vineyard between Saratoga and Los Gatos is also managed by them. In addition, they purchase two Chardonnays from Santa Cruz vineyards situated between the 1,300 and 1,700 foot level, and Pinot Noir from San Ysidro, while Pinot Blanc and an Italian blend from 1991 (with a Nebbiolo planned for 1992) complete a varied range of wines, almost all of which are made in tiny quantities.

All of the wines are made in the Pichetti Winery, which has been painstakingly restored, and which provides a super-sized cellar door sales and excellent function area in the vast upper story. The Zinfandel is as deeply concentrated and powerful as one might expect, with strong cherry fruit, the Pinot Noir from San Ysidro showing entirely unexpected verve and style, with sappy sweet fruit, minimal oak, and an unusually long finish.

WOODSIDE VINEYARDS 1960

A: 340 Kings Mountain Road, Woodside, CA 94062 **T**: (415) 851 3144 **V**: By appointment **P**: 1,800 **W**: Brian Caselden

Bob Mullen purchased his Woodside property back in 1961, building his house in 1962, following with the winery and underground cellars. Urban pressure is substantial, even though the houses are often hidden in the pretty, twisting, timbered valleys. Thus Woodside controls 40 acres of vineyards all told, but the largest (including its own estate plantings of Chardonnay and Pinot Noir) is four acres, with 15 growers involved. One of the most precious single acres is the 1882 La Questa Cabernet vineyard, which produced the utterly memorable 1938 Woodside Cabernet (under the La Questa name) served to me in 1992 by Darrell Corti. A wine of my birth year, it is in decidedly better condition than I, a flawless wine still with all of its varietal fruit flavor intact. The Woodside range comprises Chardonnay, French Colombard, Pinot Noir (all 45 cases), Gewurztraminer, Zinfandel and Cabernet Sauvignon. Winemaker Brian Caselden (who doubles up as vineyard manager) does his work well: the Chardonnay, with citric, mandarin peel and melon notes is lively and well balanced; and the Cabernet Sauvignon with plenty of attractive, clean, sweet berry fruit and well-controlled tannins, augmented by a touch of American oak.

OTHER WINERIES

CRESCINI WINES 1980
A: P.O. Box 216, Soquel, CA 95073
T: (408) 462 146 **W**: Richard Crescini

DEVLIN WINE CELLARS 1978
A: P.O. Box 728, Soquel, CA 95073
T: (408) 476 7288 **W**: Charles Devlin

FELLOM RANCH VINEYARDS 1987
A: 17075 Montebello Road, Cupertino, CA 95014 **T**: (408) 741 0307 **W**: Roy S. Fellom and Mike Daggett

MCHENRY VINEYARD 1980
A: Bonny Doon Road, Santa Cruz, CA 95060
T: (916) 756 3202 **W**: Henry McHenry

OBESTER WINERY 1977
A: 12341 San Mateo Road, Half Moon Bay, CA 94019 **T**: (415) 726 9463 **W**: Bruce Regalia

RIVER RUN
A: 65 Rogge Lane, Watsonville, CA 95076
T: (408) 726 3112 **W**: J.P. Pawloski

SALAMANDRE WINE CELLARS 1973
A: 108 Don Carlos Drive, Aptos, CA 95003
T: (408) 685 0321 **W**: F. Wells Shoemaker, M.D.

SHERRILL CELLARS 1973
A: 1185 Skyline Boulevard, Palo Alto, CA 94302
T: (415) 851 1932 **W**: Nathaniel D. Sherrill

P. & M. STAIGER 1973
A: 1300 Hopkins Gulch Road, Boulder Creek, CA 95006 **T**: (408) 338 4346 **W**: Paul Staiger

ZAYANTE VINEYARDS 1988
A: 420 Old Mountain Road, Felton, CA 95018
T: (408) 335 7992 **W**: Gregory Nolten

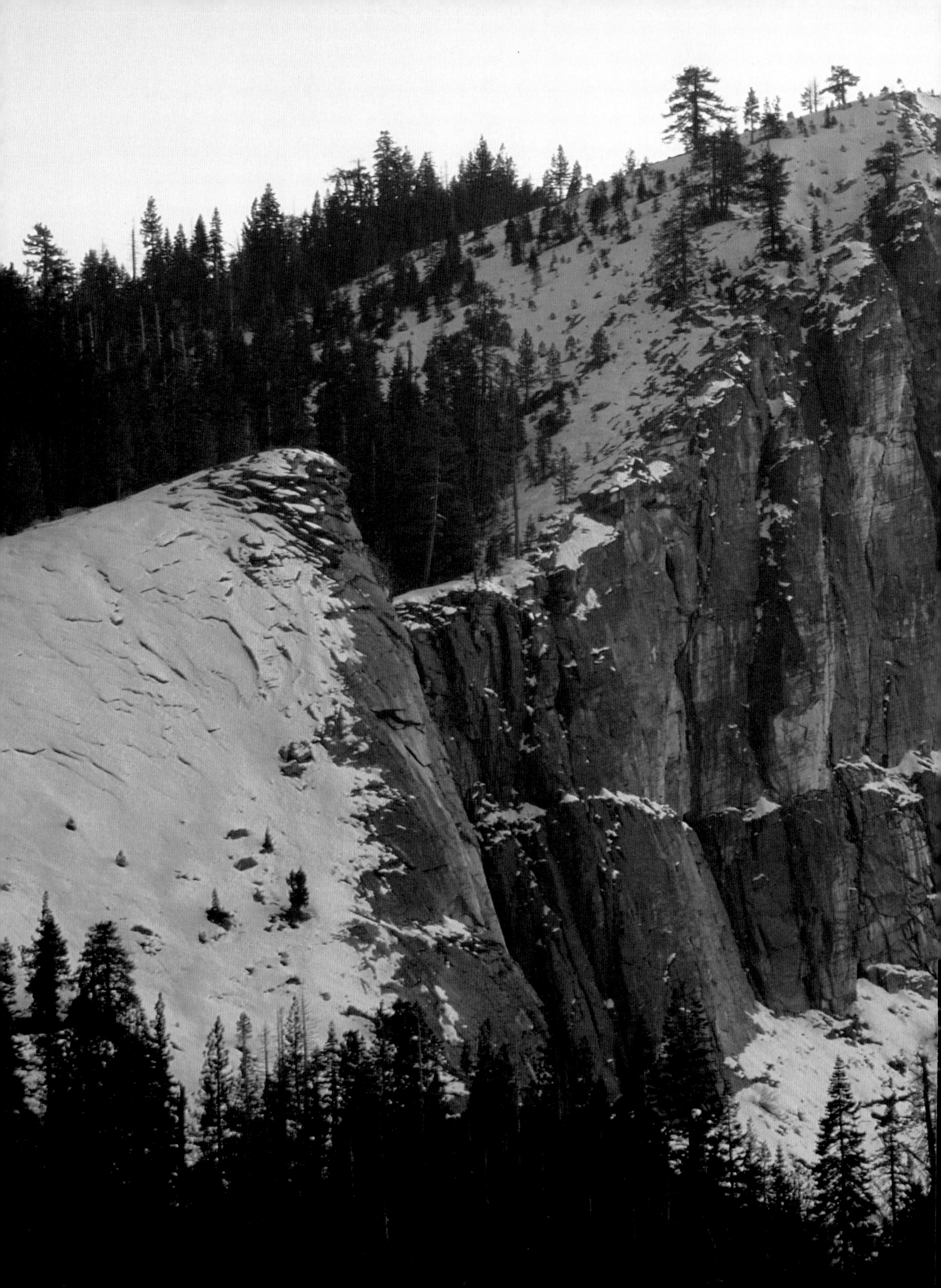

SIERRA FOOTHILLS

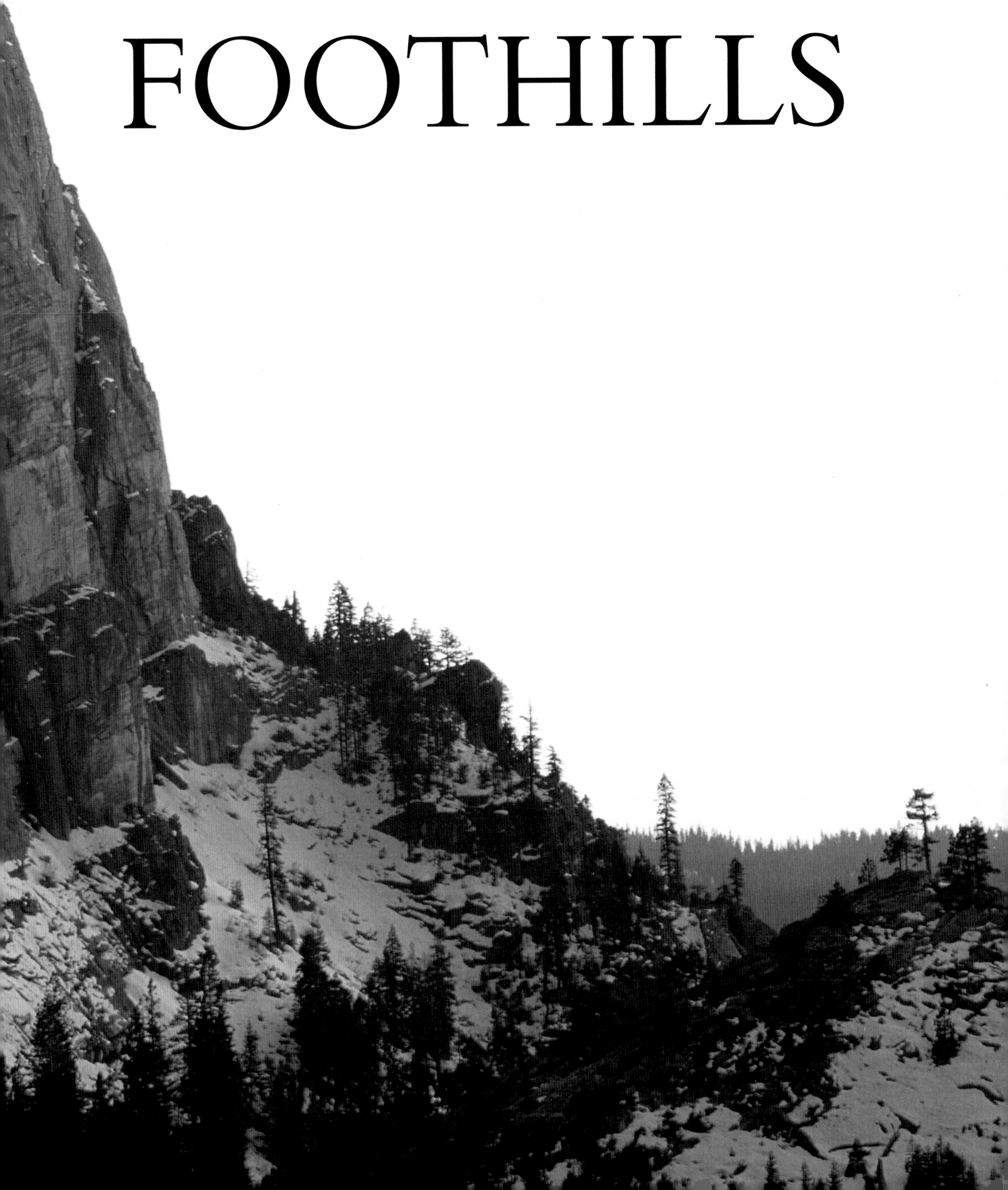

The Sierra Foothills AVA stretches like an elongated sausage 160 miles south from the northern boundary of Yuba County to the southern boundary of Mariposa County, nestling all the way in the foothills of the towering Sierra Range. Highway 49 runs more or less precisely up its center, passing through the historic gold towns of Sonora, Angels Camp, Jackson, Sutter Creek, Plymouth, Placerville, Coloma, Auburn and Nevada City. The application for an Amador AVA (coinciding with the boundaries of Amador County) scheduled to be filed with the BATF at the end of 1992 will do much to tidy up what was previously a jigsaw puzzle. It will subsume the existing Fiddletown and Shenandoah Valley AVAs and mean that the sausage will be effectively cut into four parts: North Yuba, El Dorado, Amador and Calaveras.

Driving along Highway 49 is a great experience, provided you are not in a hurry. It is easy to think that the road is a testing ground for all of America's mobile homes, usually driven by very careful retired couples whose timetable is distinctly different from that of the rest of the world. But it must be expected, for this is essentially a world of tourists, holiday makers and retirees.

The sense of history is palpable, not just in the gold towns but also in the feeling of the countryside. The road twists and turns endlessly, rising and falling, with streams and creek beds criss-crossing everywhere. It is a region of constantly changing beauty that somehow always remains intimate. History also comes in the form of the old Zinfandel vines which survived the long break between the onset of Prohibition and the renaissance of the 1970s. Only one winery of the 100 existing at the turn of the century showed the same resilience: D'Agostini's, which is now Sobon Estate and which has been turned into a wine museum (the Sobon Estate wines are made at Shenandoah Vineyards, which is under the same ownership).

The first winery in Amador to open its doors after Prohibition was Montevina, founded in 1973 by the Gott family and purchased in 1988 by Sutter Home, which has had such a profound influence on the region and its crown jewel, Zinfandel. Boeger founded El Dorado in the same year (1973), while Stevenot followed suit for Calaveras County in 1974.

Since that time there has been a modest increase in the number of wineries (and a few closures along the way). But what of the future? There is an interesting school of thought which says it just could be very bright. Napa boomed in the 1960s, Sonoma in the 1970s, the Central Coast in the 1980s; why not the Sierra Foothills in the 1990s?

The rolling hills and valleys may deter the larger companies from establishing the vast vineyards one finds in the San Joaquin Valley, but that is no bad thing. If there is to be a mini-boom in the Sierras, it is appropriate that it should be driven by small to medium sized wineries specialising in direct sales.

There has always been a tremendous synergy between wine and tourism, and the tourist industry worldwide is one of certain and continuous growth in the future. The Sierras are a prime tourist region already; land is relatively cheap, and much of the climate is ideally suited to the Italian and Rhone varietals, themselves harbingers of the future.

Sierra Foothills
1971 and 1991 Acreage/Grape Varieties

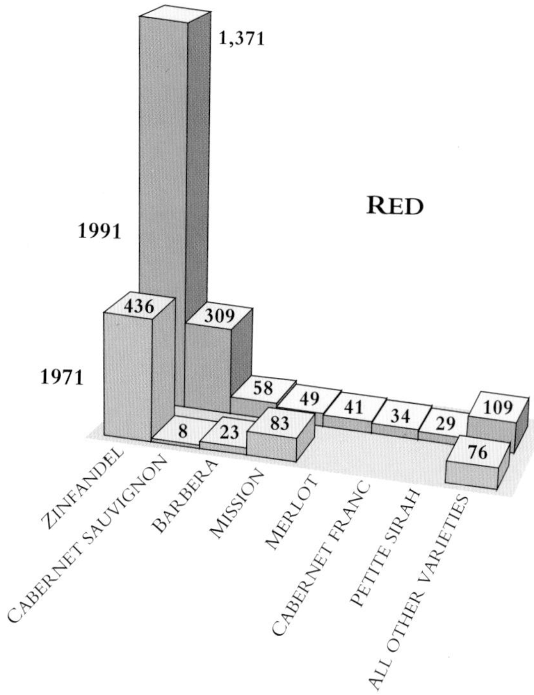
RED
1991
1971
1,371
436
309
58
49
41
34
29
109
8
23
83
76
ZINFANDEL
CABERNET SAUVIGNON
BARBERA
MISSION
MERLOT
CABERNET FRANC
PETITE SIRAH
ALL OTHER VARIETIES

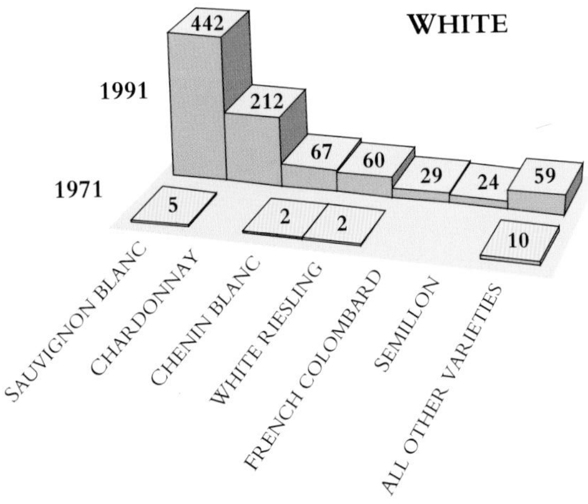
WHITE
1991
1971
442
212
67
60
29
24
59
5
2
2
10
SAUVIGNON BLANC
CHARDONNAY
CHENIN BLANC
WHITE RIESLING
FRENCH COLOMBARD
SEMILLON
ALL OTHER VARIETIES

PREVIOUS PAGE ~ *The Sierras towards Lake Tahoe: snow is seldom far away from the vines.*

ABOVE ~ *Dick Bush, founding owner of Madrona Vineyards, in the company of one of his cherished trees.*

GOLD AND WINE

The parallels between the California gold rush and that of Victoria in Australia are quite striking. In California the first discovery was made in 1848, in Victoria in 1851. The fever which gripped society at the time was vividly described by the distinguished Australian historian Professor Manning Clark in *A History of Australia:*

ABOVE ~ *Main Street, Plymouth, richly evocative of the gold rush days.*

> *A hot fit of auriferous fever took possession of the men. As in Macbeth, men stood not on their social rank in going, but went at once. Painters put on a first coat, and then vanished; plasterers mixed their mortar, then threw away their trowels; brick layers on scaffolding turned giddy with the thought of gold; carpenters shook with the fever till they flung their tools away and bolted for the fields; attendants at the Melbourne lunatic asylum rushed off; teachers at the denominational schools dropped all pretence about their higher calling and made for the fields; capitalists saddled up horses and joined the army of prospective diggers on the road.*

The city of Melbourne was literally denuded of its population; the social disruption was immense. In California gold fever heralded an unprecedented flood of new arrivals, not only from other parts of the United States but from all over the world. When gold was discovered by James Marshall, California had a population of 14,000; four years later it had risen to 224,000, almost entirely driven by the gold rush. At the height of the ephemeral boom, Nevada City boasted a greater population than San Francisco.

In both countries, miners had a powerful thirst, and those who were successful had ample money with which to slake that thirst. Some of the most intelligent arrivals decided it was better to let others do the hard work of finding and digging out the elusive bands of gold, and instead went into the business of supplying the miners with food, alcohol and female company, profiting greatly in doing so.

Thus in both countries vineyards appeared overnight in and around goldfields. In 1860 El Dorado County alone had more vineyards than either Sonoma or Napa. Even James Marshall himself owned a vineyard in Coloma County where the discovery of gold was made. Thomas Pinney in *A History of Wine in America* describes the cosmopolitan nature of the vignerons:

> *Since the Gold Rush had attracted every sort of person from every part of the world, the early wine growers were a diverse lot — Germans and Dutchmen, Frenchmen, Yankees, and Englishmen were all among the pioneers. Sutter himself, the Swiss adventurer and feudal-style landholder on whose land gold was first found, after losing most of his property in the rush that followed, turned to winegrowing on his Hock Farm, as he called it, on the Feather River south of Yuba City, where a vineyard had been set out in 1851.*

The end of easily won gold did not spell the end of the vineyards; in fact, the opposite. Former miners either started their own vineyards or were employed by others to do so. (In Victoria at Great Western, an enterprising butcher named Joseph Best, who had made his fortune feeding the gold diggers, employed former miners to construct the vast underground caves which are now the showpiece of leading sparkling wine producer, Seppelt.)

By 1890 more than a hundred wineries were operating up and down the length of the Sierra Foothills: at Nevada City, Colfax, Lincoln, Penryn, Auburn, Placerville, Coloma, Shingle Springs, Ione, Fiddletown, Volcano, Jackson, San Andreas, Sonora, Columbia and Jamestown. No doubt much of it was aimed at a relatively unsophisticated market: an 1876 advertisement for Coloma Vineyard offered "Green Hungarian (very choice)" but went on to list Catawba, Isabella, "Native (white and red), Burgundy (Port and Dry)" as well as blackberry wines, cordials and bitters.

The last word belongs to an Australian pastoralist, Lindsay Brown, who became a vigneron in 1851. A contemporary recorded that "Brown was in the habit of settling miners' discussions as to the depth to which sinking should be carried. 'To get gold,' he would say, 'you need sink only 18 inches and plant vines'."

ABOVE ~ *Ferrero Ranch Zinfandel with old gold tailings in the background, each dating from the nineteenth century.*

AMADOR AND CALAVERAS

Amador is by far the most significant region in the Sierra Foothills: its plantings of Zinfandel alone exceed the combined acreage of all varieties in Placer, El Dorado, Yuba and Calaveras counties. During the gold rush days, too, it was the center of agricultural activity; Adam Uhlinger founded his winery in 1856, and it was this property which was purchased by D'Agostini in 1911 and operated under that name until its 1988 acquisition by the Sobon family.

The reasons for the continuous history of viticulture in the region, and specifically the survival of old Zinfandel vineyards such as the Deaver Ranch and the Grand-Père Vineyard (dating from 1868 and with most of its vines surviving from that date) are threefold. First, the rainfall and the water-retentive yet well-drained soils produce reasonable yields (one and a half to three tons per acre) of dry-farmed grapes. Second, the absence of fogs and the dry summer means a low incidence of fungal disease and molds. Third, phylloxera has yet to make inroads into any of the plantings, new or old.

Until the influx of new wineries commenced in 1973, virtually all of the grapes grown in Amador were sold to wineries outside the region, but until Sutter Home became known (initially in a small way) for its Zinfandel from the Deaver Ranch — the first vintage of which was made in 1968 — no credit was given to the county. It took a home winemaker called Charles Myers to vinify Deaver Zinfandel in the mid 1960s, a wine which so impressed Darrell Corti that he arranged for Sutter Home to make the 1968 wine specifically for sale through Corti Bros.' Sacramento store (and which indirectly led to the development of the White Zinfandel market).

Calaveras County's vineyards and wineries are well to the south, away from the main tourist flow through to Lake Tahoe, and have not developed as quickly as the northern districts. Which is a pity, because Angels Camp is well named: the transition from the flat, dry plains of the San Joaquin Valley to the clear mountain streams which flow through the year, the lush vegetation and the forested hillsides is quite startling. The principal winery, Stevenot, is in its own secluded and quite beautiful tiny valley, rimmed by Ponderosa pine-clad hills. It also happens to be the largest winery in the Sierra Foothills, producing 45,000 cases drawn both from its estate vineyards and elsewhere in the Sierra Foothills. Calaveras is also notable for the fact that, alone among the Sierra Foothills regions, it produces more white and red grapes, attesting in part to its cooler climate.

ABOVE ~ *It is more economical to store maturing wine in bulk bins or stacks than to package and box it.*

OPPOSITE ~ *The 120-year-old Grand-Pere Zinfandel vineyard of Santino Wines (with bed-and-breakfast accommodation behind).*

The Region in Brief

Climate, Soil and Viticulture

Amador

Climate

As with El Dorado, elevation and site are powerful influences in determining mesoclimate. Thus the Fiddletown AVA has a cooler climate than that of the neighboring Shenandoah Valley AVA because of its higher elevation of between 1,500 and 2,500 feet (remembering that both of these AVAs will fall within the upcoming Amador AVA). This cooler climate is principally reflected in colder night-time temperatures, and in a higher rainfall which averages up to 40 inches compared to 25 inches elsewhere in the county. Daytime temperatures throughout the region during the middle and later part of the growing season range between the low 80s and 100°F, but seldom go much higher, thanks to afternoon breezes from the San Francisco Bay. The average heat summation is 3,400 degree days, high Region III, and thus not infrequently ends up well into Region IV. Night-time cool breezes emanating from the Sierra Nevada mountains play an essential role in moderating the climate and allowing the grapes to ripen with good levels of acidity.

Soil

The soils vary somewhat from north to south, but are all of volcanic origin, deriving principally from decomposed granite. In the northern (and major) sector, the soils are of the Sierra-Ahwahnee series, which in simpler language are deep to moderately deep sandy and gravelly loams. In the southeastern part of the county the soils are of the Pentz-Pardee series, consisting of phyolitic tuff and mixed alluvium, and visually are not greatly different to those of the north. Overall, the soils promote considerable vine vigor; while the higher slopes present no vigor problems, the lower slopes and benchlands tend to produce hyper-vigor, giving vignerons formidable problems in adequately controlling the canopy, particularly where irrigation is used.

The Growing Season

The danger of frost continues through to the middle of May, one of the reasons why Zinfandel (which has a late budbreak and can set a good second crop even if it is frosted) has always been so widely planted. From this point on, the conditions seldom present any problems, with harvest typically starting in early September and running through to mid October.

ABOVE ~ *Old vines do not necessarily produce great grapes: these vines, planted just prior to Prohibition, are the Mission variety.*

Amador
VINTAGE CHART 1981–91

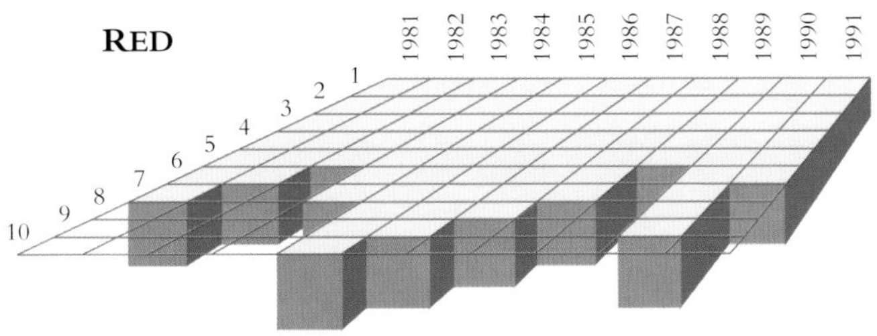
RED
1981
1982
1983
1984
1985
1986
1987
1988
1989
1990
1991
1
2
3
4
5
6
7
8
9
10

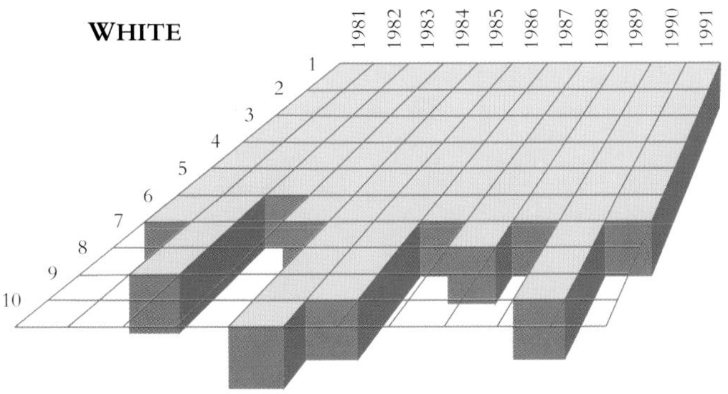
WHITE
1981
1982
1983
1984
1985
1986
1987
1988
1989
1990
1991
1
2
3
4
5
6
7
8
9
10

Amador and Calaveras
1971 AND 1991 ACREAGE/GRAPE VARIETIES

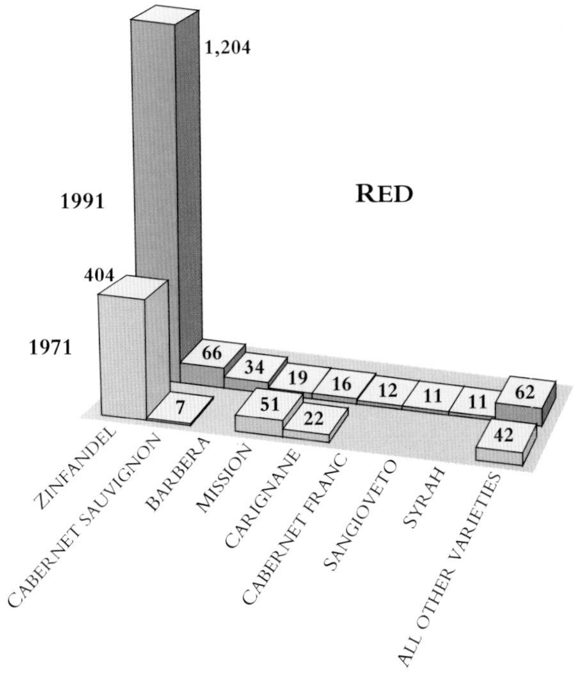
RED
1991
1971
1,204
404
66
7
34
51
19
22
16
12
11
11
62
42
ZINFANDEL
CABERNET SAUVIGNON
BARBERA
MISSION
CARIGNANE
CABERNET FRANC
SANGIOVETO
SYRAH
ALL OTHER VARIETIES

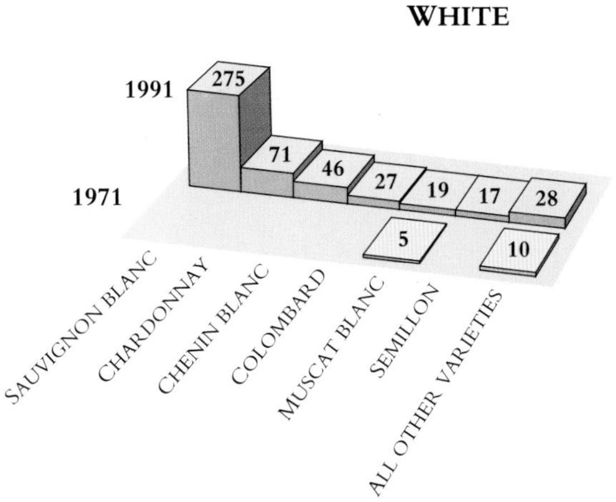
WHITE
1991
1971
275
71
46
27
19
17
28
5
10
SAUVIGNON BLANC
CHARDONNAY
CHENIN BLANC
COLOMBARD
MUSCAT BLANC
SEMILLON
ALL OTHER VARIETIES

CALAVERAS

CLIMATE

Stevenot, and several of the nearby wineries and vineyards, is at an altitude of 1,800 feet, and enjoys a distinctly cooler climate than Amador, ranging from high Region II to Region III; the cool vintages of the late 1980s and early 1990s fell into Region II. With the exception of the lower summation, the major influences on the climate are similar to those experienced in Amador and El Dorado.

SOIL

The soils are not dissimilar, with the surface soils derived from weathered volcanics, but the subsoil is quite different, being limestone impregnated and balancing the higher acidity of the surface soils. Once again, the vines grow vigorously, and modern trellising methods could well lead to continuing increases in grape quality.

THE GROWING SEASON

With budbreak for Chardonnay falling around April 1, frost protection through overhead sprinklers (fed from abundant aquifers) is essential. Stevenot commences harvest with Chardonnay in mid September, although nearby valleys can ripen up to two weeks earlier. The Bordeaux varieties come next, usually in the first weeks of October.

Contract Vineyards

Deaver Ranch Situated at 1,700 feet on Shenandoah School Road, Plymouth, planted primarily to Zinfandel and sold to Sutter Home.
Eschen Vineyard Forty acres at 1,700 feet on Ostrom Road, Fiddletown, planted to Zinfandel in 1924; sold to Amador Foothill Winery and Santino.
Esola Vineyard Ninety acres at 1,700 feet on Shenandoah School Road planted in 1910 to Zinfandel (76 acres) and subsequently to Cabernet Sauvignon; sold to Ridge and Carneros Creek.
Ferrero Ranch Fifty acres at 1,600 feet on Shenandoah School Road, planted in 1926 to Zinfandel; sold to Amador Foothill Winery and Monterey Peninsula.
Frank's Vineyard Six acres at 1,700 feet planted to seven classic Portuguese port varieties; sold exclusively to Quady.

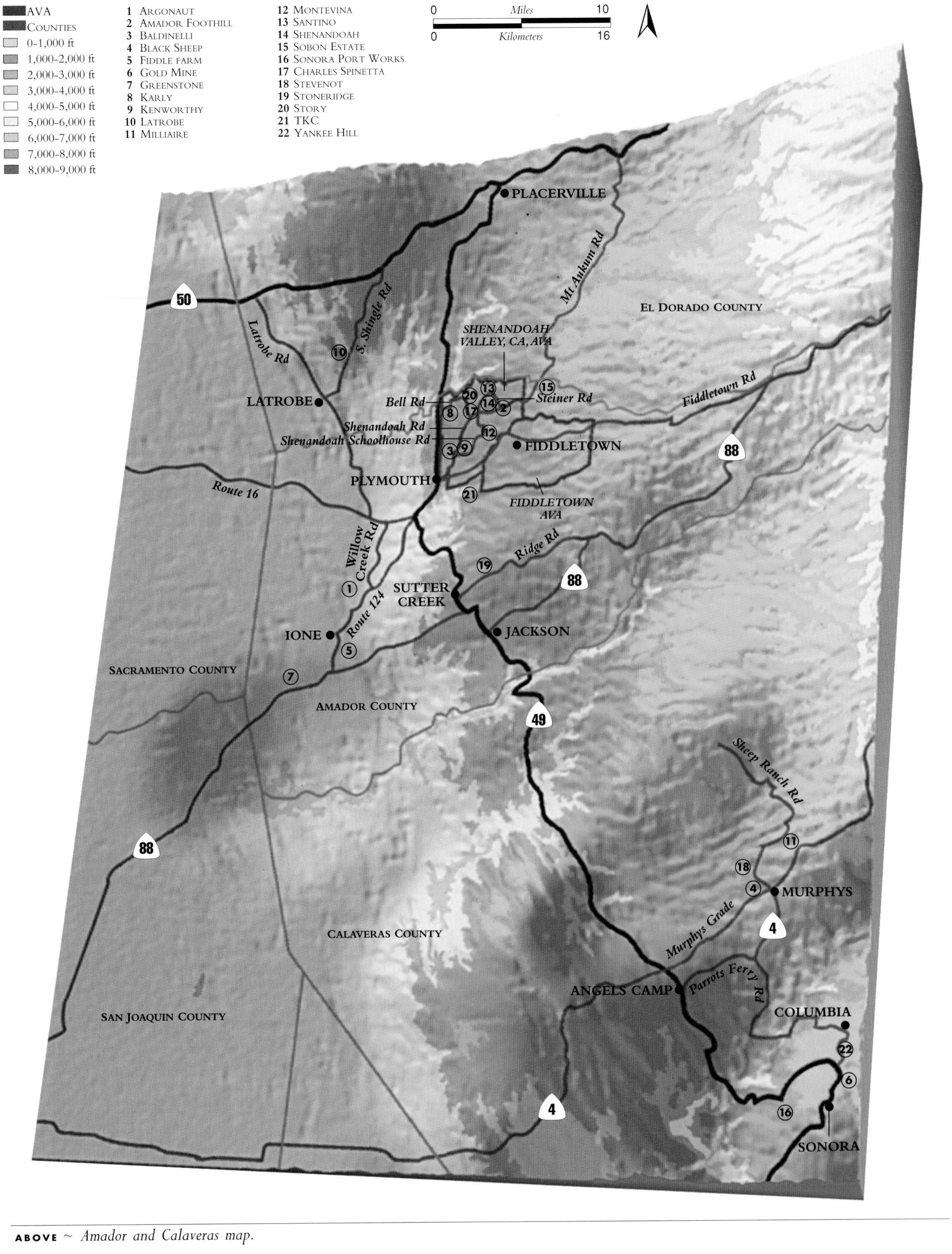

AVA
Counties
0-1,000 ft
1,000-2,000 ft
2,000-3,000 ft
3,000-4,000 ft
4,000-5,000 ft
5,000-6,000 ft
6,000-7,000 ft
7,000-8,000 ft
8,000-9,000 ft
1 Argonaut
2 Amador Foothill
3 Baldinelli
4 Black Sheep
5 Fiddle Farm
6 Gold Mine
7 Greenstone
8 Karly
9 Kenworthy
10 Latrobe
11 Milliaire
12 Montevina
13 Santino
14 Shenandoah
15 Sobon Estate
16 Sonora Port Works
17 Charles Spinetta
18 Stevenot
19 Stoneridge
20 Story
21 TKC
22 Yankee Hill
0 Miles 10
0 Kilometers 16
PLACERVILLE
50
S. Shingle Rd
Mt Aukum Rd
El Dorado County
Latrobe Rd
SHENANDOAH VALLEY, CA, AVA
LATROBE
Bell Rd
Steiner Rd
Fiddletown Rd
Shenandoah Rd
Shenandoah Schoolhouse Rd
FIDDLETOWN
88
PLYMOUTH
Route 16
FIDDLETOWN AVA
Willow Creek Rd
Ridge Rd
SUTTER CREEK
88
IONE
Route 124
JACKSON
Sacramento County
Amador County
49
Sheep Ranch Rd
88
MURPHYS
Murphys Grade
4
Calaveras County
ANGELS CAMP
Parrots Ferry Rd
COLUMBIA
San Joaquin County
4
SONORA

ABOVE ~ *Amador and Calaveras map.*

Grand-Père Vineyard Ten acres at 1,700 feet on Steiner Road planted in 1868 to Zinfandel and sold to Amador Foothill Winery and Santino.

Principal Wine Styles

ZINFANDEL

Accounting for two-thirds of the plantings in Amador County, and solely responsible for the revival of interest in the county as a wine producing region, Zinfandel stands unchallenged as the most important wine style. Given the apparent suitability of the climate, the rich heritage of old vineyards, and the dedication of the makers (both large and small) who handle these old vineyard grapes, one might think that assessment of style and quality was a foregone conclusion. But it seems that beauty is very much in the eye of the beholder: Bruce Cass is a disciple, seeing the wines as having a distinctive mineral, salty, brackish quality which he finds wholly enjoyable but admits is a learned preference; Matt Kramer sits, like myself, on the fence, ascribing to the wines a hard kernel of prune and tar flavors. For my palate, the best of the wines are impressive for their balanced depth and concentration of flavor, but the lesser wines consistently display candy, hay and straw characteristics which suggest the grapes may have been picked too ripe. For sheer consistency, but also for style, Amador Foothill Winery stands out, but Greenstone, Montevina, Santino (particularly with its older wines), Shenandoah Vineyards and Sonora Winery are all capable of producing high quality wines if conditions are right.

SAUVIGNON BLANC AND WHITE MERITAGE

Given the problems of vigor and yield which beset many of the plantings, the quality of the wines is altogether surprising, and explains why this variety should be the second most widely propagated grape in the Amador County. Once again, it defies the seeming imperatives of the climate, coming up with crisp, clean, direct wines which have distinct varietal flavor and excellent acidity. Amador Foothill Winery, Karly and Latrobe Vineyards all excel with the wine.

CHARDONNAY

This is far more important (relatively speaking) in Calaveras than it is in Amador — with remarkable perception and restraint, few growers have bothered to plant it in the latter county. In the cooler climate of Calaveras it does much better, Stevenot producing a clean, melon flavored wine which in 1990 and 1991 had good intensity and length, and which largely eschewed the props of malolactic fermentation and excessive oak.

CABERNET SAUVIGNON AND RED MERITAGE

In neither Calaveras nor Amador have these wines made much impact, even though all of the Bordeaux varieties are planted. Stevenot's Cabernet Sauvignon carries a California appellation, its Merlot a North Coast appellation — and these are among the best from wineries in either county.

ITALIAN AND RHONE VARIETALS

After Zinfandel, it is with these wines that the future may well lie, a future discussed on pages 250–1 and 326–7.

ABOVE ~ *The Shenandoah Valley in high summer, looking towards the Sierra Mountains.*

WHITE ZINFANDEL

The blush phenomenon is a fascinating one, in no small measure due to the fact that it is exclusive to the United States — yet the underlying shift in patterns of wine consumption occurred in the same fashion and at the same time right across the world. For California, that shift was from a market dominated by red wine sales up until 1975 to one in which white wines (including blush styles) reached 70% of the total sales by 1985. The change is to all intents and purposes identical to that of Australia — except for one thing: Australia has at no time looked like accepting blush wines.

Early in the piece it was by no means certain that in the United States the blush segment would flourish in the way that it has. Its origins go back to the second half of the 1960s, when Charles Myers (who still runs a small Sacramento winery called Harbor Wines) made a small quantity of Zinfandel he purchased from Ken Deaver's vineyard (which was said to also have some Mission grapes planted in 1859). Sacramento wine merchant Darrell Corti tasted Myers' wine and was so impressed he asked Bob Trinchero of Sutter Home to purchase Deaver Zinfandel and make a red wine which he (Corti) would sell. Thus the first vintage of Sutter Home Zinfandel was born (in 1968).

ABOVE ~ *Exceptionally well-ripened Zinfandel at Madrona Vineyard awaits the crusher.*

At that time Sutter Home was another small, Italian-owned business with its roots in the bulk market, tentatively moving towards own brand, bottled wine sales. The Sutter Home blush gradually established a name for itself, and by the end of the 1970s Sutter Home was making 25,000 cases a year of the wine, accounting for half its total sales. Each year from 1980 sales doubled, leaping to 550,000 cases by 1984/85, and a staggering 1.4 million cases the following year (1985/86). After the first few vintages, Sutter Home had moved from Amador to Lodi for its source of Zinfandel for blush, ostensibly because Amador's grapes were "too spicy," but no doubt also because the massive plantings in Lodi and elsewhere in the Central Valley ensured a plentiful supply of grapes at low prices.

1991 CALIFORNIA WINE PRODUCTION

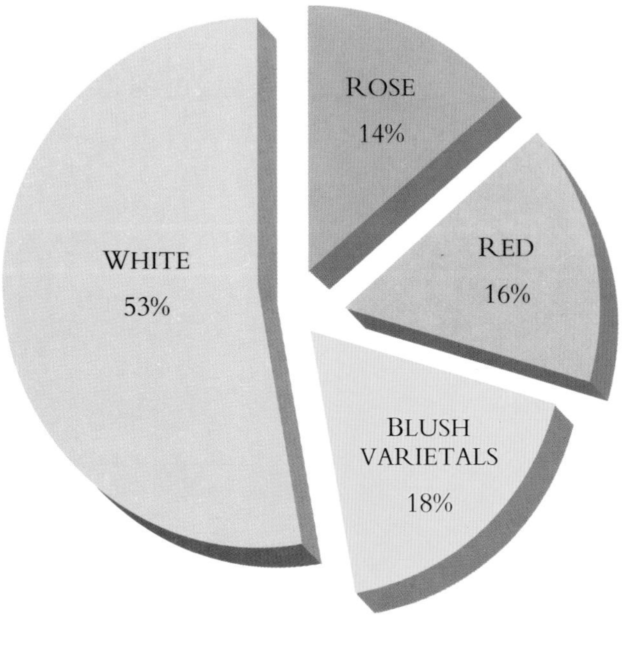
ROSE
14%
RED
16%
WHITE
53%
BLUSH VARIETALS
18%

Notwithstanding Sutter Home's success, it was not until 1984 that blush wines attracted much attention from the press. Apart from a few passing comments, the first article on blush wines appeared in the September 1984 issue of *Wines and Vines*. Its opening paragraph read, "Wine market observers predict that production of Blancs de Noir, or 'blush' wines, more-or-less white wines made from red grapes, will increase dramatically during the 1984 crush. And perhaps beyond."

Yet, curiously, many of the major companies seemed content to let Sutter Home make all the running. When tiny Shenandoah Vineyards jumped on the bandwagon in the 1980s it was one of only three labels (the other two being Sutter Home and Montevina), producing 1,000 cases in 1981 and soaring to 36,000 cases by the middle of the decade, before bowing out gracefully as the major producers came in.

Thus in 1984 Gallo, which had produced a pink Chablis in 1966, said it had no plans to produce a Blanc de Noirs as such, and the only other significant player was Beringer/Hermanos. And it was not until 1987 that separate statistics were published differentiating blush from white wines. By that year they accounted for over 9% of sales of California wines in the United States, since which time they have since increased to 18%, a share greater than that of dry red.

By the end of the decade, Sutter Home was producing three million cases of Blush Zinfandel, and had acquired 3,000 acres of vineyard — having started its blush program without a single acre to its name, and having established necessarily a vast winery to handle the production. From the maker's viewpoint, blush is a dream wine: it never sees oak (new or old), and can be on the market six weeks after harvest, months before the first grape payment is made.

It must also be said that the market is a largely uncritical one. Provided the wine has a bright pale pink color (rather than brown-tinged) and the maker gets the acid-sugar balance right, nothing else matters very much. Blush is an alcoholic beverage, selling on price, store positioning and promotional support; the questions of flavor, structure or style are of academic interest to wine show judges and the occasional wine writer, but irrelevant to the buying public.

Yet the importance of the sector cannot be over-emphasized. It is in no way like the cooler market, which bloomed precociously and briefly in the mid-1980s, nor the flavored wines of bygone eras. Blush represents an entry point for many who would otherwise never drink wine; some will graduate to more sophisticated consumption, others will be content with blush all their lives. What is important is the spread in the consumer base.

It is also a highly logical point for the development of reduced alcohol or light wines. The Australian-developed spinning cone technology licensed to Sutter Home in 1992 offers tremendous opportunities if used properly. Once again, it offers the prospect of expanding the acceptance of wine across a broader span of social circumstance, without debasing the concept of wine as coolers and such-like inevitably do.

1987–91 GROWTH IN PRODUCTION IN GALLONS

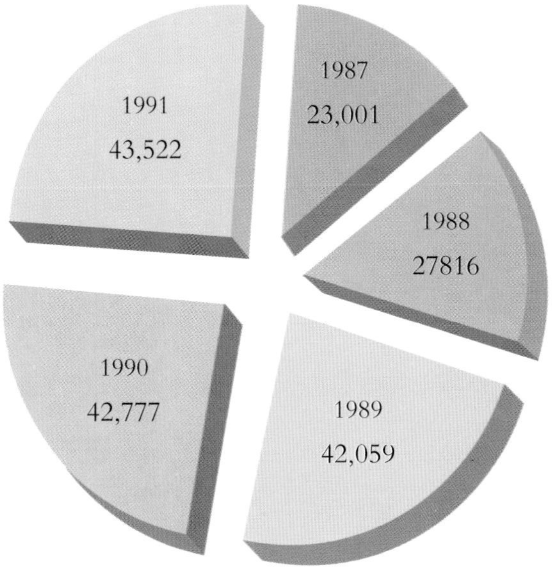
1991
43,522
1987
23,001
1988
27816
1990
42,777
1989
42,059

ABOVE ~ *White Zinfandel — it really is blush in color — on the high-speed bottling line at San Antonio Winery (in Los Angeles).*

WINERIES *of* AMADOR

AMADOR FOOTHILL WINERY 1985

A: 12500 Steiner Road, Plymouth, CA 95669
T: (209) 245 6307 **V**: 12–5 Sat–Sun or by appointment **P**: 30,000
W: Katie Quinn and Ben Zeitman

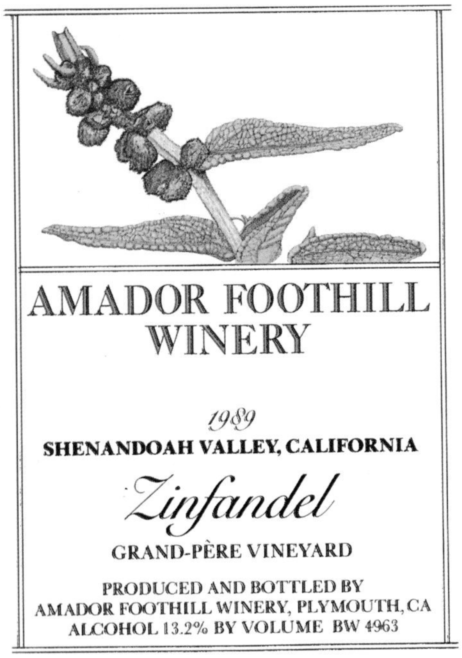
AMADOR FOOTHILL WINERY
1989
SHENANDOAH VALLEY, CALIFORNIA
Zinfandel
GRAND-PÈRE VINEYARD
PRODUCED AND BOTTLED BY
AMADOR FOOTHILL WINERY, PLYMOUTH, CA
ALCOHOL 13.2% BY VOLUME BW 4963

Former NASA research chemist Ben Zeitman started home winemaking in the early 1970s, first purchasing Zinfandel from the Grand-Père Vineyard in 1974. These winemaking activities were part of those of a group which included Leon Sobon, and when Sobon purchased land in Amador, Zeitman and wife Katie Quinn eventually purchased part of the property to establish Amador Foothill Winery. While Zeitman was (and is) without formal winemaking qualifications, Katie Quinn has dual degrees in chemistry, and her masters in enology from U.C. Davis. Into the bargain, she worked for three years at Gundlach Bundschu in Sonoma.

Though Zinfandel occupies an appropriately dominant place in the total production mix, Zeitman and Quinn decided to plant Cabernet Sauvignon (since grafted over to Sangiovese), Sauvignon Blanc and Semillon when they established ten and a half acres of vineyard on the 20-acre property. Their logic was that they wished to make Zinfandel from old vines, and that they were reasonably assured of supplies of such grapes. So it is that they purchase grapes from the Grand-Père Vineyard (which adjoins their hillside property), from the 75-year-old Eschen Vineyard in Fiddletown, and from the 27-year-old Ferrero Vineyard in the Shenandoah Valley. They treat their material very skillfully, making most attractive Zinfandels which faithfully reflect the differing vineyard sources. Thus the Grand-Père Zinfandel is immensely rich and concentrated, with sinewy power, length and intensity, overlain with a bramble character. That from the Ferrero Vineyard is much more fragrant, spicier and lighter: drink it young, and cellar the Grand-Père if you wish to. The White Meritage, made from a blend of 75% Sauvignon Blanc and 25% Semillon, is another high quality wine, with citric overtones, a fresh and crisp bouquet and palate, and excellent length and intensity to the flavor.

BALDINELLI VINEYARDS 1979

A: 10801 Dixon Road, Plymouth, CA 95669
T: (209) 245 3398 **V**: 11–4 Sat–Sun
P: 16,000 **W**: Edward Baldinelli

Ed and Kay Baldinelli acquired the historic Dixon Vineyard (planted in 1923) in the early 1970s, and in 1972 added Cabernet Sauvignon and Sauvignon Blanc to the 38 acres of existing Zinfandel. There are now 70 acres in all, and all of the production is estate-grown. In 1979 the Baldinellis, in partnership with vineyard manager John Miller, built a winery which was bonded in 1980. The Zinfandel, both in standard and Reserve form, is the outstanding wine, particularly the Reserve, a wine of massive concentration and dimension.

GREENSTONE WINERY 1980

A: 3151 Highway 88, Ione, CA 95640
T: (209) 274 2238 **V**: 10–4 Wed–Sun
P: 12,000 **W**: Stan Van Spanje

Greenstone was established on a 40-acre ranch by the Van Spanje and Fowler families in 1980. Thirty acres of French Colombard, Chenin Blanc, Sauvignon Blanc, Muscat Blanc, Palamino, Zinfandel and Cabernet Sauvignon have been established on the estate vineyards, with French Colombard and White Zinfandel accounting for over half the total production. The Chenin Blanc, made in a semi-dry style — like the White Zinfandel — is unashamedly commercial, but competently made and neatly aimed at its target market. The Dry Colombard falls in much the same category, the most interesting wines being the full-bodied dry reds. A Barbera purchased from the Delta College Vineyard (outside of Amador County) is suitably Italianate, but does show its warm origins. The full-blown, ripe Cabernet Sauvignon with rich, red berry fruit tinged with hay/straw characters, and a powerful, jammy Zinfandel made in the old style will please those who like flavor, alcohol and body in their reds.

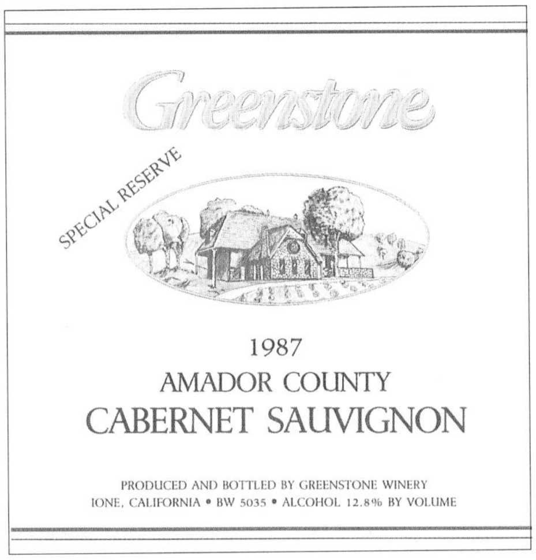
Greenstone
SPECIAL RESERVE
1987
AMADOR COUNTY
CABERNET SAUVIGNON
PRODUCED AND BOTTLED BY GREENSTONE WINERY
IONE, CALIFORNIA • BW 5035 • ALCOHOL 12.8% BY VOLUME

KARLY 1980

A: 11076 Bell Road, Plymouth, CA 95669
T: (209) 245 3922 **V**: By appointment
P: 10,000 **W**: Lawrence (Buck) Cobb

Buck Cobb and wife Karly commenced developing their 17-acre vineyard in the 1970s, planting Zinfandel, Sauvignon Blanc and Petite Sirah. The estate grapes are complemented by purchases from both within and without the Sierra Foothills, sometimes extending as far as the MacGregor Vineyard in the Edna Valley for Chardonnay.

The Zinfandel and Petite Sirah are, to put it mildly, erratic, even at their best belonging to the old, full-blooded, rustic style. Against all the odds, as it were, Karly then produces some quite lovely and very unusual white wines, including a Late Harvest Orange Muscat with pungent, citrussy fruit, bracing acid to counterbalance the sweetness, and considerable length and style. Less unusual is an even better (in 1991) Sauvignon Blanc, a no-frills version in which the varietal fruit flavor has been allowed to do all of the work — and that with total success.

LATROBE VINEYARDS 1985

A: 4861 Memory Lane, Shingle Springs, CA 95682 **T**: (916) 676 0108 **V**: By appointment **P**: 1,000 **W**: Mark Foster (Contract)

Owner Bob Clarke has elected to focus on Sauvignon Blanc, and have the wine made under custom crush arrangements by Mark Foster at Madrona Vineyards. The wines show Foster's undoubted winemaking skills, and support considerable evidence that Sauvignon Blanc can flourish and produce wines of excellent varietal character in an exceptionally wide range of climate and *terroir*. The Latrobe Sauvignon Blancs are noteworthy for their crispness, austerity, and elegance, with clean fruit, good mouthfeel and long flavor.

MONTEVINA WINERY 1973

A: 20680 Shenandoah School Road, Plymouth, CA 95669 **T**: (209) 245 6942 **V**: 11–4 daily P: 50,000 **W**: Jeffrey Meyers

Montevina played a leading role in the Amador revival of the early 1970s under the ownership and direction of the Gott family. An 81-acre vineyard was planted between 1972 and 1974, with 29 acres of Sauvignon Blanc, 22 acres of Zinfandel, 15 acres of Cabernet Sauvignon, ten acres of Semillon and five acres of Barbera. The then winemaker Cary Gott was among the innovators in the handling of Zinfandel, producing a carbonic maceration style, a bone-dry White Zinfandel, and of course Zinfandel in conventional guise.

Gott left after a family dispute in 1982, and between that date and 1988 the substantial operation lost its sense of direction, which has only been partially restored since Sutter Home purchased Montevina in 1988. The White Zinfandel is utterly unmemorable, while the proprietary Montanaro (a blend of 75% Barbera and 25% Zinfandel) gives little support to the belief that Italian varieties should do well in this area, being light and innocuous in every way. It is with the various Zinfandels that Montevina strikes form. The Amador County Reserve is heavily oaked, but is certainly distinctive; the standard Zinfandel, with a Sierra Foothills Appellation, also shows a hint of caramel oak together with gently ripe cherry fruit and soft tannins. The most striking of all, though I must say not the best, is the proprietary Brioso carbonic maceration Zinfandel, with extraordinary fruit essence aromas and flavors which range from fruit cordial to fruit pastille.

SANTINO WINES 1979

A: 12225 Steiner Road, Plymouth, CA 95669 **T**: (209) 245 6979 **V**: 12–4.30 daily **P**: 25,000 **W**: Scott Harvey

Santino Winery was established in 1979 by Nancy Santino, but is now owned in partnership by winemaker Scott Harvey and president Joseph Schweitzer. Scott Harvey received his degree in enology at Geisenheim, Germany, a background which reflects itself in some of the quite extraordinary late harvest wines produced by the winery. Whether it is because of or despite that training, I do not know, but Harvey is forthright in his views that Amador has far too warm a climate for Sauvignon Blanc and Cabernet Sauvignon, and that the varieties which make sense are Zinfandel, Syrah, Mourvedre and Barbera. Apart from stirring that controversy, Scott Harvey has also tweaked the tail of the BATF like no one else I know: the folks at Kenwood (see page 194) must still be scratching their heads in disbelief at how Santino got BATF approval for its Satyricon label, featuring a voluptuous lady and a satyr engaged in something more than foreplay.

For the time being, at least, the flagship of the winery is the Grand-Pere Vineyard Zinfandel. Scott Harvey purchased the Grand-Pere Vineyard from previous owner John Downing in 1984, and curiously elects to sell part of the grapes to other wineries, while Santino itself turns around and purchases Zinfandel from the D'Agostini Vineyard owned by Sobon Estate. Scott Harvey's philosophy and approach to Zinfandel are as challenging as one might expect: he believes the best wine is made from grapes which will produce a wine carrying between 15 and 16.5% of alcohol (assuming the yeasts are able to do their work), but having said that, rushes on to assert that he picks Zinfandel on the basis of its taste, rather than chemical analysis. The result is a suitably monumental Zinfandel which has a very strong following.

Satyricon is a classic southern Rhone blend of 38% Grenache, 22% Mourvedre, 20% Syrah, 17% Carignane and 3% Cinsault, fermented with a component of whole berries, again in the manner of the southern Rhone. The components of the wine tasted from barrel were exhilarating, but earlier bottled blends less so. The Barbera, made in similar fashion, and with 19% Zinfandel added, has genuine Italian style with flavors of plum and cedar wood, and appropriately soft tannins.

The really startling wines are the occasional late harvest wines which, over the past ten years, have won major national competitions. 1989 was a vintage custom-tailored to produce ultra-late harvest wines, and Scott Harvey duly obliged with a Late Harvest Riesling from the Sonoma Valley, picked in December at 48° Brix, and made in the style of a German Trockenbeerenauslese with only 6% alcohol. Intense dried apricot botrytis aroma and flavor obscure the varietal underlay, but with that carping criticism to one side, it is a superb example of the style. A totally bizarre wine is the Late Harvest White Zinfandel, Dry Berry Select, picked on December 6 at 52° Brix, and fermented to produce only 5.4% alcohol and 38.8% residual sugar. The only wine I have tasted on a par with this was a 1976 Trockenbeerenauslese made from Spatburgunder (or Pinot Noir) in the Rheingau. It is a "love it or hate it" style, with searingly luscious grapey flavors, and of course no hint of its varietal origin.

SHENANDOAH VINEYARDS 1977

A: 12300 Steiner Road, Plymouth, CA 95669 **T**: (209) 245 4455 **V**: 10–5 daily **P**: 40,000 **W**: Leon Sobon

CALIFORNIA
Shenandoah Vineyards
1990
AMADOR COUNTY
SAUVIGNON BLANC
ALCOHOL 12.6% BY VOLUME
PRODUCED & BOTTLED BY SHENANDOAH VINEYARDS
BW-CA 4809 PLYMOUTH CALIFORNIA
CONTAINS SULFITES

Leon Sobon spent 20 years as a research scientist in Silicon Valley, working with the Lockheed Research Laboratory, authoring numerous publications and obtaining three patents. He and a group of friends began home winemaking as a bit of light relief from the daily professional grind, homing in on Amador County Zinfandel. Within a few short years, he and wife Shirley decided on a radical lifestyle change, purchasing the Steiner Ranch in 1977 and moving (with their six children) to live on the property full time. The children have since grown up, and suffered no lasting trauma, because two sons and one son-in-law currently work for the business.

Shenandoah Vineyards found itself in the right place at the right time: at the start of the White Zinfandel boom. From an initial production of 1,000 cases, output soared to 65,000 cases, driven by 35,000 cases of White Zinfandel. They were hectic but highly profitable times, allowing the development of a substantial winery purely from cash flow. When, in due course, White Zinfandel became a low-priced commodity, the Sobons had no hesitation in scaling back production to its present level of around 7,000 cases, and can foresee the day when it largely disappears from the portfolio.

By the mid 1980s the writing was well and truly on the wall, and Shenandoah started moving the basis of its production towards Sauvignon Blanc, Cabernet Sauvignon (together with Cabernet Franc and Petit Verdot), and Syrah. In 1988 a further opening came, when the family purchased the old D'Agostini

Vineyard and established Sobon Estate, which is dealt with under a separate entry. The old vintages of Shenandoah Red Zinfandels have aged extremely well, with rich, chocolatey fruit and great texture. Similarly, the old vintages of Late Harvest Zinfandel kept in the family's cellar are delicious wines, going close to persuading me that there really is some merit in this style. The wide range of current releases are modestly priced, and adequate within their price range, but, I am afraid, little more than that.

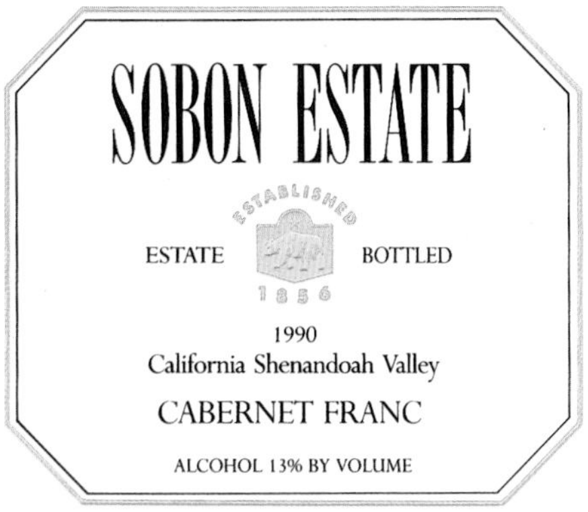
SOBON ESTATE
ESTABLISHED
ESTATE BOTTLED
1856
1990
California Shenandoah Valley
CABERNET FRANC
ALCOHOL 13% BY VOLUME

SOBON ESTATE 1988

A: 14430 Shenandoah Road, Plymouth, CA 95669 **T**: (209) 245 6554 **V**: 10–5 daily **P**: 10,000 **W**: Leon Sobon

When the Sobon family purchased the winery built in 1856 by Adam Uhlinger, it decided to establish a completely separate brand and identity for the winery which (between 1911 and 1988) was known as D'Agostini, and which produced wines of absolutely no distinction. A greater contrast between the highly colored flower and butterfly-decorated Shenandoah Vineyards label and the classic black and gold restraint of Sobon Estate could not be imagined. Shirley Sobon was also responsible for establishing a museum in the historic stone winery, which is used as a storage facility, but not for active winemaking purposes.

The wines released under the Sobon Estate label are Shenandoah Valley Cabernet Sauvignon, Chardonnay, Cabernet Franc and Syrah, and a Sierra Foothills Zinfandel. The initial release of Cabernet Franc was enthusiastically greeted, but the following vintage was rather jammy and sweet, completely overshadowed by the outstanding Syrah, with abundant dark berry, plum and spice aroma and flavor, a fleshy and round mid palate, and balancing tannins.

SONORA WINERY & PORT WORKS 1986

A: 17500 Route 5 Road, Sonora, CA 95370 **T**: (209) 532-PORT **V**: By appointment **P**: 2,500 **W**: Richard Matranga

ABOVE ~ *A balmy spring morning heralds the first growth of yet another season.*

As the name suggests, the limited partnership headed by Richard Matranga specializes in the production of port and Zinfandel. The Vintage Port is made from the classic Portuguese grape varieties of Souzao, Tinta Cao, Touriga Nacional and Alveralhao, all grown in Amador County. Notwithstanding its noble lineage, the Vintage Port simply serves to prove once again that the majority of the makers of this wine in California have a great deal of work to do before they begin to approach remotely the style and quality of Australian Vintage Ports, let alone those of Portugal. However, the Zinfandels — one made from Sonoma County fruit, the other from old vines in Amador County — are rich, robust wines, full of rustic charm and texture.

OTHER WINERIES

ARGONAUT WINERY 1976
A: 13675 Mount Echo Drive, Ione, CA 95640
T: (209) 274 4106 **W**: Stephen F. Bural

CHARLES SPINETTA WINERY 1988
A: 12557 Steiner Road, Plymouth, CA 95669
T: (209) 245 3384 **W**: Charles J. Spinetta

FIDDLE FARM 1988
A: P.O. Box 142, Ione, CA 95640
T: (209) 274 4070 **W**: Henry W. Gonzalez

KENWORTHY VINEYARDS 1979
A: 10120 Shenandoah Road, Plymouth CA 95669 **T**: (209) 245 3198
W: John Kenworthy

STONERIDGE 1975
A: 13862 Ridge Road East, Sutter Creek, CA 95685 **T**: (209) 223 1761 **W**: Gary Porteous

STORY VINEYARD 1973
A: 10525 Bell Road, Plymouth, CA 95669
T: (209) 245 6208 **W**: John Ousley

T.K.C. VINEYARDS 1981
A: 11001 Valley Drive, Plymouth, CA 95669
T: (209) 245 6428 **W**: Harold Nuffer

WINERIES *of* CALAVERAS

STEVENOT WINERY 1978

A: 2690 San Domingo Road, Murphys, CA 95247 **T**: (209) 728 3436 **V**: 10–5 daily **P**: 42,000 **W**: Chuck Hovey

Barden Stevenot was 12 years old when he was driven along San Domingo Road by his parents (the family lived at Angels Camp) and saw the house and swimming pool on what is now the Stevenot Ranch. He made his mind up there and then that one day he would own it, and be able to enjoy the seeming unattainable luxury of a swimming pool. In 1969 his childhood dream came true when he purchased the property and, with the encouragement of friends David Stare and Lou Preston, commenced planting grapes on the cattle ranch in 1974. Four years later he converted a hay barn to a rudimentary winery, and made the first 2,000 cases of wine. Since that time Stevenot has not looked back, its production increasing in line with sales to its present level of 42,000 cases. Given the relative isolation of Stevenot, it has been a remarkable achievement. True, the valley in which it nestles is extremely beautiful, as is Angels Camp, but first the tourists have to come.

Winemaker Chuck Hovey spent seven years with J. Lohr before joining Stevenot in 1983, and runs a singularly efficient and neat facility. As well as Stevenot's own production, he consults to several local wineries, making part of their wines on site at Stevenot. The California Appellation Cabernet Sauvignon and North Coast Merlot are both thoroughly professionally made wines, the former with crisp redcurrant and raspberry fruit flavors, soft tannins and good balance, the latter with ripe dark plum and chocolate fruit. The Grand Reserve Chardonnay comes primarily from estate-grown grapes, and once again is skillfully made. Hovey has deliberately put the accent on the fruit, turning his back on malolactic fermentation and using particularly subtle French oak barrels made by an outstanding Burgundy barrel maker, Dargaud & Jaegle. The Chardonnay is thus very different in style from the usual California offering, and seems to have suffered in consequence; I think it deserves greater critical recognition than it has so far been given.

OTHER WINERIES

BLACK SHEEP VINTNERS 1987
A: P.O. Box 1851, Murphys, CA 95247
T: (209) 728 2157 **W**: David Olson

GOLD MINE
A: 22265 Parrots Ferry Road, Sonora, CA 95370
T: (209) 532 3089

MILLIAIRE WINERY 1983
A: 276 Main Street, Murphys, CA 95247
T: (209) 728 1658 **W**: Steve Millier

YANKEE HILL WINERY 1970
A: 11755 Coarsegold Lane, Columbia, CA 95310 **T**: (209) 533 2417 **W**: Ron Erikson

TASTING ROOM

ABOVE ~ *The August 1992 bushfire stopped perilously close to the Stevenot vineyards.*

El Dorado and North Yuba

Highway 50 bisects the center of the El Dorado AVA, running from Sacramento to Lake Tahoe, and carrying an endless stream of tourists throughout the year. It crosses Highway 49 at Placerville, around which city the majority of the El Dorado wineries are grouped. The odd men out are Nevada City Winery, falling within the all-encompassing Sierra Foothills AVA but well north of El Dorado, and Renaissance, further north again, and sole incumbent of the North Yuba AVA.

I said earlier that D'Agostini was the only winery to survive Prohibition: it might have been more accurate to say only active winery, for the tasting room at Boeger Winery was one of California's oldest wineries, dating from 1872. Built of field stones, it is in immaculate condition, and is on the National Register of Historic Places. It serves both as tasting room and mini-museum, nestling in a little vale along with an 1857 distillery building and the winery proper, built in 1973 but so cleverly designed that it is difficult to tell which is old and which is new.

El Dorado's varied sites and mesoclimates are reflected in the diversity of grape varieties planted, and in the on-going experimentation with the full range of Italian and Rhone varieties. Zinfandel still remains the most widely planted variety, but is nowhere near as dominant as it is in Amador county.

North Yuba has but one winery and one vineyard — the wholly remarkable Renaissance, described at length on pages 278–9.

ABOVE ~ *Hand-picking Riesling on the terraced hillside vineyards at Renaissance.*

OPPOSITE ~ *Jesus Santana Garcia, a vineyard worker at Boeger Winery, relaxing on the verandah of the cellar door facility built in 1872.*

The Region in Brief

Climate, Soil and Viticulture

El Dorado

Climate

The climate is intimately linked to and affected by changes in altitude, with the appellation including areas ranging from 1,200 to 3,500 feet, although the highest vineyards so far established are those of Madrona at 3,000 feet. Rainfall rises by three to four inches for every 300 feet increment in elevation, increasing from 33 to 45 inches. As the elevation rises, so does the climate become cooler, belying the Region III summation unceremoniously slapped on the district by advisers from U.C. Davis. (It varies in fact from Region II to Region III according to elevation and year.) It was a simple observation of the trees and native vegetation which told Dick Bush that he should ignore the Davis recommendations when he started planting Madrona in 1974.

So, obviously enough, elevation, aspect and slope all play roles in influencing mesoclimate, and — interacting with *terroir* — explain the diversity of grape varieties established in the region. Throughout the year, the evenings and nights are cooled by breezes originating from the Sierra Nevada Mountains in the east; the corollary is that there are none of the maritime fogs which play such a profound role in the coastal regions of California, and a very low disease load.

The late summer enjoys warm days and cool nights (typically 90°F to 95°F in late summer, with night-time temperatures falling to 50°F), and rainfall rarely starting before late October or early November.

Soil

The geology is typically very complex, dominated by steeply dipping, faulty and folded rocks intruded by igneous rocks. The soils vary in texture and depth; they are volcanic and have not been transported by glacial or alluvial action. The one common feature is the relatively high acid and lower pH than the valley soils, a characteristic of most mountain soils which leads to a wholly desirable inbuilt vigor control.

The Growing Season

Particularly on the steeper mountain slopes, spring frost is not a major problem, and at higher elevations budbreak is, in any event, late. The effect of the Indian summer in extending the season into October is all important; while the white varieties are harvested in September, Zinfandel does not ripen until early to mid October, and Cabernet Sauvignon in the latter half of that month.

North Yuba

Climate

North Yuba is to all intents and purposes co-extensive with the splendid Renaissance Vineyards, which run from 1,700 feet up to 2,300 feet in elevation, lords of all they survey. The climate here is distinctly cooler than that of the nearby Sacramento Valley, and the wind pattern is different from both that of El Dorado and Sacramento: it does receive westerly winds of maritime origin. The diurnal temperature range is less than that of El Dorado, but can still be as much as 30°F. The rainfall averages 37 inches.

Soil

One of the features which led the BATF to grant the AVA application are the soils, described thus: "The soil associations

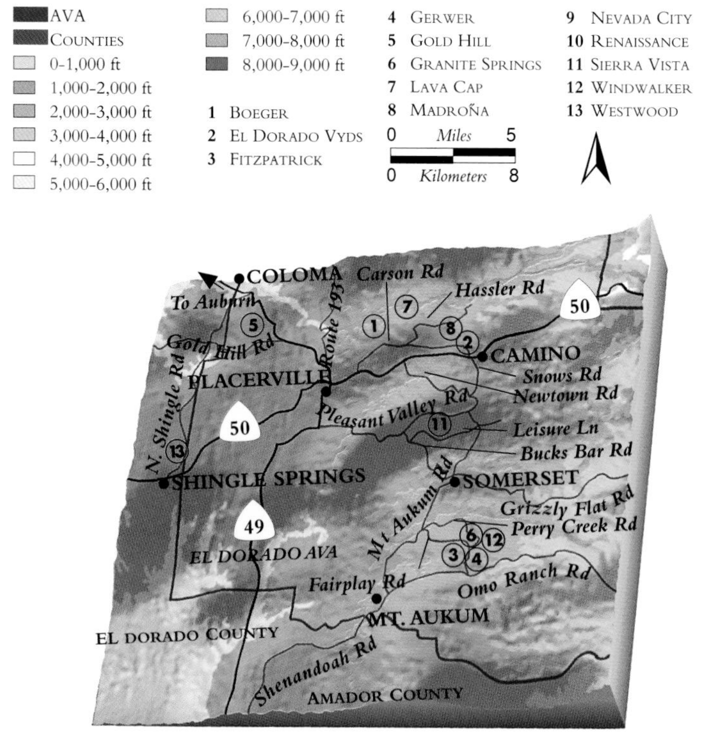
AVA
Counties
0-1,000 ft
1,000-2,000 ft
2,000-3,000 ft
3,000-4,000 ft
4,000-5,000 ft
5,000-6,000 ft
6,000-7,000 ft
7,000-8,000 ft
8,000-9,000 ft
1 Boeger
2 El Dorado Vyds
3 Fitzpatrick
4 Gerwer
5 Gold Hill
6 Granite Springs
7 Lava Cap
8 Madroña
9 Nevada City
10 Renaissance
11 Sierra Vista
12 Windwalker
13 Westwood
0 Miles 5
0 Kilometers 8
COLOMA
To Auburn
Carson Rd
Hassler Rd
50
Route 193
Gold Hill Rd
CAMINO
Snows Rd
Newtown Rd
PLACERVILLE
Pleasant Valley Rd
Leisure Ln
Bucks Bar Rd
N. Shingle Rd
SHINGLE SPRINGS
Mt Aukum Rd
SOMERSET
Grizzly Flat Rd
Perry Creek Rd
49
EL DORADO AVA
Fairplay Rd
Omo Ranch Rd
MT. AUKUM
EL DORADO COUNTY
Shenandoah Rd
AMADOR COUNTY

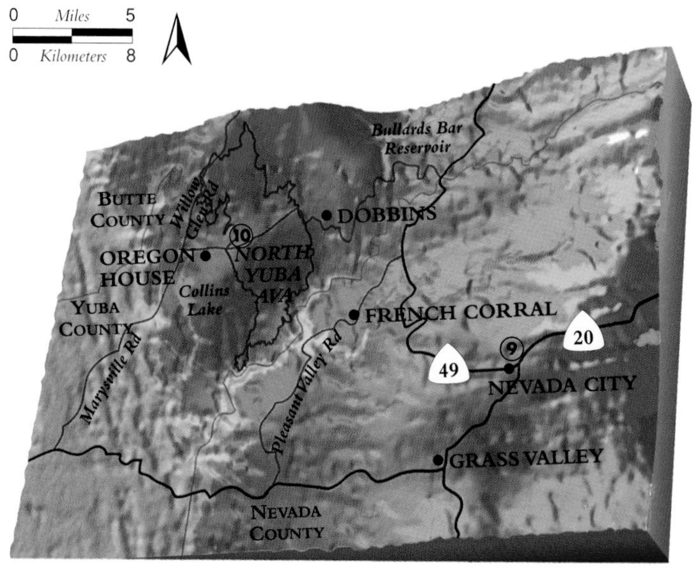
0 Miles 5
0 Kilometers 8
Bullards Bar Reservoir
Butte County
DOBBINS
OREGON HOUSE
NORTH YUBA AVA
Collins Lake
Yuba County
Marysville Rd
FRENCH CORRAL
20
49
NEVADA CITY
Pleasant Valley Rd
GRASS VALLEY
Nevada County

ABOVE ~ *North Yuba map.*
TOP ~ *El Dorado map.*

El Dorado
VINTAGE CHART 1981–91

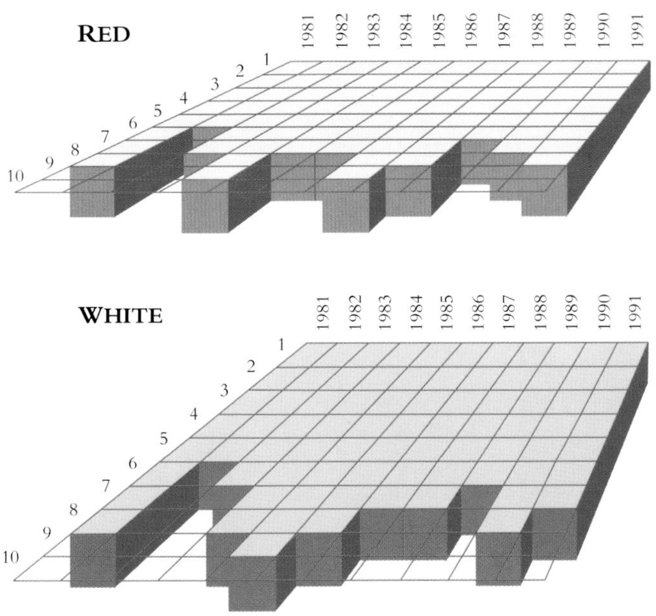
RED
1981
1982
1983
1984
1985
1986
1987
1988
1989
1990
1991
1
2
3
4
5
6
7
8
9
10
WHITE
1981
1982
1983
1984
1985
1986
1987
1988
1989
1990
1991
1
2
3
4
5
6
7
8
9
10

are ... Sierra-Auberry, Englebright-Rescue, and Dobbins. These soils are typical of those developed from granite and igneous rocks. The soils are shallow to very deep, rocky, cobbly and rocky, or non cobbly and rocky, and are generally well drained." Anyone who has visited Renaissance will simply say amen to that.

THE GROWING SEASON

An earlier budbreak and an earlier commencement to the harvest result in a relatively short growing season of 215 to 225 days. Sauvignon Blanc ripens as early as the second week of August when harvested for dry wines, Cabernet Sauvignon between August 20 and September 30, and Riesling between mid September and mid October (the latter for botrytised wines).

Principal Wine Styles

ZINFANDEL

By dint of history as much as present day convictions, this remains the most important grape, and hence wine. It is less exotic than that of Amador County, and in cooler years (and particularly from the higher elevation vineyards) can produce elegant wines with light, fresh fruit and a distinct touch of spice. Madrona and Granite Springs both produce attractive spicy wines; those of Boeger are more in the sweet, cherry jam fruit-mold.

CABERNET SAUVIGNON AND MERLOT

The Cabernet family does well in both El Dorado and North Yuba, albeit with quite different climatic (and *terroir*) inputs. Specifically, the wines do not show any overripe fruit characteristics, yet have ample weight and intensity. A range of wineries do well in various ways: Boeger with Merlot, Gold Hill and Nevada City with Meritage wines, and Renaissance with Cabernet Sauvignon.

El Dorado and North Yuba
1971 AND 1991 ACREAGE/GRAPE VARIETIES

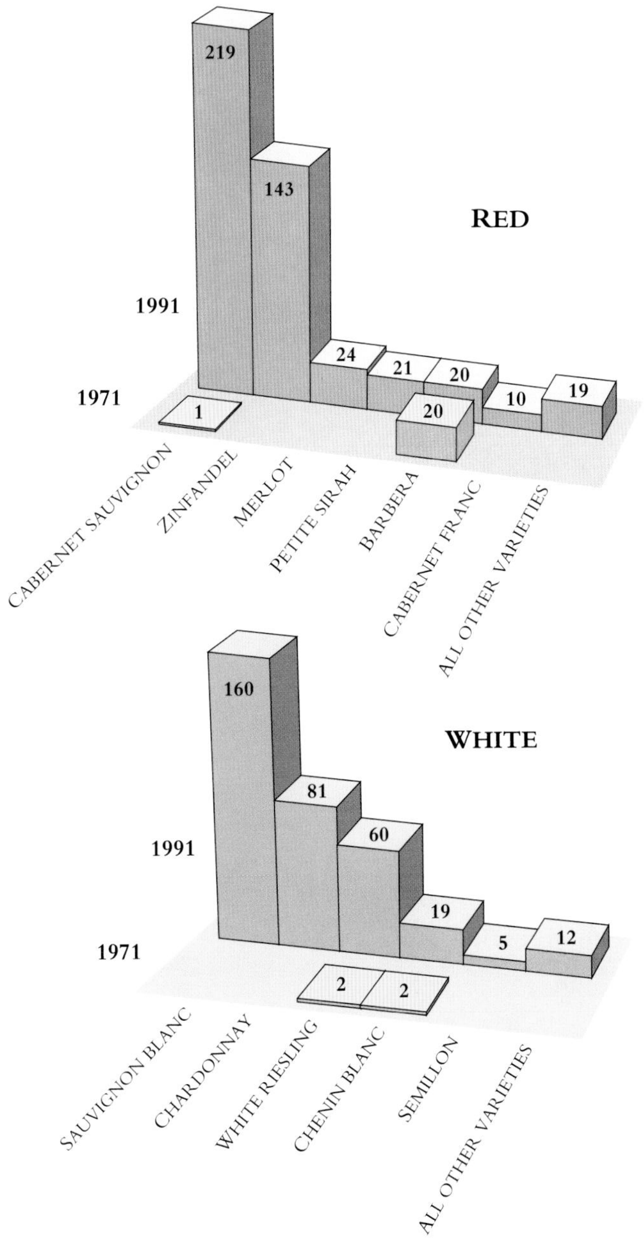
RED
1991
1971
219
143
24
21
20
20
10
19
1
CABERNET SAUVIGNON
ZINFANDEL
MERLOT
PETITE SIRAH
BARBERA
CABERNET FRANC
ALL OTHER VARIETIES
WHITE
1991
1971
160
81
60
19
5
12
2
2
SAUVIGNON BLANC
CHARDONNAY
WHITE RIESLING
CHENIN BLANC
SEMILLON
ALL OTHER VARIETIES

CHARDONNAY

While the plantings are of modest dimension, those wines made from grapes grown at higher elevations show elegance and style, with Madrona and Lava Cap among the notable producers.

BARBERA AND ITALIAN VARIETIES

Barbera is a very successful reality, with Boeger producing consistently outstanding wines from the variety. The omens for the other Italian varieties are propitious; Boeger in El Dorado and Santino in Amador will, it seems, be the leaders.

WHITE RIESLING

The leading producer of White Riesling, in both dry and late harvest manifestations, is Renaissance, which has 44 acres under vine, compared with a mere 16 acres in the whole of El Dorado County.

RENAISSANCE

If there is a more remarkable vineyard in California, I did not see it. Those who have visited the Douro in Portugal, or gazed upon the hill of Hermitage in the Rhone Valley will understand the impact Renaissance has on the first-time visitor. Indeed, the improbability, the magnitude of the labor really only has a true parallel in the Douro. How did those Portuguese construct those endless terraces, so far above the River Douro, so far from summer water and so far from civilization as we know it today, let alone 300 years ago? The same sense of the improbable, accentuated by the grandeur of the sweeping vistas, confronts one at Renaissance.

ABOVE ~ *"The court of the caravans" provides the (slightly controversial) accommodation for members of the Fellowship of Friends at Renaissance.*

It makes sense only when you understand how Renaissance came into being, and why it has the name it has. For while the winery and vineyards are incorporated into a commercial, taxpaying business (or potentially taxpaying once accumulated losses have been offset), it is owned by the Fellowship of Friends, a 1,500-strong philosophical or religious group founded in the San Francisco Bay area in the early 1960s.

The Fellowship was inspired by two Russian mystic philosophers, G.I. Gurdjieff and P.D. Ouspensky, who developed their cult in the early years of this century. Some of their central tenets were that art should be part of life, and that all of us have talents and abilities which our normal life patterns and occupations suppress — but which should be developed.

The members of the Fellowship donate 10% of their annual income, tax deductible if they are United States citizens, but not if they are from other countries (and many are). Since almost by definition most of the Fellowship of Friends are high income earners, this provided a large capital sum and on-going income.

But the Fellowship is not simply a sponge soaking up conscience income. There is an expectation, though not an absolute obligation, that members will spend up to one month a year in the active service of the aims of the Fellowship — the one concession being that during this period payment of the tithe is suspended.

So it was that in 1971 the Fellowship bought a 1,400-acre forested mountain property near the town of Oregon House, and commenced the back-breaking task of clearing the manzanita, scrub oak, pines and cedars which somehow grew out of the exceptionally rocky soil.

It took four years for the terraces to start to take shape, with granite boulders blocking the path at every turn. Indeed, to this day certain of the rows cannot be entered by machinery because the domes of vast boulders rear out of what passes for soil. Conventional planting was out of the question: 175,000 one-foot holes were drilled into the granite, filled with compost, and only then could the vines be planted.

Planting commenced in 1975, and today there are 365 acres of vines planted on over 100 miles of terraces, yielding two tons per acre with the aid of drip irrigation. The terraces were built and the vines were planted by members of the Fellowship, albeit under the supervision of foremen. During this period the Friends were allowed to stay on the estate, principally in an up-market caravan park.

Karl Werner, former winemaster at Schloss Vollrads and founding winemaker at Callaway, was retained from the outset beginning a long period of varietal experimentation in the vineyards and also helping plan and design the spectacular winery since built (though even yet not completed) on the site. What has been completed are a 300-seat auditorium in which regular concerts are held (and which are open to the public), a restaurant (available to all and in fact franchised to a professional restaurateur), and — most remarkably of all — a breathtaking museum of Chinese art, artifacts and furniture. This, too, can be visited by the public at no cost, although the fact is not widely known or advertised.

The winery is functionally complete; ancillary reception and administration areas remained to be built in 1992, but were scheduled for completion within a year or two. Chief executive James Bryant sees himself as running an economic enterprise which must justify the $16 million expenditure to date, and is in no hurry to spend further capital on non-essential programs, however much the unfinished concrete work and protruding reinforcing rods must irritate him.

The winery, with its gleaming white exterior, sits like a jewel on its hilltop, vines above (on a higher range) and below. It is circular in shape, and is built on three levels, relying largely on gravity flow. The crushing and fermentation area is on the upper level, serving three concentric rings of gleaming stainless steel fermenters. The 2,800 barrels, principally of white German oak, are on the next level, while the bottom level houses the bottling line and vast bottle storage facilities.

Experimental winemaking began in 1979, and the first commercial scale production (small in scope) in 1982, but it was not until 1988 that Renaissance made its first commercial release — the year in which Karl Werner died, passing the winemaking mantle on to his wife Diana, herself a fully qualified winemaker, and who had worked with her husband at Renaissance.

Despite early gold medal success with a Petite Sirah (released under the second label of da Vinci), and on-going experimentation with Chardonnay and Merlot, the winery now releases only Sauvignon Blanc (in dry and botrytised forms), White Riesling (likewise) and Cabernet Sauvignon (standard and Reserve).

I discuss the wines on page 281, but suffice it to say that while Renaissance may have been in no hurry to enter the market in the first place, President James Bryant and sales manager Hanns Heick have been extremely energetic in building sales both in the United States and in export markets (notably the United Kingdom and Germany) since that time.

For the time being, at least, Renaissance Winery is open to visits by appointment only. I can only suggest you move heaven and earth to make an appointment, for you will see both when you arrive.

ABOVE ~ *The picking crew at the top of the Renaissance vineyards moving to another block.*

WINERIES *of* EL DORADO AND NORTH YUBA

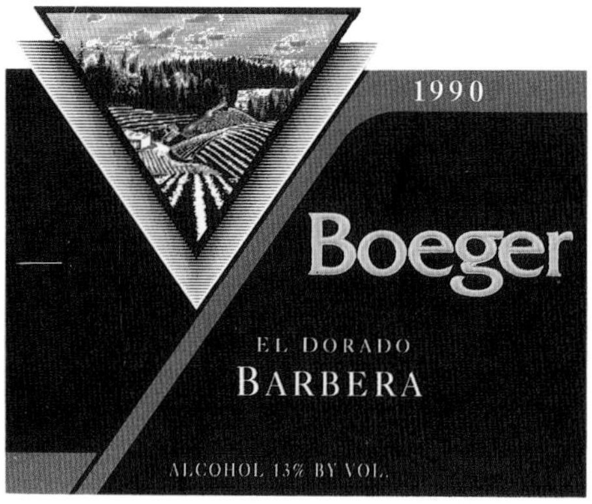
1990
Boeger
EL DORADO
BARBERA
ALCOHOL 13% BY VOL.

BOEGER WINERY 1973

A: 1709 Carson Road, Placerville, CA 95667 **T**: (916) 622 8094 **V**: 10–5 daily **P**: 15,000 **W**: Greg Boeger

Greg Boeger comes from a distinguished Napa Valley family of grape growers (the Nicholinis, with whom Boeger has recently gone back into partnership) but elected to come to El Dorado to open the first winery after the repeal of Prohibition following his graduation from U.C. Davis. The ranch he purchased was the site of a nineteenth-century winery, built in 1872 by Lombardi Fossati, and which stands (magnificently preserved) to this day, now serving as the tasting room. Together with a small rock dam, an 1850s distillery building and the winery (built in 1973), it provides an idyllic setting.

Greg Boeger candidly admits he is still determining which varieties are most suited to the region, and relied entirely upon intuition in the original selection of Cabernet Sauvignon, Merlot, Zinfandel, Chardonnay, Sauvignon Blanc and Semillon. (An additional leased vineyard nearby provides Johannisberg Riesling.) While happy with the results he has achieved from these varieties, he has recently moved to establish one acre each of Syrah, Grenache, Mourvedre, Viognier, Nebbiolo, Refosco and Sangiovese, as well as making a Barbera from grapes purchased from a nearby vineyard.

The Barbera is a particularly exciting wine, with intense yet soft sweet fruit, and quite entrancing mouthfeel. The Zinfandels are well made, and have the capacity to age, while the Merlot has lots of firm, red berry fruit, even if it is a little tough. It has to be said that I was not the least bit impressed by the Chardonnay, but Boeger has a good track record with the variety, and my judgment may be harsh.

GOLD HILL VINEYARD 1985

A: 5660 Vineyard Lane, Placerville, CA 95667 **T**: (916) 626 6522 **V**: 10–5 Sat–Sun **P**: 8,000 **W**: Hank Battjes

Gold Hill Vineyard uses Coloma Gold as its second label, signifying its connection with the town of Coloma, just south of Sutter Mill where gold was first discovered in California, and reviving memories of Coloma Vineyard which flourished in the last century. Owner and winemaker Hank Battjes has established 35 acres of vineyard (part of it first planted in the mid 1960s and purchased by him) with Chardonnay, Cabernet Sauvignon, Merlot, Cabernet Franc, Chenin Blanc and Riesling. The 1989 Meritage from Gold Hill won the top red wine gold medal for the Sierra Foothills region at the 1992 California State Fair.

GRANITE SPRINGS WINERY 1981

A: 6060 Granite Springs Road, Somerset, CA 95684 **T**: (209) 245 6395 **V**: 11–5 Sat–Sun and by appointment **P**: 10,000 **W**: Lester Russell

VINTAGE 1989
GRANITE SPRINGS
EL DORADO
Petite Sirah
GRANITE HILL VINEYARDS
PRODUCED & BOTTLED BY GRANITE SPRINGS WINERY
SOMERSET, EL DORADO COUNTY, CALIFORNIA BW 5073
ALCOHOL 13% BY VOLUME CONTAINS SULFITES

Granite Springs was established by Lynne and Les Russell on a modest ranch purchased by them in 1979 at an elevation of 2,400 feet. The relatively thin mountain soils were planted to Cabernet Sauvignon, Sauvignon Blanc and Zinfandel, with lesser amounts of Petite Sirah, Cabernet Franc and Chenin Blanc. The vineyards have been well maintained, the vines showing excellent balance between canopy and crop, and over the intervening years, Granite Springs has established a solid reputation garnering show medals with consistency along the way. Zinfandel is made in two modes, one estate-grown, the other from Higgins Vineyard. The estate wine typically shows attractive dark plum and spice fruit, with good balance and adequate concentration. The estate-bottled Cabernet Sauvignon is in fact around 80% Sauvignon and 20% Cabernet Franc, while the Petite Sirah follows a Rhone Valley approach by incorporating 5% Chenin Blanc.

LAVA CAP 1986

A: 2221 Fruitridge Road, Placerville, CA 95667 **T**: (916) 621 0175 **V**: 11–5 daily **P**: 8,000 **W**: Thomas Jones

The 30-acre Lava Cap Vineyard was established by the Jones family on the rich, volcanic soils from which it takes its name at an elevation of 2,600 feet. It is planted to Chardonnay, Sauvignon Blanc, Cabernet Sauvignon and Zinfandel, the latter two being made in both red and blush guises. The elevation results in significantly cooler growing conditions, which clearly suit the white varieties. U.C. Davis-trained Tom Jones made an exceptionally good 1990 Chardonnay, which was the top-rated Sierra Foothills white wine at the 1992 California State Fair, emulating the achievement of Gold Hill Vineyard with its Red Meritage.

MADRONA VINEYARDS 1980

A: High Hill Road, Camino, CA 95709 **T**: (916) 644 5948 **V**: 11–5 daily **P**: 12,000 **W**: Mark Foster

Madrona is said to be the highest vineyard in California; certainly the elevation of 3,000 feet dwarfs that of its neighbors in the El Dorado region. Owner Dick Bush came here in 1973, and lost no time in planting Gewurztraminer, Riesling, Chardonnay, Cabernet Sauvignon and Cabernet Franc, bowing to convention only with Zinfandel. By one of those chances of fate, Madrona was the first place which winemaker Mark Foster approached upon changing careers from biologist to aircraft systems computer programmer to winemaker, but was told there was no opening as it was a family-owned and run concern. Five years later, having worked for Smothers Brothers (in Santa Cruz) and Chalone, he was approached by Dick Bush and joined the team.

It is an exciting operation, entered by driving through a model ranch (owned by others) replete with special fishing ponds and innumerable attractions for children and those of the young at heart. Madrona itself has kept abreast of the latest viticultural techniques, and the viticulture generally is as impressive as the winemaking. The professed aim of Madrona is to make wines of consistently even quality across a wide range, and it achieves just this. The Zinfandel is the only style which shows radical vintage variation, veering from cherry/spicy fruit in the lighter years through to a big, chocolatey style in the warm years. Madrona also acts as a custom crush maker for the 2,000-case Lake Tahoe Winery.

NEVADA CITY WINERY 1980

A: 321 Spring Street, Nevada City, CA 95959
T: (916) 265 9463 **V**: 12–5 daily **P**: 8,000
W: Ron Goodspeed

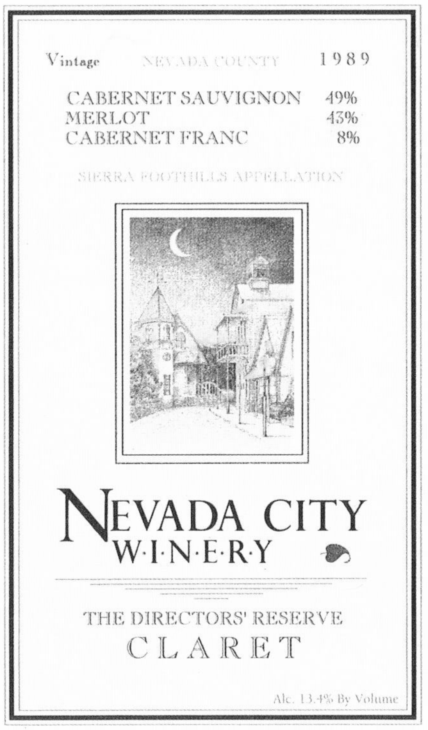
Vintage NEVADA COUNTY 1989
CABERNET SAUVIGNON 49%
MERLOT 43%
CABERNET FRANC 8%
SIERRA FOOTHILLS APPELLATION
NEVADA CITY
W·I·N·E·R·Y
THE DIRECTORS' RESERVE
CLARET
Alc. 13.4% By Volume

The town of Nevada City has to be seen to be believed, so much of it looking as if it were built yesterday as a film set. In fact, it is an unspoilt reminder from the gold mining days, which still uses gas lamps for street lights, and which has a thoroughly enlightened attitude to the finer things of life, including a local law which permits the consumption of wine in the public streets. Nevada City Winery was founded in 1980 by former lawyer Allan Hayley, who, amongst other things, had run a wine distribution business in Hawaii. Right from the outset, Nevada City Winery has targeted the tourist trade, the winery itself being situated in the center of town in a building which started life as a brewery in the last century. Its proprietary labels include Douce Noir, Alpen Glow, Rough and Ready Red, Bicycle Blanc and Victorian White; the labels are exceptionally imaginative, that of Bicycle Blanc being one of the most striking I have ever seen, without detracting from the far prettier and conventional basic label.

The winery may be market-orientated, but it is a serious wine producer, making a range of interesting wines in very small quantities (less than 200 cases of each). Douce Noir is a Rhone blend of Charbono, Mourvedre and Grenache, which is packed with ripe, luscious red berry fruit (and a fair dose of tannins). The Directors Reserve Claret (a Meritage blend of Cabernet Sauvignon, Merlot and Cabernet Franc) shows fresh red cherry and redcurrant fruit, but again finishes with rather firm tannins.

RENAISSANCE VINEYARD & WINERY 1978

A: 12585 Rice's Crossing Road, Renaissance, CA 95962 **T**: (916) 692 2222
V: By appointment **P**: 20,000
W: Diana Werner

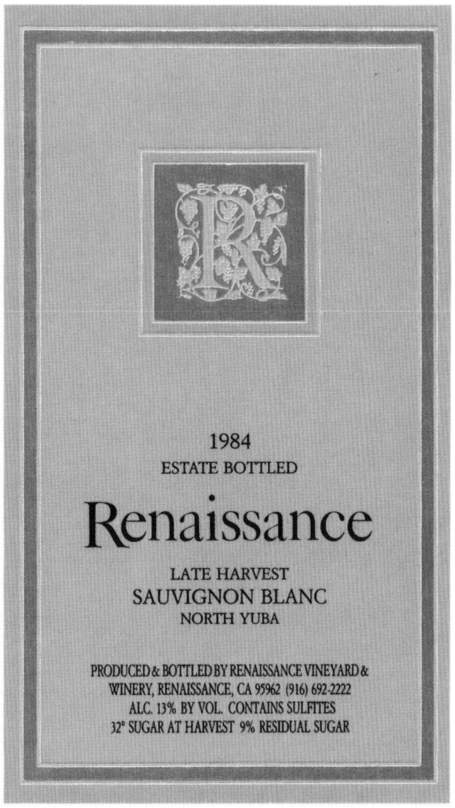
1984
ESTATE BOTTLED
Renaissance
LATE HARVEST
SAUVIGNON BLANC
NORTH YUBA
PRODUCED & BOTTLED BY RENAISSANCE VINEYARD & WINERY, RENAISSANCE, CA 95962 (916) 692-2222
ALC. 13% BY VOL. CONTAINS SULFITES
32° SUGAR AT HARVEST 9% RESIDUAL SUGAR

The story of the inspiration behind Renaissance has been told earlier (pages 278–9), but I did not there speak of the wines. These form part of a portfolio which is spartan in its simplicity: a Sauvignon Blanc (dry and Late Harvest), White Riesling (likewise) and Cabernet Sauvignon (standard and Reserve). All of the few releases made up to 1992 had received high praise, but surely none was better than the magnificent 1985 Special Select Late Harvest Riesling, a wine which even the former winemaster of Schloss Vollrads must have been particularly proud. Still available in 1992, it showed intense botrytis influence, yet retained pure, pronounced lime juice varietal character — for me always the mark of the very greatest late harvest styles. It worked much better than the Late Harvest Sauvignon Blanc, which comes as no great surprise. The dry Sauvignon Blanc is more successful, although I have some reservations about what appears to be a touch of German oak.

The Cabernet Sauvignons from 1984 to 1986, the former under a Reserve label, are wines of great elegance, with a tightness of structure which has a distinctly European cast. The 1987 Cabernet Sauvignon, the most recent release, is perceptibly lighter in style, but nonetheless shows attractive cherry/berry fruit.

OTHER WINERIES

ELDORADO VINEYARDS 1976
A: 3551 Carson Road, Camino, CA 95709
T: (916) 644 2854 **W**: John Mirande

FITZPATRICK WINERY 1980
A: 7740 Fairplay Road, Somerset, CA 95684
T: (209) 245 3248 **W**: Brian Fitzpatrick

GERWER WINERY 1982
A: 8221 Stoney Creek Road, Somerset, CA 95684 **T**: (209) 245 3467 **W**: Vernon Gerwer

SIERRA VISTA WINERY 1977
A: M/A 4560 Cabernet Way, Placerville, CA 95667 **T**: (916) 622 7221 **W**: John MacReady

WINDWALKER VINEYARDS
A: 7360 Perry Creek Road, Somerset, CA 95684
T: (209) 245 4054

WESTWOOD 1987
A: 3100 Ponderosa Road, Shingle Springs, CA 95682 **T**: (916) 666 6079 **W**: Umbert E. Urch

ABOVE ~ *Spanish born Maria Jesus picking Riesling at Renaissance Vineyard.*

CENTRAL VALLEY

The Central Valley is the unromantic business end of the industry, where wine is made in plants that look far more like petroleum refineries than wineries and is marketed as a beverage with price and store position determining its fate, while wine-maker and variety are generally unknown. But its importance cannot be overstated: after all, it contains 55% of the state's vineyards and produces 75% of its wine (yields are high in this neck of the woods). Each of the ten largest wine companies in the United States has a base here, and it is home to Gallo, the biggest wine company in the world.

Like the rest of California, it had a history of grape growing in the nineteenth century, but its present-day importance did not begin to take shape until the post-Second World War period and matured only in the 1970s. How irrelevant that history is may be gauged from the fact that in 1881 Leland Stanford purchased the Gerke Vineyard in Tehama County on the banks of the then unspoilt Sacramento River north of Chico. He expanded the vineyards to 5,000 acres, the largest in the world at that time, and built a two-million-gallon winery. Unfortunately, the table wine was so appalling that he had to become the largest brandy distiller in the world, making lesser quantities of fortified wine. Nothing remains; today Tehama County has a token 140 acres of grapes.

The areas around the Delta — notably the Solano Green Valley, Clarksburg and Lodi AVAs — have gained the greatest identity and are treated separately. Here intensive farming has always been carried out in the very rich soils washed down from the Sierras and with abundant water from the meanderings of the Sacramento, Consumnes, Mokelumne and San Joaquin Rivers.

San Joaquin County (in the northern portion of which Lodi is located) marks the start of this viticultural empire, which is basically the southern half of the Central Valley, which is often as not called the San Joaquin Valley. This region was brought to life by one of the vast irrigation schemes of the latter nineteenth and early twentieth centuries; if one wishes to have a real understanding of those schemes I can earnestly recommend Marc Reisner's brilliant book *Cadillac Desert*.

The drive from Stockton to Bakersfield down Highway 99 is as boring — and throughout summer as searingly hot — as the mind can conceive. I have often said that vineyards bring their own special beauty to a landscape. I am sorry to say that here they fail. But, at the end of the day, that is irrelevant: just as the origin of milk or orange juice on the supermarket shelf is unknown and irrelevant, so is that of the jug and wine of the Central Valley.

Central Valley
1971 AND 1991 ACREAGE/GRAPE VARIETIES

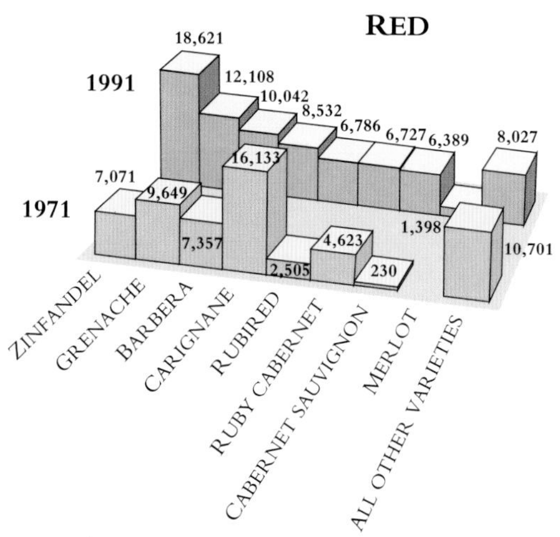
RED
1991
1971
18,621
12,108
10,042
8,532
6,786
6,727
6,389
8,027
7,071
9,649
7,357
16,133
2,505
4,623
230
1,398
10,701
ZINFANDEL
GRENACHE
BARBERA
CARIGNANE
RUBIRED
RUBY CABERNET
CABERNET SAUVIGNON
MERLOT
ALL OTHER VARIETIES

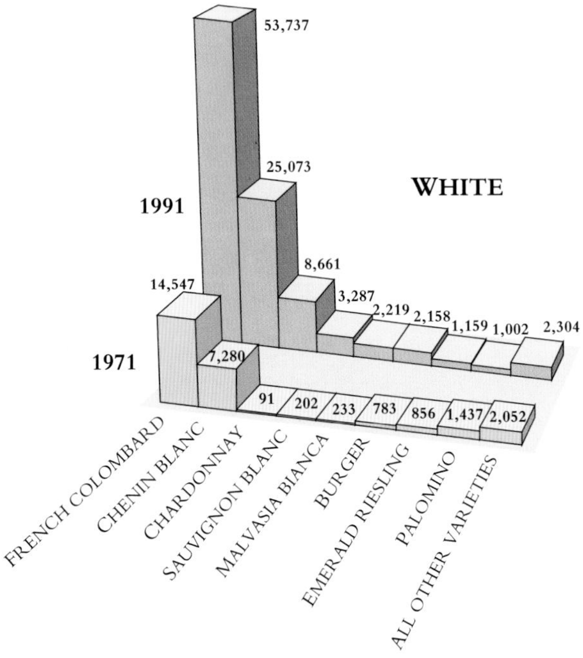
WHITE
1991
1971
53,737
25,073
8,661
3,287
2,219
2,158
1,159
1,002
2,304
14,547
7,280
91
202
233
783
856
1,437
2,052
FRENCH COLOMBARD
CHENIN BLANC
CHARDONNAY
SAUVIGNON BLANC
MALVASIA BIANCA
BURGER
EMERALD RIESLING
PALOMINO
ALL OTHER VARIETIES

PREVIOUS PAGE ~ *The deep and alluvial soils of the Central Valley needed only water to create some of the world's most productive farming land.*

ABOVE ~ *Miguel Munoz works on the Bonita Ranch in the San Joaquin Valley.*

ABOVE ~ *San Pablo Bay looking west to Mount Tamalpais.*

LODI, CLARKSBURG AND SOLANO

LODI

When the Flame Tokay was introduced to Lodi at the turn of the century, the region was known only for its watermelons and grains. Within 20 years Lodi had become the most prosperous grape district in the United States, the brilliantly colored grapes being transported fresh to the Eastern States markets in the newly developed refrigerated rail cars. Even a relatively few miles to the south at Stockton, Flame Tokay did not develop the same bright color — as if in punishment, phylloxera attacked the Stockton plantings, and Lodi was left unchallenged.

Flame Tokay served Lodi well for decades, but today is fast disappearing: in 1980 there were 18,200 acres in San Joaquin County, in 1991 there were said to be 10,994 acres (97% of the state's total), but local growers suggest there were in fact much less. With the qualified exception of base wine for brandy, it has never made wine of any quality, and its primary function as a table grape has been usurped by Flame Seedless, grown all the way south to Arizona, which gets to the market earlier.

ABOVE ~ *Winery or refinery? In the Central Valley both function in much the same way.*

Nonetheless, it remains symptomatic of a region which has basically been one of intensive, mixed farming. There are 600 growers in Lodi today, most of whom sell to a few very large producers; typically, their farm is 100 acres or less, and will include cherries, table grapes, row crops and wine grapes. In all, there are 45,000 acres of grapes (according to the local growers' association, a figure higher than the official statistics would suggest) in the total AVA land acreage of 458,000.

The one variety which has always been grown is Zinfandel. Lodi produces almost 40% of the state's total production, and there are many old vineyards alongside newer plantings. It was to Lodi which Sutter Home turned once its White Zinfandel started to

OPPOSITE ~ *The delta system west of Clarksburg near the junction of the Sacramento and San Joaquin Rivers.*

Lodi and Clarksburg
VINTAGE CHART
1981–91

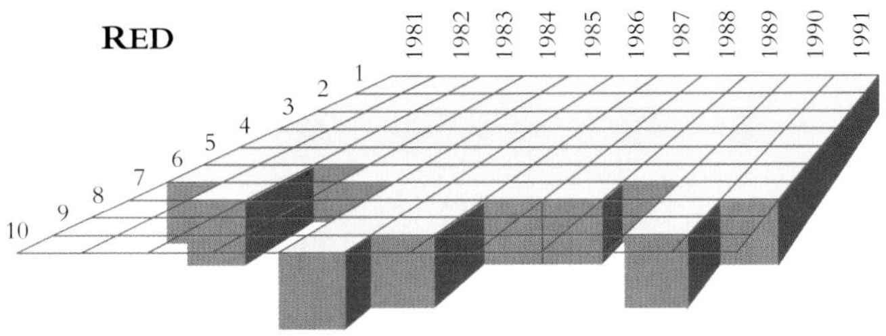
RED
1981
1982
1983
1984
1985
1986
1987
1988
1989
1990
1991
1
2
3
4
5
6
7
8
9
10

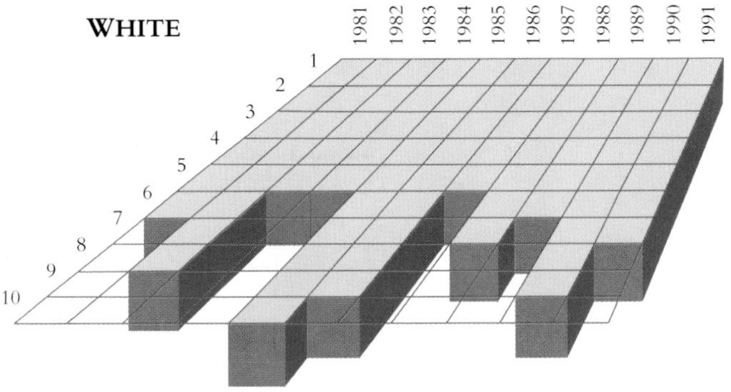
WHITE
1981
1982
1983
1984
1985
1986
1987
1988
1989
1990
1991
1
2
3
4
5
6
7
8
9
10

take hold, although the quality of the red Zinfandel wine has never been in doubt.

Driven by the demands of the market as a whole, but also by those of Mondavi Woodbridge, Sebastiani (which has a major processing plant in Lodi) and Gallo (which for long regarded Lodi as its private domain and is still hugely powerful), growers have progressively replaced Flame Tokay with Sauvignon Blanc, Chenin Blanc, Chardonnay, Cabernet Sauvignon and Merlot (amongst others, of course). Mondavi Woodbridge, in particular, is very active in its grower education programs, leading to on-going improvements in both quality and productivity.

Lodi sees itself as uniquely well placed to profit from the phylloxera invasion of the North Coast regions (and also Monterey). AxR has never been the rootstock of choice for those vineyards which have been planted on grafted stock, while the very sandy soils which prevail in much of the region harbor neither phylloxera or nematodes. With a grape production equivalent to that of Napa, Sonoma and Mendocino combined, it is a force to be reckoned with.

CLARKSBURG

Clarksburg not only has its own AVA, but has an AVA subdistrict, Merritt Island, which was in fact given AVA status first (in 1982 — Clarksburg followed in 1984). Merritt Island AVA is the home of Bogle Vineyards and Winery (which having petitioned for the AVA, does not use it on its label), but is also noteworthy for being a man-made island of some 5,000 acres created by reclaiming land from the Sacramento River Delta. This is not a district of hills, but an area reminiscent of Holland; frequently the few, ill-marked roads are placed on the top of the levee banks which hold the waters at bay, so you in fact look down on the vineyards.

The Clarksburg AVA is unique in that its one great wine is Chenin Blanc: the overwhelming majority of the best California Chenin Blancs have been made by

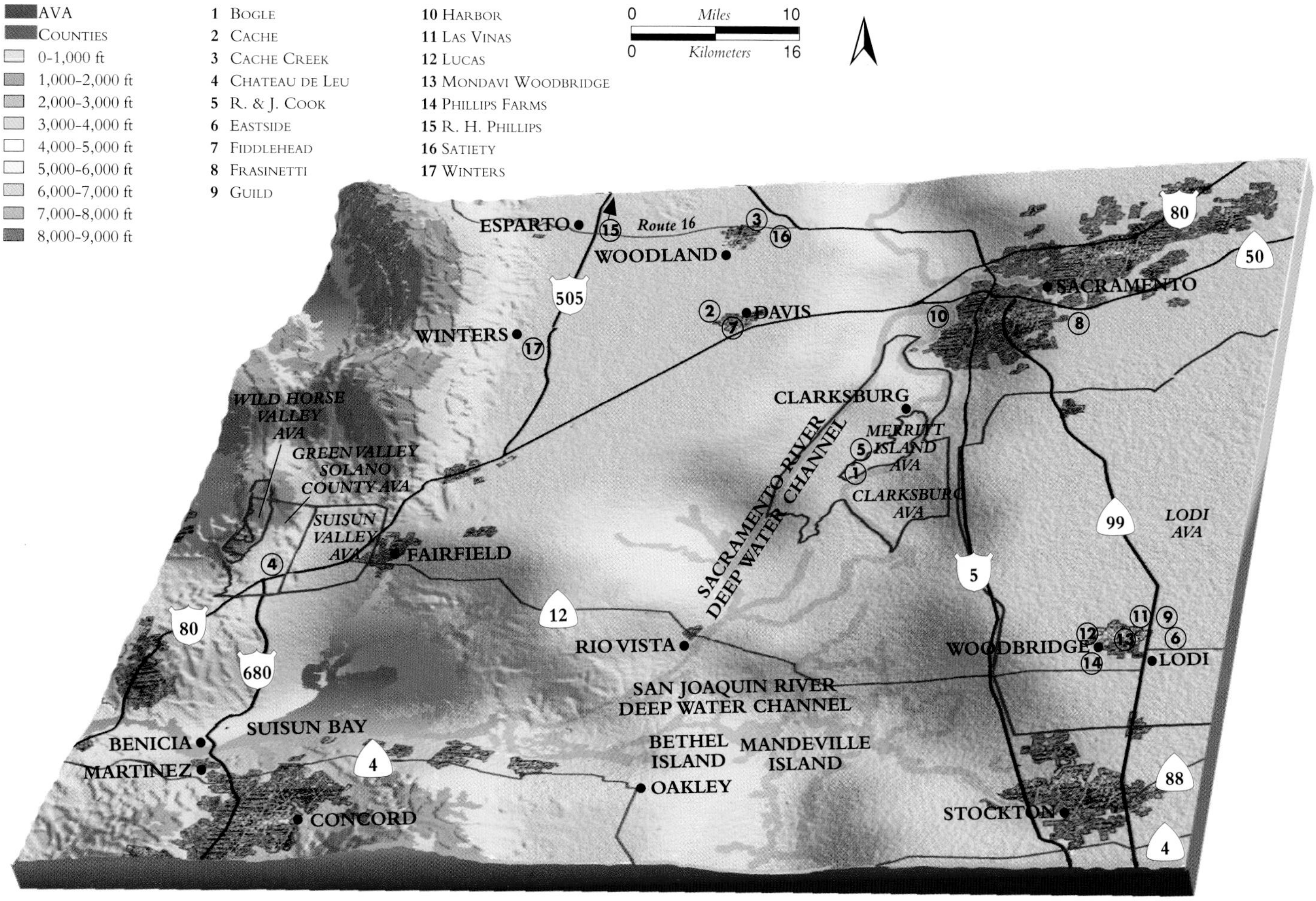
AVA
Counties
0-1,000 ft
1,000-2,000 ft
2,000-3,000 ft
3,000-4,000 ft
4,000-5,000 ft
5,000-6,000 ft
6,000-7,000 ft
7,000-8,000 ft
8,000-9,000 ft
1 Bogle
2 Cache
3 Cache Creek
4 Chateau de Leu
5 R. & J. Cook
6 Eastside
7 Fiddlehead
8 Frasinetti
9 Guild
10 Harbor
11 Las Vinas
12 Lucas
13 Mondavi Woodbridge
14 Phillips Farms
15 R. H. Phillips
16 Satiety
17 Winters
0 Miles 10
0 Kilometers 16
ESPARTO
Route 16
WOODLAND
505
WINTERS
DAVIS
SACRAMENTO
80
50
CLARKSBURG
MERRITT ISLAND AVA
CLARKSBURG AVA
SACRAMENTO RIVER DEEP WATER CHANNEL
WILD HORSE VALLEY AVA
GREEN VALLEY SOLANO COUNTY AVA
SUISUN VALLEY AVA
FAIRFIELD
99
LODI AVA
5
12
RIO VISTA
WOODBRIDGE
LODI
680
SAN JOAQUIN RIVER DEEP WATER CHANNEL
SUISUN BAY
BENICIA
MARTINEZ
4
BETHEL ISLAND
MANDEVILLE ISLAND
OAKLEY
CONCORD
STOCKTON
88

wineries across the state who have purchased grapes from Clarksburg. Conversely, it has proved to be a very ordinary district for red wines. The rich soil and the high water table mean that Cabernet Sauvignon keeps growing and will not provide adequately colored or flavored wines — although Petite Sirah has a much better track record.

ESTAB. 1890

Solano

Solano County has two AVAs: Solano Green Valley, which sits just to the east of the Napa Valley county line (but is separated from the Napa Valley by the Vaca Range as well as the exigencies of the county line), and the Suisun Valley to the east of the Green Valley.

Solano Green Valley is only four miles long and one mile wide. It is coastal influenced, with a climate which ranges between 3,500 and 3,700 degree days, or mid Region III. Fogs are prevalent between May and August, but the afternoons are warm. It is home to the remarkable Chateau de Leu, a small winery making a disproportionate impact with locally grown and Napa-sourced grapes.

Suisun Valley has more grapes than does Solano (800 acres compared to 400 acres) but likewise has only one winery. It is no warmer than Solano Green Valley, but fogs do not penetrate. Both regions share clay loam soils, although of different series.

ABOVE ~ *Lodi, Clarksburg and Solano map.*

ABOVE ~ *Around the turn of the century Lodi enjoyed enormous prosperity from its grape-growing, and in particular from Flame Tokay.*

THE REGION IN BRIEF

Climate, Soil and Viticulture

LODI

CLIMATE

Although the Central Valley south and north of the Delta (and also Lodi) is broad and absolutely flat, the climate of Lodi is distinctly different from and cooler than that of the country to the north and south. The reason lies with the Carquinez Straights, where the eastern reach of the San Francisco Bay is pinched by mountain ranges before opening up again. As the vacuum cleaner of the hot extremities of the Central Valley draws in the cool marine air, it is funneled through the Carquinez Straits, hitting first Clarksburg and then Lodi before being pulled south or north, and being rapidly warmed by the land mass across which it travels. So it is that Lodi has a ten-year mean heat summation of 3,570 degree days, putting it at the low end of Region III, and that in some years (such as 1975) it can be as low as 3,100 degree days, or low Region II — with counterbalancing hot vintages, of course. Stockton, just outside the southern extremity of the Lodi AVA, has a mid Region IV average summation of 4,386 degree days, Sacramento low Region IV at 4,185 degree days.

In typical fashion, morning summer fogs are common, while the afternoon sea breezes prevent the temperature climbing above 95°F on even the hottest days, leading to a rapid drop in temperature between 4 P.M. and 5 P.M. most days; temperatures of over 100°F are rare. The rainfall of 16 inches (all winter-spring) makes growing season irrigation essential: as in much of the San Joaquin Valley, this is typically carried out by flood irrigation of every second row, but drip irrigation will gradually become the norm as pressures on water usage increase. Interestingly, years of high rainfall (up to 26 inches have been recorded) can create problems through excessive crops which then refuse to ripen adequately; the combination of the sandy soils and controlled water application is a major quality factor.

SOIL

The soils are predominantly alluvial sandy loams in the Hannaford and San Joaquin series. They have derived from the Sierra Mountains over the millennia, and been deposited in floodplains and terraces. They are very well drained, and are tremendously deep — up to 40 feet in places. The newer plantings in the foothills at the eastern extremity of the AVA between the Consumnes and Calaveras Rivers are on far rockier mountain soils which are only five to six feet deep, and hold out hope for high quality red wine production.

THE GROWING SEASON

The season proceeds at a brisk pace, untroubled by early frosts or late rains. Zinfandel picked for blush wines comes in first, typically commencing around August 17, but as early as August 4 (in 1992) and as late as August 24 (in 1991). Chardonnay ripens mid August, and Cabernet Sauvignon from the end of September through to early October.

CLARKSBURG

CLIMATE

The climate is similar to but marginally cooler than that of Lodi, with an average summation of less than 3,000 degree days. It is affected by precisely the same maritime-sourced fogs and winds, which reach it first, but has an added mesoclimatic effect from the Sacramento River, its tributaries, backwaters and sloughs.

SOIL

The soil is radically different from that of Lodi, ranging between poorly drained clay and clay loam through to organic, peat-based soils. Here it is drainage rather than irrigation which is practiced, and the whole management of the vineyards takes on a different aspect.

THE GROWING SEASON

As one would expect, it conforms to that of Lodi except that it starts a week or so later, and the process of adequately ripening Cabernet Sauvignon can be a lengthy and uncertain one.

Principal Wine Styles

ZINFANDEL

For many, Lodi is the spiritual home of Zinfandel, however much of the vast tonnage disappears in the bland anonymity of White Zinfandel — a wine which could equally well be made from any other grape variety, and (as blush) sometimes is. It comes as no surprise to find that the few regionally identified Zinfandels on the market are made from the significant acreage of old vines dating back to the early years of this century, protected from phylloxera by the sandy soils and from replanting because of the generally low grape prices prevailing until the late 1970s. Lucas Winery is the one estate producer of significance in Lodi; Bogle does well enough in Clarksburg, while R.H. Phillips does the same in the Dunnigan Hills. As for the rest, the powerful, sweet fruit of the Lodi grapes is the anonymous cornerstone of many of the big company varietal Zinfandels, red and white.

SAUVIGNON BLANC

Yet again, a variety which makes delicious wines in Lodi, Green Valley and Clarksburg — but does best in Lodi. In its youth it produces a fragrant wine with fruity, orange-blossom aromas mixed with greener, herbal characters; with age — as long as seven to eight years — citrus characters dominate. The reality is that few consumers in the world understand that well-made Sauvignon Blanc can age as well as almost any other white wine: how many readers, I wonder, have enjoyed a ten-year-old Pouilly Fumé? Mondavi Woodbridge makes exemplary Sauvignon Blanc: I can think of few better picnic lunch wines for a summer's day. There is no artifice, just simple, direct, and deliciously crisp fruit flavor.

Cabernet Sauvignon

If the real quality — and potential — of Lodi is to be realized, it may well be through this variety. The region may be inherently better suited to Zinfandel and Sauvignon Blanc, but they do not have — nor will they ever have — the cachet of Cabernet Sauvignon. The answer here lies in part in viticultural techniques (better canopy management, moderate yields and so forth), and in site and soil selection. As it is, Las Vinas shows what can be achieved in the small winery context, Mondavi Woodbridge at the other end of the spectrum. These are not Napa Valley styles: they will never have the extract or the tannin, but one of these days people will realize that this is not necessarily such a bad thing. Sweet, soft red berry fruit can make a delicious wine, ready to drink at two to three years of age, but quite capable of retaining its freshness for twice that time.

Chenin Blanc

Clarksburg has made this variety its own, with help from such makers as David Stare of Dry Creek and recognition from writers as erudite and perceptive as Gerald Asher. The soft climate and unique soil of the district combine to produce a distinctively floral and authentically fruit-salad accented wine — evocative of pretty little girls and springtime. Ever the heretic when it comes to this variety, my only wish is that someone, somewhere in the world will make a wine which bears even a passing resemblance to the great wines of Vouvray, Montlouis, Bonnezeaux and Coteaux du Layon in the Loire Valley of France.

Chardonnay

Needless to say, this flourishes by the day, producing a wine as soft and as charming as Chenin Blanc, but lacking even its distinction.

ABOVE ~ *Gary Pylman grows Merlot and Chardonnay on Merrit Island in the Clarksburg region.*

WINERIES *of* LODI

GUILD WINERY & DISTILLERY 1934

A: Guild Avenue and Winemaster Way, Lodi, CA 95240 **T**: (209) 368 5151 **V**: 10–5 daily **P**: 5 million **W**: Mark Gabrielli

Now part of the New York-based Canandaigua Wine Co., Guild was formed in the aftermath of Prohibition by disaffected growers seeking a better price, indeed any price, for their grapes. It then went through decades of growth, purchasing Alta Vineyards, A. Mattei, Cameo Vineyards, B. Cribari & Sons, and Garrett (the last famous for its Virginia Dare brand) in 1962. Next it purchased the wineries of its co-operative members, following this with the purchase of Chen Lee's Roma and Cresta Blanca Wineries in 1970. Now, as I say, under Canandaigua ownership, its brands include Dunnewood Vineyards & Winery, Cribari, Paul Garrett Vintners Choice, Cook's Champagne and Chase-Limogere Sparkling wines.

LAS VINAS WINERY 1986

A: 5573 West Woodbridge Road, Lodi, CA 95242 **T**: (209) 334 0445 **V**: 9–5 weekends **P**: 12,000 **W**: John Cotta

The Cotta family have been grape growers in the Lodi region for a long time, with 800 acres under vine. In 1986 John Cotta persuaded his brothers that they should convert a dairy barn into a winery and start producing their own wine under the Las Vinas label. Says John Cotta, "I was convinced that super-premium wines could be made from this region, but the emphasis has always been on yield rather than quality." The string of awards that Las Vinas has won in major shows are one symbol of John Cotta's success. The other, as always, is the wine in the glass. Here the Peltier Vineyard Cabernet Sauvignon is in turn the most striking example: with a two to three tons to the acre crop, it produces a wine of real character and concentration. The Chardonnay is clean, direct and crisp, the Zinfandel with a briary cut set against the jammy sweetness of Lodi. Cotta ascribes the fruit quality to the sea breezes funneled through the Carquinez Straits, to leaf pulling in the vineyards, and to modest yields on the sandy soils.

THE LUCAS WINERY 1978

A: 18196 North Davis Road, Lodi, CA 95240 **T**: (209) 368 2006 **V**: By appointment **P**: 1,000 **W**: Dave Lucas

Dave Lucas knows all there is to know about Lodi Zinfandel. The Lucas Winery is but a hobby for him; he is the viticultural manager for the entire Robert Mondavi empire, spending most of his waking hours traveling from one end of the state to the other supervising the ever-expanding and always exciting Mondavi vineyards. But he also remembers that Robert Mondavi was born in Lodi, and that he (Mondavi) has always thought the Lodi Zinfandel to be some of the best in the state.

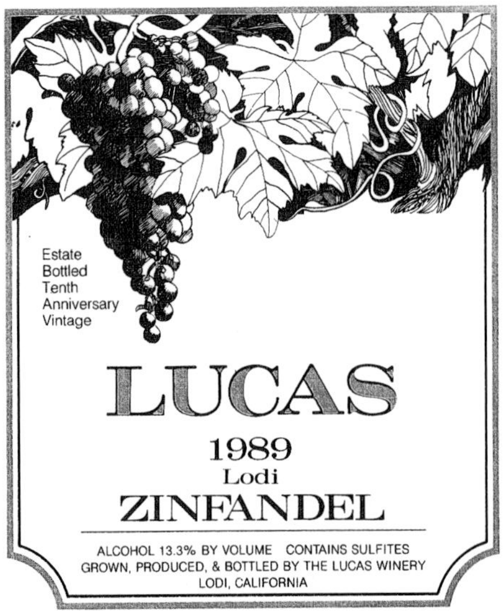
Estate Bottled Tenth Anniversary Vintage
LUCAS
1989
Lodi
ZINFANDEL
ALCOHOL 13.3% BY VOLUME CONTAINS SULFITES
GROWN, PRODUCED, & BOTTLED BY THE LUCAS WINERY
LODI, CALIFORNIA

Dave and Tamara Lucas purchased the vineyard in 1977, knowing that 18 acres of the Zinfandel had been planted in 1917, and it is from these old vines that the Lucas wines are made. Like Saucelito Canyon (and others, too, no doubt) Dave Lucas makes three distinct pickings: one, in the last week of August at 19–20° Brix; the major part of the harvest in September at 22–23° Brix; and the final picking in the first week of October. The early picking gives high acid, tart raspberry flavors; the mid season picking typical Claret flavors; the October picking gives blackberry pie flavors. Yet further complexity is gained from using the oak from five different French coopers, all from Burgundy, headed by Francois Freres. It hardly needs be said that the resulting wines are exceedingly complex, with intense varietal fruit running the gamut from strawberry through boysenberry, and black cherries, with a continuous web of vanillin spices.

MONDAVI WOODBRIDGE 1979

A: Woodbridge Road, Woodbridge, CA 95258 **T**: (209) 369 5861 **V**: 10–5 daily **P**: 2,500,000 **W**: Brad Alderson

There is something about the Mondavi touch: who else could have purchased a not-terribly-distinguished Lodi winery in 1979, and in little over ten years see it producing 850,000 cases of Cabernet Sauvignon (the largest selling

ABOVE ~ *The Mondavi Woodbridge Winery is a large and highly efficient producer of technically flawless wines.*

branded Cabernet Sauvignon in the United States), and a cool one million cases a year of Sauvignon Blanc? The facility itself is a model of functional efficiency; the aesthetics are left to Opus One. But in general manager and winemaker Brad Alderson, Mondavi Woodbridge also has a singularly perceptive and intelligent CEO. He is dispassionate about the potential of the Lodi area: Sauvignon Blanc and Zinfandel are unique stand-alones, vastly under-appreciated by the market as a whole, but at the end of the day condemned by their price positioning in the market. The Cabernet Sauvignon has improved out of all recognition over the past ten years, moving from strong tomato and vegetable characters to black cherry and black olive, a direct result of improved viticulture, and with further significant improvement possible over the next ten years. The Chardonnay is adequate, no more no less, a wine which sells because of the name on the label rather than the contents of the bottle.

Not surprisingly, Mondavi Woodbridge is looking closely at the potential for both Rhone and Italian red varietals. The much-despised Barbera has shown that, if given half a chance in the vineyard, it can do well; the Rhone varieties fall into the same camp. Whether those varieties will come out under the Mondavi Woodbridge label is another question: it has taken a huge slice of the market by producing wines which are well known and utterly reliable, and the last thing Mondavi would wish to do is confuse the customer.

Other Wineries

Oakridge Estate/Eastside Winery 1934
A: 6100 E. Highway 12, Lodi, CA 95240
T: (209) 369 4758 **W**: Lee Eichel

Phillips Farms Vineyards 1984
A: 4580 W. Highway 12, Lodi, CA 95240
T: (209) 368 7384 **W**: Michael J. Phillips

Orleans Hill
A: County Road 19, Woodland, CA 93695
T: (916) 661 6538 **W**: Jim Lapsley

Wineries *of* Clarksburg

BOGLE VINEYARDS 1979

A: 37675 County Road 144, Clarksburg, CA 95612 **T**: (916) 744 1139 **V**: 8–4 Mon–Fri **P**: 40,000 **W**: Chrisopher Smith

Chris Bogle is the fifth generation of Bogles to farm in the Delta region, but it was not until 1968 that he helped his father, Warren, plant the first vines. Bogle Vineyards was officially formed in 1973, the winery following in 1979. In the meantime, 650 acres of vines had been established, and Bogle is a major supplier to other California wineries as well as producing Chardonnay, Fumé Blanc, White Zinfandel, Merlot, Petite Sirah, Zinfandel and Cabernet Sauvignon under its own striking label.

Its production is notable for a number of things. While on the one hand it is able to claim that it is virtually self-sufficent in fruit and in total control of its quality and costs, it is in fact a grape purchaser as well as a grape seller. Thus all of its wines carry the California (rather than the Clarksburg) AVA, and we are told the Chardonnay is a blend of Napa Valley, Carneros and Clarksburg grapes; Fumé Blanc is a blend of 76% Lake County Sauvignon Blanc and 24% Clarksburg Semillon; and that the Merlot is a blend of Napa Valley and Clarksburg fruit. The regional make-up of the other wines is not specified. No less intriguingly, although it is one of only two wineries in the Clarksburg AVA, it does not produce a Chenin Blanc, the wine for which Clarksburg is most famous.

All of that said and done, the quality of its wines is consistently very good. The Sauvignon Blanc shows why Lake County has the reputation it has for this variety, the wine being presented in a direct, clean and crisp style with pleasantly herbaceous varietal fruit, good length and mouthfeel. The Merlot is precisely the weight and style which I believe Merlot should exhibit: clean and fruity but with low tannins. The Chardonnay and Zinfandel are, perhaps, not up to the exemplary quality of the Sauvignon Blanc and Merlot, but both show clear varietal fruit, the Chardonnay in a light style, the Zinfandel with fresh, simple, sweet fruit. A fairly oaky Cabernet Sauvignon rounded off the portfolio of wines I tasted; the Petite Sirah, however, has done extremely well in tastings and competitions over the years, and there is every reason to suppose it is in the same class.

R. & J. COOK 1979

A: Netherlands Road, Clarksburg, CA 95612 **T**: (916) 775 1234 **V**: 10:30–4:30 Mon–Fri, 12–5 Sat–Sun **P**: 62,000 **W**: Roger Cook

Roger and Joanne Cook, like the Bogles, come from families which have long farmed in the Delta region. Also like the Bogles, they commenced planting vines at the end of the 1960s, and now have 130 acres under vine. All of the wines are estate-grown, the range comprising Chardonnay, Chenin Blanc, Fumé Blanc, White Merlot, Cabernet Sauvignon, Merlot and Petite Sirah, together with four generics — Delta Red, Delta White, Delta Blush and Moonlight Mist. The Cook winery has also acted as a custom crush facility for other labels from time to time.

R&J Cook
CLARKSBURG
WHITE • MERLOT
EXPRESSLY 1990 FOR JOANNE
ESTATE BOTTLED
GROWN, PRODUCED & BOTTLED BY
R.&J. COOK, CLARKSBURG, CA
ALCOHOL 11.0% BY VOLUME 750ML

ABOVE ~ *Romance does not loom large in the vineyards and wineries of Lodi.*

WINERIES *of* SOLANO

CHATEAU DE LEU 1981

A: 1855 De Leu Drive, Suisun City, CA 94585 **T**: (707) 864 1517 **V**: 11–4:30 Wed–Sun **P**: 8,000 **W**: Alessio Carli

Chateau de Leu sits alone in its little three mile long by one mile wide valley north of the Suisun Delta. The vineyard site was originally planted in 1882 by Italian immigrants, and part of the existing vines are over 50 years old. The winery was established in 1980, but was purchased by Japanese owners in 1989, and placed under the management of Swiss-born and trained Bruno Welz, who has had one foot in the food and hospitality industry and one foot in the wine industry almost since he could walk. He hired former Badia e Coltibuono winemaker Alessio Carli for the 1990 vintage, Carli having come from Italy initially to work at Viansa. Bruno Welz is a fascinating character, with a deep understanding of both viticulture and wine formed with an international perspective, and Carli is a supremely talented winemaker. Together they have taken Chateau de Leu from obscurity to modest fame in a very short period of time.

Welz has started replanting the vineyard, with 32 acres being planted to Sangiovese, Dolcetto, Syrah and Merlot, all on close spacing. In the interim, and even in the future, grapes are purchased from elsewhere, and in particular Cabernet Sauvignon and Merlot from the Napa Valley, notably the Steltzner and Signorello Vineyards. The instructions to Welz from the Japanese owners are to make the best possible wine and to make the winery self-sufficient on its own vines; it has certainly achieved the first goal, and is on the way towards the second, with existing plantings providing Sauvignon Blanc and old Carignane.

The wines being produced at Chateau de Leu are, in a word, spectacular. While the 1990 Merlot tied with a 1989 Clos du Bois Marlstone for Best Wine of Show at the 1992 California State Fair, having previously won a double gold medal at the San Diego National Wine Competition, the 1990 Brunolino is the wholly exceptional wine in my view. Its proprietary blend of Carignane, Early Burgundy and Pinot Noir (a bizarre blend if ever there was one) was selling for $6.95 in 1992, but was one of the most delicious red wines I tasted during my three month sojourn in California. It has wonderful spicy, complex dark berry fruit aroma and flavor, with abundant but soft tannins, and an utterly seductive texture and structure. The Merlot is a far more sophisticated wine, with quite pronounced oak supporting the firm, clean fruit. I do not suggest for one moment that it did not deserve its gold medals, but simply that the Brunolino is one of those wholly exceptional wines one strikes every now and then. The 1990 Pinot Noir from the Kent Rasmussen Vineyard in Carneros is another beautifully made and constructed wine, with very good varietal character.

You reach Chateau de Leu by driving past a housing subdivision the like of which I have never seen: the walls around the subdivision alone must have cost millions of dollars. I devoutly trust that the Japanese owners realize what a jewel Chateau de Leu is.

ABOVE ~ *Flame Tokay and other table grapes are still grown in Lodi.*

ADDITIONAL WINERIES *of* CENTRAL VALLEY

THE R.H. PHILLIPS VINEYARD 1983

A: 26836 County Road 12A, Esparto, CA 995627 **T**: (916) 662 3215 **V**: 10–5 weekends **P**: 300,000 **W**: Ron McClenden

The
R.H. PHILLIPS
Vineyard
NIGHT HARVEST
WHITE ZINFANDEL
CALIFORNIA
ALC. 10.7% BY VOL.

Driving to R.H. Phillips is a most interesting experience. As you travel north from Davis or Sacramento, you have long since left all their vineyards behind, and it is not hard to imagine you are headed in entirely the wrong direction. In summer the rolling hills are covered in bleached grass, and nothing else: suddenly as you come over the crest of a hill on the small country road, to the left is a huge swathe of emerald-green vines, and on the right is the bleached grass country through which you have been driving. The black stripe of the road neatly bisects this green and gold canvas, with the azure-blue California sky above. Which, I suppose, is a fairly logical introduction to the other feature of R.H. Phillips: its extraordinarily imaginative packaging. Given the pricing of the wines, the amount spent on bottles, capsules and label design is extraordinary, but has no doubt had much to do with the spectacular growth in sales enjoyed by Phillips since it became seriously involved in winemaking in the mid 1980s.

Its initial foray into winemaking in 1983 was intended to be a one-off venture to help publicize the existence of the vineyards in what Phillips calls the Dunnigan Hills. Those vineyards are part of a very much larger agricultural venture owned by the Giguiere family, with 750 acres planted to vines. The success of the wines made in 1983 created its own momentum, and the large, modern winery in which the wines are made is the most obvious result of that success. Having initially concentrated on Chardonnay, Sauvignon Blanc and Chenin Blanc, which varieties still remain the volume base of the business, R.H. Phillips has hitched its marketing wagon to the Rhone star. In 1987, 55 acres of Syrah were planted and grafted, and a further 75 acres were added in 1992. Mourvedre has increased from seven to 35 acres, with contracts for the purchase of grapes from an additional 40 acres. Seven acres of Viognier have been planted, and there are plans to establish 20 acres of Grenache. It is these varieties which are used in the EXP range, strikingly packaged in ultra-modern 500ml sized Italian art-glass bottles. A fourth wine, called Alliance, and which is a blend of Syrah, Mourvedre and Grenache, is packaged in a conventional size bottle, but no less strikingly. One of its unique touches is a clear plastic capsule which exposes the cork, finishing at the bottom of the capsule with a neck-band showing the vintage of the wine.

Relative to the shelf price of the product, it is doubtful whether any company in the United States spends more on packaging than does R.H. Phillips. This might lead one to expect that the wines in the bottle are utilitarian at best; in fact, they are impressive. The small-volume barrel Cuvee Chardonnay is certainly driven by spicy, nutmeg oak, but is a most attractive, precocious wine more in Australian than typical California style. The Cabernet Sauvignon is full of sweet red berry and cassis fruit, with soft tannins, and is once again a user-friendly wine of immediate appeal. The EXP and Alliance range live up to their packaging: the Syrah with intense, reserved briary fruit, the Alliance with sweet redcurrant and plum fruit and soft tannins. The same sophisticated and expensive packaging extends to the Night Harvest series of Sauvignon Blanc, Cuvee Rouge Rhone (a non-vintage wine), and White Zinfandel.

OTHER WINERIES

CACHE CREEK WINERY 1985
A: 36380 County Road 21, Woodland, CA 95695
T: (916) 662 2578 **W**: Jacob Barth Jr.

JAMES FRASINETTI & SONS 1897
A: P.O. Box 28306, 7395 Frasinetti Road, Sacramento, CA 95828 **T**: (916) 383 2444
W: Gary and Howard Frasinetti

HARBOR WINERY 1972
A: 610 Harbor Boulevard, West Sacramento, CA 95691 **T**: (916) 371 6776
W: Charles H. Meyers

SATIETY 1981
A: P.O. Box 1056, Davis, CA 95617
T: (916) 661 0680 **W**: Sterling Chaykin

ABOVE ~ *Old vines and old buildings in the evening light at Lodi.*

The San Joaquin Valley

The first and last impression of the valley is its sheer size. The vines grow trunks as thick as an elephant's leg, bunches which are larger than life, and crops which are larger than anywhere else. The wineries are huge, and grow like mushrooms after spring rain. In 1971 the Franzia family sold Franzia to an investment group which on-sold to Coca-Cola. Within a year John Junior, Joseph S. and Fred T. Franzia had built a new winery six miles south of Modesto, glorying in the name of J F J Bronco. By 1992, J F J Bronco was the sixth largest wine producer in the United States, its single winery having a storage capacity of 43,800,000 gallons. And wineries — better called refineries — of this size are in proportion to the vast, seemingly unending horizons of the San Joaquin Valley.

While J F J Bronco is a huge winery, it is as well to put it into perspective against Gallo, the heart which pumps the life blood of the San Joaquin Valley. It has a combined capacity of 330,000,000 gallons at its four plants; I tell more of its Modesto headquarters on pages 140–1. Yet Gallo was not created until 1933; did not start selling packaged wines under its name until 1940; and it was not until the mid 1960s that Gallo outpaced Louis Petri's United Vintners. Louis Petri, incidentally, showed exquisite timing in selling United Vintners to Heublein in 1968 for $33 million, and selling his last vineyard to the same company in 1971.

The history of the San Joaquin Valley falls into three phases. The first phase ran from the turn of the century to 1945, a period during which the valley was dominated by its growers. Few significant wineries were created before Prohibition; quite obviously none during it; and in the wake of Repeal sagging grape prices led to the establishment of several large cooperative wineries (one the forerunner of Guild), and of course Gallo.

The second phase spanned 1945 and 1970 or thereabouts. It could well be called the Thompsons Seedless reign of terror: by the mid 1960s that variety accounted for almost 50% of the state's grape plantings, although mercifully much less went to make wine. It was the ideal multi-purpose grape: it could be used to make raisins (its chief purpose), fresh table grapes, brandy, fortified wine and — not entirely as a last resort — table wine. Both the first and second phases were marked by periods of excess production which would make a Frenchman blush, with state-ordered compulsory distillation into industrial alcohol the last resort.

ABOVE ~ *Rigo Rodriguez, a cellar hand at Quady Winery.*

OPPOSITE ~ *Trees such as this on Jack Tone Road (near Ripon) are a rare sight in the San Joaquin Valley.*

The wineries were by and large uncaring about the deficiencies of the grapes they were dealing with. Essentially, they were providing a form of alcohol which was weaker than spirits, stronger than beer, and sweeter than both. It was not until 1968 that sales of table wine exceeded those of fortified wine, and it must be said that — by the standards of today — the table wine of the Central Valley was crude stuff. Equally, of course, it was sold to an undiscriminating public at a price which encouraged growers to produce as much as they possibly could per acre.

The third phase marked the beginning of the end for Thompsons Seedless as a major wine grape, crystallized by Gallo's boast that since 1974 — the year in which it sold its first wine in bottles with corks, rather than screw caps — it has not used Thompsons Seedless in any of its wines. That year saw Gallo release its first seven varietally designated wines (albeit then with no Cabernet Sauvignon or Chardonnay).

Since 1970 there have been huge advances in both viticultural practices and in winemaking standards. Machine harvesting at night, temperature-controlled fermentation

WHITE FREIGHTLINER
508

ABOVE ~ *A truckload of Semillon leaves the Bonita Ranch in the San Joaquin Valley.*

in stainless steel tanks, and improved varietal selection have all played critical roles, particularly in the wake of the shift from red wine to white wine consumption.

But it would be fanciful to suggest that the San Joaquin Valley even pretends to be a premium wine producing region. Its Region IV to Region V climate, rainfall which decreases from 12 inches at Stockton to six inches at Bakersfield, its rich soils, its total dependence on flood irrigation, and its deeply ingrained ethics all militate against that. Gallo has voted with its feet by establishing its premium base in the Sonoma Valley; others have gone across to the Monterey Valley.

The double play of improved viticulture and better wine-making will go some of the way to guaranteeing the continued importance and prosperity of the valley, not to mention the massive infrastructure already in place. The next logical development is the total mechanization of viticulture, including pruning. The vast size of the Central Valley vineyards make full mechanization not only feasible but inevitable, which will mean cheaper grapes. And while the climate may be severe, it is tailor-made for organic viticulture — particularly if drip irrigation is used in place of furrow irrigation.

Finally, there will always be room for specialist makers such as Ficklin and Quady, who have cunningly made a virtue of necessity.

The San Joaquin Valley VINTAGE CHART 1981–91

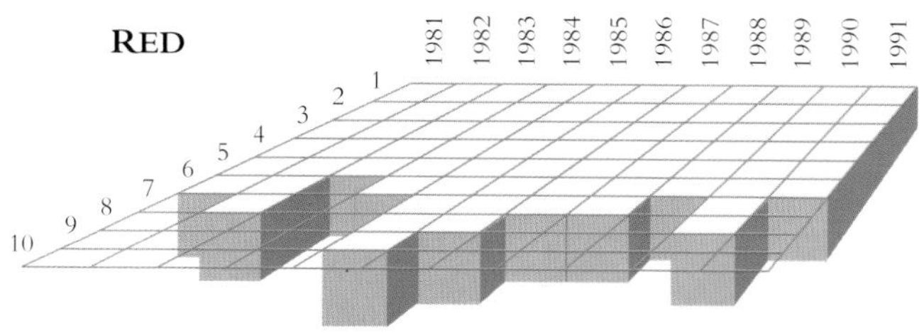
RED
1981
1982
1983
1984
1985
1986
1987
1988
1989
1990
1991
1
2
3
4
5
6
7
8
9
10

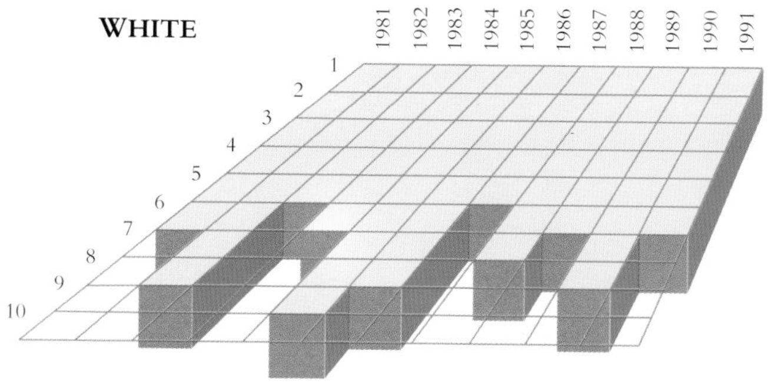
WHITE
1981
1982
1983
1984
1985
1986
1987
1988
1989
1990
1991
1
2
3
4
5
6
7
8
9
10

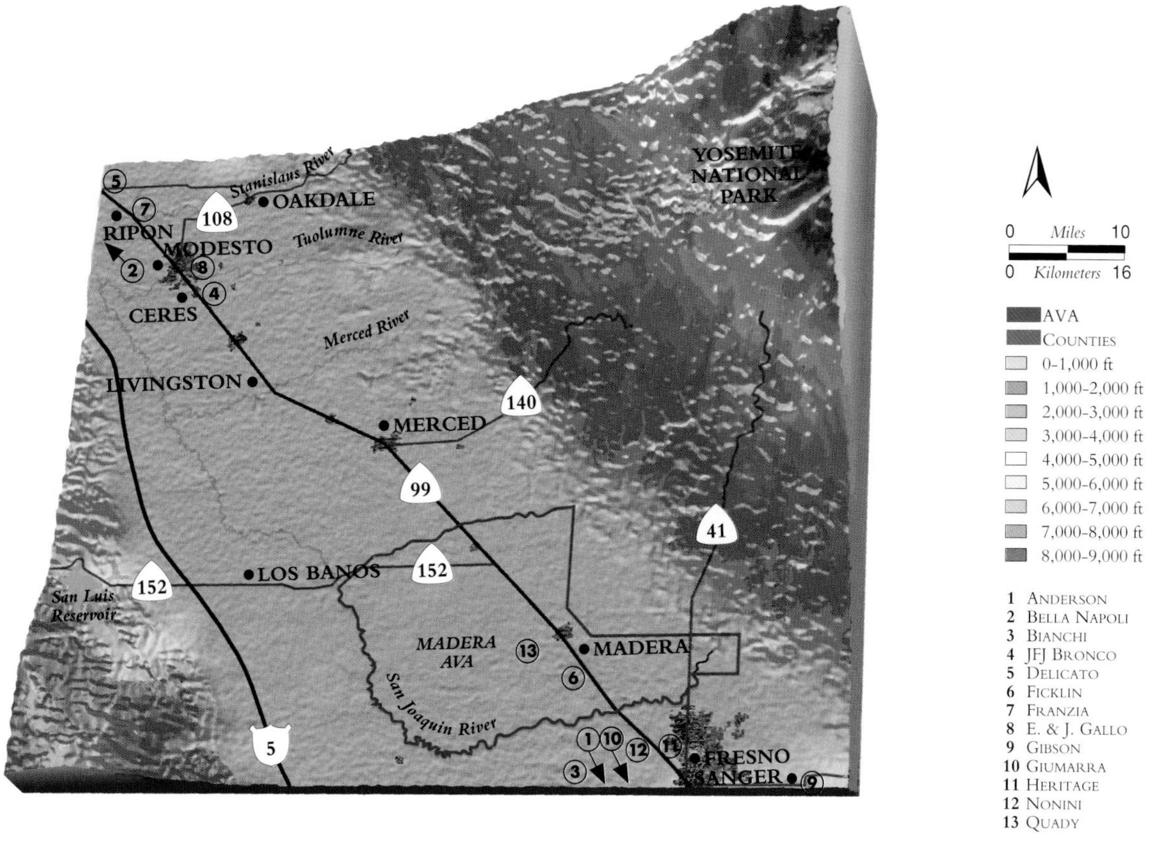
Stanislaus River
OAKDALE
108
RIPON
MODESTO
Tuolumne River
CERES
Merced River
LIVINGSTON
MERCED
140
99
41
YOSEMITE NATIONAL PARK
LOS BANOS
152
San Luis Reservoir
MADERA AVA
MADERA
San Joaquin River
5
FRESNO
SANGER
0 Miles 10
0 Kilometers 16
AVA
COUNTIES
0-1,000 ft
1,000-2,000 ft
2,000-3,000 ft
3,000-4,000 ft
4,000-5,000 ft
5,000-6,000 ft
6,000-7,000 ft
7,000-8,000 ft
8,000-9,000 ft
1 ANDERSON
2 BELLA NAPOLI
3 BIANCHI
4 JFJ BRONCO
5 DELICATO
6 FICKLIN
7 FRANZIA
8 E. & J. GALLO
9 GIBSON
10 GIUMARRA
11 HERITAGE
12 NONINI
13 QUADY

ABOVE ~ *The San Joaquin Valley map.*

WINERIES of SAN JOAQUIN VALLEY

purchase the San Bernabe Ranch at the northern end of the Salinas Valley.

In the same year it constructed a large crushing facility in Monterey, where the grapes are processed before being taken to Manteca (head office) for fermentation, although ultimately a full winery will be constructed in Monterey. Likewise, the range of Monterey County varietals of Chenin Blanc, White Grenache, Zinfandel, Sauvignon Blanc and Chardonnay will be significantly expanded by the end of the 1990s. In the meantime, and not surprisingly, White Zinfandel remains the cork-finished market leader, heading the range of generics carrying the California appellation.

FICKLIN VINEYARDS 1948

A: 30246 Avenue 71/2, Madera, CA 93637
T: (209) 674 4598 **V**: By appointment
P: 10,000 **W**: Peter Ficklin

Ficklin was founded in 1948 by Walter Ficklin, a wealthy local farmer who, recognizing the limitations of the Region V climate, planted the 40-acre property to the port varieties Tinta Madeira, Touriga, Tinta Cao and Souzao. Current winemaker Peter Ficklin is in fact the third generation to make port from the estate vineyards, which is released both as a non-vintage Tinta, and with occasional vintage-dated releases. I have tasted the wines over the years, though not recently, it must be said, and found them sadly lacking in comparison to Australian tawny and vintage port styles, let alone those of Portugal. Part of the problem has appeared to lie with the fortifying spirit used, although why this should be so I do not know.

J F J BRONCO WINERY 1973

A: 6342 Bystrum Road, Ceres, CA 95307
T: (209) 538 3131 **V**: By appointment
P: Not stated **W**: John Franzia Jr.

As I have related in the introduction to this section, J F J Bronco was founded by the Franzia cousins in the wake of the sale of the family company and winery which still bears the Franzia name to The Wine Group. It produces massive quantities of table wine and sparkling wine, with a storage capacity of over 43 million gallons and a crush capacity of 6,000 tons per day. Its brands are C C Vineyard and J F J Winery, but much of the wine is sold to others, either in bulk or bottled. It is also building export markets under brands specially developed for those markets.

DELICATO VINEYARDS 1935

A: 12001 S. Highway 99, Manteca, CA 95336
T: (209) 239 1215 **V**: 9–5:30 daily, closed holidays **P**: 2 million **W**: Pat Minnix

Delicato is now the ninth largest producer in the United States, having moved up from 16th position in 1980, and having started its major growth in the early 1970s when, for the first time, it began bottling its own wines. Prior to that time, and indeed since, a very large part of its business has been supplying wine (and grape juice) in bulk to other producers. Its most notable association was with Sutter Home, which it supplied with a considerable portion of its White Zinfandel. It was indeed the growth of that market which put Delicato into the position such that, in 1988, it was able to

E. & J. GALLO WINERY 1933

A: 600 Yosemite Boulevard, Modesto, CA 95353 **T**: (209) 579 3111 **V**: Nil
P: 75 million **W**: Julio Gallo

Gallo's dominance of the American wine industry is absolute. It is more than twice as large as the next nearest group, the Grand Metropolitan/Heublein Group, the latter showing severe strains as it absorbed its fine wine division into its Central Valley-based operations in 1992, with ominous storm clouds hanging around Inglenook and, to a lesser degree, Beaulieu. But it remains to be seen what will happen when the octogenarian Ernest relinquishes his grip on Gallo. The iron discipline with which the business has been run is wholly remarkable; whether the presence of

ABOVE ~ *Cleaning a fermentation tank at Quady Winery: hygiene is all-important.*

the children and grandchildren in the organization is good, time alone will tell. But, as I say on pages 140–1 Gallo certainly seems to be doing all the right things, and its reign at the top appears to be an exceedingly long one.

GIUMARRA VINEYARDS 1946

A: 11220 Edison Highway, Edison, CA 93220
T: (805) 395 7079 **V**: 10–5 Tues–Sat
P: 13 million gallons **W**: Mike Robertson

Giumarra is a family owned and run business, established by Giuseppe "Joe" Giumarra, who emigrated from Sicily in the early 1900s, making the classic rags-to-riches voyage which has been told so many times. The family today farms 15,000 acres, with 5,000 acres of plums, citrus, potatoes and cotton, 7,000 acres of table grapes, and 3,000 acres of wine grapes. Giumarra is the largest packer and shipper of table grapes in the world. It ventured into winemaking in 1946, but remained purely a seller in bulk to other producers until 1974. It then developed its own label, with business growing rapidly, before taking a turn towards the specialist supply of four litre, 18 litre and 60 litre kegs and containers to restaurants and hotels. Only 250,000 cases a year carry the Giumarra label; of these, 25,000 cases are the Proprietor's Reserve wines introduced in the late 1980s. The quality of these wines is as modest as their prices.

QUADY WINERY 1977

A: 13181 Road 24, Madera, CA 93637
T: (209) 673 8068 **V**: 8–5 Mon–Fri, weekends by appointment **P**: 13,500
W: Andrew Quady and Michael Blaylock

Randall Grahm turns being different into an art form; Andrew Quady does the same thing, but with a much more disciplined approach. He became interested in making fortified wine, when, as a winemaker in a large Lodi winery, he was asked by Darrell Corti (that man again) to make a vintage port from Amador County Zinfandel. When he decided to form his own winery in 1981, it was to fortified wines that he turned, and his vintage ports are comprehensively the best made in California. But it was almost by chance that he came upon a planting of Orange Muscat, and decided to make a Muscat Beaumes-de-Venise style, adding around 2% of alcohol to end up with a wine with 14–14.5% and 12–14% residual sugar. He called the wine Essencia, and gave it a striking label, looking vaguely as if it might have been designed by Ronald Searle. Essencia has been the wine which has pulled (or pushed) the Quady empire ever since, now accounting for around half of the total sales. In 1990 it spawned Electra, an ultra-low alcohol wine with only 4%, all of it added in the form of alcohol to unfermented Orange Muscat juice. Elysium, a lightly fortified Black Muscat, accounts for 3,000 cases, and the Vintage and Ruby Ports for 2,000.

None of these wines are technically easy to make, but Quady has demonstrated absolute mastery. Essencia shows all of the fragrant orange blossom aroma and fruit one could wish for in this variety. Electra is appropriately named: it is almost alive in the mouth, with a totally delicious sherbet fizz bite to the floral aromas and flavors. Even though it has only 4% alcohol, one's inclination is to blend it with 50% sparkling mineral water, and end up with the ultimate summer drink. As I have said, the vintage ports are very good, showing dark berry and chocolate fruit, soft tannins and appropriate fortifying spirit. These are sourced from Franks Vineyard in Amador County, which is planted to the traditional port varieties.

ESSENSIA
California Orange Muscat
sweet dessert wine
vintage 1989
Produced & Bottled by
Andrew Quady, Madera, California
alcohol 15% by volume
750 mL

OTHER WINERIES

ANDERSON WINE CELLARS 1980
A: 20147 Ave 306, Exeter, CA 93221
T: (209) 592 4682 **W**: Donald E. Anderson

BELLA NAPOLI WINERY 1934
A: 21128 S. Austin Road, Manteca, CA B95336
T: (209) 599 3885 **W**: Lucas G. Hat

BIANCHI VINEYARDS 1974
A: 5806 N. Modoc Avenue, Kerman, CA 93630
T: (209) 846 7356 **W**: Robert Lovell

FRANZIA
A: Highway 120, Ripon, CA 95366
T: (209) 599 4111

GIBSON WINE CO. 1939
A: 1720 Academy Avenue, Sanger, CA 95657
T: (209) 875 2505 **W**: Paul Mamika

HERITAGE CELLARS 1984
A: 2310 S. Railroad Avenue, Fresno, CA 93721
T: (209) 442 8452 **W**: Marvin Riding

NONINI WINERY 1936
A: 2640 N. Dickenson Avenue, Fresno, CA 93722 **T**: (209) 275 1936 **W**: Reno Nonini

ABOVE ~ *Old palm trees line the entrance to the Heublein facility at Madera.*

CENTRAL COAST

MONTEREY TO PASO ROBLES

Long before grapevines were planted in the Salinas Valley — for this is essentially the Monterey AVA — it was known as the Salad Bowl of the world; subdistricts gave themselves similar world titles for lettuce, celery, asparagus, artichokes, garlic, broccoli and strawberries. Indeed, even since the vine invasion those crops have flourished and at times taken back ground lost to the new pretender to the throne.

The climatic suitability of the Salinas Valley for viticulture had been pinpointed by Amerine and Winkler in their historic 1935 climate studies, but the region continued to go unnoticed. Of the 400 acres of vines in Monterey County during Prohibition, half were removed after its repeal. Prevailing wisdom was that it was too cold, too dry and too windy an area in which to grow grapes. The aesthetes would have added that it was also a singularly boring, indeed inhospitable, part of the world when judged by normal California standards. (Farmers from places such as the Dakotas would no doubt have thought quite differently.)

The impetus for reappraisal came from the progressive urbanization of the Santa Clara and Livermore Valleys and the pressure this placed on two prominent wine companies, Paul Masson and Mirassou. Realizing that their local vineyards were doomed, they began looking elsewhere, first at the Sonoma Valley and then at the Sierra Foothills. In neither area could they identify sufficiently large tracts of flat land, so — armed with the theoretical imprimatur of Winkler and Amerine — they turned in 1957 to the Salinas Valley.

Masson planted 1,000 acres on the east side of the valley on Metz Road, due east of Greenfield; it named the vineyard after the Pinnacles National Monument, those jagged peaks rearing on the skyline, a name which took a certain amount of poetic licence since the vineyard was planted on laser-flat alluvial land. On the opposite side of the valley, a little further north at the Mission Soledad, Mirassou planted 300 acres. Within three years it became clear that the gamble had been justified, and by the mid 1960s the exceptional quality of the Monterey Rieslings and Gewurztraminers was established. Leon Adams in *The Wines of America* records that in October 1966 a luncheon was held in the new winery Masson had built on its Pinnacles Vineyard to honor "the world's first fine wine district established as the direct result of scientific temperature research."

By 1971, 6,228 acres had been planted; in 1972, 1973 and 1974 plantings increased

TEXACO

ABOVE ~ *Grape pickers wait outside the Paicines general store: today they will pick Chardonnay being sold to Glen Ellen.*

PREVIOUS PAGE ~ *Looking west across the vast expanse of Monterey's Salinas Valley near San Lucas.*
OPPOSITE ~ *The Carmel coastline — and the ever-present fog.*

Monterey
VINTAGE CHART 1981-91

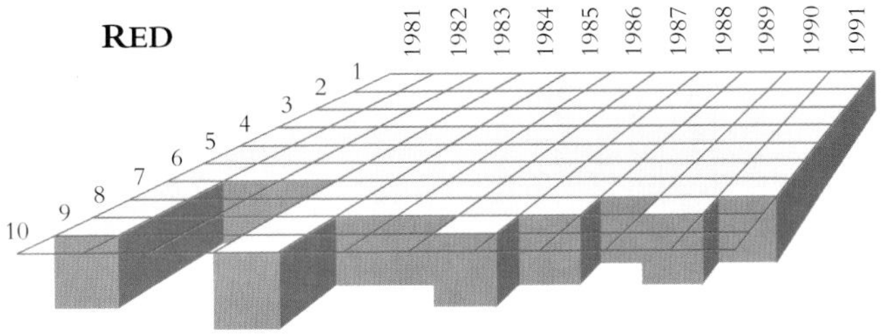
RED
1981
1982
1983
1984
1985
1986
1987
1988
1989
1990
1991
1
2
3
4
5
6
7
8
9
10

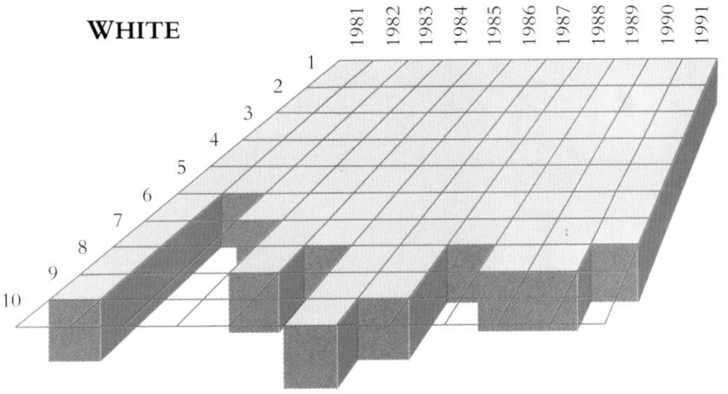
WHITE
1981
1982
1983
1984
1985
1986
1987
1988
1989
1990
1991
1
2
3
4
5
6
7
8
9
10

by 6,311, 7,832 and 6,688 acres respectively, fueled by anticipated demand and by the tax shelter incentives which led to The Prudential Insurance Company of New Jersey to provide the funds to develop the largest contiguous vineyard in the world — San Bernabe. But it was not all sheer bliss. Plantings ground to a halt and then went into decline. The 27,000 acres of 1975 dwindled to 19,500 acres in 1982 before the second boom cycle of 1987 to 1991 lifted plantings back to the 1975 level.

At the end of the day, Monterey has emerged as the third-ranking source of premium quality grapes after the Napa and Sonoma Valleys. It is the cool-climate correlative of the San Joaquin Valley, providing grapes to wineries largely situated outside its boundaries at a price which belies their quality. Experience has shown the northern two-thirds of the Salinas Valley to be suited to white wine varieties and Pinot Noir, the latter being statistically unimportant. The jury is still out on the question of whether the southern third of the valley — where the heat summation rises to Region III — can produce Cabernet Sauvignon and Merlot of a quality equal to that of the white varieties. The vignerons of the Santa Lucia Highlands AVA and the Arroyo Seco AVA all aver that they can produce high quality red wines, and Smith & Hook (in the Santa Lucia Highlands, which aren't terribly high, by the way) is putting its money where the mouth is by becoming the largest grower (in terms of acres) of Merlot and Cabernet Franc in the state.

To the east is San Benito County, with its multiplicity of minor AVAs, the most important of which is Mount Harlan, home to Josh Jensen's Calera Wine Company. These AVAs are effectively a half way house between the Salinas and San Joaquin Valleys; Mount Harlan has its own splendid mountain vineyard sites with the famed limestone-chalk soil so assiduously sought by Jensen.

At the extreme southern end of the Salinas Valley you ascend into the entirely different scenery of Paso Robles; the Salinas River, however, continues, its source even further south than the southern end of the Paso Robles AVA. It is the river which provides the umbilical cord connecting Paso Robles with Monterey, and allows the last gasp of cold air from Monterey Bay to make its presence felt.

Monterey
1971 AND 1991 ACREAGE/GRAPE VARIETIES

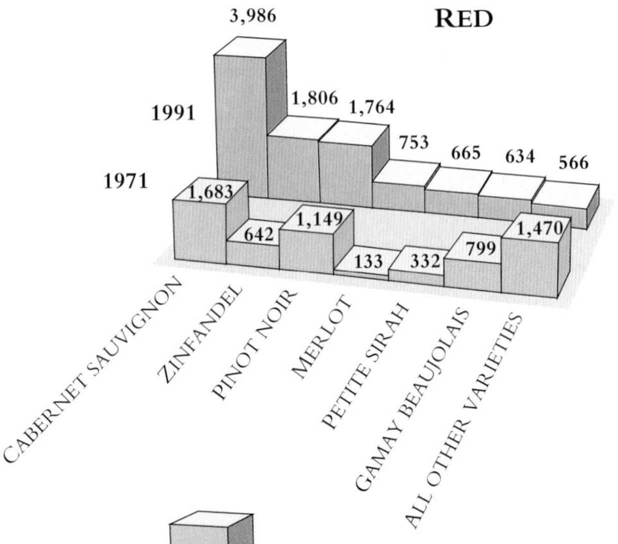
RED
1991
1971
3,986
1,806
1,764
753
665
634
566
1,683
642
1,149
133
332
799
1,470
CABERNET SAUVIGNON
ZINFANDEL
PINOT NOIR
MERLOT
PETITE SIRAH
GAMAY BEAUJOLAIS
ALL OTHER VARIETIES

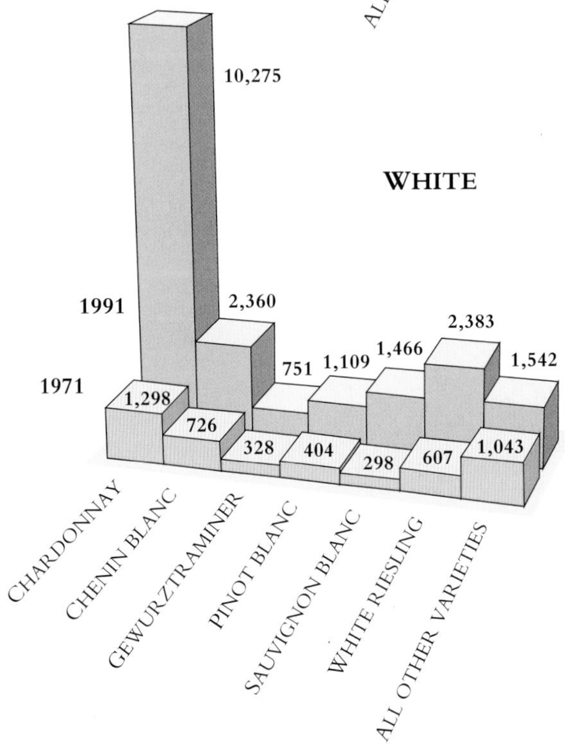
WHITE
1991
1971
10,275
2,360
751
1,109
1,466
2,383
1,542
1,298
726
328
404
298
607
1,043
CHARDONNAY
CHENIN BLANC
GEWURZTRAMINER
PINOT BLANC
SAUVIGNON BLANC
WHITE RIESLING
ALL OTHER VARIETIES

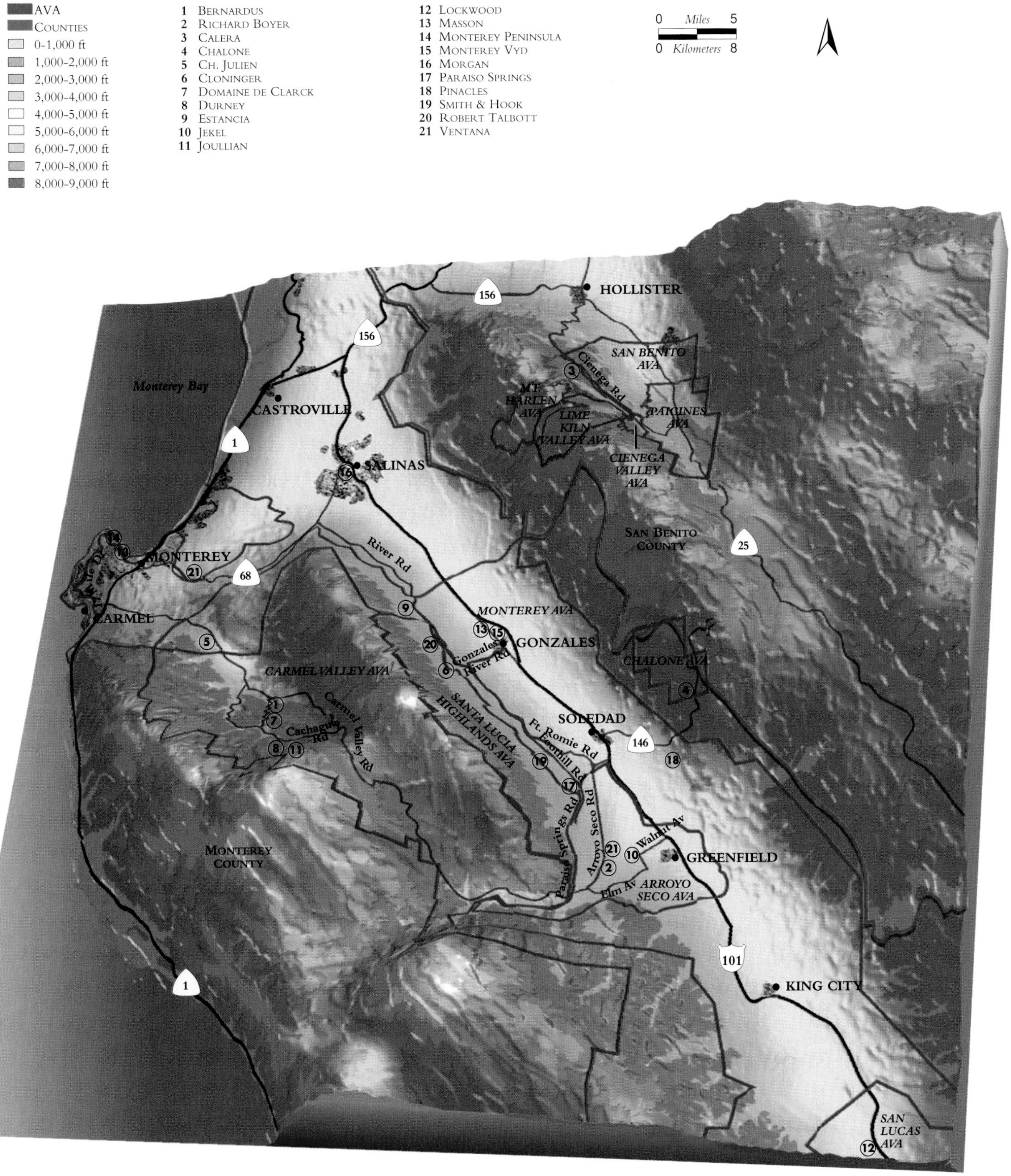
AVA
Counties
0-1,000 ft
1,000-2,000 ft
2,000-3,000 ft
3,000-4,000 ft
4,000-5,000 ft
5,000-6,000 ft
6,000-7,000 ft
7,000-8,000 ft
8,000-9,000 ft
1 Bernardus
2 Richard Boyer
3 Calera
4 Chalone
5 Ch. Julien
6 Cloninger
7 Domaine de Clarck
8 Durney
9 Estancia
10 Jekel
11 Joullian
12 Lockwood
13 Masson
14 Monterey Peninsula
15 Monterey Vyd
16 Morgan
17 Paraiso Springs
18 Pinacles
19 Smith & Hook
20 Robert Talbott
21 Ventana
0 Miles 5
0 Kilometers 8
HOLLISTER
156
Monterey Bay
CASTROVILLE
SALINAS
1
SAN BENITO AVA
Cienega Rd
MT. HARLEN AVA
LIME KILN VALLEY AVA
PAICINES AVA
CIENEGA VALLEY AVA
San Benito County
25
MONTEREY
68
CARMEL
River Rd
MONTEREY AVA
GONZALES
Gonzales River Rd
CARMEL VALLEY AVA
CHALONE AVA
SANTA LUCIA HIGHLANDS AVA
Cachagua Rd
Carmel Valley Rd
SOLEDAD
146
Ft. Romie Rd
Foothill Rd
Paraiso Springs Rd
Arroyo Seco Rd
Walnut Av
GREENFIELD
Elm Av
ARROYO SECO AVA
Monterey County
101
KING CITY
SAN LUCAS AVA

ABOVE ~ *Monterey and San Benito map.*

THE AVA MATRIX

There is a profusion of AVAs in and around the Salinas Valley, all falling within the octopus of the Central Coast AVA.

Making sense of these AVAs, and determining their relevance and importance, is not easy. For a start, a number are single-winery AVAs; some are even single vineyard AVAs, the product of naked corporate power being exerted on the BATF. The relevance of some was doubtful at the time of their creation and has waned since. I have to admit to agonizing over the inclusion of Paso Robles in this section of the book and no less to the grouping of the San Benito AVAs with the Santa Clara Valley. An eagle's eye view of the geography will perhaps explain the decisions I have made.

ABOVE ~ *The tank farm at Meridian, like tank farms at any large installation looking as much like a refinery as a winery.*

The Monterey County AVAs

MONTEREY, ARROYO SECO AND SANTA LUCIA HIGHLANDS

Monterey is the all-important AVA, dominated by the Salinas River and its vast flood plain. The Arroyo Seco and Santa Lucia Highlands AVAs have been granted because the BATF has been persuaded that, in particular, the benchland, fan and (in the case of Santa Lucia) hillside soils are different from those of the valley proper. These two AVAs also happen to accommodate vineyards now or previously owned by two particularly outspoken vignerons (Doug Meador of Ventana and Bill Jekel of Jekel), and by the nakedly ambitious Hahn family of Smith & Hook. But in terms of climate (and wine style) these AVAs fall within the mainstream of the Monterey flow.

SAN LUCAS

I treat San Lucas separately not because of any geographic distinction, nor because it is an especially important AVA, but simply because it shows just how far the temperature gradient carries the heat summation — all the way from Region I to Region IV, putting San Lucas into near Central Valley category.

CHALONE

Like Mount Harlan, Chalone is a single winery appellation and utterly distinct in terms of topography and climate, while possessing an extraordinary viticultural history. The Chalone vineyards are established at an elevation of around 1,650 feet, above the fog line, with the Pinnacles rearing in the background. If you arrive at Chalone, you will not have done so by accident, and you will marvel at its wildness and remoteness. It has summer temperatures 10°F higher than the Salinas Valley below, putting it comfortably into Region II summations, approaching Region III in hot years. And it has Miocene volcanic and Mesozoic granite soils, heavy in limestone.

CARMEL VALLEY

There was much debate at the time the Monterey AVA boundaries were established as to whether Carmel should be included within the larger AVA. In the outcome, its distinct (and very beautiful) geography won the day, and it has its own identity, even if Durney is the only winery of any significance using the AVA. It has a Region I climate (2,317 degree days) similar to the Salinas Valley, but a much higher rainfall of between 17 inches and 22 inches, and mountainside soils of shaley clay and loams.

The San Benito AVAs

As one travels south and across the San Benito County line, one passes through a series of AVAs which act as climate corridors between the Salinas Valley and the San Joaquin Valley, but which belong to neither.

PACHECO PASS

This is a supremely unimportant AVA with one equallly insignificant winery. Chiefly notable as one of the two gaps (passes) through to the Central Valley, hence playing an important role in shaping the climate of both the Salinas and (to a lesser degree) the Central Valley.

SAN BENITO, PAICINES, CIENEGA VALLEY AND LIME KILN VALLEY

The Paicines, Cienega and Lime Kiln are, or were, all single vineyard appellations (Masson, Almaden and Enz being the three sponsor-owners), and all fall within the San Benito AVA, which encompasses 95% of all the grapes grown in the infinitely larger San Benito County. It straddles the second gap through to the Central Valley, covering 45,000 acres of which 2,500 acres are planted to 23 grape varieties. The climate is mid Region II (2,750 to 2,860 degree days on long-term averages); the soils are well-drained loams underlain variously by weathered granite, dolomite, and (in the Lime Kiln Valley) limestone. Rainfall varies between 12 and 16 inches.

Mount Harlan

A single-winery (Calera) AVA created in 1990, and which in climatic and geographic terms makes absolute sense. The Jensen Vineyards are established at an altitude of 2,200 feet; the climate is cooler (the average annual temperature is 58°F to 60°F compared to 60°F to 62°F in the Cienaga Valley) and sunnier (fogs are uncommon); and harvest dates are two to four weeks later than in San Benito. Finally, there are the limestone soils for which Jensen successfully searched.

The San Luis Obispo AVAs

Paso Robles

An AVA of undoubted credentials and which I have treated separately; it has been included in this section because, at the end of the day, it has far more to do with Monterey than with the coastal AVAs to the southwest. It also provides the source of the mighty Salinas River and aquifer.

York Mountain

Again, separately discussed; another single winery though multiple vineyard AVA with a very different (and much cooler) climate.

ABOVE ~ *Looking back to the Salinas Valley and the Santa Lucia Range from the Chalone vineyards high above the valley fog.*

THE REGION IN BRIEF

Climate, Soil and Viticulture

CLIMATE

Here I content myself with describing the broad climatic parameters of the Monterey AVA as a whole, having pinpointed most of the special features of the satellite and subappellations. The marine influence is profound; the deep, crystal clear but dark green-blue waters of Monterey Bay are as cold as they look, a comfortable home for the seals which frolic in them and the source of the massive air-conditioning system which dominates the Salinas Valley. The key is the Central Valley and the gaps in the Gabilan Range: the hot air of the Central Valley rises, sucking in the stream of cold air and fog which covers the valley virtually every morning from May through to the end of August. But as it travels south over the 84-mile long valley, the land mass warms the air: thus at Gonzales, which more or less marks the northern extension of viticulture, the heat summation is a Region I, 2,350 degree days. By the time you reach Soledad it has risen to 2,880 degree days and mid Region II. King City is mid Region III at 3,389 degree days, while at San Lucas it reaches 3,734 degree days and Region IV. The higher the summation, the greater the diurnal temperature range: at the northern end of the valley it is typically between 15°F and 20°F; at the southern end in San Lucas it is as much as 40°F. Thus at the coast the average daily maximum temperature is in the low 60s°F, (the waters of Monterey Bay have a year-round temperature of 55°F), reaching the middle 90s°F at the southern end.

Technically, the Salinas Valley is a desert, with an average rainfall of ten inches. Viticulture is made possible only by the Salinas River, the largest upside down (in other words, underground) river in California, which is fed by the watersheds of the Santa Lucia, Gabilan and Diablo Ranges. Supplemented by summer discharges from the reservoirs in San Luis Obispo County, it provides a seemingly inexhaustible (and for long excessively used) supply of high quality water for all-essential irrigation.

The other feature of the Salinas Valley is the wind which replaces the fog. To Australian eyes, the strangest sight is the giant-sized telegraph poles which, on closer inspection, turn out to be eucalypts which are bereft of limbs. On the northern side they are utterly bare; on the southern side there is a carpet of leaves and minuscule branches, looking like regrowth after a bushfire. This deformed growth is the result of the winds which howl ferociously down the valley, starting at any time after 10 A.M., and making the winds of Carneros seem like zephyrs. Wind is now recognized as a potent inhibitor of photosynthesis — even at moderate to high temperatures — and there is no question that it contributes both to the long growing season and to the high acid retention of the grapes.

SOIL

The soils are generally light textured silts and loamy sands which have been derived from the mountains and hills which surround the Salinas Valley, and which have been carried downstream over a prolonged period. They are by and large low in organic matter, but are likewise low in salinity. The generally free-draining nature of the soils has played a significant role in the improved viticulture of the past decade: by reducing the amount of water applied through irrigation, vine vigor has been reduced and better fruit flavors have been the result.

THE GROWING SEASON

The season is claimed by many, including Doug Meador of Ventana Vineyard (in the Arroyo Seco) to be the longest in the world, with up to 150 days between bloom and harvest (the

ABOVE ~ *The only water available on the Smith Ranch (of Smith and Hook) came from wells accessed by ladders for maintenance.*

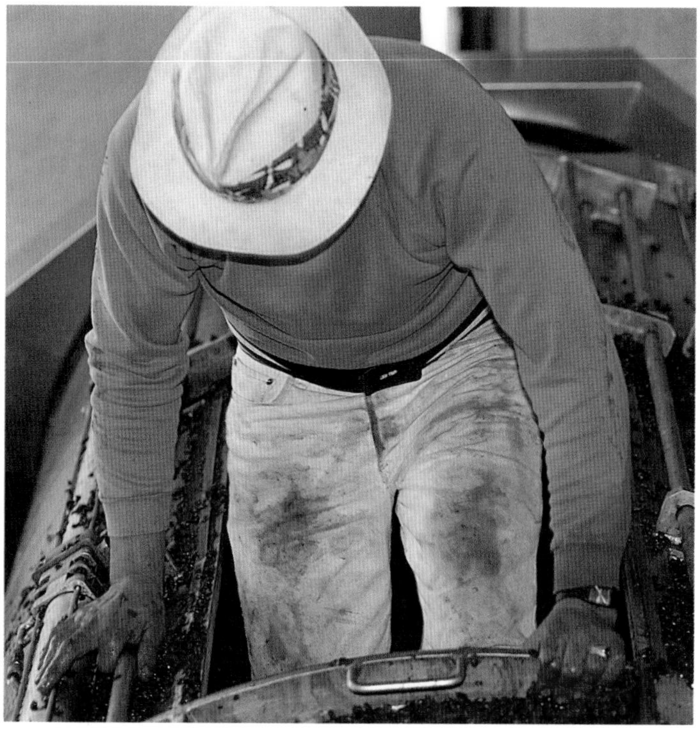

French reckon on 100 to 115). Budburst is in February, and the early ripening varieties are not picked until September, with later varieties extending through to late October. Indeed, in the early days of the Monterey Vineyard it produced a "December Harvest Zinfandel," which some might think was no particular advertisement for the suitability of the variety for the region.

Contract Growers

Lockwood Vineyard One thousand six hundred and fifty acres south of King City planted 1981/82 to Chardonnay, Cabernet Sauvignon, Riesling, Sauvignon Blanc, Semillon, Pinot Blanc, Merlot, Cabernet Franc, Chenin Blanc, Pinot Noir and Muscat Canelli. Many purchasers.

San Bernabe Vineyard Seven thousand acres planted from 1972 to 1974, but with much replanting since (see pages 312–3). Innumerable purchasers.

Sleepy Hollow Vineyard Two hundred acres at extreme northern end of the valley near Chular planted early 1970s to Chardonnay, Pinot Noir and Riesling.

Ventana Vineyard Three hundred acres in Arroyo Seco planted from early 1970s to late 1980s to Riesling, Gewurztraminer, Chardonnay, Sauvignon Blanc, Pinot Noir, Cabernet Sauvignon, Merlot and Syrah. Purchasers include Ahlgren, Cronin, Thomas Fogarty, Leeward, Sarah's Vineyard and Woodside. Ventana, of course, also has its own label.

Principal Wine Styles

Chardonnay

By sheer force of numbers, Chardonnay leads the way; clearly, it is a variety which ought to be extensively planted in the northern two-thirds of the valley at least. Yet more than one commentator has pointed out that (excluding Chalone and Jensen) while the Chardonnays are good, they are not great. It seems to me the reasons are obvious: first, the domination of the very big companies which have concentrated on the production of beverage wine at a price level which necessarily predicates relatively high yields and simple production methods. Second, hydroponic viticulture (growing vines in a sandy desert) is inherently unlikely to produce great grapes. Yet Morgan Winery (at the boutique end) and Franciscan's Estancia (at the volume end) show what can be achieved: these are wines of exemplary quality and style, with all of the citrus and melon fruit and intense, lingering finish one expects from cool climate Chardonnay. Newcomers Lockwood and Domaine de Clarck and old stagers The Monterey Vineyard and Ventana also produce creditable wines.

Riesling

More than 50% of California's Riesling is grown in Monterey County. An equilibrium seems to have been reached between supply and demand: while overall it is regarded as a difficult wine to sell, there is solid demand for the grapes, notably from Ventana Vineyard. The wines are produced in both dry and late harvest botrytis versions; all have abundant flavor and personality, with full lime juice aroma and flavor. Long-time leaders Ventana and Jekel have been joined by Lockwood.

Cabernet Sauvignon

Quite clearly, the major players have decided they can beat the soapy, weedy vegetable characters for which Monterey became so notorious in the early years. The focus of these plantings has moved to south of King City and, to a lesser degree, to the sides of the valley. One suspects that much of the demand is for blending: a touch of herbaceousness in a warmer-based wine might be all to the good. With the third-largest plantings in California (after the Napa and Sonoma Valleys) one might wish for more obvious signs of success: Lockwood and San Bernabe are the most likely locations.

Sauvignon Blanc

If eucalypts can give a eucalypt mint flavor to Cabernet Sauvignon, why shouldn't asparagus do the same for Sauvignon Blanc? I jest, but Doug Meador of Ventana Vineyard went to considerable lengths to find a clone which didn't provide an asparagus flavored wine. Indeed, I think the grape does well overall, but plantings have remained anchored over the past decade, which suggests winemakers think otherwise. Ventana and Lockwood do best.

Pinot Noir

Has the same relative position as Cabernet Sauvignon; theoretically it ought to be more secure. As with Chardonnay, Chalone and Jensen make the wines which Monterey as a whole fails to produce. The wines overall are pretty, but frail: the finger points firmly at excessive yields with a variety which is supremely intolerant of such behavior.

Gewurztraminer

As with Riesling, the leading region in the state, Thomas Fogarty consistently excels with Ventana-grown grapes, providing a spicy wine of verve and style.

ABOVE ~ *Jose Romero filling the press at Chalone with Pinot Noir skins.*

SAN BERNABE VINEYARD

What is thought to be the largest contiguous vineyard in the world (and certainly in the western world) was developed by McCarthy Farming with Prudential Insurance Company and Reader's Digest investment funds in the zenith of the tax shelter days of 1972 to 1974. The statistics go on and on. The vineyard is 11 miles long and five miles wide. Its net vineyard area (excluding access roads, reservoirs and so forth) is 7,000 acres with 8,100 acres the maximum plantable on a property which comprises 13,000 acres. There are 188 blocks ranging from ten to 300 acres in size. The vineyard is irrigated from 30 wells which pump 55,000 gallons a minute, stored in 26 reservoirs and distributed to irrigation points by 30 miles of canals.

ABOVE ~ *The many hues of Chardonnay bunches, some from the outside of the canopy, some from within, and some showing botrytis.*

The permanent staff is 70, with up to 200 seasonal workers employed during the pruning season. Picking is carried out with 11 huge machine harvesters specially developed by McCarthy Farming which pick two rows at a time. Working from 10 P.M. until noon the following day, they can harvest 2,000 tons a day, although the normal schedule sees 1,200 tons a day picked. The sulfur sprays against mildew are applied by plane; tillage and other sprays by 13 tractors. It produces over 25% of the entire Monterey County output.

In 1988 the vineyard was purchased by Delicato, an acquisition which has led to many changes. But San Bernabe remains in the business of selling grapes (largely in the form of juice of wine) to others, including the likes of Gallo. Eighty per cent of the output is now processed either at Delicato itself or at Cypress Ridge Winery, the processing facility established on the northern side of the San Bernabe Vineyard (owned by Delicato/San Bernabe). Here six Bucher presses de-juice 20,000 tons of grapes each season.

If it all sounds like very big business, it is, but there are surprising aspects. If this were an Australian vineyard, there is no question that it would be machine pruned. San Bernabe has looked at machine pruning, but has backed away for two reasons. Says San Bernabe chief executive Dana Merrill, "Our hills and side slopes make it difficult for a precision piece of equipment to operate uniformly. As well, we've worked hard to avoid being identified as a bulk grape producer which is secondarily concerned with quality."

The trend is, indeed, to have more manual labor and hand manipulation of the vines, rather than less. Notwithstanding that many purchasers take delivery of juice ex the Cypress Ridge facility or wine from Delicato, they insist on knowing from which block it came, and to have provided input into the viticulture. Merrill observes, "It's all part of the trend for the winemakers to be in the vineyard: they are starting to insist on weak shoot removal, leaf pulling, and so forth. It's very expensive, but we have to do it."

Market forces have also seen the plantings change radically in the 20 years' life of the vineyard. The original plantings were to two-thirds red, and one-third white. At one point in the late 1970s the ratio had swung to three-quarters white and one-quarter red, but (largely due to recent plantings of Cabernet Sauvignon) red varieties have come back to one-third.

Radical though those changes might appear, the arrival of Delicato as owners heralded a major shift in philosophy. In the first winter following the change of ownership 1,200 acres were grafted over to Chardonnay, and in each succeeding year 900 additional acres have been grafted (not just to Chardonnay). Between 1988 and 1992 the Chardonnay tonnage increased from 1,500 to 8,000 tons, almost all of it sold under eight-year contracts.

Merlot, planted in the early days but then removed, has been reinstated alongside the increasing Cabernet Sauvignon plantings, while Chenin Blanc (a high yielding variety much favored by the financially driven owners before Delicato) has been greatly reduced. Other plantings to make way for Chardonnay and Cabernet Sauvignon include French Colombard, Grey Riesling and Sylvaner. The portfolio has shrunk from 23 to 17 varieties, still representing an unusually wide range in a state so besotted with Chardonnay and Cabernet Sauvignon.

As one might expect, San Bernabe is moving towards reduced input agriculture. Merrill is clinical about the issue. "We have no desire to be anointed organic by the State of California, but we have moved away strongly from hot chemicals over the past five years. There are three reasons why we should have done so: cost, product liability concerns, and worker's claims, however misplaced we might believe the latter to be."

Given the massive investment in equipment designed for the 12-foot rows established in the initial plantings (not to mention the spare 1,000 acres or so), there is little prospect of radical change to the trellis design or spacing. For all that, there are 200 acres of experimental vineyard, with trials running on quadrilateral cordons, six-foot row spacing and vertical trellis designs. The only system ruled out entirely is the very expensive and labor-intensive lyre system, a system which in any event is designed for far cooler climates.

There is also a shift towards north-south row alignment; the traditional pattern in the Salinas Valley was east-west, a legacy of the San Joaquin table grape philosophy which said it was better to sacrifice a few outside rows to the wind, and have the vines produce their own windbreak. The better sunlight interception, and the increased air circulation of the north-south rows, are now seen as producing riper grapes with lower risks of disease.

Finally, while the original plantings were on their own roots, the newer plantings are on grafted stock. Phylloxera is yet to arrive, but nematodes (microscopic worms which attack the roots in much the same way as phylloxera, though without quite the same terminal effects) are very active in the sandy soils of San Bernabe. Here, too, research is continuing into the most suitable rootstocks, a choice which may well depend as much on the variety being grown as the soil type.

ABOVE ~ *The 7,000 acres of San Bernabe Vineyard stretch as far as the eye can see into the dusk.*

WINERIES *of* MONTEREY

ESTANCIA MONTEREY ESTATE

A: Soledad, CA **T**: (707) 963 7111 **V**: 10–5 daily at Franciscan, 1178 Galleron Road, Rutherford, CA 94573 **P**: 98,000 **W**: Greg Upton

I have to admit to a degree of inconsistency in not treating the Monterey Vineyards of Franciscan as being warehouse wineries or brands, because they do not have a location in Monterey other than the vineyards themselves. But there is an easily accessed place to taste the wines (at Franciscan in the Napa Valley) and there is no other warehouse winery producing 100,000 cases of wine a year. What is more, the Estancia Monterey Chardonnay is the very essence of the region, a quite lovely wine with lively, tangy, intense fruit with pronounced barrel-ferment American oak. At the price, and given its consistency, this wine must surely rate in the top echelon of California Chardonnay values. The White Meritage, a blend of Sauvignon Blanc and Semillon, is a little more erratic, with highly scented aromatic fruit and lots of oak, intermingling with spice. Not a wine one is likely to forget in a hurry, but some of the characters are non-classic. These wines come from the 500-acre estate to the northwest of Greenfield; the Pinnacles Pinot Noir comes from a vineyard within the Chalone Appellation where 50 acres are planted to Pinot Noir to the east of Soledad off Highway 146. The Pinnacles Pinot Noir has exhibited pepper and spice characteristics which, at least in Australia, are associated with incomplete physiological ripening, suggesting that in some years at least, the climate may be on the cool side.

JEKEL VINEYARD 1978

A: 40155 Walnut Avenue, Greenfield, CA 93927 **T**: (408) 674 5522 **V**: 10–5 daily **P**: 80,000 **W**: Joel Burnstein

Bill Jekel, one of the founding twins who initiated winemaking in the Monterey region in 1972, was for long a passionate and outspoken commentator on the virtues of the Arroyo Seco AVA, but a no less outspoken critic of the French concept of *terroir*. It was a curiously inconsistent position, but certainly gained Jekel (and his winery) plenty of attention and publicity. The winery has two distinct vineyards: the first is the 140-acre Gravelstone Vineyard, taking its name from the rocky soils in which it is planted, and which produces Cabernet Sauvignon, Chardonnay and Johannisberg Riesling; this was established in 1972. In 1983 a second vineyard of 187 acres was planted astride the Arroyo Seco River, with Cabernet Franc, Merlot, Cabernet Sauvignon, Chardonnay and Riesling the principal grapes, although the winery is tentatively moving back into Pinot Noir after an early and unsuccessful flirtation with the variety. There is nothing unsuccessful about its development of Riesling, which in three styles (dry, semi-sweet and intermittent luscious, botrytised late harvest) earnt Jekel a considerable reputation. The range, of course, extended further with Chardonnay, Cabernet Sauvignon, Cabernet Franc and Pinot Blanc all on offer, the Cabernet Sauvignon coming under various labels including Private Reserve and Gravelstone Vineyard.

While production grew, it was no secret that by the latter part of the 1980s Jekel was finding the financial going difficult, and in early 1990 it became part of the ill-fated Vintech group. The Jekels resumed ownership a year later, but in early 1992 found another purchaser: Brown Forman, which later in the year was to take the headlines by adding Fetzer to its portfolio.

The arrival of Brown Forman has led to urgently needed upgrading and expansion of the facilities, and will accelerate the move away from the 75/25% split between white and reds to roughly equal production of each. The wines designed to lead the reputation of the winery, and take it eventually to 125,000 cases, are Symmetry (a Cabernet-dominant Meritage blend), and Sceptre (a barrel-fermented Chardonnay). The arrival of Joel Burnstein, formerly of Sterling Vineyard, should also help.

While the Rieslings, in their various manifestations, are all that one could hope for, with quite luscious fruit and good length, the early offerings of Sceptre and Symmetry did not impress. The Symmetry showed strong herbal/grassy/tobacco characters (which the growers of Monterey are fond of insisting they have eliminated), while the Chardonnay was dominated by nutty malolactic fermentation characters and oak, with not enough fruit.

LOCKWOOD 1986

A: Steinbeck Station, 59020 Paris Valley Road, Salinas, CA 93902 **T**: (408) 753 1424 **V**: By appointment **P**: 75,000 **W**: Stephen Pessagno

In 1981, Paul Toppen, Butch Lindley and Phil Johnson, the latter two having been Monterey grape growers since the early 1970s, decided to establish a major vineyard to supply what they foresaw to be ever-increasing demand for

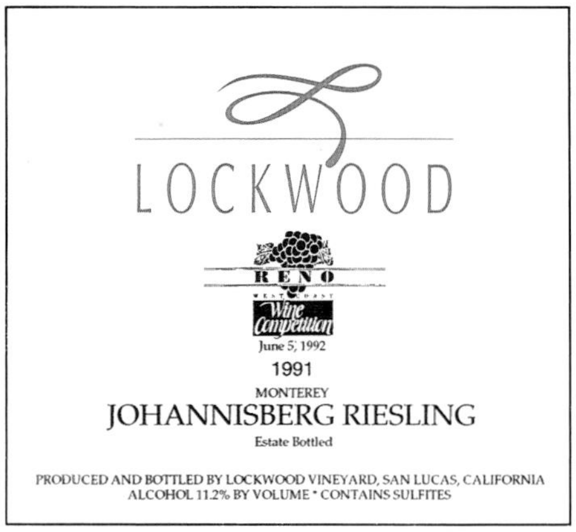
LOCKWOOD
RENO
Wine Competition
June 5, 1992
1991
MONTEREY
JOHANNISBERG RIESLING
Estate Bottled
PRODUCED AND BOTTLED BY LOCKWOOD VINEYARD, SAN LUCAS, CALIFORNIA
ALCOHOL 11.2% BY VOLUME • CONTAINS SULFITES

Monterey grapes. A large ranch was acquired at the southern end of Monterey County, and during 1981 and 1982, 1,650 acres of vines were established. There are 925 acres of Chardonnay, 500 of Cabernet Sauvignon, 100 each of Johannisberg Riesling, Sauvignon Blanc and Semillon, with Pinot Blanc, Merlot, Cabernet Franc, Chenin Blanc and Pinot Noir making up the roster.

In 1986 the partners decided to vinify small quantities of the grapes, both to learn more for themselves, and to help publicize the vineyard. By 1989, the program had been extended to the production of grapes on a commercial scale, and were so successful that in 1990 the decision was taken to build a full-scale winery, commissioned for the 1991 vintage. With a crush of 1,300 tons going through the winery in 1992, there is no question that Lockwood has entered the winemaking business in serious fashion, even if grape growing and selling remains a major part of the enterprise. The quality of the first commercial releases from Lockwood has been exemplary; it now remains to be seen whether the three marketing methods chosen by Dan Lucas will succeed. It is using an aggressive direct mail order campaign; it is selling direct to restaurants in California and Illinois via commission brokers; and in other states will follow the traditional three-tier distribution system. With 1992 prices of $8–9 for the standard wines and $19 for the very limited Reserve Chardonnay, the price seems right.

The outstanding wines in the range are the Riesling, the 1991 vintage of which was awarded a gold medal at the 1992 California State Fair, also receiving the award as Best Wine of the North-Central Coast Appellation, and the Cabernet Sauvignon. The latter reflects the Region III climate in which Lockwood is situated, with soft, full, sweet berry fruit and complementary sweet oak. It shows none at all of the vegetative characters which have been the bane of the Monterey Valley. The Pinot Blanc and Fumé Blanc from 1991 also impressed, the former with a floral, aromatic bouquet, a seductive hint of spice on the palate, and a well balanced, long finish, the latter intense and tangy. If Lockwood can maintain this early form, it will be a force to be reckoned with.

MASSON VINEYARDS 1852

A: 800 South Alta Street, Gonzales, CA 93926 **T**: (408) 675 2481 **V**: 10–8 Summer, 10–6 Winter, at 700 Cannery Row, Monterey CA 93940 **P**: 5 million **W**: Larry Brink

It is something of poetic license to show the establishment date of Masson Vineyards as 1852, for nothing remains of the wine dynasty established by Paul Masson other than his surname. The writing was on the wall from 1943, when Joseph Seagram purchased the original mountain winery established by Paul Masson. Paul Masson became a leader in the non-vintage table wine market in the 1960s, with sales peaking at 8 million cases. This expansion was partly underpinned by the acquisition of 4,500 acres of Monterey County vineyards, but wine quality remained distinctly ordinary. In 1987 Vintners International acquired Masson (along with Taylor California Cellars and Taylor of New York), moving the production base to Soledad and Madera, and introducing the Masson Vineyards label as the flagship, relegating Paul Masson to a second range of generics, sparkling wines and blush. The current releases are no better than they ought to be, with indifferent oak disfiguring the Chardonnay and Merlot, but with the Cabernet Sauvignon showing the sweet and sour side of Monterey County: an amalgam of ripe fruit and cedar/cigar/leafy characters. Improbably, the flavors work quite well in what is the best wine in the line-up, the Cabernet Sauvignon.

THE MONTEREY VINEYARD 1973

A: 800 South Alta Street, Gonzales, CA 93926 **T**: (408) 675 2481 **V**: 10–5 daily **P**: 550,000 **W**: Phil Franscioni

The Monterey Vineyard was established in 1973 by two of the best known figures in the California wine industry at that time: Dick Peterson (ex Beaulieu Vineyard) and Gerald Asher, the English-born wine merchant who had come to the United States to work for the imported wine division of Seagram, and who these days is known as the wine writer for *Gourmet Magazine* — and as such, is the most skilled and erudite wine writer in the United States. Notwithstanding the skills and experience of the management team, the venture did not prosper; in retrospect, it is clear that Monterey vignerons were still coming to terms with the particular combination of climate and *terroir* in which they were working. In 1977 the winery and vineyards were sold to Coca-Cola, which in turn passed on ownership of all of its wine interests to Joseph Seagram in 1983.

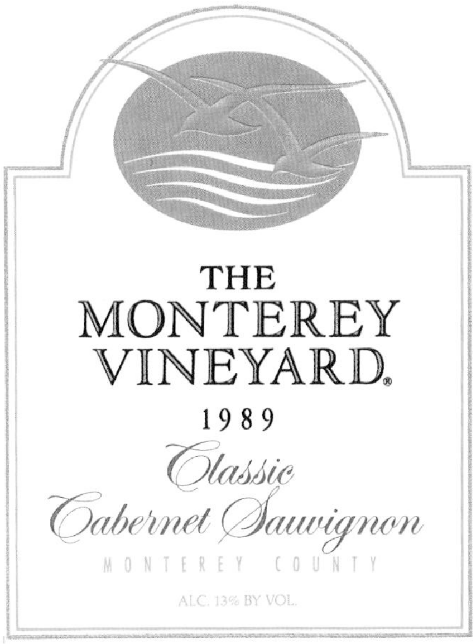
THE
MONTEREY
VINEYARD.
1989
Classic
Cabernet Sauvignon
MONTEREY COUNTY
ALC. 13% BY VOL.

Drawing upon the 100-acre Paris Valley Ranch situated in the San Lucas AVA at the far southern end of the Salinas Valley, the Monterey Vineyard has settled down to produce a reliable range of varietal wines. Since 1986 Phil Franscioni has been winemaker, having spent his entire career after graduating from U.C. Davis in the Salinas Valley, splitting his time between Ventana Vineyards, Paul Masson and Taylor California Cellars. At the head of the portfolio are three Limited Release varietals: Chardonnay, Pinot Noir and Cabernet

ABOVE ~ *Deep-ripping a Monterey vineyard before replanting with Cabernet Sauvignon, still a controversial variety in these parts.*

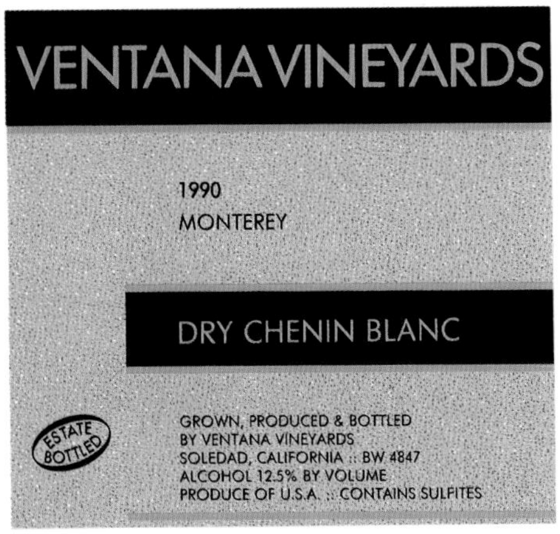
VENTANA VINEYARDS
1990
MONTEREY
DRY CHENIN BLANC
ESTATE BOTTLED
GROWN, PRODUCED & BOTTLED
BY VENTANA VINEYARDS
SOLEDAD, CALIFORNIA :: BW 4847
ALCOHOL 12.5% BY VOLUME
PRODUCE OF U.S.A. :: CONTAINS SULFITES

Sauvignon. The Classic Varietal range comprises Chardonnay, Sauvignon Blanc, Chenin Blanc, Johannisberg Riesling, White Zinfandel, Merlot, Cabernet Sauvignon and Gamay Beaujolais, with a generic white and red to round things off. Phil Franscioni is an articulate and intelligent winemaker, who has successfully introduced greater complexity into the winemaking since his arrival in 1986. The wines in the Classic range can offer exceptionally good values, the Classic Chardonnay with clean, fresh citric-tinged fruit, and the Cabernet Sauvignon with nicely balanced clear berry aromas, although showing some green olive characters on the palate — characters which many would regard as a legitimate part of Cabernet's varietal character. The Limited Release wines show more sophistication, more oak and more complexity, which is what one would expect.

SMITH & HOOK WINERY 1980

A: 37700 Foothill Road, Soledad, CA 93960 **T**: (408) 678 2132 **V**: 11–4 daily at 217 Crossroads Boulevard, Carmel, CA 93921 **P**: 25,000 **W**: Duane DeBoer

As you drive south along Highway 101 towards Soledad, and look across to the west, you will see an extensive area of vineyard terraces tucked tightly into the foothills of the Sierra de Salinas at Mission Soledad. The view is strikingly similar to that of parts of the Valais region of Switzerland, even if the mountain backdrop is less dramatic. And if you then proceed across to the 250 acres of terraced vineyards established in 1974, you will not be disappointed: the view down the hillside and back across the valley is extremely attractive.

Smith & Hook takes its name from the two ranches which were purchased to start the venture: that upon which the vineyards are established was owned by Smith (and was a horse stud), while the lower ranch was owned by Hook, and was purchased merely to give the mountainside vineyards access to the Salinas aquifer. The venture is now wholly owned by the Hahn family, who were one of the founding investors. The vineyard holdings have been extended to include the Doctors Vineyard, Lone Oak Vineyard, and a further planting in Arroyo Seco.

The Smith & Hook label has been joined by the Hahn label, the latter offering a Cabernet Sauvignon, Chardonnay and Merlot, all with the Santa Lucia Highlands Appellation. The intention is that Hahn will specialize in Merlot, as the Hahn interests are now the largest growers of Merlot and Cabernet Franc in California. The winery is established in an attractive, converted horse barn on Robert Smith's Ranch, but in the long term the intention is to establish specific wineries for each of the vineyards, and to establish different identities. This will do much to eliminate the confusion which surrounded the endless changes to the second label, variously called Polo, Goal, Deer Valley, Gabriel y Caroline and Lone Valley.

The Hahn Merlot is very distinctive, with sweet cassis fruit tinged with green, showing good weight and mouthfeel. The Smith & Hook Merlot shows more of the minty/leafy/spearmint characters, suggesting that seasonal conditions may well play a role in determining how acceptable the winestyle is in the market, and in the face of continuing belief by some that the Monterey region still produces excessively herbal Meritage-style reds.

VENTANA VINEYARDS 1978

A: Los Coches Road, Soledad, CA 93960 **T**: (408) 372 7415 **V**: 12–5 daily at 2999 Monterey-Salinas Highway, Monterey, CA 93940 **P**: 30,000 **W**: Doug Meador and Rick Boyer

No one who has met Ventana founder Doug Meador is likely to forget him. For one thing, the meeting will not have been brief; for another, you are likely to have heard more claims of "firsts" and more claims of "mosts" than ever before. The "firsts" cover an extraordinary range of viticultural innovations, the "mosts" chiefly center on medals won by Ventana Vineyards and its growers. The problem is, the more you dig, and the more you enquire, the more the claims ring true: this former Air Force jet and test pilot is as intelligent and innovative as he is fearless. Meador's viticultural expertise has been gained working 300 acres of vines established on the Arroyo Seco River in the early 1970s, initially with tax-driven investors, but then moving to Meador's sole ownership. He continued on in the wake of an expensive divorce, although wine production did dip steeply.

The vineyards are planted primarily to Chardonnay (131 acres), Johannisberg Riesling and Chenin Blanc (38 acres each) and the famous Ventana clone of Sauvignon Blanc (26 acres). Lesser plantings of Gewurztraminer are fought over by purchasers each year, with the bulk going to Thomas Fogarty Winery. Meador was into close planting, shoot positioning, vertical trellises and leaf plucking long before most mortals had even heard of the terms, largely as a self-taught response to the demands of the Monterey climate. Here again the hyperbole flows furiously: Meador is utterly contemptuous of those who claim a cooler climate or a longer growing season, demanding names and addresses so the claimants can be brought to justice.

Then there is the subject of the show awards: says Meador, "Over the last five years wines made from the grapes grown on this vineyard have received more awards than any other vineyard, cumulative, ever." Turning to Ventana itself, the 1990 Dry Riesling was the most awarded Riesling made that vintage, and every vintage of the wine has won a fistful of medals; the Sauvignon Blanc from 1985 won a medal at every show it was entered in, bar one (and there were many); and so on and so forth.

Apart from the White Riesling, a rich, high flavored lime juice-accented wine of undoubted quality, the Sauvignon Blanc stands out. Meador has spoken and written at length about the long search which led to the isolation of what he calls the "Ventana clone" of Sauvignon Blanc and which apparently originated from one of the Wente importations. It is absolutely true that it shows none of the asparagus/grass characters which some Monterey Sauvignons exhibit, instead providing powerful, tangy, gooseberry/herbal (but in the rich sense) fruit.

OTHER WINERIES

RICHARD BOYER WINES
A: P.O. Box 842, Soledad, CA 93960
T: (408) 678 3404 **W**: Richard Boyer

CLONINGER CELLARS
A: P.O. Box 5, Salinas, CA 93902
T: (408) 758 1686 **W**: John Estell

JOULLIAN VINEYARDS 1990
A: 107 Cachagua Road, Carmel Valley, CA 93924 **T**: (408) 659 2800 **W**: Ridge Watson

LA REINA WINERY
A: P.O. Box 1344, Carmel, CA 93921
T: (408) 373 3292 **W**: Charles Chreitzberg

MONTEREY PENINSULA WINERY 1974
A: 786 Wave Street, Monterey, CA 93940
T: (408) 372 4949 **W**: Elizabeth Shoenecker

PARAISO SPRINGS VINEYARDS 1989
A: 38060 Paraiso Springs Road, Soledad, CA 93960 **T**: (408) 678 1592

SAN MARTIN WINERY
A: 12900 Monterey Road, San Martin, CA 95046 **T**: (408) 683 2672

SAN SABA VINEYARD
A: 37700 Foothill Road, Soledad, CA 93960
T: (408) 678 2132

ROBERT TALBOT VINEYARD & WINERY 1983
A: P.O. Box 776, Gonzales, CA 93926
T: (408) 675 3000 **W**: Sam Balderas

ZABALA VINEYARDS
A: Route 1, Box 244, Soledad, CA 93960
T: (408) 675 0192

WINERIES *of* CARMEL

CHATEAU JULIEN 1982

A: 840 Carmel Valley Road, Carmel, CA 93921 **T**: (408) 624 2600 **V**: 8:30–5 Mon–Fri, 11–5 Sat–Sun **P**: 40,000 **W**: William Anderson

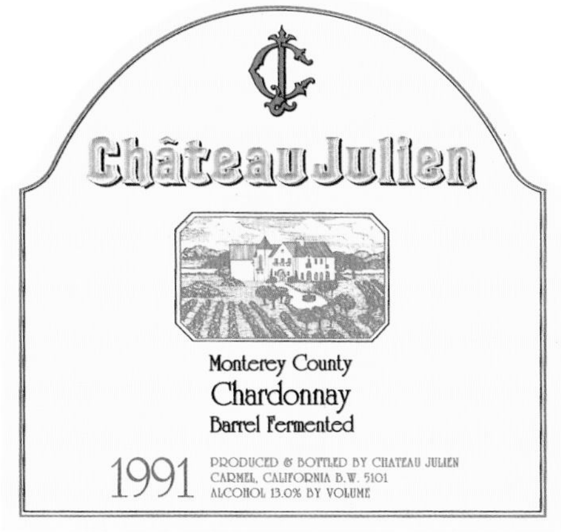
Château Julien
Monterey County
Chardonnay
Barrel Fermented
1991
PRODUCED & BOTTLED BY CHATEAU JULIEN
CARMEL, CALIFORNIA B.W. 5101
ALCOHOL 13.0% BY VOLUME

Chateau Julien is said to be named after and modeled upon the chateaux of the Haut-Medoc commune of St. Julien. The building is in fact a very curious mixture of architecture, slightly more tasteful than but reminiscent of Chateau Boswell in the Napa Valley, and with as much Spanish as French influence. The 100 or so vines planted in front of the winery are there for aesthetic reasons; Chateau Julien and its satellite brands rely entirely upon purchased grapes, with over 600 acres of Monterey County vineyards under contract, producing 2,500 tons of grapes a year. Not all of that crush finishes up under the various Chateau Julien banners; the winery has developed a thriving custom crush business for others, including Sutter Home, Guenoc and Round Hill.

The wines produced by Chateau Julien on its own account are divided into three market segments: the premium varietal range under the Chateau Julien label, the fighting varietal range under the Garland Ranch label, and what are termed to be popular price varietals under the Emerald Bay label. But let it not be thought that the Chateau Julien wines are just that: one is offered Private Reserve Cabernet Sauvignon, Private Reserve Sur Lee Chardonnay, Barrel Fermented Chardonnay, and Platinum, a White Meritage blend of Sauvignon Blanc and Semillon. The Cabernet shows ripe fruit with an interesting touch of cinnamon and spice, and is a pleasant wine; by far the best is the Private Reserve Sur Lee Chardonnay, with rich melon and fig fruit, well integrated oak, and good overall mouthfeel and structure. The other wines in the Chateau Julien line-up are adequate but unexciting.

DURNEY VINEYARD 1977

A: Cachagua Road, Carmel Valley, CA 93922 **T**: (408) 625 5433 **V**: By appointment **P**: 15,000 **W**: Peter Watson-Graff

William and Dorothy Durney commenced planting grapes in 1968 on the Rancho del Sueno (ranch of dreams) which they had purchased in 1954. The initial 20 acres of Chenin Blanc and Cabernet Sauvignon have now been increased to 150 acres, with Johannisberg Riesling and Chardonnay making up the remainder.

The winery was constructed on the exceptionally beautiful site in 1977. It and the vineyards are at an elevation of 1,200 feet on the steep slopes of the Santa Lucia mountains, with the narrow Carmel Valley way below. The vines are grown organically, and there is no irrigation. The Cabernet Sauvignon, sometimes released under a Reserve label, constitutes the major part of production, and is the best of the wines.

ABOVE ~ *The garden at Chateau Julien, reminiscent of Provence or Spain.*

WINERIES *of* CHALONE

CHALONE VINEYARD 1960

A: Box 855, Highway 146, Soledad, CA 93960 **T**: (408) 678 1717 **V**: 10–3 Sat or by appointment **P**: 30,000
W: Michael Michaud

Josh Jensen of Calera is apocryphally credited with having carried around a bottle of sulfuric acid to pour on the ground and thus determine whether or not he had indeed found limestone in his search for what became the Calera Vineyards. I am assured the story is untrue, but even if it were true, he was beaten to the punch by over 50 years by a Frenchman who found limestone soil at Chalone similar to that of Champagne. In 1919, having found his soil he elected to plant Chenin Blanc, although one cannot help but wonder whether he thought (or hoped) it was Chardonnay. The vineyards were extended in 1946, with Pinot Noir, Chardonnay, Chenin Blanc and Pinot Blanc being planted, the Pinot Noir and Chardonnay no doubt coming from Wente sources. In 1960 a tiny winery was constructed on site by a group of amateur enthusiasts, but scant attention was paid to this remote vineyard situated on the Salinas Hills with the Pinnacles National Monument rearing in the background until Richard Graff, a Harvard music graduate who had studied at U.C. Davis for a year, purchased the embryonic winery. He ensured lasting immortality for himself by driving a water truck to and from Soledad eight times a day to help the vines grow.

The first release of Chalone in 1969 won immediate fame, and Graff and partner Phil Woodward were able to attract investment funds from a tolerant group of investors for whom financial returns were secondary. While Chalone is now part of a large publicly held group, with Chateau Lafite Rothschild holding the lion's share, it is doubtful whether Chalone has ever repaid its accumulated investment and losses. What it has done, however, is create one of the most prominent quality brands in California.

In the early 1970s the vineyards were expanded with the addition of 50 acres of Chardonnay and 25 acres of Pinot Noir, and in 1974 the original winery (built in a converted chicken shed) was replaced by a more modern facility. In 1984 underground caves were built, sharing with Opus One the distinction of intercepting geothermal springs which forced the installation of air-conditioning. The vineyards have now been expanded to 187 acres in total, with the most recent plantings coming into bearing in 1992 (15 acres of Pinot Blanc).

Whatever the Chalone wines may lack, it is neither character nor flavor. There was a period around 1988 when problems with the oak barrels caused quality to waver significantly, but the oak problem has been sorted out, and Chalone has returned to the style which made it so famous. The critics aver that the Chardonnay does not age, but the remaining bottles of 1979 in my cellar suggest otherwise. In a sense it is a sterile debate, because the Chardonnay exhibits such astonishing richness of toasty flavor when young that there does not seem any pressing need to cellar it. The Pinot Noir is made in the same ripe, dense and fleshy mold. Each of the Pinot Noir and Chardonnay, incidentally, appear under the Reserve, Estate and Gavilan labels; my comments and descriptions relate to the Estate versions, which are in volume and prestige terms the most important. The Reserve wines, made from the 1946 plantings, provide even more of the same, but are seldom, if ever, seen in the marketplace.

ABOVE ~ *Dick Graff in a near-empty Pinot Noir fermentation vat at Chalone.*

ABOVE ~ *Eric Hamacher, assistant winemaker at Chalone, taking samples from first, second and third pressings.*

WINERIES *of* SAN BENITO

CALERA WINE COMPANY 1976

A: 11300 Cienega Road, Hollister, CA 95023
T: (408) 637 9170 **V**: By appointment
P: 20,000 **W**: Josh Jensen

Josh Jensen is California's high priest of Pinot Noir. Given the waywardness of the variety, it seems fitting that he should have equipped himself with degrees from Yale and Oxford, and served his vinous apprenticeship working for two years in Burgundy and the Rhone Valley. Yet life has not always been easy for Jensen since he found his limestone-based soil at an elevation of around 220 feet on the sides of Mount Gavilan. Low yields, high production costs and the typically difficult Pinot Noir market placed severe financial strains on the operation, ultimately relieved by the introduction of the Central Coast Chardonnay and the Central Coast Pinot Noir (made from purchased grapes) to provide critical volume throughout. Thus it is that of the 20,000 cases now produced, 4,000 are vineyard designated, and 16,000 cases carry the Central Coast appellation.

There are four vineyard plots, each separately named, identified and bottled. Jensen is the largest at 14 acres, followed by Mills (11 acres) and then Selleck and Reed (five acres each). In 1983, Jensen planted some of the first Viognier in California, and has since expanded those plantings to five acres.

The vineyards were established in 1974, and the winery site purchased in 1978, the site of an old rock crushing plant on a steep hillside, which lent itself to the gravity-flow system operating in the winery. Jensen had visions of establishing a visitors' center to take advantage of the spectacular views, but the authorities had other ideas, forcing him to spend a fortune in reinforcing the structure which had stood without difficulty for over half a century. There was at least some consolation when the subsequent earthquake failed to disturb a single barrel.

The gravity flow signals Jensen's wholly natural approach to winemaking. His is a strictly non-interventionist policy, with total reliance on wild yeasts, and no crushing of the grapes, the one concession to the twentieth century being a pneumatic pigeager (or plunger) for the open-top fermenters. The hands-off winemaking continues through the bottling: the wines are egg white-fined, but not filtered, and there is only one small pump in the entire winery.

The radicalists and the Robert Parkers of this world would have us believe that this is the only way in which Pinot Noir can be properly made. In some years the Jensen wines lend weight to that view; in others they most assuredly do not. Some of them have been grossly infected by lactobaccillus, and show unacceptably high levels of volatility, yet others appear as porty and overripe. But when it all comes together, the wines are majestic in their richness, texture and style, and they come together more often than they do not. 1991 was a triumph, and 1989 was not.

The Chardonnays motor along in the middle, with very ripe, lush peach and honey flavors, and strong nutty, vanillin biscuity characters coming through in the top-of-range Mount Harlan Chardonnay (from estate grapes) and soft, honey/peach fruit in the standard wine. The Viognier is truly excellent, with exotic tropical varietal fruit, and that distinctive fruit gum/pastille character which is the hallmark of the variety.

TOP ~ *Hand-picking Pinot Noir at Calera will always be the only option.*

ABOVE ~ *In the vast vineyards of the Salinas Valley floor Mexicans are inevitably yielding to machines.*

Paso Robles and York Mountain

The name Paso Robles comes from the Spanish El Paso de Robles, or The Pass of the Oaks, the name given by travelers journeying between Mission San Miguel (at the northern end of the present day region) and Mission San Luis Obispo. The records show that Mission San Miguel produced wine soon after it was founded in 1789, presumably from locally grown grapes. In 1856 a Frenchman named Adolph Siot planted vines on Vineyard Drive on a site which became the Rotta Winery.

At the very last moment, the small York Mountain AVA was excised from the much larger Paso Robles AVA, a decision which made both geographic and climatic sense, but less so from a commercial viewpoint. Simply because York Mountain has only one winery, and only a few — albeit distinguished — vineyards, I am treating it as if it were part of Paso Robles, which in any event is a sprawling region with varying *terroir* and mesoclimate.

York Mountain Winery, built in 1882, contributes its own significant history, and is one of the major tourist landmarks in the region. Much has been made of the fact that the famous pianist (and Polish President) Paderewski purchased a 2,000-acre ranch in 1914, and was persuaded to establish a vineyard on it ten years later (in the middle of Prohibition). Zinfandel was made for him at York Mountain Vineyard, which continued to purchase the grapes until his death in 1941, whereafter the vines were removed.

In 1964 Beverly Hills cardiologist Dr. Stanley Hoffman planted a 60-acre vineyard, now famous as HMR Vineyard, in the York Mountain region, and which supplies leading producers including Iron Horse with great Pinot Noir.

But, as the discussion of climate on page 324 indicates, Paso Robles is a warm region, most suited to full-bodied red wines. Those within it recognize a significant difference between "East Side" and "West Side," the dividing line being Highway 101. This is in part due to elevation (typically higher on the west) and in part to the second of the two cooling influences, which funnels up Highway 46 from Cambria.

As one goes east, the climate becomes progressively warmer, and the scenery progressively less interesting. The fact that the eastern boundary extends to Kern County (and the northern boundary to Monterey County) tells one how much a matter of

ABOVE ~ *French oak barrels awaiting refilling; space is at a premium in almost all wineries.*

OPPOSITE ~ *A pair of gnarled oak trees in silent embrace at Meridian.*

Paso Robles
VINTAGE CHART 1981-91

RED

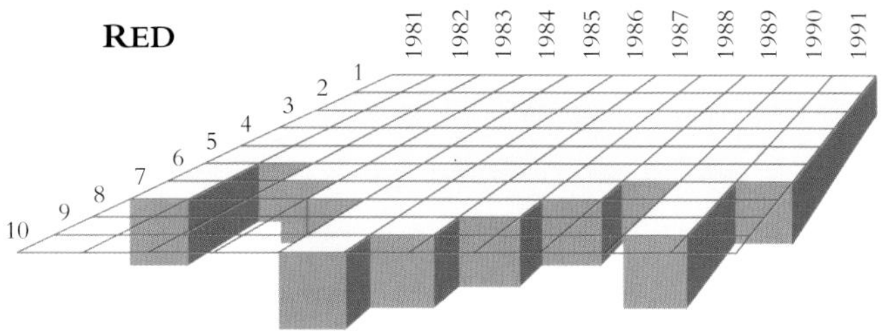
1981
1982
1983
1984
1985
1986
1987
1988
1989
1990
1991
1
2
3
4
5
6
7
8
9
10

WHITE

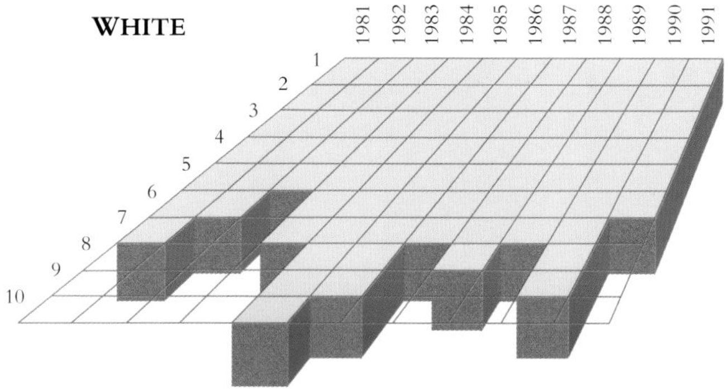
1981
1982
1983
1984
1985
1986
1987
1988
1989
1990
1991
1
2
3
4
5
6
7
8
9
10

expediency the definition of this 614,000-acre (with 9,000 acres of vines) AVA is. The one exception to this pattern is Creston Vineyard in the far southeastern corner of the AVA situated in the La Pranza Range at an elevation of 1,700 feet, and with some splendidly wild scenery en route.

Another exception, this time on the West Side, is the nascent Chateau Beaucastel (of Rhone Valley fame) vineyards, situated on a belt of near solid limestone in a Region II area. The property, which includes leading fine wine importer Robert Haas and Charles Falk as members of the partnership, lies one mile to the west of the present boundary of the Paso Robles AVA. An application to amend the boundary to follow the ridge line of the Santa Lucia Range was filed at the end of 1992, and (presumably) will ultimately be dealt with and granted.

Other moves are afoot to create an Adelaida Hills AVA (with a high Region II to low Region III climate) and a second adjacent area to the south called Templeton Hills with a Region I to mid Region II climate.

ABOVE ~ *The Italian connection: Zinfandel at Arciero.*

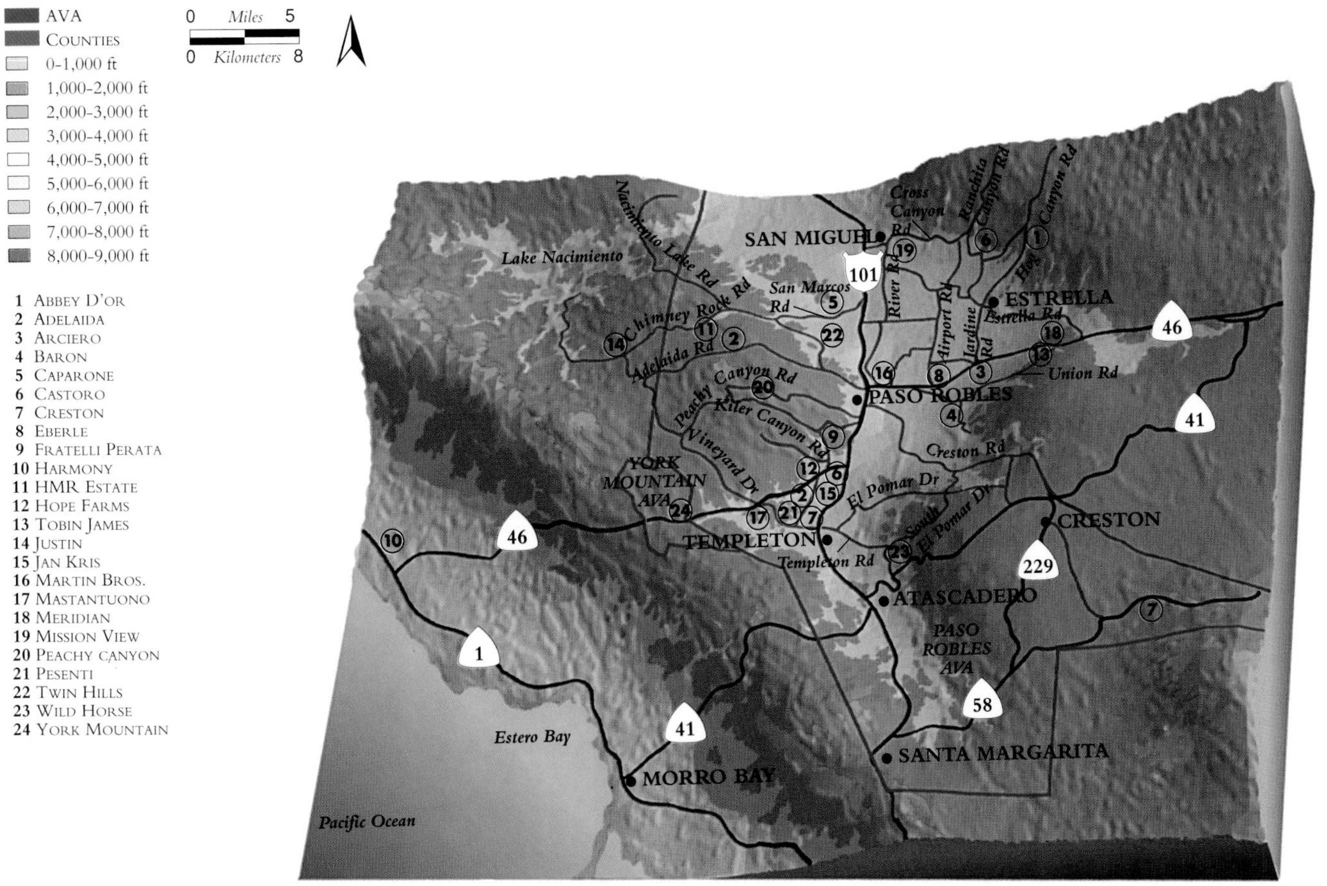
AVA
Counties
0-1,000 ft
1,000-2,000 ft
2,000-3,000 ft
3,000-4,000 ft
4,000-5,000 ft
5,000-6,000 ft
6,000-7,000 ft
7,000-8,000 ft
8,000-9,000 ft
0 Miles 5
0 Kilometers 8
1 Abbey D'or
2 Adelaida
3 Arciero
4 Baron
5 Caparone
6 Castoro
7 Creston
8 Eberle
9 Fratelli Perata
10 Harmony
11 HMR Estate
12 Hope Farms
13 Tobin James
14 Justin
15 Jan Kris
16 Martin Bros.
17 Mastantuono
18 Meridian
19 Mission View
20 Peachy Canyon
21 Pesenti
22 Twin Hills
23 Wild Horse
24 York Mountain
Lake Nacimiento
Nacimiento Lake Rd
SAN MIGUEL
Cross Canyon Rd
Ranchita Canyon Rd
Hog Canyon Rd
101
San Marcos Rd
River Rd
Airport Rd
Jardine Rd
ESTRELLA
Estrella Rd
46
Chimney Rock Rd
Adelaida Rd
Peachy Canyon Rd
Kiler Canyon Rd
Vineyard Dr
PASO ROBLES
Union Rd
41
Creston Rd
El Pomar Dr
South El Pomar Dr
YORK MOUNTAIN AVA
TEMPLETON
Templeton Rd
CRESTON
229
ATASCADERO
PASO ROBLES AVA
1
58
41
Estero Bay
SANTA MARGARITA
MORRO BAY
Pacific Ocean

Paso Robles
1971 and 1991 Acreage/Grape Varieties

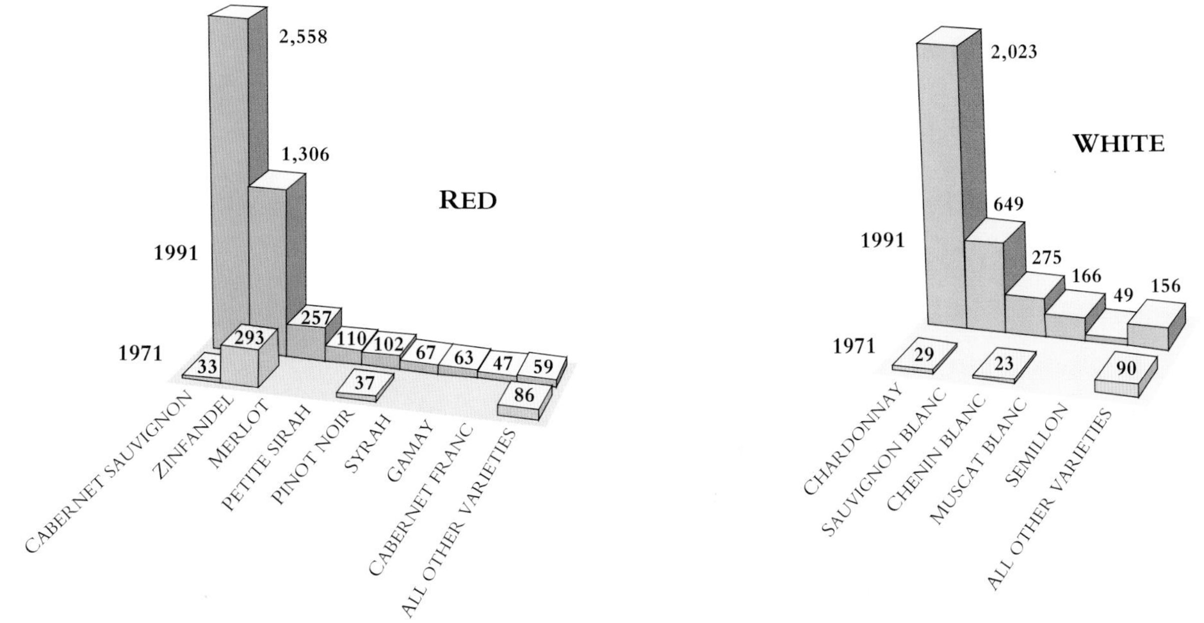
RED
1991
1971
2,558
1,306
293
257
110
102
67
63
47
59
33
37
86
Cabernet Sauvignon
Zinfandel
Merlot
Petite Sirah
Pinot Noir
Syrah
Gamay
Cabernet Franc
All Other Varieties
WHITE
1991
1971
2,023
649
275
166
49
156
29
23
90
Chardonnay
Sauvignon Blanc
Chenin Blanc
Muscat Blanc
Semillon
All Other Varieties

top~ *Paso Robles map.*

The Region in Brief

Climate, Soil and Viticulture

Climate

York Mountain is climatically utterly different from the rest of Paso Robles; at an elevation of 1,600 to 1,800 feet, and only seven miles from the Pacific Ocean, it is profoundly maritime influenced. Fogs are common, and it receives an average rainfall of 45 inches a year. Its climate is a no-holds-barred Region I, with heat summations dipping as low as 1,800 degree days, but usually sitting around 2,200 degree days.

The Santa Lucia Range, which houses York Mountain, runs east into Paso Robles proper: the vineyards established on the scenic Chimney Rock Road (including Justin) receive 30 to 35 inches of rainfall, and are in a low to mid Region II. As one comes out of the ranges, the true geographic position of Paso Robles as an inland valley at the very top of the Salinas Valley becomes apparent.

The growing season is typically punctuated by three or four days of 95° to 100°F plus peak temperatures, followed by three or four days of overcast mornings and more temperate afternoon temperatures. The periods of moderation usually come from the Salinas Valley (all the way from Monterey Bay), and the impact is necessarily modest.

The second and more localized cooling influence comes direct from the coast up Highway 46; as well as influencing the west side climate, it gives Wild Horse a mid Region II climate — but with the usual swings from year to year. Thus the ten-year average can be very different from the 100-year average.

The nights are consistently cold, with a typical diurnal range of between 40° and 50°F. Rainfall grades from 35 inches in the west to ten inches in the east, marking a transition from Region II through Region III (in which band most of the vineyards fall) to Region IV — but with elevation disrupting the neat pattern this description implies.

Soil

The soils of the Santa Lucia Mountains proper are extremely varied, with patches of dense limestone of marine origin, with pH levels ranging from 7.9 to 8.4, and requiring acidification (a rare circumstance). At Justin Winery the limestone and shale mix also has a natural pH in the 7.3 to 7.4 range, again requiring adjustment. Away from the ranges, the soils are generally alluvial and terrace deposits, usually fertile and well drained. Vine vigor is high, and proper manipulation of the trellis and canopy is important, notwithstanding the abundant warmth.

The Growing Season

Late frosts (continuing as late as mid May) make frost protection essential, usually provided by overhead sprinklers. The growing season of around 208 days sees Chardonnay typically harvested during the first few days of September (in 1991 it started three weeks late on September 23). Cabernet Sauvignon follows in late September, sometimes stretching well into October, but usually ripened by a late burst of heat. York Mountain is much later, with Zinfandel and Cabernet Sauvignon often picked at the very end of October.

Contract Growers

Abbey D'Or Vineyard Situated in the San Miguel hills planted, inter alia, to Cabernet Sauvignon; sold to Wild Horse.

Benito Dusi Ranch Forty acres on the east side of Highway 101 south of Paso Robles town planted to Zinfandel in 1923; purchased by Peachy Canyon and Ridge.

HMR Vineyard Sixty acres in York Mountain planted to Pinot Noir, Chardonnay, Zinfandel, White Riesling and Chenin Blanc. Sold to various purchasers including Wild Horse.

Perata Vineyard Planted in the Westside of Paso Robles to Cabernet Sauvignon and Merlot; sold to Wild Horse.

YORK MT. WINERY
SHADOW CANYON
MORRIS
DICK SUSAN
MOORE
CARVER
BATEMAN
LGATES RANCH →
ALVAREZ
V2 RANCH

ABOVE ~ *York Mountain Winery shares an unconventional sign post with its neighbours.*

Sauret Vineyard Five acres in Westside Paso Robles planted to Zinfandel in 1972; sold to Eberle and Byington.

Principal Wine Styles

Cabernet Sauvignon

This is undoubtedly the region's most widely acclaimed wine, perhaps most generously by Caymus Vineyards of the Napa Valley which sources all of the grapes for its early drinking Liberty School Cabernet from Paso Robles. The wines have a softness and suppleness from an early age, yet have abundant flesh and weight. The flavors run in the dark berry through dark chocolate range, with no hint of the vegetative character of the Monterey Cabernets. There are ample tannins, but these never threaten to throw the wines out of balance. Best producers are Castoro, Eberle, J. Lohr, Meridian and Wild Horse.

Zinfandel

In many ways, Zinfandel mirrors Cabernet Sauvignon, with a soft lushness which is utterly beguiling. Vineyard age, as well as location, plays the usual important role, and has been at the heart of the spectacular success of Peachy Canyon, but other makers, notably Castoro Cellars, Creston Manor, Eberle, Jan Kris and Martin Brothers, make quite lovely wines.

Chardonnay

With Meridian and Wild Horse situated in the AVA, one can hardly ignore the variety, but the fact is that Meridian (exclusively) and Wild Horse (largely though not entirely) draw their grapes from elsewhere — Santa Barbara principally, but also Monterey. The beautifully crafted wines of Wild Horse and the smooth, crispy fruity wines of Meridian are distinctly better than those wines made from Paso Robles grapes.

Merlot

Merlot is a variety which must have been given a great boost (if it needed one in the first place) by the exploits of Wild Horse, which had had an exceptional run of wines (recently augmented by its Cheval Sauvage label) made principally from Paso Robles fruit. York Mountain is another to do well with the variety.

Pinot Noir

Really a speciality of the York Mountain AVA in viticultural terms, notwithstanding the presence (in winemaking terms) of Wild Horse, one of the top ranking Pinot Noir makers in the state of California. Ken Volk is grafting some estate Cabernet Sauvignon to Pinot Noir, and did make his 1990 Cheval Sauvage Pinot entirely from HMR Vineyard fruit, but relies principally on Santa Barbara (and Arroyo Grande) grapes.

ABOVE ~ *Limestone soil occurs in many parts of Westside Paso Robles, here on Peachy Canyon Road.*

BREAKING THE TYRANNY *of* CABERNET

Paso Robles raises the question as neatly as any region: will Cabernet Sauvignon (and its hand-maiden Merlot) continue to be seen as making the only first quality red wine? And if not, where will the challenges come from?

Given the fashion industry component to wine marketing, and also having regard to its isolated position in world wine terms, it is hard to advance the cause of Zinfandel, however much one might wish to. Pinot Noir is the elusive butterfly; it is as hard to find the right place to grow it as it is to learn how to make it. Those who succeed are few in number, which is just as well, because those who really understand its beauty and grace are likewise few in number.

So, can Italy or the Rhone Valley (or both) mount the challenge? Given the amount of column inches the red grapes of these countries have already received in the wine press, and given that every second winemaker I spoke to in California had plans to become involved (if not already), it might seem that the result is a foregone conclusion.

ABOVE ~ *Rich and powerful Syrah at Santino Winery in the Sierra Foothills.*

The cold statistics suggest otherwise, and simultaneously sound a warning. For, with two exceptions, plantings of Rhone and Italian varieties are still minute, many so tiny that separate statistics are not even published. And it is those two exceptions which sound the warning: Grenache (from the Rhone) and Barbera (from Italy).

BARBERA		GRENACHE	
1971	7,499 ACRES	1971	10,986 ACRES
1980	19,305 ACRES	1980	17,560 ACRES
1991	10,243 ACRES	1991	13,088 ACRES

The chart graphically demonstrates two things: first, that both varieties have been present in a large way for a long time; second, that plantings have declined significantly since their high water mark around 1980.

Barbera may not be the greatest Italian variety, nor Grenache the best of the Rhone Valley. But each can and does make wonderful wine in its respective home. In Piedmont and elsewhere in northwest Italy, Barbera produces wines with intense purple color, mouthfilling fruit and intensity of flavor, allied with the high acidity which has so commended itself to California growers (something I return to in a moment).

In the southern end of the Rhone Valley, Grenache is capable of producing extraordinary wine: Chateau Rayas and Chapoutier's Barbe Rac are but two examples which spring immediately to mind. At less rarified levels, most growers (and consumers) would rate it at or near the top of the legendary 13 varieties which (once) went to make the wines of Chateauneuf-du-Pape.

Continuing my digression — but still painting the background — until 1960 Australia had virtually no Cabernet Sauvignon, none at all of the other Bordeaux varieties and virtually no Pinot Noir. (These varieties had flourished in the nineteenth century, but disappeared as production switched to warmer regions and concentrated on fortified winemaking.) Three red wine varieties dominated plantings well into the 1980s: they were Syrah, Grenache and Mourvedre. Even today they account for almost half of all red grape plantings, although with the exception of Syrah, their hold is steadily weakening.

The warning, then, is that no variety — be it Italian, French or Outer Mongolian — has any inherent ability to produce high quality wine which will transcend climate, *terroir* and cultural practices. The vast bulk of the Barbera and Grenache plantings were (and still are) to be found in the hot Central Valley, where the acid-retention capacity of Barbera and the high yielding attributes of Grenache have been enthusiastically exploited by growers whose sole concern was to produce as many tons per acre as humanly possible. (The same applied to Grenache and Mourvedre in Australia.)

The resulting wine was (and is) exactly what one would expect: thin, watery and extremely short lived. Yet Randall Grahm at Bonny Doon and Charlie Melton (in Australia with his Nine Popes Grenache) have shown that great wines can be made from Grenache, while Greg Boeger (among others) has done the same with Barbera.

The Italian varieties which are in fact most likely to succeed are Sangiovese (or Sangioveto, as it has been called in California), and Nebbiolo. Here again there is a note of warning: Sangiovese is subject to as much clonal variation as is Pinot Noir, and in fact falls into two main clonal groups, Sangiovese Grosso and Sangiovese Piccolo. When Cabernet Sauvignon started to threaten the identity, though not the existence, of Tuscany, the fight-back came through the clonal selection of Sangiovese.

Thus the main contributor to the 1991 California-wide plantings of 232 acres of Sangiovese is Atlas Peak. Its 120 acres are planted to a special selection of clones hand-picked by Piero Antinori, and the evaluation process for that unique site will take years to complete. If and when the preferred clones become available for planting elsewhere, the trials will have to start all over again, simply because it is certain the response will vary in differing soil and climate conditions.

It is no less certain that, regardless of clone, Sangiovese and Nebbiolo will fail to produce wines of real distinction in certain areas, because *terroir* or climate (or both) prove to be unsuitable. At the moment there is a honeymoon period: because the varieties are new, because there is much talk about them, because they are produced in very limited quantities (even by Atlas Peak) and because of the boom in Italian restaurants, the wines will sell irrespective of their real merit. But that honeymoon phase will pass, and the real business of making and marketing the wine will begin. (I should add that the handful of Sangiovese and Nebbiolo wines made in Australia to date have been extremely disappointing, but it is too early to draw any conclusions there.)

The Rhone varietals, headed by Syrah, may well have a more certain long-term future. Syrah has handsomely demonstrated its adaptability to an extraordinarily wide range of climate in Australia, producing distinctive wines of radically different style in Region I to high Region IV climate. Australia has also had success in establishing the quality (and identity) of its Syrah in the wine markets of the world.

Then there is the contribution of Randall Grahm, which I discuss on pages 250–1. But, nonetheless, the fact remains that in 1991 there were only 413 acres of Syrah planted in California, up from a 1981 base of 81 acres. These figures alone should give pause for thought, and Mourvedre (200 acres in 1981, up to a mere 300 acres in 1991) does not help the cause much.

Nonetheless, there are sufficient winemakers with the necessary talent and financial resources committed to the cause of these varieties to ensure that they are given the opportunity to succeed. When, and to what degree, they in fact succeed remains to be seen, for the market will have to play its part too.

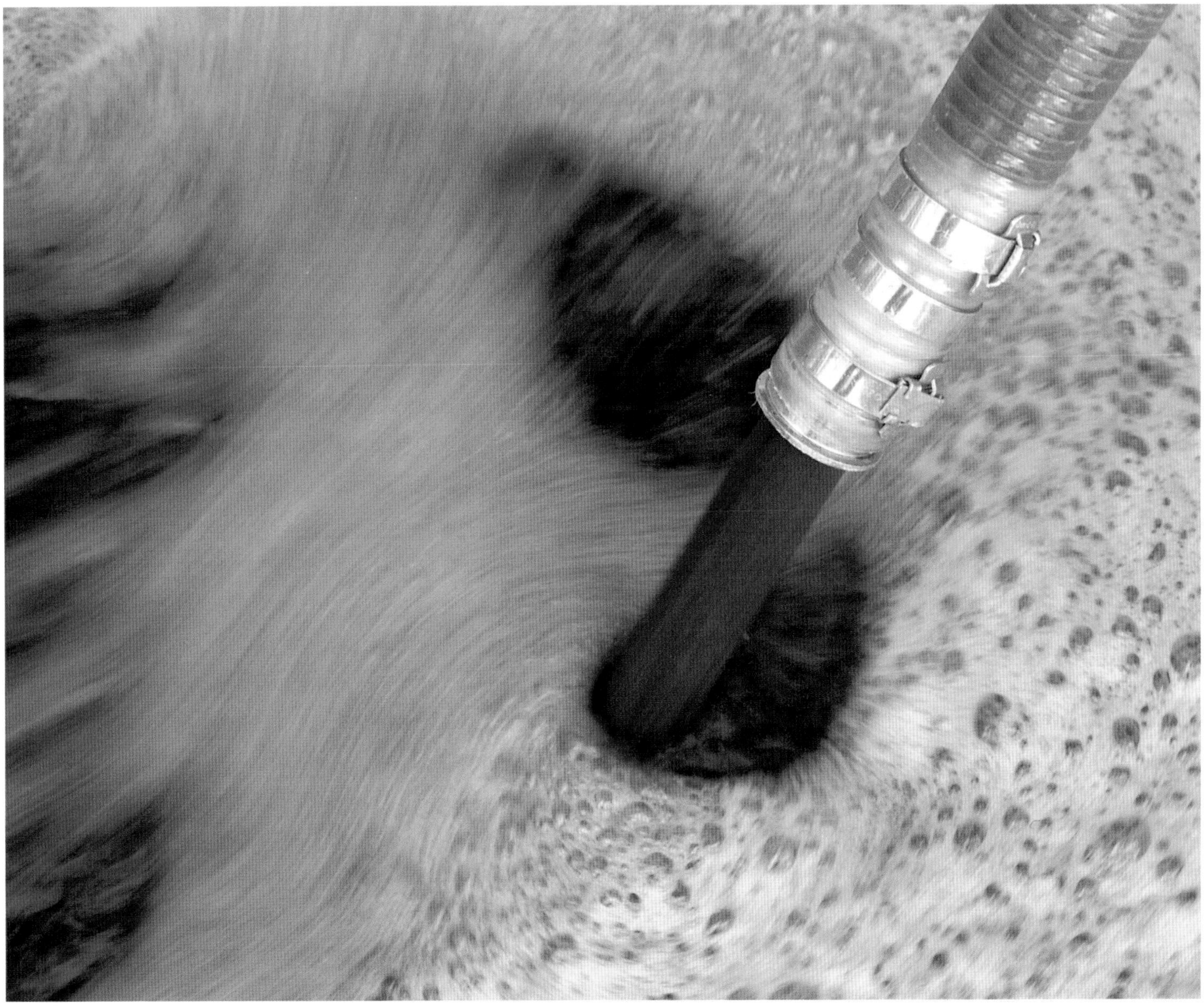

ABOVE ~ *Pumping over Sangiovese grown on experimental plantings in the Stags Leap district.*

WINERIES *of* PASO ROBLES AND YORK MOUNTAIN

ADELAIDA CELLARS 1983

A: 5805 Adelaida Road, Paso Robles, CA 93446 **T**: (805) 239 0190 **V**: By appointment **P**: 2,000 **W**: John Munch

To say that John Munch had a circuitous entry into the wine industry is a masterly understatement. Born in Costa Rica of American parents, he finished his schooling (in unspecified subjects) in the San Francisco Bay area, before traveling to Europe for a short vacation, and which ended up as a five-year stay, during which time he worked in a para-legal capacity for a Geneva investment firm, and married his Swiss wife. His employers offered to put him through law school in San Francisco, and he duly returned there, only to end up taking a masters degree in old English poetry. Employment opportunities in this particular discipline being limited, he became a part-time house renovator and finally a full-time licensed building contractor by the mid 1970s. He says, "Up to this point, my wine attention had all been directed to one side of the cork."

However, through his wife's connections, he became interested in finding viticultural land for what became the Swiss investor Chatt Bot, along the way taking a few classes at U.C. Davis. Practical experience as an assistant winemaker at Estrella River followed, and in due course, management of a new sparkling wine facility for the Swiss investors, with the wine successfully made and marketed (for a very brief time) under the Tonio Conti label. At the same time as achieving this, he also founded the Adelaida Cellars label, making the first wines at Estrella River. When Estrella River ran into difficulties, and the Swiss venture collapsed, Adelaida entered into a peripatetic existence, with limited quantities of wine being made at Castoro Cellars and at Wild Horse.

It now has a permanent location on a large ranch owned by Don Van Steenwyk, who makes a great deal of money selling specialized navigational, gyroscopic and directional drilling equipment, and who essentially grows grapes for fun. Adelaida is now a joint venture with Van Steenwyk, and a new winery was erected on the Van Steenwyk Ranch in time for the 1991 vintage. The future emphasis of Adelaida will be on Cabernet Sauvignon, Zinfandel and Syrah, although a Chardonnay does form part of the present portfolio. The Syrah will hopefully come from Adelaida's own plantings of ten acres of close-planted vines on a steep hillside. Yields will always be low, but theoretically more than the tiny crops so far achieved.

Without being unduly unkind, it might be said that the Adelaida wines reflect John Munch's career: all over the place. There are some superb wines in barrel, and some very ordinary ones, while the commercially bottled releases are likewise very inconsistent. Munch has a very good understanding of viticulture, and there is every reason to suppose the vineyards under his control will produce outstanding quality fruit; with an assistant winemaker to help him, Adelaida might just be a winery to watch.

ARCIERO WINERY 1984

A: Cnr. Highway 46 and Jardine Road, Paso Robles, CA 93446 **T**: (805) 239 2562 **V**: 10–5 daily **P**: 75,000 **W**: Malcolm Seibly

Frank and Phil Arciero arrived from Italy 45 years ago, and built one of the largest cement contracting businesses in southern California, before branching out into land development, and establishing their own Indy car racing team. In 1980 they decided to go back to their Italian roots, and purchased a large property on Highway 46 on which more than 700 acres of vineyards have since been established, planted to Chardonnay, Sauvignon Blanc, Chenin Blanc, Muscat Canelli, Zinfandel, Cabernet Sauvignon, Petite Sirah, Sangiovese, Merlot and Nebbiolo. An appropriately ornate Italianate winery has been constructed which has a capacity of 500,000 gallons.

The viticultural techniques used have been taken direct from Piedmont, with two vines planted at each stake, trained in opposite directions, increasing vine density from 500 vines to the acre to 880 vines per acre on a 9 x 11 foot spacing. The idea is that competition between the vines will reduce the crop load per vine, and likewise reduce berry and bunch size.

The production team is headed by Klaus Mathes, who joined Arciero as general manager in 1987 after 21 years with Almaden; Malcolm Seibly, who also spent 13 years at Almaden, joined as winemaker in 1990. At the present time, around 50% of the production of the vineyards is in fact vinified at Arciero, the remaining grapes being sold. There are two labels: Arciero, and the second label, Monteverde, the latter competing in the fighting varietal market with the likes of Glen Ellen.

With one or two notable exceptions, the Arciero wines have failed to excite. One of those exceptions was a 1988 Zinfandel, classically rich, with hints of mint, cherry and spice, and that highly polished texture which is so attractive. The Petite Sirah impresses with its power, if not its finesse, but the first release of Nebbiolo was rather disappointing, being somewhat stemmy and thin. The principal interest of the remaining wines in the extensive portfolio is their modest price.

CASTORO CELLARS 1983

A: 6565 Von Dollen Road, San Miguel, CA 93465 **T**: (805) 467 2002 **V**: 11–5:30 daily **P**: 15,000 **W**: Niels Udsen

The sleepy, hooded eyes of Niels Udsen should fool no one. Together with his wife Berit Udsen, he has already established a remarkable business empire, yet has only just begun. The clue comes not from the time he spent learning to make wine at J. Lohr's Paso Robles Winery, but his degree in agricultural business management. This has led to his installation of one of three of the largest Europresses ever built, with the ability to whole-bunch press 30 tons of Chardonnay delivered direct into the press from the picking bin, or up to 70 tons of axially fed, conventionally crushed grapes. This drives the very substantial custom crush and juicing business which Castoro enjoys and which generates instantaneous cash flow. Castoro also undertakes custom fermentation for other producers, as well as providing a substantial warehouse facility used by others. Another weapon in the horizontal integration armory is a high-tech mobile bottling line which numbers amongst its clients Arrowfield Wines of Australia. The bottling line does not travel to Australia, but it does go to Los Angeles or San Francisco as required. It also services those local wineries which are intelligent enough to realize that the investment in a bottling line is a poor one unless production is in excess of 50,000 cases a year. Ken Volk of Iron Horse is one of the intelligent users.

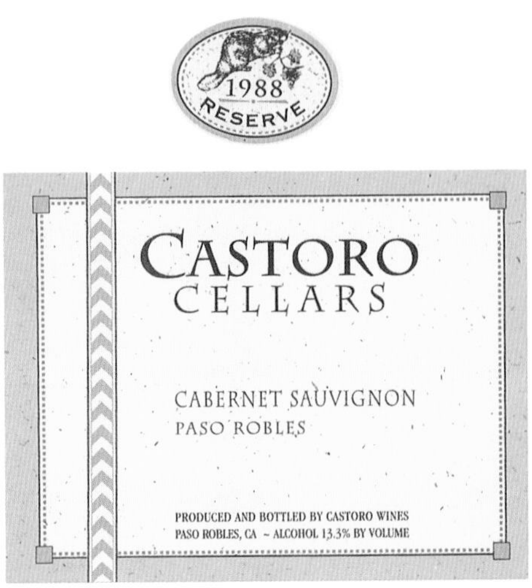
1988
RESERVE
CASTORO
CELLARS
CABERNET SAUVIGNON
PASO ROBLES
PRODUCED AND BOTTLED BY CASTORO WINES
PASO ROBLES, CA ~ ALCOHOL 13.3% BY VOLUME

Castoro Cellars' own label is a low key affair, little known in either San Francisco or Los Angeles, and even less known out of state. As one might expect, the wines are made in a large, strictly utilitarian facility; the roadside sign appears to have been painted by a Mexican vineyard worker on a piece of wood found abandoned by the roadside. But appearances are utterly deceptive. For my money, Castoro Cellars makes absolutely brilliant Gamay Nouveau, deliciously fragrant and fruity, and eerily like a first class Beaujolais (even though it is the wrong Gamay grape). Its Zinfandel is in the same Olympian class, with sensuous raspberry and redcurrant aromas, and spectacularly fresh raspberry and blackcurrant fruit. The Chardonnay (with intense, citric flavors untrammeled by oak) and the Cabernet Sauvignon (soft, chewy and fleshy with dark plum and tobacco flavors) are also very good wines, even if not in the stellar quality of the Gamay and Zinfandel. If I had money to invest, and Udsen was looking for a partner, I know where my money would go.

CRESTON VINEYARDS & WINERY 1982

A: 679 Calf Canyon Highway 58, Creston, CA 93432 **T:** (805) 238 7398 **V:** 10–5 daily, also at tasting room on Highway 101 in Templeton **P:** 35,000 **W:** Victor H. Roberts

Creston was established by a Los Angeles syndicate which included Christina Crawford, daughter of Joan Crawford. One hundred and forty acres of vineyards were planted on the 450-acre estate in a remote and high (1,700 feet average) corner of Paso Robles, reached by driving through scenery not dissimilar to that found in parts of central Australia. Ownership changed in 1987, with Stephanie and Larry Rosenbloom now having control.

Victor Roberts presides over a hard working winery, which crushed 1,000 tons of grapes in 1992, part estate-grown and part purchased from various Paso Robles wineries. The portfolio of wines comprises Chevrier Blanc, Sauvignon Blanc, Chardonnay, White Zinfandel, Pinot Noir, Merlot and Cabernet Sauvignon, the latter also released under the Winemakers Selection label. The wines are all competently made, the most interesting being the striking Pinot Noir, by no means classic, but packed with essency fruit, which is drawn from Creston Manor's own vineyards, the HMR Vineyard and Beckwith Vineyard; and the lovely Zinfandel, made from estate-grown grapes, and invested with a touch of charred oak, bursting with bright, breezy red and dark berry fruits.

EBERLE WINERY 1984

A: Highway 46 East, Paso Robles, CA 93447 **T:** (805) 238 9607 **V:** 10–5 daily **P:** 10,000 **W:** W. Gary Eberle

EBERLE
1991
PASO ROBLES
MUSCAT CANELLI
ESTATE BOTTLED
GROWN, PRODUCED AND BOTTLED BY
EBERLE WINERY, PASO ROBLES, CALIFORNIA
ALCOHOL 11.8% BY VOL. • RESIDUAL SUGAR 4.5% BY WT.

Former defensive tackle for Penn State, Gary Eberle knows the Paso Robles district better than most. He arrived in 1977 to plan the construction of Estrella River Winery (now called Meridian) as part of an ambitious family venture. Eberle left Estrella River after four years because of a family dispute, but no one has ever questioned the brilliance of the design of this very large winery now owned by Nestlé. Gary Eberle has no desire to grow beyond 10,000 cases, and least of all running a winery the size of Meridian. Which is not to say that he does not care passionately about his wines, and in particular, about the merits of Paso Robles Cabernet (and necessarily his own Cabernet Sauvignon). It comes from 41 acres of vineyard planted around the winery to just two varieties: Cabernet Sauvignon and Chardonnay. As well as the estate-grown Cabernet and Chardonnay, Eberle makes Zinfandel and an occasional Muscat Canelli.

Defensive tackles are known for their courage, and Eberle (who, incidentally, has degrees in zoology and enology from U.C. Davis to his credit) courageously put his 1982 and 1987 Cabernets in a blind tasting against the First Growth Bordeaux Chateaux of those vintages and invited the press along. The gamble paid off when the 1987 came in third, behind Chateau Margaux and Mouton-Rothschild, but ahead of Chateaux Latour, Cheval Blanc and Lafite. All of the Eberle Cabernets have been prolific show medal winners; interestingly, the 1987 having one of the less-distinguished show records, although Eberle always had ultimate faith in it. Zinfandel, which entered the list in 1989, is made in a rich, chewy, long-lived style, with abundant dark plum fruit and complex texture.

JUSTIN WINERY & VINEYARD 1981

A: 11680 Chimney Rock Road, Paso Robles, CA 93446 **T:** (805) 238 6932 **V:** 11–6 daily **P:** 6,000 **W:** Tom Westberg

Investment banker Justin Baldwin purchased an exceptionally beautiful 165-acre ranch in west Paso Robles in 1981, planting it to Chardonnay (30 acres), Cabernet Sauvignon (25 acres), Merlot (five acres) and Cabernet Franc (five acres). These early plantings have been more recently supplemented by a little Nebbiolo and Orange Muscat. All of the vines are on tightly folded, steep hillsides, offering a wide variety of aspects and mesoclimate. The generous rainfall and very alkaline limestone soil has prompted extreme vigor, even with dry-farming, but the potential of the vineyards is not in doubt.

The tasting and reception area is extremely beautiful, with landscaped gardens set amongst the natural beauty of the hilly surrounds. Rather less has been spent on the winery, with winemaking presently carried out in very cramped conditions, but with a new winery planned for 1994. The wine roster offers a Chardonnay, Merlot, Cabernet Franc, Cabernet Sauvignon and a Meritage blend of around 60% Cabernet Sauvignon, 30% Merlot and 10% Cabernet Franc (varying slightly according to the vintage). Newly arrived winemaker Tom Westberg has inherited a variable portfolio of wines, showing a range of winemaking problems and faults. The best by some distance is the 1989 Cabernet Sauvignon, with a strong, chocolate mint and sweet berry fruit. Brettanomyces, volatility and oxidation seem to jostle for position in the other wines.

MARTIN BROTHERS WINERY 1981

A: 2610 Buena Vista Drive, Paso Robles, CA 93446 **T:** (805) 238 2520 **V:** 10–5 daily **P:** 14,000 **W:** Dominic Martin

In April 1981 the Martin family purchased a run-down 83-acre former dairy, and set about creating their own wine estate. Edward Martin had been advertising manager of the Padre Vineyards in the late 1930s. Son Dominic Martin was a U.C. Davis enology graduate who had been winemaker at Lambert Bridge Winery in Sonoma from 1978 to 1981. In 1982 15 acres of Chardonnay and Sauvignon Blanc were planted, and the following year the remaining 55 acres planted to more Chardonnay and Sauvignon Blanc, and new plantings of Chenin Blanc, Zinfandel and Nebbiolo.

Right from the outset, the Martin Brothers team experimented with Italian varieties, making their first Nebbiolo in 1984 (from Amador County fruit), then switching to Central Valley sources until their own plantings came into bearing. It has now become the flagship of the winery, both in terms of production (3,000 cases) and prestige. The Italian connection is unashamedly emphasized with the labeling and branding of the other wines. The Zinfandel is labeled "Primitivo" (presumably to the annoyance of Hop Kiln), while a Red Meritage blend of 85% Cabernet Sauvignon and 15% Sangiovese is labeled "Cabernet Etrusco," with the graphics likewise Italianate. These wines sell freely through the attractive gray-painted tasting room on Highway 46; the no-less attractive wooden winery is some distance away. The fragrant, vibrantly fruity Zinfandel can be outstanding, the Nebbiolo (so far at least) being more interesting in theory than in fact. Nor should I neglect the sparkling Moscato Frizzante, a 7% alcohol wine which must sell like hot cakes at the cellar door during the summer months with its fresh citric/fruit pastille flavors.

MERIDIAN VINEYARDS 1984

A: 7000 Highway 46 East, Paso Robles, CA 93446 **T**: (805) 237 6000 **V**: 10–5 Wed–Sun **P**: 100,000 **W**: Chuck Ortman

Since what is now Meridian started life as Estrella River Winery in 1977, it has trained more winemakers in the Central Coast region than almost all other wineries put together, and looks like continuing that role well into the future. The history of Meridian is nonetheless complex. The brand was established by Chuck Ortman, who started his career at Heitz Cellars before moving to Spring Mountain and then consulting to Far Niente, Shafer, Fisher, Keenan and Cain Cellars before starting his Meridian brand in 1984, based in the Napa Valley. When Nestlé acquired Estrella River Winery in 1988 it hired Ortman as chief winemaker, and purchased the Meridian name, transforming it from boutique to major status overnight.

The production of 100,000 cases (or thereabouts) under the Meridian label is a strictly moving target. In 1992 the winery crushed 10,000 tons of grapes, the equivalent of around 750,000 cases. Much of it was processed in the form of juice for the Napa Ridge program, but the winery does have vast capacity. It sources its Chardonnay from Santa Barbara and the Edna Valley, Pinot Noir from Santa Barbara and many of the fuller-bodied reds from the 500 acres of vineyard surrounding the winery — although phylloxera is leading to an accelerated replanting program. Notwithstanding its 3,000 acres in Santa Barbara County, Meridian is slowly moving away from white wines and increasing its emphasis on reds, with particular attention being given to Syrah, Zinfandel, Cabernet Sauvignon and Mourvedre. As one would expect, the quality of the wines is utterly reliable, typified by the 1989 Cabernet Sauvignon winning the Best of Region Award at the 1992 California State Fair.

MISSION VIEW VINEYARDS & WINERY 1984

A: 13350 North River Road, San Miguel, CA 93451 **T**: (805) 467 3104 **V**: 11–5 daily **P**: 6,000 **W**: Robert Nadeau

Mission View draws upon 46 acres of estate vineyards, supplemented by grapes purchased elsewhere within San Luis Obispo County, to produce Sauvignon Blanc, Chardonnay, Zinfandel and Cabernet Sauvignon. The wines are sold under the Mission View and San Miguel Vineyard labels. Apart from some rather uncertain oak handling evident in the Sauvignon Blanc and Chardonnay, the wines are adequate; those who like ripe fruit flavors will enjoy the Zinfandel.

PEACHY CANYON WINERY 1987

A: Peachy Canyon Road, Paso Robles, CA 93446 **T**: (805) 238 7035 **V**: By appointment **P**: 2,000 **W**: Doug Beckett and Toby Shumrick (Consultant)

Peachy Canyon burst into the limelight with its 1989 Zinfandel, rated by many as one of the best — if not the best — Zinfandels produced in California in that year. It all came as something of a surprise for Doug Beckett, whose entry into wine came through the ownership of liquor stores, followed by home winemaking and ultimately the acquisition of land in Paso Robles in 1980. He and a partner then developed a commercial label, producing monstrous Zinfandel and Petite Sirah: says Beckett, "We were gorilla winemakers." His partner lost interest in the venture, and not surprisingly, the wines proved difficult to sell. Peachy Canyon rose out of the ashes, and in 1988 Toby Shumrick (former assistant winemaker at Eberle) joined Beckett as consultant winemaker on a winery share basis.

PEACHYCANYON
WINERY
1990
PASO ROBLES
ZINFANDEL
WESTSIDE
PRODUCED AND BOTTLED BY PEACHY CANYON WINERY
PASO ROBLES, CALIFORNIA
ALCOHOL: 14.7% BY VOLUME

The Zinfandel in fact comes under a number of labels, notwithstanding the very limited production. The 1989 wine which caused such a sensation was the Zinfandel Especial, while the "standard" is simply identified as "Westside," signifying that all of

ABOVE ~ *The stone office and administration centre at Meridian Winery.*

the Zinfandel for Peachy Canyon in fact comes from the western portion of the Paso Robles district.

The high praise heaped upon the 1989 was deserved: with beautifully focused cherry fruit and fine tannins, it is the sort of Zinfandel which begs not just the second glass, but the second bottle. The 1990 Westside Zinfandel showed that the 1989 was no fluke, exhibiting masses of concentrated, dark cherry fruit flavor, a hint of mint, and soft tannins.

Notwithstanding that the 1990 Zinfandel (Westside), of which there were 1,000 cases made, sold out in six weeks, Beckett is adamant that he will not increase production beyond 3,000 cases (of all labels) at the outside, and equally adamant that he will not put up the price to stifle demand. If he keeps to his word, and the wine keeps to his form, it should be one of the most eagerly sought after labels in California.

WILD HORSE WINERY 1982

A: 2484 Templeton Road, Templeton, CA 93465 **T**: (805) 434 2541 **V**: By appointment **P**: 30,000 **W**: Ken Volk

The quietly mannered, self confessed worrier Ken Volk has built a formidable reputation over the past ten years. As so many others have done, he took a circuitous route into the wine industry, studying at the Food Science department of the California Polytechnic Institute in San Luis Obispo and intending to grow oranges or avocados. His switch to grape growing still did not herald an intention to make wine: he had hopes of developing the vineyard and selling it for speculative profit. Or so he says, for he had in fact been first a home winemaker and thereafter worked at Edna Valley Vineyard during the 1981 crush, so the "forced" conversion to winemaking through the downturn in the market in the early 1980s may be something of a story. Certainly, Volk has assiduously downplayed his achievements, which have included the naming of Wild Horse as Winery of the Year by *Wine & Spirit Magazine* in 1990, the year after Wild Horse Pinot Noirs had received more awards than any other California Pinot Noir in wine shows. Just for good measure, in the same year (1989) the 1987 Wild Horse Merlot was named Best American Merlot at the American Wine Competition, winning a platinum medal there and taking gold medals in regional shows left, right and center.

But to begin at the beginning, as it were, the 64-acre home ranch is planted to 20 acres of Chardonnay, five acres of Cabernet Sauvignon, five acres of Merlot, and three acres of Cabernet Franc. It provides 20% of Wild Horse's overall production, with the leading varietals (Pinot Noir and Chardonnay) being sourced from Santa Barbara, the Edna Valley, Arroyo Grande and the HMR Vineyards on the Santa Lucia Mountains. Volk is a firm believer in blending parcels from different vineyards to give complexity, agonizing endlessly but successfully

over those blends. Thus, for example, the 1989 Paso Robles Cabernet Sauvignon came from four different vineyards which contributed 95% of the blend, and incorporated Cabernet Franc for the last 5%. His flagship Santa Barbara County Pinot Noir is usually made from grapes grown on the Sierra Madre, Bien Nacido, Rancho Venido, HMR Vineyard, Cottontail Creek and Talley Vineyards. The 1989 vintage saw the creation of what was to be a super-premium label, Cheval Sauvage, and here in 1990 Volk contented himself with a single vineyard Pinot made from the HMR Vineyard in the Santa Lucia Mountains.

The cascade of medals which has showered on all of the Wild Horse wines are no more than they deserve. The Pinot Noirs are consistently outstanding, always made in a bold, complex style, and displaying distinct Burgundian overtones as they develop in bottle. The Central Coast Chardonnay is uniformly excellent, showing superb handling of barrel fermentation, and great length and intensity of flavor.

YORK MOUNTAIN WINERY 1882

A: York Mountain Road West, Templeton, CA 93465 **T**: (805) 238 3925 **V**: 10–5 daily **P**: 6,000 **W**: Steve Goldman

When the Goldman family purchased the York Mountain Winery in 1979, it acquired an abandoned vineyard, a stone building which was still in astonishingly good condition, and a slice of quite remarkable history. The winery and mountainside vineyard had continued to operate through Prohibition, and had amongst its grape suppliers the famous pianist Paderewski, who had been persuaded by Professor Bioletti of U.C. Berkeley to plant a vineyard in 1924, right in the middle of Prohibition. Upon repeal, Paderewski had York Mountain make wine for his personal use, and for years thereafter the winery purchased Zinfandel from Paderewski's Rancho San Ignacio.

With its own AVA, and low Region I climate, the five acres of estate vineyard, planted to Pinot Noir, Cabernet Sauvignon, Zinfandel and Chardonnay, pose interesting viticultural challenges. Zinfandel does not always ripen properly, and the Cabernet likewise. However, much of the production is purchased from growers throughout warmer parts of California, primarily, though by no means exclusively, from Paso Robles and other parts of San Luis Obispo County.

The cellar door, and more particularly the winery, looks as if it has been in continuous use since the 1880s. Ancient oak barrels are stacked high to the ceiling, and the winemaking equipment comes from a bygone era. There is even a vintage forklift which looks as if it was made around the time of the first tractor. Hardly surprisingly, almost two-thirds of the wine is sold direct from the winery, with a constant stream of people passing to and fro the coast at Cambria (and Hearst Castle).

The Reserve Pinot Noir is the pick of the range, but the Merlot is also stylish, with pronounced leafy/sappy varietal character, and regularly sells out before the next release becomes available. There is also an array of fortified wines which, while of modest quality, walk out the cellar door almost as rapidly as the Merlot.

OTHER WINERIES

ABBEY D'OR
A: Star Route Box 4620, San Miguel, CA 93451
T: (805) 467 3248

BARON VINEYARDS
A: 1985 Penman Springs Road, Paso Robles, CA 93446 **T**: (805) 239 3313

CAPARONE VINEYARD 1980
A: 2280 San Marcos Road, Paso Robles, CA 93466 **T**: (805) 467 3827 **W**: Dave Caparone

FRATELLI PERATA 1987
A: 1595 Arbor Road, Paso Robles, CA 93446
T: (805) 238 2809 **W**: Eugene M. Perata

HARMONY CELLARS 1988
A: P.O. Box 2502, Harmony, CA 93435
T: (805) 927 1625 **W**: Chuck Mulligan

HMR ESTATE WINERY
A: 506 Adelaida Road, Paso Robles, CA 93446
T: (805) 238 7143

HOPE FARMS 1990
A: 2175 Arbor Road, Paso Robles, CA
T: (805) 238 6979 **W**: Stephen Rasmussen

JAN KRIS
A: Route 2, Box 40 Bethel Road, Templeton, CA 93465 **T**: (805) 434 1133

MASTANTUONO 1977
A: 46 West and Vineyard Drive, Templeton CA 93465 **T**: (805) 238 0676
W: Pasquale Mastan

PRESENTL
A: 2900 Vineyard Drive, Templeton, CA 93465
T: (805) 434 1030

TWIN HILLS RANCH WINERY 1980
A: 2025 Nacimiento Drive, Paso Robles, CA 93446 **T**: (805) 238 9148
W: James Lockshaw

ABOVE ~ *Jan Kris Winery, which now owns the excellent vineyard once called Ceres.*

SOUTH CENTRAL COAST

There is no such thing as the South Central Coast in the eyes of the BATF: there is the Central Coast, which stretches from San Francisco to Santa Barbara, and there is the South Coast, which takes in the areas south of Los Angeles. Yet, as I explained earlier, the alternative to inventing this area was to group San Luis Obispo and Santa Barbara counties together and discuss three apples (the Edna, Santa Maria and Santa Ynez Valleys) and an orange (Paso Robles) as if they had some natural affinity. The truth is that Paso Robles has nothing whatsoever to do with its county-mate, Edna Valley; that Edna Valley is a twin of the Santa Maria Valley; and that these two, together with the Los Alamos and Santa Ynez Valleys, constitute unique geographical entities in the California scheme of things.

What makes these valleys unique is that they run as any sensible coastal valley should: towards the sea — in this instance, from east to west. It is simply a freak circumstance of California's tortured and highly active geology that all the other valleys run more or less north-south, or (finally to confuse the issue) from south to north in the case of the Salinas Valley of Monterey.

With the qualified exception of the Santa Ynez Valley, not only do they run from east to west, but they travel relatively short distances and open directly to the sea. Were it not for that sea, these regions would be on a par with Cucamonga, fit only for producing table grapes and fortified wines. As it is, they contain much Region I climate and produce much of the finest Chardonnay and Pinot Noir in the state.

In the introductory pages of this book I discussed the general factors which shape the California climate (on page 13). Here it is appropriate to look at the particular factors which affect the climate of these valleys. First and foremost, there is the upwelling of cold water from the depths of the ocean which starts to occur in May and reaches its peak in August.

The fog bank which occurs when the cold air produced by the upwelling meets warmer inland air is drawn inland (although more gently) by the same mechanisms as those which operate further north, and which I have previously explained. Thus it is that the fogs start to roll in during May and continue through August into September, and thus it is that what should be a Region IV to V climate is a Region I to II.

But there is also a second factor at work, and that is the temperature gradient which exists in all of the marine-influenced regions, whatever their axis may be. This has led Richard Sanford, a trained geographer, to observe that there is a north-south band cutting across the four valleys between 15 and 25 miles inland from the coast which is ideally suited to growing Chardonnay and Pinot Noir — in other words, a Region I climate.

Closer to the coast, the climate becomes progressively cooler: Maison Deutz in the Arroyo Grande AVA may well be able to ripen its grapes for sparkling wine, but during many years it would have little hope of making table wine (which is no doubt why André Lallier of Champagne Deutz chose the site in the first place). Lompoc, just inland from the mouth of the Santa Ynez River and west of the Santa Maria AVA, has a heat summation of less than the starting point of Region I (which is 2,000 degree days) while — partly due to the initial constriction of the valley — all of the Santa Ynez Valley to the east of Buellton has a Region II climate. It is a climate, indeed, which many of the vignerons of that district are still endeavoring to come to grips with.

The other feature which unites these valleys (and ominously differentiates them from Paso Robles) is that phylloxera had not made an appearance there by 1992. Virtually all the vineyards are planted on their own roots. Byron is carrying out rootstock trials, and it would not be surprising if Cambria were doing the same, but otherwise the area is defenseless against phylloxera, be it normal or Biotype B.

Next, a word for the fourth man, the Los Alamos Valley. The San Antonio Creek creates an east-west valley as clearly defined as (but separated from) the other valleys. It also has a different soil type, closer to that of the Salinas Valley. On any view of the matter this Region I area, with more acres of vines than either the Santa Ynez or the Edna Valleys, deserves its own appellation. The lack of it reflects the fact that the largest vineyard, which once supported the now defunct Los Alamos Winery, is in the Corbett Canyon group ownership, which is no doubt satisfied with the broader Santa Barbara County appellation.

All things considered, if I were to wish to establish a winery in California, it is to the South Central Coast that I would come. In viticultural terms, its only limitation is its lack of suitability for Cabernet Sauvignon, which I would cheerfully leave to the Napa Valley (buying grapes from there or Paso Robles if I were to make the wine). It has the coast and all the tourism that this implies. It also has considerable physical beauty, and vines in a desert create a jeweled oasis in any event. Sooner or later, Los Angeles will take it to its bosom as San Francisco has taken the Napa and Sonoma Valleys.

HIRAM WALKER
Peppermint
Schnapps

PREVIOUS PAGE ~ *The large vineyards of Firestone provide oases of emerald green among the golden grasses of summer.*

ABOVE ~ *James Adelman, assistant winemaker at Au Bon Climat, topping up barrels to replace evaporative loss.*

ABOVE ~ *The 600 acres of the Bien Nacido Vineyard in Santa Maria provide 35 different wineries with some of California's finest grapes.*

EDNA VALLEY AND ARROYO GRANDE

It may come as a surprise to find that the Arroyo Grande AVA is not only almost twice the size of the Edna Valley AVA (67 square miles as opposed to 35 square miles) but that it has a much more significant viticultural history. While the books dutifully record that grapes were first planted at Mission San Luis Obispo about 1772 (presumably the Mission variety), the first recorded vineyard was planted in 1879 by Englishman Henry Ditmas and his wife Rosa on their 560-acre Rancho Saucelito. In 1883 Bostonian A.B. Hasbrouck purchased the adjoining and much larger Rancho Arroyo Grande, and — impressed by the Zinfandel and Muscat of the Ditmases — planted a 30-acre vineyard of his own, and built the St. Remy Winery.

In 1886 the Ditmases were divorced, and Rosa Ditmas married Hasbrouck three years later, moving to St. Remy. In 1915 phylloxera destroyed the St. Remy plantings, but for some strange reason spared those at Rancho Saucelito. The St. Remy Winery was closed at the onset of Prohibition, but Rancho Saucelito continued in production until the 1940s, with wine made on the Ranch (by tenants) right through Prohibition. It was the core of Zinfandel which Bill Greenough managed to revive when he purchased what he now calls Saucelito Canyon from the descendants of Mrs. Ditmas in 1972.

Back in the Edna Valley, the first move was made in 1968, when the County Farm Adviser planted a plot of premium varieties on the Righetti Ranch in 1968. In 1973 the Niven family formed Paragon Vineyards and set about planting 650 acres of vines, followed by Chamisal and then two years later by Andy MacGregor. Curiously, there was no more development until the early 1990s when a group of lawyers commenced an ambitious vineyard development on Orcutt Road, which will significantly raise the overall plantings which (prior to their involvement) stood at 800 acres.

A quick shot in parting at the AVA process. There is no question that the Edna and Arroyo Grande Valleys are distinct geographical units. For a start they run at right angles to each other, and are unusually well defined. But for the BATF to say, as it does, that "the primary characteristic distinguishing Arroyo Grande Valley from neighboring areas is climate" is arrant nonsense.

To the extent that one can generalize about the Arroyo Grande Valley climate, it is similar to that of the Edna Valley. But Maison Deutz at its western extremity is a very low Region I, while Saucelito Canyon at its eastern end has a Region III climate.

ABOVE ~ *The marc of Chardonnay and Pinot Noir, the hallmark varieties of this part of the wine world.*

OPPOSITE ~ *The new Pacific Vineyards development on Orcutt Road will significantly expand Edna Valley's production.*

THE REGION IN BRIEF

Climate, Soil and Viticulture

CLIMATE

The climate of both valleys is profoundly marine influenced: both open directly to the sea, the difference being that the Edna Valley is preceded by the Los Osos Valley which is 15 miles in length, while the Arroyo Grande Valley twists and turns (interrupted by the man-made Lopez Dam) until it reaches Saucelito Canyon. The Edna Valley is essentially flat (other than for the MacGregor Vineyards and the new Orcutt Road development) and the climate — ranging between high Region I and low II according to the season — homogeneous throughout. The typical growing season day is marked by morning fog which may last until 2 P.M., a brief period of still sunshine, followed by afternoon breezes. The humidity is high, the diurnal temperature range is low, and although 80% of the 20-inch rainfall falls between December and March, constant spraying against powdery mildew is necessary, and botrytis is an integral part of the scene (despite the use of systemic sprays).

The Arroyo Grande Valley is marked by a considerable temperature gradient along its length; fog does in fact work its way up to Saucelito Canyon (and can also come over the mountain range from the Santa Maria Valley four miles away), but July and August regularly produce days of up to 100°F, in contrast to the peak of 80°F to 85°F experienced in the western part of the Arroyo Grande and in the Edna Valley.

Edna Valley, Arroyo Grande and Santa Maria Valley
VINTAGE CHART 1981–91

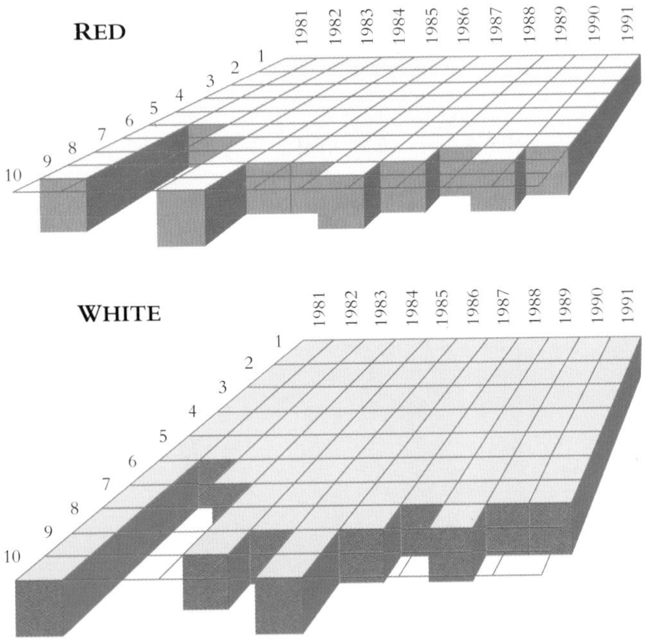
RED
1981
1982
1983
1984
1985
1986
1987
1988
1989
1990
1991
1
2
3
4
5
6
7
8
9
10
WHITE
1981
1982
1983
1984
1985
1986
1987
1988
1989
1990
1991
1
2
3
4
5
6
7
8
9
10

SOIL

There are five major soil types in the Edna Valley, but all reflect the fact that at one time in the distant past this was a marine estuary: thus they are either neutral (pH 7) or moderately alkaline, and all are calcareous at some level or the surface of subsoil. All contain a significant percentage of clay, ranging from sandy clay to

Edna Valley and Arroyo Grande
1971 AND 1991 ACREAGE/GRAPE VARIETIES

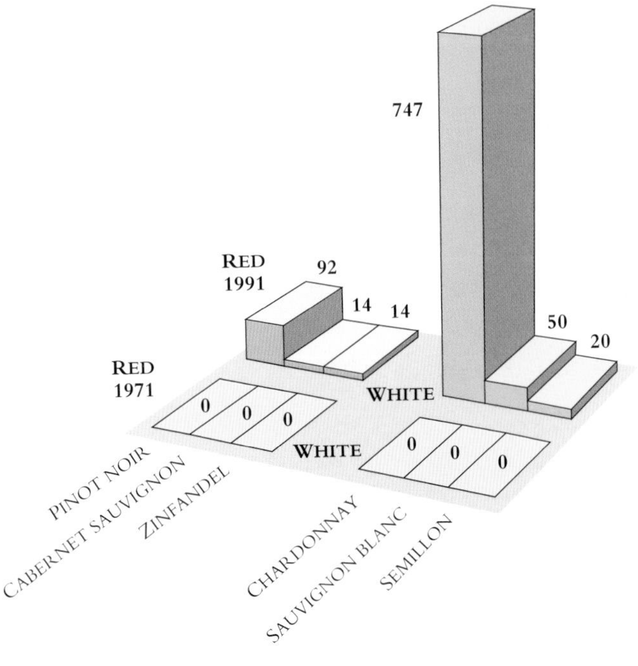
747
RED
1991
92
14
14
50
20
RED
1971
0
0
0
WHITE
WHITE
0
0
0
PINOT NOIR
CABERNET SAUVIGNON
ZINFANDEL
CHARDONNAY
SAUVIGNON BLANC
SEMILLON

ABOVE ~ *Edna Valley Vineyards, looking west.*

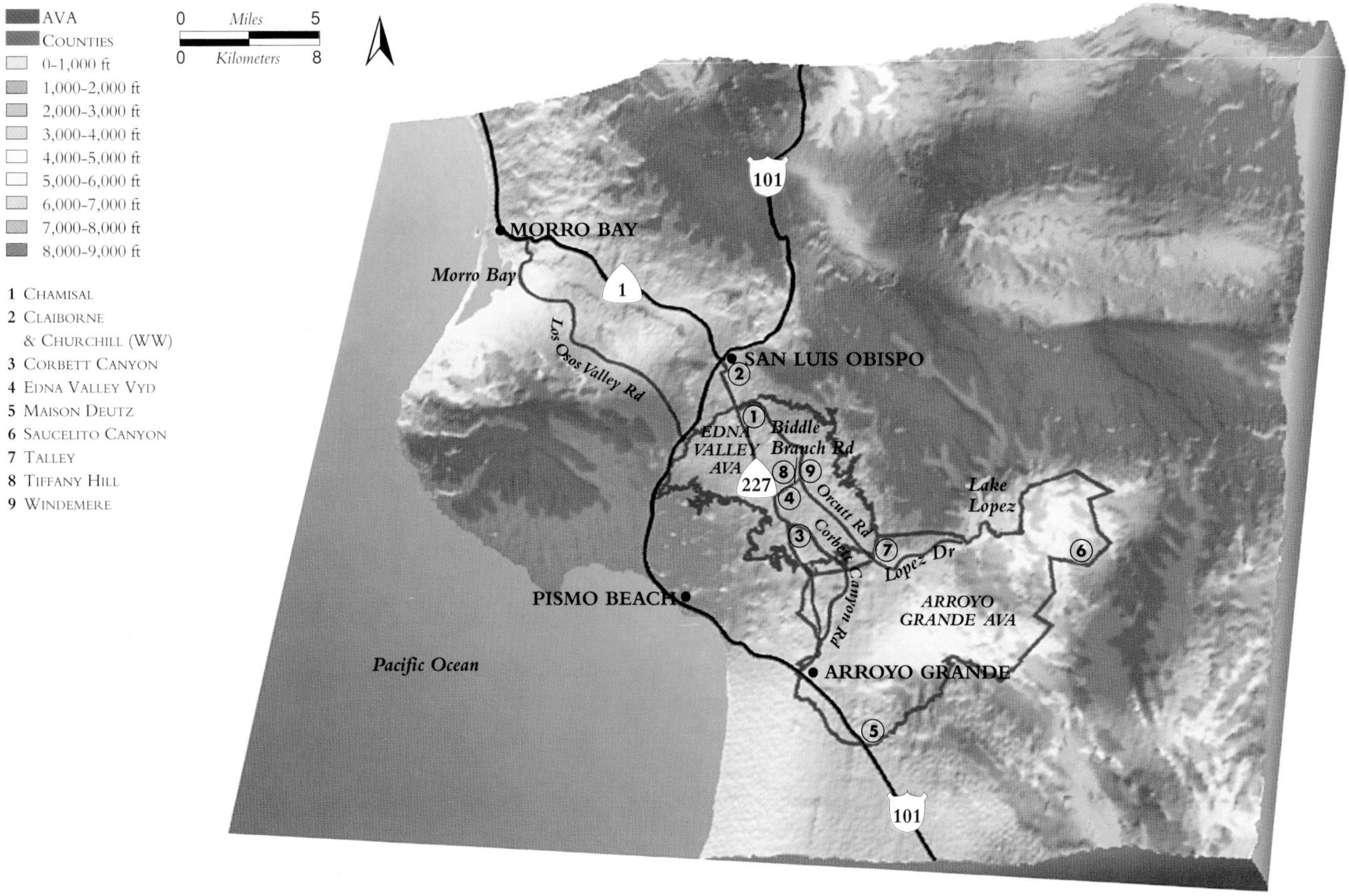
AVA
COUNTIES
0-1,000 ft
1,000-2,000 ft
2,000-3,000 ft
3,000-4,000 ft
4,000-5,000 ft
5,000-6,000 ft
6,000-7,000 ft
7,000-8,000 ft
8,000-9,000 ft
0 Miles 5
0 Kilometers 8
1 CHAMISAL
2 CLAIBORNE & CHURCHILL (WW)
3 CORBETT CANYON
4 EDNA VALLEY VYD
5 MAISON DEUTZ
6 SAUCELITO CANYON
7 TALLEY
8 TIFFANY HILL
9 WINDEMERE
MORRO BAY
Morro Bay
101
1
Los Osos Valley Rd
SAN LUIS OBISPO
EDNA VALLEY AVA
Biddle Branch Rd
227
Orcutt Rd
Corbett Canyon Rd
Lopez Dr
Lake Lopez
ARROYO GRANDE AVA
PISMO BEACH
Pacific Ocean
ARROYO GRANDE
101

clay loam through to clay, distinguishing them from the sandier soils of the Santa Ynez and Santa Maria Valleys. Those of the Arroyo Grande are similar, again showing marine sediments in the predominant silty clay loam.

THE GROWING SEASON

The season is exceptionally long, so much so that in some years there are problems with winter dormancy (the lack of it, that is), and budbreak can occur at the end of February. Frosts are not common, but a sufficient hazard to induce most vignerons to install frost protection through wind machines. Harvest commences with Chardonnay typically being picked between late September and mid October, extending into November in years such as 1991. Rain during vintage can be very damaging, as 1983 showed.

Principal Wine Styles

CHARDONNAY

In no other area of California does this variety so dominate proceedings, accounting as it does for 95% of all grape plantings; hence it has been chosen as the feature article for this chapter. In the particular circumstances of the Edna Valley, it offers both opportunities and challenges. The very cool and temperate season, and the allied slow ripening, promote the development of pronounced tropical fruit flavors which are intensified by botrytis which occurs to a greater or lesser degree in every year. It is said the grapes ripen beyond 22° Brix in one of two ways: either through the agency of a burst of heat in an Indian summer October, or through the advent of rain. In the latter circumstance botrytis can soar from 5% to 60% in a matter of days, forcing picking under very difficult circumstances. The best protection in the Edna Valley has proved to be the shoot positioning and thinning, coupled with leaf removal, practiced by Andy MacGregor at MacGregor Vineyards. The best producers are Edna Valley Vineyards, Talley and Windemere, although other purchasers make exceptionally good wines from Edna and Arroyo Grande grapes.

PINOT NOIR

While maintaining a tenuous hold in the Edna Valley (MacGregor grafted over all but an acre of his original plantings, and Edna Valley reduced its) the variety flourishes (on a small scale) at Talley Vineyards in the Arroyo Grande. The Edna Valley flavors have been described as blueberry ranging through to dark cherry; those of Arroyo Grande graduate to rich, dark plum with tremendous spicy intensity and depth. If I were making Pinot Noir in California, Talley would be one of my first ports of call. Au Bon Climat is one distinguished producer, Wild Horse another, and of course, Talley itself, while Edna Valley Vineyards does well enough with its own grapes.

ZINFANDEL

Grown and made only by Saucelito Canyon, but with sufficient distinction to ensure its representation, and to emphasize the nature of the Arroyo Grande climate, for its Zinfandel is cast in the ripe, generous mould one might expect from areas as warm as Lodi.

ABOVE ~ *Edna Valley and Arroyo Grande map.*

CHARDONNAY

Like Xerox, Chardonnay has passed into everyday language. You no longer ask for a glass of white wine, but for a glass of Chardonnay, for the two have become coextensive. And, at the risk of appearing unduly unkind, that is precisely what the consumer gets from the average Napa Valley Chardonnay: a wine which is bland, inoffensive and varietally anonymous. (For the purposes of this rhetoric, I exclude Carneros from the Napa Valley.)

There are those who would disagree with this judgment, and yet others who would (with commercial common sense) shrug their shoulders and say, "So what?" But why should it be so, if indeed it is true? The origin of the answer lies in the vineyard, primarily in the climate but also in the soil, and is completed in the winery.

ABOVE ~ *A freshly filled and vigorously fermenting Chardonnay barrel at Byron.*

Thanks to a combination of the warm (Region III) climate which prevails through all except the extreme southern portion of the Napa Valley, the generally rich soils, the large-berried and bunched heat-treated Davis clones, and (until very recently) generally lackluster viticulture, the grapes lack flavor — both in terms of intensity and in terms of varietal character. Sometimes, though not always, they lack acidity; the one thing they never lack is alcohol. Indeed, part of the underlying problem is the too-rapid accumulation of sugar.

Partly in response to the differences of the raw material, partly as a result of peer-group winemaking pressure, and partly encouraged by a frequently uncritical audience, the average Napa winery responds by taking the wine through 100% malolactic fermentation (to provide texture) and using lots of oak (to provide flavor). The same formula can be and is used with Sauvignon Blanc and, to reinforce the lesson, some makers add a little Sauvignon Blanc to their Chardonnay, while almost all add Semillon (a few Chardonnay) to their Sauvignon Blanc. Small wonder, then, that the wines all end up tasting much the same.

Lest my criticisms be seen as unfairly singling out the Napa Valley, let me also say that much the same comment applies to the majority of the Sonoma and Mendocino Chardonnays — and for precisely the same reasons. (Just as I exclude Carneros from the Napa Valley, so I exclude Russian River and the extreme southern portion of Sonoma Valley from these strictures.)

Needless to say, there are exceptions: leading the Napa Valley contingent are Grgich Hills, Freemark Abbey and Forman; Clos du Val, Matanzas Creek and even Sebastiani Reserve are the Sonoma flagbearers; and Fetzer Reserve does well for Mendocino. Before howls of rage and disbelief erupt, remember I have excluded the Russian River, and hence the superb Kistler wines and the elegant Souverain and Sonoma-Cutrer offerings, and I have likewise excluded Carneros (a great area for Merlot, says Jim Clendenen), whence many fine (perhaps too fine) wines emanate — including those of absentee makers such as Stag's Leap Wine Cellars, St. Clement, Garric-Langbehn and Sterling, and residents such as Acacia and Saintsbury. Where, then, are the best Chardonnays made or grown? First and foremost, on the Central Coast in the Edna, Santa Maria and Santa Ynez Valleys. Secondly, in spots, and with often unfulfilled potential, in Monterey, and in tiny but triumphant amounts in the Santa Cruz Mountains.

Chardonnay is an exceptionally pliant variety, growing and cropping well in almost any combination of *terroir* and climate. It is no less malleable in the winery; its identity may be obscured by the clothes it wears (oak and MLF), but it continues to strut the stage. It is thus easy to forget that for many centuries it was grown in just three places: Burgundy, Chablis (within spitting distance of each other) and Champagne.

What unites these French districts is their uncompromisingly cool climate — so cool in the case of Champagne that it only produces sparkling wine. It is not the duty of Chardonnay (or its makers) to produce a carbon copy of Burgundy or Chablis, but it is no coincidence that Chardonnay became famous in these regions long before it began its march across the Midi.

What southern France, much of Australia, much of Chile and much of California demonstrate is that Chardonnay grown in far warmer climates can be manipulated by skillful viticulture and winemaking to produce good or even great wines. But that does not mean that if those same viticultural and enological skills were applied to grapes grown in more suitable climates even better wines would not result.

As if providing an elementary lesson in logic (as taught to philosophy students) Monterey demonstrates the reverse proposition: climate alone will not produce great Chardonnay if the grower pours on the water and treats the vine as if it were a row crop. But, at the value end of the market, behold what Franciscan has achieved with its Estancia Estate label, or further up market, Smith & Hook with its Hahn brand.

The really serious action occurs, as I say, further south. Here the grapes ripen in the most temperate climate to be found in California. While the growing season is as long in Monterey, and the heat summation on the Davis scale is no greater, the diurnal (and seasonal) extremes are much larger in Monterey.

All that glitters is not gold, however. The even, moderately cool and humid climate promotes the growth of mold spores — there are few periods of heat to arrest their growth — and is ideal for botrytis activity. Powdery mildew can never be seen as advantageous, but can at least be controlled; botrytis, which can only be partially controlled, is seen as one of the contributors to complexity, provided the infection is kept within the 5% to 10% range.

This level of botrytis is part and parcel of the Burgundian landscape in most vintages; and even exceptional years (such as 1985 and 1989) in which botrytis is all but absent do not necessarily produce better Chardonnays (though they unquestionably produce better Pinot Noirs). The trick is to ensure that the other fruit flavors are there (by limiting yield) and to ensure that the handling in the winery is appropriate: if botrytis levels increase, skin contact (i.e. allowing the must to soak in contact with the skins before pressing) is as unsuitable as direct-to-press whole bunch pressing is suitable.

Wines are in fact made in surprisingly varying style through the Central Coast appellations. Au Bon Climat, Babcock, Edna Valley, Ojai, Qupe, Santa Barbara Winery, Vita Nova and Wild Horse are at the exuberant, complex end of the range; Byron, Claiborne & Churchill, John Kerr, Talley, Windemere and Zaca Mesa are more discrete and reserved. All share intensity, length of flavor and wonderful mouthfeel. Yet it is arguably the best is still to come. Clonal selection may be a matter of life and death for Pinot Noir, but it is also of great importance for Chardonnay. The quality growers are very well aware that the big-is-beautiful clones selected by U.C. Davis may suit Gallo and the growers of the Central Valley, but are disastrous for those seeking to make great wine. A huge amount of work has been done in Burgundy (chiefly by Professor Raymond Bernard) in the past few decades, yet few of the clones have become available through commercial nurseries. In this context, the clonal selection trials at Byron Vineyard assume particular significance, even if the results will not affect the wine in the bottle until the next century.

Of more immediate impact are the effects of new-generation vine spacing, trellis and canopy management techniques, the implications of which are discussed on pages 360–1. We often hear about the great wines of bygone decades; I confidently predict the greatest Chardonnays will be made in the next millennium.

California
1982–91 Acreage of Chardonnay

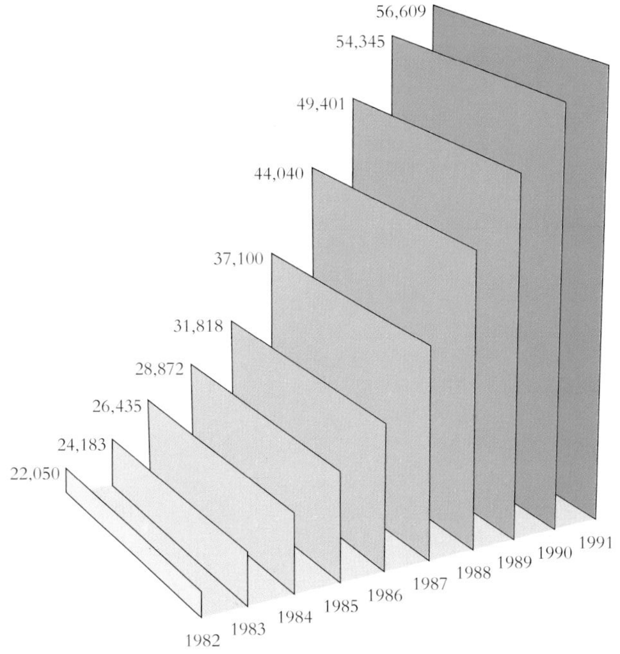
22,050
24,183
26,435
28,872
31,818
37,100
44,040
49,401
54,345
56,609
1982
1983
1984
1985
1986
1987
1988
1989
1990
1991

ABOVE ~ *Andy MacGregor (and Tillie) in his vineyard, where he conducts high-level research into the mechanisms of grape ripening.*

WINERIES *of* EDNA VALLEY

CHAMISAL VINEYARD 1979

A: 525 Orcutt Road, San Luis Obispo, CA 93401 **T**: (805) 544 3576 **V**: 11–5 Wed–Sun **P**: 3,000 **W**: Clay Thompson

This Chardonnay specialist winery, owned by well-known restaurateur Norman Goss and family, was one of the first out of the blocks in the Edna Valley, making its first wine in the same year as Edna Valley Vineyards — 1979. Its 57 acres of estate plantings are almost entirely devoted to Chardonnay, with a nominal four acres of Cabernet Sauvignon which are used to make a Cabernet Sauvignon Blanc, not a wine likely to extract praise from me. The Chamisal Vineyard Chardonnays have varied in style and quality: at their best with intense varietal fruit and well-balanced and integrated oak.

CORBETT CANYON VINEYARDS 1979

A: 2195 Corbett Canyon Road, Arroyo Grande, CA 93420 **T**: (805) 544 5800 **V**: 10–4:30 Mon–Fri, 10-5 Sat–Sun **P**: 300,000 **W**: John Clark

When Jim Lawrence built Corbett Canyon Winery in 1978, he not only constructed the largest winery in the Edna Valley, but did so with the intention of purchasing the grapes from the cheapest possible sources, including the Central Valley. History does not relate what inspired him to do this, but to a lesser or greater degree, it set the tone for Corbett Canyon which has persisted through several changes of ownership since. In 1982 it was purchased by Glenmore Distillers, and in 1988 by the Wine Group (which includes Franzia and Summit). To give the Wine Group credit, it purchased the 350-acre Los Alamos Vineyard in Santa Barbara, which now supplies Corbett Canyon with a significant part of its Pinot Noir and Chardonnay intake, although it necessarily buys grapes from other parts of California, including Sauvignon Blanc and Cabernet Sauvignon from Paso Robles, and Cabernet Sauvignon from the Napa and Sonoma Valleys. The winery is as functional and efficient as one would expect, with all of the equipment necessary to handle what is a very substantial annual crush.

The wines are released under two principal designations: the volume, value-oriented Coastal Classic range, and with limited quantities of Reserve Chardonnay, Pinot Noir, Merlot and Cabernet Sauvignon. As at 1992, the Coastal Classic Range (in 750 ml bottle configuration) sold for $8, and basically the Coastal Classic Range (and indeed the Reserve range) deliver more or less what one would expect. The Chardonnay, in both guises, shows the strong peachy/pineapple/tropical canned fruit characters of cool grown Chardonnay made without any particular artifice. Real or imagined, one can also see some botrytis at work accentuating the flavors. Unlike the disappointing Pinot Noir, the Coastal Classic Merlot and Sauvignon Blanc can rise marginally above their station, the former with a California appellation, the latter with Central Coast. Both show distinct varietal flavor, even if they are somewhat on the light and simple side of things. I must say that I tasted some exciting wines from barrel, but suspect these will get blended away.

EDNA VALLEY VINEYARDS 1980

A: 2585 Biddle Ranch Road, San Luis Obispo, CA 93401 **T**: (805) 544 9594 **V**: 10–4 daily **P**: 55,000 **W**: Steve Dooley

Paragon Vineyards, owned by the Niven family, pioneered the development of the Edna Valley when it commenced planting 650 acres in 1973. In 1977 Chalone purchased grapes from the vineyard, and released the wine under the Edna Valley Vineyards label. Three years later Paragon and Chalone Inc. formed a joint venture, Paragon providing the grapes and meeting the construction cost of the winery which is leased to the joint venture, and Chalone handling marketing and distribution. The 700 acres of vineyards are planted to over 300 acres of Chardonnay, with the balance principally comprising of Pinot Noir, Sauvignon Blanc and Semillon. Only one-third of the total production is used for the Edna Valley label; Sauvignon Blanc and Semillon are sold to Carmenet (which is in the Chalone Group ownership) with almost two-thirds going to unrelated parties. Tiffany Hill, the other label of the region, is in fact owned by Paragon, and takes a small portion of the production.

Edna Valley Vineyards is a no-holds barred Chardonnay specialist, producing exceptionally complex, Burgundian-style Chardonnays which take high quality fruit and apply sophisticated (and skilled) winemaking techniques. The facility wants for nothing: there are underground barrel caves with the patented Chalone barrel lifter, with abundant new oak, and all of the group input and expertise. It is hardly surprising that the wines are as good as they are.

It has a much lesser reputation for its Pinot Noir, but with on-going improvements in the vineyard — including trellis changes, leaf pulling and clonal trials — that situation may change. I must say that I could find nothing much wrong with the 1990 Pinot Noir, other than that it was a fraction light and simple. It has very pleasant cherry-accented fruit with a touch of charred oak, making it an above-average early drinking red wine.

WINDEMERE WINES 1985

A: 6262 Orcutt Road, San Luis Obispo, CA 93434 **T**: (805) 473 3836 **V**: Nil **P**: 2,000 **W**: Cathy MacGregor-Bryan

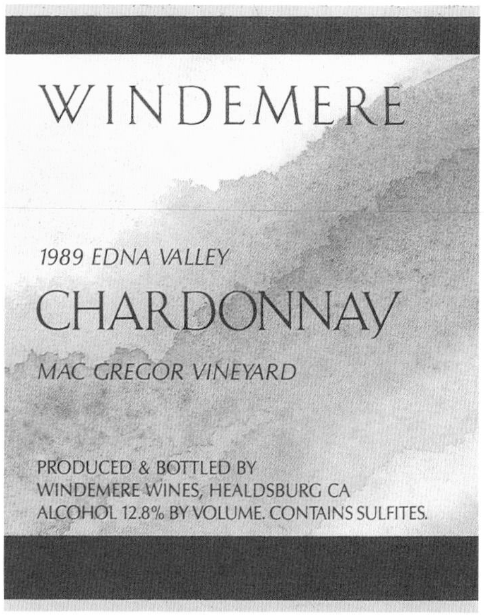
WINDEMERE
1989 EDNA VALLEY
CHARDONNAY
MAC GREGOR VINEYARD
PRODUCED & BOTTLED BY
WINDEMERE WINES, HEALDSBURG CA
ALCOHOL 12.8% BY VOLUME. CONTAINS SULFITES.

Cathy MacGregor-Bryan is the daughter of Andy MacGregor, who owns and operates the highly esteemed MacGregor Vineyard in the Edna Valley. She graduated from Davis in 1977, and subsequently worked as assistant winemaker for a number of prominent wineries including Mill Creek, La Crema and Grgich Hills. In 1985 she established her own brand, using custom crush facilities, and immediately began to make a series of award-winning Chardonnays. The 1989 wine won gold medals at both the Orange County and California State Fairs, showing strong honeyed/buttery toasty fruit with full-blown malolactic fermentation and oak characters. The range has been extended with a Cabernet Sauvignon from the Napa Valley (surprisingly elegant) and a Paso Robles Zinfandel. She and husband Larry are building a small winery at the front of the MacGregor Vineyard, ultimately aiming to produce a maximum of 10,000 cases.

WINERIES *of* ARROYO GRANDE

MAISON DEUTZ WINERY 1981

A: 453 Deutz Drive, Arroyo Grande, CA 93420 **T**: (805) 481 1763 **V**: 10–4 daily
P: 15,000 **W**: Christian Rougemant

This is a joint venture between Deutz and Geldermann of Champagne and the Nestlé-owned Wine World Inc. Having originally intended to follow the Champagne tradition of buying and blending grapes from various parts of the Central Coast, the focus has switched to 150 acres of vineyard adjacent to the winery, which is planted to Pinot Blanc, Pinot Noir and Chardonnay.

Situated so close to the coast, the heat summation rarely rises above 2,000 degree days, and is often less than that; even for sparkling wine, ripeness can hang in the balance. One imagines the 15% or so of the crush purchased from other regions plays an important role in providing balance. It will also be interesting to see the long-term fate of the Pinot Blanc.

Three wines are produced. Brut Cuvee is a blend of approximately one-third each of Pinot Noir, Pinot Blanc and Chardonnay, accounting for by far the greatest part of production. Limited quantities of a Brut Rosé, made from skin-contacted Pinot Noir, and Brut Reserve (a premium vintage-dated wine made primarily from Chardonnay and Pinot Noir, with only a touch of Pinot Blanc) are made. As one would expect, all of the wines are competently made, the 1987 Brut Reserve showing the complexity and stature one would anticipate.

SAUCELITO CANYON VINEYARD 1982

A: 1600 Saucelito Creek Road, Arroyo Grande, CA 93420 **T**: (805) 489 8762
V: By appointment **P**: 1,500
W: Bill Greenough and Richard Headwood

When Bill Greenough purchased this remote 100-acre ranch at the head of the Arroyo Grande Valley back in 1974, he acquired the remnants of a winery which had been abandoned in the 1940s, and an even more neglected three-acre patch of Zinfandel which had been planted in 1879. He resuscitated the Zinfandel by cutting it back to ground level, and then training one of the crown shoots up to constitute a new trunk. He also expanded the plantings to a total of 15 acres, adding 11 acres of Zinfandel and one of Cabernet Sauvignon.

In 1982 he bonded a simple winery, and embarked on a career as a winemaker. Over the years, the approach to the Zinfandel has become steadily more sophisticated. While the handling itself is simplicity (passed through a simple destemmer into small open-top fermenters), the approach to picking is not. The vineyard is divided into four blocks, which are picked at different times. Part is harvested around 21.5° Brix, providing a high acid, low pH and bright-fruit component. The bulk is picked at around 22.5° Brix, including part of the 1879 vines. The remainder of the old block is left to hang until it reaches 24° Brix, providing an intensely rich, jammy blend component. A big, concentrated, redcurrant and blackcurrant but rather jammy 1989 was followed by a quite glorious 1990, the latter with superb redcurrant fruit, and an exceptionally long, smooth and concentrated palate.

TALLEY VINEYARDS 1986

A: 3031 Lopez Drive, Arroyo Grande, CA 93420 **T**: (805) 489 0446 **V**: 12–5 Thur–Sat
P: 4,500 **W**: Stephen Rasmussen

The Talley family has been growing vegetables in the Arroyo Grande region for 45 years, and made its first tentative foray into grape growing in 1982, including some Cabernet Sauvignon which was speedily removed. There are now 102 acres planted, of which 70 were in production in 1992, and although the Talleys have a great deal more land, they have no intentions of planting further grapes. Says Brian Talley, "As it is, our vegetables finance the vineyard and winery, and enough is enough." Enough constitutes roughly 70 acres of Chardonnay, 15 acres of Pinot Noir, ten acres of Sauvignon Blanc and five acres of Riesling. In 1986 it was decided to have a small portion of the production vinified, principally as a sales tool to help publicize the vineyards. Nothing succeeds like success, and in 1991 a 16,000-case capacity winery was built. At the present time, the surplus capacity is used to provide custom crush and make facilities for others, and Brian Talley sees production edging up slowly. "We have always been at the premium end of horticulture, and when Dad visited Burgundy he was extremely impressed with the grower emphasis, and with the meticulous care taken with the fruit. We understand that approach, and would always wish to sell to makers such as Au Bon Climat, because we know Jim Clendenen will make great wine out of our grapes, which will in turn help build the reputation of our vineyards."

For my book, Talley is doing the job on its own account with supreme flair. It made two celestial wines in 1990 from Chardonnay and Pinot Noir, and a serviceable Sauvignon Blanc. The Chardonnay has masses of fruit, with a buttery/peachy texture, subtle oak, and wonderful finish and feel. Good though this wine is, the Pinot Noir is even better, showing sophisticated use of charred oak, strong plummy fruit on the bouquet, and an outstanding palate, with explosive plum and spice flavors, and the same length and concentration in the finish as is evident in the Chardonnay.

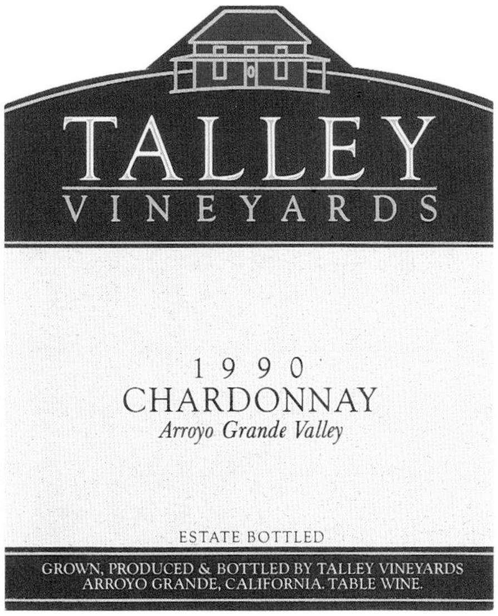
TALLEY
VINEYARDS
1990
CHARDONNAY
Arroyo Grande Valley
ESTATE BOTTLED
GROWN, PRODUCED & BOTTLED BY TALLEY VINEYARDS
ARROYO GRANDE, CALIFORNIA. TABLE WINE.

INDEPENDENCE

ABOVE ~ *Old school house in the Edna Valley, now home to the Wilson family.*

Santa Maria Valley

The first vineyard to be established after Prohibition did not appear until 1964, when San Joaquin table grape grower Uriel Nielson established 100 acres of White Riesling, Chardonnay and Cabernet Sauvignon. The first wine was vinified by the then Brother Justin (now Justin Meyer of Silver Oak) at Christian Brothers Winery, and the quality of the grapes was recognized right from the outset. Plantings grew apace during the wild, tax-driven days of the early 1970s, notably the vast Tepusquet Vineyard, since divided and sold to Kendall-Jackson (which took the lion's share of 1,200 acres), and Robert Mondavi (340 acres).

The Santa Maria AVA was granted in 1981, by which time much of the present plantings of over 5,000 acres had been established. Most of these are on the foothills of the Sierra Madre and San Rafael mountain ranges, facing southwest across the valley which is broad and open at the town of Santa Maria, but progressively funnels as one travels east up the Sisquoc River. Neither the elevation nor the slope of the vineyards is great, between 300 and 800 feet.

The region has a very low rainfall, and the water-nutrient balance of the soils induces a certain amount of stress, providing a degree of natural vigor control. It is dominated by the three great (in terms of both size and quality) vineyards of Bien Nacido (600 acres), Sierra Madre (670 acres) and Tepusquet (1,200 acres). The former two still supply premium makers across the length and breadth of California.

Scenically, it is not a particularly attractive area, but it just happens to produce some of California's finest Chardonnay, and some very good Pinot Noir. The Chardonnay imprimatur of Kendall-Jackson and Mondavi should satisfy the cynical; the wine in the glass should satisfy the critical.

ABOVE ~ *John Kerr, assistant winemaker at Bryon Winery, who also has his own (John Kerr) brand.*

OPPOSITE ~ *The massive Cambria Winery and vineyard, part of the thriving Kendall Jackson empire.*

THE REGION IN BRIEF

Climate, Soil and Viticulture

CLIMATE

The open end of the funnel-shaped valley in which the Santa Maria AVA is located meets the Pacific Ocean at the borders of the San Luis Obispo and Santa Barbara counties. The cold ocean air sweeps over the town of Santa Maria, following the path of the Sisquoc River. As the valley turns southeast, the air warms somewhat, and in the side canyons in particular (such as Rancho Sisquoc) the heat summation rises from Region I to Region II. Morning fog and afternoon sea breezes play the usual cooling role, and the midday heat load is seldom great. Indeed, the average temperature during the growing season is only 74°F, the temperate nature of the region being further emphasized by the year-round average of 64°F. The average rainfall of 12 to 15 inches makes irrigation essential, but also reduces the risk of mold and severe botrytis.

SOIL

The soils are overwhelmingly marine in origin, derived primarily as depositional soils from marine sandstones, shales and diatomaceous earth. Because of the accumulation of sea shells and other marine carbonates, the soils are alkaline. They are also well drained, ranging in texture from sandy loam to clay loam, and historically have supported intensive agriculture such as avocado and citrus growing. There have been no residual salt deposits from the marine era nor by virtue of subsequent irrigation.

THE GROWING SEASON

Some of the major growers unabashedly state Santa Maria has (and I quote) "the longest growing season for wine grapes in California, with budbreak in February and harvest as late as October, giving the grapes exceptionally high acids, low pH and intensity of flavor." Precisely the same claims are made by the mid-Monterey growers, those of the Edna Valley and those of the Santa Ynez Valley. So while the facts of the growing season are not in dispute, the uniqueness is. Spring frosts are countered by overhead sprinklers — which are also used for irrigation in some vineyards, drip irrigation elsewhere — and even helicopters. Tropical storms can interrupt harvest, doing so (for example) in both 1989 and 1990.

Contract Growers

Bien Nacido Vineyard Six hundred acres primarily planted in 1973 on the northern side of the valley near the junction of the Sisquoc and Cuyama Rivers to Chardonnay, Pinot Noir, Pinot Blanc, Riesling, Cabernet Sauvignon, Merlot and Shiraz. Numerous purchasers.

Santa Maria Vineyard One of the smaller and newer vineyards, with Chardonnay and Pinot Noir, the latter sold to Wild Horse and Babcock, the former to Sanford.

Sierra Madre Vineyard Six hundred and seventy acres planted between 1979 and 1989 at the western end of the valley (just to the east of the town of Santa Maria) to Chardonnay, Riesling, Sauvignon Blanc, Pinot Noir and Syrah. Numerous purchasers.

Santa Maria Valley
1971 AND 1991 ACREAGE/GRAPE VARIETIES

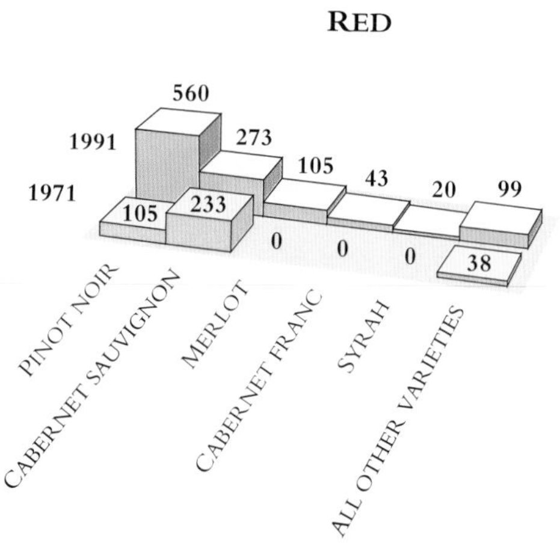
RED
1991
1971
560
273
105
43
20
99
105
233
0
0
0
38
PINOT NOIR
CABERNET SAUVIGNON
MERLOT
CABERNET FRANC
SYRAH
ALL OTHER VARIETIES

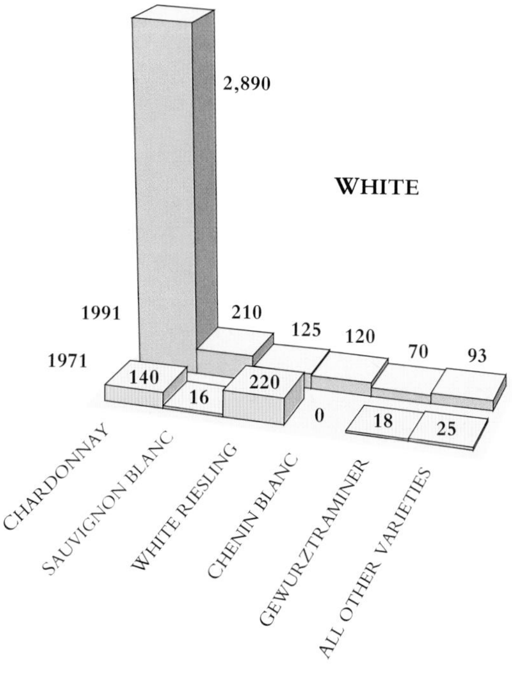
WHITE
1991
1971
2,890
210
125
120
70
93
140
16
220
0
18
25
CHARDONNAY
SAUVIGNON BLANC
WHITE RIESLING
CHENIN BLANC
GEWURZTRAMINER
ALL OTHER VARIETIES

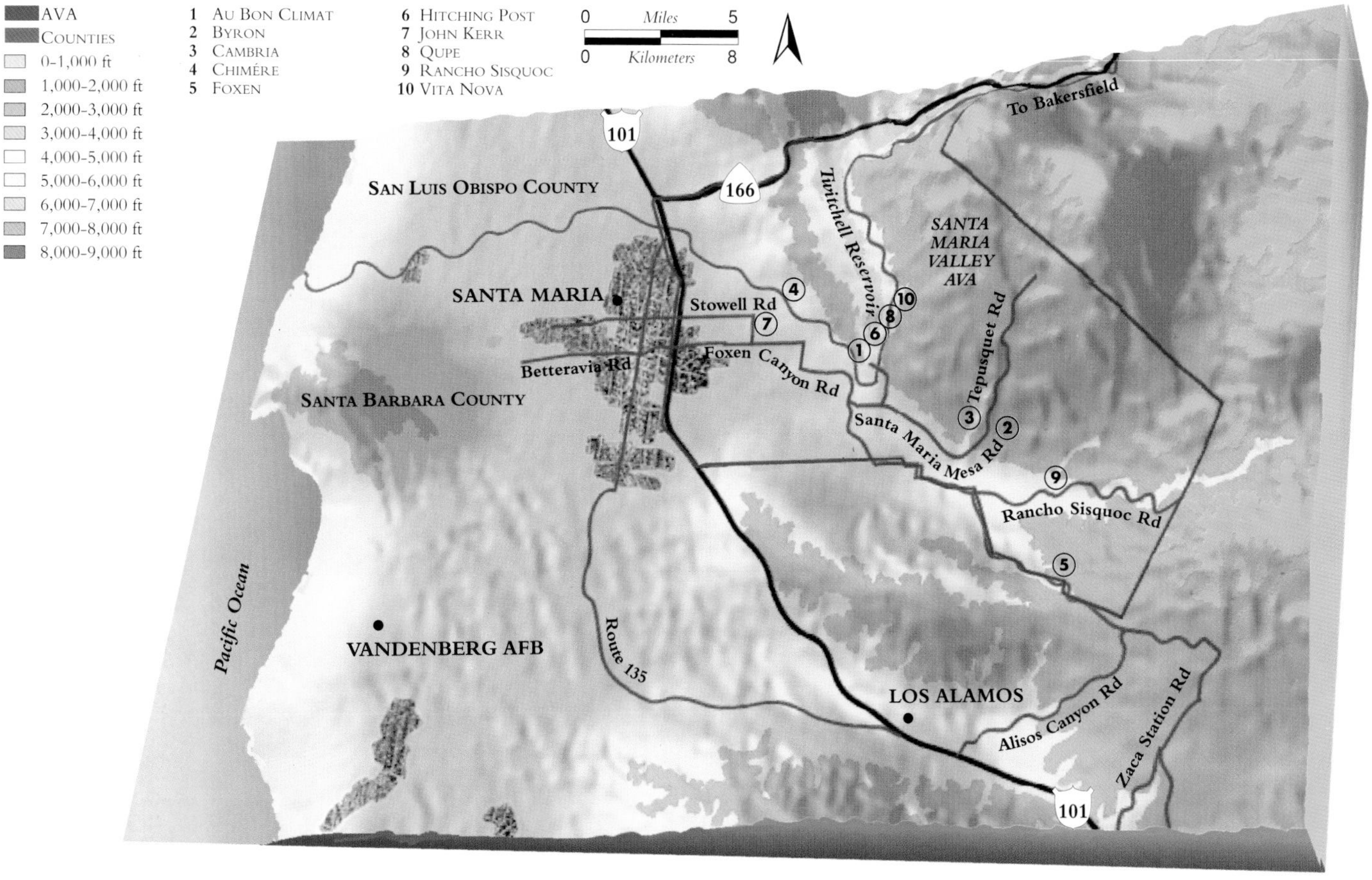
AVA
COUNTIES
0-1,000 ft
1,000-2,000 ft
2,000-3,000 ft
3,000-4,000 ft
4,000-5,000 ft
5,000-6,000 ft
6,000-7,000 ft
7,000-8,000 ft
8,000-9,000 ft
1 Au Bon Climat
2 Byron
3 Cambria
4 Chimère
5 Foxen
6 Hitching Post
7 John Kerr
8 Qupe
9 Rancho Sisquoc
10 Vita Nova
0 Miles 5
0 Kilometers 8
101
166
To Bakersfield
San Luis Obispo County
Twitchell Reservoir
SANTA MARIA VALLEY AVA
SANTA MARIA
Stowell Rd
Tepusquet Rd
Betteravia Rd
Foxen Canyon Rd
Santa Barbara County
Santa Maria Mesa Rd
Rancho Sisquoc Rd
Pacific Ocean
VANDENBERG AFB
Route 135
LOS ALAMOS
Alisos Canyon Rd
Zaca Station Rd
101

Principal Wine Styles

CHARDONNAY

Even if not quite the same degree as in the Edna Valley, Chardonnay is the master. It dominates plantings, and it is responsible for the very high reputation of the region. Due to the responsiveness of the variety to the will of the maker there are distinct styles, but the similarities far outweigh the dissimilarities: there is an almost voluptuous richness to the tropical, peach and melon fruit which is balanced and cut back by the cleansing acidity of the lingering finish to the flavor. Botrytis plays a role, although seemingly a lesser one than in the Edna Valley — but whether this is due to climate, viticulture or winemaking skills I am not so sure. That combination of richness and intensity allows makers free reign in the use of new oak and barrel fermentation; it also means the malolactic fermentation does not strip the wine of varietal fruit flavor. The outstanding makers within the region are Au Bon Climat, Byron, Foxen and Qupe; those outside include Wild Horse, Mondavi and — at a slick, commercial level — Kendall-Jackson, but there are others.

PINOT NOIR

Some may cavil at this or that manifestation of Pinot Noir, and others may fail to understand it altogether, but this is an excellent region for the variety, with Bien Nacido one of the leading sources. There is often a touch of sappiness to the wines, but I doubt whether it is fair to conclude that this is necessarily a characteristic of the region: it probably has more to do with the winemaker. In any event, I personally happen to like the cut it provides, and am less enamoured of the direct cherry style the region can also produce. For various reasons, many makers prefer to blend Santa Maria fruit with that from Santa Ynez, which makes typecasting doubly difficult. And the major item on the agenda for the future is, of course, clonal selection. In the meantime, the best producers within the region are Au Bon Climat, Byron and Hitching Post; from without, Wild Horse, Fiddlehead Cellars and Mondavi (recognizing that Santa Maria plays only a small part in Mondavi blends). If Kendall-Jackson decides to develop a major light dry red brand, it has the right vineyard resources to provide quality Pinot Noir here in Santa Maria.

SAUVIGNON BLANC, SEMILLON AND WHITE MERITAGE

These are minor players, with Semillon, in particular, struggling to reach satisfactory sugar levels — not, it must be said, a characteristic peculiar to this region. But when the conditions are right, these varieties can shine, as Byron and Vita Nova have from time to time demonstrated.

RHONE

Viognier, Marsanne and Syrah are all grown, and made in tiny quantities but — in the case of Syrah particularly — with great success. Here Qupe is the shining star, producing wines which have wonderful varietal character (spice, pepper, liquorice and dark cherries are intermingling) and equally impressive richness and texture in the mouth.

ABOVE ~ *Santa Maria Valley map.*

PINOT NOIR

Even in Burgundy, Pinot Noir is a temperamental and fickle mistress, reacting viciously to seasonal conditions which do not suit it. The truly great vintages occur less frequently than they do in Bordeaux or the Rhone Valley — seldom more than two a decade. It is also an extremely reluctant traveler: so far no other European country has succeeded with the variety, although some would argue Italy is on the brink of doing so, and Miguel Torres is trying hard in the high Penedès.

ABOVE ~ *A freshly topped barrel of Qupe Syrah; the stain will quickly dry.*

South America and South Africa have produced nothing to become excited about, and the latter, in particular, is unlikely to do so in the near future. The Martinborough region of New Zealand produces minuscule quantities of good Pinot Noir, while a ring of districts around Melbourne in Australia lead the way for that country, and are capable of producing Pinots of world class.

The combined experience of the vignerons around the world (outside of Burgundy) is that the variety is exceptionally choosy about the climatic conditions in which it is grown; and yet that it is not possible to determine in advance where it should be grown by studying climatic data. It is possible to determine where it should *not* be grown (in any climate having a greater heat summation than low Region II, or around 2,700 degree days), but it does not follow that all climates with a lower summation will suit Pinot Noir.

And whatever the beliefs of Josh Jensen (of Calera) may be, and however distinguished his best Pinots may be, soil type does not provide the answer. The limestone soils of Burgundy are not important per se; they are important because they provide particularly good drainage in a region in which rainfall is spread evenly (sometimes too evenly) throughout the growing season. In this respect at least, Pinot Noir is no different from any other grape variety: the best grapes will be grown on well-drained (but not excessively so) soils of low to moderate fertility, with subsoils which are permeable by the vine's roots but have good water holding capacity. The mineralogical composition is irrelevant except to the extent that it affects pH: unduly acid or unduly alkaline soils will need to be adjusted.

All in all, it is not surprising that so much Pinot Noir was planted in the wrong places in California in the late 1960s and early 1970s. Nor is it surprising that winemakers by and large had no idea how to make it. They and their Australian counterparts basically sought to treat it as if it were Cabernet Sauvignon or any other grape variety, and reared back in horror when this thin, soapy flavorless wine resulted, which added insult to injury by promptly turning from an insipid red color to light brown.

The solution was not unlike that adopted by the big negociant houses of Burgundy who made Englishman's Burgundy by adding a sizeable slug of the richest Algerian (and, when this ran out, Rhone) wine they could find. The result was the idea of Burgundy which permeated the world: rich, deeply colored, velvety wines with tremendous sweetness and extract, and with a soft, low tannin finish. The fact that they had little or no Pinot Noir varietal character was irrelevant, and indeed unknown.

So the Californians and Australians simply added as much full-bodied dry red made from other varieties as they judged necessary to make the wine appear conventional. If you had a particularly acute palate and mind, you would then identify it (in a blind tasting) by a process of elimination. It's not Cabernet, it's not Zinfandel, it's not Syrah ... it must be a Pinot.

The sorting out of the California regions which do suit the variety roughly coincided with the awakening of knowledge about making methods, or at least about the multitude of options open in the winery, most of which differ from those commonly used for other red varieties.

These dual strands of knowledge turned upon the realization that Pinot Noir is the most translucent, the most fragrant, the most delicate and yet intense of all red wines. For the Burgundian, the bouquet is all-important; if it is correct, the palate will take care of itself. For the Bordelaise, the palate — and in particular its structure — is all important; get it correct, give the wine time in bottle, and the bouquet will take care of itself.

This knowledge, it has to be said, was not imparted in the hallowed portals of U.C. Davis, but from the working visits made by the pioneering makers to Burgundy, and also from their consumption of substantial amounts of its wines. There was nothing to be found in books which would help: even Anthony Hanson's seminal work on Burgundy disclosed little. It was left to Matt Kramer in his book *Making Sense of Burgundy* and — even more so — Remington Norman's *Great Domaines of Burgundy* to provide such information.

The areas in which Pinot Noir succeeds (and those in which it does not) are, I think, generally agreed, although their relative order is most certainly not. My computer tells me that not a single one of the top 29 Pinots of the 95 tasted blind in bench tastings in San Francisco came from either the Napa Valley (excluding Carneros and excepting Robert Mondavi) or Sonoma County (excluding the Russian River). For the record, ten came from the Central Coast, nine from Carneros, six from the Russian River, and one each from the Santa Cruz and York Mountains, and from San Benito and Monterey.

Even at this point another difficulty arises. There is more scope for legitimate disagreement about the style of Pinot Noir than any other variety, with the possible exception of its soul-mate, Zinfandel. If the Burgundy-drinking world is divided into those (including myself) who revere the wines of the Domaine de la Romanée-Conti and those who see them as grotesque, over-extracted and over-oaked parodies of Burgundy, how can one expect agreement elsewhere?

Carneros elegantly demonstrates both this disagreement, and yet another major wild card: that of clonal selection. Were it not for the fact that I have tasted Carneros Creek's 1991 Pinot Noirs ex-barrel made from its new clonal selection blocks, I would join a band of heretics which avers that Carneros is capable of producing very good, but not great, Pinot Noirs. Saintsbury's Pinot Noir is unnervingly and consistently good; if it was the only familiar name on a wine list anywhere in the world it would be my unhesitating choice. But on the other hand, Saintsbury exemplifies what I can only describe as a singularity, a polish, which is too perfect. Where is the streak of wildness which reminds us that Pinot Noir is the most genetically unstable of all red varieties, with more utterly distinct clones?

A rhetorical question in one sense, yet in another answered by those 1991 Carneros Creek wines. Within that limitation, Acacia, Carneros Creek, Mont St. John, Richardson, Roche, Saintsbury and Schug all feature in my top-pointed wines. There are others waiting in the wings, while Robert Mondavi plays a blending game with its superlative rich Reserve Pinot Noir.

The Russian River clearly throws down the gauntlet to Santa Barbara County, with Williams-Selyem leading the way and Dehlinger, Gary Farrell and Rochioli providing strong support. The Russian River produces wines of ultimate finesse and elegance; these are not heavyweight wines (other than Dehlinger, perhaps) but they have the vinosity, that long-lingering finish which is the mark of a truly great Pinot. (To be honest, a Rodney Strong Russian River also scored highly, and should probably be added to the list.)

Monterey's potential for Pinot Noir is as great as it is for Chardonnay (and its achievement less), the obvious exceptions being the climatic oddities of Chalone and San Benito, the latter Jensen's aerie. Chalone's variability is well known, and needs no elaboration; likewise, the gulf between the vineyard-designated wines of Jensen and its Central Coast appellation wine. At their best, these producers make some of the most complex, long-lived and satisfying of all California Pinot Noirs.

But at the end of the day, it is Santa Barbara County which has its nose in front, thanks in no small measure to two vineyards, Bien Nacido, and Sanford and Benedict — although if Talley Vineyard gains the recognition it deserves, and can be persuaded to plant more Pinot Noir, it would join the list.

Whether blended or as vineyard-designated wines, these share a combination of fruit generosity and elegance exceeded nowhere else. The fruit spectrum runs the gamut from strawberry to cherry to plum, yet seldom strays over the edge to become porty or jammy. It has sufficient richness to allow makers free use of whole bunch maceration if they so desire, providing a touch of stemminess which adds to the complexity of the wine without throwing it out of balance.

On the way down to Santa Barbara one finds York Mountain Winery, the HMR Vineyard and Wild Horse (the latter drawing much of its grapes from Santa Barbara, in any event) which are significant players, Wild Horse in particular. Once in the county, Au Bon Climat, Babcock, Byron, Hitching Post, Sanford, Santa Barbara Winery, Talley and Zaca Mesa are the names to watch and follow. In so doing, be prepared for the occasional disappointing wine; Pinot Noir is like that.

California
1982–91 Acreage of Pinot Noir

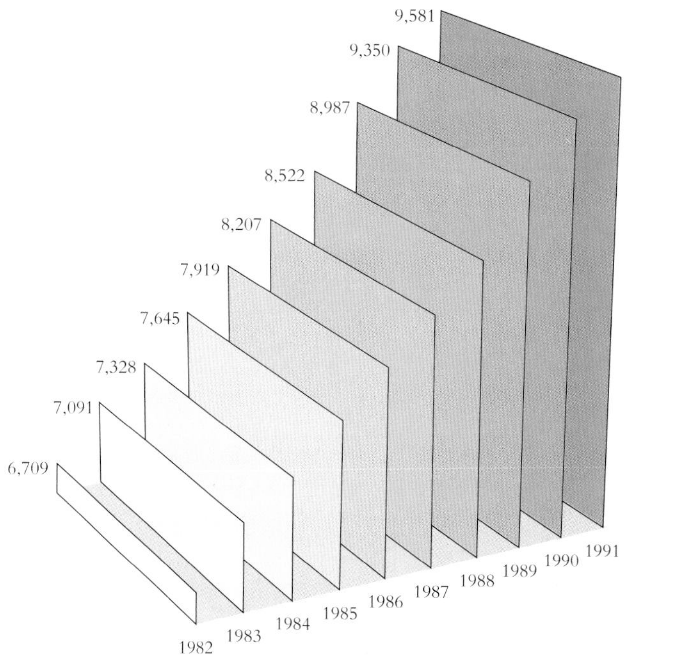
6,709
7,091
7,328
7,645
7,919
8,207
8,522
8,987
9,350
9,581
1982
1983
1984
1985
1986
1987
1988
1989
1990
1991

ABOVE ~ *Pinot Noir flourishes in the cool climate of the Russian River.*

WINERIES *of* SANTA MARIA VALLEY

AU BON CLIMAT 1982

A: Route 1, Box 1208, Santa Maria Mesa Road, Santa Maria, CA 93454
T: (805) 688 8630 **V**: By appointment
P: 10,000 **W**: Jim Clendenen

Au Bon Climat lived a peripatetic, and at times chaotic, existence until it moved to its present location on the Bien Nacido Ranch in 1988. It was founded by Jim Clendenen and Adam Tolmach at the Zaca Mesa Winery, owning neither vineyards nor winery, and initially with only the most rudimentary winemaking equipment. Tolmach has now left Au Bon Climat to develop his own Ojai Winery, but the somewhat chaotic existence continues with the Bien Nacido facility being shared by Vita Nova, in which Jim Clendenen has a proprietary interest, and by Qupe (and which are dealt with separately). Au Bon Climat is still without its own vineyards, sourcing its grapes principally from the Santa Maria Valley, but also purchasing Pinot and Chardonnay from Talley Vineyards in Arroyo Grande. Just to add a finishing touch, as it were, the winery is in fact located yards inside the San Luis Obispo County line (where it joins Santa Barbara County) simply because the authorities in San Luis Obispo are rather more cooperative than those in Santa Barbara when it comes to wineries.

Clendenen is one of the true geniuses in the California wine industry: like most of his ilk, he can be wayward, unpredictable and abrasive, albeit with a superb sense of humor which (combined with his intellect) produces an endless stream of largely unrepeatable one-liners. He is also known to suffer fools somewhat badly, and has never sought to curry favor with those he does not hold in high regard. For these reasons, Au Bon Climat has not always received the recognition its wines deserve. It is also true that the wines are uncompromisingly bold and exceedingly complex in style, the antithesis of the California food wine honed to mindless, boring perfection in the Napa Valley.

Au Bon Climat is a Chardonnay and Pinot Noir specialist. Initially, and notwithstanding varying fruit sources, there was a restricted offering each year. Now, says Clendenen, "I'm losing control, and if I don't watch out I'll be repeating Chateau St. Jean," as he discusses the possibility of releasing four or five different Pinot Noirs from the 1991 vintage, most in small quantities. In both the Chardonnay and Pinot Noir, there is a "standard" release which is distributed nationally and which enjoys substantial export markets, and then small quantities of Reserve wines which have a vineyard designation. Thus the 1991 Chardonnay will be joined by Talley Reserve and Bien Nacido Reserve, while the Pinot Noir will be joined (at the least) by Talley Reserve and Benedict Reserve.

The common thread to all of the Chardonnays is the ultra-sophisticated use of barrel fermentation oak and the voluptuousness of the fruit. These wines consistently stand out like beacons in masked tastings of California wines because they are so shockingly fruity, complex and Burgundian. Those with an international perspective find the wines extraordinarily good, those with a parochial perspective give them one star or worse.

The situation becomes even more extreme with the Pinot Noir, where individual style preferences can distort the picture even more. Here again, the connecting thread is the flavor and structural complexity, with fruit (and varietal character) to the fore, and oak — relatively speaking — playing a lesser role than it does in the Au Bon Climat Chardonnays. If I had to choose but one California producer of these two varieties, it would be Au Bon Climat.

BYRON VINEYARD AND WINERY 1984

A: 5230 Tepusquet Canyon Road, Santa Maria, CA 93454 **T**: (805) 937 7288
V: 10–4 daily **P**: 27,000
W: Byron (Ken) Brown and John Kerr

BYRON
VINEYARD & WINERY
1990
SANTA BARBARA COUNTY
PINOT NOIR
PRODUCED & BOTTLED BY BYRON VINEYARD & WINERY
SANTA MARIA, CA B.W. 5234 TABLE WINE

ABOVE ~ *Byron Vineyard's assistant winemaker John Kerr filling Chardonnay barrels due to undergo malolactic fermentation.*

Ken Brown has played a leading role in the development of the Santa Maria Valley. After a career which had encompassed business administration and real estate development, his interest in wine as a consumer led him to complete the enology program at California State University at Fresno in 1974, and in 1975 a research project brought him to Santa Maria to make wine for local growers, including Louis Ream of Zaca Mesa Ranch. The project was successful, and in 1978 the Zaca Mesa Winery was built, and Ken Brown appointed as its first winemaker. He remained at Zaca Mesa until 1986, but in 1983 began to make plans for his own winery, which was built on Tepusquet Canyon Road in 1984. In 1988 a second building was constructed, effectively doubling the size of the winery, and in 1989 Byron acquired the Nielson Vineyard, established in 1964, and the oldest commercial plantings in Santa Barbara County. The total grape acreage is now 65 acres of Chardonnay, 24 acres of Cabernet Sauvignon, 12 acres of Sauvignon Blanc, and an acre each of the Rhone varietals of Marsanne and Viognier. An additional 18 acres were planted in 1991 on ultra-close spacing (1,500 vines to the acre) to evaluate a wide selection of clones of Pinot Noir and Chardonnay, and also to compare the performance of various rootstocks as opposed to vines grown on their own roots.

Even more significant was the 1990 acquisition of Byron Winery and Vineyards by Robert Mondavi; Ken Brown remains very

much in charge of the operations, and the winery is run as a totally separate and autonomous facility, while having access to the financial resources of the Mondavi group and, no less importantly, to Mondavi's share of the Tepusquet Vineyard. With the Mondavi resources, it is planned to increase production to 50,000 cases by the end of this decade, with an ultimate target of 75,000 cases — the limit which Ken Brown believes is consistent with hand made, quality wines.

And quality wines they indeed are. The winery's two basic lines are Chardonnay (55% of total production) and Pinot Noir (30%). Each wine is offered in a standard and Reserve version, with both Chardonnays being absolutely outstanding. The emphasis is on elegance, yet the wines have intense melon/grapefruit flavors, with a long, lingering finish. The oak influence is subtle, and, as one would expect, more pronounced in the Reserve version than in the standard, but even here it is far from overwhelming. The Pinot Noirs have not been quite in the same exceptional quality, even though they are (understandably) highly regarded. It seems reasonable to expect that from the 1991 vintage and onwards, friendly advice from the Mondavi winemaking team will make its presence felt, while there is an ambitious, long-term program to replant the Nielson Vineyard with improved clones. Sauvignon Blanc and a White Meritage blend round off the portfolio, but without setting the pulse racing as does the Chardonnay.

CAMBRIA WINERY 1987

A: 5475 Chardonnay Lane, Santa Maria, CA 93454 **T**: (805) 937 1777 **V**: By appointment **P**: 70,000 **W**: David Guffy

In the twinkling of an eye, Cambria has become the biggest winery in Santa Maria, not surprising given the fact that it forms part of the Kendall-Jackson empire, and was purchased by an investment syndicate headed by Jackson's wife, Barbara Banke, and Jackson himself. What was in fact purchased were 1,200 acres of the Tepusquet Vineyard, with the remainder being simultaneously purchased by Robert Mondavi. Kendall-Jackson had bought a substantial part of Tepusquet's grapes for a number of years, so it was possible to launch the Cambria label with a 1986 Chardonnay and a 1988 Pinot Noir, the former predating the purchase and both predating the construction of the winery, completed just in time for the 1990 vintage.

The 1,200-acre vineyard included 1,000 acres of Chardonnay, in turn divided into Katherine's, Cambria and Tepusquet Vineyards, with 50 acres of Pinot Noir on Julia's Vineyard. These vineyards in turn feature on the labels of what might loosely be termed the standard releases, with the Reserve Chardonnay sitting on top. The wines are all super slick and smooth, showing the production skills for which the Kendall-Jackson Group as a whole is famed, but with that wonderful Santa Maria fruit in the background. At the end of the day, one cannot get away from the fact that the wines are made to a price (and a volume), but there are worse things in life.

FOXEN VINEYARD 1987

A: Route 1, Box 144A Foxen Canyon Road, Santa Maria, CA 93454 **T**: (805) 238 2809 **V**: By appointment **P**: 2,500 **W**: Bill Walthen and Richard Dore

Foxen Vineyard was established in 1987 by Richard Dore (a member of the Foxen family which has for a long time been engaged on a large scale in cattle ranching in Santa Maria), and Bill Walthen (former vineyard manager for Rancho Sisquoc and Chalone). A rudimentary winery has been set up in an old but attractive wooden barn on the side of Foxen Canyon Road, and a ten-acre estate vineyard has been established adjacent to the winery, planted to five acres of Chardonnay and five acres of Cabernet Sauvignon, Merlot and Cabernet Franc. The initial releases were of these two varieties, but purchased from various parts of Santa Barbara County. The quality of the wines is very good: one mark of approval is the

ABOVE ~ *Frank Ostini, proprietor of the Hitching Post Restaurant in Buellton, makes Pinot Noir under the same name (at Au Bon Climat).*

BYRON
VINEYARD & WINERY

selection of Foxen as one of the five purchasers of Pinot Noir from the Sanford and Benedict Vineyard.

THE HITCHING POST 1980

A: c/o Au Bon Climat, Route 1, Box 1208, Santa Maria Mesa Road, Santa Maria, CA 93454 **T**: (805) 688 8630 **V**: By appointment **P**: 700 **W**: Frank Ostini

Noted local restaurateur and Pinot Noir fanatic, Frank Ostini, has joined the fold at Au Bon Climat, making increasing quantities of Santa Barbara-sourced Pinot Noir which is principally sold through his restaurant — and consumed by himself and his numerous friends. Ostini has been making the wine at various custom crush locations for some time now; given his own experience and that of the Clendenen entourage, it is not surprising that very a stylish, elegant Pinot Noir is the result.

QUPE CELLARS 1982

A: Route 1, Box 1208, Santa Maria Mesa Road, Santa Maria,CA 93454
T: (805) 688 8630 **V**: By appointment
P: 3,000 **W**: Bob Lindquist

Bob Lindquist, yet another graduate of the Zaca Mesa school of winemaking, was one of the first California winemakers to become seriously interested in the making of Rhone Valley-style reds, a focus which continues to this day, although the portfolio has been increased over the past ten years. Like Au Bon Climat, Qupe had a peripatetic existence until Lindquist moved to the Bien Nacido Winery occupied by his long-time friend Jim Clendenen. Here he provides a note of pragmatism and even seriousness in proceedings, although when I visited during the first few days of vintage, I was left to wonder how on earth Au Bon Climat, The Hitching Post, Qupe and Vita Nova would not become a supernova by the end of crush. The answer is, of course, that those involved have known each other for a long time and have remained the best of friends.

Qupe buys its Syrah from Bien Nacido Vineyard, and also makes Cuvee Los Olivos, a blend of 60% Shiraz and 40% Mourvedre. A Chardonnay comes from Sierra Madre Vineyard and is offered in both standard and Reserve versions, while a Viognier has recently joined the list, along with tiny quantities of Marsanne.

The Reserve Chardonnay can reach the heights of the Au Bon Climat Reserve, with exceptional depth and intensity to the melange of grapefruit, melon and tropical fruit flavors overlain by nutty/smoky oak. The Syrah is, quite simply, the best I tasted in California, combining voluptuous, dark berry fruits and strong pepper and spice aromas and flavors in the manner of the very best Rhone Valley reds. How anyone could fail to recognize the quality of these wines is beyond my comprehension, but some critics do. The Cuvee Los Olivos is never less than striking, but I would have to agree can be controversial in style (though not in 1991 when it was superb), but the Viognier is yet to prove as exciting in the glass as it is on the label.

RANCHO SISQUOC WINERY 1977

A: Box 147 Foxen Canyon Road, Santa Maria, CA 93454 **T**: (805) 934 4332 **V**: 10–4 daily
P: 6,000 **W**: Stephan Bedford

Rancho Sisquoc is part of a very much larger diversified agricultural project, covering 38,000 acres and known as the Flood Ranch. The first vines were planted in 1968, and the first experimental wines made in 1972. Rancho Sisquoc has always been as much involved in grape growing (and selling) as winemaking, and its 211 acres are planted to a range of varieties available from few other sources in Santa Maria. They include (of course) Chardonnay, but also offer Sauvignon Blanc, White Riesling, Gewurztraminer, Chenin Blanc, Marsanne and even ten acres of Sylvaner. An attractive and functional winery was built in 1978, primarily by converting farmhouses (sitting in a grove of trees on a little hillside) on the site.

The white wines have attracted the most attention, and it is not hard to see why. The Riesling, usually made dry but occasionally botrytised, shows clearly delineated varietal character in its dry form, with floral, lime aromas, crisp limey fruit on the palate and judiciously balanced residual sugar and acidity. The Marsanne is interesting, performing much more in the manner of the Rhone Valley (and in the way it does in the Yarra Valley of Australia) producing a very dry, faintly chalky wine in its youth, which gradually fills out and softens with bottle age.

VITA NOVA 1986

A: Route 1, Box 1208, Santa Maria Mesa Road, Santa Maria, CA 93454
T: (805) 688 8630 **V**: By appointment
P: 3,000 **W**: Jim Clendenen and Bob Lindquist

Vita Nova is owned by Jim Clendenen, Bob Lindquist, Steve Arcriono and Doug Margerum, and started off life as the maker of a Red Meritage blend called Reservatum. This was joined in 1991 by the release of Reservatum Semillon, marking the first time the Semillon became sufficiently ripe to justify bottling on its own, and producing a full, soft, round and mouthfilling wine of great style. While the redcurrant and cassis-flavored Meritage Reservatum continues, a particularly voluptuous barrel fermented Chardonnay now accounts for over 50% of production. The Vita Nova style deliberately aims for very ripe fruit (between 23° and 24° Brix), which is given free play, and supported by appropriately rich oak. Sauvignon Blanc, also made as a varietal in 1991, is in the same mold: luscious, ripe, tropical with mouthfilling flavors.

ABOVE ~ *Innoculating Chardonnay barrels at Byron Winery to promote the onset of malolactic fermentation.*

ABOVE ~ *A controlled fire makes a dramatic backdrop to the Cambria Vineyard.*

36
LUFKIN
LUFKIN
507

SANTA YNEZ VALLEY

The Santa Ynez Valley AVA covers 285 square miles of ever-differing and often beautiful terrain. After the near sterile homogenity of the Edna Valley, and the constancy of climate and terrain of the Santa Maria Valley, the twists and turns of the Santa Ynez Valley signal a climate which is both variable and becomes significantly warmer than that of its sister valleys.

This is one of Los Angeles' playgrounds: it is only a hop, skip and a jump down to the city of Santa Barbara, itself a major center of both permanent and transient residents. Within Santa Ynez, the curious Danish town of Solvang provides the most outrageously calorie-filled, sugar-sweet breakfasts imaginable to the hordes of tourists who come year round. Even the little town of Los Olivos, right in the center of the wine country, has its own charm.

The vineyard renaissance began in 1969, when the first vines were planted just east of Solvang. In common with the rest of California, plantings exploded in the early 1970s, with the peak of activity in 1972/73, but then it abated. When the AVA was created in November 1982 there were 1,200 acres of vines and 20 wineries. Now there are more than 2,000 acres, and roughly the same number of wineries.

Virtually every major grape variety is planted in climates ranging from Region I to Region III, not always with the right match of climate, soil and variety. The major player, Firestone Vineyard, has been hugely successful with its Johannisberg Riesling, but has struggled mightily — not always effectively — with its red wines. Zaca Mesa, too, has fluctuated wildly in production and philosophy, helping to blur and confuse the situation further. If this were not enough, almost all of the successful wineries (other than Firestone) take a figurative drive up Foxen Canyon Road to help themselves to Santa Maria grapes which they use to great effect in their Pinot Noirs and Chardonnays.

ABOVE ~ *The doorway to La Purisma Mission at Lompoc, a reminder of the early days of viticulture in the state.*

OPPOSITE ~ *Oil wells and vines are strange bedfellows in any part of the world other than Southern California — here in Firestone Vineyard.*

The Region in Brief

Climate, Soil and Viticulture

Climate

The Santa Ynez River runs due west, descending from an elevation of 750 feet at Lake Cahuma to 125 feet at the western end of the AVA, where it wriggles its way through the western extremities of the Santa Rita Hills, before entering the broad, flat plain of Lompoc and emptying into the ocean. This toe of the Santa Rita Hills breaks the force of the marine flow which would otherwise give the Santa Ynez Valley a climate similar to the Edna and Santa Maria Valleys. Thus it is that Lompoc has a heat summation of 1,970 degree days (very low Region I), while Solvang has an average of 2,680 degree days (low Region II). At this point the valley opens up abruptly, extending due north up Alamo Pintado Creek to Los Olivos, where Foxen Canyon Road finally terminates. Here, and further east to the town of Santa Ynez, there are spots in the innumerable canyons where the climate becomes even warmer. But it would be wrong to suggest the marine influence is not the dominant effect: it is. On the interior side of the Santa Rita Hills, where the Babcock and the Sanford & Benedict Vineyards are to be found, the climate is Region I. Throughout the valley, morning fog shrouds the vines until midday, with the summer temperature slowly moving up from 50°F to peak at around 80° to 85°F before the afternoon breezes pull it back to 75°F. The winds are seldom strong, and certainly not strong enough to inhibit photosynthesis.

Soil

While largely retaining their marine origin, there are a series of distinct soil types or series. On the terraces and slopes of the northeastern sector around Los Olivos, Santa Ynez and Ballard Canyon, the Positas-Ballard-Santa Ynez series consist of well-drained, fine sandy loams to clay loams. The next major series is the Shedd-Santa Lucia-Diablo association of well-drained shaley clay loams and silty clay loams. Then there are the distinctive rocky soils of the Sanford & Benedict Vineyard; this was formed during a marine landslide, and consists of angular, hard chert which has weathered in place. The soil of the Babcock Vineyards is very different, being much lighter and sandier, though equally well drained.

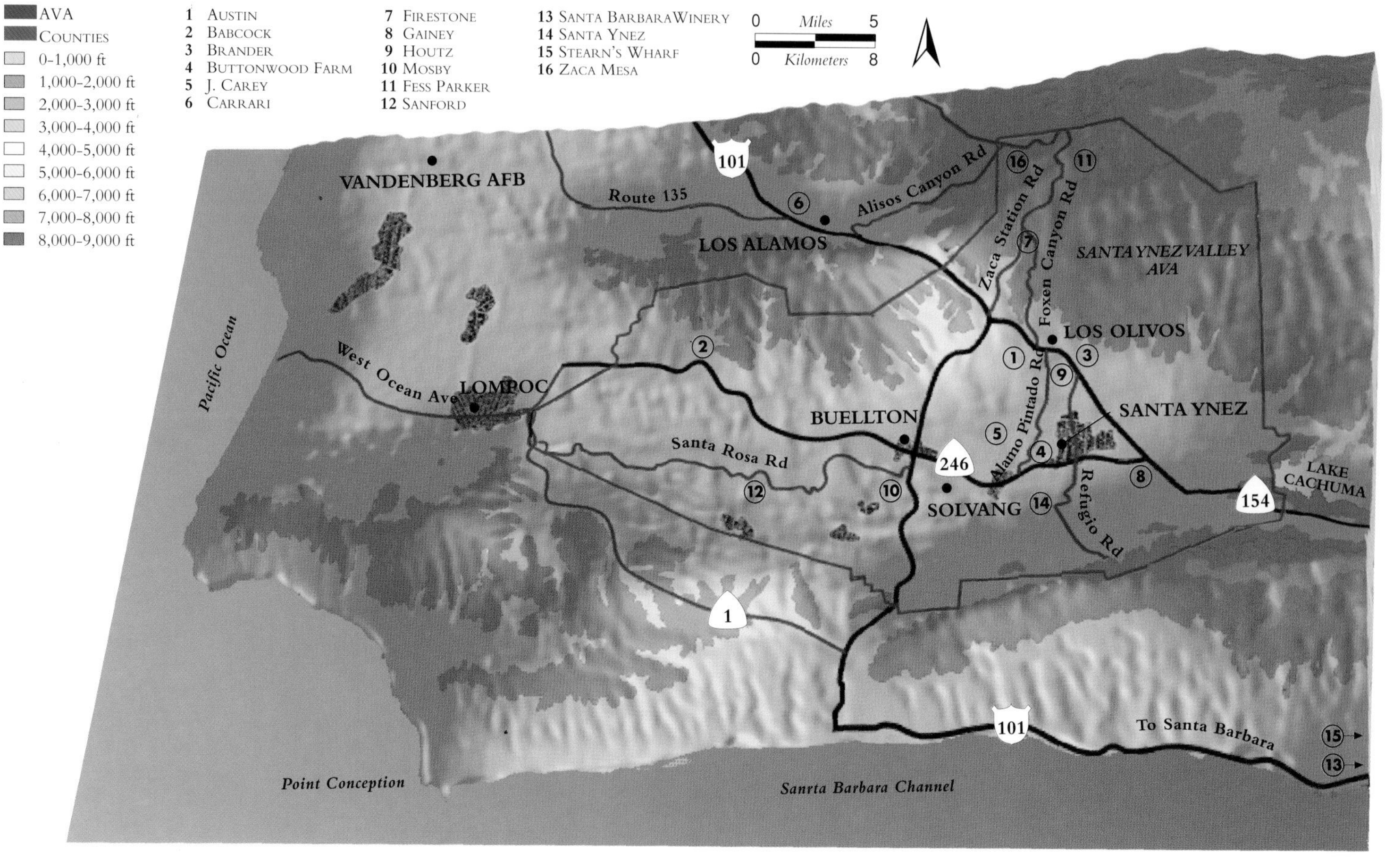
AVA
Counties
0–1,000 ft
1,000–2,000 ft
2,000–3,000 ft
3,000–4,000 ft
4,000–5,000 ft
5,000–6,000 ft
6,000–7,000 ft
7,000–8,000 ft
8,000–9,000 ft
1 Austin
2 Babcock
3 Brander
4 Buttonwood Farm
5 J. Carey
6 Carrari
7 Firestone
8 Gainey
9 Houtz
10 Mosby
11 Fess Parker
12 Sanford
13 Santa Barbara Winery
14 Santa Ynez
15 Stearn's Wharf
16 Zaca Mesa
0 Miles 5
0 Kilometers 8
VANDENBERG AFB
101
Route 135
Alisos Canyon Rd
Zaca Station Rd
Foxen Canyon Rd
LOS ALAMOS
SANTA YNEZ VALLEY AVA
LOS OLIVOS
Pacific Ocean
West Ocean Ave
LOMPOC
BUELLTON
SANTA YNEZ
Alamo Pintado Rd
246
Santa Rosa Rd
SOLVANG
Refugio Rd
LAKE CACHUMA
154
1
101
To Santa Barbara
Point Conception
Sanrta Barbara Channel

ABOVE ~ *Santa Ynez Valley map.*

Santa Ynez Valley
VINTAGE CHART 1981–91

RED

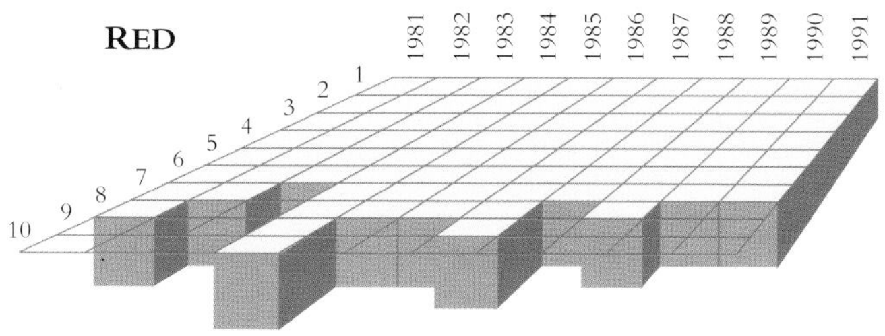
1981
1982
1983
1984
1985
1986
1987
1988
1989
1990
1991
1
2
3
4
5
6
7
8
9
10

WHITE

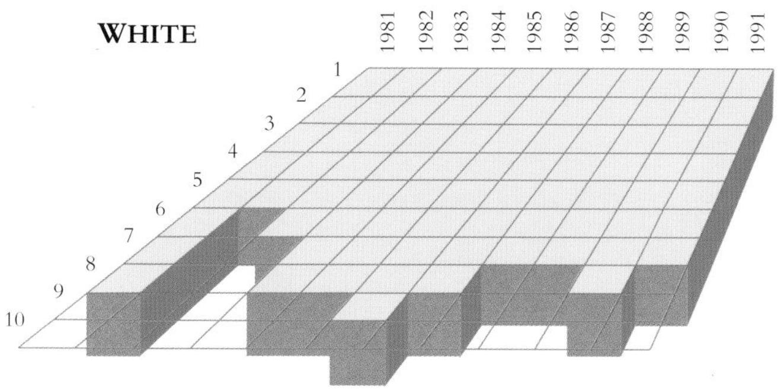
1981
1982
1983
1984
1985
1986
1987
1988
1989
1990
1991
1
2
3
4
5
6
7
8
9
10

THE GROWING SEASON

The early part of the growing season — from the end of March through to May — is largely free from morning fogs, giving plenty of sunshine hours but with moderate temperatures. The summer fogs give rise to the usual botrytis and mildew problems, but the season is not unduly long, with the early ripening varieties starting some time between the third to fourth week of August through to the first week of September, finishing with Cabernet Sauvignon in mid to late October.

Contract Growers

Buttonwood Farm Thirty-nine acres planted between 1983 and 1986 two miles north of Solvang to Cabernet Sauvignon, Cabernet Franc, Merlot, Sauvignon Blanc and Semillon, all of which it ripens well; sold to Babcock, Gainey, Wild Horse and others.

Rancho Dos Mundos Produces Chardonnay at the eastern end of the valley; sold to Babcock and Au Bon Climat.

Sanford & Benedict Vineyard One hundred and twenty-five acres (60 Pinot Noir and 65 Chardonnay) planted 1972; now independently owned but managed by and contracted to Sanford which sells three tons of Pinot Noir to each of Au Bon Climat, Foxen, Gainey and Lane Tanner.

Principal Wine Styles

RIESLING

Heads the list partly because of the sheer weight and quality of the Firestone Vineyard production, and partly because of the utterly diffuse nature of the overall Santa Ynez plantings (and the tendency to cross-blend with Santa Maria). It is made in dry, medium sweet and fully sweet versions, the latter two promoted by the ready incidence of botrytis. Austin Cellars, Babcock and Santa Barbara Winery all produce sweet versions; Mosby and Zaca Mesa sell small quantities from cellar door. At its best it shows intense, citrus lime juice aroma and flavor, with balanced acidity.

TOP RIGHT ~ *A carpet of wildflowers welcomes visitors to Zaca Mesa Winery.*

ABOVE ~ *A typical Santa Ynez vista: most of the vineyards are on the valley floor.*

Santa Ynez Valley
1971 and 1991 Acreage/Grape Varieties

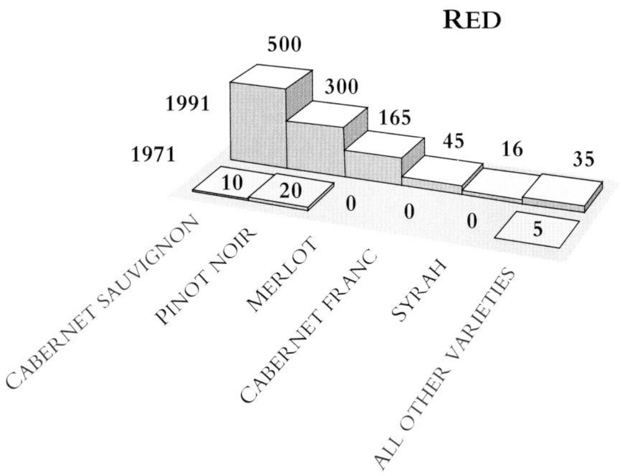
RED
1991
1971
500
300
165
45
16
35
10
20
0
0
0
5
CABERNET SAUVIGNON
PINOT NOIR
MERLOT
CABERNET FRANC
SYRAH
ALL OTHER VARIETIES

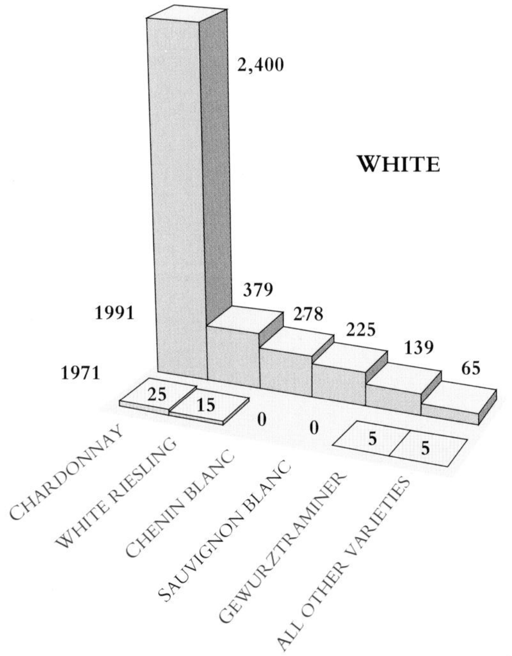
WHITE
1991
1971
2,400
379
278
225
139
65
25
15
0
0
5
5
CHARDONNAY
WHITE RIESLING
CHENIN BLANC
SAUVIGNON BLANC
GEWURZTRAMINER
ALL OTHER VARIETIES

Chardonnay

A variety which does very well at the western end of the valley and not nearly so well in the eastern and northeastern sectors. Babcock Grand Cuvee, Brander and Santa Barbara Winery Reserve are exceptional wines made entirely from Santa Ynez grapes which have the fruit intensity and natural acidity to complement and justify the complex making methods employed. Other top producers, notably Sanford and Zaca Mesa, have hitherto produced Santa Barbara County wines, although presumably Sanford will look to produce a Chardonnay from the Sanford & Benedict Vineyard.

Pinot Noir

The status of the Pinot Noirs made from the Sanford & Benedict Vineyard is beyond question. The marketing initiative of Richard Sanford (explained in the Sanford Winery entry on page 364) can only enhance that reputation, and also bring into clear focus how much Pinot Noir is shaped by the *terroir* and how much by the hand of the maker.

Sauvignon Blanc, Semillon and White Meritage

While Babcock may struggle to ripen its Semillon, there are no problems with this — or Sauvignon Blanc — in the vineyards east of Highway 101, and some complex, rich and mouthfilling wines are made. Brander, Gainey and Sanford do best.

Cabernet Family and Red Meritage

With one or two qualified exceptions, Cabernet Sauvignon has failed in the district — a view shared virtually unanimously by the makers themselves. On the other side of the coin, they are particularly impressed with the potential of Cabernet Franc and Merlot. Whether the American public can be convinced that a wine made in the image of Chinon (in the Loire Valley) is acceptable remains to be seen. Bright cherry fruit, a whisker of fresh herbs and grasses, medium body and low tannins combine to make a lovely wine, but a light year away from the style of the Napa Valley — which provides the reference point for most consumers and critics.

Syrah, Viognier and Italian Varieties

With the exception of Zaca Mesa's Petite Sirah and a few dribs and drabs of Sangiovese and Nebbiolo from Mosby Vineyards, pretty much the stuff of dreams, but with Firestone and Gainey adding substance to those dreams. Finally, as a quixotic gesture, I have thrown in Viognier: I have the feeling in my bones that parts of Santa Ynez may be ideally suited to this variety, which needs a certain degree of warmth, yet not too much.

ABOVE ~ *Training young vines is a fiddly, time-consuming task.*

ABOVE ~ *One of the three great Santa Barbara county vineyards, owned by Cambria.*

Canopy Management and the Manipulation of Microclimate

The contrast between the average California vineyard of the 1970s and that of the average French vineyard of the same era (and in the case of France, for 100 years before that) could not have been greater. Curiously, it gave both sides cause for self-congratulation, and — at least in California — did not cause any concern. California had the sun and it had the soil; it also had a tradition of row crop farming dedicated to making everything grow bigger, and the irrigation water necessary to achieve that aim.

So from the Central Valley to the Napa Valley to Sonoma, vines were planted at a density of around 500 to the acre, and encouraged to grow and grow and grow. This produced vines with a prodigious canopy, trunks as thick as an elephant's leg, and variable-sized crops of grapes which were high in alcohol but not necessarily in flavor or color. In an endeavor to achieve more flavor, some of the quality-conscious growers sought to leave the grapes on the vine for longer, thereby making the massively alcoholic wines which Frank Prial of the *New York Times* proceeded to demolish.

ABOVE ~ *Eutypa, or dead arm disease, affects vines the world over: spraying the freshly pruned vines is the only known defense.*

The real solution lay in common sense, and an understanding of what are the basic mechanisms of the vine's growth. Elsewhere I have briefly touched on the vine's forest origins, and on its primary quest to assure itself of sunlight by reaching the roof of the forest. It is this same mechanism which, in the early to mid part of the season, causes the vine to produce as much growth as it can, hence providing as many photosynthetic units (in other words, leaves) as possible. The formation of grape bunches and the accumulation of sugar in those bunches takes second place in this process.

But as the season advances, as temperatures start to wane, and particularly if and as soil moisture starts to decrease, the vine sends a signal to itself to transfer all of its energy to ripening the crop. The leaves around the bunches show the signs by turning yellow and dropping off. Well before this, active growth in the tips will have ceased, and indeed the canopy will progressively shed its leaves. Unseen, the pips inside the grapes will ripen and harden in readiness for their trip to the earth (via bird droppings).

This, at least, was what nature intended, a plan rudely interrupted by California growers to whom a big, green healthy vine was the best vine. So the water stayed on, or the vine was allowed to grow unchecked in the rich, alluvial soils with ample underground reserves. This meant the vine did not send the right signals to itself; inevitably, sugar accumulated in the grapes, but the physiological changes associated with flavor ripeness did not. Most significantly and importantly, the seeds did not mature, nor did the stems of the bunches lignify.

The second consequence was a massive imbalance between canopy and crop, and a vicious circle of increased growth and decreased crop as the buds for next year's crop were buried deep in the self-shading canopy.

The French, on the other hand, strictly limited the growth of the canopy, turning their diminutive rows into little oblong hedges by repeated trimming of the canopy. This ensured that all of the remaining leaves (and next year's bunches) received precious sunlight, and no less that the vine's energies were directed into ripening the grapes in the second half of the growing season.

The whole thrust of modern New World viticulture is to achieve the same balance as the French, albeit in very different configurations. For to copy precisely French vine spacings, trellis, pruning and canopy control systems is likely to be as counterproductive as the mindless copying of their fermentation methods by so many Napa Valley vignerons in years gone by (and in some instances, in years present).

For the French have typically established their vines on the most meagre soils, fit only for growing mustard or vines. This, certainly, was the case in Bordeaux, Burgundy and Champagne. These are what are technically known as low-potential sites. If, instead of 2,500 vines per acre, the French were to go berserk and copy California with 500 vines to the acre, they would not end up with California-sized vines. Conversely, if you were to plant 2,500 vines on an acre of Napa Valley soil and grow them to a height of three feet, you would need to be either a genius or extremely lucky not to end up with an uncontrollable jungle.

The intelligent approach is to seek to achieve the same balance as the French between the canopy and the crop, but to vary that balance where the climate and *terroir* dictate it. Thus recent research has shown that, depending on the average size of the leaf, around ten leaves are required for each bunch of grapes. The single-wire, California-sprawl canopy often provided five times that number of leaves.

There are two very important flow-on consequences from the reduced canopy: first, it will necessarily promote sunlight interception on the dormant buds formed early in the season and which determine the potential size of next year's crop, and also provide dappled sunlight on the bunches, increasing their color and flavor.

Second, it will decrease the humidity in and around the canopy by improving air movement. The reduction in the incidence of mold and botrytis is dramatic, as is the reduction in the amount of prophylactic sprays required.

It is out of this knowledge that leaf pulling, shoot positioning, vertical trellis and quadrilateral cordon have become terms familiar to virtually every grape grower and winemaker in California over the past five to ten years. Not all have been prepared to embrace these practices, mind you. For one thing, there is an inbuilt conservatism and resistance to change in many vignerons; secondly, canopy management of this kind is much more expensive in terms of labor than the old "let it grow" approach.

Phylloxera is overcoming the first barrier in many places; the second is being overcome by market forces. If the quality of the grapes from vineyard A is demonstrably better than those from vineyard B, both being neighbors and both growing the same varieties, it will not take long for A either to take away B's business or to obtain a significantly higher price for its grapes.

Leaf pulling, or removing the leaves from the area around the grapes, is the least radical of these practices, for it does not involve any alteration to the pre-existing trellis. Since 1989 it has spread like wildfire; with the ready Mexican labor pool, the leaf-plucking machines (some of the best of which were developed in New Zealand) of other parts of the world are less common than one might expect.

Retrofitting trellises is possible, but has severe limitations. It makes sense to introduce the quadrilateral cordon on high-vigor, wide-spaced plantings, but not so much the vertical trellis, which really comes into its own on closer plantings. The quadrilateral cordon involves the installation of a second wire running parallel and at the same height as the existing wire, and instead of leaving the vine with two arms, creating four. This effectively splits the canopy into two, and as many growers have found to their delight, makes it eminently possible to produce greater crops of better quality grapes.

The vertical trellis, ideally using moveable foliage catch wires, forms the canopy into a thin, vertical wall with the grapes at the base of the canopy; if perfectly done, it can eliminate the need for leaf pulling, although trimming the very top of the vine (by machine) may be necessary.

The end result is a significant change in the microclimate, or the canopy climate. It is possible thus significantly to change grape flavors — most obviously to get rid of unwanted grassy or herbal characters — while noticeably reducing the potential for disease. It is thus an integral part of the move towards organic (or sustainable) viticulture, and points the way for the future.

ABOVE ~ *This type of trellis and pruning will soon be a thing of the past.*

TOP ~ *Demonstration trellis systems at Gainey Vineyard: on the left, the Lyre, on the right, Geneva Double Curtain.*

WINERIES *of* SANTA YNEZ VALLEY

AUSTIN CELLARS 1981

A: 9100 Alisos Canyon Road, Los Olivos, CA 93441 **T**: (805) 688 8630 **V**: 11–5 daily at 2923 Grand Avenue, Los Olivos **P**: 12,000 **W**: Tony Austin

AUSTIN CELLARS
1985
SANTA BARBARA COUNTY
SAUVIGNON BLANC
SIERRA MADRE VINEYARDS
PRODUCED AND BOTTLED BY AUSTIN CELLARS LOS OLIVOS, CA :: BW5182 ALCOHOL 13.0% BY VOL.

Tony Austin came to the Santa Ynez Valley in 1975 as the first winemaker for Firestone, staying there until 1980. He left to commence winemaking on his own account in 1981, initially using custom crush facilities elsewhere, but establishing his own winery in 1983. His intention was to rely solely on purchased grapes, but he has since relented and established a vineyard between Los Olivos and Los Alamos, not far from the Nielson Vineyard. He says, quite frankly, that the decision to plant a vineyard was partly political, partly for aesthetics (it is prettier than a garden and produces income), and partly to allow him to grow varieties such as Cabernet Franc, Gewurztraminer and Orange Muscat which he would not be able to buy elsewhere, and which will provide small parcels for sale only through the cellar door.

That cellar door is a very important part of the Austin business. The town of Los Olivos may not have the obvious appeal of nearby Solvang, but it is a very attractive place, and the freshly painted wooden cellar door facility occupied by Austin Cellars likewise. The wines usually on offer are headed by a Chardonnay and Pinot Noir, the latter frequently showing very ripe red berry, mint, hay and straw characters which certainly suggest that Austin likes to pick his Pinot later than most growers. There is also a White Meritage called Cumulus, a blend of around 60% Sauvignon Blanc and 40% Semillon which is on the sharp side, and a variety of Rieslings, the most successful of which is a semi-sweet, botrytised version with attractive, soft apricot aromas and flavors, and which has a major audience at cellar door.

BABCOCK VINEYARDS 1984

A: 5175 Highway 246, Lompoc, CA 93436 **T**: (805) 736 1455 **V**: 10.30–4 Sat–Sun or by appointment **P**: 10,000 **W**: Brian Babcock

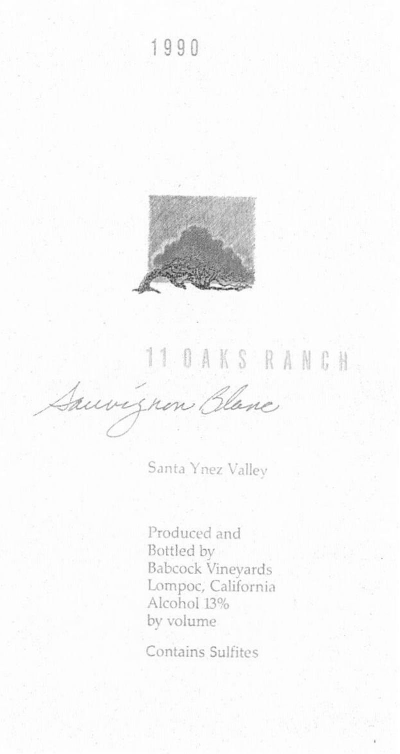
1990
11 OAKS RANCH
Sauvignon Blanc
Santa Ynez Valley
Produced and Bottled by Babcock Vineyards Lompoc, California Alcohol 13% by volume
Contains Sulfites

Walt and Mona Babcock are well-known Orange County restaurateurs, owning and operating Walt's Wharf in Seal Beach, and Oysters in Corona del Mar. Son Brian has taken the complementary course of establishing a vineyard and winery on the family-owned ranch, creating a reputation for both quality and individuality in so doing. The vineyards are situated at the western edge of the Santa Ynez Valley, close to the town of Lompoc, in the coolest part of the small valley. The lighter, sandier soils also contribute to a long growing season and to the retention of natural acidity, pointing the way to the late-maturing varieties Johannisberg Riesling, Gewurztraminer, Pinot Noir and Chardonnay. Babcock is also developing Viognier, Sangiovese and Vernaccia, and supplements the 50 acres of estate vineyards with small purchases from elsewhere in Santa Barbara County.

The wines are released under three labels: under the Babcock Vineyards label are Chardonnay, Chardonnay Grand Cuvee, Estate Pinot Noir, Riesling and Gewurztraminer; under the Eleven Oaks brand is Sauvignon Blanc and, in the pipeline, Sangiovese; while River Break is effectively a second label. Babcock is nothing if not adventurous when coming to make his Riesling and Gewurztraminer, entirely barrel fermenting the latter (in old oak) and partially barrel fermenting the former, and back blending to spatlese-sweetness with unfermented grape juice. The resulting wines are idiosyncratic, and have received high ratings, but to an Australian palate they are decidedly strange (and not terribly pleasant). At the other extreme, as it were, is the magnificently complex Grand Cuvee Chardonnay, driven by complex barrel fermentation oak handling, but supported by the intense fruit and acidity, both of which contribute to a long, classy finish. The Pinot Noir is another good wine, fractionally simple, perhaps, but showing direct varietal fruit flavor and quite certainly with the potential to gain complexity given two or three years' bottle age.

BRANDER VINEYARD 1980

A: 2401 Refugio Road, Los Olivos, CA 93441 **T**: (805) 688 2455 **V**: 10–5 daily **P**: 8,000 **W**: Fred Brander

Fred Brander is, to put it mildly, an interesting character, partly because of his unashamed regard for the wines of Bordeaux, both white and red. Since leaving Santa Ynez Winery to start his own label in 1979, bonding the Brander Vineyard winery in 1980, it is these wines which have most occupied his attention, even though he has achieved conspicuous success with other varieties. The Bordeaux influence is immediately apparent when you look at that part of the 40 acres of estate vineyard closest to the winery: here you will find some of the closest-spaced, lowest-trellised vines in California, for all the world looking like bonsai plants compared to the average California vine-cum-tree. It takes an effort to realize that the spacing and height of the vines is that which you find in the Haut Medoc. Elsewhere in the vineyard, more conventionally spaced and trellised vines are subjected to rigorous shoot thinning, with over 50% of the canopy and crop unceremoniously removed.

Over the years, Brander has caused favorable comment with Blush wines variously made from Cabernet Sauvignon and Cabernet Franc, but these days is content to focus on estate-grown Semillon and Sauvignon Blanc as one flagbearer, and a Red Meritage blend of the Bordeaux varieties as the other. It will no doubt irritate him to find that I thought the Chardonnay to be absolutely outstanding, with spicy barrel-ferment aromas and flavors, and that regional acidity and length to the finish which so distinguishes the variety. The Red Meritage blend varies according to the season, but at its best is very reminiscent of Chinon, with high-toned leafy/tobacco notes and a long, cleansing finish. Some quite superb wines were tasted from barrel, making this a singularly interesting winery, and definitely one to watch.

J CAREY CELLARS 1978

A: 1711 Alamo Pintado Road, Solvang, CA 93463 **T**: (805) 688 8554
V: By appointment **P**: 5,000
W: Alison Green and Ken Barthman

J Carey Cellars was founded by local doctor James Carey, who with his two sons shared the initial J, hence the name. Planting of the vineyards commenced in 1973, with Firestone Cellars the contractor. Firestone kept a proprietary eye on things, and when the property became available for sale in 1986, Firestone promptly acquired it. It did so for two reasons: firstly, it saw its own growth as limited, and J Carey as providing an alternative means to growth; and secondly, because it had long admired the outstanding quality of the grapes coming from the 12-acre La Questa Vineyard, planted to eight and a half acres of Cabernet Sauvignon and three and a half acres of Merlot. The estate in fact covers a total of 46 acres, with two other distinct vineyard blocks; here the plantings are Cabernet Sauvignon and Sauvignon Blanc.

Firestone injected the necessary capital into the operation, and in particular provided the new oak and the storage facilities which J Carey needed, while taking administration, finance and marketing under its own wing. It is the sort of situation which every winemaker dreams of: the resources to make first-class wine, with someone else having to worry about the ugly business of financing and marketing it.

The La Questa Vineyard produces tiny yields (three-quarters of a ton to a maximum of two tons per acre) of small-berried bunches, which produce an exceptionally concentrated and ripe wine, totally free of the vegetative characters which afflict some plantings in the region. New oak adds an extra dimension to what has the potential to become an outstanding wine.

FESS PARKER WINERY 1990

A: 6200 Foxen Canyon Road, Los Olivos, CA 93441 **T**: (805) 686 1130 **V**: 10–4 daily
P: 25,000 **W**: Mark Shannon

Owned by Daniel Boone himself, otherwise known as Fess Parker, this lavish winery (complete with the most luxurious tasting and reception center to be found in the Santa Maria Valley) was begun in 1990, and was still being completed in 1992. It draws upon 31 acres of estate vineyard, complemented by grapes purchased elsewhere through Santa Barbara County, with Chardonnay, Pinot Noir and Riesling leading the roster. Having dutifully made my way to the winery at the appointed hour on the appointed day, no one was in residence, so I am unable to comment on the wines.

FIRESTONE VINEYARD 1974

A: 5017 Zaca Station Road, Los Olivos, CA 93441 **T**: (805) 688 3940 **V**: 10–4 daily
P: 60,000 **W**: Alison Green

Brooks Firestone and English-born wife Kate pioneered the Santa Ynez Valley when they commenced planting 265 acres of vines in 1973, following that almost immediately with the erection of an 80,000-case winery, with André Tchelistcheff as consultant. Inevitably, its early releases were watched with considerable interest; I was sufficiently impressed with the 1976 Pinot Noir and 1978 Ambassador's Vineyard Johannisberg Riesling to import both commercially into Australia at the end of the 1970s. With the wisdom of hindsight, the Pinot Noir was good by the standards of its day, but not on a more permanent yardstick; however, the Ambassador's Riesling remains a glorious wine to this very point in time.

Johannisberg Riesling is still the winery's flagship. Firestone and St. Michel dominate the market in America, with Firestone selling 35,000 cases a year, and unable to keep up with the demand. It led to Firestone purchasing the adjacent vineyard, and to it continuing to buy Riesling from the White Hills Vineyard in Los Alamos. Whether produced dry or with botrytis-influenced residual sugar, the Rieslings are consistently excellent. They are very well made, with smoky, complex, tangy, spicy and crisp aromas and flavors. However, if the vigor in the vineyards could be better controlled, and the crop loads reduced, the wines might be better still. Cabernet Sauvignon and Merlot have been consistently disappointing, always showing very marked vegetative, tobacco, woody characters. As leaf roll virus takes control in the vineyard, Cabernet Sauvignon is being progressively removed, and is being replanted with Syrah and Freedom, an odd couple if ever there was one.

The Gewurztraminer is clean, direct and again very competently made, even if it too shows some dilution of fruit flavor, again, I suspect, coming from the vineyard. The Chardonnay and Sauvignon Blanc are altogether less convincing.

GAINEY VINEYARD 1984

A: 3950 East Highway 246, Santa Ynez, CA 93460 **T**: (805) 688 0558 **V**: 10–5 daily
P: 15,000 **W**: Rick Longoria

The Gainey Vineyard is but part of a much larger, 1,800-acre ranch which incorporates a horse stud and various other crops and farm animals. It is situated towards the eastern end of the Santa Ynez Valley, three miles east of Solvang with a heat summation which regularly takes the 54 acres of vineyard into high Region II. Winemaker Rick Longoria came from J Carey Cellars in the mid 1980s, and knows the region very well; he also presides over a splendidly equipped winery situated in extremely handsome, landscaped surrounds. But he is ultimately a pragmatist: only 8% of the Gainey Chardonnay comes from estate-grown grapes; the rest of the estate production of Chardonnay is sold, and grapes of the same variety are purchased from elsewhere in Santa Barbara County. Gainey, too, is one of the chosen few to receive a precious three tons of Pinot Noir from the Sanford & Benedict Vineyard, although this particular wine will be all but unprocurable outside of the mixed cases (see the Sanford & Benedict entry).

Gainey

The most successful wines for Gainey are the Johannisberg Riesling, Chardonnay (with high-toned, topical fruit), and the Sauvignon Blanc, with unusual lime citrus aromas, almost Riesling-like, but with length and intensity in its normal guise, and bigger, richer and fatter under the Reserve label. Cabernet Sauvignon disappoints, showing the distinctively stemmy, woody characters which seem to bob up all over the place in Santa Ynez, and even in warmer parts such as Gainey. On the other hand, Cabernet Franc and Merlot both show much promise, and in particular Cabernet Franc. And with over 1,000 acres of ranchland, Gainey has planted one-third of an acre each of Shiraz, Mourvedre and Grenache, preparing, says Rick Longoria, for the day when the world tires of Cabernet Sauvignon.

ABOVE ~ *The tradition of branded corks began as a means of combating fraud in France.*

MOSBY WINERY AT VEGA VINEYARDS 1979

A: 9496 Santa Rosa Road, Buellton, CA 93427 **T**: (805) 688 2415 **V**: 10–4 daily
P: 7,000 **W**: Michael Brown

The long title reflects the transition from Vega Vineyards, as the winery was originally known, to Mosby, but does not reflect a change of ownership: Bill Mosby has been in control right from the outset, having been a home winemaker since he was 17, and entering serious winemaking way back in 1959. The estate vineyards, divided into two distinct parcels, comprise 34 acres planted to Gewurztraminer, Chardonnay and Pinot Noir; the Riesling has been progressively grafted over, and there is now only one acre left. Bill Mosby says that the wine is fine; it is simply that no one wishes to buy it. In its place come Nebbiolo, Sangiovese Grosso (marketed under a Brunello label, approved by the BATF), Pinot Grigio (from 1992) and Zinfandel labeled as Primitivo. In all, two-thirds of the production comes from estate-grown grapes, the balance being purchased from within Santa Barbara County. The Primitivo Zinfandel is made in an extremely ripe, jammy style which others may enjoy more than I do; the Chardonnay is clean, smooth and pleasant, albeit without the distinction and intensity of the best wines of the region. The Pinot Noir has lots of funky, gamey barnyard characters as it develops in bottle, and is probably best drunk young while some of the fresh fruit is there to balance the barnyard.

SANFORD WINERY 1981

A: 7250 Santa Rosa Road, Buellton, CA 93427 **T**: (805) 688 3300 **V**: 11–4 daily
P: 30,000 **W**: Richard Sanford and Bruno D'Alfonso

Richard Sanford took a degree in geography from U.C. Berkeley, and when he became interested in the possibility of establishing a vineyard and making wine in the late 1960s and early 1970s, he was well placed to undertake the climatological and geographic studies which ultimately led him, with then partner Mike Benedict, to establish the 112-acre Sanford & Benedict Vineyard at the eastern end of the Santa Ynez Valley near Lompoc.

SANFORD
ELEGANT CLARKIA
Pinot Noir
SANTA BARBARA COUNTY
PRODUCED AND BOTTLED BY SANFORD WINERY
BUELLTON, CALIFORNIA, U.S.A. ALC. 13.5% BY VOL.

In 1976 the partners converted an old barn on the vineyard property and commenced winemaking, quickly establishing a reputation for high quality Pinot Noir and Chardonnay. However, tensions developed, and in 1980 the partnership was dissolved, Sanford leaving and establishing his own brand, initially made (1981 and 1982) at the Edna Valley Winery, but from 1983 in a warehouse facility at Buellton. The cellar doors and administration facilities are now established on a 738-acre property known as Rancho El Jabali, where Sanford is in the course of establishing his own vineyards. An adobe brick winery was planned for construction in 1992/93.

The very substantial Sanford production was based around Sauvignon Blanc (purchased from the Sierra Madre Vineyard), Pinot Noir (also from the Sierra Madre Vineyard, supplemented by a small amount purchased from Bien Nacido), and Chardonnay — both regular and Barrel Select — obtained from numerous different vineyards, including Paragon/Edna Valley, Bien Nacido, Sierra Madre, Cottonwood Canyon and Santa Maria Hills.

In 1990 there was a dramatic change: the vineyard which Sanford & Benedict had established way back in 1972, and which had in the meantime become known as the Benedict Vineyard, was sold to Robert and Janice Atkins of London, who in turn appointed Richard Sanford as vineyard manager; it was briefly renamed Talinda Oaks Ranch before reverting to its original name of Sanford & Benedict.

When Richard Sanford indicated he wished to use all of the production of the vineyard for the Sanford label, all hell broke loose. Partly through the intervention of highly respected Los Angeles wine writer Dan Berger, Sanford relented and hit upon one of the most enterprising marketing (and for that matter, winemaking) enterprises I have ever encountered. It is called the Signature Group, and each of Au Bon Climat, Babcock, Foxen, Gainey and Lane Tanner will receive three tons of Pinot Noir from the Sanford & Benedict Vineyard each year. Each will then provide a barrel of the wine to Sanford, who will add a barrel of his own. Half of the six barrels will be blended, and comprise six bottles in a mixed case. The remaining bottles will be the individual winery Pinots under each winery's label. The first cases (from the 1991 vintage) are due for release in mid 1993; most will be sold around the country at wine auctions, the remainder direct ex-winery.

The Sanford wines are reliably good, rich and full flavored. The Sauvignon Blanc is crammed with rich gooseberry and herbal fruit; the Chardonnays (particularly the Barrel Select) oaky but very complex, with strong supporting fruit; and the Pinot Noirs best of all. The Barrel Select shows greater charred oak impact, allied with complex plum and dark cherry fruit in a moderately (but not excessively) ripe mold, the regular bottling being very clean, leaner and spicier, with an attractive sappy cut. I await with interest the results of the reunion of Sanford with his old vineyard.

SANTA BARBARA WINERY 1962

A: 202 Anacapa Street, Santa Barbara, CA 93101 **T**: (805) 963 3633 **V**: 10–5 daily
P: 30,000 **W**: Bruce McGuire

1990
SANTA BARBARA WINERY
Santa Barbara County
Chardonnay
ALCOHOL 13.3% BY VOLUME
PRODUCED AND BOTTLED BY SANTA BARBARA WINERY
202 ANACAPA, SANTA BARBARA, CALIFORNIA, USA BW4490

When local architect Pierre Lafond took the decision to establish Santa Barbara Winery way back in 1962, it signalled the first winemaking to be carried out in the county since Prohibition. The winery itself is established in downtown Santa Barbara, only two blocks from the beach, and it was Lafond's intention to capitalize on the local tourist and cellar door trade. But by 1970 he had become convinced of the potential of the region for grape growing, and purchased 105 acres of land in the lower Santa Ynez Valley, six miles west of Buellton. In 1972, planting of 72 acres of Chardonnay, Sauvignon Blanc, Chenin Blanc, White Riesling, Zinfandel, Pinot Noir and Cabernet Sauvignon commenced. The estate production is supplemented by purchases made throughout Santa Barbara County.

Lanky Bruce McGuire became winemaker in 1981, and — while keeping cellar door specials such as Beaujour (a light, Beaujolais-style Zinfandel), Dry Chenin Blanc, White Zinfandel and Parodies (a dry White Riesling) together with a selection of late harvest wines including Zinfandel Essence on the roster — has also produced absolutely first-class Chardonnay and Pinot Noir, soaring to heights under the Reserve label. A very useful Reserve Cabernet Sauvignon from the Lafond Vineyard also flies in the face of conventional wisdom: while herbaceous and stemmy, it does have concentrated fruit to provide relief. But, as I say, it is the Reserve Chardonnay and Reserve

PREMIUM ORGANIC PRODUCE
Naturfarm
THROUGH NATURE FARMING

Pinot Noir which are worth killing for. Only 420 cases of the 1990 Reserve Pinot Noir were made, and only 1,200 cases of the Reserve Chardonnay, so the wines will not be easy to find. The Chardonnay is extremely complex, with buttery grilled hazelnut flavors, and has had the usual Reserve treatment: barrel fermentation, ten months on lees, full malolactic and 50% new wood, all of which has been swallowed up by the voluptuous fruit. The intensely complex, power-packed Pinot Noir achieves the near impossible: great intensity and strength while retaining varietal purity, and is eerily like a first-class Burgundy early in its life. If you must cellar Pinot Noir, this is the wine for you.

ZACA MESA WINERY 1972

A: 6905 Foxen Canyon Road, Los Olivos, CA 93441 **T**: (805) 688 9339 **V**: 10–4 daily **P**: 30,000 **W**: Gale Sysock

Zaca Mesa is Santa Ynez's answer to Falcon Crest. It was founded in the early 1970s by oil executive Louis Ream, who at one stage had 340 acres of vineyards under his control. With Ken Brown as chief winemaker, and a passing parade of Santa Barbara identities (including Jim Clendenen, Adam Tolmach and Bob Lindquist) as assistant winemakers, production rose to 100,000 cases by the early 1980s. Ream sold out in 1986, and a period of turmoil and reorganization followed, with production decreasing sharply, and with the estate vineyards reduced to 212 acres. The once wide range of wines produced by the winery was also slimmed down, with the focus now being on Chardonnay, Pinot Noir, Syrah and Riesling (the latter sold only at cellar door). When proprietor John Cushman became one of the owners of Sierra Madre Vineyard, Zaca Mesa commenced to source its Chardonnay and Pinot Noir from that vineyard, and quality improved sharply. Like other operations in the district, it thus finds itself in the position of being both grape seller and grape purchaser, understandable given its Region II climate at the inland tip of the Santa Ynez Valley.

The Chardonnays made by Gale Sysock are of the highest quality, with a wholly Burgundian and ultra-stylish aroma developing with bottle age. In their youth the wines show hallmark citric grapefruit/melon flavors, with all of the length, mouthfeel and style one expects from grapes grown on the Sierra Madre Vineyard. The Pinot Noir, too, is intense and lively, with a long, lingering finish and great style. If there is a criticism, it is that the stemmy characters are just a little bit obvious, but I would rather have it that way than the other. Zaca Mesa also has the oldest Syrah planting in the county, which produced its first wine back in 1983. The wine is fresh and spicy, with good varietal character, although not in the same street as that of Qupe.

OTHER WINERIES

BUTTONWOOD FARM WINERY 1989
A: P.O. Box 849, Santa Ynez, CA 93460
T: (805) 688 6160 **W**: Mike Brown

CARRARI VINEYARDS 1985
A: Santa Rosa Road, Buellton, CA 93427
T: (805) 344 4000 **W**: Joe Carrari

HOUTZ VINEYARDS 1984
A: P.O. Box 542, 2670 Ontiveros Road, Los Olivos, CA 93441 **T**: (805) 688 8664
W: David E. Houtz

SANTA YNEZ WINERY 1975
A: 343 N. Refugio Road, Santa Ynez, CA 93460
T: (805) 688 8381 **W**: Mike Blom

STEARNS WHARF VINTNERS
A: 217 Stearns Wharf, Santa Barbara, CA 93101
T: (805) 966 6624

ABOVE ~ *Certified organic farming of all types of crops is the way of the future.*

THE SOUTH

As the coast turns sharply east at Point Conception, the cold Alaskan current gives way to the body of warm water making its way north from Mexico. The marine influence still makes its presence felt in the counties in which wine grapes are grown: Ventura, San Bernardino, Riverside, Los Angeles and San Diego, but all of the regions have far warmer climates than those of Santa Barbara County.

Ventura County, with less than ten acres of vineyards all told, would not even rate a mention were it not for the presence of Adam and Helen Tolmach's Ojai Winery and its attached five-and-a-half-acre vineyard (the remaining four acres are Chardonnay planted by Leeward). Indeed, the Ojai labels are an exercise in regional self-effacement, featuring variety and vineyard designation (most of its grapes in fact come from elsewhere) and downplaying Ventura which, says Tolmach, no one has ever heard of (I think he means viticulturally.) The Ojai Valley in fact has a very useful climate, but urban pressure will almost certainly prevent the development of a meaningful viticultural presence in Ventura.

The South
1971 AND 1991 ACREAGE/GRAPE VARIETIES

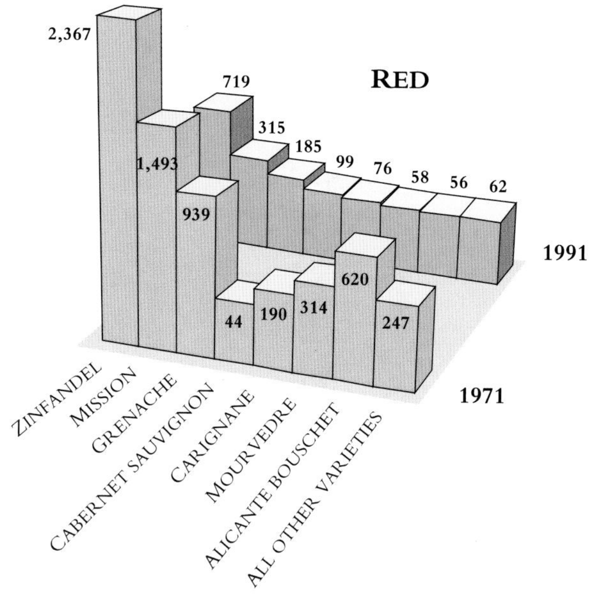
2,367
719
RED
315
185
99
76
58
56
62
1,493
939
1991
620
44
190
314
247
1971
ZINFANDEL
MISSION
GRENACHE
CABERNET SAUVIGNON
CARIGNANE
MOURVEDRE
ALICANTE BOUSCHET
ALL OTHER VARIETIES

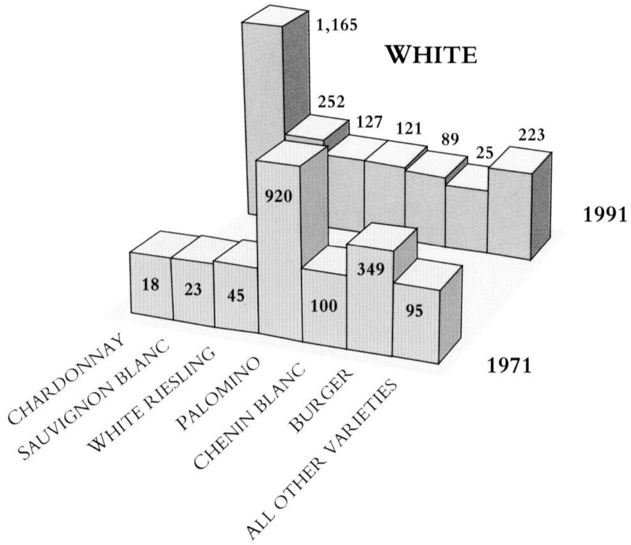
1,165
WHITE
252
127
121
89
25
223
920
1991
18
23
45
349
100
95
1971
CHARDONNAY
SAUVIGNON BLANC
WHITE RIESLING
PALOMINO
CHENIN BLANC
BURGER
ALL OTHER VARIETIES

ABOVE ~ *The acreage of Riesling vines in this area has increased in the past 20 years.*

Los Angeles County still maintains a precarious toe hold in the statistical register; as I relate on pages 370–1, it was not only the birthplace of California wine, but had a hugely successful nineteenth-century industry and still boasted 49 wineries and 5,000 acres of vineyards at the start of the Second World War. Its two utterly different but vibrant producers are San Antonio (a winery without a vineyard) and Moraga (a vineyard without a winery), with a third (Donatoni) about to move to Paso Robles.

San Bernardino County and northern Riverside County, likewise, flourished both in the last century and in this, with activities centered around Cucamonga and Mira Loma. As recently as 1966, there were almost 20,000 acres of vines; now there are less than 1,000 acres, and I suspect there will be none left by the end of the decade. The J. Filippi Winery is the only active winery, but unlike Los Angeles' San Antonio Winery has failed to move with the times.

Orange County has no vineyards now, but soared briefly to prominence between 1869 and 1883 when the Anaheim district became one of the leading producers in California before succumbing overnight to the deadly onslaught of Anaheim Disease.

San Diego County has bravely established an AVA, San Pasqual, which was proclaimed on September 16, 1991. The San Pasqual Valley lies ten to 15 miles inland from the coast, and boasts 75 acres of vines growing in a high Region III climate — but no winery.

The unifying features of all these counties (excepting Ventura) are a climate and a winemaking heritage which inevitably led to the production of fortified wines made from second-rate varieties. Thus San Bernardino still ranks with the San Joaquin Valley as the leading grower of the Mission grape in California, with (allegedly) 315 acres, or 25% of the state total. Its only other grape of consequence is Zinfandel (620 acres), which has always produced wines with a distinctly cheesy taste, according to Leon Adams. The imminent demise of Cucamonga should thus come as no surprise.

This listing leaves aside southern Riverside County and the one serious — and new — AVA of Temecula, which I deal with separately, commencing on page 375.

PREVIOUS PAGE ~ *The gentle slopes of the Temecula Valley from Baily Winery.*

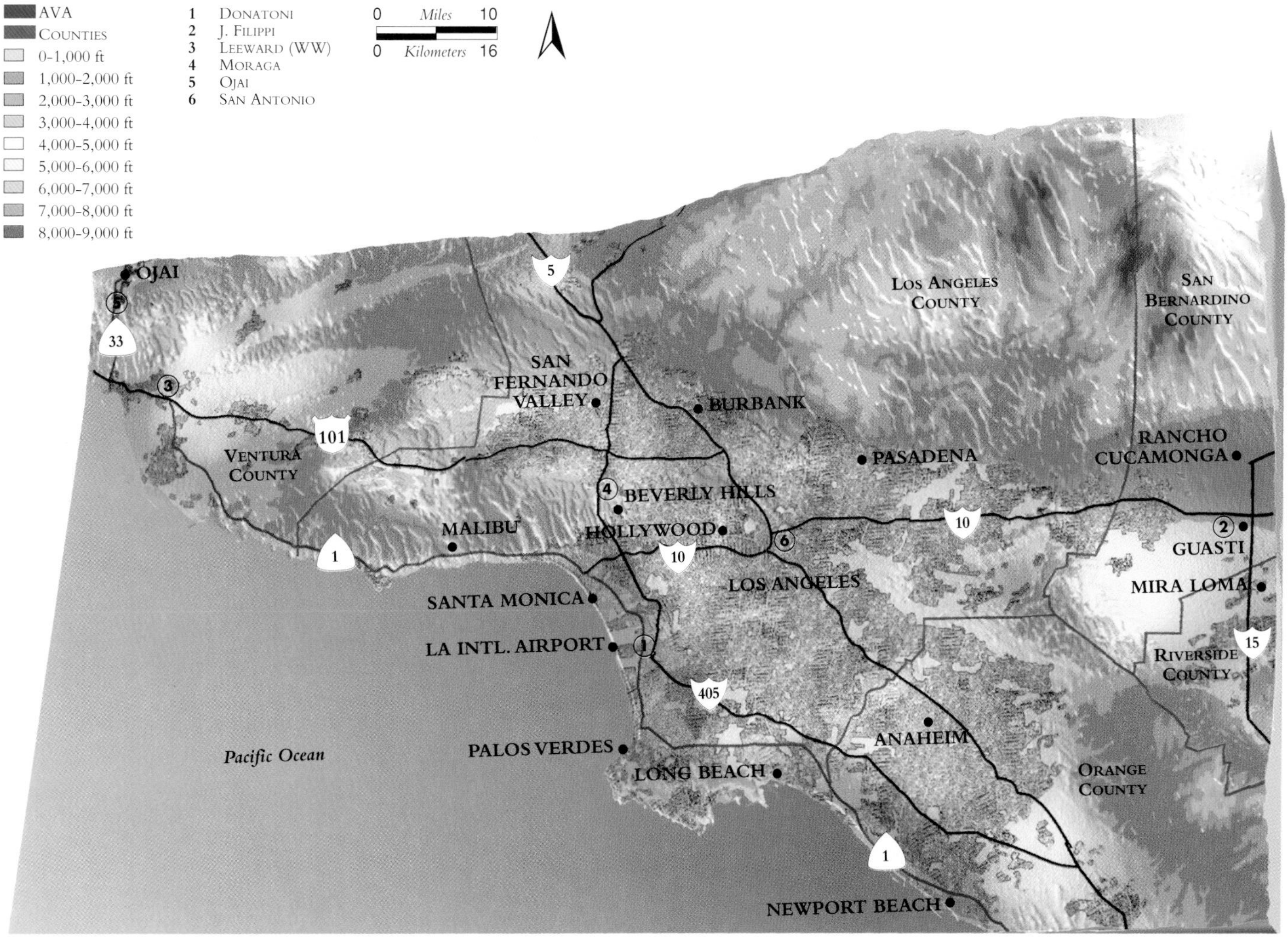

AVA
Counties
0-1,000 ft
1,000-2,000 ft
2,000-3,000 ft
3,000-4,000 ft
4,000-5,000 ft
5,000-6,000 ft
6,000-7,000 ft
7,000-8,000 ft
8,000-9,000 ft
1 Donatoni
2 J. Filippi
3 Leeward (WW)
4 Moraga
5 Ojai
6 San Antonio
0 Miles 10
0 Kilometers 16
OJAI
LOS ANGELES COUNTY
SAN BERNARDINO COUNTY
SAN FERNANDO VALLEY
BURBANK
VENTURA COUNTY
PASADENA
RANCHO CUCAMONGA
BEVERLY HILLS
HOLLYWOOD
MALIBU
GUASTI
LOS ANGELES
MIRA LOMA
SANTA MONICA
LA INTL. AIRPORT
RIVERSIDE COUNTY
Pacific Ocean
PALOS VERDES
LONG BEACH
ANAHEIM
ORANGE COUNTY
NEWPORT BEACH

ABOVE ~ *Zinfandel vines at Keyways Vineyard and Winery, Temecula.*
TOP ~ *The South map.*

Los Angeles: Birthplace *of* California Wine

If one excludes the grape-growing and wine-making carried out at the missions established by the Spanish, the birthplace of California wine is to be found buried under the railroad tracks, freeways and warehouses of downtown Los Angeles. The only clues come from the street names: Vignes, Aliso, Keller, Bouchet and Kohler Streets all recall pioneer vignerons. The original intensive vineyard area ran principally along the west (or city) side of the Los Angeles River, from Macy Street in the north to Washington Street in the south, from Los Angeles Street in the west to Boyle Heights in the east.

ABOVE ~ *In the small courtyard of San Antonio Winery, downtown Los Angeles.*

The eponymous Jean Louis Vignes is generally regarded as the founder of California viticulture. A native of the Graves region of Bordeaux, Vignes' family owned a cooperage. He suddenly left his wife and family at the age of 47, emigrating first to Hawaii in 1826, where his skills were of little consequence, and arriving in Los Angeles in 1832 or 1833.

He was somehow able to buy 100 acres of land by the Los Angeles River in the heart of what became the Los Angeles vineyard area, and which is shown in great detail on the earliest map of Los Angeles after the American annexation, dated 1849 and held in the Huntington Library. In 1833 he also arranged for the importation of French grape varieties, apparently realizing the shortcomings of the ubiquitous Mission grape. His business prospered mightily, and when he sold it in 1855 to his nephews, the Sainsevans (who had joined him from France) for $42,000, it was recorded as one of the largest commercial transactions Los Angeles had ever seen.

If Vignes was the father of California viticulture, two classical musicians, Charles Kohler and John Frohling, were the fathers of its commercial success, establishing the first national distribution in the years following their initial vintage in 1854. By 1869 they had exclusive agencies in Boston and New York, and were producing over 50,000 cases a year. Contemporary accounts of their winemaking practices are very interesting: the strong emphasis on hygiene must have been critical in helping establish the high reputation for quality which the firm enjoyed.

By the late 1850s, however, Anaheim (20 miles to the south of Los Angeles) had begun its meteoric rise. By 1883, 50 wineries were producing more than a million gallons a year from 10,000 acres of grapes. The end came even more suddenly: what is now known as Pierce's Disease (a bacterial disease spread by insects called Sharpshooters) — but was then called Anaheim's Disease — wiped out the vineyards within two years. The cost was calculated by the official government report to be ten million dollars, a comparable sum to the 500 million dollars estimate of the cost of the 1990s phylloxera epidemic.

The San Gabriel Valley, to the east of Los Angeles, had begun an equally spectacular rise (and fall) a few years earlier. Here the key players were Benjamin Wilson and his son-in-law, J. de Barth Shorb. Using the base of the Lake Vineyard which Wilson had established in the early 1850s, Shorb built a substantial wine business under the name of B.D. Wilson & Co, and by 1875 was claiming, "We are the largest wine manufacturers on the Pacific Coast," making 150,000 gallons of wine and 116,000 gallons of brandy a year.

Despite Shorb's formidable energy and persistent attempts to create lasting national and international markets, technical problems (deterioration during shipment and storage) and untrustworthy agents conspired to keep down profits, and the business branched into a range of other activities (including real estate development) to support the winery.

Seemingly not the least bit fazed by his vinous problems, Shorb floated the San Gabriel Wine Company in 1882 with $500,000 raised primarily from English investors, but with wealthy Californians also participating. At the town of Alhambra he proceeded to build what was described as "the largest winery in the world," consisting of two massive brick buildings with a fermenting capacity of one million gallons and a storage capacity of a further one and a quarter million gallons.

The irony was that much of the impetus for the investment came from a belief that phylloxera would devastate the European (and in particular the French) industry for decades to come. Not only did that belief prove unfounded, but Pierce's Disease was to come to the San Gabriel Valley — without, it is true, causing the end of viticulture as it did in Anaheim, but causing substantial damage. At the end of the day, it was not Pierce's Disease, but on-going technical problems with the quality of the wine (remedied in part by the addition of cherry juice!) and the lack of the imagined European markets which led to the liquidation of the company following Shorb's death, and to the disappearance without trace of the winery and vineyards.

The other, and more enduring, focus of viticulture was in San Bernardino County, further east. In 1839 the Cucamonga Rancho was granted to Tiburcio Tapia, and he planted vines and established a winery which in 1917 became known as the Thomas Winery, and which is now owned by J. Filippi & Sons, serving as their principal cellar door sales area.

Not far to the north on Eighth Street, Cucamonga, is Bonded Winery No. 1, the 2.5 million gallon winery which, in the years before the Second World War, was southern California's largest and most famous. Under the ownership and direction of James "Padre Jim" Vai, it made sparkling wine (from Cucamonga Burger grapes) and port in vast quantities. Its fortunes declined after Vai's death in 1961 — no doubt as the market became more sophisticated — and was purchased by Pierre Biane in 1976. Despite his plans to revive it, by 1992 it had become a polyglot warehouse facility, with an adjacent vinegar factory the only remotely vinous activity.

The other pioneer vigneron was Secondo Guasti, who in 1900 established the very large Italian Vineyard Company and the Guasti Winery. By 1917 it had 4,000 acres under vine and was advertised as "the largest vineyard in the world."

The amazing Captain Paul Garrett, who had created the Virginia Dare brand in North Carolina (using the infamous Scuppernong grape) around the turn of the century, and who had moved his winery from North Carolina, first to Virginia and then to New York State to evade the spreading tentacles of Prohibition, came to Cucamonga in 1911. He acquired 2,000 acres, and helped Cucamonga reach 20,000 acres at the onset of Prohibition, twice the size of the Napa Valley, and more than Sonoma. Prohibition did not harm Cucamonga much. It initially engaged in a vigorous trade in fresh grapes to home winemakers and bootleggers across the country. Then, super salesman that he was, Garrett added beef extract, pepsin and iron to create Virginia Dare Wine Tonic.

In the meantime, Guasti made Sacramental and Kosher wines. In 1929 Garrett and Dare joined forces to make and market "Vine Glo Grape Concentrate," providing much of the nation's home winemakers' supply during the latter Prohibition days.

But the end was in sight. The Kaiser Steel plant was built in the vineyards near Fontana in 1942; the Air Force base became the Ontario International Airport; the Ontario Speedway was built, and, most insidiously, the urban creep began. Remarkably, indeed, there were still 19,460 acres of vines in San Bernardino County in 1966; by 1977 this had shrunk to 9,658 acres; and as at 1991 there were 1,205 acres on paper (according to the California Agricultural Statistics Service 1992), a figure suspiciously unchanged since 1982. Driving up and down the Cucamonga district in 1992, as I did, searching for vineyards and wineries, was a largely unrewarding experience. Certain it is that a significant part of the 1,100 acres (if they really exist) have been abandoned, and simply await the arrival of the developer's bulldozers. Only the Filippi Winery remains conspicuous by its presence, providing a precious link with the past.

One is tempted to conjecture whether viticulture would still be flourishing had Los Angeles been located 100 miles to the north or south. In a sense it is a Catch 22 question: viticulture began and winemaking flourished precisely because it had a thirsty market on its doorstep. But its climate also suited the style of wine the market demanded. That demand was shaped in part by pragmatism and in part by taste preference, both factors favouring the production of fortified wine.

It hardly needs be said that the market share of fortified wine has shrunk dramatically since the Second World War, and is continuing to decline. The Central Valley provides all (and more) than is necessary to meet demand. So urban pressure, and the Los Angeles smog, can be convenient whipping boys, but the truth is that viticulture would have given way to orange trees (or other horticulture) in any event.

TOP RIGHT ~ *Taped fingers and a razor-sharp cutting knife mean fast picking.*

ABOVE ~ *The augur screw of the grape receival bin feeds Sauvignon Blanc into the crusher.*

WINERIES *of* THE SOUTH

DONATONI WINERY 1979

A: 10604 S. La Cienega Boulevard, Inglewood, CA 90304 **T**: (213) 645 5445
V: By appointment **P**: 1,200
W: Hank Donatoni

Until 1991, Donatoni was one of three wineries operating out of warehouse facilities adjacent to the Los Angeles international airport. When United Airlines pilot Hank Donatoni retires in 1993, there will be no wineries left. However, that is the bad news; the good news is that Hank Donatoni has every intention of continuing winemaking, but will move to Paso Robles to live and to re-establish; it is from Paso Robles that he sources his Cabernet Sauvignon.

Contrary to what one might expect, the location of the existing winery has nothing at all to do with Donatoni's profession. The site of the airport in which the warehouse is situated is just outside the Los Angeles city limits and is thus free of the planning ordinances which would otherwise prevent the making of wine. Donatoni moved there after a ten year career as an amateur winemaker, prompted by the fact that the house he purchased in 1968 had a few vines in the back garden. Armed with a home winemaking book, he made his first vintage in 1969, and was encouraged by John Daume of the Daume Winery to make the transition to professional winemaking in 1979. In one of those extraordinary stories, 70% of the production goes to a single hotel in Hawaii: it had an Italian restaurant, which the sommelier suggested be renamed Donatoni. Hank's permission was sought as a matter of courtesy, and the upshot was that Donatoni has become the surrogate house wine.

The focus is on Cabernet Sauvignon, with lesser quantities of Chardonnay (from Monterey grapes), and Sauvignon Blanc added in 1991. The range of Cabernets made over the past decade show a consistent winemaking style, in which oak is held in restraint, the grapes are picked ripe, and the maximum fruit and tannin are extracted. They reminded me very strongly of older style Barossa Valley Cabernets from Australia, warm and generous, but not the least bit sophisticated.

J. FILIPPI VINTAGE COMPANY 1934

A: 11211 Etiwand Avenue, Fontana, CA 92335 **T**: (714) 428 8630 **V**: 9–6 daily
P: Not known **W**: Joseph P. Filippi

With the demise of the Biane operations at the Brookside Winery, Filippi stands alone in holding back the inexorable creep of urbanization. It is still a substantial, if old-style business, operating not only out of the Thomas Cellars, claimed to be the oldest winery building in the state and dating back to 1839, but from other tasting and retail outlets spread through southern California. It owns 20 acres of vineyard in the Cucamonga Region, and leases a further 300 acres, crushing principally Grenache and Mission grapes which go to make a range of generic wines (Burgundy, Chablis and so forth), and also fortified wines. The "premium" varietals come from the San Joaquin Valley, and are released under the Chateau Filippi label.

MORAGA 1989

A: 650 Sepulveda Boulevard, Los Angeles CA 90031 **T**: (310) 471 8560
V: By appointment **P**: 650 **W**: Tony Soter

Tom Jones, who does not sing, but who had an outstanding career as an aeronautical engineer and ended up as head of Northrop Aviation (and helped develop the B2 Stealth Bomber), has created one of the most remarkable vineyards in the world. It is improbable in every way: it sits on 15 acres of land which, until Jones successfully had it re-zoned, was worth many more millions of dollars. It is situated in the ultra-fashionable Los Angeles bedroom suburb of Bel Air, rivaling Beverly Hills for chic. It is half an hour's drive from the center of Los Angeles, and yet it is set in a wild and craggy canyon, still inhabited by golden eagles and red-tailed hawks. And when I say craggy, I mean craggy: part of the vineyards are established on slopes as steep as the steepest face of the Bernkasteler Doktor in the Rhinegau or the steepest Swiss vineyard. Tom Jones explains that his vineyard manager Roberto Quintana comes from a hilly part of Mexico, and thinks nothing of the 1:2 slopes.

If the vineyard is remarkable, so is Tom Jones. Instead of the brash Los Angeles millionaire, there is a quiet, self-effacing man who is as deeply committed to the conservation movement as he is to his beloved vineyard. He acquired the property in 1959 from the estate of Victor Flemming, the movie director who produced such all-time classics as *Gone With the Wind* and *The Wizard of Oz*. The house had been unoccupied for three years, and the grounds had become completely overgrown, the whole canyon a wilderness.

In the ensuing years, Jones has been instrumental in ensuring that not only his property, but also the remainder of the canyon, cannot be further subdivided or developed.

Yet while he had always been an avid wine drinker, with a fabulous collection of Bordeaux and Burgundies stretching back to the 1940s, it was not until he and wife Ruth made one of their visits to France that they noted the similarity in the soil, which is an old upthrust marine seabed, rich in shale and calcareous fossils. So they commenced an experimental vineyard in 1978, consisting of a few vines of eight different varieties, thereafter extending the plantings to half an acre each of Chardonnay and Sauvignon Blanc. The quality of the grapes in 1982 was sufficiently encouraging for the Joneses to start planning a commercial-sized vineyard, only to find that the vines had been attacked by Pierce's Disease, necessitating the removal of all of the vines, ground fumigation and a new start.

Over the ensuing years six acres of densely planted vineyard (at up to 1,600 vines to the acre on a 4x6 spacing) also signalled a change of direction to Cabernet Sauvignon (80%), Cabernet Franc (15%) and Merlot (5%). Since 1989 Tony Soter has been consultant winemaker (that and the experimental early vintages, and also the subsequent vintages were physically made at the Sanford Winery), and New Zealand-based Danny Schuster has become viticultural consultant. Schuster's other principal consultancy is to Stag's Leap Wine Cellars.

The Region III climate is very soft: there are only 20 days of heavy frost a year, and the diurnal temperature range is modest, often as little as 20°F. This equable climate reflects itself in the wine: the 1989 Moraga is wonderfully silky in structure, with briary aromas, and no one fruit character predominating. The oak has been beautifully handled and woven into the wine, and the tannins are adequate but soft. Inevitably the Moraga wines will be expensive (selling for something around $40 to $50 a bottle), and will be available only by mailing list and through three selected Los Angeles restaurants.

The first vintage to be released — the 1989 — produced 400 six-bottle cases; 1990 produced 600 cases; and 1991 about three times that amount — about, because rigorous selection is practiced every year, and any substandard barrels are discarded.

THE OJAI VINEYARD 1984

A: 10540 Encino, Oak View, CA 93022
T: (805) 649 1674 **V**: By appointment
P: 3,000 **W**: Adam Tolmach

QUPE
19
87

Adam and Helen Tolmach, for long part of Au Bon Climat, always had their own venture in the form of the Ventura County Ojai Vineyard. Since the dissolution of the partnership with Jim Clendenen of Au Bon Climat, Ojai has become the sole focus of attention, with output doubling, though to a still modest 3,000 cases. The picturesque Ojai Valley in which the five and a half acres of estate vines are established has a climate very similar to that of the Santa Ynez Valley around Los Olivos, varying between Region II and Region III according to the season. While it is close to the coast, and while the marine influence certainly makes its presence felt, the twists and turns of the valley reduce the impact, with less fogs and cool air than one might expect by simply looking at a map. Indeed, another four miles up the valley and one is into Region IV to Region V climate. The relatively low incidence of fog means that there are no problems with the organic farming which has been practiced at the vineyard for many years now. Nor is botrytis a significant risk. The estate vineyards are planted to Syrah originally obtained from the Estrella River Winery in Paso Robles, thus representing a continuation of the link with Australia forged by Gary Eberle and Australia's Brian Croser during their university days. (It was Croser who persuaded Eberle to plant Syrah at what was then Estrella River.)

The wines are made in a postage stamp-sized wooden winery, but with extensions being completed over 1992/93. The expansion of the business has meant the production of 1,000 cases of Chardonnay under three different vineyard-designated labels, with a superbly rich barrel-fermented Chardonnay sourced from Talley Vineyard in Arroyo Grande leading the way, and once again underlining the tremendous potential of that vineyard. Then there are two White Meritage blends of Sauvignon Blanc and Semillon sourced from the Buttonwood Ranch, under a standard and Reserve label, both barrel fermented and enriched by malolactic fermentation. The signature wine has to be the vibrantly peppery estate-grown Syrah, a wine every bit as good as the best from Qupe. Then there are odd wines which crop up from year to year, such as an elegant, underplayed Zinfandel from Paso Robles, all fragrance and spice.

SAN ANTONIO WINERY 1917

A: 737 Lamar Street, Los Angeles, CA 90031 **T**: (213) 223 1401 **V**: 8:30–7 Mon–Sat, 10–4 Sun **P**: 350,000 **W**: Santo Riboli

San Antonio continues to operate in downtown Los Angeles partly because it is (literally) across the railroad tracks, and partly because it has been designated Cultural Historical Monument No. 42, saving it from the re-development which might otherwise have consumed it. The third generation of Ribolis now run San Antonio, which has operated continuously since it was founded. During Prohibition it provided altar wines to two of the largest churches in Los Angeles, each of which took 10,000 cases of wine a year, suggesting considerable devotion on the part of the congregations. And whereas the other wineries in and around Los Angeles seem to be headed either to extinction or relocation, San Antonio is thriving. The third generation of Ribolis can only be described as exceedingly smart, with Steve Riboli effectively driving the operation.

Over the past 20 years fermentation capacity has been increased to one million gallons, 900,000 gallons of which are in gleaming new temperature-controlled stainless steel fermenters. There is no primary processing done on site: the red wines are made under contract crush arrangements at Vichon and Wente, before being brought back to San Antonio for maturation, blending and bottling; the white wines are crushed and pressed elsewhere, and fermented on site at San Antonio. While most of the grapes are purchased, it has moved to establish 155 acres of Chardonnay in the Monterey Valley, and 20 acres of Cabernet Sauvignon in the Napa Valley, as well as having a long-term lease on 40 acres of Cabernet in the Alexander Valley. The estate plantings help produce the top-of-the-range San Simeon brand Merlot and Chardonnay, produced in limited quantities and which were selling in 1992 for around $14. The bulk of the premium end business comes under the Maddalena label, with a range of varietals selling for around $10 and which account for over 150,000 cases.

San Antonio is also unusual in that, like Gallo, it has its own direct sales force serving California, where it sells 200,000 cases a year, simultaneously acting as southern California distributor for such famous wines as Bollinger and Drouhin, as well as for several northern California wineries. Says Steve Riboli, "There are lots of reasons why we don't want to move from here. One is that I wake up in the morning, and drive direct to my major accounts." But the outlook is not myopic: San Antonio is exporting between 40–50,000 cases a year to the United Kingdom, Ireland, Germany and Japan.

While the company is sales and market driven, wine quality is consistently reliable. The Chardonnays are fresh and directly fruity, the San Simeon Merlot likewise. The Maddalena brand offers a range of wines which are all technically well handled and correct; the soaring sales of the past 15 years provide the ultimate endorsement.

ABOVE ~ *Adam Tolmach and wife Helen make tiny quantities of hand-crafted wines at Ojai Winery.*

ABOVE ~ *A decorative bunch that looks almost as good as the real thing.*

TEMECULA

ABOVE ~ *Sustained by the wine-thirsty inhabitants of San Diego and Los Angeles, plantings in Temecula continue to increase.*

The Temecula AVA falls within the vast Vail Ranch, founded in 1904 and sold in 1964 to the mammoth Kaiser-Aetna land development group. That group created the Rancho California, covering 60 square miles of rolling hillside land devoted to a planned community of country homes, avocado and citrus groves, livestock farms, a huge man-made lake — and vineyards. For, on a mesa designated for tree crops and vines, Rancho California began planting vineyards in 1965 on blocks of 40 acres and upwards in size, offering purchasers fully established vineyards, coupled with on-going viticultural management and advice for those who wished it. It was a novel idea at that time, and there have been few parallels since.

There had been sporadic ventures into viticulture in the last century: vines were planted in 1843 on the site of the existing Apis Vineyard, while Escallier's Vineyards were planted in the 1890s, and one Filipe Cazas established 30 acres in 1912. At the onset of Prohibition it is estimated 10,000 gallons of wine (almost all fortified) were made in Temecula annually, but no wineries survived.

Since 1969 Callaway has dominated production in a region driven by real estate fever and tourism. If you wish to have a country playground away from the seaside, and you live in San Diego or Los Angeles, Temecula is an obvious place to look. Until the advent of water, it must have been a barren place for much of the year, hot and dry. Now it is a somewhat brash oasis; the southern California Spanish/Latin temperament flourishes ostentatiously in these parts.

Its vignerons are exceedingly touchy on the question of its climate, producing much research which shows it is similar to and no warmer than St. Helena. What they are unable to explain is why they cannot grow Cabernet Sauvignon like St. Helena. For this is white wine country, first, foremost and last.

OPPOSITE ~ *The palatial Culbertson Winery receives thousands of visitors a day in the summer season.*

The Region in Brief

Climate, Soil and Viticulture

Climate

At 33°30' north latitude, Temecula is closer to the tropics than the commonly accepted range of 34° north for the growing of wine grapes. As in so much of California, the answer lies partly in the elevation (around 1,400 feet) and partly in the marine breezes which penetrate through the Rainbow Gap and the Deluz Gap in the afternoon. The Pacific — admittedly much warmer here than it is north of Point Conception — is only 20 miles distant, so the land warming effect is minimized. A second source of cooling is provided by cold air draining down the eastern slopes of the Santa Ana Mountains at night.

For all that, this is a warm region, mainly ranging between Region III and Region IV according to site and year, although some sites do record Region II summations, emphasizing both the rolling hillside terrain and the importance of the marine intrusions. During the full flush of the growing season, daytime temperatures typically reach 90° to 95°F, and days in excess of 100°F are far from uncommon. Under the clear skies, night-time temperatures typically fall to 55°F.

Rainfall is 16 inches, making irrigation essential. Because the region lies in a plateau surrounded by mountains, the underlying geology creates a huge basin which stores water run-off. Wells (to a depth of 500 feet) tap this resource, providing all the water which is required.

Soil

The soils east of the town of Temecula are well drained, decomposed granite which are relatively infertile. As with any hillside topography, there is considerable variation in depth, and to a lesser degree composition. Thus it is common to see vines struggle on the hilltops, but be hyper-vigorous at the bottom of the slope. Nematodes do not flourish in such soils, and — so far at least — phylloxera has not made an appearance.

ABOVE ~ *Sauvignon Blanc vines at Callaway Winery, the wines of which have nationwide distribution.*

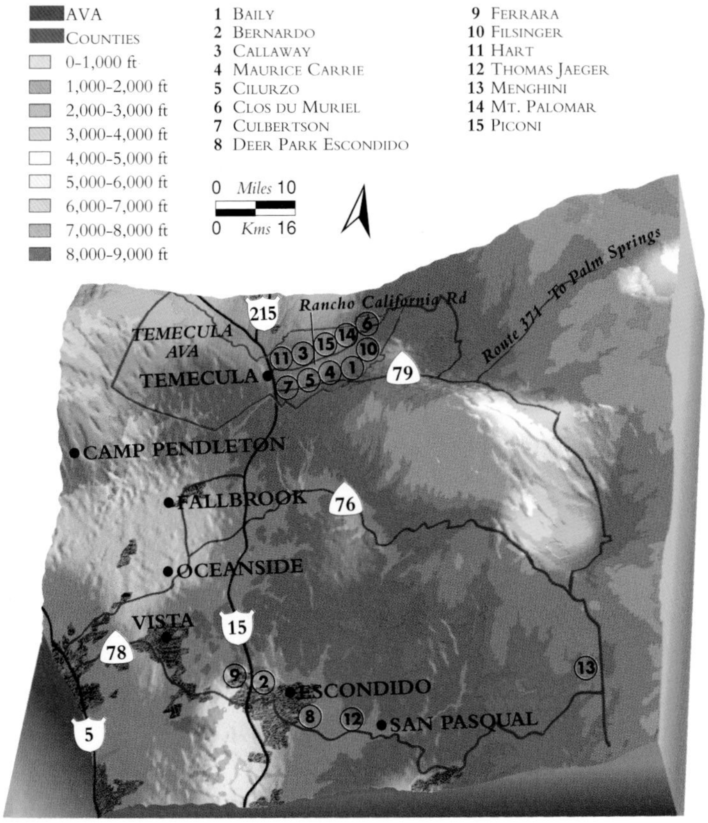
AVA
COUNTIES
0-1,000 ft
1,000-2,000 ft
2,000-3,000 ft
3,000-4,000 ft
4,000-5,000 ft
5,000-6,000 ft
6,000-7,000 ft
7,000-8,000 ft
8,000-9,000 ft
1 BAILY
2 BERNARDO
3 CALLAWAY
4 MAURICE CARRIE
5 CILURZO
6 CLOS DU MURIEL
7 CULBERTSON
8 DEER PARK ESCONDIDO
9 FERRARA
10 FILSINGER
11 HART
12 THOMAS JAEGER
13 MENGHINI
14 MT. PALOMAR
15 PICONI
0 Miles 10
0 Kms 16
Rancho California Rd
Route 371 - To Palm Springs
TEMECULA AVA
TEMECULA
CAMP PENDLETON
FALLBROOK
OCEANSIDE
VISTA
ESCONDIDO
SAN PASQUAL
215
79
76
15
78
5

Temecula
VINTAGE CHART 1981–91

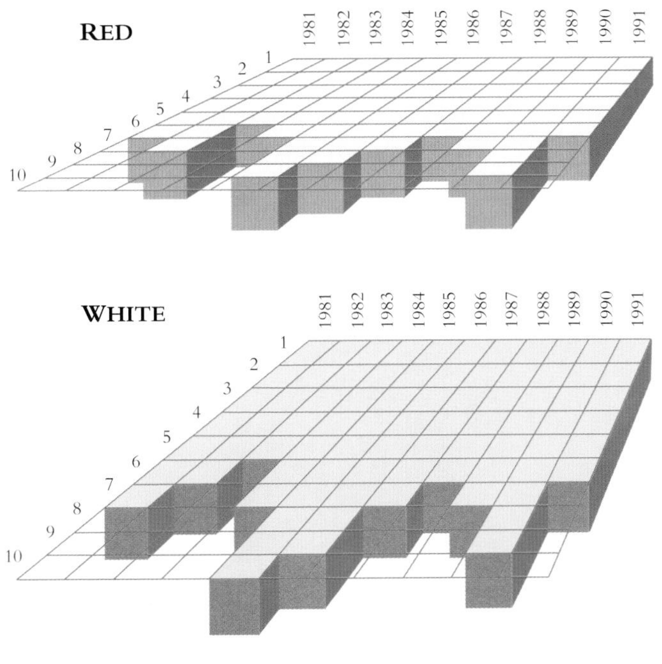
RED
WHITE
1981
1982
1983
1984
1985
1986
1987
1988
1989
1990
1991
1
2
3
4
5
6
7
8
9
10

THE GROWING SEASON

Morning fogs do play a secondary moderating influence, and are of special significance in those years in which tropical storms lead to heavy late season rainfall, causing botrytis and less noble molds to take hold. The risk of late season rainfall is partially offset by an early commencement of harvest, with Chardonnay being picked in the second half of August (and even in 1991 in early September).

Temecula
1971 AND 1991 ACREAGE/ GRAPE VARIETIES

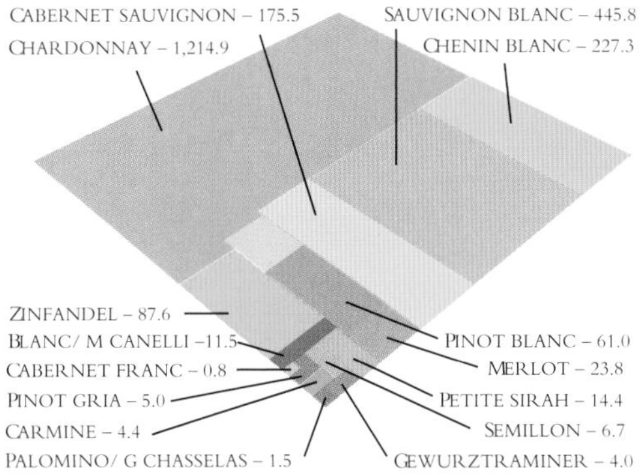
CABERNET SAUVIGNON – 175.5
CHARDONNAY – 1,214.9
SAUVIGNON BLANC – 445.8
CHENIN BLANC – 227.3
ZINFANDEL – 87.6
BLANC/ M CANELLI – 11.5
CABERNET FRANC – 0.8
PINOT GRIA – 5.0
CARMINE – 4.4
PALOMINO/ G CHASSELAS – 1.5
PINOT BLANC – 61.0
MERLOT – 23.8
PETITE SIRAH – 14.4
SEMILLON – 6.7
GEWURZTRAMINER – 4.0

Principal Wine Styles

CHARDONNAY

By a huge margin, Chardonnay is the most important wine, and Callaway in turn dwarfs all the other producers. It has consciously adopted a style which limits the possibilities: while the no-oak regime is doubtless infinitely preferable to the poor German oak which was the legacy of Karl Werner (who designed the winery for founder Eli Callaway), it is hardly likely to mask any deficiencies in the base wine. What is more, the price-positioning of the Calla-Lees brand means that production economies are paramount. Yields of four to six tons per acre (even with thinning) from quadrilateral cordon-trained vines grown in a warm, dry climate with a rapid ripening cycle may make the accountant happy, but they will not produce great wine (nor yet poor wine). But even the best Chardonnay made in the region (by Mount Palomar) is relatively soft and diffuse, with buttery/honeysuckle/ peach flavors which either fade away or end up relying on a subliminal touch of residual sugar.

SAUVIGNON BLANC AND SEMILLON

As it does in so many places in California, Sauvignon Blanc can surpass the seeming limitations of the climate, and produce crisp, clean wines with authentic varietal character. Large and small wineries alike seem to do well: Baily can be outstanding, as can Hart, while Mount Palomar looks as if it is likely to produce consistently good wines. You see, I happen to think it is Sauvignon Blanc, rather than Chardonnay, which does so nicely without oak — but then who can sell Sauvignon Blanc in the same quantity as Chardonnay?

RIESLING

While plantings are only 10% of those of Chardonnay, it is a variety which makes pleasant dry or off-dry wines, and the potential to make high class late harvest styles if growers are either willing or are forced to take the gamble.

ABOVE ~ *Temecula map.*

WINERIES *of* TEMECULA

BAILY VINEYARD & WINERY 1986

A: 36150 Pauba Road, Temecula, CA 92390 **T**: (717) 676 9463 **V**: 10–5 weekends; 10–5 daily at Tasting Room: 33833 Rancho California Road, Temecula **P**: 2,500 **W**: Phil Baily; consultant Joe Cherpin

The Baily family — father and computer expert Phil, wife Carol and sons Chris and Pat — acquired a small property in Temecula in 1981, and (inspired by Phil Baily's love of German wines) planted six acres to Riesling, and one acre to Semillon. The Riesling is made in a dry style every year, and as a late harvest wine when conditions permit; the estate production is complemented by Chardonnay, Sauvignon Blanc and Cabernet Sauvignon purchased from other Temecula growers. The Cabernet Sauvignon is also made in two guises: as a conventional red wine, and as a Cabernet Blanc. Wine quality varies from ordinary to extremely good: the 1991 Montage, a White Meritage blend of 60% Sauvignon Blanc and 40% Semillon, is as good as they come. A great seafood summer wine, it features dancing, tingling fresh and crisp fruit with subliminal oak, showing just what can be achieved with these varieties in the region.

CALLAWAY VINEYARD & WINERY 1974

A: 32720 Rancho California Road, Temecula, CA 92589 **T**: (717) 676 4001 **V**: 10–5 daily **P**: 225,000 **W**: Dwayne Helmuth

It has been said of founder Eli Callaway, former President of Burlington Industries, that his greatest virtue was knowing nothing whatsoever about wine. Be that as it may, his 1969 decision to plant vineyards in the then unknown Temecula area paid handsome dividends, for in 1981 the operation was purchased by Hiram Walker, and now forms an integral part of the Wine Alliance, until 1992 under the direction of Terry Clancy. Callaway was producing 82,000 cases when it was acquired, a substantial operation by any standards, but has since been transformed by a $3.5 million winery and warehouse expansion, and by a radical decision taken in 1981 to concentrate on the production of steel-fermented and un-oaked Chardonnay. The proprietary name "Calla-Lees" was added to the 1985 vintage, and now Calla-Lees Chardonnay makes up more than 50% of the total output. The 720 acres of vineyards have been converted to produce only Chardonnay, Chenin Blanc, Sauvignon Blanc, Muscat Canelli and Pinot Blanc, providing the basic range of Calla-Lees Chardonnay, Morning Harvest Chenin Blanc, Fumé Blanc, Sauvignon Blanc and White Riesling. Limited quantities of a sparkling wine, and an occasional Late Harvest Chenin Blanc (named Sweet Nancy by founder Eli Callaway in honor of his wife) are made from time to time.

The "Lees" in the Calla-Lees brand name signifies that the wine is indeed aged on its lees in tank for a (relatively brief) period before bottling. Whatever complexity this adds to the wine is not obvious: the nicest things one can say about the Calla-Lees Chardonnay style are that it soothes rather than excites the senses, that it has the requisite amount of alcohol, and that it is best served well chilled.

MAURICE CAR'RIE VINEYARDS & WINERY 1986

A: 34225 Rancho California Road, Temecula, CA 92390 **T**: (714) 676 1711 **V**: 10–5 daily **P**: 30,000 **W**: Steven Hagarta

Long-time Roller Rink operators Gordon (Bud) and Maurice Car'rie Van Roekel retired to Temecula in 1984, but soon tired of retirement, and purchased one of the original vineyard blocks (of 46 acres) set up at the end of the 1960s by Kaiser-Aetna. The following year they built the elaborate winery, and subsequently expanded their vineyard holdings to 110 acres, with another 110 acres held on long-term lease.

Winemaker Steven Hagarta is a former Stanford University political science graduate, who became interested in wine when he spent six months in Florence on a student exchange program while at Stanford. One might be forgiven for observing there are tougher ways of entering the wine industry. Having embarked on a post-graduate fermentation science course, Hagarta was hired as assistant winemaker at San Pasquale Vineyards in Escondido, subsequently moving to Ahern Winery and then to Piconi Winery before being installed as founding winemaker at Maurice Car'rie.

Chardonnay, Private Reserve Estate Chardonnay, Sauvignon Blanc, White Zinfandel, Muscat Canelli, Chenin Blanc, Cabernet Blanc, Fumé Blanc and Johannisberg Riesling are all made from Temecula grapes. In 1990 a Pinot Noir purchased from Santa Barbara County grapes was added to the list, and in fact provided the best wine tasted from the winery. The various Chardonnays and Sauvignon Blancs all seem to suffer from poor oak. By contrast, the Pinot Noir had complex ripe, gamey/minty aromas and tastes which, while not classic, were certainly complex.

CULBERTSON WINERY 1981

A: 32575 Rancho California Road, Temecula, CA 92390 **T**: (714) 699 0099 **V**: 10–5 daily **P**: 40,000 **W**: Jon McPherson

The grand Culbertson winery facility of today had a humble and unlikely beginning.

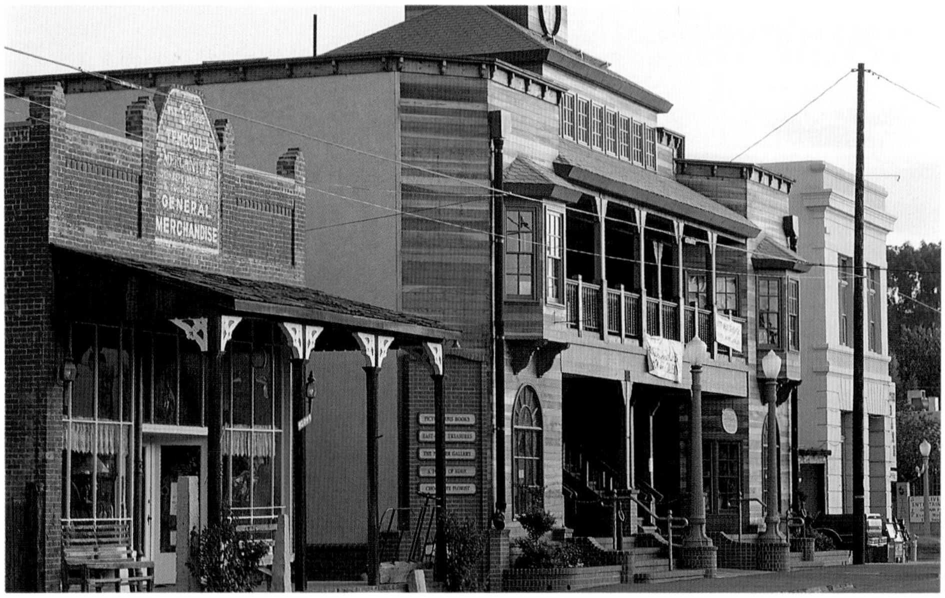
GENERAL
MERCHANDISE

ABOVE ~ *The old part of the Temecula township is in stark contrast to the new.*

Jon Culbertson owned a company providing diving and exploration services to the oil industry, and became a home winemaker in his spare time. In 1975 he purchased an avocado ranch in the north of San Diego County, and began fiddling around making sparkling wine. He caught the wave of interest in sparkling wine, and had southern California all to himself. By 1985, production had increased to 7,000 cases, and he was able to head a syndicate of investors which purchased the 20-acre property in Temecula upon which the winery, restaurant and large sales and reception area were built in time for the 1988 vintage. Production at one time soared to 80,000 cases, all from purchased grapes sourced across California, but Culbertson — like all the other sparkling wine producers — was caught in the downturn of the market. Production is now back down to 40,000 cases, and the business is owned 99% by John and Sally Thornton, who acquired it in 1991.

Culbertson, rather than Callaway, is the place to visit in Temecula. Café Champagne, the spacious restaurant, is open for lunch and dinner daily, continuously from 11 A.M. to 9 P.M., and is deservedly very popular, serving simple but stylish food in a brasserie-type atmosphere. The tasting room, otherwise known as the Champagne Bar, runs from 10 A.M. to 5 P.M. on all days except Friday and Saturday, when, for some strange reason, it closes at 4 P.M. Winery tours are run on the hour throughout the day, and then there is the obligatory gift shop offering every tourist bauble imaginable.

The Culbertson wines have always had a strong hold on the Los Angeles and San Diego markets, and the winery capitalizes fully on the fact that it is the only southern California winery specializing in sparkling wine. All of the wines are based upon combinations of Pinot Noir, Chardonnay and Pinot Blanc. For reasons I do not profess to understand, a number of them seem to have Muscat-like overtones, giving a rather cosmetic character. Nonetheless, they have been consistent medal winners in the show circuit, even if most often at the bronze and silver level. Indeed, in 1992, Culbertson was able to claim that for the two preceding years it had received more medals than any other *methode champenoise* winery in the United States, a commendable record, but one which should be put into the context that few of the French-owned California wine producers enter their wines in shows.

The best of the range is the Vintage Natural, a proprietary name for a blend of 80% Chardonnay and 20% Pinot Blanc, and which avoids those cosmetic characters. It must be said that, for the majority of consumers, a little bit of Muscat-like character may be no bad thing.

HART WINERY 1980

A: 41300 Avenida Biena, Temecula, CA 92593 **T**: (714) 676 6300 V: 9–4:30 daily **P**: 4,500 **W**: Joe Travis Hart

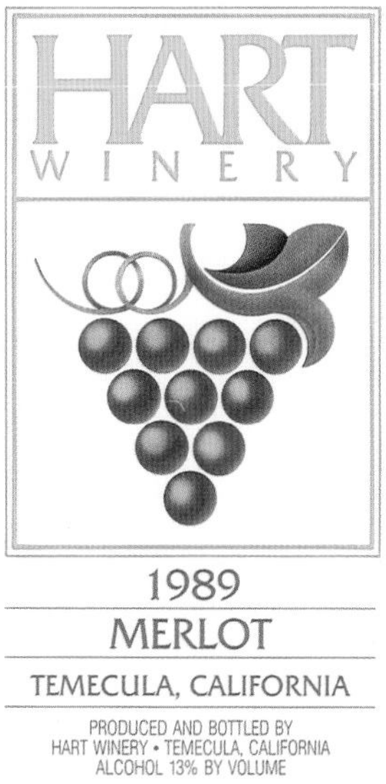
HART
WINERY
1989
MERLOT
TEMECULA, CALIFORNIA
PRODUCED AND BOTTLED BY
HART WINERY • TEMECULA, CALIFORNIA
ALCOHOL 13% BY VOLUME

Travis and Nancy Hart selected the Temecula district in which to establish their vineyard and winery because it was within easy commuting distance of Carlsbad, where they were both school teachers. In 1973 they purchased a 20-acre property and commenced developing an 11-acre vineyard, selling the grapes in the initial years until they built the now very full winery in 1979.

The estate provides Hart with its Sauvignon Blanc and much of its Chardonnay; four acres of Cabernet Sauvignon, which used to provide a Cabernet Blanc, are being grafted to equal amounts of Syrah and Viognier. The Cabernet Sauvignon produced under the Hart label comes from the Hanson Vineyard, 20 miles from Temecula (although still within the AVA) in a far cooler, coastal hill subdistrict. In 1991 Hart also sourced Grenache and Mourvedre from Cucamonga, heralding a move towards Rhone Valley styles. Any expansion in volume will be restricted by the size of the winery, every inch of which is occupied with barrels and winemaking equipment.

The wines are by and large pleasant, if unremarkable; a 1991 Meritage blend of Sauvignon Blanc and Semillon ex-barrel held considerable promise, but overall the white wines seem to lack intensity.

MOUNT PALOMAR WINERY 1975

A: 33820 Rancho California Road, Temecula, CA 92390 **T**: (714) 675 5047 **V**: 9–5 daily **P**: 15,500 **W**: Etienne P Calper

Mount Palomar was founded by John H. Poole, known to many southern Californians as the founder of radio station KBIG. In 1969 he sold the radio station and moved to Temecula to become one of the viticultural pioneers, establishing his Long Valley Vineyard. At one point the vineyard covered 150 acres, but has changed in both varietal composition and size since 1981. It now comprises 100 acres, planted to Chardonnay, Sauvignon Blanc, Johannisberg Riesling, Cabernet Sauvignon, Cabernet Franc and Sangiovese — the last a variety for which Mount Palomar holds much hope. Whether, in the fullness of time, the ability of Sangiovese to retain acid in such a warm climate is sufficient recommendation remains to be seen; there are those who say it will only produce high quality wine in a cooler climate.

The winery was commissioned in time for the 1975 vintage with John Poole acting as winemaker. Joe Cherpin was subsequently appointed as winemaker, and prior to the 1991 harvest was replaced by Etienne Calper, who had spent three years as assistant winemaker at Kendall-Jackson and two years as winemaker at Konocti, bringing with him a wealth of experience. The results are obvious in the 1991 vintage wines, all of which are very competently made. The accent is on Chardonnay and Sauvignon Blanc (both in Reserve and standard forms), Johannisberg Riesling and Cabernet Sauvignon (the last purchased from grapes grown in Dry Creek Valley). It may be a little unkind to say it, but the white wines have a distinct Kendall-Jackson stamp about them, being very soft in the mouth, and a strong tropical fruit influence. The lime-juice and passionfruit Johannisberg Riesling and the Reserve Chardonnay, in particular, would clearly have very wide appeal: Mount Palomar extended its tasting room and picnic facilities in 1982, in 1985 and again in 1990. With wines such as this on offer, a further expansion may well prove necessary.

OTHER WINERIES

BERNARDO WINERY 1889
A: 13330 Paseo Del Verano Norte, San Diego, CA 92128 **T**: (619) 487 1866 **W**: Ross Rizzo

CILURZO VINEYARD & WINERY
A: 41220 Calle Contento, Temecula, CA 92390 **T**: (714) 676 5250

CLOS DU MURIEL
A: 40620 Calle Contento, Temecula, CA 92591 **T**: (714) 676 2938

DEER PARK ESCONDIDO 1990
A: 29103 Champagne Boulevard, Escondido, CA 92026 **T**: (619) 749 1666 **W**: Robert and Lila Knapp

FERRARA WINERY 1932
A: 1120 W. 15th Avenue, Escondido, CA 92025 **T**: (619) 745 7632 **W**: Gasper D. Ferrara

FILSINGER VINEYARDS & WINERY 1980
A: 39050 DePortola Road, Temecula, CA 92390 **T**: (714) 676 4594

THOMAS JAEGER WINERY 1988
A: 13455 San Pasqual Road, Escondido, CA 92025 **T**: (619) 745 3553 **W**: Douglas A. Braun

MENGHINI WINERY 1982
A: P.O. Box 1359, 1150 Julian Orchards Drive, Julian, CA 92036 **T**: (619) 765 2072 **W**: Michael Menghini

JOHN PICONI WINERY 1981
A: 33410 Rancho California Road, Temecula, CA 92390 **T**: (714) 673 5400 **W**: John Piconi

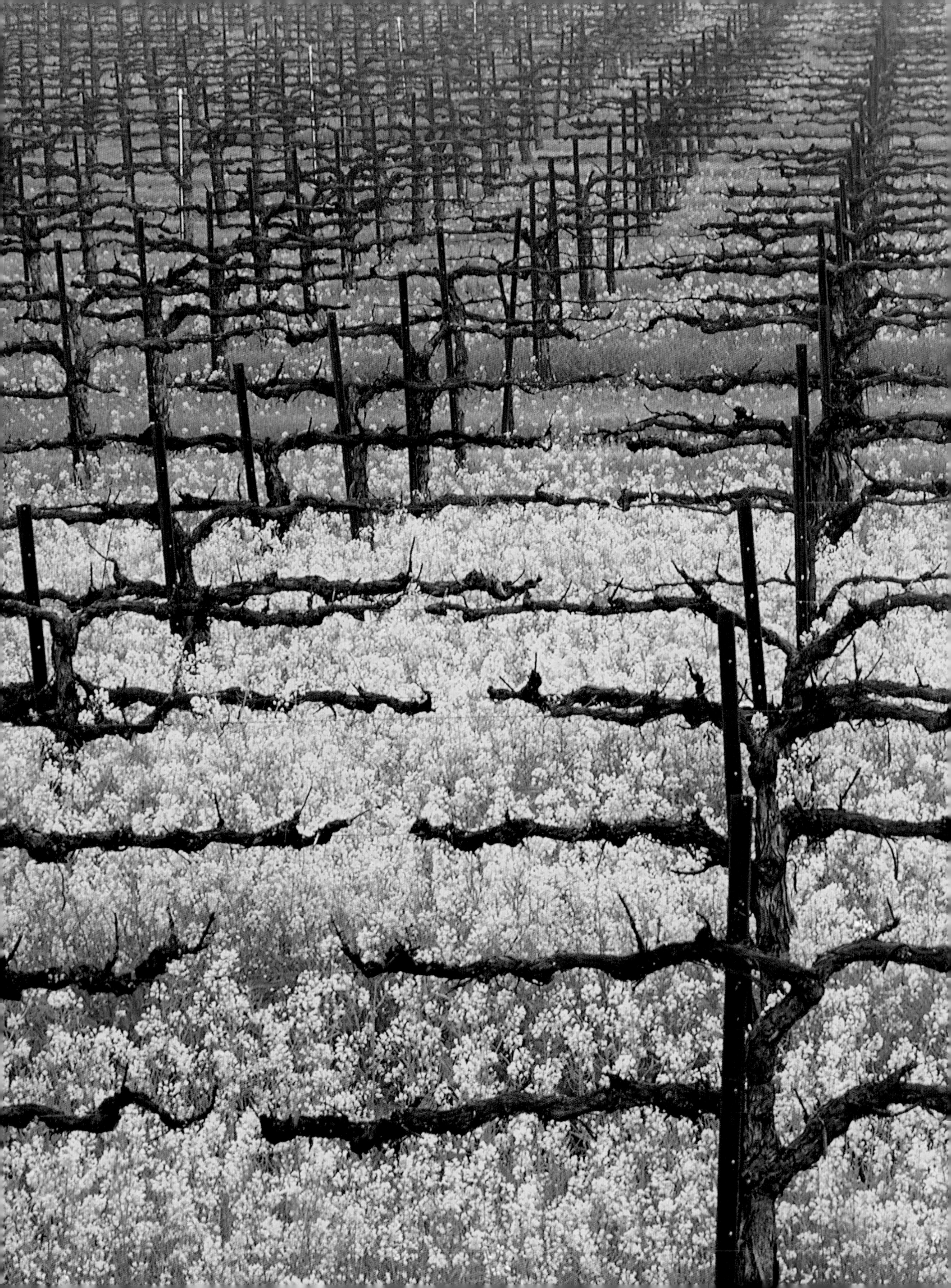

WAREHOUSE WINERIES

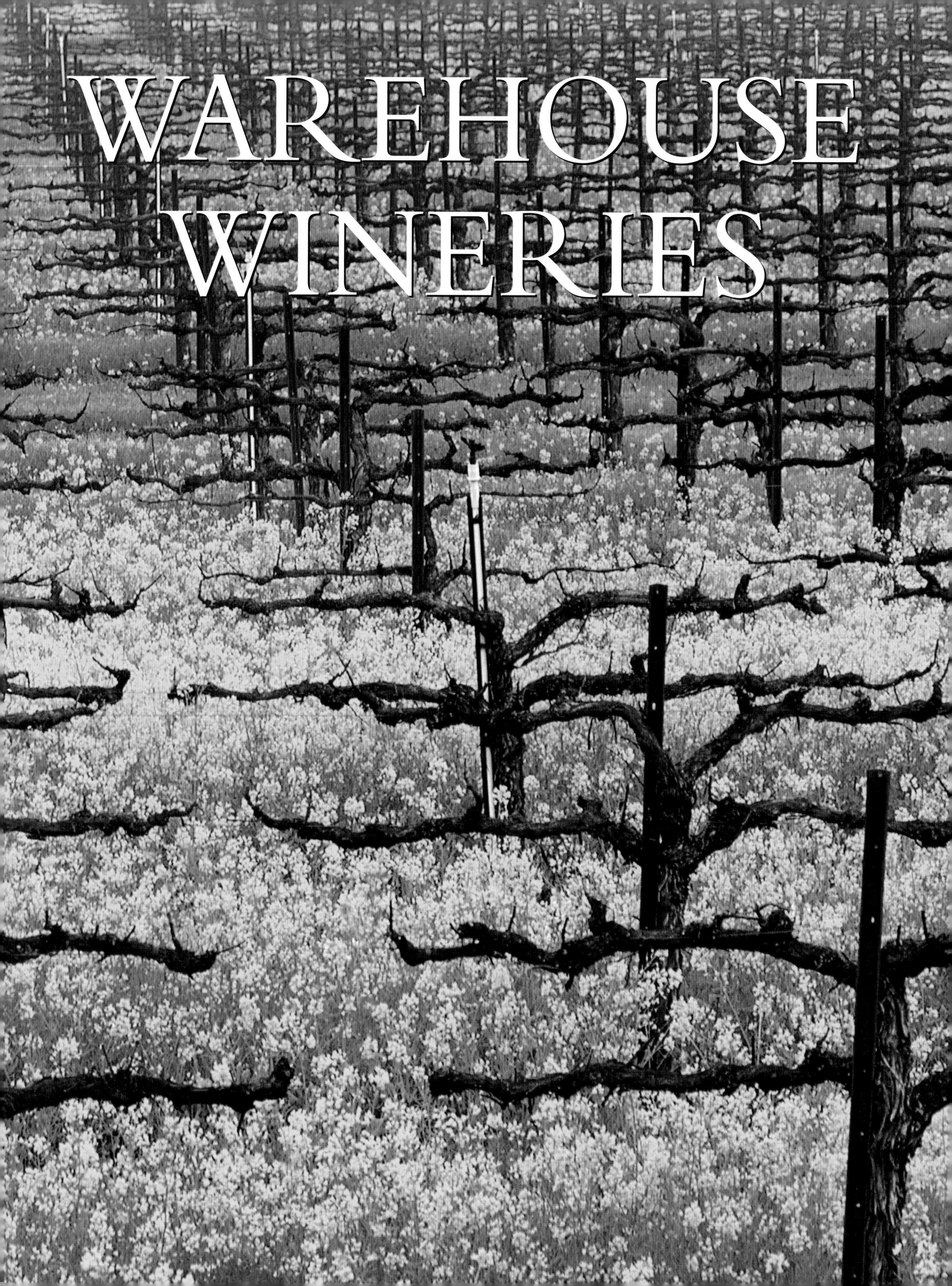

This small chapter brings together a strange assortment of people and places, bonded by the State of California and by the Pied Piper who calls them to make wine. Most of them are winemakers without a winery or a vineyard; those who do have wineries of their own do so in downtown warehouses. Others anonymously rent space in the corner of someone else's winery or even several wineries. For most, the arrangement is one of necessity: lack of capital means that they cannot afford to purchase or erect their own buildings.

For a few it is a strategic decision: why invest the capital in a winery (and a vineyard) when an alternative is available? It is better to spend whatever money is available on new oak barrels and top quality grapes. For some it represents a transitional phase, ultimately leading, they hope, to a permanent home in a winery in wine country.

Another common bond is the blend of practical experience and technical expertise these winemakers share. Many are fulltime winemakers for well-known wineries or carry on active consultancy practices; making their own wine is the ultimate busman's holiday.

Few have cellar door sales or any visitors' facilities; the notable exceptions are Leeward and Rosenblum and, to a lesser extent, Claiborne & Churchill and Weinstock. This lack of physical presence — coupled with typically limited production — restricts the avenues of sale. Around the world, retailers are irrationally jealous of those wineries which have an active cellar door sales business: it is a form of advertising which directly benefits the retailer and which costs that retailer nothing. The obverse, then, is the lack of recognition accorded many of these warehouse wineries. This is a pity, because among them are some singularly talented makers, producing many fine wines.

PREVIOUS PAGE ~ *The winter-flowering mustard has beautified the vineyards of the world since time immemorial.*

ABOVE ~ *Bay Bridge, as evocative at night as the Golden Gate, the end of the journey home.*

WAREHOUSE WINERIES

CACHE CELLARS 1978

A: Pedrick Road, Davis, CA 95616
T: (916) 756 6068 **V**: 10–4 weekends
P: 5,000 **W**: Charles Lowe

Charles Lowe explains the location of his winery this way: "If you buy good French oak and good Napa Valley grapes, it really doesn't matter a damn where the wine is made." Thus it is that this Davis graduate (1974–76), who worked at Inglenook for two years before setting up his own winery, found an old dairy barn near Davis and converted it into a small but functional winery — yet not so small that he does not have room to move, as he does have the capacity to ultimately increase to 10,000 cases if he wishes. Since 1989 he has elected to buy organically grown grapes, which has meant a change in his fruit sources, but one he believes is for the better. He also conducts a somewhat unusual custom crush facility, or at least provides the equipment therefor: in the corner of the winery is a fenced-off area in which kosher wine is made, under Rabbinical supervision, and using Rabbinical labor for all of the key handling processes.

The Cache wines comprise a Chardonnay, Sauvignon Blanc and Cabernet Sauvignon from the Napa Valley, with a Pinot Noir which includes some Monterey fruit. The Napa wines are solid, mainstream styles with good flavor and structure.

CAFARO 1975

A: c/o Robert Sinskey, 6320 Silverado Trail, Napa, CA 94558 **T**: (707) 944 9090 **V**: Nil
P: 600 **W**: Joe Cafaro

Joe Cafaro is a Napa Valley veteran, having made wine for Charles Krug, Chappellet, Keenan and Acacia before joining Robert Sinskey Vineyards, and all along he has quietly plugged away making a few hundred cases a year under his own label. Production these days is equally split between Merlot and Cabernet Sauvignon, purchasing the Cabernet from Carneros, Mount Veeder and the Stags Leap District. The wines are concentrated and powerful, with a touch of astringency which needs time in bottle (and sometimes aeration) to soften.

CRICHTON HALL VINEYARD 1983

A: P.O. Box 187, 1100 Rutherford Road, Rutherford, CA 94573 **T**: (707) 224 4200
V: Nil **P**: 10,000 **W**: Richard Crichton

Richard Crichton specializes in Chardonnay, producing tiny quantities of barrel-fermented wine which ages extremely well into a distinctly Burgundian mold, with toasty oak, citrus and melon fruit, and an attractive tangy edge.

CLAIBORNE & CHURCHILL 1983

A: 860 E. Capitolio Way, San Luis Obispo, CA 93401 **T**: (805) 544 4066 **V**: By appointment **P**: 4,000 **W**: Clay Thompson

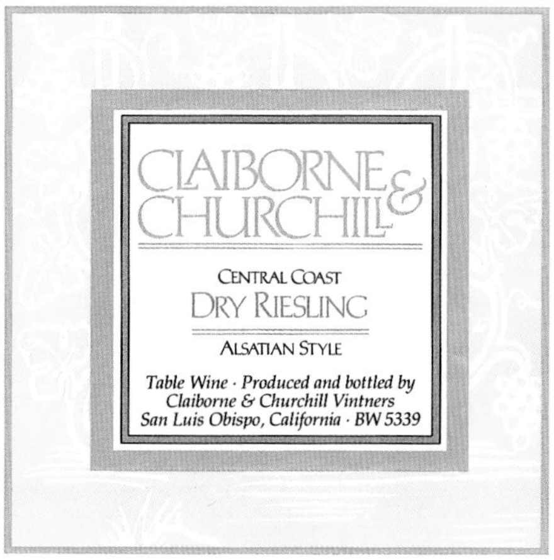
CLAIBORNE & CHURCHILL
CENTRAL COAST
DRY RIESLING
ALSATIAN STYLE
Table Wine · Produced and bottled by
Claiborne & Churchill Vintners
San Luis Obispo, California · BW 5339

Many of those in the wine industry have gravitated there from different and unusual occupations, but few of which are more esoteric than that of Claiborne (Clay) Thompson. He was a college lecturer in old Norse and Scandinavian languages in Michigan before the internecine battles of academia persuaded him a change of lifestyle was necessary for his health. He adds, with a wry grin, "It was also a classic midlife crisis of a 40 year old, heightened by re-marriage." He moved to California, and got a job working as a cellar hand (at the lowest level) at Edna Valley Vineyards, where he stayed for several years. He and wife Fredericka Churchill had always loved the wines of Alsace, and Edna Valley Vineyards grew some Riesling which always struggled to find a buyer. A chance conversation with Dick Graff led to the formation of Claiborne & Churchill and to the first three vintages at Edna Valley Vineyards on a use and pay basis.

When the time came to set up their own winery location, there really wasn't much choice. Academics and cellar hands are not particularly well paid, and, says Clay Thompson, "Many have made a fortune in one industry, and then proceeded to spend it in the wine industry building Taj Mahals; even if I had wanted to, I was not able to do so." So he rented a small warehouse unit in a downtown industrial complex in San Luis Obispo, and eked out an existence which was not particularly remunerative but was very satisfying. Then, several years ago, his wines started to receive recognition from Dan Berger and others, and production has increased.

Between 1983 and 1987 Riesling and Gewurztraminer were purchased from Edna Valley Vineyards; it then grafted over those two varieties, forcing Thompson to source from other vineyards in Santa Barbara and Monterey (Ventana providing whatever Gewurztraminer Thompson is able to buy). He briefly plunged into Chardonnay, exhorted to do so by his distributors, but has since pulled back and refocused his attention on the Riesling and Gewurztraminer which he makes so well, with tiny quantities of Pinot Noir and Chardonnay from MacGregor Vineyard — a whole half a ton of Pinot Noir, although a little more Chardonnay, which he fashions into an extremely stylish and complex wine. The Rieslings and Gewurztraminers are made genuinely dry, a welcome change from the all-pervasive sweetness of so many producers.

CORISON WINES 1987

A: P.O. Box 344, Oakville, CA 94562
T: (707) 963 7357 **V**: Nil **P**: 2,000
W: Kathy Corison

Kathy Corison is a long-term Napa Valley winemaker who spent her early years at Freemark Abbey, then at the Yverdon Winery, before moving to Chappellet where she stayed for ten years, succeeding Tony Soter in 1981. In 1990 she resigned from Chappellet, and began taking an active role in Soter's consultancy business in which she had in fact been a long-term silent partner. But she also had another string to her bow: Corison Wines. Starting in 1987 she had rented space, first in Chappellet, then Robert Pepi and now Robert Sinskey

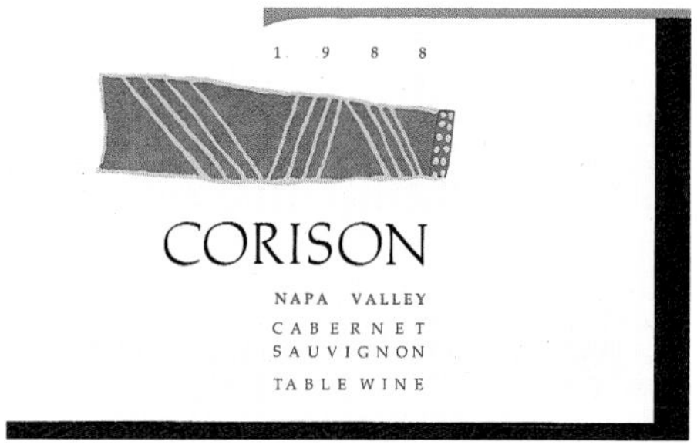
1 9 8 8
CORISON
NAPA VALLEY
CABERNET SAUVIGNON
TABLE WINE

Wines, to crush, ferment and barrel mature between 1,800 and 2,000 cases of Cabernet Sauvignon a year. The Yverdon experience was a salutory one: while it was not her winery, she was responsible for everything, from making to marketing, and it gave her a first-hand insight into the financial requirements and constraints under which a small winery operates. So she is content with spending her money on 50% new French oak every year, and on top quality grapes to produce truly excellent Cabernet Sauvignon in a full-blown, concentrated style; the fruit is sufficiently rich to swallow up the oak, although the latter is certainly present. The complexity and concentration evident in the three vintages so far released come in part from the blending of Cabernet grown in Yountville, Rutherford and St. Helena benchlands, some of the finest sites in the Napa Valley.

DOMINUS ESTATE 1982

A: Yountville, Napa Valley, CA 94599
V: Nil **P**: 10,000 **W**: Christian Moueix

In many ways, Dominus is the ultimate warehouse winery. And if it has any intention of building Opus Two, it has given no intention of doing so to date. It represents a joint venture between Christian Moueix, who runs the fabulous array of Pomerol chateaux headed by Chateau Petrus, and John Daniel's daughters, Robin Lail and Marcia Smith. Lail and Smith own the 125-acre Napanook property, which is planted to 50 acres of Cabernet Sauvignon, Merlot and Cabernet Franc, and 20 acres of Chardonnay. Only part of the production of the Napanook Vineyard goes to make Dominus, the first vintage of which was 1983. Over the years I have tasted most of the Dominus wines, and have to admit that they march to a different tune. I find the tannins and other forms of astringency overwhelm the fruit, and much though I wish it were otherwise, I cannot see that time will bring the wines back into balance, or ever allow me to enjoy them.

ETUDE 1985

A: P.O. Box 344, Oakville, CA 94562
T: (707) 963 7357 **V**: Nil **P**: 4,000
W: Tony Soter

Tony Soter established his very considerable reputation as a winemaker during his long tenure at Spotteswoode Vineyards. He has now retired as executive winemaker at Spotteswoode, concentrating on his flourishing wine consultancy business (which numbers Spotteswoode, Niebaum-Coppola and the new Eisele Winery among its clients), and Etude, the label which he commenced to develop in 1985. Tony Soter is acutely intelligent, and with that intelligence comes a remarkable degree of humility. He says, "When I embarked on Etude I knew it would take me ten years of hard work, constantly refining and changing winemaking techniques to find the perfect balance between the material I am working with and the winestyle I would like to achieve — a style which I believe can only be understood by using the classics as my yardsticks." Modestly, he says he thinks he is on the right track, implying he may get there by 1995. Many would argue he has already done so. It may also be that this wandering hermit crab will have found and established his own winery site by then: it, and even the possibility of a vineyard, was under active consideration in 1992.

Production is split between 2,500 cases of Pinot Noir sourced from Carneros, and 1,500 cases of Cabernet Sauvignon sourced from various Napa Valley vineyards. Every year, the Pinot Noir seems to get better, with typically subtle, ripe cherry and plum fruit complexed by a touch of spice, a touch of stemminess (wholly desirable), and a hint of oak. One can see the complex fermentation techniques used, yet at the end of the day it is the fruit which speaks. Best of all is the feel in the mouth: silky soft, yet with a very long, lingering finish. If there is work to be done, I think it is with the Cabernet Sauvignon, which can be distinctly variable, however supreme Soter's mastery was (and is) at Spotteswoode and elsewhere.

GARY FARRELL WINES 1981

A: P.O. Box 342, Forestville, CA 95436
T: (707) 433 6616 **V**: By appointment
P: 4,500 **W**: Gary Farrell

Gary Farrell started his career as winemaker for the Davis Bynum Winery in 1978, where he has remained ever since, although between 1982 and 1986 he doubled up as consultant winemaker for Rochioli. He makes the Gary Farrell range of wines at Davis Bynum, and is particularly anxious not to be seen to bite the hand that feeds him. In particular, he is sensitive to the fact that while the Davis Bynum wines are very good, those of Gary Farrell are usually that little bit better. The answer is simple: greater expenditure on new oak. The cascade of show awards in recent years has been reflected in Gary Farrell Winery being voted one of the U.S. Wineries of the Year by *Wine & Spirit Magazine* in 1990, and receiving the coveted Dan Berger accolade as Winemaker of the Year for 1991.

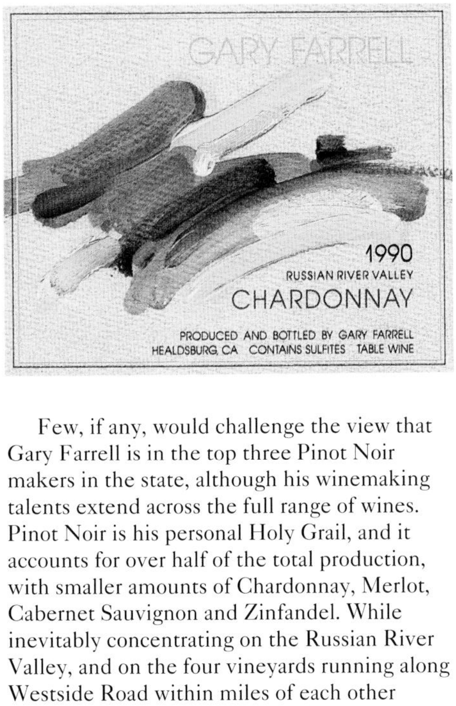
GARY FARRELL
1990
RUSSIAN RIVER VALLEY
CHARDONNAY
PRODUCED AND BOTTLED BY GARY FARRELL
HEALDSBURG CA CONTAINS SULFITES TABLE WINE

Few, if any, would challenge the view that Gary Farrell is in the top three Pinot Noir makers in the state, although his winemaking talents extend across the full range of wines. Pinot Noir is his personal Holy Grail, and it accounts for over half of the total production, with smaller amounts of Chardonnay, Merlot, Cabernet Sauvignon and Zinfandel. While inevitably concentrating on the Russian River Valley, and on the four vineyards running along Westside Road within miles of each other

ABOVE ~ *Pneumatic secateurs take some of the pain out of pruning — and speed up the process.*

(Allen, Rochioli, Bacigalupi and Kaiser), producing these either as vineyard-designated wines (Allen Vineyard in particular) or as Russian River Valley, Farrell has also turned his hand to Santa Barbara Pinot Noir from the Bien Nacido Vineyard.

The results are very interesting: near perfect winemaking techniques produce wines which, tasted blind, provoked near-identical style tasting notes, emphasizing elegance and finesse. However, as one would expect, the flavor notes are different: those of the Russian River Valley being very pure, of almost crystalline clarity, in the red cherry spectrum, while Bien Nacido shows much darker fruits, with dark plums and ripe strawberries. The points were so high that to differentiate between the two seems churlish, but as a matter of record, the Bien Nacido shaded the Allen Vineyard wine by a whisker. Others would no doubt reverse that order, something which would not worry me in the least. These are quite beautiful Pinot Noirs of world class.

The Chardonnays show the same sophistication, with wonderful length and intensity, and that touch of wildness which is sometimes absent from Russian River Chardonnay; I cannot imagine finding a French Burgundy of similar quality at the same price. The extraordinary thing is that the Gary Farrell Cabernet Sauvignon (1988 Ladi's Vineyard) was the second highest-rated wine in the 1991 Wine Show Schedule, winning four gold, one silver and two bronze medals. With a Russian River Zinfandel to round things off, Gary Farrell has a superb portfolio.

FIDDLEHEAD CELLARS 1986

A: 515 Eleventh Street, Davis, CA 95616
T: (916) 756 4550 **V**: Nil **P**: 1,000
W: Kathy Joseph

Kathy Joseph makes wine during the day for others, and for herself at night and on weekends. She produces but two wines: Sauvignon Blanc and Pinot Noir. Despite the fact that she works in the Napa Valley, she purchases her Pinot Noir from the Sierra Madre Vineyard in the Santa Maria Valley, moving the wine to Napa for maturation and ultimate bottling. Kathy Joseph is one of those who has been caught by the spell of Pinot Noir, and understands very well the complicated handling techniques needed to bring the best out of the variety. Thus she uses the full range of techniques, including two days pre-fermentation cold soak, 25% whole bunches, six days fermentation, seven days extended maceration, and does not pump the must (or pomace). The wine is typically matured in 50% new Allier and Troncais oak. These techniques, coupled with the quality of the Sierra Madre fruit, produce a Pinot of genuine distinction and style.

FREMONT CREEK 1988

A: 1127 Pope Street, St. Helena, CA 94574
T: (707) 963 9471 **V**: Nil **P**: 10,000
W: Dimitri Tschelistcheff and Judy Matulich-Weitz

Andy Beckstoffer comes through as one of the largest of the larger-than-life figures portrayed in James Conway's book *Napa*. He came to the Napa Valley in 1968 as a Heublein Inc. employee to help in the negotiations which led to the purchase of Inglenook and the Italian Swiss Colony. He returned the following year to negotiate the purchase of Beaulieu, and then founded a Heublein subsidiary, Vinifera Development Corporation, which developed and managed new vineyards. Two years later, he negotiated a leveraged buy-out of the vineyards from Heublein, and in 1978 became sole owner of the operation, which now has 1,500 acres of vineyards in Napa and Mendocino Counties. Beckstoffer Vineyards also acts as a viticultural consultant for some of the great names of the California industry. The eight vineyards in the Napa Valley, four in Mendocino and one in the Russian River are acknowledged to provide some of the best contract-grown grapes in California.

In 1988 Beckstoffer decided to have a small quantity of wine vinified under the Fremont Creek label. It is contract made at Beaulieu, with consultant help from Dimitri Tschelistcheff, and offers the big three: Chardonnay, Sauvignon Blanc and Cabernet Sauvignon. The wines are very modestly priced, and consistently offer excellent value.

DANIEL GEHRS 1991

A: 1412 E. Zayante Road, Felton, CA 95018
T: (408) 356 4455 **V**: Nil **P**: 1,000
W: Dan Gehrs

Dan Gehrs is a Santa Cruz Mountains veteran, with a deep and abiding love for the region and a great knowledge of it. He spent many years reviving the old Congress Springs Vineyard, and the financial failure of that operation (owned by a British investment syndicate) came as a great disappointment and blow. He is now a consultant on both viticulture and winemaking, with his winemaking operations carried out at the old Noble Hill Winery which is now to be called Elliston's home. In return for consultancy, he uses a small corner of the winery to produce the Daniel Gehrs wines, all of which are from grapes purchased elsewhere. His three sources are a block of old Zinfandel in Sonoma, grown by his brother; a Muscadet (or Melon) from the cool, northern edge of Monterey County; and an old Rhone mixed block in the Paicines AVA south of Hollister. The Rhone mixed block is sold under the proprietary Masquerade label, the Melon labeled as Muscadet. Not that there are many such wines, but for what it is worth, the Muscadet is the best that I have tasted in California. It has strong citrussy melon fruit, and a crisp, tangy finish. Muscadet is meant to be a seafood and summer wine, and that is precisely what this is. Masquerade is made in a Chinon style, with clean, firm but light bodied fruit.

DOLCE WINERY 1985

A: P.O. Box 327, Oakville, CA 94562
T: (707) 944 8868 **V**: Nil **P**: 1,000
W: David Cronen

Dolce is owned by Far Niente, but owner Gil Nickel is going to considerable lengths to give Dolce not only its own personality but its own separate existence. It makes but one wine: a single, late harvest blend of Semillon and Sauvignon Blanc, produced from grapes grown on Dolce's own 15-acre vineyard in the Coombsville area of the Napa Valley.

For the time being, the wines are made by Far Niente, but the long-term plan is to establish a separate winery. Even in the financial fantasy land of Far Niente, production levels at the present time could not possibly justify a separate winemaking operation. The 1985 vintage produced six barrels, 1986 nine barrels, but no wine was made in either 1987 or

MUSCADET
DANIEL GEHRS
1991
1991
MUSCADET
Monterey County ~ California
Produced & Bottled by Daniel Roland Gehrs
Felton, Santa Cruz County, California
Grapes Grown at Carmel Vineyard
Alcohol 12.5% by Volume
We are a very small winery producing scarce quantities of wine in the unique style of the famed "Garden of France": the Loire Valley. They are grown under unusually cool conditions in the northernmost vineyards of California's Monterey region. Typically late ripening, these grapes are carefully nurtured in meager soils to yield superior wines combining youthful charm, rich complexity and fine ageability.
Muscadet "Sur Lie" This smooth, dry white wine is made in a fresh, direct style featuring the Burgundian grape best known in France as Muscadet. The wine is aged from the vintage through the cold Winter months and is bottled directly from its yeast lees early the following Spring. Immensely popular in the bistros of Paris, it is best enjoyed in its youth and served well chilled both as an aperitif and with seafoods.
Want to know more? Call us toll free at 1-800-275-8138

1988. Making high quality botrytis wine places one at the mercy of the elements, and in those two years botrytis failed to do its work. The first commercial release was from 1989, with 500 cases made.

Dolce is and will always be expensive. Scarcity too, will play a powerful role in assisting the marketing effort. The first release was a pleasant wine, but far from remarkable, although further time in bottle should see the development of greater complexity.

HAVENS WINE CELLARS 1984

A: 3234 Old Sonoma Road, Napa, CA 94559 **T**: (707) 253 7153 **V**: Nil **P**: 4,500 **W**: Michael Havens

Michael Havens, in his own words, "ran away to Europe after school," there acquiring a lifelong fascination with things European and, in particular, wine. With a PhD in disciplinary humanities, he became a college professor, spending his evenings and weekends making home wine from grapes grown in the nearby Finger Lakes district. As the bug bit harder, he arranged a transfer to UCLA to teach English, and ultimately enroled in viticulture and enology at Davis. By 1984 he was into commercial winemaking, renting space and using custom crush facilities, and he purchased a small property next to Truchard to establish his own vines. He still uses storage facilities at the old William Hill Winery in 8th Street, Napa, but now makes the wine at Truchard's new winery (for which he is also winemaker).

Merlot accounts for 75% of his production, principally from the Truchard Vineyard but incorporating some Napa Valley proper grapes; Syrah and Chardonnay come from the Hudson Vineyards in Carneros, and Sauvignon Blanc from the Clock Vineyard at Calistoga.

TOBIN JAMES 1984

A: PO Box 2459, Paso Robles, CA 93447 **T**: (805) 239 2204 **V**: Nil **P**: 3,500 **W**: Toby Shumrick

When the Shumrick family moved from San Francisco to Indiana, Toby Shumrick's father — a physician — could not resist planting a vineyard, reversing the normal pattern. There are nine Shumrick children in all, and half now work in the wine industry, the other half in the medical field. Toby Shumrick's arrival in the Paso Robles area was entirely fortuitous: while studying at Ohio State University, he met Gary Eberle during a visit. Somehow or other a chord was struck, and Toby Shumrick found himself working at the Eberle Winery next vintage, leaving only to establish his own Tobin James brand. To date it has been a winery without a home, between 1988 and 1992 occupying a corner of Peachy Canyon (in Paso Robles) where Shumrick worked as winemaker, creating the great 1989 and 1990 Peachy Canyon Zinfandels. In 1992 the first steps were taken to establish a permanent residence: he has purchased a 41-acre property across the road from Meridian, which includes the remains of an old stagecoach stop building which will be refurbished as a cellar door sales area, and where a 9,000 square foot winery will be built.

Estate production is some distance off; in the meantime, Shumrick purchases fruit from selected vineyards across Paso Robles and Monterey (the latter for Pinot Noir), but then proceeds to give them exotic names such as Solar Flare, Blue Moon, Sunshine, Inspiration, and so forth. The primary emphasis is on Zinfandel, in three forms: standard, Reserve and Late Harvest, but with Pinot Noir, Chardonnay and Cabernet Sauvignon also in the portfolio. The 1989 Zinfandel was a double gold medal winner at the San Diego National Wine Competition, and there is no questioning either the quality or the style of the Tobin James Zinfandels. The Pinot Noir, which in 1990 moved from Monterey to Santa Barbara for its source, is also a commendable wine, with strong strawberry and dark cherry-accented fruit.

KALIN CELLARS 1977

A: 61 Galley Drive, Suite F. & G., Novato, CA 94949 **T**: (415) 883 3543 **V**: Nil **P**: 6,000 **W**: Terry Leighton

Terry Leighton is a microbiologist at U.C. Berkeley, from whence derives his all-consuming interest in the function and effect of yeasts in the fermentation of wine. He has developed such a reputation in the field that he was asked to deliver a paper at the 1992 International Masters of Wine Symposium in Bristol, England, and is of the same basic school of thought as Steve Kistler. In other words, the greatest complexity will be gained from the slowest-fermenting yeasts. Leighton seems to take this theory (and practice) to a far extreme, with fermentations which can last up to six months. He is also an incorrigible and inveterate experimenter, and a lengthy conversation with him leaves you with the distinct feeling that you have been lost in an intellectual maze. The wines are made in the unromantic surroundings of a Novato warehouse, but there is nothing unromantic or boring about the wines.

There is a bewildering array on offer. He sources Chardonnay from the Livermore Valley, Potter Valley, Russian River Valley, Sonoma Valley and, occasionally, Dry Creek Valley. These are all separately made, and are additionally identified by initials denoting the grower. The wines are extraordinarily full, rich and complex, with very soft buttery, nutty characters; if one searches for a criticism, it is to suggest a little less opulence and a little more finesse, a little less honey and a little more acid. The Livermore Valley Semillon is particularly interesting: again, the texture and structure are voluptuous, but the wine has character which takes one back to its Bordeaux origins. Like true Semillon, it also matures superbly in bottle. The Pinot Noirs variously sourced from the Alexander and Potter Valleys, are, quite simply, not my style. They are good red wines, no doubt, but have little or nothing to do with varietal Pinot in the classic sense.

JOHN KERR 1986

A: 900 E. Stowell Road, Suite A., Santa Maria, CA 93456-739 **T**: (805) 688 5337 **V**: Nil **P**: 1,600 **W**: John Kerr

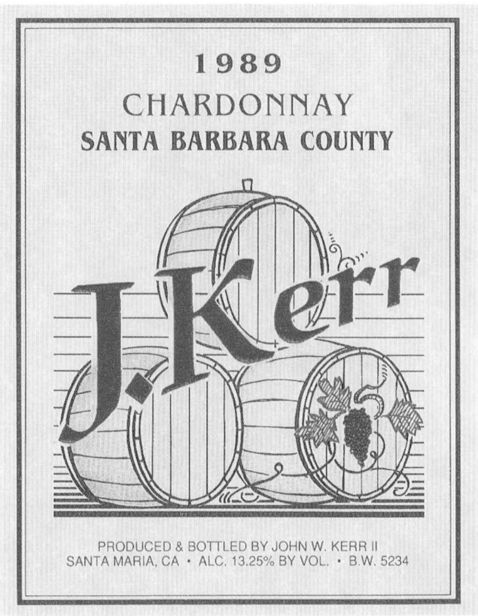
1989
CHARDONNAY
SANTA BARBARA COUNTY
J.Kerr
PRODUCED & BOTTLED BY JOHN W. KERR II
SANTA MARIA, CA • ALC. 13.25% BY VOL. • B.W. 5234

John Kerr, who grew up quickly as a helicopter gunship crew member in Vietnam, began his winemaking at the historic Brookside Winery near Los Angeles in 1972, where he worked for four years. He then left the industry to become a stereo salesman, maintaining a passing interest by selling wine on the side. In 1980 the lure of the industry took him to Monterey, where he successively worked for Chalone, Jekel and then Ventana before moving to Santa Barbara County in 1984, assisting Babcock, Brander and Houtz, also becoming a consultant winemaker to Byron Vineyards. Since Byron was acquired by Mondavi in 1990, his role there has been expanded to that of assistant winemaker.

Production for his own label has risen from 1,000 cases of Chardonnay made in 1986 to its current level of 1,300 cases of Chardonnay and 300 cases of Pinot Noir. Both wines, inevitably, are Santa Barbara sourced; half the Chardonnay comes from the Nielson Vineyard in the Santa Maria Valley, the other half from the La Presa and Houtz Vineyards in Santa Ynez. The Pinot Noir comes wholly from the Sierra Madre Vineyards. The Chardonnay has been consistently good from the outset, and seems to go from strength to strength. It shows very stylish use of oak (barrel fermentation and

partial malolactic fermentation) allied with scented, aromatic fruit, with the palate showing all of the length, finesse and style of Santa Barbara; Kerr manages to combine intensity with delicacy, no mean achievement. On the other hand a degree of volatile acidity has impinged on the Pinot Noir.

LEEWARD WINERY 1979

A: 2784 Johnson Drive, Ventura, CA 93003
T: (805) 656 5054 **V**: 10–4 daily **P**: 15,000
W: Brooks Painter

Leeward achieved unwanted fame in 1992 when the full fury of the BATF fell upon it for daring to give a factual account of the information presented in the *60 Minutes* program "The French Paradox" in one of its newsletters. Castigated, chastised and humiliated, Leeward agreed to figuratively burn the few remaining copies of the newsletter which had not been distributed, and the BATF withdrew triumphant to its fortress. However, some sanity ultimately prevailed, and finally the BATF relented and conceded, with appropriate counterbalancing warnings, that it was just possible that wineries could mention the overwhelming medical evidence which shows a sharply reduced incidence of coronary heart disease among moderate wine drinkers. Whether increased sales compensated for the legal costs incurred by founding partners Chuck Gardner and Chuck Brigham, I do not know, but I doubt whether they regret the incident.

Gardner and Brigham, respectively owners of a grocery store and a clothing store, started making wine at home for fun, and between 1979 and 1982 took the transition to commercial winemaking in their garages and basements. In the latter year Leeward moved into its warehouse complex in Ventura, where it carries on winemaking to this day. It has been a Chardonnay specialist from the outset, purchasing fruit from Santa Clara (45 tons), Monterey (55 tons), Edna Valley (25 tons) and Santa Ynez (35 tons), making minuscule quantities of Pinot Noir (from Santa Barbara) and Merlot (from the Napa Valley) to satisfy cellar door trade.

Three Chardonnays are produced: the principal wine has a Central Coast appellation, utilizing a blend of all of the vineyard sources, with lesser quantities of Monterey County and Edna Valley wines. Life being as it is, Brigham and Gardner have been unable to resist establishing four acres of Chardonnay in Ventura County, and limited releases under this label will be made. The Chardonnays have been consistently reliable, the Central Coast representing an especially good value with its ripe fruit, balancing acidity and well-handled touch of oak.

MORGAN WINERY 1982

A: 526 Brunken Avenue, Salinas, CA 93901
T: (408) 422 9855 **V**: By appointment
P: 27,000 **W**: Dan Lee

Dan Lee undertook his Monterey apprenticeship as winemaker at Jekel and Durney Vineyards, commencing to make small amounts of wine under his own label in 1982, converting that to a full-time occupation when he established his warehouse facility in downtown Salinas in 1986. In many ways this is the ultimate warehouse winery: the winery is one of a series of seemingly identical units in a development, but Dan Lee entered into the lease before the warehouses were built. He was thus able to have sloping concrete floors and drains (and the other special requirements of a winery) incorporated into the building. It is a near perfect example of function over aesthetics: spotlessly clean and ordered, and without a single inch of wasted space. On the day I visited, there was a group of obviously bemused German visitors, who had come down from the Napa Valley specifically to see the "winery." But whatever it may lack in atmosphere and aesthetics, it makes up in hard, financial common sense: Dan Lee has had to make no capital investment in winery buildings, and none in vineyards. The consequence has

ABOVE ~ *Barrel cradles facilitate every aspect of handling and accessing wine in barrels.*

been a winery which has enjoyed continuous growth and which, I venture to think, is more profitable than most.

At the end of the day, however, it is the quality of the wines that matters, and Dan Lee has established a formidable reputation for the quartet he produces: Chardonnay (in both standard and Reserve forms), Sauvignon Blanc, Pinot Noir, and Cabernet Sauvignon. The Chardonnay is drawn from multiple vineyard sources across Monterey, and is the wine for which Morgan is best known. However, the Sauvignon Blanc has been so successful that its production now is almost equal to that of Chardonnay (8,500 cases compared to 10,000 for the Chardonnay). Cabernet Sauvignon and Pinot Noir used to make up 2,500 cases each, but Lee is significantly increasing the amount of Pinot Noir, drawing 50% from Monterey and 50% from Carneros.

Notwithstanding the reputation of the Chardonnay, I have to admit that I found the Cabernet Sauvignon to be the outstanding wine, with strongly flavored dark chocolate and black cherry fruit, and persistent but well balanced tannins. The Chardonnays are elegant, with the Reserve showing that appropriately greater edge of complexity, but they are not particularly intense, albeit with pleasant apple flavors.

PAHLMEYER 1985

A: P.O. Box 2410, Napa, CA 94558
T: (707) 255 2131 **V**: Nil **P**: 1,000
W: Randy Dunn

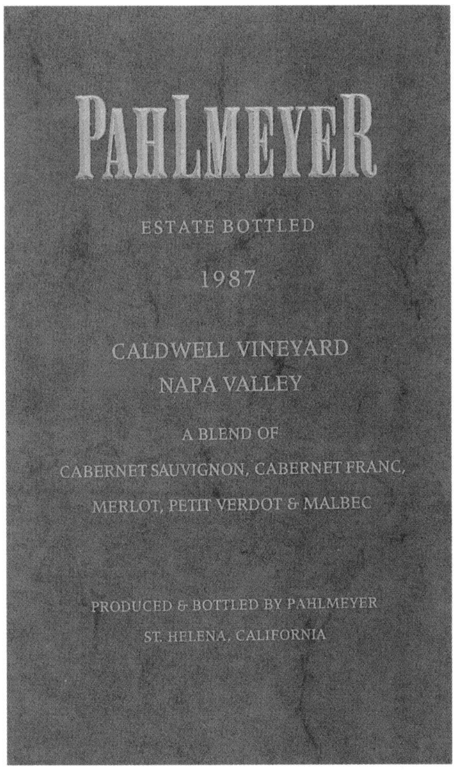
PAHLMEYER
ESTATE BOTTLED
1987
CALDWELL VINEYARD
NAPA VALLEY
A BLEND OF
CABERNET SAUVIGNON, CABERNET FRANC,
MERLOT, PETIT VERDOT & MALBEC
PRODUCED & BOTTLED BY PAHLMEYER
ST. HELENA, CALIFORNIA

Jason Pahlmeyer is a self-confessed wine fanatic. In the early 1980s he began developing a 55-acre steep hillside property in the Coombsville region east of Napa to 65% Cabernet Sauvignon, 20% Merlot, 10% Cabernet Franc and a touch of Petit Verdot and Malbec. That vineyard carries the name of his vineyard manager and partner, John Caldwell. All of the skills of the trial attorney come to the fore as Pahlmeyer relates how Randy Dunn happened to taste some of the early, experimental wines made from the property, returning several times to retaste them, and finally offering not only to purchase the fruit, but to act as contract winemaker for a small part of the production.

The wines are made in what I describe as the "fortress style," hugely complex and massively concentrated. A vertical tasting of all wines made to date showed some vintage variation — and an absolutely fascinating micro-batch of 1987 "Minty Cabernet," which raises once again the eucalypt-mint relationship — but all are variations within a theme. One can readily imagine why Randy Dunn is so enamoured of the vineyard. But the wines do have an enormous depth of sweet fruit to go with tannin and other extract, and I would not be surprised if they aged very well.

ROSENBLUM CELLARS 1978

A: 2900 Main Street, Alameda, CA 94801
T: (510) 865 7007 **V**: 12–5 weekends
P: 10,000 **W**: Kent Rosenblum

Veterinarian Kent Rosenblum came to California in 1970 from his native Minnesota, and promptly caught the California wine virus. His initial foray into winemaking resulted in five gallons of Riesling in 1973, and in the ensuing years he and 20 or so of his friends had a great time messing up each other's driveways, winning awards and ultimately giving the wine away because they could not drink it all. In 1978 he had a great idea: become a bonded winery, sell some of the wine, and take trips to France and Australia at the expense of the revenue authorities. With the dual constraints of an on-going veterinarian practice (Bruce Cass swears he has rung up to be told by Kent Rosenblum that he is dealing with a client, meaning a cat) and an ever-expanding wine business, Rosenblum has never got around to making those trips. The initial vintage of 400 cases has grown year by year, forcing a move to the large warehouse in the industrial suburbs of Alameda in 1987; there is sufficient space here for even more production.

Kent Rosenblum, with the help of his brother Roger and a wide circle of friends who appear during vintage, runs an extraordinary operation. Not for nothing is Rosenblum regarded as one of the Zinfandel specialists: he made eight different Zinfandels in 1990, and I tasted them all, as well as older wines from 1989 back to 1985. The quality and consistency is wholly exceptional. The wines have tremendous fruit concentration, depth and structure, but are never astringent or excessively tannic. That is not to say that some of them do not have tannins; they do, but the tannins are essentially soft and always have the fruit to provide balance. They are sourced from Sonoma County, Paso Robles, Contra Costa County, Alameda and the Napa Valley; in some instances they are also vineyard designated. Typically these wines are made in 500 to 800 case lots, and Rosenblum has such an outstanding reputation that these days growers with old Zinfandel plantings actually offer the grapes to him, knowing that he is prepared to pay high prices (over $1,000 a ton or more) and will make and market the wine under the vineyard name if the quality justifies it.

The wines are marketed in a novel way: the thrice yearly release attracts 800 people a day, and many of the wines sell out within days of release. To provide variety, as it were, Kent Rosenblum also makes a strongly flavored Napa Valley Merlot, and a quite awesome Napa Valley Petite Sirah, redolent with dark cherry and plum fruit, massive concentration and strong tannins. This is the cellaring special in the Rosenblum stable, and if those tannins start attacking, there is also always the Rosenblum Sparkling Cuvee, or the fortified Black Muscat to fall back on (or over, as the case may be).

STEPHEN ZELLERBACH 1970

A: 3001 S. State Street #48, Ukiah, CA 95482
T: (707) 462 2423 **V**: Nil **P**: 40,000
W: William Baccala

Stephen Zellerbach is barely a warehouse winery, and in truth simply a brand, but it is a stand alone brand, and it does have an interesting history. It was founded in 1970 by Stephen Zellerbach, a member of the well-known Crown Zellerbach family (which established Hanzell). He planted 70 acres of Sonoma Cabernet Sauvignon and Merlot, and built a winery. In 1986 he sold the brand (but not the real estate) to William Baccala, who not long before had sold his winery to what is now Jepson. Managed by partners William and Bob Baccala and Steve Situm, the Stephen Zellerbach range is partially contract crushed, and partially negociant-purchased in bulk, and matured and bottled at various locations. The range comprises a Sauvignon Blanc, Chardonnay, Chardonnay Reserve and Cabernet Sauvignon. The partners know what they are doing, for the quality of the wines relative to their price is very good indeed, the Chardonnay not infrequently outstanding, as it was in 1986, and again in 1990.

THACKREY & CO. 1982

A: P.O. Box 58, Bolinas, CA 94924
T: (415) 868 1781 **V**: Nil **P**: 3,000
W: Sean Thackrey

Over the past 35 years I have visited literally thousands of wineries in many parts of the world. With any sort of luck, I still have many hundreds to go. But I have never seen, nor am I ever likely to see, a more extraordinary winery than that of Thackrey. I suppose it can be called a winery, for parts of it would be recognizable as such; much of it is not. Sean Thackrey, a San Francisco art dealer, boasts he has the largest outdoor winery in the world, and I do not for one moment disbelieve him. For dotted around the relatively small bare earth grounds surrounding his Bolinas home are a series of sheds, lean-tos and blue, plastic-covered mounds which turn out to contain barrels of wine, many of them blackened by exposure to the elements. The crusher and press likewise sit on the earth, and it is here Thackrey makes the wine. With a display of insouciance which only an art dealer could muster, he says the only problem arises if he drops a hose or other piece of winemaking equipment. "It's a dreadful bore having to wash everything so much." To be fair, there is also a conventional barrel storage area in a strangely under-occupied shed built by a neighbor; all the new barrels (and no doubt the best wine) are stored here.

Thackrey is one of the Rhone Rangers, producing Syrah, Petite Sirah, Mourvedre and a proprietary blend thereof. He is also an astrologer: the Syrah is called Orion, the Mourvedre Taurus, and the proprietary blend Pleaides (a non-vintage wine). The wines are as unique as their surroundings, and their highly eccentric maker, suggest they should be. Carrying either the Napa Valley or California appellation, they are of monstrous weight and dimension. It is beyond my comprehension how anyone could even contemplate drinking the wines at less than ten years of age, and beyond my knowledge to guess how well they will repay the 20 years or so they appear to need. The curious thing is that the wines tasted from barrel seemed less tannic than those tasted from bottle, possibly because the fruit was fresher. Somehow or other, I think those tannins will outlive the fruit in many, but perhaps not all, of the wines.

VIADER VINEYARDS 1989

A: P.O. Box 280, Deer Park, CA 94576
T: N/A **V**: Nil **P**: 2,000 **W**: Tony Soter

Argentine-born Delia Viader has established a remarkable 18-acre vineyard on 30 degree slopes on Howell Mountain, planted at a density of 2,000 vines per acre running straight up and down the hillside. The low trellis, too, is European in design, and yields are not expected to ever exceed two tons to the acre. The first release (from 1989), a blend of 60% Cabernet Sauvignon and 40% Cabernet Franc, is soft, supple and spicy, reflecting the skills of consultant winemaker Tony Soter.

WEINSTOCK CELLARS 1984

A: 308B. Centre Street, Healdsburg, CA 95448 **T**: (707) 433 3186 **V**: 10–5 weekends **P**: 25,000 **W**: Robert Weinstock

The Weinstock wines are made under the supervision of the Union of Orthodox Jewish Congregations of America, supervised by Avrohom Rabbi Teichman. They are thus fully kosher, and are principally marketed to Sabbath observant (or orthodox) Jews. The wines are made in the Vinwood facility, with Robert Weinstock acting as winemaker; the irony is that he is not an orthodox Jew, so that the key handling operations have to be carried out by delegates of the rabbi. These delegates are also responsible for cleaning all of the winemaking equipment, and to ensure that all products used in making the wine are naturally based, and contain no animal proteins of any kind.

Weinstock produces Chardonnay, Gamay Beaujolais, White Zinfandel, Sauvignon Blanc, Pinot Noir and Cabernet Sauvignon. While the Chardonnays show fairly ordinary oak, and the Pinot Noir is eminently forgettable, the other wines are all good examples of their kind. The Sauvignon Blanc is strongly fruit driven, crisp and well made; the Gamay Beaujolais with lively, fresh, tingling fruit; the White Zinfandel neatly balances crisp acidity against a touch of residual sugar, and within the limitations of its style, is pleasant; while the Cabernet Sauvignon is elegant and pleasantly leafy. The address given, incidentally, is the tasting facility operated in the center of the town of Healdsburg.

WINTERS WINERY 1980

A: 15 Main Street, Winters, CA 95694
T: (916) 795 3201 **V**: By appointment
P: 5,000 **W**: David Storm

Dave Storm is known to practically everyone in the California industry as the expert in designing systems for dealing with winery waste water. A lifetime of experience in and around wineries inevitably led him to home winemaking, and ultimately to establishing his own winery in a historic nineteenth-century building in the main street of Winters. Originally a hotel, it housed a small theatre on the upper floor, and a meat store in the cellar. He and three partners purchased the building in 1978, and with his family converted the underground section (which in fact opens out to an alley at the rear) into a fully functional winery. The usual town planning problems were overcome, partly because of Storm's professional experience, and partly because Winters is, more than anything else, a farming community.

The first vintage at Winters was in 1980, 20 years after Dave Storm had made his first home wine. By great good fortune, he discovered the 1907 Naismith Vineyard, from which he made the Petite Sirah which has been the hallmark of the winery. At 11 years of age, the 1981 vintage still had extraordinary scented, ripe and sweet fruit, with years in front of it. The variable roster of wines includes Cabernet Sauvignon, Pinot Noir, Sauvignon Blanc and Chardonnay, the majority sourced from in and around the Napa Valley.

OTHER WINERIES

AUDUBON 1982
A: 600 Adison Street, Berkeley, CA 94710
T: (510) 540 5384 **W**: Barry Grushkowitz

BAY CELLARS 1982
A: 2413 Fourth Street, Berkeley, CA 94710
T: (510) 526 0469 **W**: Richard L. Rotblatt, John Reynolds, Carole Rotblatt

PENARD
A: 1370 Trancas Street, Suite 117, Napa, CA 94558 **T**: (800) 888 5316

ABOVE ~ *Rows of Shiraz-filled barrels.*

GLOSSARY

AGRAFE: a metal clip used to secure the cork during the secondary fermentation of champagne

ALDEHYDE: the stage between an alcohol and an acid, formed during oxidation; removed by adding sulfur dioxide

ALEMBIC: a still, usually a pot still

ALLELOPATHIC COVER CROP: plant with natural weed suppression abilities

ANAHEIM'S DISEASE, *see* PIERCE'S DISEASE

ANTHOCYANINS: coloring matter, concentrated just under the outer layer of the grape's skin

BACK BLEND: to add fresh, unfermented grape juice to fermented wine or (for example) to add unoaked wine to barrel-fermented wine

BALANCE: the harmonious relationship between wine's natural components with none dominating or deficient

BARREL FERMENTATION: the fermentation process carried out in oak barrels which produces a distinctive flavour and is different from wines only matured in barrels

BARRIQUE: standard wooden barrel of 225 litres (c. 60 gallons U.S.) capacity; should yield 22 to 24 cases of finished wine

BENCHLAND: the flat land between two slopes

BENTONITE: a fine clay containing volcanic ash used as a fining agent

BLIND TASTING: where the identity of the wines is unknown to the taster

BLUSH WINE: a pale rosé

BOTRYTIS: a fungus or rot present in humid conditions which shrivels the grapes, concentrating the flavour

BOUQUET: a term applied to the smell of wine as opposed to the aroma of the grape

BRETTANOMYCES: a type of yeast which reacts with amino acids in wine to produce a particularly distinctive (and usually unpleasant) mousy (or mice-like) aroma and taste

BRIX: a scale for measuring soluble solids, mostly sugar, of grape juice

CANE: one of the annually renewed arms of the vine which bear the current season's crop

CARBONIC MACERATION: fermentation of whole, uncrushed grape bunches in an atmosphere saturated with carbon dioxide

CASSIS: rich concentrated blackcurrant flavor

CEPAGE: a variety of vine or grape

CHARMAT PROCESS: method of making sparkling wine; the wines are not fermented in the bottle but in sealed tanks, and drawn off into the bottle under pressure

CLONAL SELECTION: deliberate selection of clones according to preordained criteria

CLONE: genetically identical population of vines of a particular variety, propagated asexually from a single source

CLUSTER: a bunch of grapes

COLD FERMENTATION: fermentation of white must at controlled low temperatures resulting in fresher, lighter wine

CRUSH: breaking the grape open to release the juice; grapes may not necessarily be crushed prior to pressing

CUVEE: blend or special selection

DISGORGEMENT: removing the sediment created during the second fermentation of sparkling wine made by the *methode champenoise* before it receives its final cork

DOWNY MILDEW: fungus disease of the vine producing a white mildew on the underside of the leaves

DRIP IRRIGATION: at its most sophisticated is a computer-controlled watering system delivered through a complex system of pipes and calibrated emitters

DRY FARMING: a type of farming practiced without irrigation by maintaining surface mulch which protects the natural moisture of the soil from evaporation

EGG WHITE: used as a fining agent

ENOLOGY: the science of wine

FERMENTATION: process by which sugar is converted by yeast into alcohol and carbon dioxide and by which grape juice becomes wine

FILTRATION: removal of solids and impurities from wine prior to bottling

FINING: addition of substances to the surface of wine which, as they settle, take suspended particles with them and leave the wine clear

FINISH: the impression a wine leaves in the mouth immediately after it has been swallowed; it precedes the aftertaste

FIRST GROWTH: the highest rank of the five growths (or groups of chateaux) established by the 1855 classification of the red wines of Bordeaux

FORTIFIED: the addition of high strength spirit to wine

FREE-RUN JUICE: the juice obtained before the pressing operation begins

GRAFT: a vine growing on disease resistant rootstock

HAND MADE WINES: a term of art applied to those made in small wineries and which, by reason of scale, in fact involve much manual labor

HYDROPONIC VITICULTURE: the cultivation of vines in gravel or other soil-less substances through which water containing dissolved inorganic nutrients is pumped

IMPERIAL: an over-size bottle equal to eight ordinary bottles

JEROBOAM: an over-size bottle equal to six ordinary bottles

KOSHER WINE: prepared according to Jewish dietary laws

LACTOBACCILLUS: ferments carbohydrates (glucose) to produce lactic acid

LEES: sediment left in the cask or vat during fermentation and left behind when the wine is racked

LENGTH: indicative of the time during which flavor of the wine lingers in the mouth after swallowing

MAGNUM: a bottle which is double normal capacity

MALIC ACID: a green apple taste in grapes which lowers as grapes ripen

MALOLACTIC FERMENTATION (MLF): secondary to alcoholic fermentation, it converts harsh malic acid into softer lactic acid

MESA: a flat-topped elevation with one or more cliff-like sides

METHODE CHAMPENOISE: producing effervescence through a second fermentation in the bottle

METHOXYPYRAZINES: substances which give Cabernet Sauvignon and Sauvignon Blanc their distinctive herbaceous taste when partially ripe

MUST: unfermented grape juice; when red, includes skins, pips and possibly stalks

NEMATODES: microscopic worms which attack the roots in much the same way as phylloxera, but without the same terminal effects

NOBLE ROT, *see* BOTRYTIS

NON-VINTAGE: a wine without a stated vintage year, usually a blend of harvests

OAK: the wood used for barrels in which wine can be counted on to develop and improve

OPEN LYRE TRELLIS: system where two posts are driven diagonally into the ground, creating two canopies from a single vine. It produces higher yields but is expensive to maintain

ORGANIC VITICULTURE: growing grapes without chemical fertilizers, pesticides or herbicides

ORGANIC WINES: made from organically grown grapes without the addition of chemicals

OXIDATION/OXIDIZED: when wine has been over exposed to the air

PATHOGEN: any agent that causes disease

PH: measure of strength of acidity/alkalinity; the higher the pH the weaker the acid

PHYLLOXERA: a louse which feeds on the roots of the vine ultimately causing the vine to die or become incapable of bearing fruit; new vines must be grafted onto phylloxera-resistant rootstock

PIERCE'S DISEASE: a bacterial disease spread by insects called Sharpshooters; originally known as Anaheim's Disease after the location 20 miles south of Los Angeles

PIGEAGE: originally foot-crushing of grapes, now refers to most forms of manual mixing (or plunging) of red wine musts

PRESSING: applying pressure to express and separate grape juice from the skins and pips prior to fermentation in the case of white wines and after fermentation in the case of red wines

PROHIBITION: In 1920 the 18th Amendment to the United States Constitution was put into effect forbidding "the manufacture, sale or transport of intoxicating liquors." It was repealed in 1933.

PUNCHEONS: barrels four times the size of the usually encountered barrique

RACKING: draining a wine off its lees into another barrel

RESIDUAL SUGAR: unfermented sugar remaining in wine

ROOTSTOCK: the lower rooting part of a grafted vine, usually phylloxera-resistant

SCION: the part of the graft that belongs to the producer vine rather than the rootstock

SKIN CONTACT: allowing the must to soak in contact with the skins before pressing

SMUDGE POTS: little fuel stoves set out in the vineyard as frost protection

SULFUR DIOXIDE: added to wine as a bactericide and a preservative

SUR LEES: wine that has been kept on the lees and not racked or filtered before bottling

SUSTAINABLE VITICULTURE: uses minimal chemical sprays, usually naturally synthesised, to ensure no long-term land degradation

TANNIN: derived from the skins, stalks and pips of grapes as well as wooden casks; harsh and bitter when young but crucial to a red wine's ability to age

TERROIR: the complete growing environment that may affect the life of a vine

TOPPED: the regular refilling of casks or barrels to ensure there is no air space between the wine and the bung

TYPICITE: typicality, a wine's sense of place

VARIETAL: the grape variety used in the making of the wine

VERAISON: the ripening period when the grapes begin to gain color and sugar

VERTICAL TASTING: comparing a run of consecutive vintages

VIGNERON: grape grower or vineyard worker

VIN DE PAILLE TECHNIQUE: cutting grapes and allowing them to dry in the sun

VINIFY: the process of turning grapes into wine

VINTAGE: the harvest year when the grapes are picked

VITICULTURE: the process of growing grape vines

VOLATILE: excessive amounts of unwanted acids in wine

YEAST: release enzymes which are necessary for fermentation of grape juice into wine

INDEX

(Numbers in *italics* refer to illustrations; numbers in **bold** refer to main entries)